Reading Diagnosis and Improvement

# Reading Diagnosis and Improvement

## Assessment and Instruction

MICHAEL F. OPITZ
University of Northern Colorado

DOROTHY RUBIN
The College of New Jersey

JAMES A. EREKSON
University of Northern Colorado

Boston  Columbus  Indianapolis  New York  San Francisco  Upper Saddle River
Amsterdam  Cape Town  Dubai  London  Madrid  Milan  Munich  Paris  Montreal  Toronto
Delhi  Mexico City  Sao Paulo  Sydney  Hong Kong  Seoul  Singapore  Taipei  Tokyo

Vice President, Editor-in-Chief: Aurora Martínez Ramos
Editorial Assistant: Amy Foley
Executive Marketing Manager: Krista Clark
Production Editor: Janet Domingo
Editorial Production Service: Susan McNally/Nesbitt Graphics, Inc
Manufacturing Buyer: Megan Cochran
Electronic Composition: Nesbitt Graphics, Inc
Interior Design: Nesbitt Graphics, Inc
Photo Researcher: Annie Pickert
Cover Designer: Elena Sidorova

For related titles and support materials, visit our online catalog at www.pearsonhighered.com.

Printed in the United States of America

**Photo Credits:** p. 1 (CH 01), Shutterstock; p.16 (CH 02), Bob Daemmrich Photography; p. 33 (CH 03), Annie Pickert/Pearson Education; p. 43 (CH 04), Pearson Learning Photo Studio; p. 61 (CH 05), Bob Daemmrich Photography; p. 91 (CH 06), Shutterstock; p. 103 (CH 07), Annie Pickert/Pearson Education; p. 147 (CH 08), Shutterstock; p. 182 (CH 09), Anthony Magnacca/Merrill Education; p. 208 (CH 10), Bob Daemmrich Photography; p. 254 (CH 11), IndexOpen; p. 285 (CH 12), iStockPhoto.com; p. 315 (CH 13), Corbis RF; p. 337 (CH 14), Krista Greco/Merrill Education; p. 349 (CH 15), Composite of (CH 01), Shutterstock, (CH 06), Shutterstock, and (CH 14), Krista Greco/Merrill Education.

10 9 8 7 6 5 4 3 2 1 [EDW] 14 13 12 11 10

www.pearsonhighered.com

ISBN-10:     0-13-705639-7
ISBN-13: 978-0-13-705639-2

To Mom and Dad,
Two of my best teachers
**M.F.O**


With love to my understanding and very supportive husband, Artie;
my precious daughters, Carol and Sharon;
my delightful grandchildren, Jennifer, Andrew, Melissa, and Kelsey;
and my special sons-in-law, Seth and Dan.
**D.R.**


To Nancy Erekson
**J.A.E**

# BRIEF CONTENTS

**PART 1** Setting the Stage  1

1 What Is Reading Diagnosis and Improvement?  1

2 Teaching for Reading Diagnosis and Improvement  16

3 Developing a Knowledge Base about Assessment, Measurement, and Evaluation  33

4 Factors that Affect Reading Performance  43

**PART 2** Assessing Reading  61

5 Using Informal Assessment Techniques across the Grades  61

6 Using Standardized Tests across the Grades  91

7 Assessing and Teaching Early Literacy  103

8 Listening in on Students' Oral Reading  147

**PART 3** Reading Content and Instruction 182

9 Using Texts to Help Children Advance as Readers 182

10 Helping Children Comprehend 208

11 Helping Children Acquire and Apply Vocabulary 254

12 Helping Children Apply Phonics 285

13 Learning Strategies and Study Skills 315

14 Partnering with Parents 337

15 Putting it All Together 349

## APPENDICES

Appendix A Constructing An IRI 357

Appendix B Informal Reading Inventory 361

Appendix C Teacher's Resource Guide of Language Transfer Issues for English Language Learners 407

Appendix D Response to Intervention: Guiding Principles for Educators from the International Reading Association, 2010 421

Glossary 427

Name Index 433

Subject Index 441

# CONTENTS

*Preface*   *xix*

## PART 1   Setting the Stage   1

### 1   What Is Reading Diagnosis and Improvement?   1

**SCENARIO: A READING DIAGNOSIS AND IMPROVEMENT PROGRAM IN ACTION**   2
Chapter Objectives   2
What Is Reading Diagnosis and Improvement?   2
What Is Diagnosis?   3
Ten Principles of Diagnosis   3
What Is a Diagnostic Pattern?   4
What Is Response to Intervention (RTI)?   4
What Is Balanced Reading?   5
**SCENARIO: BALANCED READING**   5
What Is Developmental Reading?   5
What Is Remedial Reading?   6
What Is Reading?   6
  *How Is Reading a Total Integrative Process?*   7
  *What Are Characteristics of Good Readers?*   8
What Are Models of the Reading Process?   10
Who Are English Language Learners?   11
What Are Ages and Stages of Literacy Development?   12
**REVISITING THE OPENING SCENARIO**   14
  **Authors' Summary**   14
  **Suggestions for Thought Questions and Activities**   14
  **Web Sites**   14
  **Selected Bibliography**   15

### 2   Teaching for Reading Diagnosis and Improvement   16

**SCENARIOS: EXTREMES DON'T WORK!**   17
Chapter Objectives   18
The Role of the Teacher in Reading Diagnosis and Improvement   18
The Teacher as the Key to a Good Reading Program   18

Characteristics and Practices of Good Reading Teachers   20
   *Ongoing Teacher Improvement in Reading*   20
Teacher Expectations   21
Four Teacher Roles   22
   *Role 1: Planner*   22
   *Role 2: Explicit Reading Teacher*   24
   *Role 3: Organizer and Manager*   25
   *Role 4: Self-Evaluator*   26
**REVISITING THE OPENING SCENARIOS**   30
   **Authors' Summary**   31
   **Suggestions for Thought Questions and Activities**   31
   **Web Sites**   31
   **Selected Bibliography**   32

**3   Developing a Knowledge Base about Assessment, Measurement, and Evaluation**   33

**SCENARIO: MS. SMITH LEARNS ABOUT ASSESSMENT**   34
Chapter Objectives   34
Testing in Reading Diagnosis   34
Assessment, Measurement, and Evaluation   35
Criteria for Good Tests   37
**REVISITING THE OPENING SCENARIO**   40
   **Authors' Summary**   41
   **Suggestions for Thought Questions and Activities**   41
   **Web Sites**   41
   **Selected Bibliography**   41

**4   Factors That Affect Reading Performance**   43

**SCENARIO: ANGELIQUE AND SARA—A STUDY IN CONTRAST**   44
Chapter Objectives   45
Differentiating between Educational and Noneducational Factors   45
Educational Factors   47
   *Reading Models*   47
   *Instructional Materials*   47
   *The Teacher*   48
   *Instructional Time*   48
   *School Environment*   49
Noneducational Factors   49
   *Home Environment*   49

*Language Differences*   50

*Intelligence*   51

*Gender*   51

*Physical Health*   52

*Perceptual Factors*   53

*Emotional Well-Being*   57

**REVISITING THE OPENING SCENARIO**   58

**Authors' Summary**   58

**Suggestions for Thought Questions and Activities**   59

**Web Sites**   59

**Selected Bibliography**   59

# PART 2   Assessing Reading   61

## 5   Using Informal Assessment Techniques across the Grades   61

**SCENARIO: TEACHERS TALKING**   62

Chapter Objectives   62

Authentic, Performance-Based Assessment   64

*Record Keeping*   66

Portfolio Assessment   66

The Uses of Observation   67

*Making Observations Objective*   67

Anecdotal Records   69

**SCENARIO: MR. JACKSON CHECKS AND WRITES**   70

Checklists   72

*Group and Individual Checklists*   72

*Checklists and Rating Scales*   76

Other Helpful Informal Assessment Techniques   79

*Informal Student Interviews*   79

*Interest Inventories*   82

*Reading Attitude Surveys*   82

*Projective Techniques*   84

*Reading Autobiography*   87

**REVISITING THE OPENING SCENARIO**   88

**Authors' Summary**   89

**Suggestions for Thought Questions and Activities**   89

**Web Sites**   89

**Selected Bibliography**   90

# 6 Using Standardized Tests across the Grades  91

**SCENARIO: MR. JAMES—A TEACHER WHO KNOWS THE PURPOSE OF TESTS**  92

Chapter Objectives  92

Standardized Tests  92

Norm-Referenced Tests  92

*Limitations of Norm-Referenced Measures*  93

Reading Survey Tests and General Achievement Survey Tests  93

*Selecting a Standardized Test*  95

*Test Score Terminology*  95

Criterion-Referenced Tests  97

*Limitations of Criterion-Referenced Tests*  98

Teacher-Made Tests  99

Administering Individual Tests  99

Administering Group Tests  99

Diagnostic Reading Tests  100

**REVISITING THE OPENING SCENARIO**  100

Authors' Summary  100

Suggestions for Thought Questions and Activities  101

Web Sites  101

Selected Bibliography  101

# 7 Assessing and Teaching Early Literacy  103

**SCENARIO: HELPING CHILDREN ADVANCE AS LANGUAGE LEARNERS**  104

Chapter Objectives  104

Building an Understanding of Early Literacy  105

*Areas of Early Literacy*  106

Assessing Early Literacy  106

*Pre-Reading Assessment*  106

*Uses of Group-Administered Standardized Pre-Reading Assessments*  106

*Suggestions for Choosing and Using Required Pre-Reading Tests*  109

*Current Ways to Assess Early Literacy*  109

Understanding, Assessing, and Teaching Concepts  111

*What Is a Concept?*  111

*How Do Concepts Develop?*  112

*How Does Concept Development Relate to Language and Reading?*  113

*How Can Oral Language Concepts Be Assessed?*  113

*How Can Print Concepts Be Assessed?*   116

*Teaching Oral Language and Print Concepts*   118

Understanding, Assessing, and Teaching Phonological Awareness   123

*What Is Phonological Awareness?*   123

*How Can Phonological Awareness Be Assessed?*   124

*Teaching Phonological Awareness*   124

Understanding, Assessing, and Teaching Letter Identification   128

*What Is Letter Identification?*   128

*How Can Letter Identification Be Assessed?*   130

*Teaching Letter Identification*   130

Understanding, Assessing, and Teaching Writing   133

*What Is Writing?*   133

*What Is Developmental Spelling?*   135

*How Can Writing Be Assessed?*   136

*Teaching Writing*   138

Understanding, Assessing, and Teaching Story Sense   138

*What Is Story Sense?*   138

*How Can Story Sense Be Assessed?*   138

*Teaching Story Sense and Story Comprehension*   141

Putting it All Together: Who Is in Most Need of Early Intervention?   141

*What Is Early Intervention?*   141

*Who Is in Most Need of Early Intervention?*   142

**REVISITING THE OPENING SCENARIO**   144

**Authors' Summary**   144

**Suggestions for Thought Questions and Activities**   144

**Web Sites**   144

**Selected Bibliography**   145

**Children's Literature Cited**   145

# 8 Listening in on Students' Oral Reading   147

**SCENARIO: USING ORAL READING TO LEARN MORE ABOUT VICKI**   148

Chapter Objectives   148

An Overview of the Informal Reading Inventory   149

*What Is an Informal Reading Inventory?*   149

*What Are the Purposes of an Informal Reading Inventory?*   151

*Determining Reading and Listening Capacity Levels*   151

*Reporting Students' Reading Levels*   153

*Code for Marking Oral Reading Errors*   154

*Scoring Oral Reading Errors*   154

*Using a Diagnostic Checklist for Oral and Silent Reading*   156

Administering and Scoring the IRI   156

   *Step 1: Establishing Rapport*   156

   *Step 2: The Word Recognition Inventory*   156

   *Step 3: Oral and Silent Reading Passages*   158

   *Step 4: The Listening Capacity Test*   159

   *When Is a Listening Capacity Test Given?*   159

IRI Selection Criteria   164

An Overview of Miscue Analysis   167

   *What Is Miscue Analysis and What Is its Purpose?*   167

   *How Can Miscue Analysis Be Used?*   168

   *Modified Miscue Analysis*   168

An Overview of the Running Record   170

   *What Is a Running Record?*   170

   *What Are the Purposes of a Running Record?*   170

   *How Are Running Records and IRIs Similar?*   170

   *How Are Running Records and IRIs Different?*   172

Administering a Running Record   172

Scoring a Running Record   176

Interpreting a Running Record   178

**REVISITING THE OPENING SCENARIO**   178

  **Authors' Summary**   180

  **Suggestions for Thought Questions and Activities**   180

  **Web Sites**   180

  **Selected Bibliography**   180

## PART 3   Reading Content and Instruction   182

## 9   Using Texts to Help Children Advance as Readers   182

**SCENARIO: MR. HALL'S TEXT-PACKED CLASSROOM**   183

Chapter Objectives   183

Reasons for Using a Variety of Texts   184

Text Types   185

   *Commercial Books*   187

   *Children's Literature*   189

   *Other Texts*   197

**REVISITING THE OPENING SCENARIO**   203

  **Authors' Summary**   203

Suggestions for Thought Questions and Activities   203
Web Sites   204
Selected Bibliography   204
Children's Literature Cited   205

# 10   Helping Children Comprehend   208

SCENARIO: ALAN'S COMPREHENSION   209
Chapter Objectives   209
Building Background about Comprehension   209
  *Comprehension*   209
  *Listening Comprehension*   209
  *Reading Comprehension*   211
  *Reading Comprehension Taxonomies*   213
Oral Reading, Fluency, and Reading Comprehension   214
  *Guiding Principles*   215
Comprehension Skills   215
  *Main Idea of a Paragraph*   216
  *Finding the Central Idea of a Group of Paragraphs*   222
  *Drawing Inferences*   225
Comprehension Strategies   229
Assessing Comprehension   229
  *Questioning as a Diagnostic Technique*   230
  *Cloze Procedure*   231
  *Maze Procedure*   234
  *Meta-Comprehension Strategy Index*   234
Teaching Comprehension   235
  *The Directed Reading–Thinking Activity*   238
  *Think Aloud*   238
  *Repeated Reading*   239
  *Reciprocal Reading Instruction*   239
  *Literature Webbing*   240
  *Questioning Strategies*   240
  *Question–Answer Relationships (QARs)*   242
  *Re-Quest*   243
REVISITING THE OPENING SCENARIO   250
  Authors' Summary   250
  Suggestions for Thought Questions and Activities   251
  Web Sites   251
  Selected Bibliography   251
  Children's Literature Cited   252

# 11 Helping Children Acquire and Apply Vocabulary    254

**SCENARIO: MR. JACKSON AND VOCABULARY EXPANSION**    255

Chapter Objectives    255

Vocabulary Development    256

*Acquiring Vocabulary*    256

*Vocabulary Consciousness*    257

*Levels of Knowing a Word*    257

*Types of Words*    258

*Sight Vocabulary*    258

*Defining Word Part Terms*    258

*Context Clues*    260

*Categorization*    262

*Analogies*    263

Assessing Vocabulary    264

Teaching Vocabulary    264

*Guidelines for Effective Vocabulary Instruction*    264

*Teaching Strategies*    265

**REVISITING THE OPENING SCENARIO**    282

**Authors' Summary**    282

**Suggestions for Thought Questions and Activities**    282

**Web Sites**    282

**Selected Bibliography**    283

**Children's Literature Cited**    283

# 12 Helping Children Apply Phonics    285

**SCENARIO: UNDERSTANDING JORGE**    286

Chapter Objectives    286

Phonics Content Knowledge    287

A Developmental Sequence of Phonics    287

*Auditory and Visual Discrimination*    288

*Consonants*    289

*Consonant Blends*    290

*Vowel Sounds*    291

*Phonograms*    295

*Syllables*    295

Assessing Phonics    295

*Five Meaningful Ways to Assess Phonics*    295

Teaching Phonics    303

*Guidelines for Exemplary Phonics Instruction*    303

*Synthetic and Analytic Phonics Instruction*   304

*Seven Ways to Teach Phonics*   306

**REVISITING THE OPENING SCENARIO**   312

**Authors' Summary**   312

**Suggestions for Thought Questions and Activities**   312

**Web Sites**   313

**Selected Bibliography**   313

**Children's Literature Cited**   314

# 13   Learning Strategies and Study Skills   315

Chapter Objectives   316

What Are Some Good Study Procedures?   316

*Building Good Study Habits*   317

How to Study   318

**SCENARIO: MODELING THE SQ3R APPROACH FOR FOURTH-GRADE STUDENTS**   323

*Teaching SQ3R*   324

Knowing the Textbook   324

Concentration   325

Following Directions   326

Skimming   327

Asking Questions   328

Reading and Writing as Modes of Learning   329

*Note Taking for Studying*   329

**SCENARIO: NOTE TAKING, STUDYING, AND SQ3R**   329

**SCENARIO: SEMANTIC MAPPING AND STUDYING**   330

*Summaries as a Mode of Learning*   331

Test Taking   331

*Test-Taking Principles*   333

The School Media Center and Media Literacy Skills   333

*Primary Grades*   334

*Intermediate and Upper-Elementary Grades*   334

**Authors' Summary**   335

**Suggestions for Thought Questions and Activities**   335

**Web Sites**   335

**Selected Bibliography**   336

# 14   Partnering with Parents   337

**SCENARIO: DAVID'S FATHER TALKS WITH MR. GONZALEZ**   338

Chapter Objectives   338

Parental Involvement in the Schools   338

Research on Parental Involvement in their Children's Education   339

Parental Involvement in Regular School Reading Programs   341

Television, Computers, Parents, Children, and Reading   344

*Television*   344

*Computers*   345

**REVISITING THE OPENING SCENARIO**   346

**Authors' Summary**   346

**Suggestions for Thought Questions and Activities**   347

**Web Sites**   347

**Selected Bibliography**   347

**15   Putting it All Together**   349

Chapter Objectives   350

**SCENARIO: CASE REPORT OF CHILD**   350

**SCENARIO EXPLANATION**   351

Five Scenarios   352

## APPENDICES

**Appendix A** Constructing an IRI   357

**Constructing Your Own Informal Reading Inventory**   357

Graded Word Lists   357

Graded Oral and Silent Reading Passages   358

The Comprehension Questions   359

**Appendix B** Informal Reading Inventory   361

**Special Notes**   363

**Appendix C** Teacher's Resource Guide of Language Transfer Issues for English Language Learners   407

Grammar Transfer Issues for Ten Languages   407

Phonics Transfer Issues for Seven Languages   416

Sound Symbol Transfer (Phonics)   418

**Appendix D** Response to Intervention: Guiding Principles for Educators from the International Reading Association, 2010   421

Background   421

Guiding Principles   423

**Glossary**   427

**Name Index**   433

**Subject Index**   441

# PREFACE

*Reading Diagnosis and Improvement: Assessment and Instruction*, Sixth Edition, is based on the premise that diagnosis and improvement are essential parts of reading instruction and that when both assessment and instruction are centric to a reading program, children's reading improvement can occur. We have designed this book to help pre-service and in-service teachers acquire or add to their knowledge the skills necessary to make diagnosis and improvement an integral part of their reading programs. To achieve this goal, we combine theory, basic knowledge and skills, and practical application.

The new millennium continues to demand knowledgeable teachers who know why they do what they do when teaching reading. Therefore, in the first part of the book, we emphasize the importance of teachers and explain the many roles they play when assessing and teaching reading. Good teachers must be knowledgeable of the many factors that affect the reading process and of the many assessment measures they can use to better understand these factors. This knowledge includes how to select, administer, score, and interpret information from measurement instruments. Teachers must also fully understand how to use information that they glean from assessments to design appropriate instruction that will help students become proficient readers. Finally, teachers need to understand basic developmental reading skills and strategies and have a wealth of teaching strategies. To help teachers be as knowledgeable as possible, nothing should be taken for granted. In this book, nothing is.

In Part 1, we set the stage for effective reading diagnosis and improvement. We begin by explaining reading diagnosis and improvement. We then discuss the teacher in terms of four roles. We also present assessment terminology with which a classroom teacher should be familiar. Finally, we present and discuss the many factors that affect reading performance.

In Part 2, we present various assessment measures that teachers can use to assess and diagnose students' reading strengths and needs. In this part, we explain that asking and answering three guiding questions helps teachers choose the most appropriate assessment measure: *What Do I Want to Know? Why Do I Want to Know? How Can I Best Discover This Information?* We also give special attention to assessing early literacy because there are several unique ways of identifying young children's strengths and needs from the onset of instruction.

In Part 3, we present reading content and instruction. Each chapter follows the same format and is written as a stand-alone chapter; each can be read in any order. In Chapter 9 we offer many kinds of texts that children can read and offer titles and teaching suggestions for each. In Chapters 10, 11, and 12 we explain comprehension (including fluency as a related component), vocabulary, and phonics and provide many assessment and teaching strategies that teachers can use to help children advance as readers. In Chapter 13, we provide ideas for helping children acquire and apply study skills. In Chapter 14, we discuss partnering with parents and offer specific suggestions to help teachers do just that. Our intent with Chapter 15 is to provide readers with opportunities to apply what they have learned from the entire text.

As a further aid to teachers, we include four appendixes. Appendix A offers suggestions for constructing an informal reading inventory. Appendix B contains a complete informal reading inventory. The instructions on how to administer it, mark it, and score it are presented in Chapter 8. Appendix C shows language transfer issues that impact reading. These assessment forms can also be found in the MyEducationLab.

## NEW TO THIS EDITION

*Reading Diagnosis and Improvement: Assessment and Instruction* is a teacher-friendly book designed to boost teachers' confidence. Using a variety of teaching and assessment strategies, teachers can understand their students and help them reach their maximum reading potential. We kept this goal in mind in writing this sixth edition and made substantial changes from previous editions. These are as follows:

- We **updated all lists of children's literature** and added an additional 100 titles that teachers can use to engage students during reading diagnosis and improvement, every step along the way.
- The tone of the book has been changed to **respect the teachers' voice.** All scenarios are designed to show professional teachers making every effort to serve their students.
- At the beginning of each chapter readers will find a **new chapter outline** to help guide their reading. The section headers play off of what researchers have discovered and reported make texts more reader-friendly. This new structure will aid students and instructors as they preview the chapters.
- New to this edition is a **name index** designed to help instructors guide students to specific researchers of seminal studies and researchers central to specific topics.
- We added **50 new Internet resources** that teachers can use to further their understanding of the various topics within this text. Some of the sites also provide teachers with additional teaching ideas.
- Given that phonics is a perennial topic in reading and that teachers are flooded with information, we have sifted through all of this information and have pared it down to **what is most essential for teachers to understand for reading diagnosis and improvement.** We also included **three meaningful ways to assess phonics**, complete with assessment forms and procedures, so that teachers can be confident in their interpretations of data. This confidence naturally leads to higher quality decisions as teachers design phonics lessons focused on students' strengths and needs.
- **Teachers face many contemporary demands. We addressed these contemporary demands head on.** For example, in Chapter 1, we added new information about English Language Learners including the new TESOL standards for English Proficiency levels and descriptors and teaching ideas to facilitate growth at each proficiency level. Also in Chapter 1 we provided the newest information about *Response to Intervention* and **added a new appendix that showcases the commission statement on RtI** issued by the *International Reading Association.* We believe that this appendix will be of great help to busy teachers.
- Based on reviewer's feedback and on our use of the text, **we split the chapter on formal assessment into two chapters, one on assessment in general and one on testing.** Both chapters (3 and 6) emphasize the teachers' growing role as interpreters and users of data.
- In accordance with reviewers comments, **we reordered the chapters for easier reading:**
  - The four chapters in Part 1 provide teachers with the necessary background for understanding and applying information gleaned from succeeding chapters.
  - The four chapters in Part 2 help teachers to thoroughly understand reading assessment.
  - The seven chapters in Part 3 provide teachers with a wealth of ideas for how to teach various reading content topics and provide ideas for communicating with parents.
- **In Part 3, we ordered the chapters to emphasize comprehension and to put vocabulary and phonics in their appropriate places—as tools for comprehension.**
- **New to this edition is the MyEducationLab** in which readers are directed to online resources provided by Pearson. We selected these resources and placed them in the margins to coincide with specific topics as a way to enrich readers' understanding of

these topics. As often as possible, we selected video clips so that readers could see ideas in action and hear teacher and student voices.

- **The book is comprehensive in scope so that it can be used in two college courses.** Half of the content can be used to teach a reading methods course and the other half can be used in a reading diagnosis course.
- **The instructor manual has been substantially revised to reflect the changes of this edition.** It is packed full of teaching ideas for college instructors who teach reading methods, reading diagnosis courses, or both.

In *Reading Diagnosis and Improvement: Assessment and Instruction*, Sixth Edition, we have made every effort to give principles in practical, comprehensible language. **When we use a technical term, we define the term and then use it. We also provide a glossary of these terms.**

# SUPPLEMENTS FOR INSTRUCTORS AND STUDENTS

The following supplements comprise an outstanding array of resources that facilitate learning about literacy instruction. For more information, ask your local Allyn & Bacon Merrill Education representative or contact the Allyn & Bacon Merrill Faculty Field Support Department at 1-800-526-0485. For technology support, please contact technical support directly at 1-800-677-6337 or http://247.pearsoned.com.

## INSTRUCTOR'S MANUAL AND TEST BANK

For each chapter, the instructor's manual and test bank features a chapter outline, chapter summary, chapter objectives, key terms, classroom activities, online activities, discussion topics and essay questions, multiple choice and/or true/false questions, and activity handouts. (Available for download from the Instructor Resource Center at www.pearsonhighered.com/irc.)

**PEARSON**
**myeducationlab**
**The Power of Classroom Practice**

"Teacher educators who are developing pedagogies for the analysis of teaching and learning contend that analyzing teaching artifacts has three advantages: it enables new teachers time for reflection while still using the real materials of practice; it provides new teachers with experience thinking about and approaching the complexity of the classroom; and in some cases, it can help new teachers and teacher educators develop a shared understanding and common language about teaching. . . ."[1]

As Linda Darling-Hammond and her colleagues point out, grounding teacher education in real classrooms—among real teachers and students and among actual examples of students' and teachers' work—is an important and perhaps even an essential, part of training teachers for the complexities of teaching in today's classrooms. For this reason, we have created a valuable, time-saving website—MyEducationLab—that provides the context of real classrooms and artifacts that research on teacher education tells us is so important. The authentic in-class video footage, interactive skill-building exercises, and other resources available on MyEducationLab offer a uniquely valuable teacher education tools.

[1]Darling-Hammond, L., & Bransford, J., Eds. (2005). *Preparing Teachers for a Changing World*. San Francisco: John Wiley & Sons.

MyEducationLab is easy to use and integrate into assignments and courses. Whenever the MyEducationLab logo appears in the text, follow the simple instructions to access the interactive assignments, activities, and learning units on MyEducationLab. For each topic covered in the course you will find most or all of the following resources:

## CONNECTION TO NATIONAL STANDARDS

Now it is easier than ever to see how coursework is connected to national standards. Each topic on MyEducationLab lists intended learning outcomes connected to the appropriate national standards. All of the Assignments and Activities and all of the Building Teaching Skills and Dispositions in MyEducationLab are mapped to the appropriate national standards and learning outcomes as well.

## ASSIGNMENTS AND ACTIVITIES

Designed to save instructors preparation time and enhance student understanding, these assignable exercises show concepts in action (through video, cases, and/or student and teacher artifacts). They help students synthesize and apply concepts and strategies they read about in the book.

## BUILDING TEACHING SKILLS AND DISPOSITIONS

These learning units help students practice and strengthen skills that are essential to quality teaching. They are presented with the core skill or concept and then given an opportunity to practice their understanding of this concept multiple times by watching video footage (or interacting with other media) and then critically analyzing the strategy or skill presented.

## IRIS CENTER RESOURCES

The IRIS Center at Vanderbilt University (http://iris.peabody.vanderbilt.edu – funded by the U.S. Department of Education's Office of Special Education Programs (OSEP)) develops training enhancement materials for pre-service and in-service teachers. The Center works with experts from across the country to create challenge-based interactive modules, case study units, and podcasts that provide research-validated information about working with students in inclusive settings. In your MyEducationLab course we have integrated this content where appropriate.

## TEACHER TALK

This feature links to videos of teachers of the year across the country discussing their personal stories of why they teach. This National Teacher of the Year Program is sponsored by the Council of Chief State School Officers (CCSSO) and focuses public attention on teaching excellence.

## GENERAL RESOURCES ON YOUR MYEDUCATIONLAB COURSE

The Resources section on MyEducationLab is designed to help students pass their licensure exams, put together effective portfolios and lesson plans, prepare for and navigate the first year of their teaching careers, and understand key educational standards, policies, and laws. This section includes:

- *Licensure Exams*: Contains guidelines for passing the Praxis exam. The *Practice Test Exam* includes practice multiple-choice questions, case study questions, and video case studies with sample questions.
- *Lesson Plan Builder*: Helps students create and share lesson plans.
- *Licensure and Standards*: Provides links to state licensure standards and national standards.
- *Beginning Your Career*: Offers tips, advice, and valuable information on:
  - Resume Writing and Interviewing: Expert advice on how to write impressive resumes and prepare for job interviews.
  - Your First Year of Teaching: Practical tips on setting up a classroom, managing student behavior, and planning for instruction and assessment.
  - Law and Public Policies: Includes specific directives and requirements educators need to understand under the No Child Left Behind Act and the Individuals with Disabilities Education Improvement Act of 2004.

*Visit www.myeducationlab.com for a demonstration of this exciting new online teaching resource.*

Speak with your Allyn & Bacon Merrill sales representative about obtaining these supplements for your class!

# ACKNOWLEDGMENTS

The number of individuals who work to make a book possible never ceases to amaze us. We are greatly indebted to all who helped us complete this sixth edition. We thank two doctoral candidates at the University of Northern Colorado: Krista Fiedler, for compiling the children's literature selections and adding new titles to the suggested bibliographies, and Veronica M. Richard, for rounding up the web sites. We thank Dr. Michael Ford, University of Wisconsin, Oshkosh, for his co-authorship on professional writings cited in this text. We also thank the many publishers who provided us with the numerous children's literature titles we showcase in this edition. We would also like to thank the many individuals at Pearson including our editor, Aurora Martínez Ramos; her editorial assistant, Amy Foley; and production editor, Janet Domingo; and Susan McNally from Nesbitt Graphics.

We are grateful to the following individuals for their careful review of the manuscript. We found their suggestions insightful and helpful: Debbie East, Indiana University; Dr. Rebecca C. Faulkner, University of South Carolina Upstate; Dr. Judy C. Lambert, University of Wisconsin, Oshkosh; James E. McGlinn, University of North Carolina, Asheville; and Kelly Neylon, Benedictine University.

I thank Dorothy Rubin for inviting me to revise this edition and for her support and encouragement; James Erekson for the many keen insights he brought to this edition. Finally, I thank Sheryl Opitz, my wife, for her support.

**MFO**

Thanks to both Michael Opitz and Dorothy Rubin for inviting me to revise this edition. Michael's mentoring during the writing has been invaluable. It is wonderful to be working on a book that may have direct impact on how teachers work with readers. Many thanks to my wife, Nancy, and my children Bela, Alma, and Pearl who gave up time with me during the months of this revision.

**JAE**

**PART 1**
Setting the Stage

# What Is Reading Diagnosis and Improvement?

1

## CHAPTER OUTLINE

- Scenario: A Reading Diagnosis and Improvement Program in Action
- What Is Reading Diagnosis and Improvement?
- What Is Diagnosis?
- Ten Principles of Diagnosis
- What Is a Diagnostic Pattern?
- What Is Response to Intervention (RTI)?
- What Is Balanced Reading?
- Scenario: Balanced Reading
- What Is Developmental Reading?
- What Is Remedial Reading?
- What Is Reading?
- What Are Models of the Reading Process?
- Who Are English Language Learners?
- What Are Ages and Stages of Literacy Development?
- Revisiting the Opening Scenario

**SCENARIO:** A READING DIAGNOSIS AND IMPROVEMENT
PROGRAM IN ACTION

When you walk into Ms. Johnson's third-grade classroom, you realize that something
special is taking place; you can sense the excitement of learning. Often no one notices
your arrival because the children are so engrossed in what they are doing.

Ms. Johnson's classroom is not quiet. It's a room in which children and teacher are
involved in a dynamic, interactive teaching–learning program, which includes a reading
diagnosis and improvement program.

At various times on any one day, you can observe Ms. Johnson working with an
individual child, a group of children, or a whole class. In Ms. Johnson's room, grouping is tailored to the needs of children and is very flexible. Children flow from one
group to another depending on need. It's not unusual to find a child in more than one
reading group, working individually, or working in a one-to-one relationship with
Ms. Johnson. Ms. Johnson tries to correlate reading with all the other language arts
and sees to it that she meets individually with each child in a special conference at
least once during the week. She believes in "nipping problems in the bud," so she
keeps very close tabs on her students. Whether children are reading from trade
books or from their basal readers, she keeps records of their progress in word
recognition and comprehension.

Ms. Johnson is always probing, questioning, and keeping a sharp eye out for what
her students do well and for potential problems; she interweaves diagnosis with instruction. When she notices a problem, she talks to the child to try to determine whether the
child recognizes that there is a problem. She then sets up a student conference to meet
and discuss the issue further.

## CHAPTER OBJECTIVES

After reading the chapter, you should be able to:

- Discuss the importance of a reading diagnosis and improvement program.
- State ten principles of diagnosis.
- Describe what a total integrative reading program entails.
- Discuss how a definition of reading influences the reading diagnosis and improve-
  ment program.
- Discuss what is usually meant by a balanced reading program.

## WHAT IS READING DIAGNOSIS AND IMPROVEMENT?

**Reading
diagnosis and
improvement**
Reading instruction
interwoven with
diagnosis and
intervention.

*Reading diagnosis and improvement* consists of reading instruction interwoven with
diagnosis and intervention. It is based on the premise that both ongoing diagnosis and
intervention are integral parts of a daily developmental reading program (i.e., a
program that addresses all reading skills and strategies that are systematically and
sequentially developed to enable children to become readers) and that knowledgeable
teachers can and should implement such a program once they have the necessary skills.
It is also based on the premise that early intervention (i.e., identifying students'
strengths and needs as early as kindergarten) is essential.

## WHAT IS DIAGNOSIS?

**Diagnosis**
The act, process, or result of identifying the nature of a disorder or disability through observation and examination. In education, it often includes the planning of instruction and an assessment of the strengths and weaknesses (i.e., needs) of the student.

Some educators are disturbed by the term *diagnosis* because it seems to connote illness or disease, and they do not like the analogies that are often made between medicine and education. *Diagnosis* is a term that has been borrowed from medicine. In the field of reading, it is used to discuss how to identify children's reading strengths and needs. The definition of *diagnosis* offered in *The Literacy Dictionary* (Harris & Hodges, 1995) is most often used:

> The act, process, or result of identifying the nature of a disorder or disability through observation and examination. . . . As the term is used in education, it often includes the planning of instruction and an assessment of the strengths and weaknesses (i.e., needs) of the student. (p. 59)

Let us analyze the definition further.

1. The first step in diagnosis is the identification of strengths and needs by observing certain signs or symptoms as the child is reading throughout the day and by administering informal reading assessments. (See Chapters 5, 7, and 8.) Some examples of these signs or symptoms would be a child's ability or inability to read fluently, to decode words, or to comprehend.
2. The second step is to determine possible reasons for reading difficulties. This is accomplished by analyzing the results of assessments that are used to shed light on a child's reading performance. It may also include looking for some of the underlying factors, noneducational or educational, that could be contributing to the reading problem.

Note that in the first step, teachers look for both strengths and needs. Knowledge of what a child can do is often helpful in providing insight into a child's reading problem. Teachers can also use what the child knows to teach new strategies. The second step generally reveals that a reading problem is caused by a number of factors rather than just one. (See Chapter 4.)

## TEN PRINCIPLES OF DIAGNOSIS

Ten principles underlie the type of diagnosis and improvement we propose in this text. These principles are reflected in *Excellent Reading Teachers*, a position statement issued by the International Reading Association's board of directors (IRA, 2000).

1. Diagnosis underlies prevention.
2. Early diagnosis is essential in order to ameliorate reading problems from the start.
3. Diagnosis is continuous.
4. Diagnosis and instruction are interwoven.
5. Diagnosis is a *means* to improvement; it is not an end in itself.
6. Teacher-made as well as published reading assessment instruments are used in diagnosis.
7. Noneducational as well as educational factors are considered.
8. Diagnosis identifies strengths as well as needs.

9. Diagnosis is an individual process; that is, in diagnosis, the teacher focuses on an individual child. (Diagnostic information can be obtained from various contexts: working in a one-to-one relationship with a child, observing a child in a group, or observing a child doing seatwork.)
10. The teacher works to establish rapport and treats each student as an individual worthy of respect.

## WHAT IS A DIAGNOSTIC PATTERN?

**Diagnostic pattern**
Consists of three steps: identify, assess and set goals

**Identification**
Part of diagnostic pattern; the act of determining the student's present level of performance in word recognition and comprehension for screening purposes.

Appropriate instruction stems from and is interwoven with accurate and pertinent diagnostic information for each child in the regular classroom. We also stress that diagnosis is ongoing and is necessary for prevention as well as for continued growth. In a reading diagnosis and improvement program, the teacher is interested in determining the student's reading strengths and needs, as well as the factors contributing to them, as soon as possible in order to plan and provide appropriate instruction. Three steps to accomplish this are given below.

Step 1: *Identify* the student's present level of performance in comprehension and word recognition by using a variety of reading assessments (see Part 2, Chapters 5–8).

Step 2: *Assess* specific student strengths and needs, especially if a discrepancy exists between a student's present reading status and reading potential. Doing so allows the teacher to discover specific factors that affect the student's reading performance.

Step 3: *Set goals* to help students maximize their reading potential.

Identification, assessment, and goal setting are three steps in a diagnostic pattern.[1]

## WHAT IS RESPONSE TO INTERVENTION (RTI)?

To hear an expert discuss RtI and cultural considerations, go to the IRIS Center Resources section of Topic 11: Reading Difficulties and Intervention Strategies in the MyEducationLab for your course and listen to the Podcast entitled "Leonard Baca on RtI and Cultural Considerations."

The latest version of the Individuals with Disabilities Education Improvement Act (IDEIA), which was passed by Congress in 2004, specifies that it is no longer necessary to show a discrepancy in order to determine who has a learning problem (e.g., learning to read) that is severe enough to be classified as a learning disability. In its place is a process called *Response to Intervention* (RtI). See Appendix D for the International Reading Association's Guiding Principles on RtI. The IRA commission on RtI summarizes the actual laws and provides clear principles on how to put the intent of the laws into action.

The three-step process entails providing children who appear to be struggling with the best possible instruction and taking a look at how they perform under such conditions. This first round of instruction takes place in the classroom context and is provided by the classroom teacher. If the child makes little or no progress in comparison to his or her peers, the second step involves providing supplementary instruction, either individually or in a small group. The classroom teacher or another professional provides this instruction. If the child still makes little progress, additional tests are administered to determine whether there is a specific learning disability. If there is, the child is placed in special education classes and given more intensive intervention.

*Intervention* is a key word here. Just as with reading diagnosis and improvement, RtI insists that identifying a problem early on and doing something to ameliorate it better ensures that students will continue to progress in reading. And, as discussed in Chapters 5, 7, and 8, there are numerous reading assessment techniques

[1]These terms are adapted from Ruth Strang, *Diagnostic Teaching of Reading*, 2nd ed. (New York: McGraw-Hill, 1969).

teachers can use to identify student strengths and needs beginning in kindergarten. Each technique is accompanied by teaching suggestions that will assist teachers with planning appropriate instruction.

## WHAT IS BALANCED READING?

Balanced reading is defined in many different ways. We view it as a program that incorporates various philosophies, teaching strategies, and materials to achieve the best possible reading instruction for children.

Balanced reading programs are concerned with early intervention and with helping students gain the skills that they need to become effective readers as quickly as possible. Balanced reading programs are designed to help students improve their higher-order thinking skills, as well as gain needed comprehension and word recognition skills and strategies. Teachers also use these programs to nurture in their students a love of books that will help them become lifelong readers. A good reading diagnosis and improvement program includes a balanced reading program.

A balanced reading diagnosis and improvement program can help to stop the "failure cycle." If children continually have reading difficulties, they begin to see themselves as failures, destroying their self-concept. The more they perceive themselves as failures, the more they fail. And so the cycle continues.

Instead, teachers must help to create a success cycle (Cullinan, 2000). The basic idea is that the more students read, the more their reading ability improves and the more they enjoy the reading experience. Because students enjoy the experience, they will spend more time reading.

##  SCENARIO: BALANCED READING

Ms. Hill has a balanced reading program in her classroom. Let's look at what she does.

Ms. Hill uses explicit teaching, that is, she presents an intentional program designed to teach skills and strategies. She realizes that just reading aloud to the children is not enough. She teaches phonics skills systematically because she believes in a sequential development of this skill. When appropriate, she also teaches spelling generalizations and vocabulary skills.

For those children who have difficulty with phonics, she uses a whole word approach. Ms. Hill uses many different approaches. Her goal is to help her students become good, strategic readers; consequently, she presents them with word recognition and comprehension strategies. She incorporates a program that uses both oral and silent reading. She models oral reading for her students to help them gain and recognize good adult reading fluency.

A good balanced reading program helps her students become lifelong readers.

## WHAT IS DEVELOPMENTAL READING?

**Developmental reading**
Reading skills and strategies that are systematically and sequentially developed to help students become effective readers.

In our view, *developmental reading* refers to all those reading skills and strategies that are systematically and sequentially developed to help students become effective readers throughout their schooling. "All those reading skills and strategies" refers to learning-to-read skills and strategies as well as reading-to-learn skills and strategies and reading for appreciation. Developmental reading is the major reading program, and the diagnostic improvement program that takes place in the regular classroom is part of the developmental reading program; all other programs are adjuncts to the developmental program.

## WHAT IS REMEDIAL READING?

**Remedial reading program**
Takes place inside or outside the regular classroom and is handled by special personnel.

*Remedial reading programs* can take place outside the regular classroom and are handled by special personnel such as a special reading teacher, a therapist, or a clinician. The special reading teacher usually works with students who have severe reading problems that cannot be handled in the regular classroom. The students are usually referred for help by the regular classroom teacher. Regardless of where the remedial instruction occurs, it dovetails into the developmental reading program.

For example, the prime purpose of the remedial reading program that takes place outside the regular classroom is to help students attain the developmental skills and strategies that they lack. This program is not a replacement for the student's classroom developmental instruction in reading; it is reading instruction that is given *in addition to* the reading instruction in the regular classroom; therefore, it must be related to or considered part of the developmental program. This is imperative because studies show that there is a consistent negative relationship between the time students spend in "pull-out" classes and reading.[2] Many times the "pull-out" program becomes the complete reading program for students with severe reading problems, and rather than spending more time, the students spend less time in reading. Also, if the remedial program is looked on as separate from the developmental reading program, there is usually a lack of congruence between the instruction of the regular classroom teacher and that of the remedial reading teacher. This lack of congruence can confuse children who are already struggling.[3]

## WHAT IS READING?

The relationship of reading to diagnosis is important in a reading diagnosis and improvement program. To fully understand this relationship, it is first essential to define reading. Clearly, the definition that we choose will influence both the instructional and diagnostic components of the program. For example, if we see reading as a total integrative process, diagnosis will also be seen as a total integrative process.

**Reading**
A dynamic, complex act that involves bringing meaning to and getting meaning from the printed page.

There is no single, set definition of reading. A broad definition is that *reading* is a dynamic, complex act that involves bringing to and getting meaning from the printed page. This definition implies that readers bring their backgrounds, experiences, and emotions into play. It further implies that students who are upset or physically ill will bring these feelings into the act of reading, and these feelings will influence their interpretative processes. Yet another implication is that a person well versed in the subject matter at hand will gain more from reading the material than someone less knowledgeable. For example, a student who is a good critical thinker will gain more from a critical passage than one who is not. A student who has strong dislikes will come away with different feelings and understandings than a student with strong likings related to a given text. Under a global (i.e., integrative) definition, a diagnosis acknowledges that a reading problem is often caused by multiple factors. Therefore, the diagnosis would include considerations of ecological (environmental), personal, and intellectual factors. Educational factors, as well as noneducational ones, are considered. A global definition also recognizes that not all children respond in the same way to either teachers or instruction. An atmosphere conducive to growth is important, as is the maxim that success breeds success. Diagnosis is looked on as continuous, as underlying prevention as well as remediation, and

[2]G. V. Glass and M. L. Smith, *Pull-Out in Compensatory Education*, paper prepared for Office of the Commissioner, U.S. Office of Education, 1977.

[3]See R. L. Allington and M. C. Shake, "Remedial Reading: Achieving Curricular Congruence in Classroom and Clinic," *The Reading Teacher* (March, 1986): 648–654.

as interwoven with instruction. The emphasis in diagnosis is on determining the child's reading problems and the conditions that contribute to them. This is the definition we advocate in this text. The following section further explains our view.

## HOW IS READING A TOTAL INTEGRATIVE PROCESS?

**Reading process**
Concerned with the affective, perceptual, and cognitive domains.

By using a broad or global definition of reading, we see reading as a total integrative process that starts with the reader and includes the affective, perceptual, and cognitive domains.

### The Affective Domain

**Affective domain**
Part of the reading process that involves an individual's feelings and emotions.

The *affective domain* includes our feelings and emotions. The way we feel greatly influences the way we look at stimuli on a field. It may distort our perception. For example, if we have adverse feelings about certain things, these feelings will influence how we interpret what we read. Our feelings also influence what we decide to read. Attitudes exert a directive and dynamic influence on both our readiness to respond to and our willingness to read a given text.

### The Perceptual Domain

**Perceptual domain**
Part of the reading process that depends on an individual's background of experiences in using the body's sensory receptors and interpreting sensory input.

The *perceptual domain* involves giving meaning to sensations and the ability to organize stimuli on a field. *Perception* is a cumulative process based on an individual's background of experiences in using the body's sensory receptors and interpreting the sensory input. If, for example, an individual's eyes are organically defective, perceptions involving sight will be distorted. In the act of reading, visual perception is a very important factor. Children need to be able to control their eyes so that they move from left to right across the page. Eye movements influence what the reader perceives.[4]

**Perception**
A cumulative process based on an individual's background of experiences. It is defined as giving meaning to sensations or the ability to organize stimuli on a field.

Although what we observe is never in exact accord with the actual physical stimuli,[5] we must be able to accurately decode the graphemic (written) representation of those stimuli. If readers have learned incorrect associations, this will affect their ability to read. For example, if a child reads the word *gip* for *pig* and is never shown the difference between these words, this may become part of his or her perceptions. Whether children perceive words as a whole, in parts, or as individual letters will also determine whether they will be good or poor readers. More mature readers are able to perceive more complex and extensive graphemic patterns as units. They are also able to give meaning to mutilated words such as

As noted above, the perceptual process is influenced by physiological factors as well as affective ones. Therefore, a person's biases toward a topic may result in deleting from, adding to, or distorting what is actually written.

### The Cognitive Domain

**Cognitive domain**
Hierarchy of objectives ranging from simplistic thinking skills to the more complex ones.

The *cognitive domain* includes the areas involving thinking. Under this umbrella we place all the comprehension skills (see Chapter 10). Persons who have difficulty thinking (the manipulation of symbolic representations) will have difficulty reading. Although the cognitive domain goes beyond the perceptual domain, it builds and depends on a firm perceptual base. That is, if readers have faulty perceptions, they will also have faulty concepts. (See Chapter 7 for a discussion of concept development.)

[4]Eric J. Paulson and Ann E. Freeman, *Insight from the Eyes* (Portsmouth, NH: Heinemann, 2003).

[5]Julian E. Hochberg, *Perception* (Englewood Cliffs, NJ: Prentice-Hall, 1964), p. 3.

**TABLE 1.1   Summary of Proficient and Less Proficient Reading Behaviors**

| *Proficient Reading Behaviors* | *Less Proficient Reading Behaviors* |
| --- | --- |
| Attempt to make what is read sound like language and make sense | Attempt to identify all of the words correctly |
| Monitor what is read for sense and coherence | Monitor what is read for correct letter/sound and word identification |
| Build meaning using the text, their purpose, and their background | Build meaning by attempting to identify the letters and words correctly |
| Use a variety of strategies when meaning breaks down: reread, rethink, read on and return if necessary, substitute, skip it, sound it out, seek assistance, use text aids (pictures, graphs, charts), ignore it, stop reading | Use a limited range of strategies when meaning breaks down: sound it out, skip it |
| Selectively sample the print; use a mixture of visual (print) and nonvisual (background) information | Use most of the visual (print) information |
| Use and integrate a variety of systems of language to create meaning | Rely heavily on graphemes, graphophonemics, and morphemes |
| Vary the manner in which texts are read based on purpose | Read all texts in a similar manner regardless of purpose |
| Typically correct one in three miscues | Typically correct one in twenty miscues |
| Attempt to correct miscues that affect meaning | Attempt to correct miscues that fail to resemble the word |
| "Chunk" what is read | Process letter by letter, which results in tunnel vision |

*Source:* Kucer, S. *Dimensions of Literacy: A Conceptual Base for Teaching Reading and Writing in School Settings,* 2nd ed. Mahwah, NJ: Erlbaum, 2005, p. 142.

**Metacognition**
Thinking critically about thinking; refers to students' knowledge about their thinking processes and ability to control them.

The findings of research on the brain and cognitive processes have implications for teaching and instruction. By regarding the brain as an active consumer of information, able to interpret and draw inferences as well as ignore or selectively attend to other information, the learner is "given a new, more important active role and responsibility in learning from instruction and teaching."[6]

Metacognition relates to the cognitive domain. The term *metacognition* is used "to refer to both students' knowledge about their own cognitive processes and their ability to control these processes."[7] It literally means thinking critically about thinking.

## WHAT ARE CHARACTERISTICS OF GOOD READERS?

Proficient readers have a large repertoire of strategies at their disposal, which they use to help them better comprehend the text at hand (see Table 1.1). The strategies they

[6]Merlin C. Wittrock, "Education and the Cognitive Processes of the Brain," *The National Society for the Study of Education Seventy-Seventh Yearbook,* Part II (1978), p. 101.

[7]Claire E. Weinstein and Richard E. Mayer, "The Teaching of Learning Strategies," *The Handbook of Research on Teaching,* 3rd ed. (1986), p. 323.

**TABLE 1.2  Explanations of Good Reader Attributes**

| Good Reader Attributes | Explanation |
| --- | --- |
| Active | Readers bring their own experiences to reading the text and to constructing meaning. They make predictions and make decisions such as what to read and reread, and when to slow down or speed up. |
| Purposeful | Readers have purposes in mind when they read a text. They then read with these purposes in mind. For example, they might choose to read for enjoyment or entertainment. At other times, they might read to discover specific details. |
| Evaluative | Readers evaluate what they are reading, asking themselves whether the text is meeting their initial purposes for reading it. They also evaluate the quality of the text and whether it is of value. They react to the text both emotionally and intellectually. Readers also evaluate their interaction with others in different instructional groupings as well as their ability to function as both leaders and followers in the group. |
| Thoughtful | Readers think about the text selection before, during, and after reading. *Before reading*, they think about what they might already know. *During reading*, they think about how the current text relates to what they already know. *After reading*, they think about what the text offered and formulate their interpretations of it. |
| Strategic | Readers use specific strategies such as predicting, monitoring, and visualizing to ensure that they are comprehending the text. |
| Persistent | Readers keep reading a text even when it might be rather difficult if they feel that the text is helping them to accomplish a set purpose. |
| Productive | Readers are productive in more than one way. For instance, they bring their own experiences to the text at hand to construct or *produce* their understanding of it. Because they are engaged with reading, they are more productive in terms of the amount of reading they do. |

*Source:* Adapted from Duke, N. K., and Pearson, P. D. "Effective Practices for Developing Reading Comprehension," in A. E. Farstrup and S. J. Samuels, eds., *What Research Has to Say about Reading Instruction*, 3rd ed. Newark, DE: International Reading Association, 2002, pp. 205–242.

employ will shift depending on their background for the text and the manner in which the text is written. If they have read and heard stories, for instance, they most likely have an understanding of story structure (i.e., the pattern used to write stories). This text structure poses few if any difficulties, so they are able to read with greater ease.

In essence, then, good readers are active, purposeful, evaluative, thoughtful, strategic, persistent, and productive.[8] We explain each of these attributes in Table 1.2. When you hear someone exclaim, "He is a good reader!" this is what it means.

But what do we do with children who do not carry this label? Can we teach them the "good reader" characteristics? Thanks to the work of several researchers who have designed metacognition training programs to explore this question, we know that the answer is "yes." But the characteristics must be explicitly taught; for whatever reason, less proficient readers do not acquire them with as little explicit instruction as do many of the good readers.

Regardless of a child's level of proficiency, helping all children to maximize their full potential as readers is more important than assigning a label, a view that is supported

[8]N. K. Duke and P. D. Pearson, "Effective Practices for Developing Reading Comprehension," in *What Research Has to Say about Reading Instruction,* 3rd ed., eds. A. E. Farstrup and S. J. Samuels (Newark, DE: International Reading Association, 2002), pp. 205–242.

by the Council for Exceptional Children.[9] Remember that the goal of a reading diagnosis and improvement program is to discover children's strengths and needs and to design appropriate instruction to address these. Put another way, children are always ready to learn something and our job as teachers is to figure out what that something is. Learning is what we're after. The success of education depends on adapting teaching to the individual differences among learners. That children vary is natural; what is unnatural is to assume that all children are the same.[10]

## WHAT ARE MODELS OF THE READING PROCESS?

**Top-down reading models**
Models that depend on reader's background of experiences and language ability in constructing meaning from the text.

**Bottom-up reading models**
Models that consider the reading process as one of grapheme-phoneme correspondences; code emphasis or subskill models.

**Interactive reading models**
Models that consider the top-down processing of information as dependent on the bottom-up processing, and vice versa.

The field of reading is replete with theories, and different catch phrases are sometimes assigned to the same general theories, further confusing those who try to understand the various theories. One area that has caused much disagreement and debate among reading theorists is that of beginning reading. Controversy has centered on whether the reading process is a holistic one (emphasis on meaning), that is, a *top-down model;* a subskill process (code emphasis), that is, a *bottom-up model;* and, more recently, whether it is an *interactive model.* The interactive model is somewhat but not entirely a combination of the top-down and bottom-up models in that both processes take place simultaneously depending on the difficulty of the material for the individual reader. (See Figure 1.1.)

Classroom practices are based on the theories that teachers embrace. Those who believe in a bottom-up model will emphasize decoding to the exclusion of meaning; those who believe primarily in a top-down model emphasize meaning. Those who believe in an interactive model will probably use a combination of both.

Reading theorists often tend to be exclusive; they promote their own theory and generally neglect others. The classroom teacher, however, need not accept an either-or dichotomy, but rather should seek a synthesis of all the elements that have proven workable; that is, the classroom teacher can take elements from each theory based on the individual needs of students. Good teachers realize that the reading process is very complex and that there are no simple answers.

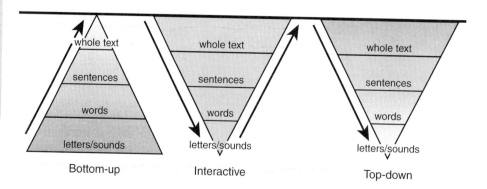

**FIGURE 1.1**    Models of Reading

[9]Council for Exceptional Children, *What Every Special Educator Must Know: Ethics, Standards, and Guidelines for Special Educators,* 5th ed. (Upper Saddle River, NJ: Pearson/Merrill/Prentice-Hall, 2003).

[10]A. Flurkey, "What's 'Normal' about Real Reading?" in *The Truth About DIBELS: What It Is and What It Does,* ed. K. Goodman (Portsmouth, NH: Heinemann, 2006), pp. 40–49.

# WHO ARE ENGLISH LANGUAGE LEARNERS?

English Language Learners are those who are fortunate to know a language other than English.[11] In fact, sometimes these learners may know more than one language. Regardless, the language they seek to acquire is English, hence the label *English Language* Learner. And just as with all learners, ELLs are constantly showing what they know and what they need to learn. There is much variability among them, which is not to be confused with disability.[12]

Researchers have identified different levels of language proficiency through which language learners progress.[13] Figure 1.2 draws on these initial delineations of levels as well as others' adaptations of them.[14] Through it, we show the levels as delineated in the TESOL standards,[15] and provide a brief description of each. Keep in mind that when learning a new language, any individual, regardless of age, progresses through these levels. To assume that the levels coincide with specific grade levels is problematic.

**FIGURE 1.2   Levels of Language Proficiency, Descriptions, and Implications**

| Levels of Language Proficiency | Description |
| --- | --- |
| Level 1: Starting | Students have a limited understanding of English. They may respond using nonverbal cues in an attempt to communicate basic needs. They begin to imitate others and use some single words or simple phrases. |
| Level 2: Emerging | Students are beginning to understand some phrases and simple sentences. They respond using memorized words and phrases. |
| Level 3: Developing | Students' listening comprehension improves, and they can understand written English. Students are fairly comfortable engaging in social conversations using simple sentences, but they are just beginning to develop their academic language proficiency. |
| Level 4: Expanding | Students understand and frequently use conversational English with relatively high accuracy. They are able to communicate their ideas in both oral and written contexts. They are also showing the ability to use academic vocabulary. |
| Level 5: Bridging | Students comprehend and engage in conversational and academic English with proficiency. They perform at or near grade level in reading, writing, and other content areas. |

[11]M. F. Opitz and L. M. Guccione, *Comprehension and English Language Learners: 25 Oral Reading Strategies That Cross Proficiency Levels* (Portsmouth, NH: Heinemann, 2009).

[12]C. Roller, *Variability, Not Disability* (Newark, DE: International Reading Association, 1996).

[13]S. Krashen and T. Terrell, *The Natural Approach: Language Acquisition in the Classroom* (Oxford: Pergamon, 1983).

[14]D. E. Freeman and Y. S. Freeman, *Teaching Reading in Multilingual Classrooms* (Portsmouth, NH: Heinemann, 2000). See also J. Kendal, and O. Khuon, *Making Sense: Small Group Comprehension Lessons for English Language Learners* (Portland, ME: Stenhouse, 2005).

[15]TESOL, *Pre-K-12 English Language Proficiency Standards* (Alexandria, VA: Teachers of English to Speakers of Other Languages, 2006).

Also problematic is seeing language learning as a linear process. As Freeman and Freeman[16] make clear, it is anything but. When using language in less formal settings, such as when having conversations with friends, ELLs may demonstrate that they have acquired Basic Interpersonal Communicative Skills (BICS) and be functioning at level 5 (bridging), an advanced level of language acquisition. However, these same learners can and do have difficulty using language in more formal settings, such as school, where they may demonstrate that they are functioning at level 3 (developing), the middle level of language proficiency. They need assistance in acquiring academic language. In other words, these ELLs need help in acquiring Cognitive Academic Language Proficiency (CALP). The same children who appear to be functioning at a given level in the classroom are instead functioning at different levels depending on how they are called on to use language.

## WHAT ARE AGES AND STAGES OF LITERACY DEVELOPMENT?

Reading ability continues to develop throughout life. For that matter, so do writing, speaking, and listening abilities. In fact, we might say that reading ability grows with exposure to oral language and print. In general, children at given ages share common characteristics in terms of reading and writing abilities. Different reading researchers and educators cast these characteristics into stages of growth (e.g., Chall, 1983; International Reading Association and the National Association for the Education of Young Children, 1998; Cooper & Kiger, 2005) to help teachers determine who is displaying age-appropriate reading behaviors.[17] Knowing some of these behaviors can also be extremely helpful in trying to determine who might need further assistance with learning to speak, listen, read, or write.

Table 1.3 shows the stages of literacy growth and some of their descriptors. Keep in mind that stages can overlap and that students rarely display every characteristic of one stage before they move into another. Many of the characteristics stay the same from stage to stage, but they become more sophisticated. Also, as when anyone is learning something new, there can be plateaus. So, while the table shows a neat linear process that happens in a smooth tempo, in reality the tempo is more halting at times.

**TABLE 1.3   Stages and Descriptors of Literacy Growth**

| Stage | Brief Description | Sample Benchmarks |
| --- | --- | --- |
| *Early Emergent* | Viewed as a foundation on which children develop oral language and a curiosity about print. | • Attends to read-alouds |
| Typically before kindergarten | | • Uses oral language for different purposes<br>• Likes playing with movable or magnetic letters<br>• Knows several nursery rhymes<br>• Uses paper and writing utensils to attempt writing |
| *Emergent Literacy* | Children show more interest in all aspects of literacy. | • Retains oral directions<br>• Enjoys tongue twisters |

---

[16]D. E. Freeman and Y. S. Freeman, *English Language Learners: The Essential Guide* (New York: Scholastic, 2007).

[17]Jean Chall, *Stages of Reading Development* (New York: McGraw-Hill, 1983). International Reading Association and the National Association for the Education of Young Children, "Learning to Read and Write: Developmentally Appropriate Practices for Young Children," *The Reading Teacher*, 52 (1998): 193–216. J. D. Cooper and N. Kiger, *Literacy Assessment: Helping Teachers Plan Instruction,* 2nd ed. (Boston: Houghton Mifflin, 2005).

**TABLE 1.3**

| Stage | Brief Description | Sample Benchmarks |
|---|---|---|
| Typically kindergarten; may overlap into the beginning of first grade | | • Knows some concepts about print such as book parts, word boundaries, and how to handle a book<br>• Recognizes and names most letters<br>• Shows evidence of being phonemically aware<br>• Can write own name<br>• Uses some punctuation |
| *Beginning Reading and Writing* | Oral language facility expands. Children develop word analysis skills, start to show fluency in reading and increased understanding of many words. Their writing begins to follow print conventions. | • Uses increased oral vocabulary<br>• Participates in discussions |
| Typically first grade; continues into second and third grade for some | | • Recognizes and names all letters in any order<br>• Identifies many sight words<br>• Uses phonics to determine word pronunciation<br>• Uses a variety of comprehension strategies<br>• Reads and retells stories<br>• Enjoys writing<br>• Uses a computer to write |
| *Almost Proficient Reading and Writing* | Children grow in their understanding of literacy. Oral language shows increased vocabulary, writing is more frequent, and silent reading increases. | • Grows in use of standard English<br>• Uses new oral vocabulary<br>• Uses context to determine word meaning |
| Typically begins at end of second grade and continues into fourth or fifth grade | | • Self-corrects<br>• Reads independently<br>• Reads for many purposes<br>• Begins learning research skills<br>• Writes for many purposes<br>• Writing conventions show growth<br>• Chooses to write in free time |
| *Proficient Reading and Writing* | Children use reading and writing for a variety of purposes. The majority of skills are acquired and used as appropriate. | • Listens to presentations with understanding<br>• Uses oral language for a variety of purposes<br>• Seldom needs help with word recognition |
| Typically begins in fourth grade and continues through life. | | • Uses several comprehension strategies<br>• Enjoys reading<br>• Writes for many purposes<br>• Edits own writing<br>• Experiments with different writing forms |

*Source:* Adapted from Cooper & Kiger, *Literacy Assessment: Helping Teachers Plan Instruction.* Boston, MA: Houghton Mifflin, 2005.

# REVISITING THE OPENING SCENARIO

Ms. Johnson plans a one-on-one conference with a student to elicit the child's perception of his strengths and needs. Ms. Johnson also contacts the parents to discuss with them what is taking place and to solicit their help. She believes strongly that parents should be partners in their children's school learning and that their help and support are important and needed. Using what you have learned in this chapter about reading and readers, decide what will help Ms. Johnson in her student conference and in the parent conversation.

# AUTHORS' SUMMARY

Chapter 1 is an introduction to a reading diagnosis and improvement program that includes balanced, developmental, and remedial perspectives. How a teacher defines reading has a direct impact on the reading diagnosis and improvement program. Defining reading as a total integrative process involves attention to the affective, perceptual, and cognitive domains. Knowing the characteristics of proficient and less proficient readers helps teachers to focus on desired behaviors of readers. Models of reading show teachers how their definitions of reading influence their programs.

# SUGGESTIONS FOR THOUGHT QUESTIONS AND ACTIVITIES

1. You have been assigned to a special committee to develop a reading program in your school that would help reduce the number of reading problems that now exist. You have decided to advocate the implementation of a reading diagnosis and improvement program. Give your rationale for doing so. How would you go about implementing such a program?

2. Ask a number of teachers how they define reading. Observe their classes and try to discern whether their reading program reflects their stated definition of reading. Discuss whether your observations show top-down, bottom-up, or interactive models of reading.

3. Observe teachers to ascertain how their reading program is balanced, according to the definitions of reading and the explanation of balanced reading in this chapter.

4. Use Table 1.1, "Summary of Proficient and Less Proficient Reading Behaviors," to observe a reader. Highlight the characteristics you notice and provide an example of what you see.

# WEB SITES

http://www.readwritethink.org/resources/index.asp

A partnership between the International Reading Association (IRA) and the National Council of Teachers of English (NCTE), this site provides professional resources.

http://www.readingonline.org/newliteracies/lit_index
.asp?HREF=/newliteracies/jaal/5-04_column_lit/

The electronic journal of the International Reading Association provided this article that explores what it means to be a reader. The author identifies and discusses various types of readers. This article will help teachers (pre-service or in-service) to gain awareness of the various readers they will/do encounter every day. An IRA membership is required to access this web site.

http://www.ncrel.org/sdrs/areas/issues/content/
cntareas/reading/li7lk1.htm

This site provides a definition of reading. See how well your personal definition coincides with that of the authors and then think about the implications of the similarities and differences between your definition and the one on this site.

http://www.sedl.org/reading/framework/

Providing a cognitive framework for reading comprehension, this site offers information on cognitive elements of reading, a glossary of reading terms, instructional resources, research, and much more.

## SELECTED BIBLIOGRAPHY

Allington, Richard L., and Mary C. Shake. "Remedial Reading: Achieving Curricular Congruence in Classroom and Clinic." *The Reading Teacher* (March, 1986): 648–654.

Anderson, Richard C., Elfrieda H. Hiebert, Judith A. Scott, and Ian A. G. Wilkinson. *Becoming a Nation of Readers.* Washington, DC: National Institute of Education, 1985.

Cullinan, Bernice. *Read to Me: Raising Kids Who Love to Read.* Rev. ed. New York: Scholastic, 2000.

Harris, Albert J., and Edward R. Sipay. *How to Increase Reading Ability*, 9th ed. New York: Longman, 1990.

Johnston, Peter H., Richard Allington, and Peter Afflerbach. "The Congruence of Classroom and Remedial Reading Instruction." *Elementary School Journal* 85, no. 4: 465–477.

Paulson, Eric J., and Ann E. Freeman. *Insight from the Eyes: The Science of Effective Reading Instruction.* Portsmouth, NH: Heinemann, 2003.

Pinnell, Gay Su, Mary D. Fried, and Rose Mary Estice. "Reading Recovery: Learning How to Make a Difference." *The Reading Teacher* 43 (January 1990): 282–295.

Samuels, S. Jay, and Michael L. Kamil, "Models of the Reading Process." In *Handbook of Reading Research,* Vol. I, edited by P. D. Pearson, R. Barr, M. K. Kamil, and P. Mosenthal. Mahwah, NJ: Lawrence Erlbaum, 2000.

Snow, Catherine E. et al., eds. *Preventing Reading Difficulties in Young Children.* Washington, DC: National Academic Press, 1998.

Wittrock, Merlin C. "Learning and the Brain." In *The Brain and Psychology*, edited by Merlin C. Wittrock, New York: Academic Press, 1980.

Now go to Topic 11: "Reading Difficulties and Intervention Strategies" in MyEducationLab (www.myeducationlab.com) for your course, where you can:

- Find learning outcomes for "Reading Difficulties and Intervention Strategies" along with national standards that connect to these outcomes.
- Complete Assignments and Activities that can help you more deeply understand the chapter content.
- Examine challenging situations and cases presented in the IRIS Center Resources.
- Access video clips of CCSSO National Teacher of the Year award winners responding to the question, "Why Do I Teach?" in the Teacher Talk section.
- Apply and practice your understanding of the core teaching skills identified in the chapter with Building Teaching Skills and Dispositions learning units.

# 2

**CHAPTER OUTLINE**

- Scenarios: Extremes Don't Work!
- The Role of the Teacher in Reading Diagnosis and Improvement
- The Teacher as the Key to a Good Reading Program
- Characteristics and Practices of Good Reading Teachers
- Teacher Expectations
- Four Teacher Roles
- Revisiting the Opening Scenarios

# Teaching for Reading Diagnosis and Improvement

# SCENARIOS: EXTREMES DON'T WORK!

## Scenario 1

Mrs. Brown, the mother of Lisa, a first grader in Ms. Clay's class, noticed that her daughter was bringing home books that she could not read independently. She told her child that she liked reading to her but that she wanted Lisa to read to her sometimes. She asked Lisa to bring home two books the next time—one that she wanted her mom to read to her and one that she could read on her own. The next week, Lisa brought home two books. When Lisa was reading her book aloud, Mrs. Brown noticed that it sounded as though Lisa had memorized the story. Mrs. Brown tested her theory by taking a number of the story's words out of the context of the book and asking Lisa to read them. What she suspected was true. Lisa had memorized the story, but was unable to identify the words out of context. Was this natural for beginning readers? Mrs. Brown didn't know, so she scheduled an appointment with Ms. Clay to discuss Lisa's reading program.

Ms. Clay told Mrs. Brown she believes strongly that if she immerses her first graders in lots of print, they will learn to read. She said that she first reads a story aloud to them and then has the whole class read the story aloud in unison, while she plays a tape of the story. She has her students do this many times. She uses trade books—that is, library books—in class, and for independent reading, she allows children to choose whatever book they would like to read. She said that she doesn't believe in explicit instruction. She felt that a teacher should be a guide or facilitator. "After all," she asked, "would you rather have 'beguiling stories' or 'drill'?" Ms. Clay assured Mrs. Brown that Lisa was learning to read.

Do you agree with the way Ms. Clay is using her views on explicit instruction to teach Lisa to read? Do you think she has an adequate understanding of explicit instruction?

## Scenario 2

Rachael started the third grade reading very well. According to her test scores, she was at grade level. Consequently, she was confused because she didn't understand why her teacher, Ms. Graves, kept having her read with children who appeared to be struggling. She started to dislike reading.

Toward the end of March, Rachael came home hysterical. Ms. Graves was sending her and her whole group to the "resource room" with a special reading teacher while the other groups stayed in the regular classroom and had reading with Ms. Graves. Rachael's mother phoned the teacher to find out what was happening.

Ms. Graves said that the children would be taking the standardized achievement tests soon and she feared that Rachael would not do well in reading, so she wanted her to go to the resource room for extra help with reading. Rachael's mother explained that her daughter was very upset about going out of the classroom and asked why Ms. Graves couldn't give her the help she needed in the regular classroom. Ms. Graves said that Rachael's whole group was going to the resource room and if Rachael didn't go, she'd be the only one left from her group. Obviously, she did not have the time to work with Rachael. Rachael's mother said that she would be happy to come in and work with her daughter if Ms. Graves would tell her what to do. She explained that her daughter was very, very upset and did not want to go out of the classroom to the "dummy" room. Ms. Graves said that under no circumstances could she come to class and work with Rachael.

Meanwhile, Rachael was becoming more and more upset. In the mornings she would have dreadful stomachaches. At times she would cry and beg her mother to let her stay home. She said that she felt like a dummy and she couldn't do the work. Rachael's mother wondered how a cheery, happy little girl who loved school and reading could change so radically.

Do you agree with the way Ms. Graves is handling Rachael and her mother? If you were Ms. Graves, would you have sent Rachael to the "resource room"? For that matter, would you have sent a whole group to the "resource room"? What insights can you draw from this scenario about Ms. Graves's ability as a reading teacher? How might Ms. Graves's attitude toward Rachael be affecting Rachael?

In this chapter we discuss the teacher's role in reading diagnosis and improvement and focus on the characteristics of a good reading teacher in the regular classroom.

## CHAPTER OBJECTIVES

After reading the chapter you should be able to:

- Describe the kinds of skills that teachers need to implement a reading diagnosis and improvement program.
- Describe the characteristics of a good reading teacher.
- Discuss what is meant by *self-fulfilling prophecy.*
- Explain the four roles of a reading teacher: *planning, explicit instruction, organization and management,* and *self-assessment.*
- Discuss why and how a teacher can use self-assessment.

## THE ROLE OF THE TEACHER IN READING DIAGNOSIS AND IMPROVEMENT

The role of a teacher in a reading diagnosis and improvement program is complex. The teacher must observe individual children, understand individual differences and the factors that influence them, build readiness for reading at various reading levels, identify children who are having reading difficulties, combine diagnosis and improvement with everyday reading, and help children gain an appreciation of reading. Teachers must have knowledge of the various word recognition and comprehension skills and strategies at their fingertips and be able to teach them effectively. They must know observation techniques and be aware of the factors that influence children's reading behaviors. Teachers must be able to administer and interpret a variety of assessments such as informal reading inventories and word analysis tests. If teachers are not able to construct their own informal diagnostic tests, they should be aware of those that are commercially available. Clearly, teachers in a reading diagnosis and improvement program must be well prepared and well informed.

## THE TEACHER AS THE KEY TO A GOOD READING PROGRAM

Although a school may have the best equipment, the most advanced school facility, a superior curriculum, and children who want to learn, "good teachers" are crucial for the desired kind of learning to take place. With today's emphasis on accountability, the spotlight is even more sharply focused on the teacher. Although there is no definitive agreement on how to evaluate teachers, researchers and educators agree that teachers influence students' behavior and learning.

Researchers have discovered that it is difficult to compare different methods or sets of materials and that students seem to learn to read from a variety of materials and methods.[1] More important, researchers consistently point to the teacher as the key to improving reading instruction. For example, the authors of *Becoming a Nation of Readers* state that "studies indicate that about 15 percent of the variation among children in reading achievement at the end of the school year is attributable to factors that relate to the skill and effectiveness of the teacher."[2] In contrast, "the largest study ever done comparing approaches to beginning reading found that about 3 percent of the variation in reading achievement at the end of the first grade was attributable to the overall approach of the program."[3] The teacher is the key to improving reading instruction:

> The main lesson, it seems to me, is that the teacher is of tremendous importance in preventing and treating children's reading and learning disabilities . . . good teaching is probably the best way to help children.[4]

Most professional reading organizations, educators, and the public at large agree that the teacher is the key to improved instruction. While the precise factors may vary according to grade level and individual students, effective reading teachers share some general qualities.[5]

For example, researchers on teacher dispositions have found that effective teachers tend to:

- Perceive others as competent and able to solve their own problems.
- Perceive themselves as identified with their students, sharing in success and failure.
- Have a broad sense of purpose that goes beyond the immediate events or requirements.
- Keep a frame of reference on people and their overall well-being as opposed to orienting themselves based on content objectives, tasks, and requirements.

The National Center for Research on Teacher Learning (NCRTL) identified three basic abilities today's schools demand of their best teachers:[6]

- Good teachers know how to identify and work on changing assumptions and beliefs they hold about teaching and learning.
- Good teachers work to improve their knowledge of content and their knowledge of how to teach diverse learners.
- Good teachers learn to reason and reflect on their work while they are doing it.

Notice how some of these general characteristics appear more specifically in the next section, which describes research on good reading teachers.

---

[1]Guy L. Bond and Robert Dykstra, "The Cooperative Research Program in First-Grade Reading Instruction," *Reading Research Quarterly* 2 (Summer 1967): 1–142. Albert J. Harris and Coleman Morrison, "The CRAFT Project: A Final Report," *The Reading Teacher* 22 (January 1969): 335–340.

[2]Richard C. Anderson, Elfrieda H. Hiebert, Judith A. Scott, and Ian A. G. Wilkinson, *Becoming a Nation of Readers* (Washington, DC: National Institute of Education, 1985), p. 85.

[3]Ibid.

[4]Jeanne Chall, "A Decade of Research on Reading and Learning Disabilities," *What Research Has to Say about Reading Instruction* (Newark, DE: International Reading Association, 1978), pp. 39, 40.

[5]M. Waczisko, "The Perceptual Approach to Teacher Dispositions: The Effective Teacher as an Effective Person," in *Dispositions in Teacher Education,* eds. M. E. Diez and J. D. Raths (Charlotte, NC: Information Age Publishing, 2007), pp. 53–89.

[6]National Center for Research on Teacher Learning (NCRTL), "About the NCRTL," http://www.nctrl.org (accessed October 12, 2009).

# CHARACTERISTICS AND PRACTICES OF GOOD READING TEACHERS

Go to the Assignments and Activities section of Topic 1: Reading Instruction in the MyEducationLab for your course and complete the activity entitled "Students to Students: Ups and Downs of Teaching." As you watch the video and answer the accompanying questions, think of questions you might like to ask these teachers.

Reading researchers have identified the practices and beliefs of teachers whose students demonstrated the highest reading achievement. For example, among first-grade teachers, eight characteristics have emerged:

1. Coherent and thorough integration of skills with high-quality reading and writing experiences.
2. A high density of instruction (i.e., integration of multiple goals in a single lesson).
3. Extensive use of scaffolding (i.e., support).
4. Encouragement of student self-regulation (i.e., solving their own problems).
5. A thorough integration of reading and writing activities.
6. High expectations for all students.
7. Masterful classroom management.
8. An awareness of their practices and the goals underlying them.[7]

In research among fourth-grade teachers, the following eight characteristics of exemplary teachers emerged:

1. Extensive reading.
2. Diverse grouping patterns.
3. Attention to skills.
4. Background development.
5. Writing instruction.
6. Diverse assessments.
7. Content integration.
8. Attention to motivation.

While these lists look rather different on the surface, what they have in common is that teachers who are deliberate about content, instruction, and individual students' strengths and needs are likely to use effective practices to maximize students' reading potential.[8]

Since some investigators suggest that teachers who have a good educational background and verbal ability are usually better teachers than those who do not, teachers should constantly be improving their own background and skills in reading.[9] A good place to begin would be to look at the characteristics listed above. For example, a teacher who learns to be more attentive to the affective domain is in a better position to motivate students.

## ONGOING TEACHER IMPROVEMENT IN READING

A four-and-a-half-year study measuring the reading skills of almost 350 teachers led researchers to conclude that practicing teachers do have room for improvement in their own reading skills.[10, 11] This finding sets an agenda for ongoing, lifelong learning for

---

[7] R. Wharton-McDonald, M. Pressley, and J. Hampston, "Literacy Instruction in Nine First-Grade Classrooms: Teacher Characteristics and Student Achievements," *The Elementary School Journal* 99 (1998): 101–128.

[8] Richard Allington and Peter Johnson, eds., *Reading to Learn: Lessons from Exemplary Classrooms* (New York: Guilford, 2002).

[9] Charles E. Bidwell and John D. Kasarda, "School District Organization and Student Achievement," *American Sociological Review* 40 (February, 1975): 55–70. Eric Hanushek, "The Production of Education, Teacher Quality and Efficiency," paper presented at the Bureau of Educational Personnel Development Conference, How Do Teachers Make a Difference?, Washington, DC.

[10] Lance M. Gentile and Merna McMillan, "Some of Our Students' Teachers Can't Read Either," *Journal of Reading* 21 (November, 1977): 146.

[11] Eunice N. Askov, et al., "Study Skill Mastery among Elementary School Teachers," *The Reading Teacher* 30 (February, 1977): 485–488.

reading teachers. New literacies continue to emerge, changing the priorities of what kind of reading is valued and the ways readers engage with different kinds of texts. For example, teachers who know how texting works (with mobile phones and instant messaging) are better equipped to understand the literacy their their students voluntarily participate in. A second example is the way magazines encourage readers to browse for information and read in a circular fashion, rather than reading from start to finish. Yet another example is the process of reading cybertext, with its links, menus, sidebars, and other ways to leave the current page in search of connections. And yet, despite these new developments, novels and other conventional texts are still immensely important. Novels, for example, are one of the best ways to encourage reading stamina—the ability to stick with a text, to build a larger picture of comprehension, and to make complex connections. While we all want to become better readers for our own sakes, we also know that when we energize our own minds, we provide models for our students to do the same.

Another researcher found that teachers scored low on tests of study skills intended for children completing elementary or junior high school. If teachers feel insecure about a subject, they will tend to avoid teaching it, and when they do cover it, they may rely on packaged materials rather than their own knowledge. If teachers lack a broad vocabulary, are unable to read critically, and have not acquired study skills, their students will suffer. How can teachers construct questions that challenge students' higher levels of thinking if they lack the ability to read at high levels of comprehension themselves? They can't. How can teachers diagnose students' problems if they do not know what skills the students are supposed to have? They can't. How can teachers instill a love of books in students if they themselves do not enjoy reading? They can't. If students perceive their teachers as not placing a high value on reading, they may not value it either. The reverse is also true. (Chapters 9–13 present reading skills that teachers should have at their fingertips and ways teachers can interest their students in books.)

## TEACHER EXPECTATIONS

**Self-fulfilling prophecy**
Teacher assumptions about children become true, at least in part, because of the attitude of the teachers, which in turn becomes part of the children's self-concept.

A positive expectation of good reading teachers is that all children can read age-appropriate texts if they are provided with the support they need for that text. The more teachers know about their students, the better able they are to plan for them. Teachers influence students' learning through their expectations about students' abilities.[12] Teachers must always be mindful of the *self-fulfilling prophecy*—where assumptions about children become true, at least in part, because of teacher attitudes and because of the structure of schooling itself (e.g., ability grouping, curriculum mandates, high-stakes testing). Over time, these kinds of hidden assumptions define a child's reading identity and school career. Leigh Hall[13] found that a child's identity as a reader can actually override reading ability when he or she is working on authentic reading. Also, "the social consequences of failing to learn to read in the early grades are severe. Longitudinal studies find that disadvantaged third graders who have failed one or more grades and are reading below grade level are extremely unlikely to complete high school."[14] Rather than shape a child's identity by assuming that past scores or performance

[12]Robert Rosenthal and Lenore Jacobson, *Pygmalion in the Classroom* (New York: Holt, Rinehart and Winston, 1968). Douglas A. Pidgeon, *Expectation and Pupil Performance* (London: National Foundation for Educational Research, in England and Wales, 1970).

[13]Leigh Hall, *Improving Middle School Students' Ability to Understand, Apply, and Talk about Comprehension Strategies*, poster session presented at the International Reading Association Convention, Phoenix, AZ, 2009.

[14]Robert E. Slavin, Nancy L. Karweit, and Barbara M. Wasik, "Preventing Early School Failure: What Works," *Center for Research on Effective Schooling for Disadvantaged Students: The Johns Hopkins University,* February, 1992, http://www.successforall.org/_images/pdfs/preventfail.htm (accessed October, 2009).

on curriculum materials define a competent reader, a good reading teacher will start with a positive perception that all students are capable.

## FOUR TEACHER ROLES

Teaching is a complex behavior that requires teachers to perform different but related roles. We see the teacher as planner, explicit reading teacher, organizer and manager, and self-evaluator (see Figure 2.1). In the following sections, we explain each role.

### ROLE 1: PLANNER

*"I read the word problem but I still don't know if I am supposed to add or subtract,"* *John, a second-grade student in Bill's class, comments.*

*"Read it to me," Bill responds. As John reads, Bill notes that John reads the problem so quickly that he pays little attention to understanding the words that signal which mathematical operation to use. In fact, he miscues on a key word, saying "today" for the printed word "together." Once John is finished reading, Bill comments, "I think I see why you might not know what you are supposed to do to solve this problem, John. Try reading it to me again, but this time I want you to read it like you are talking to me to help me understand the problem. Please read it more slowly so that I can better understand." John begins rereading the text following Bill's advice and before he is finished, he smiles.*

*"Why the smile, John?" Bill asks.*

*"I know I am supposed to add because I see the words "and" and "all together,"* *John responds.*

*"So you figured out the problem by slowing down and paying attention to understanding what you are reading. It's not enough to read quickly, is it? What's most*

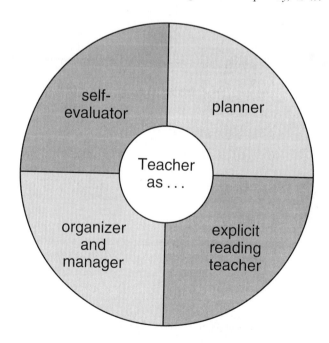

**FIGURE 2.1** Teacher Roles

*important is understanding what you read and this means that sometimes you need to read more slowly. And especially when reading word problems, you need to read every word just as it is printed."*[15]

*Mathematics word problem solved, John returns to his desk to complete the computation and to read and solve other word problems. But the reading problem is anything but resolved for Bill. He is pleased that John is aware of speed when reading because this is one aspect of fluency that he has been teaching his students. He is also pleased to see that John is able to detect where the understanding breaks down and that he uses appropriate fix-up strategies to take care of the problem.*

*But Bill also sees that he needs to help students like John to further understand how readers need to adjust the speed of reading according to the purpose for reading. He recognizes that in his future instruction, he needs to show students how to best use elements of fluency, not to mention comprehension, across all content areas including mathematics. In showing his students how fluency fits into the larger reading scheme and how reading extends to different content areas, in this case mathematics, Bill feels certain that his students will be better able to comprehend.*

Teachers in a reading diagnosis and improvement program must also be good planners. Planning helps guide teachers in making choices about instruction; clarifying their thinking about objectives; discerning their students' needs, interests, and developmental levels; and determining what motivating techniques to use.

The teacher in a reading diagnosis and improvement program bases instruction on continuous analysis of students' strengths and needs. The teacher is flexible and is always alert to student feedback to determine whether to proceed with instruction, slow down instruction, or stop to correct or clarify some misconception. In other words, the teacher uses *diagnostic teaching,* "the practice of systematic trial and evaluation of a variety of instructional strategies (including materials, methods of presentation, and methods of feedback) with individual students as part of their everyday educational program."[16] Teachers use a number of assessment instruments and techniques in such teaching, and they make whatever modifications they want based on feedback from their students.

The teacher in a reading diagnosis and improvement program must wisely plan time allotments for reading. And as Durkin (1993) noted nearly two decades ago, there are different ways to do just that. Sometimes the instruction will be *planned and intentional.* This is the type of instruction in which the teacher has designed a lesson that focuses on a specific reading skill or strategy. The lesson includes a specific objective, teaching procedures that will enable students to attain the objective, and an individual assessment that will help the teacher to determine how well the students learned the objective of the lesson.

*Unplanned, intentional* instruction is another way to plan time. This type of planning requires teachers to be responsive to what students are doing and to think on their feet. For example, sometimes students might show a misunderstanding of a topic through their oral responses. As a result, the teacher may decide to clear up any misunderstandings; this requires on-the-spot thinking of intentional ways to teach students in order to clear up their confusion. At other times, something might happen that will encourage the teacher to seize the moment to teach students. Take, for example, an experience I (Michael) encountered when the lights unexpectedly went out during the school day. The students lost all focus in the lesson I was conducting, so I decided to abandon it altogether. Instead, I used the occasion

**Diagnostic teaching**
The practice of continuously trying a variety of instructional strategies and materials based on the current needs of students.

[15]Adapted from Michael F. Opitz, *Don't Speed. READ! 12 Steps to Smart and Sensible Fluency Instruction,* (Michael F. Opitz, New York: Scholastic, 2007).

[16]John Salvia and James Ysseldyke, *Assessment in Special and Remedial Education,* 4th ed. (Boston: Houghton Mifflin, 1988), p. 525.

to teach something about electricity. I first had students talk about everyday objects that use electricity. I recorded their words on a semantic map using "electricity fuels objects" as the defined center, and we read the chart together. I then read them a book about electricity and had them compare our chart to what was mentioned in the book.

## ROLE 2: EXPLICIT READING TEACHER

Go to the Assignments and Activities section of Topic 4: Oral Language in the MyEducationLab for your course and complete the activity entitled "Language Experience Activity." As you watch the video and answer the accompanying questions, think about why a teacher would use this type of activity with students. What would students learn about how oral language connects with print?

*A teacher and five students in a fourth-grade class are engaged in a reading comprehension lesson. They are reading a trade book about the Civil War. They have been studying the Civil War, and this is a short novel depicting the lives of two different families during that period. Mr. Rojas, the teacher, prepares his students for the book by showing them a picture of President Lincoln reading the Gettysburg Address and using this as a stimulus to discuss what they have learned about the Civil War. He then presents some key vocabulary words that he feels students may need to read the chapter. Next he tells them that they will be acting as investigative reporters. Even though they had previously discussed what investigative reporters do, he wants to review it with them because he wants to read as if they are investigative reporters.*

*Today he will help them become better investigative reporters. He tells the students that before they return to their seats to read the first chapter silently, he wants to make sure they know how to collect information, especially if the information is not directly stated. Mr. Rojas hands out a short selection to each of the students and asks them to read it to try to determine how many soldiers had started out on the mission and in what direction they were headed. (None of the information is directly stated.) After the students finish reading the short selection, Mr. Rojas says that he will tell them how he figures out the answers. He tells them that he will "think out loud" to show them his thought process.*

*Mr. Rojas says that as he reads the selection to answer the first question, he notices some key information, namely, that the remaining one-third of the soldiers were exhausted. It also says that the nine remaining ones could not last much longer. From this information, he can determine that two-thirds have died or are missing. If nine equals one-third of the original number, then there were twenty-seven soldiers at the beginning of the special mission. The selection also states that the soldiers were walking toward the mountain range, and in another sentence it states that the sun was setting behind the mountain range. He says that he knows the sun rises in the east and sets in the west. Since the soldiers are walking toward the mountain range and the sun is setting behind the mountain range, they are heading west.*

*Mr. Rojas has students read another selection and has them answer questions based on information that is not directly stated. He asks for volunteers to explain how they went about answering the questions.*

*He then tells them that he wants them to go back to their seats and read silently the first chapter in their books. While they are reading, he wants them to collect evidence from this chapter to make some predictions about the two main characters introduced in the chapter and to record their predictions. He also lets them know that tomorrow they will discuss their predictions, and as they read the book, they will check to see what kind of thinking their predictions were based on.*

Mr. Rojas understands that most students need help in acquiring reading skills and strategies; they do not gain these through osmosis. The kind of instruction teachers use to teach reading explicitly will affect how well their students learn to read.

To help students become good readers, teachers must have metacognitive ability, so they know when to do what and how. In other words, they must know a number of teaching strategies and consistently monitor their teaching to help students become active consumers of information and good strategic readers.

Good teachers recognize that good readers interact with the text and bring their background of experiences to the act of reading. Good teachers also become part of the interactive process by using explicit instruction.

### What Is Explicit Instruction?

> **Explicit instruction**
>
> Instruction guided by a teacher, who uses various strategies to help students understand what they are reading.

*Explicit instruction* is guided by a teacher, who uses different kinds of strategies to help students gain understanding of what they are reading. There are several instructional strategies that teachers can use to teach reading explicitly, and the techniques teachers employ transcend the kinds of materials they use. For example, in one class, a teacher may use a published reading program, whereas in another, a teacher might use trade books, that is, library books. In yet another class, a teacher might use a combination of different printed matter including newspapers. All these teachers can still employ similar instructional strategies to help students achieve.

Explicit instruction requires the following:

1. Goals are well stated and activities are designed to accomplish these goals.
2. Students know what the goals are.
3. Students are given clear opportunities to learn.
4. Teachers assess and give prompt feedback.
5. Teachers arrange ways to assess and adjust to successes and failures at reaching goals.

As noted in the previous section, explicit instruction is most often planned and intentional.

## ROLE 3: ORGANIZER AND MANAGER

*One teacher and six children are engaged in reading at a round table. The rest of the class is involved in a variety of activities: a number of children are working individually at their seats or at learning centers; one child, sitting in a rocking chair, is reading; two children are working together; and a group of children are working together in the back of the room.*

*The teacher says to his group at the round table, "We've talked about what inference means, and we've given examples of it. Who can tell us what we mean by inference?" A few children raise their hands. Mr. Mills calls on one, and he gives an explanation of inference. "Good," says Mr. Mills. "Now, I'd like you to read the paragraph about Mr. Brown and then tell us what inferences you can make about Mr. Brown. Be prepared to support your inferences with evidence from the paragraph."*

*Mr. Mills looks at each of the children as they are reading. He then glances around the room. He says, "Judy, may I see you for a moment?" Judy comes to Mr. Mills. The teacher asks Judy in a very quiet tone if he can help her. He says, "Judy, you look confused. What's wrong?" Judy says that she is having trouble figuring out a question. Mr. Mills tells Judy to work on something else for about ten minutes, and then he will help her. As Judy goes back to her seat, Mr. Mills again quickly glances around the room. As his eyes meet those of some of the children, he smiles at them. Mr. Mills then looks at the children in his group. He sees that they are ready and asks them what inferences they can make about Mr. Brown. All raise their hands. Mr. Mills calls on one student, who makes an inference about Mr. Brown. Mr. Mills asks the rest of the group if they agree with the inference. Two students say that they do not agree. Mr. Mills asks everyone to skim the paragraph to find clues that would support their position. Mr. Mills again looks around the room. A child approaches and asks him a question. He answers the question and then goes back to the group. After a while, Mr. Mills and the group discuss whether they have accomplished what they were supposed to. They then discuss, for a moment, what they will be doing next time. They all go back to their seats. Before Mr. Mills calls another group, he checks off in his plan book the objectives that the group has accomplished. He also makes some remarks in his record book about the individual children in the group. Mr. Mills puts down his book and walks around the room to check on what the students are doing. He smiles at a number of the students, says "good" to some others, helps Judy with her problem, and listens in on the group that has been working together on a special project. Mr. Mills asks the group members how they are doing and how much more time they will need before they will be ready to report their progress to him and the class. Mr. Mills then goes back to the reading table and calls the next group.*

Go to the Assignments and Activities section of Topic 1: Reading Instruction in the MyEducationLab for your course and complete the activity entitled "Instructional Grouping: Guided Reading." As you watch the video and answer the accompanying questions, think about what information the teacher used to place children in this group. Also watch how she interacts with the children and how she has them interact with one another. Are all students provided time to read?

Experienced reading diagnosis and improvement teachers like Mr. Mills are good organizers and managers. They know how to work with large groups, small groups, the whole class, and individual students. As Table 2.1 shows, each type of grouping has advantages and disadvantages. When thinking about grouping students, teachers need to think through what they are using as a basis for grouping. Usually the basis for placement in reading groups is the student's achievement level. In this case, during the first few weeks of the term, teachers collect data concerning the achievement levels of each of the students in their classes through observation, teacher-made tests, and standardized tests. After evaluating the collected data, the teacher organizes tentative groups. The number of groups in a skill area depends on the amount of variability within the class. For some areas, there may be three or four groups; for some, there may only be two groups; for some, the teacher may decide to work with the whole class as a unit; and for some areas, the teacher may have a number of children working individually. The grouping pattern is flexible, and the groups themselves are recognized as flexible units; children can easily flow from one group to another. When the purpose for the group has been met, the group dissolves.

The teacher as a good manager is able to deal with more than one situation at a time. A teacher working with a group should be aware of what is going on not only in that group but also with the other children in the class. A teacher cannot "dismiss" the rest of the class because he or she is working with a particular group. Even though the children have been given challenging work based on their individual needs, the teacher must be alert to what is happening to ensure safety for all children and to keep children on task. The alert teacher is able to prevent problems. The scenario above about Role 3: Organizer and Manager presents an example of a good manager. Notice especially how Mr. Mills is able to manage a number of ongoing activities at the same time. Notice how he is always aware of what is going on in his class, and notice how he prevents problems from arising.

## ROLE 4: SELF-EVALUATOR

*Sarah decides to administer a word test to ascertain whether students have a store of words that they can identify instantaneously (i.e., sight words). When analyzing the results of the test, she discovers that according to this measure, several students appear to have a limited store of words. She decides to form a special needs group, placing all students who need to acquire more words into the group. Sarah then designs a lesson to teach the words she wants them to know. Several of the students have difficulty with the lesson as indicated by their inability to identify the words at the conclusion of the lesson and Sarah finds this troubling. Without a doubt, the lesson should have set students up for success and by the conclusion of it, all of the students should have been able to show that they accomplished the objective. Why didn't they? She takes a close look at her lesson to see if there is anything she might have done differently to help her students. Her examination helps her to see that the words she was trying to teach needed context because they are very abstract: is, the, of, was. Yet another look at the lesson helps her to see that students may have little or no understanding of how these words relate to reading texts. She had not provided them with time to read books that could have been selected with these words in mind. As a result of her analysis, Sarah realizes that she needs to redesign the lesson. Her self-assessment plays a role in helping students to succeed.*

**TABLE 2.1   Group Size for Guided Reading Experiences**

| Group Size | Description | Advantages | Disadvantages | When It Works |
|---|---|---|---|---|
| Whole Class | Teacher works with the whole class and everyone participates in similar activities. In one way or another, the same text is often read by all students. | • Builds a community of learners<br>• Provides a common knowledge base for all | • Differentiating instruction is more difficult<br>• Some students can get frustrated or bored depending on the level of instruction<br>• Students may not interact as planned | • Different learners are considered when planning instruction<br>• All members of the class are provided with a similar experience |
| Small Group | Groups of two to five students work together to accomplish a given task. | • Provides for focused instruction<br>• Engages more learners<br>• Students learn to work with one another | • Students may not interact<br>• Creates a higher noise level<br>• Students might be grouped together for too long<br>• Student perceptions of the group can be negative | • Group membership changes on a regular basis<br>• Students are taught how to respond to one another |
| Partners | Students are paired up with one another to read text in one or more ways. | • Students stay focused<br>• Enables relationships to develop<br>• Encourages independent learning so the teacher can help those who need it | • One of the two students may become too dependent on the other<br>• One of the two may dominate | • Partners are switched on a regular basis<br>• Procedures are clearly understood by both |
| Individual | Students work by themselves and each often reads a different text. | • Allows students to read at a comfortable level and to develop their own understandings<br>• Enables teacher to evaluate individual progress to determine what students know and need to know | • Can be hard to organize<br>• Students may become distracted and/or lose focus<br>• Little sense of community | • Reading is at the appropriate level<br>• Students understand procedures<br>• An effort is made to bring students back together either as a small or large group to discuss what they've learned |

---

**FIGURE 2.2    Human Relations Incidents for Assessing Teacher Dispositions**

---

**Write a Human Relations Incident** (HRI) from personal experience:
FIRST: Describe the situation as it occurred at the time.
SECOND: What did you do in the particular situation?
THIRD: How did you feel about the situation at the time you were experiencing it?
FOURTH: How do you feel about the situation now? Would you wish to change any part of it?

**Score incidents** - After you are familiar with the perceptual factors below and have written your own HRIs, infer your perceptual orientation on a scale similar to the one shown.

---

### Perception of Others

| *Able* | *Unable* |
|---|---|
| The teacher sees others as having the capacities to deal with their problems. S/He believes others are basically able to find adequate solutions to events in their own lives. | The teacher sees others as lacking the necessary capacities to deal effectively with their problems. S/He doubts their ability to make their own decisions and run their own lives. |

7    6    5    4    3    2    1

---

### Perception of Self

| *Identified* | *Unidentified* |
|---|---|
| The teacher feels a oneness with all people. S/He perceives him/herself as deeply and meaningfully related to persons of every description. | The teacher feels generally apart from others. His/her feelings of oneness are restricted to those of similar beliefs. |

7    6    5    4    3    2    1

---

### Sense of Purpose

| *Larger* | *Smaller* |
|---|---|
| The teacher views events in a broad perspective. His/her goals extend beyond the immediate to larger implications and contexts. | The teacher feels generally apart from others. His/her feelings of oneness are restricted to those of similar beliefs. |

7    6    5    4    3    2    1

---

### Frame of Reference

| *People* | *Things* |
|---|---|
| The teacher views events in a broad perspective. His/her goals extend beyond the immediate to larger implications and contexts. | The teacher views events in a narrow perspective. His/her purposes focus on immediate and specific goals. |

7    6    5    4    3    2    1

---

*Source:* From Waczisko, M. "The Perceptual Approach to Teacher Dispositions: The Effective Teacher as an Effective Person." In M. E. Diez and J. D. Raths, eds., *Dispositions in Teacher Education,* Charlotte, NC: Information Age Publishing 2007, pp 53–89.

Although the major goal of this text is to provide you with an understanding of the many ways to assess and evaluate children's reading growth, teacher self-assessment plays an important part in the diagnosis cycle. Taking time to reflect on lessons and how students perform can help you to measure the effectiveness of the lesson. Did all students attain the lesson objective? If not, why not? Asking questions such as these can illustrate that sometimes the problem resides with the teacher rather than with the student.

There are many ways to self-evaluate. Videotaping and reviewing lessons using specific criteria is one. Evaluating student performance is another. In addition, a checklist can be designed to help evaluate the entire diagnostic reading and improvement program in general. Another checklist can be constructed to reflect on reading lessons. In Figure 2.2 we provide a self-evaluation rubric for the beliefs and dispositions effective teachers bring to their work. Another method is to write notes on the lesson itself, either during the lesson or afterward. The underlying assumption is that there is a written plan for the lesson, which indicates that the teacher has thought through the lesson and the many associated considerations such as the students who will be receiving the lesson, the materials, and teaching strategies.

Figure 2.3 is an example of a checklist that can be used to look at the diagnostic reading and improvement program in general. Figure 2.4 shows a sample checklist that can be used to reflect on reading lessons. After reading each question, teachers using this checklist can rate themselves on a scale, with 1 being poor and 5 being excellent, and then write out any thoughts and/or ideas related to each question.

---

### FIGURE 2.3   All Children Survey

**"All children can learn in a system that respects their abilities."**
                                                                  **—C. Roller**

| *Statement* | *Yes* | *No* |
|---|---|---|
| 1. All children are provided the same amount of time to read authentic books and /or stories throughout the day. | | |
| 2. All children spend the same amount of time on skill/drill work. | | |
| 3. All children are permitted to read without interruptions. | | |
| 4. All children are expected to solve problems when reading. | | |
| 5. All children are provided time to solve problems when reading. | | |
| 6. All children are provided the same amount of time to read books during guided reading instruction. | | |
| 7. All children are provided many "just right" books. | | |
| 8. All children are engaged with high-level questions. | | |
| 9. All children preread silently before reading orally in front of a group. | | |
| 10. All children appear to enjoy reading. | | |
| 11. All children have the opportunity to self-select books. | | |
| 12. All children are provided time to read independently. | | |

*Source:* From *Flexible Grouping in Reading* by Michael Opitz. Published by Scholastic Teaching Resources/ Scholastic, Inc. Copyright © 1998 by Michael Opitz. Reprinted by permission.

---

**FIGURE 2.4**   **Sample Checklist for Teacher Self-Assessment of a Reading Lesson**

Reading Lesson: _____    Date: _____

| Question | Rating Scale | Thoughts / Ideas |
|---|---|---|
| 1. Did I capitalize on students' interests? | 1  2  3  4  5 | |
| 2. Was I enthusiastic about the lesson? | 1  2  3  4  5 | |
| 3. Was I clear in presenting the lesson objective? | 1  2  3  4  5 | |
| 4. Did all activities relate to the objective and did they progress from concrete to abstract? | 1  2  3  4  5 | |
| 5. Did I provide for individual differences? | 1  2  3  4  5 | |
| 6. Did my assessment of students align with the objective for the lesson? | 1  2  3  4  5 | |
| 7. Did I allow enough time for students to complete the activities under my guidance? | 1  2  3  4  5 | |
| 8. Did I use positive reinforcement? | 1  2  3  4  5 | |
| 9. Did I give specific feedback so that students knew how well they were progressing? | 1  2  3  4  5 | |
| 10. Did I alter the lesson as needed? | 1  2  3  4  5 | |

## REVISITING THE OPENING SCENARIOS

By now you should be able to answer the questions posed at the end of the introductory scenarios. Before reading our comments, take time to look at your answers. Then read our comments. Do you agree with them? Why or why not?

Ms. Clay's belief that explicit instruction and drill are synonymous is faulty. As noted earlier in this chapter, explicit instruction calls on the teacher to show students how to do a given task. It is much more than simply giving children practice with a particular skill or strategy. She needs to develop an understanding that most beginning readers need direct help in learning to read. She also needs to become aware of the many teaching strategies she can use to help students gain important word recognition, comprehension, and study skills. (See Chapters 10, 11, 12, and 13 for a review of these.)

To best help Lisa, Ms. Clay needs to use some explicit teaching. She should choose a few books at Lisa's independent reading level and then let Lisa choose one for independent reading. In addition, Ms. Clay should make sure the trade books she is using for reading instruction are based on graduated levels of difficulty; that is, each subsequent trade book should be more challenging than the preceding one. She also needs to encourage Lisa to do a lot of easy reading when reading independently.

Ms. Graves is also a teacher who needs to further understand effective teaching. She appears to be insensitive to Rachael's needs. If she had had a reading diagnosis and improvement program in her classroom, she would have been more likely to notice Rachael's reading strengths. Rather than send Rachael or her whole group to the "resource center," she would have worked with them in the regular classroom; she would understand the importance of making sure that all children feel that they are a part of one community. These children needed additional help and encouragement. She would have sought help from the special reading teacher and worked closely with Rachael's mother, as well as with the other parents. She would have created a nonthreatening atmosphere in which children feel they can learn and succeed—an atmosphere where the children are the center of the curriculum and tests are not used as ends in themselves.

## AUTHORS' SUMMARY

In this chapter, we focused on the characteristics of an effective teacher in a reading diagnosis and improvement program. The teacher is the person who needs to help children when they come to school, regardless of their backgrounds. The role of a teacher in a reading diagnosis and improvement program is multifaceted, so a good reading teacher is well prepared and well informed. We discussed research findings that show competent teachers are what make the difference, rather than materials or programs. Characteristics a good teacher of reading should have include knowledge of the content of reading, an ability to read, and positive expectations of and attitudes toward students. We called attention to the potential harm of the self-fulfilling prophecy. Teachers who accept and develop the four roles of planner, organizer and manager, explicit reading teacher, and self-evaluator recognize the complexity of teaching students in a reading diagnosis and improvement program.

## SUGGESTIONS FOR THOUGHT QUESTIONS AND ACTIVITIES

1. Think of one of the best teachers you have ever had. Discuss the characteristics of the teacher you remember best. Compare and contrast this teacher with other teachers you remember as being less effective.
2. Use the information in this chapter to create an observational checklist. Observe a teacher during a reading lesson, or videotape yourself teaching one. Check off all the characteristics you observe. What do you notice?
3. You have been assigned to a special committee that is concerned with teacher professional development. Based on your understanding of teacher characteristics and roles, what suggestions would you have for the committee?

## WEB SITES

http://www.k8accesscenter.org/training_resources/readingdifferentiation.asp

This site provides information on what differentiated instruction looks like from a reading perspective. The authors provide a great implementation guide addressing tiered planning that includes specific reading strategies, the focus of the differentiation, definition, and an example.

http://readingrockets.org/article/c64/

This site contains a definition of differentiated instruction pertaining to reading as well as articles geared toward defining this concept. The site includes an extensive annotated list of articles on the importance of differentiated instruction and various other relevant topics. The articles are geared toward teachers and parents. Each article also provides links to strategies and articles on related topics.

http://eduscapes.com/tap/topic43.htm

This site explores three different types of instructional approaches: project-based learning, problem-based learning, and inquiry-based learning. The authors provide various resources in each section, enabling teachers to choose which approach, or which combination thereof, might work in their specific classrooms.

http://www.readwritethink.org/lessons/index.asp

Providing a wealth of lesson plans centered on literacy, learning language, learning about language, and learning through language, this site enables teachers to search for lessons targeting specific grades (K–12) and literacy topics. The site also offers various student materials designed to enhance literacy learning and engagement.

http://www.teachervision.fen.com/classroom-man agement/curriculum-planning/6281.html?detoured=1

In addition to having an entire section on teaching methods, this site provides sections on standards for good teaching, adapting lessons for all students, multiple intelligences overview, and much more. Limited free access.

## SELECTED BIBLIOGRAPHY

Ashton-Warner, Sylvia. *Teacher.* New York: Simon & Schuster, 1963.

Baumann, James F., and Ann M. Duffy-Hester. "Making Sense of Classroom Worlds: Methodology in Teacher Research." In *Handbook of Reading Research,* Vol. III, edited by Michael L. Kamil, et al. Mahwah, N.J: Lawrence Erlbaum, 2000.

Donahue, Patricia L. et al., eds. *NAEP 1998 Reading Report Card for the Nation and the States.* Washington, DC: U.S. Department of Education, March 1999. http://nces.ed.gov/naep.

*Do Teachers Make a Difference?* Department of Health, Education and Welfare Report No. OE 58042. Washington, DC: U.S. Government Printing Office, 1970.

Durkin, Dolores. *Teaching Them to Read.* Boston: Allyn and Bacon, 1993.

Jackson, Phillip W. *Life in Classrooms.* New York: Teachers College Press, 1990.

Opitz, Michael. *Flexible Grouping in Reading: Practical Ways to Help All Students Become Better Readers.* New York: Scholastic, 1998.

Opitz, Michael, and Michael Ford. *Reaching Readers: Flexible and Innovative Strategies for Guided Reading.* Portsmouth, NH; Heinemann, 2001.

Report of the National Reading Panel: Teaching Children to Read. "Findings and Determinations of the National Reading Panel by Topic Areas," Bethesda, MD: National Institute of Child Health and Human Development, April 2000. www.nichd.nih.gov/publications/nrp/findings.htm.

Rosenthal, Robert, and Lenore Jacobson. *Pygmalion in the Classroom.* New York: Holt, Rinehart and Winston, 1968.

Woolfolk, Anita E. "Teachers, Teaching, and Educational Psychology," in *Educational Psychology,* 8th ed. Boston: Allyn and Bacon, 2001, pp. 2–21.

PEARSON
**myeducationlab**

Now go to Topic 1: "Reading Instruction" and Topic 4: "Oral Language" in MyEducationLab (www.myeducationlab.com) for your course, where you can:

- Find learning outcomes for "Reading Instruction" and "Oral Language" along with national standards that connect to these outcomes.
- Complete Assignments and Activities that can help you more deeply understand the chapter content.
- Access video clips of CCSSO National Teacher of the Year award winners responding to the question, "Why Do I Teach?" in the Teacher Talk section.
- Apply and practice your understanding of the core teaching skills identified in the chapter with Building Teaching Skills and Dispositions learning units.

# Developing a Knowledge Base about Assessment, Measurement, and Evaluation

## 3

### CHAPTER OUTLINE

- Scenario: Ms. Smith Learns about Assessment
- Testing in Reading Diagnosis
- Assessment, Measurement, and Evaluation
- Criteria for Good Tests
- Revisiting the Opening Scenario

## SCENARIO: MS. SMITH LEARNS ABOUT ASSESSMENT

Go to the Assignments and Activities section of Topic 2: Reading Assessment in the MyEducationLab for your course and complete the activity entitled "The Test, Part 1." As you watch the video and answer the accompanying questions, think about how the information applies to your experiences with being assessed with high-stakes tests.

Ms. Smith is a new teacher. She's excited about her job and wants to be the best teacher possible; however, she's a little overwhelmed and confused. At the orientation meeting at the beginning of the school term, the principal talked about the school district's testing program, and then the reading specialist talked about the various kinds of reading tests that the teachers were expected to give. They talked about norm-referenced tests, informal tests, and criterion-referenced tests. They also talked about group and individual tests. In addition, they mentioned performance-based tests and said that their school district personnel were committed to authentic assessment and that teachers would be hearing much more about this during the school year.

Toward the end of the meeting, two teachers raised their hands and said that they felt all standardized reading tests should be outlawed. The silence that followed was deafening. Then, as if on cue, everyone started talking at once.

Ms. Smith listened carefully to the heated debate between those who felt there should be no standardized testing and those who disagreed. Most teachers spoke harshly against the use of standardized reading achievement tests as high-stakes tests. Others claimed that these tests did not measure the kinds of behaviors they are supposed to.

Taking his cue from the teachers' discussion, the principal said that he was aware of the testing controversy. He then told them that there would be more rather than less testing because of the increased emphasis on accountability. He went on to say that their school district administration was always open to new ideas and change if changes were warranted. He also said that regardless of an individual's teaching position, all teachers must know what is taking place and be knowledgeable about the various types of tests being used in the school. He reminded the teachers that in a reading diagnosis and improvement program, they must know how to use various types of teacher-made and commercial tests to best assess their students' reading.

Ms. Smith recognized her lack of knowledge regarding assessment and decided to gain as much background information as possible.

## CHAPTER OBJECTIVES

After reading the chapter, you should be able to:

- Give a rationale for using tests in reading diagnosis.
- Describe some of the criteria of good tests.

## TESTING IN READING DIAGNOSIS

A good testing program tells part of a student's educational story. Such a program includes a variety of measurements such as student self-assessment, teacher-made tests, criterion-referenced standardized tests, and norm-referenced standardized tests. Reading is a complex behavior, and, as Ruth Strang noted years ago, "diagnosis is as complex as the reading process itself."[1] Without a doubt, a good testing program takes time, but it is time well spent when the goal is to help all children maximize their full reading potential. This is what a reading diagnosis and improvement program is all about. And a sound testing program that uses a variety of measures should help teachers to focus on individual improvement.

[1]Ruth Strang, *Diagnostic Teaching of Reading,* 2nd ed. (New York: McGraw Hill, 1969), p. 27.

One of the unfortunate byproducts of the high-accountability era has been that the terms "testing" and even "assessment" now feel synonymous with standardized tests and the accountability policies that accompany them. But in reading diagnosis, assessment and testing must encompass broader concepts that are more interesting and vital than those addressed by state tests. In this chapter we provide clear definitions, we discuss the purposes for different types of tests, and we begin the discussion with a classroom approach to testing.

## ASSESSMENT, MEASUREMENT, AND EVALUATION

Go to the Assignments and Activities section of Topic 2: Reading Assessment in the MyEducationLab for your course and complete the activity entitled "The Test, Part 2." As you watch the video and answer the accompanying questions, decide whether you would or would not use high-stakes tests given the choice.

**Assessment**
Asking questions about students' knowledge and skills, and the process of getting answers.

The terms *assessment, measurement, evaluation,* and *test* are often treated as synonyms. But they are not. This chapter is your chance to reclaim the testing process and make it work for you. We show these four terms as a hierarchy, with assessment as the primary category, measurement and evaluation underneath, and testing connecting to both measurement and evaluation (see Figure 3.1). We intend for Figure 3.1 to show that having good assessment questions is the starting point. They lead to measurement, or collection of evidence. Tests are common collection instruments. Teachers must evaluate test results and check their interpretation against their original assessment questions.

*Assessment* is a term with powerful potential. In everyday language it means figuring out what is going on. For example, when we walk into a room full of people, we assess the situation. When we are looking at buying a home, we might assess its condition or location. When someone bumps our fender, we get out and assess the damage. Assessment in school must preserve some of this everyday meaning: Assessment helps teachers figure out what students know, what skills they have, what they can do, and whether they are learning anything. Because knowing someone else's mind can be tricky, instruments of measurement and evaluation exist to help teachers gain confidence in what they know about students' minds. There are three basic questions in assessment:

- What do I want to know?
- Why do I want to know it?
- How can I discover this information with confidence?

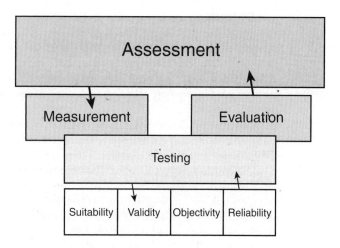

**FIGURE 3.1** Assessment Hierarchy

What makes answering the third question so difficult is that assessment uses a variety[2] of ways to measure and evaluate knowledge. Tests are a part of this larger process, all of which should lead us to confident statements about our students' minds.

*Measurement* is how educators obtain evidence to evaluate. It is parallel to evaluation in the hierarchy because without measurement, there would be no evidence to interpret (i.e., evaluate). The educational community leans heavily on the metaphors of scales and rulers. These are literally "instruments" of measurement. Once we have the evidence of putting something on a scale or laying down a tape measure, then we can begin to evaluate what its weight or length means to us. Usually when we are measuring something, we have a desired "fit" in mind, a plan or purpose—that is, we don't usually just walk around weighing and measuring things for no apparent reason. It should be so with educational assessment. First, we must decide *what* our goals are; second, we must consider *why* we value those goals; and third, we must decide *how* we might proceed toward attaining those goals. Any means we use to achieve these goals is an "instrument" of measurement. Measurement instruments are our answer to the question of the "how" of assessment. In tests, one type of measurement instrument, the emphasis is often on question/answer sequences as a means of figuring out what someone else knows. We find this narrow emphasis unfortunate. There are other important values in testing, which we discuss later in this chapter.

The positive values of measurement outweigh the negative connotations often associated with it. Measurement is useful for diagnostic, review, and predictive purposes. It can be used as a motivating technique for students, as well as a basis for discussing achievement with parents and other community members. Through ongoing measurement, teachers are also able to reevaluate their own teaching methods. Smart diagnosis means we puzzle out what data are needed and then figure out how to gather them. When planning to teach an individual student, tests are only a part of the assessment picture because they may not provide the kind of evidence we want or need. For example, if we want to know whether a past traumatic experience is still affecting a child's reading performance, we might use test data, but we would also use our own observations and reports from counseling and parent conferences, which are less easy to quantify.

In order for measurement to be an effective part of the evaluative process, teachers must know varied instruments and be able to select, administer, and interpret them. Such instruments include standardized tests and teacher-made tests. Direct observation of student behavior is also necessary in order to collect data for valid evaluations. These other assessment methods are discussed in more detail in Chapter 5.

*Evaluation* is the interpretation of evidence gathered through measurement. When we have gathered evidence with measurement instruments, we return to the assessment question of "what do we want to know?" and see whether the evidence provides a reasonable answer. The scores on a test are one type of evidence, but they mean nothing in and of themselves. They have to be interpreted with respect to *why* we used the test as a measurement in the first place and *what* we hoped to learn about our students. When we write our own tests, we can track student responses back to individual items and also look for trends across items. By contrast, most standardized test authors keep individual test items and participant responses private. Teachers rely on the testing company to score and provide a written interpretation of participant responses.

Evaluation involves passing personal judgment on the truthfulness, consistency, and validity of the evidence. Basic principles of test design are supposed to give us confidence when we finish gathering evidence and begin to interpret it. The *teacher* is the one who makes the diagnosis; no test can. Once again, it is the knowledgeable professional who is at the core of instruction that will lead to reading improvement.

**Measurement**
Ways of gathering evidence for evaluation.

**Evaluation**
Evaluation is interpreting evidence.

---

[2]W. James Popham, *Classroom Assessment: What Teachers Need to Know,* 2nd ed. (Boston: Allyn and Bacon, 1999), p. 2.

**Test**
An assigned set of tasks to be performed.

Society changes its demands on schools to produce knowledge and skills, (e.g., the standards movement of the past twenty years). This demand has created a crisis of confidence, and tests have been used and abused for a variety of reasons. Especially for reading diagnosis, a test's main worth is its usefulness in solving problems and creating a path to improvement for individual students.

A *test* is one way to provide evidence for evaluation. We use tests when other instruments do not give us confidence in what we know about our students. For example, we might have rich classroom discussions but still be worried that only some of the students are participating. A test is a way to give each individual a chance to provide evidence of knowledge. If previously silent students respond well on written tests, our confidence in their knowledge increases.

We might experience doubt when we try new methods or curricula, when our school is compared to other schools, or when our country is compared to other countries. We might even have doubts when we compare one student's skill to other students' skills. A variety of assessment methods, including tests, can help us alleviate these doubts and inspire confidence in our students' knowledge, abilities, and performance. One of the best reasons for using tests is that good test design provides us with confidence that the responses are good representations of students' thinking. Criteria for good tests are discussed below.

## CRITERIA FOR GOOD TESTS

Anne Anastasi wrote, "[T]he most effective tests are likely to be those developed for clearly defined purposes and for use within specified contexts."[3] We wholeheartedly agree. And, like Anastasi, we believe teachers must select a test that will help them to assess a specific aspect of the reading process. Usually, misuse of tests comes from taking evaluation out of context. Evaluation is meant to serve the purposes of assessment. One way to ensure appropriate selection is to ask and answer three assessment questions: What do I want to know? Why do I want to know? Which test will help me best discover this information? Test users must also be able to administer and interpret the results. After all, it is the test administrator and not the test itself that makes the diagnosis. Regardless of the tests that are chosen, there are four criteria that all good tests should meet:

**Suitability**
The appropriateness of a test for a specific population of students.

**Validity**
The degree to which a test instrument leads to valid inferences—that is, the degree to which it really measures what it claims to measure.

1. *Suitability:* In selecting or preparing a test, the teacher must determine not only whether it will yield the type of data desired but also whether the test is suitable for the age and type of students and for the locality in which they reside.

2. *Validity:* Educators often talk about the validity of a test and generally define validity as the degree to which a test measures what we hope for it to measure. We can question a test's validity (i.e., whether the items relate well to the purposes we are measuring). But we can also question the validity of inferences people make from the test. Individual student factors can affect the validity of evaluation, or the inferences educators make from tests. For example, consider the four students described below who each got 4/20 correct on a true/false test. How confident are we that the score measures the students' knowledge of content?

> *Student A: English Language Learner.* For this student, the true/false format is new and confusing. The test may have measured her comfort with the format rather than her content knowledge.

---

[3]Anne Anastasi, "Mental Measurements: Some Emerging Trends," *The Ninth Mental Measurements Yearbook* (Lincoln, NB: Buros Institute of Mental Measurements, University of Nebraska, 1985), p. xxix.

To hear an expert discuss testing culturally and linguistically diverse learners, go to the IRIS Center Resources section of Topic 14: English Language Learners in the MyEducationLab for your course and listen to the Podcast entitled "Alfredo Artiles on Testing Culturally and Linguistically Diverse Learners."

*Student B: Difficulty at home.* This student's parents may have filed for divorce and are in a heated custody battle. This affective challenge is likely to affect a student's performance on a test, and thus the test may not be measuring the content knowledge it purports to measure in its objectives statement. Instead, for this student, it may have simply measured stress.

*Student C: Does not care about the test.* This student has already taken dozens of tests this year and is questioning their value. She chooses true/false items randomly. When a student's effort and engagement in the test is low, the score has not measured content but rather may have provided evidence about motivation.

*Student D: Does not understand what the test is asking for.* This student is genuinely confused by the test items themselves. He thinks they are worded strangely, and gets confused by words that might mean more than one thing. Item for item, we are really not sure what we have measured for this student. It may be we have measured nothing. We wonder whether other low-scoring students had similar problems with the wording of the items. The randomness of responses for this type of student makes us question validity, but as noted below, this example also prompts us to question reliability.

Validity is among the main concerns diagnostic teachers have when the balance of assessment tips toward standardized testing. First, the standardized testing organization has almost 100 percent of the responsibility for ensuring the validity of the structure of the test and the individual items on the test. Teachers usually cannot examine the actual tests and items at any length. Second, teachers seem to have few opportunities to explain or provide a rationale for individual student scores. Larger trends in score manipulation have revealed these frustrations. In the past, school administrators were known to purposefully exclude English Language Learners and students with diagnosed disabilities from standardized testing. They knew the standardized system would not allow them to explain the special circumstances of these individuals, so they met this frustration by taking those students out of the scoring pool.

According to the *Standards for Educational and Psychological Testing,* "Validity is the most important consideration in test evaluation. The concept refers to the appropriateness, meaningfulness, and usefulness of the specific inferences made from test scores. Test validation is the process of accumulating evidence to support such inferences."[4] If a test or test items are not valid, then one of two things has happened: (a) we measured something else, or (b) nothing really got measured.

3. *Objectivity:* The ways of giving an answer are controlled (such as true/false, multiple-choice, multiple-response, and matching questions). The range of answers is limited, usually to one acceptable response. The same score must result regardless of who grades the test. Since essay questions allow for a variety of ways to express an answer in language, each scorer is likely to interpret essay responses differently. Developers of less controlled tests should give specific training for scorers and should make the essay questions as explicit and as plain as possible.

Objective testing puts strict limits on student responses. This constrains our ability to learn what they might know. So why would we want an objective test? The key reason we administer objective tests is to eliminate our own biases. Many of our biases are hidden to us. For example, many teachers are surprised the first time they observe themselves on video and learn that they tend to favor one side of their classroom when calling on students. Similar biases are likely to influence our scoring (measurement)

**Objectivity**
The same score must result regardless of who grades the test.

---

[4]*Standards for Educational and Psychological Testing,* prepared by the Committee to Develop Standards for Educational and Psychological Testing of the American Educational Research Association, the American Psychological Association, and the National Council on Measurement in Education (Washington, DC: American Psychological Association, 1985), p. 9.

and the inferences we make from scores (evaluation). For example, sometimes teachers change their pattern of scoring essays from the beginning of a pile of papers to the end. Reading the early essays can affect the teacher's interpretation of those that follow. The scorer might also just be more tired at the end. Objectivity is an important principle to help us rule out biases in assessing student knowledge.

**Reliability**
The extent to which a test instrument consistently produces similar results.

4. *Reliability:* Reliability is about consistency. It is highly related to objectivity because reliable instruments help us control the influence of outside factors on the score. When educators design and administer a reliable test, they can be more confident that factors in the test items, instructions, or administration do not create variation in answers. In testing reading, we want to ensure that the differences in individual scores actually come from a student's reading skill and not from how they received the instructions. What if one of our students showed radical growth from test to test, but later we found out that our way of reading the instructions the second time gave students inadvertent clues? To control this kind of bias, standardized tests often come with extremely rigid scripts for delivery. If teachers want reliability for a teacher-made test, they need to follow this same principle and write a script for delivery. These scripts should ensure that they do not have one way of giving the instructions on one day and another way the next. When a test is rewritten in a foreign language, its reliability must be rechecked to ensure that translation (differences in how the items are actually expressed) does not affect the way students answer items.

Another way of defining reliability is that we want to ensure that the *same thing* happened to all the students. Otherwise, what we are really testing may be the difference in how the test is presented.

Why is reliability important? If we use an objective test and the items on it get unpredictable responses, it is not a worthwhile part of our assessment program. For example, on a teacher-made multiple-choice test we might see the following analysis of items:

*Test item 25:* 85% of students mark response B, which is the correct response. When given to a different group of students, the results come back roughly similar: 82% correct and 88% correct. I am therefore reasonably confident that when most students see this item they have a good chance of getting it correct. I do further investigation into the 15% (or so) who respond incorrectly and see that they also scored poorly on classroom assignments correlated with item 25. I am confident that students who have learned this material will answer the question correctly, and that those who do not know it will answer it incorrectly.

*Test item 18:* 25% of students mark C, the correct response. 27% mark B. 23% mark D. 25% mark A. When I reinstruct students on the principle involved and retest the item, the results are different: 40% mark C, 27% mark B, 25% mark D, and 11% mark A. And it looks like many of those who originally answered the question correctly are now answering it incorrectly. I am therefore not very confident that this item will get me reliable results. When I administer it the next semester, I get 55% marking C, 30% marking B, 10% marking D, and 5% marking A. I am now pretty suspicious about this item, because the percentages do not look similar at all. I don't know why students are getting the item right or wrong. With item 25, I was pretty sure about why students were giving the responses they did. I take item 18 out of the test and try to write another one that gets me more predictable results for my purposes across students and across time.

When a student takes a test, teachers hope the score will remain consistent, even if the conditions under which the test are taken change slightly, even if different scorers are used, or even if similar but not identical test items are used.

In Figure 3.2 we provide a diagram of the types of tests we introduce in Chapter 6 and discuss throughout the book.

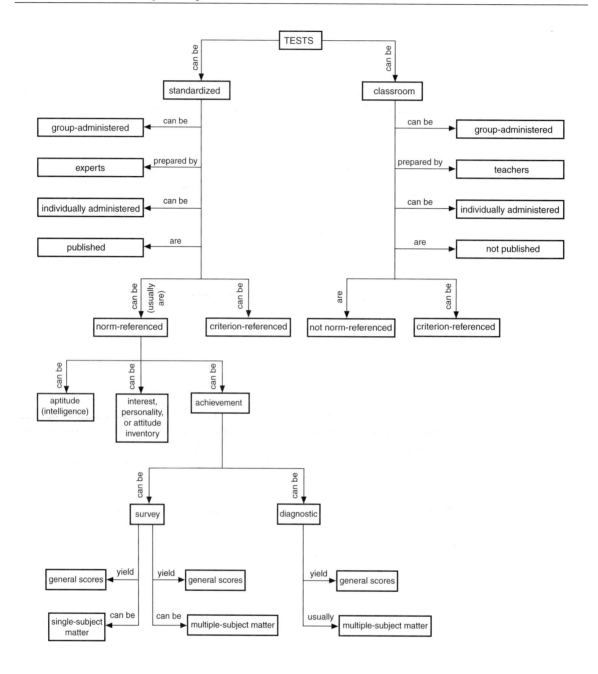

**FIGURE 3.2**   A Free Diagram of the Various Types of Tests. This diagram is a simplification, showing the relationship of the tests.

## REVISITING THE OPENING SCENARIO

Remember that Ms. Smith agreed with the principal and reading specialist that a good teacher must be able to administer and interpret various types of tests, not only for evaluation but also for diagnostic purposes. She made a decision to learn how to do both in the coming year with the help of both the reading specialist and the principal. What general knowledge about assessment will help her study and make decisions?

## AUTHORS' SUMMARY

In this chapter, we presented general information about what teachers should know concerning assessment, measurement, and evaluation. Good evaluators use tests and other measurement techniques to avoid bias in their judgments. We discussed criteria that all good tests should have: suitability, validity, objectivity, and reliability. We introduced the fact that many different kinds of assessment instruments exist. We emphasized that teachers in a reading diagnosis and improvement program must be knowledgeable about the various kinds of assessment tools so that they can make a wise selection for the proper purpose. To that end, we proposed that teachers ask and answer three important questions: What do I want to know? Why do I want to know it? Which test will help me discover this information?

## SUGGESTIONS FOR THOUGHT QUESTIONS AND ACTIVITIES

1. Discuss assessment, measurement, evaluation, and test as a hierarchy in reading diagnosis.

2. Discuss some of the important criteria that good tests must have.

## WEB SITES

http://teams.lacoe.edu/reading/assessments/assessments.html

This site provides assessment tools for K–3. Topics include but are not limited to spelling inventories, phonemic awareness tasks (such as the Yopp-Singer Test of Phonemic Segmentation and rhyming), and concepts about print.

http://www.teachervision.fen.com/assessment/new-teacher/48353.html?detoured=1

This site contains limited free articles (i.e., three free). This particular article discusses the difference between assessment and evaluation. Also included are criteria for teachers to consider in their own classrooms. Users can sign up for a 7-day free trial for access to over 20,000 + resources for Pre-K–12 teachers, downloadable materials, and over 180 printable books.

http://www.ncrel.org/sdrs/areas/issues/students/earlycld/ea500.htm

Focusing on a variety of topics such as developmentally appropriate assessments and standardized tests, this site explains the various concepts and shares information on the ways they are applied in different educational contexts.

http://nces.ed.gov/nationsreportcard/

Known as the Nation's Report Card, the National Assessment of Educational Progress (NAEP) is one of the primary assessments referenced when looking at our nation's educational progress. This site will keep teachers informed regarding the current educational state of affairs.

## SELECTED BIBLIOGRAPHY

McMillan, James H. *Classroom Assessment: Principles and Practice for Effective Instruction,* 3rd ed. Boston: Allyn and Bacon, 2004.

Popham, James W. *Classroom Assessment: What Teachers Need to Know,* 2nd ed. Boston: Allyn and Bacon, 1999.

Salvia, John, James F. Ysseldyke, and Sara Bolt, *Assessment,* 10th ed. Boston: Houghton Mifflin, 2007.

*Standards for Educational and Psychological Testing.* Prepared by the Committee to Develop Standards for Educational and Psychological Testing of the American Educational Research Association, the American Psychological Association, and the National Council on Measurement in Education. Washington, DC: American Psychological Association, 1985, 1986.

Woolfolk, Anita E. "Standardized Testing," in *Educational Psychology,* 10th ed. Boston: Allyn and Bacon, 2007.

**PEARSON**
**myeducationlab**

Now go to Topic 2: "Reading Assessment" and Topic 14: "English Language Learners" in MyEducationLab (www.myeducationlab.com) for your course, where you can:

- Find learning outcomes for "Reading Assessment" and "English Language Learners" along with national standards that connect to these outcomes.
- Complete Assignments and Activities that can help you more deeply understand the chapter content.
- Examine challenging situations and cases presented in the IRIS Center Resources.
- Access video clips of CCSSO National Teacher of the Year award winners responding to the question, "Why Do I Teach?" in the Teacher Talk section.
- Apply and practice your understanding of the core teaching skills identified in the chapter with Building Teaching Skills and Dispositions learning units.

# Factors That Affect Reading Performance

## CHAPTER OUTLINE

- Scenario: Angelique and Sara—
  A Study in Contrast
- Differentiating Between Educational
  and Noneducational Factors
- Educational Factors
- Noneducational Factors
- Revisiting the Opening Scenario

**4**

SCENARIO: ANGELIQUE AND SARA—A STUDY IN CONTRAST

Angelique and Sara are both in Mrs. Brown's first-grade class. Angelique is a bubbly, inquisitive, alert child who is excited about learning and looks upon every day as an adventure. She loves books and reads well. She asks good questions and likes to learn about things in depth. She talks about nocturnal birds and how she saw an owl one evening. She converses knowledgeably about wild animals and tame animals, and she is always eager to show anyone the stories she has written about different animals.

Angelique is quite verbal. She has an extensive vocabulary and uses words correctly. She can talk about animals, books she has read, books that have been read to her, other parts of the country, and many other things. She can give you word opposites and words similar in meaning. She can tell if you are being "funny." In addition, she can relate present information or experiences to past ones and make predictions about various things.

Angelique is an only child, and her college-educated parents adore her. They feel she is the joy of their lives. When she was born, her mother left her job to stay home with Angelique until she started school. Her parents read to her, talk to her, and interact with her. They take trips together and have flown to various other parts of the country. She has eaten different kinds of food in various restaurants, gone to zoos, farms, museums, and so on.

Sara, on the other hand, comes from a home in which she is the oldest of six children. At seven years of age, she has had a great amount of responsibility thrust upon her. Her mother works outside of the home, and often Sara has to stay home to help take care of the other children. Her father does not live at home with them. Sara is a "put upon" child. She is very mature for her age and is gaining many experiences. However, she has never traveled, has never been to a zoo or a farm, and she has never had anyone read to her. In short, Sara and Angelique's home environments and life experiences are quite different.

Here are composites of these two children. Which child would you predict will succeed in school? Why?

*Angelique L.*

Only child.
Upper socioeconomic status.
College-educated parents.
Standard English is dominant language.
Parents read to Angelique.
Many books are available for Angelique.
Newspapers, books, and magazines are available for parents.
Parents read for pleasure.
Angelique sees parents writing.
Television is supervised.
Parents discuss books and television shows with Angelique.
Family does many things together.
Angelique has pets.
Angelique helps take care of pets.
Family travels together to "fun" places.
Child has her own computer.
Time on computer and computer sites is supervised.

*Sara M.*

Oldest of six children.
Low socioeconomic status.
Mother has a seventh-grade education.
There is no father present.

Nonstandard English is spoken.
No newspapers, magazines, or books are visible.
Television is unsupervised.
No one reads to Sara.
Mother does not read for pleasure.
Sara is responsible for younger brothers and sisters.

You probably answered "Angelique," and if you did, you would probably be correct. You are also probably saying that the deck has been stacked in Angelique's favor. It has been; however, many children have backgrounds similar to those of Sara and Angelique. Most Angeliques do well in school because they have the background and experiences that seem to correlate well with school success. The Saras, who lack such backgrounds and experiences, are considered at-risk children. Unless they are identified early and helped, they will remain at high risk of failing in school; some may eventually drop out of school altogether. Certainly there are many children who come from low socioeconomic home environments who do well both in school and in life. The portrait of Sara M. is not meant to imply that all children who live in disadvantaged areas will not do well in school. We provide it to raise the awareness of the possibility.

As Angelique and Sara's profiles help to illustrate, there are many factors associated with learning to read. In this chapter, we present several of these factors and explain how they affect reading performance. Although there may be some factors over which educators have little control (e.g., low-income home, little or no reading material in the home, lack of being read to), there are several factors over which teachers do have control (e.g., time spent reading at school, developing requisite background necessary for understanding a given concept, developing an ear for different ways to use language via reading aloud and other forms of classroom communication). Understanding these factors puts teachers in better positions to set their students up for success. In other words, teachers can do much to help children overcome any shortcomings, and they are obligated to do so.

## CHAPTER OBJECTIVES

After reading the chapter, you should be able to:

- Differentiate between educational and noneducational factors.
- Discuss some factors that influence children's reading performance, such as home environment, intelligence, gender, health and well-being, or birth order.
- Discuss the relationship of language and dialect to the development of standard English.
- Discuss the relationship of physical health to reading.

## DIFFERENTIATING BETWEEN EDUCATIONAL AND NONEDUCATIONAL FACTORS

There are many ways to classify the many factors that affect children's reading performance. For purposes of this text, we classify the different factors as either *educational* or *noneducational* factors. In Table 4.1, we provide an overview of these categories, a

**TABLE 4.1   Factors Affecting Reading Performance**

| Category | Definition | Factors |
|---|---|---|
| Educational | Those factors that come under the domain or control of the educational system and influence learning | • Teaching methods<br>• Instructional materials<br>• The teacher<br>• Instructional time<br>• School environment |
| Noneducational | Those factors that do not come under the domain or control of the educational system and cannot be influenced by it | • Home environment<br>• Dialect and language differences<br>• Intelligence<br>• Gender<br>• Physical<br>   Illness<br>   Nutrition<br>• Perceptual<br>   Visual perception<br>   Auditory perception<br>• Emotional<br>   Self-concept<br>   Learned helplessness<br>   Motivation<br>   Attitude |

**Educational factors**
Those factors that come under the domain or control of the educational system and influence learning.

**Noneducational factors**
Those factors that do not come under the domain or control of the educational system and that supposedly cannot be influenced by it.

definition of each category, and a list of the specific factors we discuss in this chapter. When people talk about *educational factors*, they generally are referring to those factors that come under the domain or control of the educational system and influence learning. In this category, we would usually include the various methods and materials that the child has been exposed to, the teacher, the instructional time, and the school environment. Under *noneducational factors*, we generally would include physical health (general), vision, hearing, personality, and gender. Noneducational factors are supposedly those that do not come under the domain or control of the educational system and cannot be influenced by it. Although the two categories appear distinct at first glance, a second look shows that they are not necessarily; some factors overlap. For instance, although gender cannot be influenced by the schools, sex roles can. A case could even be made for general physical health as being influenced by educational practices. For example, children who are doing poorly in school may wish to avoid school to such an extent that they become ill every morning. The children's emotional health influences their physical health so that they actually get a stomachache, headache, or throw up. Their emotional state may so affect them that they cannot eat or sleep. The physical symptoms are real, even though the cause may not be a virus or bacterium.

Rather than spending time debating which factors belong in one category or the other, the important idea here is the interrelatedness of the many factors that affect reading performance. A child who has difficulty learning to read usually has many accompanying emotional and social problems, and these are compounded as the child goes through school if he or she is not helped as soon as a problem is detected or suspected. Clearly, when using a reading diagnosis and improvement program, many factors need to be considered in order to help all children advance in their ability to read.

## EDUCATIONAL FACTORS

Educational factors in learning come under the domain or control of the educational system. Examples are teaching methods, instructional materials, instructional time, teachers, and school environment. If a child is experiencing difficulty in reading, it is generally a good idea to check his or her school record to see if there is any information that might shed light on the child's problem. From the records, the teacher may be able to learn about the methods and materials the child has been exposed to in previous years. It may be that these were not effective, and something different should be tried. For example, a third-grade student might appear to have difficulty with decoding. Yet examination of school records might reveal that this child has been in systematic phonics programs since kindergarten. Rather than continuing to use systematic phonics as a primary mode of instruction, another approach (e.g., literature-based phonics, chunking strategies, whole word, language experience) seems warranted. The National Reading Panel's review of research on phonics has shown that the effectiveness of systematic, sequential phonics instruction decreases each year after first grade.[1] In this case, the *reading model* could be a major contributing factor to the problem.

### READING MODELS

As mentioned in Chapter 1, three models of learning to read inform and guide instructional decisions. For example, if teachers subscribe to a top-down view of reading, they will be likely to use a whole-to-part approach to instruct students. While many students may flourish in such a classroom, some may need the incremental steps of a bottom-up program in order to progress. The same holds true if a teacher favors a bottom-up model of reading. Some students will learn and others will not. A program based on an interactive model would work from both directions. The good news is that, like other educational factors, schools and often individual teachers usually have control over the reading models they use. If a child is not progressing, we can examine our lessons to determine why, and then alter our plans. Allowing beliefs about a model to trump our interest in the child's progress is unfair to the child. All children deserve better.[2] Many programs are organized based on belief in a particular model, and teachers should examine the programs they use to determine the model on which it is based.

### INSTRUCTIONAL MATERIALS

A former third-grade student of mine (MO) helped me to understand the importance of instructional materials—in this case the use of hardcover books instead of softcover books. We were provided multiple copies of the same text, some hardcover and others softcover. In the distribution, he was given a softcover text. Seeing this, he broke into loud sobs, saying that he couldn't read the book. In my effort to calm him, I assured him that of course he could read the book, and I pointed out the similarities of the versions. It didn't work. He kept crying, telling me I didn't understand. He was correct; I didn't understand, so I asked him to explain. He pointed out that in the softcover book, there wasn't as much space around the sides of the page and the lines were all squished together. Taking another look at the books, I saw what he was explaining and once again had to admit that he was correct. The hardcover book appeared much easier

[1]National Institute of Child Health and Human Development, *Report of the National Reading Panel, Teaching Children to Read: An Evidence-Based Assessment of the Scientific Research Literature on Reading and Its Implications for Reading Instruction* (Washington, DC: U.S. Government Printing Office, 2000).

[2]Richard Allington and Peter Johnson, eds., *Reading to Learn: Lessons from Exemplary Classrooms* (New York: Guilford, 2002). Elaine M. Garan, *In Defense of Our Children: When Politics, Profit, and Education Collide* (Portsmouth, NH: Heinemann, 2004). Elaine M. Garan, *Resisting Reading Mandates: How to Triumph with the Truth* (Portsmouth, NH: Heinemann, 2002).

to read because of the extra space devoted to the margins and the line spacing. The problem was resolved by letting him read from a hardcover version—which he did with ease. The point here is that instructional materials matter more than we might think. We need to pay attention to this. Not only should the materials be in alignment with the teaching approach but also they should entice children to read. When given the choice, students very rarely opt to read a page of print on poor quality paper over a trade book.

When a student resists reading, we need to take a look at what we are putting before the child to better understand whether this resistance is a problem with the child or a problem with the instructional materials. We then need to make any necessary changes to keep the child reading.

## THE TEACHER

In the words of Albert Harris and Edward Sipay, "Teacher effectiveness has a strong influence on how well children learn to read."[3] Like other scholars, we could not agree more.[4] This is one reason that we devoted Chapter 2 to the teacher's role in a reading diagnosis and improvement program. Listed below are some teaching practices that reading educators believe contribute to reading problems:

1. Failing to ensure that students are prepared to learn the skill or strategy.
2. Using materials that are too difficult.
3. Pacing instruction either too fast or too slow.
4. Ignoring unsatisfactory reading behaviors until they become habits.
5. Rarely expecting a certain child to perform the same tasks required of others.
6. Asking questions and then answering them without giving students time to respond.
7. Failing to acknowledge students when they do try.
8. Expressing disapproval or sarcasm when a mistake is made.
9. Allowing other children to disparage another child's efforts.
10. Expecting a child to perform a task that he or she cannot do in front of others.
11. Expecting a child to do poorly because older brothers and sisters did.

## INSTRUCTIONAL TIME

Sometimes research is needed to prove what common sense would tell us. A case in point is instructional time. As the result of Rosenshine's findings related to academic engaged time (i.e., the time students spend on academically relevant activities at the right level of difficulty), we now have proof that the more time students spend on a task, the higher their academic achievement will be.[5] And, as other researchers have reported, students spend more time on task when they are engaged with the teacher. Let us always remember teacher enthusiasm! It can go a long way toward keeping students focused.[6] When students are not receiving instruction, individual work still needs to be meaningful and engaging. Independent activities need to extend and refine their reading abilities.

[3]Albert J. Harris and Edward R. Sipay, *How to Increase Reading Ability: A Guide to Developmental and Remedial Methods,* 9th ed. (New York: Longman, 1990), p. 355.

[4]Richard L. Allington and Mary C. Shake, "Remedial Reading: Achieving Curricular Congruence in Classroom and Clinic," *The Reading Teacher* (March, 1986): 648–654. R. Wharton-McDonald, M. Pressley, and J. Hampston, "Literacy Instruction in Nine First-Grade Classrooms: Teacher Characteristics and Student Achievements," *The Elementary School Journal* 99 (1998): 101–128. International Reading Association Board of Directors, "Excellent Reading Teachers: Position Statement," http://www.reading.org/General/AboutIRA/PositionStatements/ExcellentTeachersPosition.aspx (accessed October 2009).

[5]Barak V. Rosenshine, "Academic Engaged Time, Content Covered, and Direct Instruction," *Journal of Education* 60 (1978): 38–66.

[6]Edward M. Bettencourt, et al., "Effect of Teacher Enthusiasm on Student On-Task Behavior and Achievement," *American Educational Research Journal* 20 (1983): 435–450.

## SCHOOL ENVIRONMENT

Context matters. If children feel safe, they are more likely to take the necessary risks on their way to becoming proficient readers.

Beyond safety, though, the actual physical environment of the classroom has a great influence on learning. In order to become readers, children need to be exposed to a lot of print and in many forms. A classroom that is full of print, such as children's literature, magazines, brochures, and so on, sends a powerful message to students. A classroom littered with print helps demonstrate that there are many reasons to read (and write).

## NONEDUCATIONAL FACTORS

## HOME ENVIRONMENT

**Home environment**
Socioeconomic class, parents' education, and the neighborhood in which children live are some factors that shape children's home environments.

Socioeconomic class, parents' education, and the neighborhood in which children live are some of the factors that shape children's *home environments*. The results of studies have led researchers to conclude that the higher the socioeconomic status, the better the verbal ability of the child[7] and the better children usually achieve in school.[8]

Children who have good adult language models and are spoken to and encouraged to speak will have an advantage in the development of language and intelligence. Similarly, children who come from homes where there are many opportunities to read; where there are many different types of text such as magazines, encyclopedias, books, and newspapers; and where they discuss what they read with their parents will be better readers than children without these advantages.[9] Parents who behave in a warm, democratic manner and provide their children with stimulating, educationally oriented activities; challenge their children to think; encourage independence; and reinforce their children are preparing them very well for school. The National Assessment of Educational Progress reports have consistently shown that "parental education and student achievement are positively associated."[10]

Children who come from homes where parents have only an elementary school education, where there are few reading materials available, where no one reads, where many people live in only a few rooms, and where unemployment among the adults in the home is common will usually be at a disadvantage in learning language and in reading. (See Chapter 14 for more on the importance of parental involvement.)

The adult composition of the child's home environment also has an impact on the child. Whether a child is reared by both parents, a single parent, a nanny, grandparents, or foster parents will affect the child's attitudes and behavior. For instance, a child who is raised by a female single parent may behave differently from one raised by a male single parent. The death of one parent or of another family member will usually cause emotional stress for the child. Divorce can also be a traumatic experience for children.

Go to the Assignments and Activities section of Topic 15: Parents and Families in the MyEducationLab for your course and complete the activity entitled "Emergent Literacy Development." As you watch the video and answer the accompanying questions, think about how teachers need to work with students who come from a variety of home environments.

[7]Walter D. Loban, *Language Development: Kindergarten through Grade Twelve* (Urbana, IL. National Council of Teachers of English, 1976), Research Report 18.

[8]Statement of Emerson J. Elliot, Commissioner of Education Statistics, at the Release of *National Assessment of Educational Progress 1994 Reading Assessment: A First Look,* April 27, 1995, p. 2. Shirley Brice Heath, *Ways with Words: Language, Life, and Work in Communities and Classrooms* (New York: Cambridge University Press, 1983). V. Purcell-Gates, *Other People's Words: The Cycle of Low Literacy* (Cambridge, MA: Harvard University Press, 1995). P. A, Edwards, H. M. Pleasants, and S. H. Franklin, *A Path to Follow: Learning to Listen to Parents* (Portsmouth, NH: Heinemann, 1999).

[9]B. D. Rampey, G. S. Dion, and P. L. Donahue, *NAEP 2008 Trends in Academic Progress* (NCES 2009). National Center for Education Statistics, Institute of Education Sciences, U.S. Department of Education, Washington, DC, http://nces.ed.gov/nationsreportcard/pubs/main2008/2009479.asp, (accessed October 2009).

[10]Rampey et al., p. 72.

The number of children in a family and the order of birth also affects achievement levels of individuals, at least to some degree. While studies are still being done on these factors, several researchers have noticed that firstborn children and only children do better both in school and in life than other children in the family.[11] Other researchers have reported that the only child, who is more often in the company of adults, has more chances of being spoken to by the grown-ups around him or her than is the case when there are many children in the family. Twins seem to have less need to communicate with others because they usually have a close relationship with one another. A child with siblings likewise has "interpreters" close at hand. Often, older siblings can understand a brother's or sister's messages so well that younger children do not need to express themselves clearly. All these factors form part of the learning climate in the home and influence the degree and amount of learning the child will do in school.[12]

## LANGUAGE DIFFERENCES

To hear an expert discuss cultural and linguistic differences, go to the IRIS Center Resources section of Topic 11: Reading Difficulties and Intervention Strategies in the MyEducationLab for your course and listen to the Podcast entitled "Donna Ford on Cultural and Linguistic Differences."

We live in a pluralistic society.[13] In a reading diagnosis and improvement program, teachers must recognize that most classes will be a composite of children who speak many different languages. For example, one student might grow up with two non-English languages spoken at home (such as Spanish and Quechua), and another student in the same class may have grown up with both English and another heritage language spoken at home (such as in a Navajo community). Still others come from homes where only one language is spoken (Korean, Russian, Vietnamese, Somali). English language learners from various backgrounds face unique problems in phonology, orthography, grammar, usage, and pragmatics[14] (see Teacher's Resource Guide of Language Transfer Issues for English Language Learners, in Appendix C, pp. 405–417).

The challenge teachers face is one of helping all students to value and develop their home language(s) while at the same time learning English as a new language.[15] Spanish is an important and widespread language in the United States. And yet we do ourselves and our students a disservice when we prepare only for Spanish-English diversity. Imagine a school where 65% of parents identify their children as coming from Spanish-speaking homes, and 34% from English-speaking homes. That leaves 1% of students who are not from either group. Good teachers learn how to design reading instruction for these students as well as for those speaking the dominant languages of the school population. They understand that ELLs are constantly showing what they need to know and learn, and that there is much variability among them. Good teachers do not confuse variability with disability.[16]

In the United States, standard English is considered the "prestige" dialect, and where regional dialects differ very little from each other, perhaps almost exclusively in pronunciation, we would be more likely to speak of an "accent" than a "dialect."[17] Children who speak a variation or dialect of English or another language are not inferior to children speaking standard English, nor is their language inferior. Research

[11]Mildred A. Dawson and Miriam Zollinger, *Guiding Language Learning* (New York: Harcourt, 1957), pp. 36–37. Didi Moore, "The Only-Child Phenomenon," *The New York Times Magazine,* January 18, 1981, pp. 26–27, 45–48.

[12]James P. Byrnes and Barbara Wasik, *Language and Literacy Development: What Educators Need to Know* (New York: Guilford Press, 2008).

[13]Office of English Language Acquisition (OELA). *The Growing Number of Limited English Proficient Students 1995–96, 2005–06* (Washington, DC: Office of English Language Acquisition, 2007).

[14]M. Swan and B. Smith, *Learner English: A Teacher's Guide to Interference and Other Problems* (London: Cambridge University Press, 2001).

[15]Kathy Escamilla, "Considerations for Literacy Coaches in Classrooms with English Language Learners," Literacy Coaching Clearinghouse, http://www.literacycoachingonline.org, (accessed October 8, 2007).

[16]C. Roller, *Variability Not Disability* (Newark, DE: International Reading Association, 1996).

[17]John P. Hughes, *The Science of Language* (New York: Random House, 1962), p. 26.

by linguists has shown that many variations of English are highly structured systems and not accumulations of errors in standard English. Noted scholar William Labov states that "it is most important for the teacher to understand the relation between standard and nonstandard and to recognize that nonstandard English is a system of rules, different from the standard but not necessarily inferior as a means of communication."[18]

We want children to be flexible language users—that is, we want to help them develop the understanding that every "club" has a language. To successfully communicate with members of any given club, one needs to speak the language of that club.

## INTELLIGENCE

Intelligence includes problem-solving ability and the ability to do abstract reasoning. Since reading is a thinking process, we might assume that students who have the ability to think at high levels of abstraction and who have strategies for processing information will be good readers. To a large degree this assumption is true. However, investigators have reported that not all children who are deemed "highly able" become good readers.[19] These findings suggest that there are factors besides intelligence, such as those shown in Table 4.1 on page 46 that contribute to success in reading and, consequently, to achievement in school.

Most intelligence tests are highly verbal, and persons who do well on vocabulary tests also seem to do well on intelligence tests. In addition, there is a research base that indicates a high positive correlation between reading achievement test scores and intelligence quotients.[20] Therefore, a child with a low IQ score would not be expected to do as well on a standardized reading achievement test as one with a high IQ score. Although intelligence is one factor to consider, reading educators Marjorie Lipson and Karen Wixson[21] note that there are several important points to keep in mind:

1. The components of intelligence cannot be observed, and there is disagreement about what components contribute to overall intelligence.
2. Intelligence has been expanded to include more than verbal skills. For example, Gardner's multiple intelligences theory posits that there are eight different kinds of intelligences.
3. Some researchers have reported that intelligence can be affected by experience and instruction.[22]
4. Culture influences how children show their intelligence. Some cultures, for example, teach students to provide more global answers rather than factual answers to posed questions.

While intelligence test scores might provide some direction and insight, we need to remember that they represent only one of many factors that can affect reading potential.

## GENDER

A review of research on gender differences shows that even though the data on gender differences studies are inconclusive and sometimes contradictory, there are a few

---

[18]William Labov, *The Study of Nonstandard English* (Urbana, IL: National Council of Teachers of English, 1970), p. 14.

[19]Leigh Hall, "Improving Middle School Students' Ability to Understand, Apply, and Talk about Comprehension Strategies," poster session presented at the International Reading Association Convention, Phoenix, AZ, 2009.

[20]Keith Rayner and Alexander Pollatsek, *The Psychology of Reading* (Hillsdale, NJ: Erlbaum, 1994), p. 395.

[21]Marjorie Y. Lipson and Karen K. Wixson, *Assessment and Instruction of Reading and Writing Difficulty: An Interactive Approach*, 3rd ed. (Boston: Allyn and Bacon, 2003).

[22]Carnegie Corporation, *Starting Points: Meeting the Needs of Our Youngest Students* (New York: Carnegie Corporation, 1994). Robert Slavin, *Educational Psychology* (Englewood Cliffs, NJ: Prentice Hall, 1991).

generalizations that can be made.[23] The reviewers report that "the largest differences appear in tests of mathematical or quantitative ability, where males tend to do better than females, particularly in secondary school and beyond. In recent years, there is some evidence that this gap may be narrowing. Females have tended to do better than males in many tests of verbal skills (particularly writing), but a number of studies indicate that this superiority has diminished since the early 1970s.[24] However, an extensive Educational Testing Service (ETS) study suggests that female superiority in writing and language skills still persists, and the investigators report that "research shows that females have closed the gap significantly on math and science scores."[25]

Investigators conducting the ETS gender study found that there are "many similarities and some genuine differences between how females and males perform in educational settings."[26] As Cole notes, "Differences are the result of many factors, and they widen particularly between the 4th and 12th grades."

Even well-meaning teachers might show gender biases in how they interact with students, and this can play out in reading instruction as well as in other areas of the classroom. Self-analysis of video or peer observation are important ways for teachers to learn to recognize gender-based patterns in how they call on students, how they respond to them, and what opportunities they give students to learn.[27]

## PHYSICAL HEALTH

### *Illness*

A child who is ill is not able to do well in school. This statement is obvious; however, it may not be obvious that a child is ill. A teacher needs to be alert for certain symptoms that may suggest a child is not well or is not getting enough sleep. For example, a child who is listless, whose eyes are glazed, who seems sleepy, and who actually does fall asleep in class may need a physical checkup.

The reason a child who is ill does not usually do well in school is not necessarily the child's illness, but the child's frequent absence from school. Children who have recurrent illnesses are generally absent from school a lot. This lack of attendance can contribute to reading problems because it causes the child to miss important reading instruction. In fact, such long absences, especially in first and second grade, are often the reason children struggle with reading.[28]

### *Nutrition*[29]

The effects of nutrition, and particularly malnutrition, on learning have been evident for a long time. It should come as no surprise that children who are hungry and malnourished

---

[23]Amram Scheinfeld, *Women and Men* (New York: Harcourt, 1944), pp. 58–71. Peg Tyre, *The Trouble with Boys: A Surprising Report Card on Our Sons, Their Problems at School, and What Parents and Educators Must Do* (New York: Crown, 2008).

[24]"The Gender Gap in Education: How Early and How Large?" *ETS Policy Notes,* vol. 2, no. 1 (Princeton, NJ: Educational Testing Service, 1989).

[25]Nancy S. Cole, *The ETS Gender Study: How Females and Males Perform in Educational Settings* (Executive Summary). (Princeton, NJ: Educational Testing Service, 1997), p. 26. Debby Zambo and William G. Brozo, *Bright Beginnings for Boys: Engaging Young Boys in Active Literacy* (Newark, DE: International Reading Association, 2009).

[26]Ibid.

[27]Ibid.

[28]Albert J. Harris and Edward R. Sipay, *How to Increase Reading Ability: A Guide to Developmental and Remedial Methods,* 9th ed. (New York: Longman, 1990).

[29]M. D. Florence, M. Asbridge, and P. J. Veugelers, "Diet Quality and Academic Performance," *Journal of School Health* 78 (2008): 209–215. D. Satcher, "School Wellness and the Imperative of Leadership," in *Progress or Promises? What's Working for and Against Healthy Schools: An Action for Healthy Kids Report* (Skokie, IL: Action for Healthy Kids, 2008), pp. 8–10.

have difficulty learning. They cannot concentrate on the task at hand; they also lack drive. They simply lack the energy to perform at their best. For several decades some researchers have suggested that severe malnutrition in infancy may lower children's IQ scores.[30] Several other researchers have found that the lack of protein in an infant's diet may adversely affect the child's ability to learn.[31] Still others have found that the effects of certain food additives may be a deterrent to learning for certain children.[32]

And consider the current state of affairs regarding nutrition. Childhood obesity is in the media spotlight; some even call it an epidemic and point to possible reasons why children are becoming obese in increasing numbers. Not surprisingly, nutrition is a major factor, as is the type of food that children consume. Is it any wonder that many children have trouble performing in school when they eat processed foods that contain a lot of sugar?[33]

## PERCEPTUAL FACTORS

In Chapter 1 we noted the importance of perception (giving meaning to sensations) as part of the process of reading. We stated that a child who has problems in the perceptual domain will most assuredly encounter difficulty in concept development and consequently in reading. Vision and hearing are two key areas of perception in reading. Ruling out visual and auditory issues as factors that contribute to reading problems is important. For example, a struggling reader who also has astigmatism is at a heightened disadvantage. The same holds true for readers with auditory perception problems.

### Visual Perception

Visual problems are not always obvious and, as a result, are not always detected (See Figure 4.1). Most schools have some kind of visual screening. The most common screening is for *myopia,* or nearsightedness. The Snellen chart test is usually done by the school nurse. In this familiar test, a child must identify letters of various sizes with each eye. A score of 20/20 is considered normal. A score of 20/40 or 20/60 means that a child has defective vision because the child with normal vision can see the letters at a distance of forty or sixty feet, whereas the child with defective vision can only see these letters at a distance of twenty feet. Other tests are used to identify farsightedness (*hypermetropia*) and *astigmatism.*[34]

### Visual Discrimination

*Visual discrimination* is the ability to distinguish between written symbols. If children have difficulty discriminating between and among letters, they will experience difficulty when learning to read. In learning to read, children need to be able to make fine discriminations, and therefore need activities involving letters rather than geometric figures or pictures. Transfer of learning is greater if the written symbols children work with are similar to those they will meet in reading.[35]

### Phonological Processing

Phonological processing refers to the way a person's brain processes speech sounds. Among the key issues for those with difficulty are breaking down whole words into

**Myopia**
Nearsightedness; difficulty with distance vision.

**Hypermetropia**
Farsightedness; difficulty with close-up vision.

**Astigmatism**
A defect of vision that causes blurred vision.

**Visual discrimination**
The ability to distinguish differences and similarities between written symbols.

[30]Merlin C. Wittrock, "Learning and the Brain," in *The Brain and Psychology,* ed. Merlin C. Wittrock (New York: Academic Press, 1980), pp. 376–377.

[31]Nevin S. Scrimshaw, "Infant Malnutrition and Adult Learning," *Saturday Review,* March 16, 1968, pp. 64–66, 84.

[32]Eleanor Chernick, "Effect of the Feingold Diet on Reading Achievement and Classroom Behavior," *The Reading Teacher* 34 (November, 1980): 171–173.

[33]Michael F. Opitz, *Literacy Lessons to Get Kids Fit and Healthy,* (New York: Scholastic, 2010).

[34]Albert J. Harris and Edward R. Sipay, *How to Increase Reading Ability,* 9th ed. (New York: Longman, 1990), p. 347.

[35]Albert Harris and Edward Sipay, *How to Increase Reading,* 9th ed. (New York: Longman, 1990). Marie Clay, *Early Detection of Reading Difficulties* (Portsmouth, NH: Heinemann, 1985).

---

FIGURE 4.1   **Symptoms of Vision Problems**

Child's Name: _____

Date of Observation: _____

**Symptoms**
**The child . . .**                                                                     *Yes*      *No*

| | | |
|---|---|---|
| 1. Complains of constant headaches | | |
| 2. Eyes show some of the following: red rims, swollen lids, crusted lids, redness, frequent sties, watering | | |
| 3. Squints while reading | | |
| 4. Asks to sit closer to the board | | |
| 5. Can't seem to sit still while doing close-up tasks | | |
| 6. Holds reading material very close to face when reading | | |
| 7. Skips many words and/or sentences when reading | | |
| 8. Makes many reversals when reading | | |
| 9. Confuses letters | | |
| 10. Avoids reading | | |
| 11. Mouths words or lip-reads | | |
| 12. Confuses similar words | | |
| 13. Makes many repetitions while reading | | |
| 14. Skips lines while reading | | |
| 15. Has difficulty remembering what was read silently | | |

---

parts of sound, and blending parts of sound into whole words. This factor is discussed in detail in Chapter 7, including ways to diagnose and teach children with phonological processing issues.

### Auditory Perception

Like visual perception, auditory perception involves several abilities. While auditory perception is important, we need to remember that it is just one factor that may affect reading performance. Many children with hearing impairments read quite well.

### Auditory Acuity

**Auditory acuity**
Physical response of the ear to sound vibrations.

*Auditory acuity* is concerned with the physical response of the ear to sound vibrations. If individuals have organic ear damage, they will not be able to hear properly, if at all, depending on the extent of the damage. Auditory acuity is the ability to respond to various frequencies (tones) at various intensities (levels of loudness).

---

**FIGURE 4.2   Symptoms of Hearing Problems**

---

Child's Name: _____

Date of Observation: _____

---

| Question | Yes | No |
|---|---|---|
| 1. Does the child appear to be straining to push himself or herself closer to the speaker? | | |
| 2. Does the child speak either very softly or very loudly? | | |
| 3. Does the child have difficulty following simple directions? | | |
| 4. Does the child turn up the sound of the CD player or tape player? | | |
| 5. Does the child have difficulty pronouncing words? | | |
| 6. Does the child seem disoriented? | | |

---

Human speech comprises frequencies ranging from 125 to 8,000 hertz (Hz).[36] The intensity or loudness level found in everyday speech will typically range from 55 decibels (faint speech) to 85 decibels (loud conversation). When hearing is tested, a person's ability to hear is checked across the entire speech-frequency range. If more than the normal amount of volume (dB level) is required to hear sounds at certain frequencies, the individual is most probably exhibiting a hearing loss.

Many states and doctors are advocating that newborns' hearing be tested before they leave the hospital because hearing loss is so common. This makes sense, because a hearing loss that is undetected and therefore untreated will usually affect children's speech and all other language arts areas. This can be especially detrimental to children when learning to read.

Children who have difficulty hearing high frequencies generally have problems discerning differences between and among consonants, whereas those who have problems hearing low frequencies usually have difficulties discriminating between and among vowels. Such problems with consonants and vowels could cause great difficulties for children learning to read.

While audiologists have many tools for measuring various aspects of hearing, teachers can make informal measurements on their own. They can use the observational checklist in Figure 4.2 to make notes that may lead to further testing.

According to audiologist William Jones, it is possible for a child to have a normal result from auditory testing but still have significant difficulties in cognitive processing of speech sounds. A child's inability to consistently follow directions when they are presented loudly enough to be clearly understood is one sign of such a problem. These children should be referred to a specialist for further testing, including a complete audiological assessment.[37]

---

[36]*Hertz* is the accepted international scientific word for cycles per second, named after the great nineteenth-century German physicist who proved the existence of electromagnetic waves.

[37]Dr. William O. Jones, Professor Emeritus, The College of New Jersey, 2001.

### Binaurality
The ability of listeners to direct both ears to the same sound.

### Masking
Factor inhibiting hearing as other sounds interfere with the spoken message.

### Auditory discrimination
Ability to distinguish differences and similarities between sound symbols.

### Auditory memory span
Amount of information able to be stored in short-term memory for immediate use or reproduction.

### *Binaural Considerations*

*Binaurality* is the ability of listeners to increase their reception sensitivity by directing both ears to the same sound. This can be an issue for readers, especially when they are listening to someone else read or when they are reading aloud to themselves. For example, they may not be able to tune out outside noises to hear the teacher reading a book, or ambient noise may distract them even when they are reading to themselves.

### *Masking*

*Masking* occurs when other sounds interfere with the message being spoken. Background noises drowning out a speaker, noisy classrooms, or simultaneous group discussions all interfere with hearing ability.

### *Auditory Discrimination*

*Auditory discrimination*, which is the ability to distinguish among sounds, is important for the acquisition of language and for learning to read. Following is a summary of what speech clinicians have learned about auditory discrimination:[38]

1. There is evidence that the more nearly alike two phonemes are in structure, the more likely they are to be misinterpreted (such as /f/ and /v/).
2. Individuals differ in their ability to discriminate among sounds.
3. The ability to discriminate begins at birth, yet frequently matures when the child turns eight. A few individuals never develop this capacity to any great degree.
4. There is a strong positive correlation between slow development of auditory discrimination and inaccurate pronunciation.
5. There is a positive relationship between poor auditory discrimination and poor reading.
6. Although poor discrimination may be at the root of both speech and reading difficulties, it often affects only reading or speaking.
7. There is little if any relationship between the development of auditory discrimination and intelligence, as measured by most intelligence tests.

For children who speak languages other than English at home, the acquisition of speech sounds for any given language is learned very early in life and is usually established before the child starts school. Distinguishing among English phonemes may be difficult for these children, especially at the beginning of English language learning (see Appendix C).

The *Wepman Auditory Discrimination Test,* which was developed by Joseph M. Wepman and published by Language Research Associates, is a norm-referenced test that teachers use to discern whether students have auditory discrimination problems. The teacher asks the student to turn around so that he or she cannot lip-read; then the teacher very distinctly pronounces each pair of words. The student must determine if the words are the same or different. There are two forms of the test, each one consisting of forty pairs of words.

### *Auditory Memory Span*

*Auditory memory span* is essential for individuals who must judge whether two or more sounds are similar or different. In order to make such comparisons, the sounds must be kept in memory and retrieved for comparison. Auditory memory span is defined as "the number of discrete elements grasped in a given moment of attention and organized into a unity for purposes of immediate reproduction or immediate use."[39] A deficiency in memory span will hinder effective listening.

[38]Joseph M. Wepman, "Auditory Discrimination, Speech and Reading," *Elementary School Journal* 60 (1960): 326.

[39]Virgil A. Anderson, "Auditory Memory Span as Tested by Speech Sounds," *American Journal of Psychology* 52 (1939): 95.

Individual intelligence tests, such as the *Stanford-Binet* and the *Wechsler,* have subtests called "Digits Forward"and "Digits Backward" that measure an individual's memory span. The individual is told to listen carefully, and then the examiner says some numbers at the rate of one per second. After the entire series of numbers has been given, the individual must repeat them in the exact order for the "Digits Forward" sub-test. For the "Digits Backward" subtest, the individual must repeat the digits in reverse order after the examiner has stopped.

## EMOTIONAL WELL-BEING

Self-concept, learned helplessness, motivation, and attitude are four aspects related to emotional health. Each needs to be considered when thinking about a child's emotional well-being and how it can affect reading performance.

### Self-Concept

Self-concept is the way an individual feels about himself or herself. Although the verdict is still out on specific origins of self-concept, our lives are a testament to the fact that it exists and that it can change depending on the task at hand. For example, if we feel adequate, confident, and self-reliant about reading, we are more apt to be good readers. We would say that we have a positive self-concept as it relates to reading. However, if we are feeling less than adequate, have little confidence, and are not self-reliant about reading, we are more likely to be poor at reading and to have a negative self-concept about it. One factor to consider, then, is how children feel about themselves as readers. Asking students the following questions is one way to discern students' perceptions of themselves as readers:

1. Do you think you are a good reader? Why or why not?
2. How do you feel when you are expected to read?
3. Do you read at home?
4. Do you like to read?

### Learned Helplessness

Related to self-concept is learned helplessness. If we repeatedly experience failure at a task regardless of how hard we try, we are apt to develop the idea that we simply cannot perform the task; this is called *learned helplessness*. As a result, any time we are expected to perform the task, we become passive. This should come as no surprise, because few of us like to feel like failures! Avoidance is one way to block these feelings of failure. Thus, children who feel that they simply cannot perform well at reading are likely to show avoidance behaviors. Even if others, such as a well-meaning teacher, believe that a child can perform quite well, the important point to keep in mind is that learned helplessness is the child's viewpoint. The questions presented earlier can help to reveal children's perceptions of themselves as readers. Watching what children do when they are called on to read in various ways can also shed light on how they feel about reading. For example, during independent reading time, when children are to read a book of their choosing, those who feel less than adequate tend to act as if they are reading when in fact they are doing everything they can to avoid it.

### Motivation

Like Paris and Carpenter, we believe there are several components that facilitate *motivation* to read. These include how readers perceive their ability to read, the text, the reason for reading, and the surrounding environment.[40] Take, for example, children who attend a sleepover at school and are told to bring their favorite book for reading

---

[40]Scott G. Paris and Robert D. Carpenter, "Children's Motivation to Read," in James V. Hoffman and Diane L. Schallert, eds., *The Texts in Elementary Classrooms* (Mahwah, NJ: Erlbaum, 2004), pp. 61–85.

and sharing with others. Children who elect to attend the event are sure to be motivated to read. After all, they get to choose the text with the purpose in mind. Self-selection means that they are likely to pick out a text they feel they can read with ease. They need not be embarrassed when they share a part of it aloud with another person. Likewise, because everyone will be reading, the environment encourages all children to do the same. The child who chooses not to follow suit will be the odd one out and is likely to feel uncomfortable.

### Attitude

If we simply take a look at ourselves and our relationship to reading, we can fully understand what researchers have concluded over the years: *Attitude* is a major factor that affects reading performance.[41] In fact, a positive attitude can override missing skills,[42] enabling a reader to perform far better than expected based on past reading performances. A former student of mine (MO) helped me to understand this. She selected a book that presented many challenges for her—too many from my perspective. As much as I tried to persuade her to read other, easier texts, she kept returning to "her" book and simply would not give it up. For whatever reason, she wanted to read the book and, after continual assistance, she read it with ease. What seemed like a miracle was a positive attitude in action. Deep down, she wanted to read the book and felt that she could get it, and so she did. Excited about her new-found reading ability, I wondered whether she could read other texts at a similar level of complexity. My subsequent observations revealed that she could not. In fact, she often chose to read much easier books after she did a repeated reading of her more difficult book.

## REVISITING THE OPENING SCENARIO

Having read about several factors that can affect reading, return to the scenario at the beginning of the chapter. Which of the factors discussed might be affecting each of these girls? Which factors are educational and which are noneducational?

## AUTHORS' SUMMARY

In this chapter, we presented a variety of educational and noneducational factors that can affect a child's reading performance. Educational factors, those factors that come under the domain or control of the school, include teaching methods, instructional materials, the teacher, and the school environment. Noneducational factors include home environment, language differences, gender, physical condition, visual and auditory perception, and emotional state.

Teachers can do nothing about many of these individual differences, such as home environment, family makeup, and languages/dialects spoken. However, if teachers are aware that some of their children come from environments that may present obstacles to learning, they can provide experiences in school to help these children become successful readers. Teachers can also be ready to diagnose and provide appropriate instruction for children with physical, perceptual, or emotional difficulties, should these difficulties become apparent.

[41]Marjorie Y. Lipson and Karen K. Wixson, *Assessment and Instruction of Reading and Writing Difficulty: An Interactive Approach,* 3rd ed. (Boston: Allyn and Bacon, 2003).

[42]Scott G. Paris, G. Olson, and H. Stevenson, eds., *Learning and Motivation in the Classroom* (Hillsdale, NJ: Erlbaum, 1983).

## SUGGESTIONS FOR THOUGHT QUESTIONS AND ACTIVITIES

1. You have been asked to give a talk to your colleagues about why there are more reading disabilities among boys than among girls in the United States. What will you say?
2. Why would the community be considered an educational factor that could affect children's reading?
3. Imagine a child who has multiple noneducational factors impeding her reading success. How would you determine all the contributing factors?
4. A colleague is throwing up her hands in despair over her class's reading problems. Many of her students have multiple noneducational factors that hinder their reading. Explain how she can balance out noneducational factors by strengthening educational factors.
5. There are many educational and noneducational factors that could affect reading success. Think of others that go beyond those already listed, and describe how they would affect reading.

## WEB SITES

http://bookadventure.com/

Although primarily devoted to children, this site also provides information for parents and teachers. For children, this site offers book lists, quizzes, and prizes, addressing external motivational factors. For teachers, the site presents activities and resources for engaging young readers.

http://www.readingrockets.org/helping/target/

The site provides information about the five components of reading and the difficulties occurring in each area. Within each section, the component is defined and described as to what the problem looks like from students', parents', and teachers' perspectives.

http://www.readingrockets.org/helping/target/otherissues

This page includes information on noneducational factors affecting reading, including processing (auditory processing, phonological processing, and language processing), memory, attention, and English language learning.

http://kidsreads.com/features/great-books-boys.asp

This site provides an extensive list of books for boys. Included are series titles and stand-alone fiction that cover a variety of genres: fantasies, mysteries, thrillers, action/adventure novels, and historical fiction. While many of these selections also will appeal to girls, they are especially geared toward capturing the attention of boys, who are often much more reluctant readers.

## SELECTED BIBLIOGRAPHY

Bennett, Christine I. *Comprehensive Multicultural Education: Theory and Practice,* 4th ed. Boston: Allyn and Bacon, 1999.

Cole, Nancy. *ETS Gender Study: How Females and Males Perform in Educational Settings.* Princeton, NJ: Educational Testing Service, 1997.

Grohens, Joe. "Nutrition and Reading Achievement." *The Reading Teacher* 41 (May, 1988): 942–945.

Horgan, Dianne D. *Achieving Gender Equity: Strategies for the Classroom.* Boston: Allyn and Bacon, 1994.

Piaget, Jean. *The Language and Thought of the Child.* New York: Harcourt, 1926.

Rigg, Pat, and Virginia G. Allen, eds. *When They Don't All Speak English: Integrating the ESL Student into the Regular Classroom.* Urbana, IL.: National Council of Teachers of English, 1989.

Smith, Nila Banton. "Early Language Development: Foundation of Reading." *Elementary English* 52 (March, 1975): 399–402, 418.

Sutton, Christine. "Helping the Nonnative English Speaker with Reading." *The Reading Teacher* 42 (May, 1989): 684–688.

Tiedt, Pamela L., and Iris M. Tiedt. *Multicultural Teaching: A Handbook of Activities, Information, and Resources,* 5th ed. Boston: Allyn and Bacon, 1999.

Woolfolk, Anita E. "Cognitive Views of Learning," in *Educational Psychology,* 8th ed. Boston: Allyn and Bacon, 2001.

**PEARSON**
**myeducationlab**

Now go to Topic 15: "Parents and Families" and Topic 11: "Reading Difficulties and Intervention Strategies" in MyEducationLab (www.myeducationlab.com) for your course, where you can:

- Find learning outcomes for "Parents and Families" and "Reading Difficulties and Intervention Strategies" along with national standards that connect to these outcomes.
- Complete Assignments and Activities that can help you more deeply understand the chapter content.
- Examine challenging situations and cases presented in the IRIS Center Resources.
- Access video clips of CCSSO National Teacher of the Year award winners responding to the question, "Why Do I Teach?" in the Teacher Talk section.
- Apply and practice your understanding of the core teaching skills identified in the chapter with Building Teaching Skills and Dispositions learning units.

# Using Informal Assessment Techniques across the Grades

## CHAPTER OUTLINE

- Scenario: Teachers Talking
- Authentic, Performance-Based Assessment
- Portfolio Assessment
- The Uses of Observation
- Anecdotal Records
- Scenario: Mr. Jackson Checks and Writes
- Checklists
- Other Helpful Informal Assessment Techniques
- Revisiting the Opening Scenario

**SCENARIO:** TEACHERS TALKING

Read the following conversation overheard in the faculty lounge:

*MS. ANDERSON:* I don't know what to do with Billy. His behavior is driving me crazy.

*MR. JOHNSON:* Why? What does he do?

*MS. ANDERSON:* What doesn't he do? He's forever getting up from his seat. He can't seem to sit still for a moment. He's always disturbing his neighbor. If there is any commotion or problem in the room, you can be sure that Billy is the cause of it.

*MR. JOHNSON:* Have you spoken to Billy's parents about his behavior?

*MS. ANDERSON:* Yes, but they say that they do not see the same kind of behavior at home, so they feel that it's something related to school. I've just about had it.

*MR. JOHNSON:* I've had Billy in my class, and I remember him as a pretty bright boy. I think that you should try to observe when Billy starts to act up. I know that I had another child who acted just as Billy does, and I thought that she was misbehaving all the time, just to make my life miserable. Fortunately, I had just finished a course in reading diagnosis, and the professor had discussed the uses of observation techniques to learn about the behavior of students. I decided to try it, and I was surprised at the results! Using observation techniques made me aware of how unfounded my statements about Susan were. Let's go to my room, and I'll show you what I did.

What do you think Mr. Johnson showed Ms. Anderson? Make a few guesses before continuing to read.

We propose three questions that teachers need to ask related to assessment: What do I want to know? Why do I want to know? How can I best discover the information? The focus in this chapter is on asking and answering these questions using various informal measures of reading behaviors. Although these instruments may appear to be less objective than the tests presented later in Chapter 6, they actually provide the foundation for interpreting and better understanding any test data you collect. The specific purpose (the "What do I want to know" and the "Why do I want to know?") is what guides our choice of which type of measure to use (the "How can I best discover the information?"). In Table 5.1 we provide an overview of informal assessment techniques.

## CHAPTER OBJECTIVES

After reading the chapter, you should be able to:

- Describe the difference between a reading portfolio assessment and authentic observation assessment.
- Explain how teachers can use portfolios as part of the reading diagnosis and improvement program.
- Discuss when teachers should and should not make generalizations about students' behavior.
- Discuss how observation and anecdotal records can be made more objective.
- Describe some of the various kinds of checklists, and explain how a rating scale can be used with a checklist.
- Explain what you can learn by using various types of interviews, interest inventories, and surveys.
- Discuss the uses of projective techniques and reading biographies in the classroom.

**TABLE 5.1   Authentic and Performance-Based Assessment Techniques**

| *What Do I Want to Know?* | *Why Do I Want to Know?* | *How Can I Best Discover?* |
| --- | --- | --- |
| Do the children use what they know about reading regardless of what they read? | To show competence in reading, children need to show that they can use what they have learned. I need to see if they can do this, and if they cannot, I need to determine why. | Performance Assessment (p. 64)<br>Project (p. 64) |
| Do children show growth over time? | Children continue to grow as readers and I need to provide evidence of that growth. I want to be able to show the kind of progress the children are making. | Portfolio (pp. 66–67) |
| How do children perform in a variety of contexts? | Watching children as they perform a variety of reading-related tasks is an excellent way for me to see firsthand what they are able to do. I can also develop intuitions about what they do well and what might need additional work. I can use these observations as a way of selecting additional reading assessments that will help me to better understand the children. | Direct Observation (pp. 67–69) |
| How can I remember everything I see when observing? | Watching children can help me to learn more about them, but I simply cannot remember everything. I also need a way to document what I have actually observed as a way of showing others that I have detected a pattern of behavior that sheds light on a student's performance. | Anecdotal Record (pp. 69–72) |
| What specific behaviors do the children show when they complete reading tasks? | There are a variety of behaviors that children need to exhibit on their way to becoming accomplished readers. I need to determine which they show and those they need to learn, and be able to document this in a quick and clean way. I can then use the results to plan appropriate instruction. | Checklists (pp. 72–78) |
| How do the children view reading? | Faulty perceptions of what it means to read can inhibit reading growth. Uncovering the children's views can help me to see which are correct and which need to be added to or altered. | Informal Student Interview (pp. 79–88) |
| What reading strategies do children think they use when they are reading? | Good readers use a variety of strategies to assist them as they try to comprehend a text. Relying on one or two strategies to the exclusion of others can prevent growth. I need to know which strategies readers do and do not use so that I can help all the children to develop a full array of strategies. | Informal Student Interview (pp. 79–88) |

*(continued)*

**TABLE 5.1**   (*continued*)

| What Do I Want to Know? | Why Do I Want to Know? | How Can I Best Discover? |
|---|---|---|
| What do children like to read? | We are more prone to read if we are interested in the reading material. Identifying the children's interests can help me to select texts for instruction and inclusion in the classroom library. I can also use interests to group children in different ways, making it possible for them to work with a variety of peers. | Interest Inventories (pp. 82–83) |
| How do children feel about themselves as readers? | Feelings of self-efficacy play a big part in reading success. I need to know how students feel about themselves as readers. Then I can identify children who view themselves as failures and work to help them gain confidence as competent readers. | Projective Strategies (p. 84–87) Reading Autobiography (pp. 87–88) |
| What kind of attitudes do the children have about reading? | Attitude has a big impact on reading. Identifying (attitudes) will help me to see if I need to help a child develop a more positive outlook, which will make reading a more enjoyable experience. Children with a positive attitude are more likely to attempt reading. | Primary Reading Survey (p. 85) Reading Attitude Survey for Grades 3 and up (p. 86) |

# AUTHENTIC, PERFORMANCE-BASED ASSESSMENT

**Authentic assessment**
Using authentic, "real-life" materials to assess students' reading.

**Performance assessment**
Using a situation or project where learners can demonstrate knowledge.

Authentic, performance-based assessment is often called "alternative" assessment, because it does not measure reading proficiency with standardized tests. While test situations are often contrived, we can learn much about readers through "direct, 'authentic' assessment of student performance on important learning tasks."[1]

*Authentic assessment* (sometimes called *naturalistic assessment*) helps teachers to measure students' "important abilities using procedures that simulate the application of these abilities to real-life situations."[2] Therefore, a magazine article or a children's literature title might be used to assess how well students read different types of text. To assess students' ability to use phonics to decode words, individual students might be given a class roster such as the one shown in Chapter 12 and asked to read the names aloud while the examiner makes notes about what the child says in relation to the actual names.

*Performance assessment* is often used as a synonym for authentic assessment because it calls on the learner to show understanding by completing tasks like those "required in the instructional environment."[3] These demonstrations are sometimes documented in a *portfolio* (i.e., a selection of the student's work that is meant to show

[1]Shelby J. Barrentine and Sandra M. Stokes, eds., *Reading Assessment: Principles and Practices for Elementary Teachers,* 2nd ed. (Newark, DE: International Reading Association, 2005). Suzanne Bratcher, with Linda Ryan, *Evaluating Children's Writing: A Handbook of Grading Choices for Classroom Teachers,* 2nd ed. (Mahwah, NJ: Erlbaum, 2004).

[2]Robert E. Slavin, *Educational Psychology: Theory and Practice,* 6th ed. (Boston: Allyn and Bacon, 2000), p. 469.

[3]Shirley-Dale Easley and Kay Mitchell, *Portfolios Matter: What, Where, When, Why and How to Use Them* (Portland, ME: Stenhouse, 2003).

learning progress) or by having students complete a project. For both portfolios and projects, a scoring system (i.e., rubric) is used to help teachers determine how well students have achieved specified standards. The *rubric* is a set of criteria that places a value on students' performance in certain areas. Students are usually given these rubrics—or invited to help construct one—in advance of the performance task so that they can see how they are going to be evaluated. They can use this rubric as a guide when preparing for the performance. Figure 5.1 shows a sample rubric. As you can see, certain criteria are established, but the teacher must still determine how well students have met the criteria. In other words, rubrics can help to reduce subjectivity, but they cannot completely do away with it. In fact, we would say that rubrics are "objective subjectivity."

---

**FIGURE 5.1   Rubric for Writing to Learn**

| Criteria / Quality | 3 | 2 | 1 |
| --- | --- | --- | --- |
| Ideas & Content | Clear and focused. Provides several relevant examples from the text and own experiences. Shows own thinking about the topic. | Beginning to develop the paper. Some examples. Own thinking is starting to become evident but full explanation is lacking. | No real focus. Few examples are cited and original thinking is not evident. |
| Organization | Paper written with an introduction, body, and conclusion. Written in format as explained in class. | Paper has two of the three: introduction, body, conclusion. Written in the format as explained in class. | Paper has one of the three: introduction, body, conclusion. The format explained in class is not used. |
| Voice | Speaks to the reader; shows attention to audience. | Beginning to speak to the reader but still rather general; not always aware of audience. | Passive; writing appears distant; lack of attention to audience. |
| Print Conventions | Makes use of all print conventions: spelling, grammar, punctuation. | Most print conventions are used but occasional misspellings and incorrect grammar and/or punctuation are evident. | Little attention to print conventions as evidenced by misspelled words, incorrect grammar, and/or misuse of punctuation. |
| Legibility | Neat—easy to read. One side of paper is used and there are no crossouts. | Semilegible—can be read but takes some effort. One side of paper is used; occasional crossouts. | Sloppy—hard to read. Both sides of the paper are used and there are several crossouts. |
| Totals | _____ | _____ | _____ |

_____ ÷5 = _____ (Total earned for this assignment)

Go to the Assignments and Activities section of Topic 2: Reading Assessment in the MyEducationLab for your course and complete the activity entitled "Forms of Assessment." As you watch the video and answer the accompanying questions, ask yourself how Mr. Johnson in the opening scenario might respond to this information.

There are some limitations associated with performance assessments. First, they can be costly both in terms of time and human resources because performance assessments are individually administered. Teachers who videotape students' performances for further analysis can spend enormous amounts of time on each assessment. Second, some students might not perform at their best when others are watching. Third, teachers must have excellent classroom management skills because the performance assessment activity can take the teacher away from the rest of the class. Students need to be able to function independently while the teacher is working on the assessments.

Performance assessments are an excellent way to learn about students' reading behaviors, and they must be used in the type of reading diagnosis and improvement program we describe and explain in this text. As a result of watching students complete a task, we can note strengths and needs and design tomorrow's instruction accordingly. Authentic, performance-based assessment is based on a set of assumptions, which include:

1. Authentic contexts are appropriate for answering assessment questions about individual learners.
2. Learners are active participants who should be made aware of their growth and learning and to value both.
3. Ongoing evaluation and teacher guidance occur simultaneously.
4. Both the end product and the means of arriving there (i.e., the process) are important.
5. A body of evidence from many sources needs to be collected, interpreted, and used over time.
6. Interpretation focusing on students' strengths and needs should be used to plan appropriate instruction.
7. The teacher is not the only contributor to the body of evidence. Others, including the students themselves, can provide valid input.

## RECORD KEEPING

Using many different kinds of informal assessment techniques necessitates having a manageable system for keeping track of students' data. Establishing a record-keeping system such as a folder for each student in the class is one way to get started. Use the folder to gather and store data from different sources. For example, Mr. Davies, after meeting with Pearl, goes back to his file drawer to pull her folder. He wants to record that she is attempting to answer inference questions. While looking, he notices that Pearl's folder already contains a number of items he has collected: a checklist of activities, a writing sample, test scores, and a sheet listing specific skills and strategies she has already attained with the dates these were accomplished. In the folder there is also a sheet listing the objectives that Pearl has attempted to accomplish. He adds a note to this list about her recent work on inference questions.

Mr. Davies takes the opportunity to invite Pearl over to look at her folder. He tells her she can also make contributions and suggestions about what should be in the folder to show her progress. Like Mr. Davies, students can also keep records that contain valid assessment data. Encouraging students to keep records and look at assessment data is one way to encourage them to take ownership of their learning.

## PORTFOLIO ASSESSMENT

Many educators have promoted portfolios as a way to enhance students' reading and writing, and today portfolios are used for a variety of purposes. However, confusion sometimes exists between the general concept of portfolios and portfolio assessment.

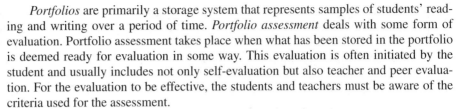

**Portfolio**
A storage system that represents samples of students' reading and writing over a period of time.

**Portfolio assessment**
Material in a portfolio is evaluated in some way.

*Portfolios* are primarily a storage system that represents samples of students' reading and writing over a period of time. *Portfolio assessment* deals with some form of evaluation. Portfolio assessment takes place when what has been stored in the portfolio is deemed ready for evaluation in some way. This evaluation is often initiated by the student and usually includes not only self-evaluation but also teacher and peer evaluation. For the evaluation to be effective, the students and teachers must be aware of the criteria used for the assessment.

Portfolios can be a powerful tool for reading diagnosis because they provide teachers with an ongoing record of their students' reading and writing behavior; however there are several questions that need to be asked and answered in order to get the most from using portfolios (see Figure 5.2).

Portfolios do not give students the reading and writing skills they need to become good readers and writers. They help teachers gain an idea of the kinds of skills students have and need. A close examination can help teachers to design appropriate instruction that will increase student learning.

The use of portfolios can give students more decision-making power. In this sense, they can give more "ownership" to students. They can also be a good way for students, teachers, and parents to see the progression of the students' learning over a period of time.

## THE USES OF OBSERVATION

Go to the Assignments and Activities section of Topic 12: Progress Monitoring in the MyEducationLab for your course and complete the activity entitled "Portfolio Assessment." As you watch the video and answer the accompanying questions, think about how engaging students in the assessment process leads to their ownership.

Direct observation is an essential part of any reading program, and it is especially helpful in diagnosing reading strengths and needs. Observation is also useful for evaluation because it helps teachers become aware of students' attitudes and interests. It is one thing for students to say that they enjoy reading, but quite another for them to actually read. Through observation, teachers can observe many reading-related behaviors such as whether students are voluntarily choosing to read in their free time and how they approach silent reading, oral reading, selecting books, completing assignments, and writing in response to reading. Most often, the best method for determining whether students have learned something is to observe whether they are actually using what they have been taught. Moreover, watching children in a variety of contexts reveals additional information not provided by other assessment measures.[4]

## MAKING OBSERVATIONS OBJECTIVE

*Observation* is a technique; it is a means of collecting data. For observations to be of value, teachers must be as objective as possible and avoid making premature generalizations about a student's behavior. For example, by observing that Sharon on one or two occasions is reading mystery stories, Sharon's teacher might conclude that Sharon likes mysteries. This may be so, but it may be that she is just trying them out. Sharon may actually like only a few mystery writers, and she may read only one or two mysteries a year. Here are some suggestions on how to make observations as objective and useful as possible:

**Observation**
A technique that helps teachers collect data about students' behavior.

1. Use checklists and anecdotal records (observed behavior without interpretations) to record observations (see the next two sections).

[4]J. Choate and L. Miller, "Curricular Assessment and Programming," in J. Choate, J. Bennett, B. Enright, L. Miller, J. Poteet, and T. Raledy, *Assessing and Programming Basic Curriculum Skills* (Boston: Allyn and Bacon, 1987), pp. 35–50.

## FIGURE 5.2  Portfolio Checklist

The following questions are those you may wish to pose to yourself as you go about implementing portfolios. Remember that more than one item may be "checked" to answer each question. Also note that your ideas are also important! These are **suggestions!**

***How will the portfolio be used?***
_____ for student self-reflection
_____ as part of regular school evaluation/report card
_____ at parent conferences
_____ in IEP meetings
_____ in communicating to next year's teacher(s)
_____ in curricular planning
_____ in acknowledging students' accomplishments

***How will the portfolio be organized?***
_____ for finished pieces only from several subject areas
_____ to show progress from first idea to final copy
_____ to show samples of a week/month/year's work
_____ "best" work only
_____ group work included

***How will the items in the portfolio be arranged?***
_____ chronologically
_____ by student: from worst to best (reasons stated for each)
_____ by teacher: from worst to best (reasons stated for each)
_____ from beginning of idea to final product
_____ by subject area

***What procedures will be used to place items in the portfolio?***
_____ select specific times for pulling student work
_____ show students how to select items
_____ pull items that meet established criteria
_____ random

***What will the portfolio look like?***
_____ two pieces of posterboard stapled or taped together
_____ box or other container (e.g., milk crate with a hanging file for each student)
_____ scrapbook
_____ manila folder or some other large envelope
_____ CD-ROM or DVD

***Who will do the evaluating?***
_____ teacher
_____ several teachers
_____ student self-evaluation
_____ peer evaluation
_____ parent evaluation

***How will the portfolio be evaluated?***
_____ number of entries
_____ use of benchmarks or standards
_____ degree of self-reflection
_____ demonstrated improvement from past performances
_____ achievement of preset goals (student, teacher, and/or school)
_____ combination of products, perceptions, reflections

*Source:* Tom Armstrong. *Multiple Intelligence in the Classroom.* Alexandria, VA: Association for the Supervision of Curriculum Development (ASCD), 1994.

2. Observe the student over an extended period of time before making any inferences about the student's behavior.
3. Avoid projecting feelings or attitudes onto the student's behavior.
4. Use observations in conjunction with other measurement techniques, including those that allow students to report about themselves.

5. Allow someone else to observe.
6. Make sure that only observed behavior is recorded and record it immediately, or as soon as possible.
7. Look for a pattern of behavior before making any inferences about behavior.
8. Remember that checklists and anecdotal records do not reveal causes of the observed behaviors; they only help to identify patterns of behavior from which a teacher can try to deduce the existence of possible strengths and needs.
9. Note the date and time on all observations.

As valuable and powerful as observation is, for some teachers, it can seem overwhelming. There are so many skills needed to observe accurately that they hardly know where to begin. For example, oral reading can help a teacher to observe much about a child's reading ability. Questions such as the following can guide the observation:

Does the child read for meaning?
What does the child do when meaning is not maintained?
How well can the child retell what was read?
Does the child read with a sense of meaning, expression, and fluency?

Focusing on all the possible questions through observation at any one time can seem daunting. When teachers consider the unique needs of English language learners, the task may appear even more complex.

Our suggestion is this: Less is more. That is, rather than trying to use all questions at once, choose one question that best fits your purpose. What is it that you want to know most about this student? Once you have determined this, you can record your observations on a form such as the one shown in Figure 5.3

## ANECDOTAL RECORDS

**Anecdotal record**
A record of observed behavior over a period of time.

Another way to lessen any anxiety related to observation is to use *anecdotal records,* a record of *observed behavior* that is as objective as possible. When recording observed behavior, make every attempt to put down exactly what has taken place *as soon as possible.* Record the date and time of the event, as well as an interpretation of the observed behavior; however, the teacher's interpretation should be put in brackets or set off in some way to avoid confusion with the actual observed behavior. Recording and observing the student over an extended period of time is best. Look for a pattern of behavior, rather than making conclusions based on one observation. Figure 5.4 shows one example of an anecdotal record.

What information should be recorded? This is a difficult question to answer, and can be overwhelming for any teacher. Because teachers using this method record everything that happens, anecdotal records sometimes capture unusual behavior. For example, you might observe a student taking a break from reading and staring into space. Making a note that the student was staring and then overinterpreting the staring could lead to a false assumption about the learner. However, recording common behaviors *over an extended period of time* can be very helpful. Consider the following scenario.

FIGURE 5.3   **Observation Guide**

**Class Observation Form**

Focal Question: _____

Date: _____

| *Name of Student* | *Notes* |
| --- | --- |
|  |  |
|  |  |
|  |  |
|  |  |
|  |  |
|  |  |
|  |  |
|  |  |
|  |  |
|  |  |
|  |  |
|  |  |
|  |  |
|  |  |
|  |  |
|  |  |

 # SCENARIO: MR. JACKSON CHECKS AND WRITES

Mr. Jackson has a reading checklist for each student, and after each reading lesson and at other appropriate times, he checks off what he has observed. To supplement his checklist, Mr. Jackson also employs anecdotal information. Whenever he notices anything unusual, he records the observed behavior. For example, yesterday Joshua started a fight with his best friend, and then for the rest of the day, he refused to do any work. Mr. Jackson made note of this.

Mr. Jackson also observed and noted that Joshua rested his head on his desk during reading.

1/9 Joshua puts head on desk—reading period
1/13 Joshua puts head on desk—reading period
1/16 Joshua puts head on desk—reading period
1/20 Joshua puts head on desk—reading period

1/23 Joshua puts head on desk—reading period
1/27 Joshua puts head on desk—reading period

Joshua's behavior of putting his head on the desk has become such a normal occurrence that Mr. Jackson could have overlooked it. Only by recording when Joshua put his head on the desk could Mr. Jackson see that it was always during a reading period. By recording the dates, Mr. Jackson could check to see what kinds of reading lessons were involved. It may be that Joshua was tired or sleepy, but that is most unlikely. It is more probable that by checking further, Mr. Jackson will find that Joshua is bored because the work is too easy for him or that he is frustrated because the work is too hard for him. It may be that Joshua cannot do sustained silent reading because of an eye problem. Joshua's resting behavior may be related to any number of factors. The point is that Mr. Jackson would not be aware of these problems had he not recorded what appeared to be "common" behavior.

---

**FIGURE 5.4 Rachael's Anecdotal Record**

| *Strategies Implemented* | *Result* |
|---|---|
| **Spelling** | |
| 3/11 Start a list of trouble words and tape to desk. These become no excuse words. | 3/11 She refers to list and keeps it out. Because of CSAP we didn't do any writing. |
| 3/17 Go through published pieces and find words she wants to use as spelling words. (Find 5) | 3/17 She said in a conference "I was writing and noticed I spelled **her** and it didn't look right. I meant it to be **here.** The list helped and I know that her is **her** not **here.**" |
| 3/19 Do **look, say, cover, write,** and **check** practice. | 3/17 We added 3 words to her list (their, there, and white). |
| 3/23 Had her look through writing and check to see all no excuse words were spelled correctly. | 3/19 She was able to do the list she has on her desk. She is also working on definitions. |
| | 3/23 No words misspelled from her list. |
| **Sentence Starters** | |
| 3/17 Conference with her about past writings and discuss how authors start sentences in different ways. Ask her to try to vary her sentences as she writes today. | 3/17 I showed her examples of her writing, and we went over strengths and weaknesses. I had her read a past piece where she repeated the beginning. I had her identify and highlight what was repeating. We took 1 paragraph and rewrote to change the sentences. |
| 3/22 We focused on one sentence beginner and changed old sentences from past writing into new ones (used Writer's Express). | 3/22 Sample two shows how she was working on using introductory phrases. |
| | 3/23 Shared with me that she noticed an old piece was too repetitive. She changed the sentence beginnings as she typed. |

While there are no specific guidelines about what should or should not be recorded, teachers should be sure to record a variety of types of behavior, including physical, verbal, and social. As with any other assessment, the focus of observation should be: "What do I want to know?" and "Why do I want to know it?" However, alert teachers who are aware of the individual differences of the students in their classes will recognize those situations that warrant recording.

Here are some examples:

1. Bela always seems to want to go to the restroom. Recording when and how often she goes may point to a physiological problem or an emotional problem, or it may be that she wants to "escape" from a certain situation.
2. Michael is always causing disruptions in class. Recording when Michael acts up will help to determine whether there is a pattern. Are there any immediate antecedents to his acting up? It may be that causing disruptions is Michael's way of avoiding reading. What is he avoiding? Is he bored or is he frustrated?

Remember that observations and the resultant anecdotal record do not explain causes of behavior. Observation is a technique for gathering data; it helps teachers learn more about the behavior of students. When used with other assessment techniques discussed in this chapter, as well as test data (see Chapter 6), anecdotal records can help teachers hypothesize about causes.

## CHECKLISTS

**Checklist**
A means for systematically and quickly recording behavior; the observer checks items as present or absent.

*Checklists* usually consist of lists of important and typical behaviors that the observer marks as being present or absent. Checklists are a means of systematically and quickly recording a student's behavior. For example, to ascertain students' reading interests, I (MO) administer a reading interest inventory to each student. I then compile the results on a class profile, which is shown in Figure 5.5. At a glance, I can see who has common interests. I can use the results to group students when I have them do investigations. I can also use the list to make sure the classroom library reflects the interests of the class.

Checklist formats may vary. Some use rating scales, some are used for a whole class or group, and some are used for an individual child. The purpose for the checklist should determine what kind of checklist is used. An example of a diagnostic checklist for a child's speech problems is shown in Figure 5.6.

### GROUP AND INDIVIDUAL CHECKLISTS

Group checklists can be used to follow up on hunches or to find general trends among a whole class of learners. At a glance, a teacher can see who might need help in a specific area and who obviously does not. A group checklist can be helpful in planning instruction for the group as well as for the individual, whereas an individual checklist is useful in assessing the strengths and weaknesses of an individual student only.

Figure 5.7 shows a group checklist I (MO) used to record how my kindergarten students performed on a language concepts test. At a glance, I was able to see that some children understood the majority of concepts, whereas others did not. I used this chart to design lessons for the children who needed some explicit

## FIGURE 5.5 Reading Interest Inventory

| Names \ Interests | animals | true stories | science fiction | fantasy | mysteries | stories about people | poetry | funny books | science topics | series books | magazines (sports) | magazines (computers) |
|---|---|---|---|---|---|---|---|---|---|---|---|---|
| Hank | ✔ | | | | | | | | | ✔ | ✔ | |
| Meredith | | | ✔ | | ✔ | | | | | | | ✔ |
| Brenda | ✔ | ✔ | | | | | ✔ | ✔ | | | | |
| Jay | ✔ | | ✔ | ✔ | | ✔ | | | | ✔ | | |
| Corey | | ✔ | | | | ✔ | | | | | | |
| Kamal | | | ✔ | | | | | | ✔ | | | |
| Jason | ✔ | | | | | | | | | | | |
| Joel | | | | | ✔ | | | ✔ | | | | ✔ |
| Holly | ✔ | | ✔ | | | | ✔ | | ✔ | | | |
| Marni | ✔ | | | | | ✔ | | | | | ✔ | |
| Sarah | | | | ✔ | | | ✔ | ✔ | | | | ✔ |
| Derrick | | ✔ | ✔ | ✔ | | | | | ✔ | | | |
| Ryan | | | | | | | | | | | | |
| John | | ✔ | | | ✔ | | | | | ✔ | | |
| Sandi | | | | | | | | | | ✔ | | |
| Robyn | ✔ | | | | | | | | | ✔ | | |
| Annie | | ✔ | | | | | | | | ✔ | | |
| Kurt | | | | ✔ | | | | | | ✔ | | |
| Jeff | | | | | | | | | | | | ✔ |
| Tina | | | ✔ | ✔ | | | | | | | | |
| Hailey | ✔ | | | | | | | | ✔ | | | |
| Bo | | | | | ✔ | | | ✔ | | | ✔ | |
| Jake | | | ✔ | | | | | ✔ | | | ✔ | |
| Shari | | | | | | | | ✔ | | | ✔ | |
| Jessie | ✔ | | | | | | | ✔ | | ✔ | | |

**FIGURE 5.6   Diagnostic Checklist of Speech Problems**

Child's Name: _____

Grade: _____

Date: _____

|  | Yes | No |
|---|---|---|
| 1. Is child's voice | | |
|    a. loud? | | |
|    b. too low? | | |
|    c. nasal? | | |
|    d. hoarse? | | |
|    e. monotonous? | | |
|    f. pitched abnormally high? | | |
|    g. pitched abnormally low? | | |
| 2. Is child's rate of speech | | |
|    a. too slow? | | |
|    b. too rapid? | | |
| 3. Is child's phrasing poor? | | |
| 4. Is child's speech hesitant? | | |
| 5. Does the child show evidence of articulatory difficulties such as | | |
|    a. the distortion of sounds? | | |
|    b. the substitution of one sound for another? | | |
|    c. the omission of sounds? | | |
| 6. Does the child show evidence of vocabulary problems such as | | |
|    a. the repetition of phrases? | | |
|    b. a limited vocabulary? | | |
| 7. Does the child show evidence of negative attitudes toward oral communication such as | | |
|    a. not engaging in discussions or conversations? | | |
|    b. not volunteering to give a talk or oral report? | | |

teaching. While the other children were engaged with free exploration, I worked with those students who needed to learn a given concept. I also made sure that I used these terms when teaching the whole class as a way of reinforcing the language concept.

A teacher who wishes to see a complete profile of a child may prefer the individual checklist. A teacher who wishes to see a profile of the strengths and weaknesses of an entire class for instructional planning will prefer a group checklist. For example, when listening to a student read, I (JE) record notes and observations on a photocopy of the passage the student is reading. Once all students in the class have read, I note the scores

### FIGURE 5.7 Whole Class Language Concepts Checklist

Boehm Basic Language Concepts

| Names | 1. top | 2. through | 3. away from | 4. next to | 5. inside | 6. same, not many | 7. middle | 8. few | 9. farthest | 10. around | 11. over | 12. widest | 13. most | 14. between | 15. whole | 16. nearest | 17. second | 18. corner | 19. several | 20. behind | 21. row | 22. different | 23. after |
|---|---|---|---|---|---|---|---|---|---|---|---|---|---|---|---|---|---|---|---|---|---|---|---|
| Vanessa | ✔ | ✔ | ✔ | ✔ | ✔ | ✔ | ✔ | ✔ | ✔ | ✔ | ○ | ✔ | ✔ | ✔ | ✔ | ✔ | ✔ | ✔ | ✔ | ✔ | ✔ | ✔ | ✔ |
| Jessica | ✔ | ✔ | ✔ | ✔ | ✔ | ✔ | ✔ | ✔ | ✔ | ✔ | ✔ | ✔ | ✔ | ✔ | ✔ | ✔ | ✔ | ✔ | ✔ | ✔ | ✔ | ✔ | ✔ |
| Diamond | ✔ | ✔ | ✔ | ✔ | ✔ | ✔ | ✔ | ✔ | ✔ | ✔ | ✔ | ✔ | ✔ | ✔ | ✔ | ✔ | ✔ | ✔ | ✔ | ✔ | ✔ | ✔ | ✔ |
| James | ✔ | ✔ | ✔ | ✔ | ✔ | ✔ | ✔ | ✔ | ✔ | ✔ | ○ | ✔ | ✔ | ✔ | ✔ | ✔ | ✔ | ✔ | ✔ | ✔ | ✔ | ✔ | ○ |
| Renee | ✔ | ✔ | ✔ | ✔ | ✔ | ✔ | ✔ | ✔ | ✔ | ✔ | ✔ | ○ | ✔ | ✔ | ✔ | ✔ | ✔ | ✔ | ✔ | ✔ | ○ | ✔ | ○ |
| Victoria | ✔ | ✔ | ✔ | ✔ | ✔ | ○ | ○ | ○ | ○ | ✔ | ○ | ✔ | ✔ | ✔ | ✔ | ○ | ✔ | ○ | ✔ | ✔ | ○ | ✔ | ✔ |
| Tatiana | ✔ | ✔ | ✔ | ✔ | ✔ | ✔ | ✔ | ✔ | ✔ | ✔ | ✔ | ✔ | ✔ | ✔ | ✔ | ✔ | ✔ | ✔ | ✔ | ✔ | ✔ | ✔ | ✔ |
| Kelly | ✔ | ✔ | ✔ | ✔ | ✔ | ✔ | ✔ | ✔ | ✔ | ✔ | ✔ | ○ | ✔ | ✔ | ✔ | ✔ | ✔ | ✔ | ✔ | ✔ | ○ | ✔ | ✔ |
| Rory | ✔ | ✔ | ✔ | ✔ | ✔ | ○ | ✔ | ○ | ✔ | ✔ | ✔ | ✔ | ✔ | ✔ | ✔ | ✔ | ✔ | ✔ | ✔ | ✔ | ✔ | ✔ | ✔ |
| Tiffany | ✔ | ✔ | ✔ | ✔ | ✔ | ✔ | ✔ | ✔ | ✔ | ✔ | ✔ | ✔ | ✔ | ✔ | ✔ | ✔ | ✔ | ✔ | ✔ | ✔ | ✔ | ○ | ○ |
| Ethan | ✔ | ✔ | ✔ | ✔ | ✔ | ✔ | ✔ | ✔ | ✔ | ✔ | ✔ | ✔ | ✔ | ✔ | ✔ | ✔ | ✔ | ✔ | ✔ | ✔ | ✔ | ✔ | ✔ |
| Genevieve | ✔ | ✔ | ✔ | ✔ | ✔ | ✔ | ✔ | ✔ | ✔ | ✔ | ✔ | ✔ | ✔ | ✔ | ✔ | ✔ | ✔ | ✔ | ✔ | ✔ | ✔ | ✔ | ✔ |
| Robert | ✔ | ✔ | ✔ | ✔ | ✔ | ✔ | ✔ | ✔ | ✔ | ✔ | ✔ | ✔ | ○ | ✔ | ○ | ✔ | ✔ | ○ | ✔ | ✔ | ○ | ✔ | ✔ |
| Marcelino | ○ | ✔ | ✔ | ✔ | ○ | ○ | ✔ | ✔ | ✔ | ✔ | ○ | ○ | ✔ | ○ | ○ | ○ | ○ | ○ | ○ | ○ | ✔ | ○ | ○ |
| Christopher | ✔ | ✔ | ✔ | ✔ | ✔ | ✔ | ✔ | ✔ | ✔ | ✔ | ✔ | ✔ | ✔ | ✔ | ✔ | ✔ | ✔ | ✔ | ✔ | ✔ | ✔ | ✔ | ✔ |
| Margaret | ✔ | ✔ | ✔ | ✔ | ✔ | ✔ | ✔ | ✔ | ✔ | ✔ | ✔ | ✔ | ✔ | ○ | ✔ | ✔ | ✔ | ✔ | ✔ | ✔ | ✔ | ✔ | ✔ |
| Mindy | ✔ | ✔ | ✔ | ✔ | ✔ | ○ | ✔ | ○ | ✔ | ✔ | ✔ | ✔ | ✔ | ✔ | ✔ | ✔ | ✔ | ✔ | ✔ | ✔ | ✔ | ✔ | ✔ |
| Ben | ✔ | ✔ | ✔ | ✔ | ✔ | ✔ | ✔ | ✔ | ✔ | ✔ | ✔ | ✔ | ✔ | ✔ | ✔ | ✔ | ✔ | ✔ | ✔ | ✔ | ✔ | ✔ | ✔ |
| Megan | ✔ | ✔ | ✔ | ✔ | ✔ | ✔ | ✔ | ✔ | ○ | ✔ | ✔ | ✔ | ✔ | ✔ | ✔ | ✔ | ✔ | ✔ | ✔ | ✔ | ✔ | ✔ | ✔ |
| Natasha | ✔ | ✔ | ✔ | ✔ | ✔ | ○ | ✔ | ✔ | ✔ | ✔ | ○ | ✔ | ✔ | ✔ | ○ | ✔ | ○ | ✔ | ✔ | ✔ | ✔ | ○ | ○ |
| Jack | ✔ | ✔ | ✔ | ✔ | ✔ | ✔ | ✔ | ✔ | ✔ | ✔ | ✔ | ✔ | ✔ | ✔ | ✔ | ✔ | ✔ | ✔ | ✔ | ✔ | ✔ | ✔ | ✔ |

on a class profile. Figure 5.8A shows an individual's performance and Figure 5.8B shows the group's performance.

Regardless of whether a group or individual checklist is used, it should contain an itemized list of behaviors in a domain of reading, a space for dates, and a space for special notes. An example of an individual diagnostic checklist for comprehension in oral and silent reading is shown in Figure 5.9.

---

**FIGURE 5.8A   Individual Performance Checklist**

---

Name: *Brenda*

---

### *Pettranella*

Long ago in a country far away lived a little girl named Pettranella. She lived with her father and mother in the upstairs of her grandmother's tall, narrow house.

Other houses just like it lined the street on both sides, and at the end of the street was the mill. All day and all night smoke rose from its great smokestacks and lay like a grey
blanket over the city. It hid the sun and choked the trees, and it ~~withered~~ the flowers that                II
tried to grow in the window boxes.

One dark winter night when the wind blew cold from the east, Pettranella's father
came home with a letter. The family gathered around the table in the warm yellow circle of          I
the lamp to read it; even the grandmother came from her room downstairs to listen.

"It's from Uncle ~~Cris~~ in America," began her father. "He has his homestead there now,          II
and is already clearing his land. Someday it will be a large farm growing many ~~crops~~ of          II
~~grain.~~" And then he read the letter aloud.                                                          I

When he had finished, Pettranella said, "I wish we could go there, too, and live on a homestead."

Her parents looked at each other, their eyes twinkling with a secret. "We *are* going,"
said her mother. "We are sailing on the very next ship."                                                I

1. ⎱
2. ⎰  *couldn't remember anything for*
3.    *sure – even w/ prodding*
4.

---

## CHECKLISTS AND RATING SCALES

A checklist that uses a *rating scale* is actually an evaluation instrument. This type of checklist is different from one that records observed behavior. A rating scale is used by the teacher to quantify a student's progress. These numbers can also be used to make students aware of their progress in a specific reading domain. While children may not completely understand reading theory and terms, progress from a 2 to a 3 is easy to grasp.

Rating criteria need to be set up beforehand to help teachers give a valid rating to a particular student. For example, during a retelling of a passage, the established expectation for a rating of 3 is that students can identify setting and character traits. Therefore, a student whose retell includes clear statements about story setting and character traits will receive a rating of 3.

**FIGURE 5.8B   Group Performance Checklist**

**Level 1 — Pettranella**

| Name | W. Rec. 0–12 | Comp 3–4 | P/F | Comments |
|---|---|---|---|---|
| Hank | 10 | +2 | F | because of comp. |
| Meredith | 4 | +4 | P | very fluent |
| Brenda | 9 | +0 | F | looks like comp. needs work but could be expressive voc. |
| Jay | 3 | +3 | P | fairly fluent; could retell a bit |
| Corey | 3 | +4 | P | fluent |
| Kamal | 1 | +4 | P | very fluent |
| Jason | 26 | +3 | F | applies knowledge of phonics |
| Jack | 4 | +0 | F | looks like comp. but most likely expression is what needs work |
| Holly | 7 | +2 | F | very fluent; comp. appears weak |
| Marni | 3 | +4 | P | very fluent |
| Sarah | 3 | +4 | P | |
| Derrick | 3 | +4 | P | |
| Ryan | 1 | +3 | P | fluent |
| John | 13 | +2 1/2 | P | —marginal |
| Sandi | 0 | +4 | P | |
| Robyn | 7 | +4 | P | fairly fluent |
| Annie | 0 | +4 | P | |
| Kristy | 1 | +4 | P | very fluent; good intonation |
| John | 4 | +4 | P | very fluent |
| Jeff | 0 | +4 | P | |
| Zack | 21 | +2 1/2 | F | will need curr. adap. to read this text successfully |
| Jeff | 11 | +3 | P | fairly fluent |
| Sara | 0 | +4 | P | |
| Haitley | 0 | +3 | P | |
| Tina | 0 | +4 | P | |
| Kyle | 1 | +4 | P | |

*Source* [for Figures 5.8A and B]: From *Flexible Grouping in Reading* by Michael Opitz. Published by Scholastic Teaching Resources/Scholastic, Inc. Copyright © 1998, by Michael Opitz. Reprinted by permission.

## FIGURE 5.9 Comprehension Observation Checklist

|  | Date | Text | Comments |
|---|---|---|---|
| Can put an easy sentence or passage in own words _____ |  |  |  |
| Makes simple inferences putting in own words _____ |  |  |  |
| Can explain what just happened _____ |  |  |  |
| Can do blow-by-blow repetition of a story _____ |  |  |  |
| Can retell a story in a different context _____ |  |  |  |
| Self-monitors when lost in a story: with help _____ without help _____ |  |  |  |
| Asks questions when self-monitoring: with help _____without help _____ |  |  |  |
| "Gets" stories that demand "big picture" inferences: with help _____ without help _____ |  |  |  |
| Looks back at details to "get" stories that demand "big picture" inferences: with help _____ without help _____ |  |  |  |
| Uses relevant prior knowledge to "get" stories that demand "big picture" inferences: with help _____ without help _____ |  |  |  |
| Can explain where information to "get" stories came from: with help _____ without help _____ |  |  |  |
| Anticipates what will happen later in story _____ |  |  |  |
| Explains reasons for anticipation: with help _____ without help _____ |  |  |  |
| Makes relevant connections between book and personal experience: with help _____ without help _____ |  |  |  |
| Can distinguish between relevant and irrelevant personal experience connections: with help _____ without help _____ |  |  |  |
| Projects self into situations in book: with help _____ without help _____ |  |  |  |
| Extracts important information from book: with help _____ without help _____ |  |  |  |
| Can organize information from a book: with help _____ without help _____ |  |  |  |
| True summary: with help _____ without help _____ |  |  |  |

*Source:* James Erekson and Eliot A. Singer, Observational Checklist for Reading, 1996. Reprinted by permission.

## OTHER HELPFUL INFORMAL ASSESSMENT TECHNIQUES

There are some important student characteristics that cannot be discerned through direct observation. Attitudes, perceptions, feelings, and interests are examples of essential characteristics that cannot be directly observed. Cognitive structures such as concepts and schemata also cannot be observed directly. Projective techniques, informal interviews, and inventory-type measures can help reveal these aspects. Students can also provide valid information about their own learning that cannot be gleaned from other sources.

In a reading diagnosis and improvement program, looking at both the cognitive and affective characteristics of students is important. Students' attitudes and interests will affect what they learn and whether they learn. Reading helps reading; unfortunately, many students are not choosing to read. The reasons for this lack of interest in reading are varied. Understanding students' attitudes and interests enables teachers to motivate students and instill in them a positive attitude toward reading. For example, if a student is interested in sports, the teacher can find books about sports to motivate the student to read.

### INFORMAL STUDENT INTERVIEWS

> **Informal interviews**
> Teachers converse with students to learn about their interests and feelings.

The easiest way to learn about students' likes or dislikes is to ask them. Teachers have many opportunities during the school day to converse with their students and learn about their feelings and interests. Teachers can also set up special times during the school day to meet with students for a consultation in the form of an *informal interview*. Doing so helps to build rapport with students, as well as to gain information about them.

Another purpose for interviewing students who are having difficulty with reading is to gain insight into how they perceive reading. Because perception determines behavior, a change in behavior follows rather than precedes implicit perceptions. In order to change reading behaviors, the students' perceptions of reading must first change. Thus, gaining an insight into students' existing perceptions assists the teacher in better understanding why students function as they do and knowing which, if any, additional aspects of the reading process students need to perceive and employ to increase their own reading ability.

A third purpose for interviewing students is to enable them to explore their own reading behaviors—to help them understand themselves. In talking about their reading, students become more aware of how they perceive and approach reading. Self-awareness is essential because it is the first step toward change. Thus, becoming aware of their perceptions about reading can help students realize whether their perceptions are accurate and, if not, which additional aspects need to be incorporated into their understanding of the reading process. For example, the first three questions in Figure 5.10 are designed to elicit students' perceptions of reading. A student who responds, "I'm trying to understand the story" or "Sound out the words I'm reading so I'll understand the book" is showing a perception that emphasizes comprehension.

In addition, becoming more conscious of the strategies that they presently use in reading may, with teacher guidance, lead students to see that there are additional strategies they can and may need to learn. Once aware of these options, students can decide which strategies to use and when to use them to ensure comprehension. In other words, they can exercise control over their cognitive actions.

Figure 5.10 is an example of a protocol that can reveal both perceptions of reading and strategies used in reading. The first four questions focus on perceptions of reading, whereas the last three are designed to elicit strategies used in reading.

---

FIGURE 5.10   **Student Interview Protocol**

Name: _____

*Student Interview*

1. What is the most important thing about reading?

   _____

   _____

2. When you are reading, what are you trying to do?

   _____

   _____

3. What is reading?

   _____

   _____

4. When you come to a word you don't know, what do you do?

   _____

   _____

5. Do you think it's important to read every word correctly? Why? Why not?

   _____

   _____

6. What makes a person a good reader?

   _____

   _____

7. Do you think good readers ever come to a word they don't know? If yes, what do you think they do?

   _____

   _____

---

The following are some suggestions for managing interviews:

1. Count on spending about ten minutes for each interview.
2. Because the interviews require one-to-one attention, plan independent activities for the other children to minimize interruptions.
3. Interview children more than once. You might consider interviewing students at the beginning, middle, and end of the year, making note of shifts in their perceptions of reading and the repertoire of strategies they use on the form shown in Figure 5.11.
4. Interpret the responses. Do they primarily focus on reading as a meaning-seeking activity? Do the responses primarily focus on reading as being an act of pronouncing

**FIGURE 5.11** **Student Interview Summary**

Name: _____ Interviewer: _____

Grade: _____ Age: _____ School: _____

_____

***Beginning of School Year*** **Date:** _____

Perceptions of Reading Strategies Used

***Middle of School Year*** **Date:** _____

Perceptions of Reading Strategies Used

***End of School Year*** **Date:** _____

Perceptions of Reading Strategies Used

words with no attention to their meanings? Do the responses focus on something other than understanding of words? Do the responses show that the reader has a limited set of strategies?

5. Make a list of the strategies that students mention. Some strategies they might mention are: sound it out, ask, use other words, break it into parts, skip it, use a dictionary, spell it, wait for the teacher, stop reading.

The following are some suggestions for using information revealed from the interviews:

1. Use what you discover to plan appropriate instruction. For example, if students comment that the purpose of reading is to say the words, prepare and teach lessons that emphasize the meaning aspect. Such a lesson might begin like this: "Today I want to teach you another way of figuring out words. When you come to a word you cannot pronounce, say 'blank' and keep reading until the end of the sentence. When you get to the end of the sentence, go back to the word that caused you some problems and ask yourself what word might make sense that looks like the word that is actually printed."

2. Consider using a whole class brainstorming session to create a chart showing what to do to gain pronunciation of a word and what to do to gain the meaning of a word when reading.

3. If the interviews as a whole seem to indicate that students lack understanding about what good readers do when they read, create a list and post it in the classroom.

## INTEREST INVENTORIES

**Interest inventory**
A statement or questionnaire method that helps teachers learn about students' likes and dislikes.

The purpose of an *interest inventory* is to help teachers learn about their students' likes and dislikes. In this book, we are particularly invested in finding out about students' likes or dislikes so that we can use this information to help stimulate them to read.

Interest inventories usually employ statements, questions, or both to obtain information. The statement or questionnaire method enables the teacher to gain a great amount of information in a relatively short period of time. Teachers who have good rapport with their students will be able to gain the trust of their students, and can often get them to speak more candidly. Before administering the inventory, teachers can discuss its purpose and ask students to speak frankly.

Interest inventories are most often individually administered. Teachers can use a checklist type of questionnaire, where they read the question aloud and the children mark the appropriate space. Figure 5.12 shows an example. One way to compile the results of individual inventories was shown earlier (see p. 73). As with other instruments above, teachers use the inventory to answer basic assessment questions: "What do I want to know?" and "Why do I want to know it?" When the inventory is finished, it should be treated like other data or information. Using the results is essential.

## READING ATTITUDE SURVEYS

Attitude has a significant impact on reading; this should come as no surprise if we take a minute to think about ourselves as readers. When we have a positive outlook on our ability to read, we are more likely to read because we enjoy it and we are successful. We are also more likely to comprehend any given text when we have a positive attitude about it. The reverse is true for negative attitudes.

Teachers can uncover student attitudes by using an attitude survey. Figure 5.13 is a reading attitude survey intended for primary grades, and Figure 5.14 is for intermediate grades.

**FIGURE 5.12   Interest Inventories**

LOWER PRIMARY GRADES (Read aloud by teacher)

Name _____          Grade _____

1. Do you like to read?   Yes _____  No _____  Sometimes _____

2. What kinds of books do you like to read? Books about  a. animals _____ b. children _____
   c. sports _____ d. adventure _____ e. fairy tales _____

3. What do you like to do after school?  a. watch TV _____ b. read a book _____ c. play _____
   d. do schoolwork _____ e. work around the house _____ f. work on a hobby _____
   g. work with computer if available _____

4. What do you like to do when there is no school? a. watch TV _____ b. read a book _____
   c. play _____ d. do schoolwork _____ e. work around the house _____
   f. go shopping with parents _____ g. visit the zoo _____
   h. work with computer if available _____

5. What are your favorite television shows? a. cartoons _____ b. comedy shows _____
   c. movies _____ d. mysteries _____ e. musicals _____ f. game shows _____
   g. adventure _____

6. What are your favorite games? a. group games played outside _____ b. indoor games _____
   c. electronic (television) games _____ d. computer games _____

(For numbers 2 through 6, the child may check more than one.)

UPPER PRIMARY GRADES

Name _____          Grade _____

1.  Do you like to read? _____

2.  When do you like to read the best? _____
    _____

3.  What is your favorite subject?  _____
    _____

4.  What is your favorite book?  _____
    _____

5.  What do you like to do after school? _____
    _____

6.  What is your favorite game? _____
    _____

7.  What is your favorite television show?  _____
    _____

8.  What kinds of books do you like to read? _____
    _____

(*continued*)

**FIGURE 5.12**   *(continued)*

9.  What is your hobby? _____

_____

10.  Do you take out books from the library? _____

_____

INTERMEDIATE GRADES

Name _____   Grade _____

1.  Do you like to read? _____
2.  What kinds of books are your favorites? _____

_____

3.  What do you like to do after school? _____

_____

4.  What are your favorite subjects? _____

_____

5.  Name your favorite hobby. _____
6.  How often during the month do you go to the public library? _____
7.  How often during the week do you go to your school library? _____
8.  Name your favorite book. _____
9.  What do you enjoy doing the most? _____
10.  What is your favorite television show? _____
11.  Name your favorite movie. _____
12.  What is your favorite sport? _____
13.  If you could go anywhere in the world, where would you like to go? _____
14.  If you could visit any book character you wanted to, whom would you like to visit? _____

_____

15.  Name the magazines and newspapers that you read. _____
16.  What part of the newspaper do you like to read the best? _____
17.  What book is the most popular among you and your friends? _____
18.  What would you like to be when you grow up? _____

## PROJECTIVE TECHNIQUES

**Projective technique**

A method in which the individual puts himself or herself into a situation and reveals how he or she feels.

*Projective techniques* are subtle procedures in which individuals put themselves into a situation and reveal how they feel. On a projective test, students are more likely to give the answer that is natural for them and, as a result, reveal how they really feel.

Projective techniques have definite benefits in reading diagnosis and improvement. They can help teachers gain insights into the way students feel about themselves. Teachers can also gain information about why students think they have a reading problem. The teacher could then use this information to plan appropriate instruction.

Here are some examples of projective tests that can be administered either to a group or individually.

### Sentence Completion Test

The sentence completion test is easy to administer in a relatively short period of time. Students are given some unfinished sentences that they are asked to complete as rapidly as

---

**FIGURE 5.13   Primary Reading Survey**

Name: _____

| *How do you feel when:* | 😊 | 😐 | ☹️ |
|---|---|---|---|
| 1. your teacher reads a story to you? | | | |
| 2. your class has reading time? | | | |
| 3. you can read with a friend? | | | |
| 4. you read out loud to your teacher? | | | |
| 5. you read out loud to someone at home? | | | |
| 6. someone reads to you at home? | | | |
| 7. someone gives you a book as a present? | | | |
| 8. you read a book to yourself at home? | | | |

*How do you think:*

| | | | |
|---|---|---|---|
| 9. your teacher feels when you read out loud? | | | |
| 10. your family feels when you read out loud? | | | |

*How do you feel about how well you can read?*

Make this face look the way you feel.

FIGURE 5.14 **Reading Attitude Survey for Grades 3 and Up**

Name: _____

**Directions:** The 20 statements that follow will be read to you. After each statement is read, circle the letter that best describes how you feel about that statement. Your answers will not be graded because there are no right or wrong answers. Your feeling about each statement is what's important.

SA = Strongly Agree    A = Agree    U = Undecided
D = Disagree    SD = Strongly Disagree

SA  A  U  D  SD    1. Reading is for learning but not for enjoyment.

SA  A  U  D  SD    2. Money spent on books is well spent.

SA  A  U  D  SD    3. There is nothing to be gained from reading books.

SA  A  U  D  SD    4. Books are a bore.

SA  A  U  D  SD    5. Reading is a good way to spend spare time.

SA  A  U  D  SD    6. Sharing books in class is a waste of time.

SA  A  U  D  SD    7. Reading turns me on.

SA  A  U  D  SD    8. Reading is only for students seeking good grades.

SA  A  U  D  SD    9. Books aren't usually good enough to finish.

SA  A  U  D  SD    10. Reading is rewarding to me.

SA  A  U  D  SD    11. Reading becomes boring after about an hour.

SA  A  U  D  SD    12. Most books are too long and dull.

SA  A  U  D  SD    13. Free reading doesn't teach anything.

SA  A  U  D  SD    14. There should be more time for free reading during the school day.

SA  A  U  D  SD    15. There are many books that I hope to read.

SA  A  U  D  SD    16. Books should not be read except for class requirements.

SA  A  U  D  SD    17. Reading is something I can do without.

SA  A  U  D  SD    18. A certain amount of summer vacation should be set aside for reading.

SA  A  U  D  SD    19. Books make good presents.

SA  A  U  D  SD    20. Reading is dull.

*Source:* From *Improving Reading: Strategies and Resources,* 3rd ed., by Jerry L. Johns and Susan Davis Lenski. Copyright © Kendall/Hunt Publishing Company. Used by permission.

possible. This test can be given orally to those students who have trouble reading or writing, or it can be given to a whole group at once. Here are some typical incomplete sentences:

> Reading is . . .
> I believe I can . . .
> I prefer . . .
> My favorite . . .

### Wish Test

The wish test is similar to the sentence completion test except that the phrase *I wish* precedes the incomplete sentence. Here are some typical examples:

> I wish I were . . .
> I wish I could . . .
> I wish reading were . . .
> I wish school were . . .
> I wish my friends were . . .
> I wish my teacher . . .

## READING AUTOBIOGRAPHY

**Reading autobiography**
Students write or tell about their feelings and attempt to analyze their reading problems.

The *reading autobiography* is not as subtle as a projective technique because the students are aware that they are writing or telling about their feelings and trying to analyze why they have a reading problem. It is a helpful technique, however, and probably more accurate than responses on an interest inventory because the students are partners in an attempt to analyze their reading difficulties. The reading autobiography is the student's own life story of his or her reading experiences. It can be presented in a number of ways, and it can be administered individually or to a group.

### Open-Ended Reading Autobiography

One technique that could be used is simply to have the students write their reading autobiography. They are given the following instructions:

> Since this is the life story of your reading experiences, you must go back as far as you can remember. Try to recall your earliest reading experiences, what they were, and how you felt about them. Try to recall what books you liked when you were very small, and whether you still like those kinds of books. Try to remember when you first started to read. How did you feel? Try to recall how you first learned to read, and what you think helped you the most in learning to read. If you have a reading problem, try to remember when you think it first started and why it started. Put down anything that you feel is important in helping others to understand your reading problem if you think you have one.

Students who have trouble writing could orally relate their autobiographies to the teacher, or they could tape-record them.

### Questionnaire Reading Autobiography

The questionnaire autobiography is also helpful in gaining information about a student's reading history, but it is more limiting than the open-ended reading autobiography. Also, it is only as good as the questions on it because students' responses are determined by the way the questions are written and what kinds of questions are included. Figure 5.15 provides an example.

**FIGURE 5.15   Reading Autobiography**

|  | Yes | No | Sometimes |
|---|---|---|---|
| 1. Do you like to read? |  |  |  |
| 2. When do you like to read? |  |  |  |
| 3. Do you like someone to read to you? |  |  |  |
| 4. Do you feel you understand what you read? |  |  |  |
| 5. Did anyone try to teach you to read before you came to school? |  |  |  |
| 6. Did anyone read to you when you were younger? |  |  |  |
| 7. Are there lots of books in your house? |  |  |  |
| 8. Do you think you have a reading problem? |  |  |  |

If you answered *yes* to question 8, answer the following questions:

1. What do you think your reading problem is?

2. Why do you think you have a reading problem?

3. Has anyone tried to help you with your problem?

4. When do you feel your reading problem began?

5. Who do you think has helped you the most in reading?

6. What do you think has helped you the most in reading?

7. Have you ever left the class to attend a special reading class?

If you answered *yes* to question 7, answer questions 8 and 9.

8. How do you feel about being in a special reading class?

9. Do you think the special reading class has helped you?

10. Are your parents interested in helping you in reading?

11. Do you like to read to anyone?

12. What do you do when you come across a word you do not know?

13. What do you do when you do not understand something you are reading?

14. Do you have a library card?

15. If you have a library card, how often do you go to the library?

16. What kinds of books do you like to read?

## REVISITING THE OPENING SCENARIO

Now that you have had a chance to read about many different instruments for informal assessment, take a look back at the opening scenario in this chapter. Take on the role of Mr. Johnson and think about what you would say to Ms. Anderson about how to use different informal assessment techniques to inform her instruction.

## AUTHORS' SUMMARY

In this chapter, we presented several informal assessment techniques that can be used across grades. Three questions need to be asked and answered to select the best possible technique: What do I want to know? Why do I want to know? How can I best discover the information? Cognitive and affective factors need to be considered when determining how to best help children with reading. We provided a wealth of ideas about how to acquire insight into both cognitive and affective domains. Observation is a way of gathering information, but teachers must document and interpret what they see, because observations by themselves cannot explain the causes of reading behaviors. Informal assessment techniques can provide valid information about student characteristics that cannot be garnered from other sources.

## SUGGESTIONS FOR THOUGHT QUESTIONS AND ACTIVITIES

1. Construct a checklist for a specific reading skill to use for instruction; create a rating scale for the checklist; expand it to include other reading behaviors.
2. Use one of the checklists in this chapter to learn more about the behavior of a particular child.
3. Observe a child at various times in class. Record his or her behavior by using a checklist or anecdotal record.
4. Discuss portfolios with a teacher who uses them.
5. Develop a plan to use portfolios in your class. Discuss how the portfolios would help you diagnose your students' reading strengths and needs.

## WEB SITES

http://rubistar.4teachers.org/index.php

This site provides the space for teachers to create and store their own rubrics using numerous templates and topics. It also enables users to search a vast store of rubrics by topic, author, or author email.

http://www.teachervision.fen.com/classroom-management/curriculum-planning/6281.html?detoured=1

Having an entire section on assessment tools, this site provides information on portfolio evaluation, alternative assessments, group evaluations, rubrics, and much more. Limited free access.

http://teams.lacoe.edu/reading/assessments/assessments.html

The TEAMS Educational Resources provide a multitude of assessment tools. Topics include but are not limited to spelling inventories, phonemic awareness tasks—including the Yopp-Singer Test of Phonemic Segmentation—and concepts about print.

http://www.ncrel.org/sdrs/areas/as0cont.htm/

This site provides a collection of alternative assessments designed by the North Central Regional Educational Laboratory (NCREL). Topics explored include equity in assessments, formative assessment, what research has to say about assessment, and much more.

http://www.teach-nology.com/currenttrends/alternative_assessment/

TeAchnology offers numerous sources for teaching including various alternative assessment information, Includes research literature, knowledge mapping, performance-based assessment, portfolios, and rubrics. This source also provides information and/or tools on authentic assessment, assessment and accountability programs, and more.

## SELECTED BIBLIOGRAPHY

Barrentine, Shelby J., and Sandra M. Stokes, eds. *Reading Assessment: Principles and Practices for Elementary Teachers,* 2nd ed. Newark, DE: International Reading Association, 2005.

Bratcher, Suzanne, with Linda Ryan. *Evaluating Children's Writing: A Handbook of Grading Choices for Classroom Teachers,* 2nd ed. Mahwah, NJ: Erlbaum, 2004.

Cohen, Dorothy H., and Virginia Stern. *Observing and Recording the Behavior of Young Children.* New York: Teachers College Press, 1978.

Easley, Shirley-Dale, and Kay Mitchell. *Portfolios Matter: What, Where, When, Why and How to Use Them.* Portland, ME: Stenhouse, 2003.

Gillespie, Cindy S., et al. "Portfolio Assessment: Some Questions, Some Answers, Some Recommendations." *Journal of Adolescent & Adult Literacy* 39 (March, 1996): 480–491.

Goodrich, Heidi. "Understanding Rubrics." *Educational Leadership* 54 (December/January, 1996/1997: 14–17.

Popham, James W. "Portfolio Assessment," in *Classroom Assessment: What Teachers Need to Know,* 2nd ed. Boston: Allyn and Bacon, 1999.

Salvia, John, and James E. Ysseldyke. "Assessing Behavior Through Observation," in *Assessment,* 8th ed. Boston: Houghton Mifflin, 2001.

Now go to Topic 2: "Reading Assessment" and Topic 12: "Progress Monitoring" in MyEducationLab (www.myeducationlab.com) for your course, where you can:

- Find learning outcomes for "Reading Assessment" and "Progress Monitoring" along with national standards that connect to these outcomes.
- Complete Assignments and Activities that can help you more deeply understand the chapter content.
- Examine challenging situations and cases presented in the IRIS Center Resources.
- Access video clips of CCSSO National Teacher of the Year award winners responding to the question, "Why Do I Teach?" in the Teacher Talk section.
- Apply and practice your understanding of the core teaching skills identified in the chapter with Building Teaching Skills and Dispositions learning units.

# Using Standardized Tests across the Grades

**6**

## CHAPTER OUTLINE

- Scenario: Mr. James—A Teacher Who Knows the Purpose of Tests
- Standardized Tests
- Norm-Referenced Tests
- Reading Survey Tests and General Achievement Survey Tests
- Criterion-Referenced Tests
- Teacher-Made Tests
- Administering Individual Tests
- Administering Group Tests
- Diagnostic Reading Tests
- Revisiting the Opening Scenario

## SCENARIO: MR. JAMES—A TEACHER WHO KNOWS THE PURPOSE OF TESTS

Mr. James, a sixth-grade teacher, loves to teach. He chose this profession over others because he likes to work with children, and he feels he can make a difference. He remembers his own sixth-grade teacher who helped him through rough times and he feels good about being able to do the same for his students. Mr. James is never defensive about having chosen teaching as his career and resents others who are. When he is asked, "And what do you do?" he proudly replies, "I am a teacher."

However, there is one period of time during the school year that bothers Mr. James; it probably disturbs many others, also. In schools across the nation, you can always tell when it's time for the dreaded standardized achievement tests. A hush seems to envelop the school; it's as if everyone is walking on tiptoe. Doors are closed, and anxious students and teachers are captives within. Everyone waits with apprehension for the results. Will they be an embarrassment to the school district, or will the students score substantially above the national norms? It's a tense time for all involved.

## CHAPTER OBJECTIVES

After reading this chapter, you should be able to:

- Give a rationale for using tests in reading diagnosis.
- Define key terms in testing, including types of tests and test scores.
- Discuss the variety of reading tests available.

## STANDARDIZED TESTS

**Standardized tests**
Tests that have been published by experts in the field and have precise instructions for administration and scoring.

Standardized tests are commercially published tests most often constructed by experts in the field. They are developed in a very precise fashion, and have specific instructions for both administration and scoring. These instructions are supposed to be followed exactly by everyone who administers the tests.

Confusion may exist concerning the definition of standardized tests. In the past, the term *standardized* referred mainly to *norm-referenced* tests; however, a standardized test may or may not be norm-referenced. We consider a test to be standardized if it is a published test with specific instructions for administration and scoring.[1, 2]

## NORM-REFERENCED TESTS

**Norms**
Average scores for a given group of students, which allow comparisons to be made among different students or groups of students.

Although not all standardized tests have norms, most do. *Norms are average scores for a given group of students*, which allow comparisons to be made among different students or groups of individuals. The norms are derived from a random sampling of a cross-section of a large population of individuals.

Norm-referenced tests are used to help teachers learn where their own students stand in relation to others in the class, school system, city, state, or nation. Although a child may be doing average work in a particular class, the child may be above average when compared to

[1]Teacher's Guide, *California Diagnostic Reading Tests Levels A and B* (Monterey, CA: CTB/McGraw-Hill, 1989), p. 7.

[2]Michael Zieky, Executive Director, Officers Division, Educational Testing Service (ETS), Princeton, NJ, 2001.

other norms. Similarly, it is possible for a child to be doing above average work in a particular third-grade class but to be below average compared to all third-graders in the nation.

Also keep in mind that norm-referenced tests have limitations. Identified by Otto (1973) and paraphrased by us, these limitations are listed in the following section.

**Norm-referenced tests**
Standardized tests with norms so that comparisons can be made to a sample population.

## LIMITATIONS OF NORM-REFERENCED MEASURES

1. The measure may be inappropriate for use with some groups or individuals. It might be too hard for some and not challenging enough for others.
2. Allocated time limits may be unrealistic, which means that the scores of students who work slowly but with precision are most likely not accurate.
3. Items may sample breadth of reading rather than depth, which results in a superficial view of the student's reading behaviors.
4. Administering the test in a group setting might invalidate the results in that children who fail to understand the directions may be unable to answer any of the items they actually know.
5. The test format limits the kinds of items used. Multiple-choice formats are often used and these do not measure some reading behaviors appropriately.
6. Norm-referenced tests generally provide an overestimate of the students' appropriate instructional reading level.[3]

Go to the Assignments and Activities section of Topic 11: Reading Difficulties and Intervention Strategies in the MyEducationLab for your course and complete the activity entitled "The Challenge of Standardized Tests." As you watch the video and answer the accompanying questions, determine what you think is most important for you as a classroom teacher.

Teachers must be cautious when they use these tests. In addition to the limitations mentioned above, teachers must use the three assessment questions to determine whether a test is appropriate for their students: What do I want to know? Why do I want to know? How can I best discover this information?

Another important factor concerns the students themselves. Students who feel comfortable, alert, well-fed, rested, and highly motivated are better prepared to perform at their best. Such factors do affect test performance. Teachers want to administer tests under the best possible circumstances. Good teachers remind students and parents before a test that students need to sleep well, eat breakfast, pay attention, and expect to do well on a test.

Standardized tests are often referred to as *high-stakes tests*. The term "high stakes" implies undesirable consequences for those who fail. Performance benchmarks for these tests are usually determined by policy, not by students' needs. While evaluation and interpretation is out of the hands of teachers, the results are often used to reward or penalize students, teachers, and schools. Without a doubt, the political use of high-stakes testing data affects the lives of students and teachers.

## READING SURVEY TESTS AND GENERAL ACHIEVEMENT SURVEY TESTS

Publishers differentiate between reading survey tests such as the *Gates-MacGinitie Reading Tests* and the reading subtest of a general achievement survey such as the *TerraNova CAT.* As shown in Figure 6.1, the reading survey test and the reading subtest of an achievement survey test battery are quite similar and serve the same purposes. Both measure a student's overall reading achievement. The major difference between the two types of tests is that a standardized reading survey test, such as the *Gates-MacGinitie Reading Tests,* only measures reading and therefore can be somewhat more comprehensive. The reading achievement subtest of an achievement test, such as the *TerraNova CAT,* is part of a survey battery of achievement tests; that is, the reading

[3]Wayne Otto, "Evaluating Instruments for Assessing Needs and Growth in Reading," in *Assessment Problems in Reading,* ed. W. MacGinitie (Newark, DE: International Reading Association, 1973), pp. 14–20.

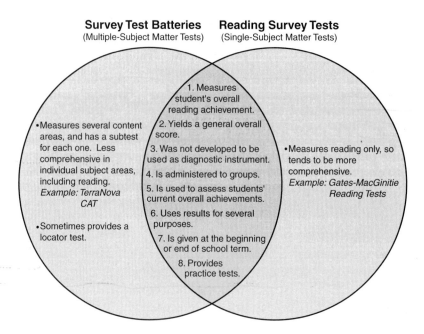

**Survey Test Batteries**
(Multiple-Subject Matter Tests)

**Reading Survey Tests**
(Single-Subject Matter Tests)

- Measures several content areas, and has a subtest for each one. Less comprehensive in individual subject areas, including reading.
  *Example: TerraNova CAT*

- Sometimes provides a locator test.

1. Measures student's overall reading achievement.
2. Yields a general overall score.
3. Was not developed to be used as diagnostic instrument.
4. Is administered to groups.
5. Is used to assess students' current overall achievements.
6. Uses results for several purposes.
7. Is given at the beginning or end of school term.
8. Provides practice tests.

- Measures reading only, so tends to be more comprehensive.
  *Example: Gates-MacGinitie Reading Tests*

**FIGURE 6.1**   Comparison of Standardized Tests: Survey Batteries and Reading Surveys.

achievement test is one of many tests that measure different curricula. For example, the *TerraNova CAT* is designed to measure achievement in the basic curricular areas of reading, spelling, language, mathematics, study skills, science, and social studies. Both reading survey tests and reading achievement tests from survey test batteries yield a general or overall score and were not developed to be used as diagnostic instruments; however, they play an essential role in any diagnostic program. These are group tests that are usually very easy to administer in a relatively short period of time, and they are useful for screening or identification, which is the first step in a diagnostic pattern. Standardized norm-referenced reading achievement or survey tests are used to assess the students' present achievement status. The results of these kinds of tests are used for a number of purposes. One use is usually to make comparisons among other schools in the district, state, or nation. Another use is to identify which children are doing well, and which children may need help. If the test is used to identify these children, the instrument is being used in a positive manner.

You are probably most familiar with standardized achievement tests such as the *Metropolitan Achievement Tests*, the *Stanford Achievement Tests*, and the *TerraNova CAT* because most schools employ these kind of tests. They are generally given either at the beginning or the end of the school year by the classroom teacher. It's usually a good idea to give the test at the same time that the test was given to the students who determined the norms for the test. For example, if you wish to give an achievement test in the fall to help determine how to group for instruction, you should choose a test in which the norms were gathered in the fall. Standardized achievement tests that are given in the fall are generally used for instructional purposes and screening, whereas standardized achievement tests that are given at the end of the year are generally used for comparison purposes.

Before giving any tests, study the accompanying test manual. The manual usually contains information about the test, such as how norms were gathered, instructions on how to administer and score the test, and what the test measures.

### Locator Tests

**Locator test**
Used to determine at what level a student should begin testing.

Some of the achievement batteries supply a *locator test*, which is used to determine the level at which a student should begin testing when testing out-of-level, because the U.S. Office of Education for Title I testing recommends functional level testing. Locator tests are used to provide students with tests to which they can relate well. Students in sixth grade reading at a fourth-grade level will not relate well to a sixth-grade reading test. The locator test is used to determine the approximate functional level of these students, and it is recommended that those students who test out-of-level on the locator test be given the achievement test at the approximate functional level at which they tested on the locator test. Therefore, the sixth-grade students who score at the fourth-grade level on the locator test would be tested with a fourth-grade level test.

Locator tests may be individually or group administered. The developers of *Terra Nova* recommend that their locator tests be used with special education students.

### Practice Tests

**Practice test**
Ensures that the actual test measures what students know rather than their test-taking ability; it familiarizes students with the test.

Most standardized achievement tests provide a *practice test*. These are designed to ensure that students know how to mark an answer *before* they take the actual test. The practice tests are supposed to ensure that the actual test measures what students know and not their previous familiarity with test-taking procedures. Practice tests are supposed to help "level the test-taking playing field."

## SELECTING A STANDARDIZED TEST

Like it or not, teachers are often left out of the loop when it comes to selecting a standardized test. Generally, administrators select these tests and teachers are told rather than asked to administer them.

There are times, however, when teachers are in a position to select a test with the three questions posed earlier at the forefront of their minds: What do I want to know? Why do I want to know? Which test will best help me to discover this information? Some teachers might feel a bit lost when it comes to answering the last question, but fortunately, there are references that provide much assistance.

The *Mental Measurements Yearbooks* are excellent resources for teachers intent on choosing standardized reading tests that best suit their purposes. The books help acquaint teachers with most tests in the field, except the very recent ones. Frank, critical evaluations of tests are written by authorities in the field. Test users are also warned about the dangers of standardized tests and are told of their values. An essential contribution that the books make is to "impress test users with the desirability of suspecting all standardized tests—even though prepared by well-known authorities—unaccompanied by detailed data on their construction, validity, uses, and limitations."[4]

*The Seventeenth Mental Measurements Yearbook,* published in 2007, continues in the tradition of the others by providing valuable information about tests. Other sources of test information that teachers would find helpful are *Tests in Print; Tests: A Comprehensive Reference for Assessments in Psychology, Education, and Business;* and *Test Critiques,* as well as journals such as *The Reading Teacher* and the *Journal of Adolescent & Adult Literacy* (formerly the *Journal of Reading*) that periodically review various tests.

## TEST SCORE TERMINOLOGY

There are many potentially confusing terms test makers use in discussing standardized achievement tests. Following is a guide to some of the terms teachers will probably encounter at one time or another.[5]

[4]Oscar Buros, ed., *Reading: Tests and Reviews* (Highland Park, NJ: Gryphon Press, 1968), p. xvi.

[5]Adapted from *Test Interpretation Guidelines, Comprehensive Tests of Basic Skills,* 4th ed. (Monterey, CA: CTB/McGraw-Hill, 1988). *Comprehensive Tests of Basic Skills* now comes under the umbrella of *TerraNova.*

### Raw Score

| |
|---|
| **Raw score**<br>The number of items that a student answers correctly on a test. |

The *raw score* is the number of items that a student answers correctly on a test. (The number of test items, as well as the difficulty of the items, may vary from one section of a test to another; therefore, the weighting of the test items should vary.) The raw score is usually not reported because it does not convey meaningful information. Test makers use the raw scores to derive their scale scores.

### Standard Scores

| |
|---|
| **Standard Scores**<br>Used to compare test takers' assessment scores. Presented in terms of standard deviations. |

Standard scores are used to compare test takers' assessment scores. They are presented in terms of standard deviations (measures that define a range of scores around the mean, that is, "how widely the scores vary from the mean."[6]). If the standard deviation is large, it means that the scores are more scattered in relation to the mean. Conversely, if the standard deviation is small, the scores are more clustered around the mean.[7]

### Standard Deviation

| |
|---|
| **Standard Deviation**<br>Deals with how widely scores vary from the mean. |

Measurement experts like to work with *standard deviations* because they feel that they produce more accurate appraisals of a student's scores in relation to others, and they are exceptionally helpful in understanding test results. For example, on one test, the standard deviation is 10, and the *mean* or average of all the scores is 100. On another test, the standard deviation is 5, and the mean or average of all the scores is 100. Two students take the two different tests. Student A scores 110 on one test and Student B scores 105 on the other test. Even though the students have different scores, they both have scored one standard deviation above the mean. The 110 score is therefore equivalent to the 105 score.

| |
|---|
| **Mean**<br>Arithmetical average. |

The same logic would apply to tests with different means. It is beyond the scope of this book to discuss the various kinds of standard scores that exist. For more information on standard and scale scores, consult one of the many excellent measurement textbooks that are available.

### Normal Curve

| |
|---|
| **Normal curve**<br>Scores are symmetrically distributed around the mean. |

Many teachers are familiar with the bell-shaped symmetrical curve (*normal curve*) in which the majority of scores fall near the mean (average) of the distribution, and the minority of scores appear above or below the mean. In Figure 6.2 we show a sample of a bell-shaped symmetrical curve.

### Grade Equivalent

| |
|---|
| **Grade equivalents**<br>Description of year and month of school for which a given student's level of performance is typical. |

A *grade equivalent* is a description of the year and month of school for which a given student's level of performance is typical. A grade equivalent of 6.2 on the *TerraNova California Achievement Test (CAT)* is interpreted as the score that is typical of a group of students in the third month of the sixth grade. (September is designated as month .0, October as .1, November as .2, December as .3, and so on up to June, which is .9.) These scores are useful in the elementary grades because fairly regular gains are expected in basic skill development at each grade level.

Extreme grade equivalents, those that are more than two years above or below grade level, must be interpreted with great caution because they are based on "extrapolations" rather than actual student performance. A very low or a very high score just means that the student scored far below or far above the national average. A grade

[6]Anita E. Woolfolk, *Educational Psychology,* 10th ed. (Boston: Allyn and Bacon, 2007), p. 527.

[7]Ibid.

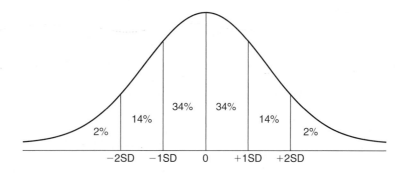

**FIGURE 6.2** A Bell-Shaped Symmetrical Curve.

equivalent score of 6.6 by a third-grader does not mean the third-grader is able to do sixth-grade work or should be in the sixth grade. It does mean that this student is scoring well above the average for third-grade students.

### Percentile

**Percentile**
A point on the distribution below which a certain percentage of the scores fall.

A *percentile* is a point on the distribution below which a certain percent of the scores fall. A test score equivalent to the 98th percentile means that the student's score is higher than that of 98 percent of others who took the test.

Remember that the 50th percentile score is the middle score, or the median; it is the point above and below which half of the students scored. Likewise, remember that percentile and percent correct are not the same. A percentile score of 75 on an achievement test by a fifth-grader means that the fifth-grader obtained a score higher than 75 out of every 100 students in a representative sample of fifth-graders in the nation who took the test. A student might get 60 percent of the test items correct and still be in the 75th percentile.

## CRITERION-REFERENCED TESTS

**Criterion-referenced tests**
Based on an extensive inventory of objectives in a specific curriculum area; they are used to help assess an individual student's performance with respect to his or her mastery of specified objectives in a given curriculum area.

**Objective**
Desired educational outcome.

*Criterion-referenced reading tests* are based on an extensive inventory of reading objectives. These tests are designed to help teachers learn about students' specific strengths and needs. Teachers use them to gain more information about students' various skill levels. The information they get from the test is used in conjunction with other valid assessment data to plan appropriate instruction.

Criterion-referenced tests are considered standardized if they are published tests that have been prepared by experts in the field and have precise instructions for administration and scoring. They can be administered individually or to a group, and they can be teacher-made or standardized. Criterion-referenced tests are concerned primarily with mastery of predetermined *objectives*, which are based on content material. On criterion-referenced tests, an individual is supposed to compete only with himself or herself. While there may be very little difference in appearance between a norm-referenced test and a criterion-referenced test, differences do exist in the objectives of the tests.

**Content domain**
Term that refers to
subject matter
covered.

For a criterion-referenced test to be valid, a *content domain* must be specified, and the test items must be representative of the content domain. Test makers identify various content area domains and write measurable objectives within each domain; then they develop detailed item specifications to ensure detailed measurement of the skills stated in the objectives. Usually, there are several items written for each objective.

Criterion-referenced tests are not norm-based; however, as odd as it may sound, "criterion-referenced tests and norm-referenced tests are no longer seen as a strict dichotomy."[8] When a criterion-referenced test has equated norms, it means that "the scores on one test have been statistically matched to the scores on a normed test."[9]

Some test makers are including a "cutoff or passing score" with criterion-referenced tests, perhaps because the term *criterion* implies a benchmark for performance. With a criterion-referenced interpretation of scores, the focus is on what students can do and the comparison should be to a content domain, not to other students.

Teachers can write their own criterion-referenced tests, such as the example shown here. The test item is correlated to the objective for a specific skill. The important factor is whether we can infer that the test item does indeed measure what it is supposed to—in this case, the ability of the child to draw inferences. In other words, is the test item a valid representation of its content domain? Let's take a look.

- **Content domain:** Reading comprehension
  **Skill:** Drawing inferences
  **Objective:** The student will draw inferences about the personality of the main character based on the content of reading material.

- **Administration Procedure:** The child is asked to read a short story carefully. After finishing the reading, the child is asked to answer questions based on the story.

- **Question:** What can you infer about the personality of Dennis?

The child is then asked to choose the best answer from the given statements. In criterion-referenced testing *every* test item is related to a corresponding objective.

## LIMITATIONS OF CRITERION-REFERENCED TESTS

1. Some qualities, such as appreciation or attitudes about reading, are difficult to assess using content objectives.
2. Stated objectives are sometimes considered mastered if the student can perform them one time. Retention and transfer of what the student has learned may not be considered as important.
3. Determining specific instructional objectives to be taught and tested can be difficult.
4. Establishing the mastery standard can be difficult. Performance standards may need to fluctuate depending on the objective being assessed.

[8]Ibid.

[9]Michael Zieky, Executive Director, Officers Division, Educational Testing Service (ETS), 2001.

## TEACHER-MADE TESTS

**Teacher-made tests**
Tests prepared by the classroom teacher for a particular class and given by the classroom teacher under conditions of his or her own choosing.

*Teacher-made tests* are sometimes called *classroom tests* or *informal tests*. These are prepared by the classroom teacher for a particular class and given under conditions of the teacher's choosing. Usually, teacher-made tests are the primary basis for evaluating students' school progress. Teachers can get quick feedback on learning behaviors by constructing appropriate classroom tests. The tests with which you are probably the most familiar are those used to determine students' grades; these tests are generally classified into essay and objective tests and are mostly administered to groups of students.

In the field of reading, classroom tests are generally used to help diagnose a student's reading problem or to learn more about a student's weaknesses and strengths. Many of the teacher-made tests used for diagnosis are individually administered. For example, the informal reading inventory, which can be commercially produced or teacher-made, is a valuable aid in helping a teacher to diagnose reading problems.

## ADMINISTERING INDIVIDUAL TESTS

**Classroom tests**
Teacher-made tests; also called informal tests.

**Informal tests**
Teacher-made tests.

**Individual tests**
Administered to one person at a time.

Individual tests in reading are usually given when the teacher feels there is some inconsistency between a student's classroom reading performance and test scores on a group-administered standardized reading achievement test. Teachers also administer individual tests when they want to learn more about a student's reading behaviors. An individual test can also be given if the teacher suspects that a child has difficulty following directions. When giving an individual test, the tester can also make notes about whether a student understands a question, or is tired, hungry, or not feeling well.

There are two guiding principles to follow when administering an individual test. The first is privacy. When students are reading orally, for example, most often they will be encountering the text for the first time. They don't need the added pressure of performing for an audience. One suggestion for a way to adhere to this principle is to take students aside one at a time to a designated area of the room and have them read to you. This can be accomplished when the other students are completing independent activities, or when they are reading a given selection silently. As the rest of the students read to themselves, individuals can be taken aside to read a given segment of text privately for the teacher.

Another principle is to observe the children during the reading experience. Make notations of your observations on a copy of what the child is reading. Your notes can then be used for further analysis.

Individually administered tests are more useful than group tests for students who have reading difficulties. Teachers can learn more about a student in a one-to-one testing situation than in a class. This individual attention increases the chances of the test's validity.

## ADMINISTERING GROUP TESTS

Teachers usually administer *group tests* when they are looking for reliability. That is, they test a whole group when they want to ensure that differences in performance are

**Group tests**
Administered to a group of students at the same time.

not due to the way they explain or administer the test. Group tests may be more reliable, but this may come at the cost of validity. We want to know as much about individual students as possible in a diagnosis and improvement program. This knowledge is more difficult to attain through a group test.

## DIAGNOSTIC READING TESTS

**Diagnostic reading tests**
Provide subscores discrete enough that specific information about a student's reading behavior can be obtained and used for planning instruction.

A *diagnostic reading test* is designed to break a complex skill down into its component parts to help teachers gain information about a student's specific reading strengths and weaknesses. It is generally given after an analysis of a group standardized reading survey test. The analysis helps the teacher to determine which children seem to be reading below their ability. Unclear as to *why* a child appears to be struggling, the teacher decides to explore further through the use of a diagnostic reading test.

Diagnostic reading tests can be either standardized or teacher-made tests. Most reading diagnostic tests are individually administered and given by a special reading teacher rather than by the regular classroom teacher. However, many of these diagnostic tests can be given by the regular classroom teacher, and in a reading diagnosis and improvement program, many should be. Informal reading inventories are examples of diagnostic tools that are indispensable to the classroom teacher (see Chapter 8).

A good diagnostic test battery provides subscores discrete enough that specific information about a student's reading behavior can be attained and used for instructional purposes. It may consist of oral reading, silent reading, comprehension, phonics analysis, structural analysis, sight vocabulary, phonemic awareness, visual and auditory discrimination, reading and study skills, or rate of reading.

The diagnostic test teachers choose must fit the criteria for good assessment (see Chapter 3). Most importantly, the test should help the teacher interpret the student's performance, and then determine strengths and needs. Once again, three questions can help guide teachers in selecting an appropriate diagnostic test: What do I want to know? Why do I want to know? Which test will help me discover this information?

## REVISITING THE OPENING SCENARIO

Mr. James is interested in the timing of testing times because he feels that fall results would be more indicative of the children's present developmental levels and more useful for grouping and teaching. How can Mr. James use standardized reading tests as a screening device to identify students who have potential problems?

## AUTHORS' SUMMARY

In this chapter, we defined *standardized* tests. We explained the terms *norm-referenced* and *criterion-referenced*. We introduced specific types of standardized reading tests and emphasized that teachers must be knowledgeable of the various kinds of tests so that they can best choose the appropriate ones. To that end, we proposed that teachers ask and answer three important questions: What do I want to know? Why do I want to know it? Which test will help me discover this information?

## SUGGESTIONS FOR THOUGHT QUESTIONS AND ACTIVITIES

1. Your school is interested in using criterion-referenced tests. You have been appointed to explain the differences between criterion-referenced and norm-referenced tests. What will you say?

2. Choose a reading content domain that is not likely to be represented on a current published test, for example, text messaging. Create a criterion-referenced measure to assess students' understanding of this domain.

3. Many teachers in your school are confused about the many different types of tests that exist. You can help them by drawing a tree diagram showing the relationships among tests.

4. Explain some of the differences between teacher-made tests and published or commercially produced tests.

## WEB SITES

http://teams.lacoe.edu/reading/assessments/assessments.html

This site provides assessment tools for K–3. Topics include but are not limited to spelling inventories, phonemic awareness tasks—including the Yopp-Singer Test of Phonemic Segmentation—rhyming, and concepts about print.

http://www.teachervision.fen.com/assessment/new-teacher/48353.html?detoured=1

This site contains limited free articles (i.e., three free). This particular article discusses the difference between assessment and evaluation. Also included are criteria for teachers to consider in their own classrooms. Teachers can sign up for a 7-day free trial for access to over 20,000 resources for Pre-K–12, downloadables, and over 180 printable books.

http://www.ncrel.org/sdrs/areas/issues/students/earlycld/ea500.htm

Focusing on a variety of topics such as developmentally appropriate assessments and standardized tests, this site explains the various concepts and provides information on the ways they are applied in different educational contexts.

http://nces.ed.gov/nationsreportcard/

Known as the Nation's Report Card, the National Assessment of Educational Progress (NAEP) is one of the primary assessments referenced when looking at our nation's educational progress. Navigating this site will prove informative and keep teachers up to date regarding the educational state of affairs.

## SELECTED BIBLIOGRAPHY

McMillan, James H. *Classroom Assessment: Principles and Practice for Effective Instruction*, 3rd ed. Boston: Allyn and Bacon, 2004.

Popham, James W. *Classroom Assessment: What Teachers Need to Know,* 2nd ed. Boston: Allyn and Bacon, 1999.

Salvia, John, James F. Ysseldyke, and Sara Bolt, *Assessment,* 10th ed. Boston: Houghton Mifflin, 2007.

*Standards for Educational and Psychological Testing.* Prepared by the Committee to Develop Standards for Educational and Psychological Testing of the American Educational Research Association, the American Psychological Association, and the National Council on Measurement in Education. Washington, DC: American Psychological Association, 1985, 1986.

Woolfolk, Anita E. "Standardized Testing," in *Educational Psychology,* 10th ed. Boston: Allyn and Bacon, 2007.

**PEARSON**
**myeducationlab**

Now go to Topic 11: "Reading Difficulties and Intervention Strategies" in MyEducationLab (www.myeducationlab.com) for your course, where you can:

- Find learning outcomes for "Reading Difficulties and Intervention Strategies" along with national standards that connect to these outcomes.
- Complete Assignments and Activities that can help you more deeply understand the chapter content.
- Examine challenging situations and cases presented in the IRIS Center Resources.
- Access video clips of CCSSO National Teacher of the Year award winners responding to the question, "Why Do I Teach?" in the Teacher Talk section.
- Apply and practice your understanding of the core teaching skills identified in the chapter with Building Teaching Skills and Dispositions learning units.

# Assessing and Teaching Early Literacy

## CHAPTER OUTLINE

- Scenario: Helping Children Advance as Language Learners
- Building an Understanding of Early Literacy
- Assessing Early Literacy
- Understanding, Assessing, and Teaching Concepts
- Understanding, Assessing, and Teaching Phonological Awareness
- Understanding, Assessing, and Teaching Letter Identification
- Understanding, Assessing, and Teaching Writing
- Understanding, Assessing, and Teaching Story Sense
- Putting It All Together: Who Is In Most Need of Early Intervention?
- Revisiting the Opening Scenario

**7**

# SCENARIO: HELPING CHILDREN ADVANCE AS LANGUAGE LEARNERS

Ms. Berger is a highly qualified early childhood teacher who believes that literacy is an ongoing, dynamic process and that children are often at different places in their literacy acquisition. Rather than waiting for children to show that they are ready for literacy instruction, she uses what she knows about her students to plan developmentally appropriate instruction. She wholeheartedly believes that assessment drives instruction, but she recognizes that she must use a variety of assessment measures, each designed to evaluate different aspects of early literacy. She can then interpret the results to plan lessons and to determine which children might need additional instructional time so that they can learn essential literacy skills.

As is often the case, Ms. Berger's students come from a variety of backgrounds. Some come from high-poverty areas, whereas others come from middle-class neighborhoods. When she looks at the results of the many different assessment measures she uses, she recognizes that some children perform poorly when compared to their peers. That is, some are lagging in oral vocabulary, print concepts, letter identification, and phonological awareness. She knows that she will be able to offer some children additional instruction in each of these areas, while others will be better served by teachers who are specially trained in early intervention. She fully understands that children who don't do well on the assessments need more rather than less help. Their progress must be accelerated in order for them to function at the same level as their peers.

Ms. Berger recognizes that there are noneducational factors such as parental support, socioeconomic status, and nutrition that affect school performance. She also knows that there are several educational factors such as teacher experience, curriculum rigor, and time on task that affect how children fare in school. Although all factors are important, she focuses on what she can control—the educational factors—and strives to teach children to the best of her ability.

Recent government mandates have Ms. Berger quite concerned. Even though she is an advocate of accountability, she also understands that the results of early literacy tests are not supposed to be used as high-stakes tests by which children are labeled and sorted into various groups. Yet this is what she sees happening. She is concerned that too much time is being spent on labeling children and not enough time is being spent on helping them advance as language learners.

Go to the Assignments and Activities section of Topic 4: Oral Language in the MyEducationLab for your course and complete the activity entitled "Literacy." As you watch the video and answer the accompanying questions, reflect on the narrative voiceovers. Do you agree with the narrator? Why or why not?

# CHAPTER OBJECTIVES

After reading this chapter, you should be able to:

- Discuss the essential components of early literacy, and the differences between the terms *early literacy, reading readiness,* and *emergent literacy.*
- Provide an example of a specific assessment measure and explain what it is designed to reveal.
- Discuss early intervention and provide an example of an early intervention program.
- Explain the pros and cons of three different ways to determine who is most in need of early intervention.

In this chapter, we focus on the different aspects of literacy that young children enrolled in kindergarten and first grade need to acquire. Our purpose is to explain these essential components and provide some ways to assess and teach each one. Whereas several of the assessment measures explained throughout this text are suitable for all ages, those in this chapter are especially appropriate for evaluating essential components related to early literacy.

# BUILDING AN UNDERSTANDING OF EARLY LITERACY

**Emergent literacy**
The development of the association of print with meaning that begins early in a child's life and continues until the child reaches the stage of conventional reading and writing.

**Reading readiness**
Children demonstrate behaviors that show they are ready for reading instruction.

Many terms are used to describe the beginning stages of literacy. One of the most common is *emergent literacy*, defined by Harris and Hodges as "the development of the association of print with meaning that begins early in a child's life and continues until the child reaches the stage of conventional reading and writing."[1] This definition suggests that children's involvement with language begins long before they come to school and that it continues to evolve over time. For example, what appears to be a young child's scribbling is really more than scribbling; it is the child's attempt at using written language. In the past, behaviors such as these were often thought of in terms of *reading readiness*. That is, children were showing that they were ready for reading instruction.

Although some may argue that emergent literacy and reading readiness are basically synonymous, they are not at all. Emergent literacy connotes an ongoing process that is developmental in nature. Reading readiness seems to connote a "waiting period." The notion of waiting in literacy development violates the spirit and essence of literacy as a developmental process.

Some make the distinction between emergent literacy and *beginning reading* by noting that once children show a certain amount of understanding about how print functions, they are no longer emergent but actually beginning to read in the formal sense. Therefore, they are beginning readers. But exactly how much do children have to know to move from being emergent to beginner? At what age does this shift happen?

Although kindergarten is usually considered to be the bridge between emergent literacy and beginning reading, using kindergarten as a yardstick can be problematic for a couple of reasons. First, not all children attend kindergarten because it is not required in several states. Therefore, lack of exposure to a language-rich environment could mean that the children will not exhibit several emergent literacy behaviors until first grade.

Second, there are still differences of opinion about the purpose and curriculum of kindergarten. Those who believe that children will grow or mature into reading provide children with many opportunities to learn all areas of literacy (speaking, listening, reading, and writing), yet do very little explicit teaching. Others believe that children are continually developing and that they need some help as they develop. Consequently, like their counterparts, they provide children with a language-rich environment, but they also believe in offering children explicit instruction based on what they have discovered as a result of using several different assessment techniques and interpreting what they reveal.

We base our view on the latter opinion, for which the International Reading Association is using the broader term "early literacy." We believe that children are always showing us what they know and what they need to learn. Children change over time in the way they think about literacy and the strategies they employ as they attempt to comprehend and/or produce text. Like Teale, we believe that children are always trying to make sense of their world and that there is a logic behind what they do that drives their attempts to solve the literacy mystery. Once we understand this logic, we are in a better position to plan instruction that will foster their development toward conventional language use.[2]

One of the best ways to take a look at children's attempts at using language in meaningful ways is to create a language-rich environment and observe what the children do. Such an environment needs to employ authentic language experiences and much

---

[1]T. Harris and R. Hodges, *The Literacy Dictionary* (Newark, DE: International Reading Association, 1995).

[2]W. Teale, "Emergent Literacy," in *The Literacy Dictionary,* eds. T. Harris and R. Hodges (Newark, DE: International Reading Association, 1995), pp. 71–72.

support. Cambourne provides a useful way to think about such an environment. His conditions of learning are shown in Figure 7.1.

## AREAS OF EARLY LITERACY

In Chapter 1, we provided some sample benchmarks that show some specific behaviors that we would expect to see from children. Whereas a number of the behaviors overlap and continue through different stages, many manifest themselves early on. In a broader sense, there are specific areas of emergent literacy that are viewed as the foundation for future reading and writing success. In Table 7.1 we provide an overview of these components.

## ASSESSING EARLY LITERACY

### PRE-READING ASSESSMENT

Before the label *emergent literacy* surfaced and replaced *reading readiness,* most school systems administered whole group reading readiness tests to their students, usually at the end of kindergarten, to determine whether the children were "ready for reading." These tests were usually the first types of standardized tests that the children encountered in their lives at school.

**Pre-reading**
Precursor to reading; before formal reading begins.

Group-administered standardized tests are still being used. Most major standardized achievement assessment batteries still have some types of *pre-reading* tests that are usually administered to children at some point in kindergarten. Some school district personnel use these tests to predict reading success, as well as to determine those children who will be "at risk" in school. One example is the *Gates-MacGinitie Reading Test,* 4th edition (2000). This test is a group-administered standardized reading test. There is a pre-reading test (PR), which contains four subtests: literacy concepts, oral language concepts, letters and letter/sound correspondences, and listening comprehension. According to the authors, the purpose of the test is to determine "a student's background for reading instruction."[3] The authors also note that the test is designed to help teachers learn "what each student already knows about important background concepts on which beginning reading skills are built and which concepts students may need additional help with as they begin to receive reading instruction."[4] A close examination of the testing manual provides the authors' rationale for the subtests and other important information. A separate volume entitled *Linking Testing to Teaching: A Classroom Resource for Reading Assessment and Instruction* provides teachers with some ideas about interpreting test scores as well as teaching suggestions related to each subtest.

Unfortunately, there are some dangers attached to pre-reading tests if they are misused. One danger is a self-fulfilling prophecy. If a child does poorly on such a test, the teacher may feel that the child cannot benefit from reading instruction; the child is not expected to be able to learn to read, and, as a result, the teacher defers instruction in reading. Eventually, the teacher's feelings concerning the child's inability to read become part of the child's own self-concept (see "Teacher Expectations" in Chapter 2).

## USES OF GROUP-ADMINISTERED STANDARDIZED PRE-READING ASSESSMENTS

Studies have suggested that the predictive validity of pre-reading tests is not very high, that they could not predict with accuracy how well nonreaders would learn to read, and

---

[3]Walter H. MacGinitie, Ruth MacGinitie, Katherine Maria, Lois G. Dreyer, and Kay E. Hughes, *Gates-MacGinitie Reading Tests,* 4th ed. (Itasca, IL: Riverside Publishing, 2000).

[4]Ibid.

**FIGURE 7.1 Cambourne's Conditions of Learning**

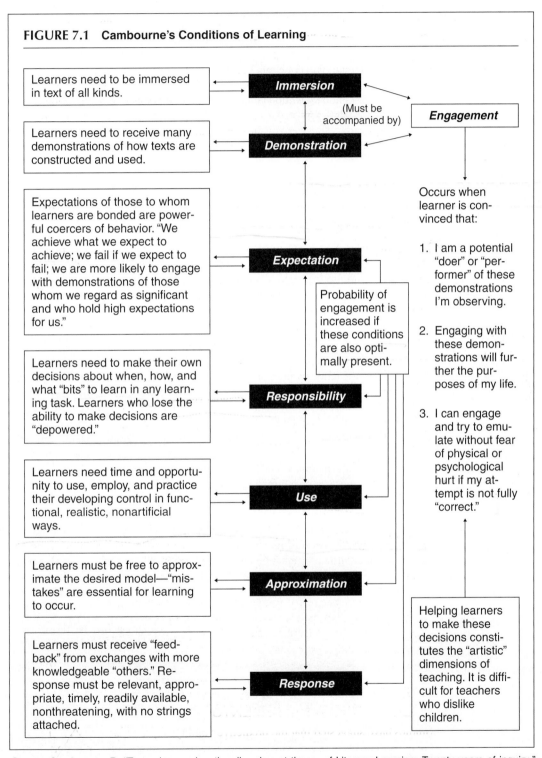

*Source:* Cambourne, B. "Towards an educationally relevant theory of Literacy Learning: Twenty years of inquiry." *The Reading Teacher,* 49 (3): 182–202. 1995.

**TABLE 7.1    Early Literacy Components and Their Definitions**

| *Early Literacy Component* | *Brief Definition* |
| --- | --- |
| Oral language concepts | Understanding concepts that are used in spoken language |
| Print concepts | Understanding written language related to books and some of the terms associated with it |
| Phonological awareness | Awareness that spoken language is made up of words, syllables, and phonemes |
| Letter identification | Understanding of the symbols used to form the alphabet |
| Alphabetic principle | Understanding that there is a systematic relationship among letters and sounds and that this code can be used to communicate with others |
| Story sense | Awareness of the structure used to create narrative stories; understanding that stories have to make sense and that books contain stories |

*Source:* Snow, C., S. M. Burns, and P. Griffin, eds. *Preventing Reading Difficulties in Young Children.* Washington, DC: National Academy Press, 1998.

Go to the Assignments and Activities section of Topic 1: Reading Instruction in the MyEducationLab for your course and complete the activity entitled "Creating a Print-Rich Environment." As you watch the video and answer the accompanying questions, notice how many ways that a teacher can create a print-rich environment. How might the teacher encourage children to participate in creating a print-rich environment?

that teachers' ratings were just as accurate in predicting reading success.[5] On the other hand, there is a great amount of evidence available to support the relationship between young children's letter naming and their later reading achievement, as well as school achievements.[6] This is also true of phonological awareness. Studies have shown that the alphabet subtest of the *Metropolitan Readiness Tests* "has consistently been the best predictor of scholastic achievement."[7]

It has been stated that "a great saving in testing time could well stem from using only the letters and numbers subtests or, perhaps, by not testing readiness at all. In either case, the sacrifice in information would be minimal."[8] Such statements continue, and educators still decry the misuses of pre-reading tests.[9] Despite many expressions of concern, test makers continue to produce such tests, and many teachers are required to use them.

Why is a test needed to predict future reading success? We already know from voluminous research that high-achieving readers usually come from homes with enriched verbal environments, whereas low-achieving readers usually come from homes in which little conversation takes place. We also know that a rich verbal environment is more likely to be found among middle and upper socioeconomic classes than in lower socioeconomic classes.

[5]Max Coltheart, "What Can Children Learn to Read—and When Should They Be Taught?" in *Reading Research: Advances in Theory and Practice,* Vol. 1, eds. T. Gary Waller and G. E. MacKinnon (New York: Academic Press, 1979), p. 15.

[6]Daniel J. Walsh, Gary Glen Price, and Mark G. Gillingham, "The Critical but Transitory Importance of Letter Naming," *Reading Research Quarterly* 23 (Winter, 1988): 110. Steven A. Stahl, Jean Osborn, and Fran Lehr, *"Beginning to Read: Thinking and Learning about Print" by Marilyn Jager Adams: A Summary* (Urbana, IL: Center for the Study of Reading, 1990), p. 10.

[7]Ibid., p. 110.

[8]Robert L. Hillerich, *Reading Fundamentals for Preschool and Primary Children* (Columbus, OH: Merrill, 1977), p. 25.

[9]See "NAEYC Position Statement on Standardized Testing of Young Children 3–8 Years of Age," *Young Children* 43 (March, 1988): 42–47. Sue Bredekamp and Lorrie Shepard, "How Best to Protect Children from Inappropriate School Expectations, Practices, and Policies," *Young Children* 44 (March, 1989): 14–24. Constance Kamii, ed., *Achievement Testing in the Early Grades* (Washington, DC: National Association for the Education of Young Children, 1990).

Pre-reading tests, like other assessment measures, have their problems. Here are three that come to mind:

1. As any teacher who has ever tried to get a group of twenty kindergarten students all focused on the same item on the same page knows, actually administering the test can be extremely time-consuming. When test developers estimate how long it will take to administer the test, they do not take classroom management into account.

2. More often than not, there are too many prompts from the teacher. Therefore, a child's performance score may be inflated. Take, for example, a subtest that is designed to determine whether students can identify words. There is a sentence with one word missing, and four choices are given below the sentences. The examiner's manual directs the test administrator to read the sentence *and* the words under the sentence. Students are then supposed to choose the word to complete the sentence so that the sentence will make sense. The problem? Although the test is designed to shed light on how well students can identify words, it does not do this at all because the teacher does all of the reading. All the students have to do is *recognize* a word, which is much easier than identifying it. The only conclusion that can be drawn about students who successfully complete a subtest such as this is that they appear to be able to recognize some words. But can they read them independently, as their performance on this test is supposed to indicate? We cannot say.

3. Yet another problem is the lack of congruence between *emergent literacy* and the best way to assess it. Because children are constantly emerging and changing, it can be extremely difficult to obtain valid and reliable scores indicative of their development and learning from a one-time group-administered standardized test.

## SUGGESTIONS FOR CHOOSING AND USING REQUIRED PRE-READING TESTS

Here are some suggestions on how to choose and use pre-reading tests if they are required in your school system:

1. Use a test that can provide you with information on a child's present level of literacy development.

2. Check the subtests to determine how directly the tasks required are related to reading. For example, some tests require children to match pictures and geometric figures rather than letters. Those children who do well in matching pictures and geometric figures may not do well in matching letters. Check to see if the subtests are similar to the activities presented in the beginning reading program.

3. Check the administration time of the test. Make sure that it is suited to the attention span of your students.

4. Make sure children comprehend the terminology used on the test and understand the directions.

5. Use the results of the test and your interpretation of them to gain information about the child's present level of development so that you can provide the best possible program for him or her.

6. Use the pre-reading test as one measure; also use informal assessments and your judgment to make decisions concerning the child's literacy development. (See Chapter 1.)

## CURRENT WAYS TO ASSESS EARLY LITERACY

One of the recommended policies set forth by the authors of the joint position statement of the International Reading Association (IRA) and the National Association for

the Education of Young Children (NAEYC) calls for "appropriate assessment strategies that promote children's learning and development." Because children are constantly changing, obtaining a valid and reliable score indicative of a child's development and learning from a one-time, group-administered, timed standardized test can be extremely difficult.

Does this mean that there is no place for standardized tests in assessing and teaching early literacy? Not necessarily. Standardization doesn't automatically make a test evil. Many times it is the *content* of these standardized tests juxtaposed with a teaching philosophy and a district or state policy that causes problems. For example, one test that appears to be sweeping the nation is the *Dynamic Indicators of Basic Early Literacy Skills (DIBELS)* (2000).[10] This battery of tests was created by researchers at the University of Oregon. (For more information, visit the web site at *dibels.oregon.edu.*) The tests begin in kindergarten and continue through sixth grade. The creators use the word "fluency" a lot when they actually mean "proficiency." Thus, the letter recognition subtest is called "fluency of letter recognition" (LRF). Students are given one minute to say the displayed letters. Their performance is then interpreted as a reading level. The problems we see with this battery of tests in general, and the letter recognition test in particular, stem from their lack of congruence with our view of what it means to be a reader (see Chapter 1). First, when assessing fluency, students need time to rehearse; a "cold" read tells us nothing about how fluently a child reads. Second, who cares how quickly a child can say letters of the alphabet? What we want to know is which letters does the child know and which need to be learned? Third, good readers adjust their rate of reading to their purpose for reading. But will students be left with this most important learning if they are constantly timed on all subtests? Not likely. Instead, tests such as these can potentially distort what it means to read, leaving children with many misconceptions about reading. In reality, the one-minute time standard on DIBELS is a standardized way of keeping the test simple and quick to administer. Yet interpreting the results as "fluency" creates a misconception of what fluency is about. The misconceptions surrounding the protocols and labeling on this test can prevent children from becoming willing and able readers.[11]

We all want to be efficient with our use of time. But speed is not what matters, especially for early reading. Instead, what matters is asking and answering these assessment questions: What do I want to know? Why do I want to know it? How can I best learn this information? When making decisions about selecting assessment strategies, staying focused on the purpose of the assessment and how the results will be used to inform instruction is essential. With standardized measures, teachers need to find and understand the statements of purpose usually provided by test authors in training materials.

And let's remember that most often teachers are told rather than asked about using standardized measures. Fortunately, there are several standardized measures that can be used to meaningfully and appropriately assess different aspects of early literacy. For example, the *Yopp-Singer Test of Phonemic Segmentation*[12] is a useful standardized tool to help ascertain how well children can segment phonemes in spoken words. *Concepts About Print*[13] is another useful tool that is designed to tap students' understanding of books and terminology related to them. Rathvon[14] lists additional standardized measures.

---

[10]*Dynamic Indicators of Basic Early Literacy Skills (DIBELS)* (Eugene, OR: University of Oregon. 2001).

[11]Kenneth S. Goodman, *The Truth About DIBELS What It Is–What It Does.* (Portsmouth, NH: Heinemann, 2006).

[12]H. Yopp, "A Test for Assessing Phonemic Awareness in Young Children," *The Reading Teacher* 49, no. 1 (1995): 20–29.

[13]M. Clay, *The Early Detection of Reading Difficulties,* 3rd ed. (Portsmouth, NH: Heinemann, 1985).

[14]N. Rathvon, *Early Reading Assessment: A Practitioner's Handbook* (New York: Guilford, 2004).

**TABLE 7.2   What, Why, How of Early Literacy Assessment Techniques**

| What Do I Want to Know? | Why Do I Want to Know? | How Can I Best Discover It? |
|---|---|---|
| Do the children have an understanding of basic language concepts? | Knowing the language concepts children understand and need to learn will better help me to explain instruction. | Informal Inventory of Concepts (pp. 114–116) |
| Do the children have an understanding of how print functions? | Understanding how print functions and knowing the terminology associated with reading are essential for effective reading. | Print Concepts (p. 117) |
| Do children display phonological awareness? | Having phonological awareness can assist reading success. | Phonological Awareness Test  (p. 125) |
| Can children identify letters of the alphabet? | Knowing letters appears to be associated with competent reading. | Letter Identification (pp. 131–132) |
| To what degree do students write? | Understanding about the alphabetic principle and using other print conventions are essential for writing success. | Writing Vocabulary (p. 137) Message Writing (p. 137) |
| Do children understand how stories are structured, and do they show listening comprehension? | Understanding how stories are structured will facilitate future reading success. Showing listening comprehension indicates that students realize that understanding is essential for reading. | Wordless Picture Story (p. 139) |

The majority of these measures are individually administered and they can be given several times so that the teacher can note progress over time. When contrasted with group-administered tests, these individual assessment measures can also yield much more information because the examiner can watch what the child does on given tasks. For example, after reading a passage, a child might stop and talk about something that happened to him or her that is similar to what happened in the story. This type of response indicates that the child is making some self-to-text connections, that he is comprehending.

To standardize or not to standardize is not the question. Instead, the pertinent question is "What are the children showing they know and what do they need to know to advance as language users?" Addressing these strengths and needs at the onset is about ensuring that children get a fair start, rather than needing to catch up later on. Just as regular maintenance can prevent costly car repairs, so, too, early intervention saves resources, human as well as monetary.

Because there are different aspects of early literacy, we need to use a variety of measures to assess them. However, variety can be a bit overwhelming if we aren't sure what it is we're looking for. This leads us once again to ask three important questions: What do I want to know? Why do I want to know? How can I best discover it? Table 7.2 provides some help in answering these questions.

# UNDERSTANDING, ASSESSING, AND TEACHING CONCEPTS

## WHAT IS A CONCEPT?

A *concept* is a group of stimuli with common characteristics. These stimuli may be objects, events, or persons. Concepts are usually designated by their names, such as *book,*

**Concept**
A group of stimuli with common characteristics.

*war, man, woman, animal, teacher,* and so forth. All these concepts refer to classes (or categories) of stimuli. Some stimuli do not refer to concepts; Ms. Jones, the lawyer, Hemingway's "The Killers," World War II, and the Empire State Building are examples. These are specific (not classes of) people, stimuli, or happenings.

Concepts are needed to reduce the complexity of the world. When children learn that their shaggy pets are called *dogs,* they tend to label all other similar four-footed animals as "dogs." Young children overgeneralize, tending to group all animals together, and have not yet perceived the differences between and among various animals. Unless children learn to discern differences, the classes of words that they deal with will become exceptionally unwieldy and unmanageable. However, if children group each object in a class by itself, this too will create difficulties in coping with environmental stimuli because it will also be unwieldy.

The first step in acquiring concepts concerns oral vocabulary because concepts are based on word meanings: Without vocabulary there would be no base for concept development. The second step is gathering data, that is, specific information about the concept to be learned. In doing this, students use their strategies for processing information—they select data that are relevant, ignore irrelevant data, and categorize items that belong together. Concepts are formed when the data are organized into categories.

## HOW DO CONCEPTS DEVELOP?

**Concept development**
Refers to development of thinking.

*Concept development* is closely related to cognitive (thinking) development. Jean Piaget, a renowned Swiss psychologist, has written on children's cognitive development in terms of their ability to organize (which requires conceptualization), classify, and adapt to their environments.

**Schemata**
These structured designs are the cognitive arrangements by which the mind is able to categorize incoming stimuli.

According to Piaget, the mind is capable of intellectual exercise because of its ability to categorize incoming stimuli adequately. *Schemata* (structured designs) are the cognitive arrangements by which this categorization takes place. As children develop and take in more and more information, it becomes necessary for them to have some way to categorize all the new information. At the same time, their ability to categorize by means of schemata grows, too. That is, children should be able to differentiate, to become less dependent on sensory stimuli, and to gain more and more complex schemata. Children should be able to categorize a cat as distinct from a mouse or a rabbit. They should be able to group cat, dog, and cow together as animals. Piaget calls the processes that bring about these changes in children's thinking *assimilation* and *accommodation.*[15]

**Assimilation**
A continuous process that helps the individual to integrate new incoming stimuli into existing concepts—one aspect of what Piaget refers to as cognitive development.

Assimilation does not change a concept, but allows it to grow. It is a continuous process that helps the individual to integrate new, incoming stimuli into existing schemata or concepts. For example, when children tend to label all similar four-footed animals as dogs, they are assimilating. They have assimilated all four-footed animals into their existing schema.

If the child encounters stimuli that cannot be made to fit into the existing schema, then the alternative is either to construct a new category or to change the existing one. Accommodation occurs when a new schema or concept is developed, or when an existing schema is changed.

**Accommodation**
Developing new categories for stimuli that do not fit into into existing ones—another aspect of what Piaget refers to as cognitive development.

Although both assimilation and accommodation are important processes that the child must attain in order to develop adequate cognition, a balance between the two processes is necessary. If children overassimilate, they will have categories that are too large to handle; similarly, if they overaccommodate, they will have too many categories. Piaget calls the balance between the two *equilibrium.* A person having equilibrium would be able to see similarities between stimuli and thus properly assimilate

[15]Jean Piaget, *The Origins of Intelligence in Children* (New York: International Universities Press, 1952).

**Equilibrium**
According to Piaget, a balance between assimilation and accommodation in cognitive development.

them, and would also be able to determine when new schemata are needed for adequate accommodation of a surplus of categories.

As children develop cognitively, they proceed from more global (generalized) schemata to more particular ones. For the child, there are usually no right or wrong placements, but only better or more effective ones. That is what good education is all about.

## HOW DOES CONCEPT DEVELOPMENT RELATE TO LANGUAGE AND READING?

Concept development is closely related to language development. Unless children attain the necessary concepts, they will be limited in reading as well as in all other aspects of the language arts (listening, speaking, writing, and viewing).

Knowledge of what concepts are and how children attain them is especially essential in a reading diagnosis and improvement program. Teachers in such a program must recognize early when a child is lacking certain concepts and help that child to attain them.

The quality of language development depends on the interrelationships of factors such as intelligence, home environment, sex differences, and family makeup. The factors that influence language development also influence concept development. As a result, children who are more advanced in language development are also usually more advanced in concept development, and these children tend to be better readers than those who are not as advanced.[16]

## HOW CAN ORAL LANGUAGE CONCEPTS BE ASSESSED?

Concepts are necessary to help students acquire increasing amounts of knowledge. For example, as students proceed through the grades in school, their learning becomes more abstract and is expressed in words, using verbal stimuli as labels for concepts. Many teachers take for granted that those spoken concept labels are understood by their students, but this is not always so. Young children's literal interpretation of oral and written discourse and their limited knowledge of the world around them affects their comprehension and ability to form correct concepts. If not enough information is given, concepts are often learned either incompletely or incorrectly.

When children enter school, the teacher must assess their concept development level, and then help them to add the attributes that are necessary and relevant for the development of particular concepts. At the same time, the teacher must help students to delete all those concepts that are faulty or irrelevant.

One way to assess language concepts is to use an informal inventory test of concepts, such as the one shown in Figure 7.2. It can be given orally to individual students.

Another method to determine whether children have a concept such as opposites is to ask each child to give some opposites for words such as these:

| | | |
|---|---|---|
| no | good | fat |
| boy | mommy | go |
| happy | early | fast |

A third way to determine whether the children understand language concepts is to play games. For example, to see if children understand the concepts of left and right, play the game "Simon Says" with the children and use directions with the words *left* and *right*.

A fourth way to observe whether children understand specific language concepts is to use these concepts as part of classroom routines. For example, the concepts of *first* and *last* can be assessed by asking children to name who is first or who is last in line.

---

[16]Walter D. Loban, *Language Development: Kindergarten through Grade Twelve,* Research Report #18 (Urbana, IL: National Council of Teachers of English, 1976).

**FIGURE 7.2** **Example of an Informal Inventory Test of Concepts for Early Primary-Grade Students**

For each concept the teacher will orally state the tested term in the context of a sentence. The children will show they understand the concept by correctly checking or putting a circle around the picture that best describes the concept. Before beginning, the teacher should make sure that all children understand the symbol for a check (✓) and that they can draw a circle around an object.

    1. Concept *over.* Concept in sentence: The check (✓) is over the ball.

*Directions*

Put a circle around the picture that shows a ✓ is over a ball. (Again, the teacher should put a ✓ on the board to make sure children understand this term. The teacher should make a circle on the board to make sure children understand this concept as well.)

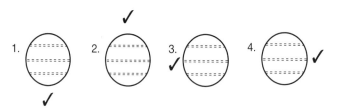

    2. Concept of *under.* Concept in sentence: The check (✓) is under the ball.

*Directions*

Put a circle around the picture that shows a ✓ is under a ball.

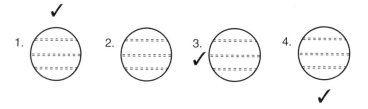

    3. Concept of *square.* Sentence: Which picture shows a square?

*Directions*

Put a check in the square.

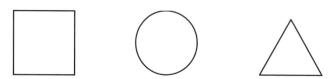

**FIGURE 7.2**

4. Concept of *triangle.* Sentence: Which picture shows a triangle?

*Directions*

Put a check in the triangle.

5. Concept of *most.* Sentence: Which box has the most balls?

*Directions*

Draw a circle around the box that has the most balls.

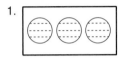 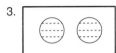

6. Concept of *least.* Sentence: Which box has the least number of balls?

*Directions*

Draw a circle around the box that has the least number of balls.

 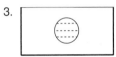 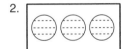

7. Concept of *smallest.* Sentence: Which ball is the smallest?

*Directions*

Draw a circle around the smallest ball.

   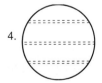

8. Concept of *largest.* Sentence: Which ball is the largest?

*Directions*

Draw a circle around the largest ball.

*(continued)*

---

**FIGURE 7.2**    *(continued)*

---

9. Concept of *opposites.*

*Directions*

Draw a circle around the picture that is the opposite of the word that I am going to say. (For example, the teacher says, "What is the opposite of girl?")

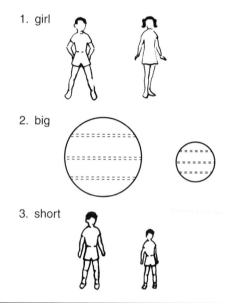

1. girl

2. big

3. short

---

A fifth, more formalized way of assessing oral language concepts is to use a standardized, norm-referenced test such as the *Boehm Test of Language Concepts,* 3rd edition (2000), which is published in both English and Spanish. The test is designed to help teachers determine which of the 50 most frequently occurring concepts children know or need to learn.

## HOW CAN PRINT CONCEPTS BE ASSESSED?

Some concepts relate to print and books. Children's understanding of these concepts is important to their early reading success. These concepts include: print carries a message, left-to-right progression, return sweep, and terms such as "word," "letter," "beginning," and "ending."

One way to assess for these print concepts is to use the *Print Concepts Test* shown in Figure 7.3. It is a modification of the original *Concepts About Print* test developed by Marie Clay.[17] The main difference between this version and Clay's is that this one is not standardized. It also permits the examiner to use just about any children's literature selection.

*Print Concepts Administration Procedures*

1. Choose a book that is relatively short. *The Hungry Monster* by Phyllis Root (Candlewick, 1997) is one example.
2. Make a copy of the *Print Concepts* form for each child (Figure 7.3).

---

[17]Clay (1985).

---

**FIGURE 7.3   Print Concepts**

---

Name: _____

***Directions:*** Using the book that you have selected, give the following prompts to encourage the child to interact with it. Read the story aloud as you proceed. Place a ✔ next to each item answered correctly.

| *Prompt* | *Response* *(✔ = correct)* | *Print Concept* |
|---|---|---|
| 1. Hand the child the book upside down, spine first, saying something like: "Show me the front of this book." Then read the title to the child. | | layout of book |
| 2. Say: "I would like to begin reading the story, but I need your help. Please open the book and point to the exact spot where I should begin reading." | | print conveys message |
| 3. Stay on the same page and say: "Point to where I need to start reading." | | directionality: where to begin |
| 4. Say: "Point to where I should go after I start reading." | | directionality: left-to-right progression |
| 5. Say: "Point to where I go next." Read the pair of pages. | | directionality: return sweep |
| 6. Turn the page and say: "Point to where I should begin reading on this page. Now point to where I should end." Read the page. | | terminology: beginning and end |
| 7. Turn the page and say: "Point to the bottom of this page. Point to the top of it. Now point to the middle of it." Read the page. | | terminology: top, bottom, middle |
| 8. Using the same page, say: "Point to one letter." | | terminology: letter |
| 9. Again using the same page, say: "Point to one word." | | terminology: word |
| 10. Turn the page. Make sure that this page contains words that have corresponding upper- and lowercase letters. Read the page. Then point to a capital letter and say: "Point to a little letter that is like this one." | | matching lower to uppercase letters |
| 11. Turn the page and say: "Let's read these pages together. I'll read and you point." Read the pages. | | speech-to-print match |
| 12. Finish reading the book. Then turn back to a page that has the punctuation marks you want to assess. Point to the punctuation mark and say: "What is this?" "What is it for?" | | punctuation: period, question mark, quotation marks |

*Source:* From *Flexible Grouping in Reading* by Michael Opitz. Published by Scholastic Teaching Resources/Scholastic, Inc. Copyright © 1995 by Michael Opitz. Reprinted by permission.

3. Read through the form to become familiar with what you will be asking and to make sure that the book you will be using has the appropriate examples as noted on the form.
4. Individually administer the *Print Concepts* assessment using the prompts shown on the *Print Concepts* form.

*Scoring Procedures*

1. Look at the responses that the child provides.
2. Record your observations on the *Summary of Print Concepts* form shown in Figure 7.4.
3. Use the results to plan instruction.

As noted in Chapter 5 compiling the results of individual assessment measures on a class matrix can be helpful in terms of seeing the class at a glance. The *Concepts about Print: Class Profile* form shown in Figure 7.5 can be used for this purpose. The form is also helpful in that it shows which items are related to directionality, terminology, and punctuation.

Those who need to use a norm-referenced standardized test will want to use Clay's *Concepts About Print* test. Standard prompts are used, and the literature selections used to assess the print concepts are specified.

## TEACHING ORAL LANGUAGE AND PRINT CONCEPTS

A rich oral language program is a necessary first step to prevent reading failure because it helps prepare children for reading. The closer the children's language is to the written symbols encountered in reading, the greater their chance of success. Hearing English in the context of something meaningful with which they can identify helps children gain "facility in listening, attention span, narrative sense, recall of stretches of verbalization and the recognition of new words as they appear in other contexts."[18]

Teachers using a reading diagnosis and improvement program understand that one main reason for assessing students is to determine what students know and what they need to learn. Teachers can then use the results to plan appropriate instruction. There are several ways to teach language and print concepts.

### Read Aloud to Children

Numerous researchers investigating the power of the read-aloud have arrived at the same findings: Reading aloud increases children's listening vocabularies.[19] Other researchers have discovered that children who speak nonstandard English make significant gains toward standard English when they are involved in a rich oral program, one that stresses reading stories aloud and actively involving children in related activities. In terms of language and print concepts, there is much teacher can do:

- Before reading, the teacher can emphasize "front" by saying something like, "The title of our book is on the front cover."
- The teacher can also point to the words while reading, which helps children to see that print carries the message and that there is a match between what is said and the print on the page (i.e., speech-to-print match).
- Upon completion of the story, the teacher can emphasize language concepts such as "first" and "last" by using the terms as children tell what happened first and last.

[18]Dorothy H. Cohen, "The Effect of Language on Vocabulary and Reading Achievement," *Elementary English* 45 (February, 1968): 217. See also David B. Yaden, Jr., Deborah W. Rowe, and Laurie MacGillivray, "Emergent Literacy," *Handbook of Reading Research,* III (Mahwah, NJ: Lawrence Erlbaum Associates, Inc. 2000), p. 429.

[19]Warwick B. Elley, "Vocabulary Acquisition from Listening," *Reading Research Quarterly* 24 (Spring, 1989): 174–187.

FIGURE 7.4  **Summary of Print Concepts**

Title of Book: _____

**Directions:** Use this form to summarize your observations of print concepts.

**Observations**

The child demonstrates knowledge of the following print concepts (✔ the appropriate spaces)

_____ layout of books (item 1)

_____ print conveys written message (item 2)

_____ directionality (items 3, 4, 5)

_____ terminology associated with reading (items 6, 7, 8, 9)

_____ uppercase letters (item 10)

_____ lowercase letters (item 10)

_____ speech-to-print match (item 11)

_____ punctuation (item 12)

**Comments/Notes**

_____

_____

_____

_____

_____

_____

_____

_____

_____

_____

_____

_____

_____

_____

_____

_____

_____

_____

## FIGURE 7.5  Concepts about Print: Class Profile

| Name | Directionality | | | | | Terminology | | | | | Punctuation |
|------|---|---|---|---|---|---|---|---|---|---|---|
| | 1 | 2 | 3 | 4 | 5 | 6 | 7 | 8 | 9 | 10 | 11 | 12 |
| | layout of books | print conveys message | where to begin | left-to-right progression | return sweep | beginning, end | top, bottom, middle | letter | word | upper- and lower-case matching | speech-to-print match | period, question mark, quotation marks |
| | | | | | | | | | | | | |
| | | | | | | | | | | | | |
| | | | | | | | | | | | | |
| | | | | | | | | | | | | |
| | | | | | | | | | | | | |
| | | | | | | | | | | | | |
| | | | | | | | | | | | | |
| | | | | | | | | | | | | |
| | | | | | | | | | | | | |
| | | | | | | | | | | | | |
| | | | | | | | | | | | | |
| | | | | | | | | | | | | |
| | | | | | | | | | | | | |
| | | | | | | | | | | | | |
| | | | | | | | | | | | | |
| | | | | | | | | | | | | |
| | | | | | | | | | | | | |

*Source:* From *Flexible Grouping in Reading* by Michael Opitz. Published by Scholastic Teaching Resources/ Scholastic, Inc. Copyright © 1995 by Michael Opitz. Reprinted by permission.

- Concepts such as "pair" can be emphasized by telling students to pair up. Each pair can then be invited to chime in during a rereading of the story at their designated time.

As you can see, there are many ways that language concepts can be reinforced through read-alouds. There are several children's literature titles that actually focus on language concepts that you can choose to use for read-aloud sessions. *A Pair of Protoceratops* by Bernard Most (Harcourt, 1998), *Parts* by Shelley Rotner (Walker, 2001), *Over, Under, Through* by Tana Hoban (Macmillan, 1973), and *What's Opposite?* by Stephen Swinburne (Boyds Mills, 2000) are a few of the many available titles.

Reading a story to children can be a rewarding, interactive learning experience if it is done properly. Here are some suggestions to ensure your success when reading aloud to children.

*Preparing for the Story*

1. Choose a short storybook that is at the attention, interest, and concept development levels of the children and that has large pictures that can be easily seen.
2. Have the children sit comfortably and in a position that allows them to see the pictures easily.
3. Make sure there are no distractions in the room.
4. State the title and show the book to the children. Ask them if they can figure out what the story will be about from the title.
5. Tell them to listen carefully for certain things. (Of course, this will be based on the story being read.)

*Reading the Story*

1. Read the story aloud to the children.
2. Stop at key points and have them predict what will happen or have them state the refrain if the story contains one.
3. State more questions for them to think about while they are listening to the story.
4. If children interject comments during the story, you should acknowledge these by saying "good thinking," if it shows they are thinking, and then continue reading.

*After the Story*

When the story is finished, have the children answer some of the unanswered questions and do some of the following based on their attention and interest levels:

1. Tell what the story is about.
2. Retell the story in sequence.
3. Discuss whether the story is based on fantasy or reality.
4. Act out the story.
5. Make up another ending for the story.

### Engage Children in Language Play

Learning language can and should be fun. Fun allows for a positive association with learning language. Games such as "Simon Says" are perfect for developing further understanding of specific language concepts. And playing the "Hokey Pokey" is a perfect way to help children to better understand specific language concepts. A rich oral language classroom should involve singing songs, reciting poems and verse, oral storytelling, dramatizations (including reader's theater, student-authored plays, puppet shows). All oral language play can be accompanied by print in some form to help children make the connection between their playfulness and printed text.

### Do Some Focused, Explicit Teaching

You might decide that in addition to focused story reading, you want to design some lessons that teach specific language concepts. Looking at the class matrix described earlier can help you to see who needs some extra instruction in certain areas so you can teach them the needed concepts. In Chapter 5, we provide an example of a teacher who did just that.

### Use Language in a Variety of Ways

Several years ago, Halliday identified seven distinct functions that children often use for language. However, some children appear to be limited language users. Knowing about these functions can help teachers to create classroom situations in which children need to use all seven functions, which will help them become flexible language users.[20] In Table 7.3 we show these functions and provide sample classroom activities.

**TABLE 7.3**  Halliday's Functions of Language and Sample Instructional Activities

| Function of Language | Use | Sample Instructional Activities |
|---|---|---|
| Instrumental ("I want") | To satisfy needs or desires | Check out library books<br>Sign in for attendance<br>Provide directions for others |
| Regulatory ("Do as I tell you!") | To control behavior of others | Establish guidelines for taking care of classroom equipment<br>Play follow-the-leader type games |
| Interactional ("Me and You") | To establish and maintain relationships | Write messages to one another<br>Have children share work areas and/or materials<br>Have children work together to plan a project |
| Personal ("Here I Come!") | To express one's personal feelings or thoughts | Provide time for students to talk with one another<br>Read stories and ask students to share their thoughts about the story |
| Heuristic ("Tell me why.") | To discover and find out why something happens | Create problems for students to solve<br>Conduct simple experiments |
| Imaginative ("Let's pretend.") | To create an imaginative world of one's own | Use puppets<br>Have a dress-up center |
| Informative ("I have something to tell you.") | To provide information to others | Provide time for students to share announcements<br>Provide time for students to tell current events |

*Source:* From Halliday, M., *Exploration in the Functions of Language,* 1975.

[20]M. Halliday, *Explorations in the Functions of Language* (London: Arnold, 1975).

# UNDERSTANDING, ASSESSING, AND TEACHING PHONOLOGICAL AWARENESS

## WHAT IS PHONOLOGICAL AWARENESS?

**Phonological awareness**
Awareness of spoken words, syllables, and phonemes.

**Phonemic awareness**
Awareness that words are made up of individual sounds.

Although the terms phonological awareness and phonemic awareness are sometimes used as synonyms, this is incorrect. *Phonological awareness* refers to awareness of three aspects of spoken language: words, syllables within words, and sounds or phonemes within syllables and words. *Phonemic awareness* is the awareness that words are made up of individual sounds. It is one aspect of the larger category of phonological awareness. One way to remember the difference between the terms is to visualize an umbrella adorned with tassels. Phonological awareness would be the fabric and the frame holding the umbrella together. Phonemic awareness would be one of the tassels hanging from the end of one of the umbrella's sections. Both terms, however, refer to spoken language. A child who is phonologically and phonemically aware is not necessarily able to connect the sound units with written symbols.

Phonological awareness develops in stages. Learners first become aware that their spoken language is composed of words. They then progress to the stage in which they become aware that words are constructed of syllables. The last stage is the one in which learners become aware that words and syllables are made up of individual sounds (i.e., phonemes). Children who end up being proficient readers usually have developed a strong sense of phonology, whereas children who end up struggling with reading and writing often have needs in this area during early literacy. Table 7.4 shows the different stages of phonological awareness and sample tasks associated with each.

### Phonemic Awareness Tasks

There are many tasks associated with phonemic awareness; some are more difficult than others. When children can perform all of these tasks, they are considered to have phonemic awareness. Identifying and producing rhyme appears to be the least difficult of these tasks. Another phonemic awareness task is *phoneme matching*, which calls for the learner to identify words that have a given sound or to generate a word that has a given sound. When children are expected to listen to a sentence and then state the sound that they hear at the beginning of a word or to state some words that begin like a given word, they are performing phoneme matching.

**TABLE 7.4   Stages of Phonological Awareness**

| *Phonological Awareness Level* | *Sample Activity* |
| --- | --- |
| Recognizing that words represent a sound unit—word awareness | Provide children with some sort of counter. After reading a story, select one sentence and say it aloud. Repeat the sentence slowly and instruct students to drop a counter into a cup every time they hear a word. |
| Detecting that words are made up of different parts—syllable awareness | After reading a story, select some words that have single and multiple syllables. Invite students to clap out the parts as words are read. |
| Recognizing that words are made up of individual sounds—phoneme awareness | State a given word from a story and ask students how many sounds they hear in the word. |

*Source:* From *Rhymes and Reasons: Literature and Language Play for Phonological Awareness* by Michael Opitz. Copyright © 2000. Published by Heinemann.

In a *phoneme blending* task, students are expected to put sounds together to form a given word. For example, the teacher might say, "I'm thinking of a word that names something we have at lunch. It's /m/ ilk. What's the word?" Children must blend the first sound with the rest of the sounds to state the word "milk."

In a *phoneme segmentation* task, children are given a word and asked to tell how many sounds they hear in it. They are also often expected to produce the actual sounds. For example, the teacher might say, "Tell me the sounds you hear in the word 'mom.'" Learners might be expected to drop a counter into a cup that represents the sounds heard in the word.

*Phoneme manipulation* entails manipulating the sounds within a given word in different ways. Sometimes, children are expected to substitute one sound for another as in "What word do we have if we change the /m/ in *man* to /p/?" Other times, children are asked to add sounds to a given word as in "Add /s/ to *nail*. What's the new word?" Another task requires children to delete a sound within a word such as when the teacher says, "Take away the first sound in *gate*. What's the new word?"

## HOW CAN PHONOLOGICAL AWARENESS BE ASSESSED?

Go to the Assignments and Activities section of Topic 5: Phonemic Awareness and Phonics in the MyEducationLab for your course and complete the activity entitled "Assessing Phonological and Phonemic Awareness." Watch the video to see how phonological awareness plays out in some classrooms. Pay close attention to the narrators' comments and see which, if any, connect to what we mention about phonological awareness.

Phonological awareness in general and phonemic awareness in particular appear to be important for reading success. Recently, the National Reading Panel performed a meta-analysis of several studies and concluded that phonemic awareness is an important reading skill and that some children needed explicit instruction.[21] Likewise, the Board of Directors of the International Reading Association published a position statement on phonemic awareness and the teaching of reading.[22] By posing several questions and answers in the statement, the group explains the intricacies of phonemic awareness.

There are both informal and formal ways of assessing the different levels of phonological awareness. The one shown in Figure 7.6 is an informal measure that Michael Opitz created for *Summer Success Reading*.[23]

*Administering the Phonological Awareness Test*

1. Make a copy of the score sheet shown in Figure 7.6 for each student to be assessed.
2. Individually administer the test following the prompts shown on the score sheet.

*Scoring the Phonological Awareness Test*

1. Write the number correct for each subtest in the Summary section shown on the form in Figure 7.6.
2. Write any pertinent comments in the space provided.

A second way to assess phonological awareness is to use a norm-referenced measure such as the *Test of Phonological Awareness* (TOPA),[24] which is a group-administered test.

## TEACHING PHONOLOGICAL AWARENESS

For most children, phonological awareness is more caught than taught. Children who come to kindergarten or first grade with this awareness have been raised in a rich language environment where they were exposed to read-alouds, songs, nursery rhymes,

---

[21]National Institute of Child Health and Human Development, *Report of the National Reading Panel: Teaching Children to Read,* NIH Publication 00-4654 (Washington, DC: Government Printing Office, 2000).

[22]"Phonemic Awareness and the Teaching of Reading: A Position Statement from the Board of Directors of the International Reading Association" (Newark, DE: International Reading Association, 1998).

[23]Michael Opitz, *Summer Success Reading* (Boston, MA: Great Source Education Group, 2001).

[24]J. K. Torgesen and B. R. Bryant, *Test of Phonological Awareness* (Austin, TX: PRO-ED, 1994).

FIGURE 7.6 **PRETEST: Part A: Phonological Awareness Score Sheet**

Name: _____ Date _____

For each item, circle + for each correct response and – for each incorrect response. Give one point for each +.

**1. Word Level: Counting Words in Sentences**

***Directions:*** "I am going to say a sentence to you. I want you to clap every time you hear a word. Let's try one: 'I am here.'" (Pause for child to clap or repeat the sentence and clap.) "Good! You clapped three times! Now do the same for these sentences."

| *Sentence* | *Response* | |
|---|---|---|
| I like you. (3) | + — | |
| Summer is fun. (3) | + — | |
| The boy likes to read. (5) | + — | |
| Can you write? (3) | + — | |
| Tom drinks his milk. (4) | + — | Score _____ |

**2. Syllable Level: Counting Syllables in Words**

***Directions:*** "I am going to say some words to you, and this time I want you to tap on the table for each word part, for example, *cat* (tap once), *mother* (tap twice). Try some with me: *pig* (pause for response), *letter* (pause), *bunny* (pause). Good! Let's do some more words."

| *Word* | *Response* | |
|---|---|---|
| Dad (1) | + — | |
| funny (2) | + — | |
| animal (3) | + — | |
| toy (1) | + — | |
| sidewalk (2) | + — | Score _____ |

**3. Phoneme Level: Rhyming**

***Directions:*** "I am going to say two words. If they rhyme, say 'yes.' If they don't, say 'no.' Let's try a couple: *mat/cat* (pause for response). Yes! They rhyme. Now try another: *man/bet* (pause). Good! Let's do some more."

| *Word Pairs* | *Response* | |
|---|---|---|
| fish/wish (*yes*) | + — | |
| said/pet (*no*) | + — | |
| look/book (*yes*) | + — | |
| come/some (*yes*) | + — | |
| nine/name (*no*) | + — | Score _____ |

*(continued)*

---

**FIGURE 7.6** *(continued)*

---

**4. Phoneme Level: Matching**

**Directions:** "Now let's think of words that begin with the same sound. For example, dad, dog, and door begin with /d/." (Be sure to state the sound rather than the name of the letter.) "Let's try one. I'll say a sound and you tell me a word that starts with that sound: /s/." (Accept any word that begins with /s/.) "Good! Let's do a few more."

| *Sound* | *Response* | |
|---------|------------|---|
| /l/ | + — | |
| /p/ | + — | |
| /r/ | + — | |
| /t/ | + — | |
| /m/ | + — | Score _____ |

**Summary**

| | |
|---|---|
| 1. Word Level: Counting Words in Sentences | _____ |
| 2. Syllable Level: Counting Syllables in Words | _____ |
| 3. Phoneme Level: Rhyming | _____ |
| 4. Phoneme Level: Matching | _____ |
| | Total _____ /20 |

---

poems, and other forms of language play. The reverse is true for those children who are lacking in phonological awareness. More than likely, they have not been afforded a rich language environment that facilitates an understanding of spoken language.

Here are six specific suggestions drawn from the work of many individuals who have shed light on how best to help children acquire phonological awareness.[25] Keep in mind that while much unintentional instruction occurs throughout a school day, planned deliberate instruction in phonemic awareness is most effective when it is kept within short time frames (the National Reading Panel suggests about 200 minutes per school year, or about 7 minutes per day).

1. *Embed phonological awareness into everyday reading and writing experiences.* Doing so helps children understand how this awareness of sounds relates to reading and writing. Table 7.5 provides a list of typical reading and writing experiences, a sample activity for each, and an explanation of how the experience promotes phonological awareness.
2. *Provide children with time to write using invented spelling.* Although it is true that phonological awareness is focused on sounds of language rather than its printed form, there is a wealth of research that points to the value of having children write to develop phonological awareness. As children write, they learn to represent spoken language with written symbols and hone their skills at segmenting phonemes.

[25]M. Opitz, *Rhymes and Reasons: Literature and Language Play for Phonological Awareness* (Portsmouth, NH: Heinemann, 2000).

**TABLE 7.5　Reading and Writing Experiences That Foster Phonological Awareness**

| Typical Reading/ Writing Experiences | Sample Activity | Phonological Awareness |
|---|---|---|
| Read-aloud | Reading books that emphasize language features such as rhyme and alliteration | Words are made up of sound elements that sometimes sound alike. |
| Shared reading | Reading a big book and asking children to clap every time they hear a word | Words are separate units in the speech stream. They can be used to create stories and sentences. |
| Guided reading | Providing children with a text to read and directing them to point to each word as they read | Stories are made up of words. Spaces show where a word starts and ends. |
| Independent reading | Providing time for children to read their own books | Stories are a written form of language. There are units of sound in the speech stream— including words, syllables, and sounds—that are used to write these stories. |
| Modeled writing | Inviting children to watch as words are written on a chart or on the board, saying each word slowly to stretch them out—either by syllable or by sound | Several word parts/sounds can be used to create a word. These need to be put in a specific sequence. |
| Interactive writing | Encouraging children to participate in creating a message by stating their ideas | Speech can be written. It is written in chunks. |
| Independent writing | Providing time for children to write | Sounds are used to create words to communicate an idea to others. |

3. *Read aloud books that use specific language features.* These kinds of texts draw the learners' attention to given language features such as rhyme, alliteration, phoneme substitution, and phoneme segmentation. As a result of being exposed to books such as these, children learn to make distinctions among sounds and may develop phonological awareness in general and phonemic awareness in particular in meaningful contexts. Fortunately, several such titles are written every year. *Clickety Clack* (Spence & Spence, 1999) is a rhyming story about what happens when many different kinds and numbers of animals decide they want to ride a train. Much initial consonant substitution is used to create the rhymes, making this an excellent book not only for exposing children to rhyme but also for providing some meaningful practice with phoneme substitution. *Pignic* (Miranda, 1996) is an example of alliterative text in which each member of the pig family brings to the pignic something that begins with the same sound that begins their name. Children can join in the fun by going on their own imaginary picnic and bringing along some item that begins with the same sound as their name. *Things That Are Most in the World* (Barrett, 1998) is a repetitive text that tells about some of the silliest, heaviest, and smelliest things in the world! Once they have finished reading the book, children can learn more about phoneme deletion by playing the take-away game. Using words from the text, children might be asked to "Take -*est* away from wiggliest. What's the new word?" *Earthsong* (Rogers, 1998) is a poetry text that includes a rhythmic, rhyming pattern in the dialogues between parents and their offspring. It is an excellent book to help children further understand rhyme.

Songs can also be used to further children's understanding of phonological awareness. Song picture books have been created to illustrate specific songs. For example, *Hush Little Baby* (Frazee, 1999) is true to the original song, but uses updated illustrations. Once children have sung the song, each word can be framed on a second reading to help children understand word boundaries.

Finally, texts that use language in humorous ways, such as those written by Dr. Seuss, help children to see that we often play with the sounds in our language. Along with this learning comes a heightened sense of phonological awareness. For example, in *Altoona Baboona* (Bynum, 1999), the author inserts a sound at the end of several words, making this a perfect book to help children further understand sound deletion or sound addition. Children can be directed to take the last sound off the word and say the remaining word (i.e., phoneme deletion), or to add a sound to the end of their names (i.e., phoneme addition). Additional books that invite language play are listed in Table 7.6.

4. *Involve children in fun oral language activities.* Some children may need more explicit instruction to develop all levels of phonological awareness. These children need to be engaged with the three points listed above as well as with activities that will stimulate their curiosity about and understanding of their spoken language. If children need to understand the concept that words represent a sound unit, they can be provided with some sort of counter. Once a story has been read, students can be directed to pick up a counter for each word they hear. If children need to better understand that words are constructed of syllables, they can be invited to clap out the parts as words are read aloud. If students need additional practice with recognizing that words are made up of individual sounds (i.e., phonemes), they can be asked to tell the sounds they hear in given words from the story.

5. *Assess to see where children need the most help.* This can be accomplished through observing children as they participate in literacy-related activities such as writing. Observations during writing could reveal those children whose writing shows spaces between words or words that have representative symbols for sounds. These would indicate that the child has developed a sense of all levels of phonological awareness. And the results of assessments such as those shown and mentioned above can be used to detect which children might need some additional help.

6. *Get families involved!* One way to accomplish this is to provide a book and a brief explanation of how to complete an accompanying activity. For example, if the book that is being sent home contains much alliteration, the letter can explain how to point out to the child that all of the words on a given page begin with a certain sound. The child can then be asked to listen for the sound and to state it after a page has been read. The parent can then be instructed to have the child think of other words that begin with the same sound. The letter must focus on exactly what the parent needs to do when working on the book with the child.

# UNDERSTANDING, ASSESSING, AND TEACHING LETTER IDENTIFICATION

## WHAT IS LETTER IDENTIFICATION?

Letter identification is just that—identifying the letters of the alphabet. Although common sense would tell us that being able to identify and name the letters of the alphabet is important for reading and writing tasks, there is also ample evidence that being able to name letters is a predictor of end-of-year achievement for kindergarten students.[26]

[26]G. Bond and R. Dykstra, "The Cooperative Research Program in First-Grade Reading Instruction," *Reading Research Quarterly* 2 (1967): 5–142.

**TABLE 7.6   Additional Books That Invite Language Play**

*Rhyme*

Burleigh, R. 2009. *Clang! Clang! Beep! Beep! Listen to the City.* Simon & Schuster. 978-1-4169-4052-4.
Downey, L. 2000. *The Flea's Sneeze.* Holt. 0-805-061037.
Marshak, S. 1999. *The Absentminded Fellow.* Farrar, Straus, & Giroux. 0-374-300135.
Martin, B. 1999. *A Beasty Story.* Harcourt. 0-15-201683-X.
Morrow, B. 2009. *Mr. Mosquito Put on His Tuxedo.* Holiday House. 0-8234-2072-8.
Thomas, J. 2009. *Rhyming Dust Bunnies.* Beach Lane Books. 978-1-4169-7976-0.

*Alliteration*

Barron, R. 2000. *Fed Up! A Feast of Frazzled Foods.* Putnam. 0-399-234500.
Duncan, P. 1999. *The Wacky Wedding: A Book of Alphabet Antics.* Hyperion. 0-7868-2248-1.
Pavey, P. 2009. *One Dragon's Dream.* Candlewick Press. 978-0-7636-4470-3.
Shapiro, Z. 2009. *We're All in the SAME BOAT.* G.P. Putnam's Sons. 978-0-399-24393-6.

*Repetition*

Bauer, M. 2002. *Sleep, Little One, Sleep.* Aladdin. 0-689-85269X.
Collicut, P. 1999. *This Train.* Farrar, Straus, & Giroux. 0-374-37493-7.
Hamilton, K. 2009. *Police Officers on Patrol.* Viking. 978-0-670-06315-4
Weinstein, E. 2008. *Everywhere the Cow Says "Moo!"* Boyds Mill. 978-1-59078-458-7.

*Poetry*

Lobel, A. 2009. *The Frogs and Toads All Sang.* Harper Collins. 978-0-06-180022-1.
Rylant, C. 1998. *Bless Us All: A Child's Yearbook of Blessings.* Simon & Schuster. 0-689-823703.
Schertle, A. 2009. *Button Up!* Houghton Mifflin Harcourt. 978-0-15-205050-4.
Stevenson, R. 1999. *My Shadow.* Harcourt. 0-7636-0923-4.

*Song*

Hoberman, M. 2000. *The Eensy-Weensy Spider.* Little, Brown. 0-316-363308.
Norworth, J. 1999. *Take Me Out to the Ballgame.* Aladdin. 0-689-82433-5.
Scieszka, J. 2009. *Truckery Rhymes.* Simon & Schuster. 978-1-4169-4135-4.
Tobin, J. 2009. *Sue MacDonald Had a Book.* Henry Holt and Company. 978-0-8050-8766-6.

*Goofy*

Feldman, E. 2009. *Billy & Milly Short & Silly.* G.P. Putnam's Sons. 978-0-399-24651-7.
London, J. 2001. *Crunch Munch.* Harcourt. 0-15-202603-7.
Palatini, M. 2009. *Boo-Hoo Moo.* Harper Collins. 978-0-06-114375-5.

Letter identification also helps students learn letter–sound associations (i.e., alphabetic principle). This should come as no surprise because it would be pretty difficult to make any kind of association if one part of the equation is unknown! And, as Rathvon notes, "Only when children have developed the insight that written word forms are related to the sounds rather than the meaning of language can they learn the specific correspondences between letters and phonemes."[27]

Many games teachers are likely to play with words depend on children being able to identify letters from their names. Therefore, children will have much more fun and are more likely to participate well in such games when they can identify letters early on.

## HOW CAN LETTER IDENTIFICATION BE ASSESSED?

Ask any kindergarten or first-grade teacher and he or she will tell you that a good way to assess letter identification ability is to individually ask children to name the letters in random order. Both uppercase and lowercase letters are assessed because knowing one form of the letter doesn't necessarily mean that a child knows the other form.

The protocol in Figure 7.7 shows one informal way of assessing letter identification.

*Administering the Letter Identification Test*

1. Place the letter identification page in front of the child. Say something like, "Here are some letters. Take a look at each one and tell me what it is. You may say 'pass' if you cannot remember the name of the letter."
2. Use index cards to cover everything but the lines being read. If necessary, point to each letter with your finger (or have the child point).
3. As the child responds, use your copy of the assessment to note correct responses (1) and incorrect responses (2). When responses are incorrect, record the actual response or "DK" (doesn't know) if the child doesn't know the specific letter. If the child self-corrects, write OK. Remember that self-corrections can be made at any time and should not be counted as errors.

*Scoring the Letter Identification Test*

1. Count the number of responses for the uppercase letters and lowercase letters.
2. Note the scores in the box on the scoring form in Figure 7.8.

Marie Clay's *Observation Survey* (Heinemann, 1985) provides a formal, norm-referenced standardized way of assessing letter identification. The assessment is similar to the one described above and it is individually administered. However, norms are provided, as are some additional assessment procedures.

## TEACHING LETTER IDENTIFICATION

Many children come to school already knowing the letters of the alphabet, so the suggestions given here simply enhance their understanding. We catch others right in the middle of the process. However, there are some children who are just beginning to learn to identify letters. This is not to say that these children haven't already noticed letters. Few can escape environmental print and most understand at an intuitive level that certain marks are used to record their names. They simply cannot put a label with the squiggle. Here are a few suggestions for helping children to identify letters:

1. *Use their names!* Meaningful association is necessary for any of us to learn anything, and this is also true of children learning letters. That is why many kindergarten and first-grade teachers use children's names when thinking about which letters to teach first. In other words, the fact that children can identify their names

Go to the Assignments and Activities section of Topic 5: Phonemic Awareness and Phonics in the MyEducationLab for your course and complete the activity entitled "Name Lotto." As you watch the video and answer the accompanying questions, pay close attention to how the teacher uses what children know to teach them something they need to know. How might using children's names to teach letter identification facilitate children's success?

[27]N. Rathvon, *Early Reading Assessment: A Practitioner's Handbook* (New York: Guilford, 2004).

**FIGURE 7.7   PRETEST: Part A: Letter Identification, Student Copy**

| C | U | S | I | N | Q |   |
|---|---|---|---|---|---|---|
| Z | K | E | M | L | D | V |
| P | T | R | B | F | G |   |
| Y | X | W | O | H | A | J |

| d | w | e | t | f | p |   |
|---|---|---|---|---|---|---|
| j | u | h | k | n | r | i |
| x | b | o | y | c | a |   |
| g | m | v | l | q | z | s |

*Source:* From *Summer Success: Reading, Kindergarten* by James F. Baumann, Michael F. Opitz, Laura Robb. Text copyright © 2001 by Great Source Education Group, a division of Houghton Mifflin Company. Reprinted by permission. All rights reserved.

**FIGURE 7.8   PRETEST: Part A: Letter Identification, Score Sheet**

Name: _____   Date: _____

## Capital Letters

| | | | | | |
|---|---|---|---|---|---|
| C | U | S | I | N | Q |
| Z | K | E | M | L | D | V |
| P | T | R | B | F | G |
| Y | X | W | O | H | A | J |

Number Correct _____

## Lowercase Letters

| | | | | |
|---|---|---|---|---|
| d | w | e | t | f | p |
| j | u | h | k | n | r | i |
| x | b | o | y | c | a |
| g | m | v | l | q | z | s |

Number Correct _____

TOTAL CORRECT ____/152

is no guarantee that they know every letter in the name. Because names are meaningful, teachers often begin by having children learn these letters.

2. *Use alphabet books.* One sure way to help children see the connection between letters and reading is to share alphabet books with them. Different letters can be pointed out along the way. There are numerous alphabet books that would appeal to just about any interest. *ABC Disney* by Robert Sabuda (Hyperion, 1998) is a pop-up book that features different characters from Disney movies. Others include *The Accidental Zucchini* by Mary Grover (Harcourt, 1997), *Flora McDonnell's A B C* by Flora McDonnell (Candlewick, 1997), and *ABC Kids* by Laura Ellen Williams (Philomel, 2000).

3. *Create an alphabet book.* Staple enough pages together for each letter of the alphabet. You might print one letter on each page in alphabetical order or you may decide to have the children write the letters in the order they learn them. In either case, the letter can be written at the top of the page and children can find pictures associated with the letter. These pictures can be labeled and children can trace over the letter shown at the top of the page.

4. *Be newspaper detectives.* Tear pages of the local newspaper into four parts and give each child a part. Have them search out letters that match the ones they are learning. They can use a yellow marker to highlight the letters.

5. *Use objects.* Have children bring in toys or other objects whose names begin with letters they are learning. These could be put in a big tub and could be used for sorting into different pockets, each labeled with a different letter. Likewise, labels from cans and other food products can be brought into the classroom and students can identify the letters shown on the various labels.

## UNDERSTANDING, ASSESSING, AND TEACHING WRITING

### WHAT IS WRITING?

**Emergent writing**
Nonconventional writing that includes scribbling and nonphonetic letterings.

When young children of about two and one-half first put pencil or crayon to paper, they are in the initial, or emergent, stage of writing. Children in the *emergent writing* stage write in preconventional or emergent forms (scribbling, drawing, nonphonetic letterings, and phonetic spellings) before they write conventionally. The desire to create something of one's own is a very important and necessary first step.

Teachers and parents can create a stimulating environment for preschoolers, so that children will scribble and express themselves. After preschoolers have put something down on paper, they can be encouraged to tell about what they have drawn or "written." A number of preschoolers try their skills at writing stories, even though they do not have specific hand motor control. (See Figures 7.9 and 7.10) Showing enthusiasm about the child's efforts will encourage him or her to continue.

Teachers and parents are good role models for their children. Those who write will be more likely to have children who write. Teachers and parents who value and model writing invite children to do the same.

Children who are motivated to write, and who value it intensely, will master the control of specific muscles needed to write. Three-year-olds are often able to make circles, showing that they are gaining control of specific hand muscles. By age five, many can construct other geometric figures, such as squares, which require more precision. Some kindergarten children, who have the necessary coordination and desire, are able to construct letters or words. Some can print their names in some legible form and write a story about themselves or their families. See Figure 7.11 for an example of such a story. Early childhood writing can be one of the most engaging and rewarding aspects of early literacy.

As you can see, children attempt to use writing at a very young age and they progress over time toward conventional writing. Taking a look at their writing enables

**FIGURE 7.9** Melissa, who is 4, knows "M" is for "Mom."

**FIGURE 7.10** Melissa at 4½ includes Kelsey, her sister, in her stories. She also likes to draw and tell stories about her neighbor's kitten. (Melissa tells you that she is the one with the bow in her hair.)

**FIGURE 7.11** A kindergarten child's story.

us to identify their progress. We can also get a glimpse of the words a child has in his or her writing vocabulary—those words the child can write conventionally without any prompting from the teacher. Finally, we can see what the child understands about the alphabetic principle by noting the symbols the child uses to represent sounds in words; this indicates where the child is in terms of developmental spelling.

## WHAT IS DEVELOPMENTAL SPELLING?

Learning to spell is a complex undertaking that involves more than simply memorizing words; it is developmental in nature and requires the acquisition and application of knowledge of spoken and written language.[28] By *developmental, we mean that learning to spell is ongoing and based on the cognitive development of the child.* Conventional spelling is learned gradually as a child writes over the years.

Young children's spelling is based on their present knowledge of the language system, so when they spell, they may use *invented spelling.* When young children begin asking about adults' writing, it is often a signal that they want to write, too. They may begin by using invented spelling. The pattern of invented spelling will vary from one child to another. However, an analysis of children's invented spelling indicates that they

**Developmental spelling**
Learning to spell is ongoing and based on the cognitive development of the child.

[28]Richard E. Hodges, "The Language Base of Spelling," in *Research in the Language Arts: Language and Schooling,* eds. Victor Froese and Stanley B. Straw (Baltimore: University Park Press, 1981), p. 218.

progress through stages that make use of their years of experience with oral language. Some researchers claim that children's spelling development parallels earlier stages of oral language development. This language-based hypothesis about how children learn to spell argues that children "internalize information about spoken and written words, organize that information, construct tentative rules based on that information, and apply these rules to the spelling of words. "[29]

Gentry has developed a model to show four stages children often go through before they develop standard or correct spelling.[30] The first is called the *precommunicative stage* (formerly known as the deviant stage) because the appearance of the child's spelling attempts shows that the child has no knowledge of letter–sound correspondence. At the *semiphonetic stage* the child demonstrates some letter–sound correspondences; that is, the child is beginning to gain the concept that letters represent sounds and that these are used to write words. Semiphonetic spelling is abbreviated spelling in which one, two, or three letters usually represent the word; for example, U = *you*, B = *Be*, and LEFT = *elephant* show that the "speller represents words, sounds, or syllables with letters that match their letter name."[31] At this stage, the child is also gaining the concept that letters are arranged in a left–right orientation, knows the alphabet, and can form the letters.

At the *phonetic stage,* the child's spelling is characterized by an almost perfect match between letters and sounds. The child's spelling includes all sound features as he or she hears and says them. As a result, the child's spelling at this stage does not resemble standard spelling, for example, "MONSTR" = *monster* and "DRAS" = *dress*. The *transitional stage,* which is the final stage in this model, precedes standard spelling. At this stage, the child is better acquainted with standard spelling, and words look like English, even though they are misspelled. The child includes vowels in every syllable, so phonetic "EGL" for *eagle* at this stage becomes "EGUL." It is at this stage that the child moves from phonological to morphological and visual spelling (e.g., EIGHTEE instead of the phonetic ATE [*eighty*])[32] and begins to use more conventionally spelled words in writing.

If children are given many opportunities to write for many different purposes, they will progress through these stages with teacher guidance. Forcing the child to move into the next stage without time to develop the concepts in the current stage can actually thwart progress rather than advance it. Correction of spelling during these early stages is ineffective. Children need long time periods to "live" and figure things out in each stage.[33]

## HOW CAN WRITING BE ASSESSED?

To find out whether children have a writing vocabulary, we can give them a blank sheet of paper and ask them to write all of the words they know.

To get a view of the children's understandings about the alphabetic principle, we can give them a blank piece of paper and tell them to write a message. We can then watch what they do and make note of our observations using a form such as the one shown in Figure 7.12.

[29]James W. Beers, "Developmental Strategies of Spelling Competence in Primary-School Children," in *Developmental and Cognitive Aspects of Learning to Spell,* eds. Edmund H. Henderson and James W. Beers (Newark, DE: IRA, 1980), p. 36.

[30]J. Richard Gentry, "An Analysis of Developmental Spelling in GYNS at WRK," *The Reading Teacher* 36 (November, 1982): 192–200.

[31]Ibid., p. 194.

[32]Ibid., p. 197.

[33]S. Kucer, *Dimensions of Literacy*, 3rd ed. (Mahwah, NJ: Lawrence Earlbaum, 2009).

**FIGURE 7.12   Writing Observation Form**

**Brief Directions:** Give the student paper and pencil. Ask the student to do some writing. Record qualitative judgments, observations, and insights below.

|  | *Not Evident, Low, Seldom, Weak, Poor* | *Very Evident, High, Always, Strong, Excellent* |
|---|---|---|

**Directionality**

Left to right

Top to bottom

**Writing**

Scribbles or "cursivelike" scribbles

Letterlike formations

Repeated letters, numbers, words

Variety of letters, numbers, words

Knowledge of first (F) and last (L) name

**Letter–Sound Relationships**

Represents sounds heard at word beginnings

Represents sounds heard at word endings

Represents sounds heard in middle of words

**Writing Conventions**

Use of word boundaries

Use of punctuation

**Overall Message Intent (check one)**

_____ Student indicated no message intent.

_____ Student talked about but did not read or pretend to read what was written.

_____ Student was able to read what was written.

Teacher could make sense of writing independently. _____ yes _____ no

*Observations, Comments, Notes, and Insights*

*Source:* From Jerry Johns, *The Basic Reading Inventory,* 8th edition, p. 425. Copyright © 2001 by Kendall/Hunt. Reprinted by permission.

Teachers who need a norm-referenced standardized writing test might want to use the writing assessments in Clay's *Diagnostic Survey* (1993).[34] The writing vocabulary test is used to reveal a child's writing vocabulary, whereas the dictation test is used to shed light on a child's understanding of the alphabetic principle.

## TEACHING WRITING

In early literacy teaching, we want to encourage children to express and share their own ideas. This gives them confidence in themselves and makes them feel that what they have to write is worth sharing with others. Teachers need to capitalize on children's creativity. They can do this by giving children the time and opportunity to write and by respecting their ideas. Although the writing may be scant at first, it is the child's own creation. When children feel supported as writers, the volume and frequency of writing will increase.[35]

### *Writing Environment*

An inviting classroom, filled with books and children's "published" works and well organized into a number of learning centers, can be a catalyst for students' writing. A classroom where exciting things are happening and where children are involved in reading, observing, manipulating, and experimenting, is a place that encourages written self-expression. The quality of the teacher–student and student–student relationships is important in setting the emotional climate. If students and teachers are engaged in cooperative endeavors and students feel secure, they will want to write and share their written ideas with others.

### *Time for Writing*

Writing helps students become better writers. They need adequate time to write in class. As with all writers, expressing themselves takes time. Good writing requires teachers to provide students with enough time to write. After getting the proper start in class, many children will work on their own during free time and at home, finishing compositions because they have become involved with the creative act and want to see the finished product.

## UNDERSTANDING, ASSESSING, AND TEACHING STORY SENSE

### WHAT IS STORY SENSE?

**Story sense**
The understanding that there is a structure used to tell stories and that stories are written to be understood.

*Story sense* is the understanding that there is a structure used to tell stories and that stories are written to be understood. In other words, not only does it involve understanding a simple story line, it also includes comprehension.

### HOW CAN STORY SENSE BE ASSESSED?

Probably the best way to assess story sense and story comprehension is to use a wordless picture book such as *Good Dog, Carl* by Alexandra Day (Green Tiger, 1985). As students tell the story, note whether they are able to tell it with any kind of order that flows from one page to the next. This is the most authentic assessment, but it is time-consuming.

Another way to assess story sense and story comprehension is to use the wordless picture story shown in Figure 7.13. After giving the student time to preview the pictures, have him or her tell you the story. Follow the directions stated on the score sheet in Figure 7.14 to score the storytelling. To check comprehension, ask the questions shown on the score sheet in Figure 7.14 and score them as directed.

[34]M. Clay, *The Early Detection of Reading Difficulties* (Portsmouth, NH: Heineman, 2003).

[35]J. Hansen, *When Writers Read* (Portsmouth, NH: Heinemann, 2002).

**FIGURE 7.13   PRETEST: Part B: Wordless Picture Story #1**

**1.**

**2.**

**3.**

**4.**

*Source:* From *Summer Success: Reading, Kindergarten* by James F. Baumann, Michael F. Opitz, Laura Robb. Text copyright © 2001 by Great Source Education Group, a division of Houghton Mifflin Company. Reprinted by permission. All rights reserved.

FIGURE 7.14   PRETEST: Part B: Wordless Picture Story #1 Score Sheet

Name _____   Date _____

### Storytelling

Check the details the child mentions for each picture. Accept any logical interpretation. Give one (1) point for each detail the child includes. Make sure the student understands each picture before going on to the next.

#### Frame 1

1. a **man** (dad, brother, uncle, etc.) _____

2. is giving a **package** (box, present, gift, etc.) _____

3. to a **girl** (child, his daughter, etc.) _____

#### Frame 2

4. the **girl** (child . . .) _____

5. is **tearing the paper off** (unwrapping) _____

6. the **package** (box . . .) _____

#### Frame 3

7. the **girl** _____

8. **opens the box** (package . . .) _____

9. **inside** the box _____

10. is a **ball** (basketball . . .) _____

#### Frame 4

11. the **girl** _____

12. and the **man** _____

13. **play with the ball** (play catch, play basketball . . .) _____

*Score* ____ /13

### Story Comprehension

Ask these questions. Give 1 point for each correct answer.

1. Who is this story about? *a girl (child . . .)* _____

2. What happens to the girl? *She gets a package with a ball in it.* _____

3. What does the girl do with the ball? *plays with the man (her dad . . .)* _____

4. How do you think the girl felt when she opened the package? How can you tell? *This response requires inferential thinking based on prior knowledge. Accept any reasonable opinion and explanation. Probably the girl is happy. She is smiling and she goes right out to play.* _____

*Score* ____ /4

**TABLE 7.7   Directed Listening/Thinking Approach (DLTA) Chart**

| *What Teachers Do* | *What Children Do* | *What Teachers Need to Observe* |
| --- | --- | --- |
| Relate talk to children's past experiences | Listen carefully; relate to past experiences | Students' attentiveness and their interest level based on the kinds of questions that students ask |
| Present motivating technique and vocabulary necessary to understand talk | | |
| Present questions as guide before, during, and after talk | Answer and ask questions | Students' responses to questions |

## TEACHING STORY SENSE AND STORY COMPREHENSION

Reading aloud to children is perhaps one of the best ways to help them develop a sense of story. Likewise, giving them time to share their thoughts about the story after the read-aloud can be a good way to check their comprehension.

What's really going on here has to do with listening comprehension, however, because students are listening to the text rather than reading it for themselves. Using the *Directed Listening/Thinking Activity* shown in Table 7.7 is an excellent way to teach students how to listen and to work on story sense and comprehension simultaneously.

### The Directed Listening/Thinking Approach

They *directed listening/thinking approach* requires teachers to ask questions before, during, and after a talk. The steps in this approach are as follows:

**Directed listening/thinking approach**
Requires teachers to ask questions before, during, and after a talk; consists of a number of steps; requires students to be active participants.

*Step 1: Preparation for talk, lecture, audiotape, or film.* The teacher relates to students' past experiences, gives an overview of the talk and presents any special vocabulary and questions at various difficulty levels that students should try to answer while listening to the talk.

*Step 2: Students listen to the presentation.* During the presentation, the teacher stops, asks students to answer some of the previously given questions, and interjects some more thought-provoking questions to guide students.

*Step 3: After the presentation.* The children answer unanswered questions and are presented with some more challenging questions. In addition, the teacher asks the children to identify the central idea of the talk, as well as to give a short summary.

*Step 4: After the discussion.* The teacher asks students to devise some good questions that could be used as test questions.

# PUTTING IT ALL TOGETHER: WHO IS IN MOST NEED OF EARLY INTERVENTION?

## WHAT IS EARLY INTERVENTION?

*Early intervention* is just what the term suggests: helping children to become successful as early as possible. Once their strengths and needs are identified, children receive specialized instruction that focuses on their strengths and addresses their needs.

Go to the Assignments and Activities section of Topic 11: Reading Difficulties and Intervention Strategies in the MyEducationLab for your course and complete the activity entitled "Early Intervention." As you watch the video and answer the accompanying questions, think about what you can do as a teacher to prevent reading problems.

Accelerating foundational knowledge through rich early literacy experiences sets students up for success in attaining proficient reading. Teachers using a reading diagnosis and improvement program will often provide this instruction themselves, but they may also call on others to help them.

Extra reading help sometimes comes in the form of an early intervention program such as *Reading Recovery*.[36] The purpose of this program is to identify those children who are experiencing difficulty in their first year of reading instruction. In this short-term curriculum, children who are the lowest achieving readers in a given first-grade class receive daily individualized 30-minute lessons from a specially trained *Reading Recovery* teacher in addition to the regular classroom reading instruction. Every individualized lesson is tailored to engage children in authentic reading and writing activities that will help them catch up with their peers.

## WHO IS IN MOST NEED OF EARLY INTERVENTION?

But how do we determine which children could benefit from additional instruction and assessment? The most obvious way is to make a class composite of each of the subtests shown in this chapter. The class composite will show how children performed and can signal which children need the most help with a given aspect of early literacy.

A second way is to follow a process similar to the one used by *Reading Recovery* teachers. Children complete each test of Clay's *Diagnostic Survey*: letter identification, word test, concepts about print, writing vocabulary, dictation, and text reading. The examiner then adds the scores together to get an overall score. However, combining scores in this way is useful only for identifying a student with needs. To design appropriate instruction, the teacher will need to take a look at the child's performance on each subtest. Doing so will help to reveal where the child needs some additional instruction.

As it relates to the measures we show in this chapter, teachers can use the form shown in Figure 7.15 to note scores for each test. As with the *Diagnostic Survey* noted above, the scores can be added together and the students with the lowest overall scores can then receive the individualized additional reading instruction designed to address their reading needs.

A third way to identify those children who need the most help is to use a rating tool such as the *Teacher Rating of Oral Language and Literacy (TROLL)*,[37] which was created to guide observations of children's literacy skills in all areas of the language arts (speaking, listening, reading, and writing). This instrument provides a way for teachers to record what they see. The authors note that the TROLL also does something that a direct assessment cannot capture—it enables the teacher to observe children's interests in a variety of oral language and written language activities.

Another advantage of the TROLL is that teachers can use the results to inform instruction (e.g., to identify children who are showing evidence of oral language delay, those who may need further testing to explore learning needs, and those who are functioning above average and need additional stimulating activities). For further explanation about TROLL and its development, see the article by Dickinson, McCabe, and Sprague. The authors include the entire instrument, along with an explanation about what the scores mean.

---

[36]Clay (1993).

[37]D. Dickinson, A. McCabe, and K. Sprague, "Teacher Rating of Oral Language and Literacy (TROLL): Individualizing Early Literacy Instruction with a Standards-Based Rating Tool," *The Reading Teacher,* 56, no. 6 (2003): 554–564.

**FIGURE 7.15    Summary of Early Literacy Test Results**

| Child's Name | Oral Language Concepts (9 possible) | Print Concepts (12 possible) | Phonological Awareness (20 possible) | Letter Identification (52 possible) | Story Sense (17 possible) | Total (110 possible) |
|---|---|---|---|---|---|---|
| | | | | | | |
| | | | | | | |
| | | | | | | |
| | | | | | | |
| | | | | | | |
| | | | | | | |
| | | | | | | |
| | | | | | | |
| | | | | | | |
| | | | | | | |
| | | | | | | |
| | | | | | | |
| | | | | | | |
| | | | | | | |
| | | | | | | |
| | | | | | | |
| | | | | | | |
| | | | | | | |
| | | | | | | |
| | | | | | | |
| | | | | | | |
| | | | | | | |
| | | | | | | |
| | | | | | | |
| | | | | | | |
| | | | | | | |
| | | | | | | |
| | | | | | | |
| | | | | | | |
| | | | | | | |
| | | | | | | |
| | | | | | | |
| | | | | | | |
| | | | | | | |

## REVISITING THE OPENING SCENARIO

Describe the various assessments that Ms. Berger uses to figure out how best to advance her students in oral language and early literacy. How can she simultaneously demonstrate accountability to those concerned with meeting government mandates?

## AUTHORS' SUMMARY

The major focus in this chapter was how to best assess and teach various aspects of early literacy. After providing background for each component of early literacy, we presented some assessment and teaching suggestions intended to give teachers ways to work with students on the various components in early literacy. We concluded the chapter with three suggestions for determining who is most in need of early intervention.

## SUGGESTIONS FOR THOUGHT QUESTIONS AND ACTIVITIES

1. Observe a kindergarten classroom, making note of the classroom environment. How do you see Cambourne's conditions of learning exemplified?
2. Create a list of alphabet books that could be used to help children learn more about the alphabet, and identify different features that each book brings to students.
3. Using the guidelines on pages 126–128, develop a list of books that can be used to teach children about the different aspects of phonological awareness.
4. During your interview for a teaching position, the committee members ask you to explain how you would determine kindergarten students' strengths and needs. Construct your response.

## WEB SITES

http://www.starfall.com/

This colorful site provides information and activities for teachers, parents, and children. Geared toward emergent literacy, the site includes printable books, downloadables for teachers and parents, and information and activities on phonemic awareness, systematic phonics, vocabulary, and so on. Also contains a scope and sequence page lining up texts with objectives.

http://www.readinga-z.com/assess/other.html#reading

Although the site requires a subscription for access to its extensive resources, it does offer some assessment ideas without the subscription that are worth checking out. For example, this resource includes assessment tips on student talk, observation checklists, and running records. Also included in the larger site are resources on guided reading, fluency, poetry, and more.

http://10ss.qtp.nsw.edu.au/elo/stage1/assesrecord.html

This Early Literacy Online site includes various teaching and assessment resources. The assessments include talking and listening, reading behaviors, writing, and more. The site also contains links to scope and sequences and points to consider when planning lessons. Including various downloadable sources, Early Literacy Online also provides units (e.g., http://10ss.qtp.nsw.edu.au/elo/stage1/Assets/pdfs/Eng_TRS1_oneworld.pdf).

http://www.readingrecovery.org/reading_recovery/facts/index.asp

In this portion of the Reading Recovery Council of North America site, teachers have access to basic information regarding Reading Recovery. Other links in the site offer access to lessons, professional development, and information on a comprehensive literacy plan.

http://www.eric.ed.gov/ERICWebPortal/contentdelivery/servlet/ERICServlet?accno=ED272922

Defining invented spelling and its development, this site covers the developmental stages of spelling and the implications for teachers and their instructional planning. The site provides useful background research for teachers interested in developing students' strategies for learning Standard English spelling as opposed to memorization as the key to mastery.

# SELECTED BIBLIOGRAPHY

Elley, W. "Vocabulary Acquisition from Listening to Stories." *Reading Research Quarterly* 24 (1989): 174–187.

Johns, J. *The Basic Reading Inventory,* 9th ed. Dubuque, IA: Kendall/Hunt, 2005.

"Learning to Read and Write: Developmentally Appropriate Practices for Young Children: A Joint Position Statement of the International Reading Association and the National Association for the Education of Young Children." Newark, DE: International Reading Association, 1998.

O'Connor, R. E., and J. R. Jenkins. "Prediction of Reading Disabilities in Kindergarten and First Grade." *Scientific Studies of Reading* 3 (1999): 159–197.

Opitz, M. *Flexible Grouping in Reading: Practical Ways to Help All Students Become Better Readers*. New York: Scholastic, 1998.

Rubin, D. *Teaching Elementary Language Arts: A Balanced Approach,* 6th ed. Boston: Allyn and Bacon, 2000.

# CHILDREN'S LITERATURE CITED

Barrett, Judi. *Things That Are Most in the World.* New York: Atheneum, 1998.

Barron, Rex. *Fed Up! A Feast of Frazzled Foods.* New York: Putnam, 2002.

Bauer, Marion. *Sleep, Little One, Sleep.* New York: Aladdin, 2002.

Burleigh, Robert. *Clang! Clang! Beep! Beep! Listen to the City.* New York: Simon & Schuster, 2009.

Bynum, Janie. *Altoona Baboona.* San Diego: Harcourt, 1999.

Collicut, Paul. *This Train.* New York: Farrar, Straus, & Giroux, 1999.

Day, Alexandra. *Good Dog, Carl.* New York: Green Tiger, 1985.

Downey, Lynne. *The Flea's Sneeze.* New York: Holt, 2000.

Duncan, Pamela. *The Wacky Wedding: A Book of Alphabet Antics.* New York: Hyperion, 1999.

Feldman, Eve. *Billy & Milly Short & Silly.* New York: G.P. Putnam's Sons, 2009.

Frazee, Marla. *Hush Little Baby.* San Diego: Browndeer/Harcourt, 1999.

Grover, Mary. *The Accidental Zucchini.* San Diego: Harcourt, 1997.

Hamilton, Kersten. *Police Officers on Patrol.* New York: Viking, 2009.

Hoban, Tana. *Over, Under, Through.* New York: Macmillan, 1973.

Hoberman, Mary. *The Eensy-Weensy Spider.* New York: Macmillan, 1973.

Lobel, Arnold. *The Frogs and Toads All Sang.* New York: Harper Collins, 2009.

London, Jonathan. *Crunch Munch.* San Diego: Harcourt, 2001.

McDonnell, Flora. *Flora McDonnell's ABC.* Cambridge, MA: Candlewick, 1997.

Marshak, Samuel. *The Absentminded Fellow.* New York: Farrar, Straus, & Giroux, 1999.

Martin, Bill. *A Beasty Story.* San Diego: Harcourt, 1999.

Miranda, Anne. *Pignic.* Honesdale, PA: Boyds Mills, 1996.

Morrow, Barbara Olenyik. *Mr. Mosquito Put on His Tuxedo.* New York: Holiday House, 2009.

Most, Bernard. *A Pair of Protoceratops.* San Diego: Harcourt, 1998.

Norworth, Jack. *Take Me Out to the Ballgame.* New York: Aladdin, 1999.

Palatini, Margie. *Boo-Hoo Moo.* New York: Harper Collins, 2009.

Pavey, Peter. *One Dragon's Dream.* Somerville, Ma: Candlewick, 2009.

Rogers, Sally. *Earthsong.* New York: Dutton, 1998.

Root, Phyllis. *The Hungry Monster.* Cambridge, MA: Candlewick, 1997.

Rotner, Shelley. *Parts.* New York: Walker, 2001.

Rylant, Cynthia. *Bless Us All: A Child's Yearbook of Blessings.* New York: Simon & Schuster, 1998.

Sabuda, Robert. *ABC Disney.* New York: Hyperion, 1998.

Schertle, Alice. *Button Up!* New York: Houghton Mifflin Harcourt, 2009.

Scieszka, Jon. *Truckery Rhymes.* New York: Simon & Schuster, 2009.

Shapiro, Zachary. *We're All in the SAME BOAT.* New York: G.P. Putnam's Sons, 2009.

Spence, Rob, and Amy Spence. *Clickety Clack.* New York: Viking, 1999.

Stevenson, Robert. *My Shadow.* San Diego: Harcourt, 1999.

Swinburne, Stephen. *What's Opposite?* Honesdale, PA: Boyds Mills, 2000.

Thomas, Jan. *Rhyming Dust Bunnies.* New York: Beach Lane Books, 2009.

Tobin, Jim. *Sue MacDonald Had a Book.* New York: Henry Holt, 2009.

Weinstein, Ellen Slusky. *Everywhere the Cow Says "Moo!"* Honesdale, PA: Boyds Mills, 2008.

Williams, Laura. *ABC Kids.* New York: Philomel, 2000.

**myeducationlab** )
PEARSON

Now go to Topic 4: "Oral Language," Topic 1: "Reading Instruction," Topic 5: "Phonemic Awareness and Phonics", and Topic 11: "Reading Difficulties and Intervention Strategies" in MyEducationLab (www.myeducationlab.com) for your course, where you can:

- Find learning outcomes for "Oral Language," "Reading Instruction," "Phonemic Awareness and Phonics," and "Reading Difficulties and Intervention Strategies" along with national standards that connect to these outcomes.
- Complete Assignments and Activities that can help you more deeply understand the chapter content.
- Examine challenging situations and cases presented in the IRIS Center Resources.
- Access video clips of CCSSO National Teacher of the Year award winners responding to the question, "Why Do I Teach?" in the Teacher Talk section.
- Apply and practice your understanding of the core teaching skills identified in the chapter with Building Teaching Skills and Dispositions learning units.

# Listening in on Students' Oral Reading

## CHAPTER OUTLINE

- Scenario: Using Oral Reading to Learn More about Vicki
- An Overview of the Informal Reading Inventory
- Administering and Scoring the IRI
- IRI Selection Criteria
- An Overview of Miscue Analysis
- An Overview of the Running Record
- Administering a Running Record
- Scoring a Running Record
- Interpreting a Running Record
- Revisiting the Opening Scenario

## SCENARIO: USING ORAL READING TO LEARN MORE ABOUT VICKI

Vicki is a new student in Ms. Mills's fifth-grade class. She and her family just moved into the school district. Ms. Mills is trying very hard to make Vicki feel at home because she knows how difficult it is for a young person to leave all her friends and come to a new school where she does not know anyone. Ms. Mills makes a point of speaking to Vicki informally during recess and at other times so that she can get to know her. During some of their conversations, Ms. Mills tries to find out what Vicki's interests are and what kinds of books she likes to read.

Vicki's records from her other school haven't arrived yet, so Ms. Mills has to do some informal testing to determine at what level Vicki is reading. Ms. Mills prefers to do her own informal testing before looking at a child's past records. She feels that records can bias a teacher.

Ms. Mills chooses a passage from the middle of the basal reader, which is equivalent to a fifth-grade level. She tells Vicki that she wants her to read the passage aloud and that she should concentrate because she will be asked some questions about what she has read. She tells Vicki something about the story before Vicki begins to read. As Ms. Hill listens, she notices Vicki reads word by word. She sounds out every word she comes to. It's as if she does not recognize any word or as if she does not trust herself to say it correctly unless she first sounds it out. When Ms. Mills asks Vicki questions about the passage, Vicki is able to answer most of the literal questions, but she has difficulty answering any at the interpretive level. Ms. Mills decides to choose another passage from the same basal reader and read it aloud to Vicki. She wants to see if Vicki would do better in comprehension if she did not have to concentrate so hard on decoding. Ms. Mills tells Vicki to listen carefully. After Ms. Mills finishes reading the passage, she asks Vicki some questions. Again, Vicki is able to answer most of the literal questions but not the ones requiring a higher level of thinking.

Ms. Mills asks Vicki to tell her about her reading experiences. She asks Vicki how she learned to read. Vicki tells Ms. Mills that she had learned to sound out every word and that all they did at her other school was work with words. She says very proudly that she could figure out lots of words by herself. Ms. Mills replies that she can see this and it is very good, but she tells Vicki that she wants her to try to go beyond the words and concentrate more on the message that the words have.

Ms. Mills thinks that Vicki is a capable child who should be doing much better than she is. She believes that Vicki needs to focus on higher-level thinking skills, so she will plan a program for her that will help her to develop such skills. Ms. Mills also feels that Vicki needs practice in reading for meaning rather than for pronunciation and that she needs to gain confidence in herself.

Fortunately for Vicki, Ms. Mills knows how to use oral reading to gain a better understanding of how children read. She also knows how to use the results of the reading to identify strengths and needs as well as to plan appropriate instruction.

## CHAPTER OBJECTIVES

After reading this chapter, you should be able to:

- Describe the components of an informal reading inventory (IRI) and state the purpose of each.
- Describe how oral reading errors are coded and scored.
- Explain modified miscue analysis and discuss reasons for using it.
- Discuss the similarities of and differences between the running record and IRI.
- Discuss some advantages of using a running record instead of an IRI, and vice versa.

Learning how to use oral reading to assess children's reading is the focus of this chapter. Oral reading can help teachers gain insight into both what students do well and

**TABLE 8.1   What, Why, and How of Oral Reading Assessment**

| *What Do I Want to Know?* | *Why Do I Want to Know?* | *How Can I Best Discover It?* |
|---|---|---|
| What are the children's functional reading levels? | All readers have three reading levels: independent, instructional, and frustration. I want to help children read books of varying difficulty to become strong readers. A majority of what they read should be at their independent and instructional reading levels. | Informal Reading Inventory (pp. 156–164) Running Record (pp. 172–176) |
| What strategies do children use when reading? | Using a variety of reading strategies rather than relying on one or two is a hallmark of a good reader. I need to discover which strategies students are using to determine other strategies that I should explicitly teach. | Modified Miscue Analysis (pp. 167–170) Running Record (pp. 172–176) IRI (pp. 156–164) |
| How well do children comprehend? | Comprehension is the essence of reading. I need to make sure that children are comprehending at all levels and explicitly teach those children who are having difficulty. | IRI (pp. 156–164) Retelling (p. 175) |
| Are students able to identify words when reading connected text? | Word identification is one part of successful reading. I need to determine if students have a large store of words to draw on when reading. | IRI (pp. 156–164) Modified Miscue Analysis (pp. 167–170) Running Record (pp. 172–176) |

what needs more attention. As with the assessment procedures mentioned in previous chapters, teachers need to ask and answer three important questions to guide their selection of the most appropriate oral reading measure: What do I want to know? Why do I want to know? How can I best discover it? In Table 8.1, we ask and answer these questions. The table also serves as an overview of the three assessment techniques we will explain in this chapter: the informal reading inventory, the modified miscue analysis, and the running record.

# AN OVERVIEW OF THE INFORMAL READING INVENTORY

## WHAT IS AN INFORMAL READING INVENTORY?

> **Informal Reading Inventory (IRI)**
> A valuable aid in helping teachers determine a student's reading levels and his or her strengths and needs. It usually consists of oral and silent reading passages and comprehension questions.

The *Informal Reading Inventory (IRI)* originated from the work of Emmett A. Betts and his doctoral student Patsy A. Killgallon, and is used to determine three reading levels and a listening capacity level. An IRI is individually administered and usually consists of oral and silent reading passages selected from basal readers from the preprimer to the eighth-grade levels (some exist up to the twelfth grade). Factual, inferential, and word meaning questions accompany each passage.

Teachers use graded word lists to determine at what grade level the student should begin reading the oral passages. The student begins by reading the word list at two levels below his or her present grade level. The highest grade level at which the student has few errors on the graded word list is the grade level at which he or she begins reading the oral passage. The student reads the oral passage aloud, and the teacher records omissions, substitutions, insertions, pronunciation errors, repetitions, and hesitations (see Table 8.2).

**TABLE 8.2    Code for Marking and Scoring Errors**

| Type of Error | Rule for Marking | Examples | Error Count |
|---|---|---|---|
| Omissions—leaves out a word, part of a word, or consecutive words | Put circle around omitted word or part of word. | She went in(to) the store.<br>The (big) black dog is here. | 1<br>1 |
| Substitutions—substitutes a whole word | Put line through substituted word, and insert word above. | home<br>She went into the ~~house~~.<br>along.<br>She went ~~alone~~. | 1<br><br>1 |
| Insertions—adds a word, part of a word, or consecutive words | Put caret to show where word or word part was inserted, and write in inserted part of word or word(s). | big<br>The ˄ dog is black.<br>very big<br>The ˄ dog is black. | 1<br><br>1 |
| Mispronunciations—mispronounces a word to produce a nonsense word (unlike substitution where an actual word is substituted) | Put line through word that was mispronounced, and insert phonetically the word, if possible. | herz<br>A ~~horse~~ went into the barn.<br>ka rōt′<br>It weighed a ~~carot~~. | 1<br><br>1 |
| Words pronounced by examiner after four-second pause by child | Put *P* over word or words pronounced by tester. | P<br>The anecdote was funny. | 1 |
| Hesitations—a pause of less than five seconds | Put an *H* above the word on which the hesitation occurs. | H<br>She reiterated that she wouldn't go. | 0 |
| Repetitions—a word, part of a word, or a group of words repeated | Draw a wavy line under the part of word or word(s) repeated. | She mumbled her acceptance. We were reluctant to go. His probation would be up soon. | 0<br><br>0<br>0 |
| Reversals—word order is changed | Enclose words in a horizontal *S*. | The (big black) cat drinks milk. | 1 |
| Self-corrections—error is spontaneously corrected | Enclose incorrect word in parentheses. | (brought)<br>He bought something. | 0 |

When the student reads the oral passage at the independent or instructional level, the teacher asks comprehension questions; the student then reads the silent passage at the same grade level and the teacher asks questions about the silent passage. The student continues to read increasingly difficult passages until he or she reaches a frustration level. If the student makes so many word recognition errors in oral reading that he or she is close to a frustration level, the teacher stops the student and reads passages aloud and then continues asking comprehension questions. This continues until the student's listening comprehension reaches frustration level. This is called a listening capacity test.[1]

---

[1] A listening capacity test may also be referred to as a listening comprehension test.

Go to the Assignments and Activities section of Topic 2: Reading Assessment in the MyEducationLab for your course and complete the activity entitled "Informal Reading Inventory." As you watch the video and answer the accompanying questions, notice how the teacher uses a retelling checklist as the student mentions story events.

## WHAT ARE THE PURPOSES OF AN INFORMAL READING INVENTORY?

An informal reading inventory is probably one of the most valuable diagnostic aids because of the amount of information it can convey. An essential function of an IRI is to help the teacher determine the child's functional reading levels: independent, instructional, frustrational. Teachers also use it to get an estimate of a student's listening capacity. All are needed to make a proper match between the child and appropriate texts.

Another important reason for administering and interpreting an IRI is to learn about a student's reading strengths and needs so that the teacher can design appropriate instruction for the student. For example, if while giving a child an IRI the teacher observes that the child has difficulty answering inference comprehension questions, the teacher can develop lessons for the child to help build skill in this area. From listening to the student reading orally, the teacher can discover whether the student has word recognition problems that may be interfering with comprehension when the child is reading silently. (See Chapter 10.)

Yet another function of the IRI is to give the student feedback on his or her reading behavior. As the student reads passages at graduated levels of difficulty, he or she becomes aware of the reading level that is appropriate. It helps the student recognize his or her word recognition and comprehension strengths and needs. The IRI is an excellent instrument for estimating students' reading levels and for helping teachers to diagnose their strengths and needs, but the IRI is only as good as the person administering it and interpreting its results. That is, the IRI does not diagnose; the teacher does!

## DETERMINING READING AND LISTENING CAPACITY LEVELS

The criteria for reading levels on the IRI were determined by Betts, and many informal reading inventories still use the same levels or modifications of them. The reason for this is that even though there is disagreement on what the quantitative reading levels should be, the research on determining reading levels is not conclusive.[2] Also, it is imperative to restate, "the valid and reliable use of IRIs must rely upon the accurate professional judgments of the person conducting the evaluation. The accurate use of IRIs requires judgment and interpretation, not the mechanical calculation or application of scores."[3]

In designating these levels Betts gave not only percentage determinants but also other criteria that teachers should look for at each level.[4] The levels (as determined by Betts) and his percentages that designate the levels follow:

### Betts Reading Levels

| | | |
|---|---|---|
| Independent Level* | Children read on their own without any difficulty. | Word Recognition—99% or above<br>Comprehension—90% or above |
| Instructional Level | Teaching level. | Word Recognition—95% or above<br>Comprehension—75% or above |
| Frustration Level | This level is to be avoided. It is the lowest level of readability. | Word Recognition—90% or less<br>Comprehension—50% or less |
| Listening Capacity Level* | Highest level at which a pupil can comprehend when someone reads to him or her. | Comprehension—75% or above |

*Betts also called the *independent level* the *basal level,* and the *listening capacity level* the *capacity level.*

[2]Majorie Seddon Johnson, Roy A. Kress, and John Pikulski, *Informal Reading Inventories,* 2nd ed. (Newark, DE: International Reading Association, 1987), p. 13.

[3]Ibid.

[4]Adapted from Emmett A. Betts, *Foundation of Reading Instruction* (New York: American Book Company, 1946), pp. 445–454.

### Independent Level

**Independent reading level**
Level at which child reads words without any assistance and comprehends the text.

The *independent reading level* "is the highest level at which an individual can read and satisfy all the criteria for desirable reading behavior in silent- and oral-reading situations."[5] At the independent level the child can read words without any assistance and comprehend the text. When the student is reading orally or silently at this level, a minimum comprehension score on literal and interpretive questions of at least 90 percent should be achieved. Look for signs that the experience is enjoyable and rewarding.

The independent level is an important one for the child, teacher, parents, and librarian. Functional reading levels are centered in the child's independence, need for help, or frustration. Teachers and librarians should help students find any texts and portions of texts they can read independently.

### Instructional Level

**Instructional reading level**
The teaching level.

The *instructional reading level* is the one at which explicit teaching is done. This level must not be so challenging that it frustrates the student nor so easy that the student needs no assistance. This level is sometimes referred to as the "zone of proximal development" or ZPD.[6] At this level there should be a minimum comprehension score of at least 75 percent for both oral and silent reading on literal and interpretive questions, and in the oral reading there should be accurate pronunciation of at least 95 percent of the running words. Watch for signs of tension such as fidgeting, distraction, and facial expressions.

Children can have an instructional level that spans more than one grade level. When this happens, the instructional level is reported as a range; see "Reporting Students' Reading Levels." A student may read passages beyond an identified grade level for a number of reasons, including interest, background information, and content. You will address a variety of student interests and backgrounds when you use an IRI that has passages from different content areas and types of writing.

### Frustration Level

**Frustration reading level**
The child reads with many word recognition and comprehension errors. It is the lowest reading level and one to be avoided.

The *frustration reading level* is when the balance of effort outweighs the value of the return. At this functional level, the child reads with many comprehension and word errors; this may appear observably frustrating to the child. It is helpful for teachers to know what this level is so that they can determine a child's reading range. A teacher would have to spend so much time in instruction and scaffolding for this type of passage that the return would not warrant the amount of time and energy spent by both teacher and reader. A teacher can tell that a child has reached his or her frustration level when the child attains a comprehension score of 50 percent or less on literal and interpretive questions for oral and silent reading and is unable to pronounce 10 percent of the words in the oral reading passage. Watch for signs of tension such as fidgeting, distraction, and facial expressions.

During silent reading, the child reads at a slow rate, uses lip movements, and makes audible vocal utterances. During oral reading, the child may lose fluency.

### Listening Capacity Level

**Listening capacity level**
The highest level at which a learner can understand material when it is read aloud to him or her.

The *listening capacity level*, as first determined by Betts, is the "highest level of readability of material which the learner can comprehend when the material is read to him."[7] Betts also established the minimum comprehension score of at least 75 percent, based on both factual and inferential questions for listening capacity. He noted that the term "*level* refers to the grade level at which the material was prepared for use; for example, preprimer, primer, first reader, second reader, and so on."[8] The listening capacity level is often called a *listening comprehension level*.

[5]Ibid., p. 445.

[6]Lev S. Vygotsky, *Mind in Society* (Cambridge, MA: Harvard University Press, 1978).

[7]Betts (1946), p. 452.

[8]Ibid., p. 439.

### The Buffer Zone of the IRI

**Buffer zone**
The area that falls between the instructional and frustration levels.

The *buffer zone* of the IRI is the area that falls between the instructional and frustration levels. For word recognition it is 94 percent to 91 percent, and for comprehension it is 74 percent to 51 percent (Betts's criteria). When a child's score falls in the buffer zone, the teacher must decide whether to continue testing. If the child appears interested in continuing, testing should continue. If, on the other hand, the child exhibits symptoms of frustration, testing should be stopped. Even though the decision of whether to continue testing is subjective, there are some factors that the teacher can take into consideration; for example, the types of errors the child has made, the child's personality, the child's prior reading record, the child's health, and whether the child speaks another language at home.

A student who stays in the buffer zone for more than one reading level and does not exhibit signs of frustration will probably be able to gain the skills that he or she lacks more readily and quickly than a student who goes from the instructional level directly to the frustration level. Staying in the buffer zone shows that the student has enough skills to be able to continue.

Teacher judgment plays an important role in determining whether to continue testing. For example, it is possible to stop testing, even though the child has not reached a frustrating passage, when the child appears nervous or upset. Also, even though minimum criteria are usually given for estimating the various reading levels of IRIs, these are actually general standards. Remember, the teacher is the final judge, not the mechanical calculation or application of scores.

## REPORTING STUDENTS' READING LEVELS

The independent level is reported as one level only: the highest level at which the child can read and satisfy the criteria for the independent level. If a child reads independently from passages at level 1 (1st grade), $2^1$ (first semester of second grade), $2^2$ (second semester of second grade), and $3^1$ (first semester of third grade), the child's independent level will reported as the highest level, in this case reader level $3^1$.

The frustration level is also reported as one level only. The first passage at which the child reaches frustration is reported as the frustration reading level. The teacher does not continue to have the child read passages after reaching the frustration reading level.

The instructional reading level is often reported as more than one level. A child's instructional reading level can span several grade levels, and is reported as a range instead of a single number. For example, if a child reads at the instructional level at passage levels 4, 5, and 6 before going into the buffer zone or reaching the frustration level, the child's instructional reading level is reported as a 4–6 range.

To determine a child's independent and instructional reading levels, the criteria for both word recognition and comprehension must be met. For the independent level, the student should meet the criteria of 99 percent accuracy in word recognition and 90 percent in comprehension. For the instructional level, the student should meet the criteria of 95–98 percent for word recognition and 75–89 percent in comprehension. For the frustration level, however, only one of the criteria has to be met, that is, 50 percent or less in comprehension or 90 percent or less in word recognition.

The silent reading comprehension score on an informal reading inventory is more indicative of what a student does in a directed reading lesson than the oral reading comprehension score; therefore, teachers may use the silent reading comprehension score combined with the oral reading word recognition score to engage children with appropriate independent and instructional texts.

Also, teachers should be aware that on informal reading inventories, students must rely heavily on their short-term memories, so those who have difficulties in this area will probably not do well when answering comprehension questions. Clearly, the teacher must use judgment in making these determinations.

## CODE FOR MARKING ORAL READING ERRORS

Becoming proficient in marking oral reading errors is beneficial so that you can focus on what the child is doing when reading. The code is a shorthand method you can use to record information quickly; it is an aid. Table 8.2 on page 150 presents a common marking code that you can use when administering an IRI.

## SCORING ORAL READING ERRORS

The scoring scale is based on the philosophy that good readers make miscues when they read. Miscues are intended to point you toward what a reader is doing well, rather than focusing on what students cannot do. In the scoring scale of errors, multiple errors on the same word will only count as one error; mispronunciations due to dialect differences will not count as an error; mispronunciations of difficult proper nouns will not count as errors; hesitations of less than five seconds and repetitions will not count as errors; and an immediate self-correction will not count as an error. All other errors that are made will count one point. If a child meets the same word a few times in a selection and makes a substitution, omission, or mispronunciation error on it each time, it would count as *one error* the first time and as *one-half error* each subsequent time. After the third time, the teacher should pronounce the word for the child.

The teacher should keep a record of errors made so that he or she can determine what kinds of strategies the student is using to figure out words, whether a pattern exists among the errors made, and whether the student relies on graphic, semantic, or syntactic clues. We cannot overstate the importance of using the score to figure out what the child *can* do well, instead of dwelling on what the child *cannot* do. The Summary Sheet in Figure 8.1 has a checklist of possible errors, which should be helpful in recording a student's specific errors.

### Sample Markings of Oral IRI Passages

*Sample 1*

                   *H* polet
"What is making the lake ~~polluted~~?" asked Jill.

                 *s*
"It could be a lot ∧ things," said Mr. Brown.

"Let's go down to the lake and look at it."

                            big
Mr. Brown and the children went to the ∧ lake.

They looked into the water. It wasn't clean. They

         about               was
walked ~~around~~ the lake. Then they ~~saw~~ why it wasn't clean.

*Total Error Count = 7 (Polluted counts for one error only.)*

*Sample 2*

      Fritz and Anna lived on a farm. It was a small farm. It was also very dry, and things did not grow well. So Fritz and his wife, Anna, were poor.

      One day there was a tap, tap, tap on the door. A woman had come to the farm. She had been walking most of the day, and she was hungry. She asked Fritz and Anna to give her something to eat. Fritz and Anna had a pot of soup. They let the woman come in to eat.

*Total Error Count = 3 (The repetitions on hungry and something do not count as errors.)*

FIGURE 8.1   **Diagnostic Checklist for Oral and Silent Reading**

| *Oral Reading* | *Yes* | *No* | *Specific Errors* |
|---|---|---|---|

1. Word recognition errors
   The teacher listens to the child while he or she
   is reading orally and records whether the child
   makes any of the following errors.

| | Yes | No | Specific Errors |
|---|---|---|---|
| a. omissions | | | |
| b. insertions | | | |
| c. substitutions | | | |
| d. repetitions | | | |
| e. hesitations | | | |
| f. mispronunciations | | | |
| g. reversals | | | |

2. Manner of reading
   The teacher observes the child while he or she
   is reading aloud and records whether the child
   exhibits any of the following behaviors:

| | Yes | No | Specific Errors |
|---|---|---|---|
| a. word-by-word phrasing | | | |
| b. finger pointing | | | |
| c. head movement | | | |
| d. fidgeting | | | |
| e. voice characteristics | | | |
| high-pitched | | | |
| loud | | | |
| soft | | | |
| monotonous | | | |
| f. other | | | |

3. Comprehension
   (*See* Comprehension Diagnostic Checklist
   in Chapter 10.)

| *Silent Reading* | *Yes* | *No* |
|---|---|---|

1. Comprehension
   (*See* Comprehension Diagnostic Checklist
   in Chapter 10.)

2. Manner of reading
   The teacher observes the child while he or she
   is reading silently and records whether the child
   exhibits any of the following behaviors.

| | Yes | No |
|---|---|---|
| a. lip movement | | |
| b. reads aloud | | |
| c. head movement | | |
| d. continually looks up | | |
| e. finger pointing | | |
| f. other | | |

*Word Recognition Formula for Percent Correct*

Here is a formula to help you to figure out the percent correct for word recognition:

$$\frac{\text{Number of words in passage} - \text{number of errors}}{\text{number of words in passage}} \times 100\% = \text{percent correct}$$

**Example: 150 words in passage**

**7 errors**

$$\frac{150 - 7}{150} \times 100\% = 95\%$$

(This is at the instructional level using Betts's criteria.)

## USING A DIAGNOSTIC CHECKLIST FOR ORAL AND SILENT READING

Complete coding is necessary to determine a student's word recognition strengths and needs. If, however, you are only interested in quickly determining a student's reading level, you can simply check (✓) errors, because all you need is an error count. Diagnostic checklists are useful in recording errors, especially if you are only interested in an error count.

A checklist you can use is shown in Figure 8.1. Note that this checklist is helpful in recording students' manner of reading, as well as their strengths and needs in comprehension and word recognition.

# ADMINISTERING AND SCORING THE IRI

## STEP 1: ESTABLISHING RAPPORT

Establishing rapport with the child who is to be tested is an important first step. Since you are the child's teacher, you should know this child quite well and should be able to allay any fears or apprehensions that the child may have about taking the test. Make sure the child understands that the IRI is not a test that will give him or her a grade; it is a test to help both of you learn more about the child's reading. The IRI will provide information so that you can work together to overcome any reading problems.

## STEP 2: THE WORD RECOGNITION INVENTORY

The Word Recognition Inventory (WRI) is used to determine at what level to begin the oral reading passages of the IRI. It evaluates a student's ability to recognize (state) words in isolation and is administered to one student at a time.

*Preparation*

1. The WRI begins two grade levels below the student's grade level.
2. Duplicate the word lists for at least three grade levels above and below the grade level at which you will begin.

3. Decide how you will show the words to the student and prepare the necessary materials. Here are two possible methods. Both require index cards.

   a. Cut out a rectangle no more than ⅜ inch by 1½ inches in the center of an index card. Expose the words being tested, one at a time, through the rectangular opening.

   b. Use one index card to cover any printed matter that appears above the word the student is being asked to state. Use a second index card to cover all matter below the card. Continue this procedure for each word on the list.

*Administration*

1. Because you will be working with students on an individual basis, use a relatively isolated part of the classroom when administering the WRI.

2. Keep the word lists covered as you explain the method of presentation to the student.

3. Begin the WRI by showing the first word. The student should respond immediately.

   a. If the student's response is correct, place a check (✓) beside the word and proceed to the next word.

   b. If an initial response is incorrect but the student makes an immediate, independent correction, place a check with a plus sign (✓+) beside the word and proceed to the next word.

4. When the student's response is incorrect and is not independently corrected, reexpose the word. Allow a reasonable length of time for the student to study the word and to apply, without assistance, any word analysis skills he or she may have.

   a. If this response is correct, place a check with a minus sign (✓−) beside the word and proceed to the next word.

   b. If the student is unable to decode the word, record a zero (0) and proceed to the next word. For later reference, you may want to record what the child says, for example, *run* for *ran*.

5. After the student has responded to all words for a particular level, record the total number of correct responses. This total is the student's WRI score for that level.

6. Continue administering the WRI until the student misses four or more words at any level. Start the oral reading at the highest level at which the child has made 0 errors.

*Examples*[9]

1. Student: John X, fifth grade (the beginning)
   Begin WRI at third-grade reader level (beginning)

### Results

| Reader Level* | No. of Errors |
| --- | --- |
| $3^1$ | 4 |
| $2^2$ | 2 |
| $2^1$ | 1 |
| First | 0 |

*Refers to the grade level at which the material was prepared for use. Also, note that authors of reading programs have different ways of keying book levels to reader grade levels. In one series *Level 7* is equivalent to an IRI level $2^2$, whereas in another program their *Level 6* is equivalent to IRI $2^2$.

*Interpretation of results:* Begin oral reading passages at first reader level.

[9]Examples are based on the WRI presented in Appendix B.

2. Student: Nancy E, fifth grade (middle)
   Begin WRI at third-grade reader level (middle)

**Results**

| Reader Level | No. of Errors |
|---|---|
| $3^2$ | 0 |
| 4 | 0 |
| 5 | 1 |
| 6 | 4 |

*Interpretation of results:* Begin oral reading passages at fourth-grade reader level.

3. Student: Alma J, fourth grade (beginning)
   Begin WRI at second-grade reader level (beginning)

**Results**

| Reader Level | No. of Errors |
|---|---|
| $2^1$ | 0 |
| $2^2$ | 0 |
| $3^1$ | 1 |
| $3^2$ | 0 |
| 4 | 2 |
| 5 | 5 |

*Interpretation of results:* Begin oral reading passages at third-grade reader level (middle).

## STEP 3: ORAL AND SILENT READING PASSAGES

The student begins to read the oral passage at the highest reader level matched to the Word Recognition Inventory score (see examples given in Step 2). The teacher introduces the passage and asks the child to read it aloud and then answer questions about it. The child is asked to read the passage aloud without first looking at it, a "cold read."

While the child is reading aloud, the teacher records oral reading errors (refer back to Table 8.2). If the child's word recognition in oral reading is at the independent or instructional levels, the child is asked the comprehension questions. If the child's response is correct, the teacher puts a check (✓) next to the question. If the answer is not correct, the teacher records the student's response. The child is then asked to read the silent passage. Again, the student is not given an opportunity to look over the passage before reading it. After finishing the silent reading passage, the child is asked the comprehension questions. If the response is correct, a check (✓) is put next to the question. If the answer is incorrect, the student's response is recorded next to the question.

The student then goes to the oral passage at the next reader level. The same procedure continues until the child reaches his or her frustration level.

If the student makes many word recognition errors while reading aloud, and the teacher feels the errors will interfere with the child's ability to answer the comprehension questions, the teacher usually does not have the child read the silent reading passage at the same reader level. Instead, the teacher administers a listening capacity test; that is, the teacher reads aloud to the child and then asks the comprehension questions.

## STEP 4: THE LISTENING CAPACITY TEST

**Listening capacity test**
Given to determine a child's comprehension through listening. Teacher reads aloud to child and then asks questions about the selection.

A *listening capacity test* is given to determine a child's comprehension through listening. Also, a listening capacity test can help to identify those students who seem to comprehend information better through listening than through reading. This knowledge is important in planning proper modes of instruction for each child.

The teacher reads passages from the IRI to determine a child's listening capacity. The passages are evaluated in the same way as the oral and silent reading passages except that the teacher is doing the reading. If the passages have already been read by the child, choose different ones. Some commercially produced IRIs have a separate set of selections for the listening capacity test for this reason.

## WHEN IS A LISTENING CAPACITY TEST GIVEN?

A listening capacity test is usually given when a child is reaching frustration level in word recognition on the oral reading passages. If a child has difficulty with a large number of words at a certain passage level, the teacher usually does not use the silent reading passage at the same level (see Example 1). If a child does not have any extensive word recognition problems, the listening capacity test is usually given when the child is reaching frustration level in silent reading on the IRI.

*Example 1*[10]
Student: Jim, fifth grade (beginning). Begin Word Recognition Inventory at $3^1$ level.

| Reader Level | Number of Errors |
|:---:|:---:|
| $3^1$ | 2 |
| $2^2$ | 0 |
| $3^2$ | 4 |

Jim begins oral reading at the $2^2$ level because he has 0 errors at that level. The following chart shows his reading behavior.

| | Oral Reading | | | Silent Reading Comprehension | | Listening Capacity | |
|:---:|:---:|:---:|:---:|:---:|:---:|:---:|:---:|
| | Word Recognition | Comprehension | | | | | |
| Reader Level | No. Errors/ Total No. Words | % Errors | % Correct | % Errors | % Correct | % Errors | % Correct |
| $2^2$ | 4/131 | 0 | 100 | 0 | 100 | | |
| $3^1$ | 7/151 | 0 | 100 | 0 | 100 | | |
| $3^2$ | 10/171 | 20 | 80 | 25 | 75 | | |

### Listening Capacity

| Reader Level | % Errors | % Correct |
|:---:|:---:|:---:|
| 4 | 0 | 100 |
| 5 | 0 | 100 |
| 6 | 0 | 100 |
| 7 | 20 | 80 |
| 8 | 40 | 60 |

[10]Examples are based on the IRI presented in Appendix B.

At the $3^2$ level the teacher must decide whether to let Jim read silently or to give him a listening capacity test. His word recognition errors may be interfering with his ability to answer the comprehension questions. The teacher decides to let him read silently, even though he is in the "buffer" zone in word recognition, because she wants to see how well he uses context clues. Even though Jim has a word recognition problem, he seems to do quite well in comprehension. He scores 25 percent errors. The teacher has Jim read at the next level, which is the fourth-grade reader level, because he does not appear to be frustrated. At the next level, however, Jim makes 19 errors in oral reading, and he has difficulty answering the comprehension questions. The teacher decides to give him a listening capacity test. She starts to read aloud the silent reading passage at the fourth-grade reader level. Then she continues to read aloud one passage from each level. The chart above shows Jim's listening capacity scores. (It doesn't make any difference whether the passage was chosen from the oral or silent reading selections.) From the listening capacity test, the teacher sees that Jim has excellent comprehension but his word recognition might be hindering him from working at his ability level. The teacher had decided to give Jim an IRI because his verbal behavior in class belied his reading achievement test scores.

The teacher continues administering the oral reading part of the IRI to determine Jim's independent oral reading level and to gain some more insight into the types of errors that he makes in word recognition so that she can develop a program to help him. (Jim reads the oral passage at the $2^1$ level. He makes one error out of 112 words. This is his independent oral reading level.) She will probably also give Jim another word analysis diagnostic test.

A summary sheet in Figure 8.2 shows a complete record of Jim's reading behavior on the IRI.

*Example 2*
Student: Susan, fifth grade (beginning). Begin WRI at $3^1$ level.

| Reader Level | No. of Errors |
| --- | --- |
| $3^1$ | 0 |
| $3^2$ | 0 |
| 4 | 0 |
| 5 | 0 |
| 6 | 4 |

Susan begins oral reading at the 5 level because that is her highest level of zero errors. She immediately reaches the frustration level in oral reading comprehension (see the chart on page 163). Because of this, the teacher would be justified in not having her read the silent reading passage and start going down to lower grade levels to find her instructional and independent levels for comprehension. However, the teacher decides to have Susan read the silent reading passage because she wants to see if Susan was concentrating so hard on pronunciation that she didn't pay

**FIGURE 8.2 Summary Sheet**[*]

Name _Jim_     Age _10_

Grade _5_     Teacher _Mrs. Smith_

| Reader Level | Word Recognition in Isolation (No. of Errors) | Oral Reading | | | Silent Reading | | Listening Capacity | |
|---|---|---|---|---|---|---|---|---|
| | | W.R. | Comp. | | Comp. | | | |
| | | No. of Errors/ Total No. Wds[†] | % Errors | % Correct | % Errors | % Correct | % Errors | % Correct |
| Preprimer | | | | | | | | |
| Primer | | | | | | | | |
| First | | | | | | | | |
| $2^1$ | | 1/112 | | | | | | |
| $2^2$ | 0 | 4/131 | 0 | 100 | 0 | 100 | | |
| $3^1$ | 2 | 7/151 | 0 | 100 | 0 | 100 | | |
| $3^2$ | 4 | 10/171 | 20 | 80 | 25 | 75 | | |
| 4 | | 19/187 | 40 | 60 | | | 0 | 100 |
| 5 | | | | | | | 0 | 100 |
| 6 | | | | | | | 0 | 100 |
| 7 | | | | | | | 20 | 80 |
| 8 | | | | | | | 40 | 60 |

[*] For use with the IRI in Appendix B.

[†] Percentages can be easily calculated using the word recognition formula on page 156, or see the IRI in Appendix B for corresponding reading levels, that is, independent, instructional, or frustration levels.

Level at which WRI was begun     $3^1$

Level at which oral reading was begun     $2^2$

Oral reading—word recognition

    Independent level     $2^1$

    Instructional level     $2^2$–$3^1$ (range)

    Frustration level     4

(continued)

**FIGURE 8.2**    *(continued)*

Oral reading—comprehension
    Independent level          $3^1$
    Instructional level         $3^2$
    Frustration level
Silent reading—comprehension
    Independent level          $3^1$
    Instructional level         $3^2$
    Frustration level
Listening capacity level       7

Word analysis
    Consonants—single
      initial
      medial
      final
    Consonants—double
      blends
      digraphs         *ch, sh, ph*
    Consonants—silent
    Vowels—single
      short            $\breve{a}, \breve{e}$
      long
    Vowels—double
      digraphs         *oa, ea*
      diphthongs       *ou in bough*
    Effect of final *e* on vowel
    Vowel controlled by *r*
    Structural analysis
      prefixes
      suffixes
      combining forms
      inflectional endings    *ignores most*
    Compound words
    Accent

Special Notes on Strengths and Needs

*Jim appears to use semantic and syntactic clues very well. He appears to need additional help with understanding how to use visual cues and with word identification.*

Comments on Behavior During the Testing

*Jim seemed to like working in a one-to-one relationship. He said that he didn't like to read, but he liked to listen to others read aloud.*

Recommendations

*Design a program that emphasizes using visual cues and word identification, all the while focusing on Jim's strengths of using syntactic and semantic clues.*

attention to what she was reading. Susan is asked to read the fifth-grade silent reading level passage. She makes 60 percent errors. The following chart shows Susan's reading behavior:

| Reader Level | Oral Reading | | | Silent Reading Comprehension | | Listening Capacity | |
| | Word Recognition | Comprehension | | | | | |
| | No. Errors/ Total No. Words | % Errors | % Correct | % Errors | % Correct | % Errors | % Correct |
|---|---|---|---|---|---|---|---|
| 5 | 2/208 | 60 | 40 | 60 | 40 | | |
| 4 | 2/187 | 60 | 40 | 60 | 40 | | |
| $3^2$ | 2/171 | 50 | 50 | 50 | 50 | | |
| $3^1$ | 2/151 | 40 | 60 | 50 | 50 | 50 | 50 |
| $2^2$ | 1/131 | 25 | 75 | 25 | 75 | 40 | 60 |
| $2^1$ | 1/112 | 10 | 90 | 10 | 90 | 25 | 75 |
| 6* | 9/252 | — | | — | | | |

*Susan was asked to read orally only at the sixth level to find her instructional oral reading word recognition level.

From the results, we can see that Susan has excellent word recognition, but she has severe difficulties in reading comprehension. A listening capacity test is given to determine the level at which she can listen to material and comprehend it at the instructional level. After looking at the results of Susan's reading performance, the teacher decides to start reading aloud to Susan at the $3^1$ level because this is the level at which she had reached frustration in silent reading. Since Susan is also at her frustration level on the listening capacity test at the $3^1$ level, the teacher moves to the $2^2$ level and reads the passage aloud. At this level, Susan is still approaching frustration. The teacher then reads the $2^1$ level passage and finds Susan's listening capacity level. (The selections read aloud to Susan to determine her listening capacity level were different from those in the IRI because Susan had already read those.) It is interesting to note that Susan's listening capacity score is lower than her oral and silent reading scores. She probably has more difficulty concentrating while listening than when reading silently or orally. Her oral and silent reading scores appear to be comparable. The teacher must analyze the kinds of comprehension errors that Susan made. It seems obvious that Susan's ability to read well orally has obscured her comprehension problems. Susan's teacher had decided to give her an IRI because she had noticed the discrepancy between Susan's verbalizing in class and her inability to answer even literal questions correctly. Susan can pronounce words very well, but she doesn't know the meanings for many of them. Even when she knows the meaning of the words used in a paragraph, she can't tell you what the paragraph is about. The IRI will give Susan's teacher some insights into Susan's comprehension. The listening capacity test that was administered to Susan indicates that her reading potential may be at a $2^1$ grade level. Susan's teacher will have to develop a program for Susan based on her strengths and needs.

Figure 8.3 on pages 165–167 is a summary sheet, showing a complete record of Susan's reading behavior on the IRI.

## IRI SELECTION CRITERIA

Researchers have identified the following criteria for selecting an appropriate IRI instrument.[11]

1. There should be two forms (sets of passages), so the inventory can be used more than once per child.
2. There should be different passages for oral and silent reading.
3. The comprehension questions should consist of a variety of literal and interpretive questions. Critical reading questions are also desirable.
4. All questions should be text-driven; that is, all questions including inferential and word meaning questions should be text-dependent.
5. The passage should be cohesive; it should be one for which it is possible to state the main or central idea.
6. The graded word lists should be representative of the grade levels from which they have been taken.
7. The passages selected for oral and silent reading should be representative of the reading material in the book; that is, the readability level should not be higher or lower than the level from which the passages have been selected.
8. Specific directions should be given for administering and scoring the inventory.
9. There should be a separate set of passages and comprehension questions for the listening capacity inventory.

[11]R. F. Flippo, D. Holland, M. McCarthy, and E. A. Swinning, "Asking the Right Questions: How to Select an Informal Reading Inventory," *Reading Teacher* 63, no. 1 (2009): 79–83.

**FIGURE 8.3** **Summary Sheet**[*]

Name _Susan_                                   Age _10_

Grade _5_                                       Teacher _Mr. Jones_

| Reader Level | Word Recognition in Isolation (No. of Errors) | Oral Reading | | | Silent Reading | | Listening Capacity | |
|---|---|---|---|---|---|---|---|---|
| | | W.R. | Comp. | | Comp. | | | |
| | | No. of Errors/ Total No. Wds[†] | % Errors | % Correct | % Errors | % Correct | % Errors | % Correct |
| Preprimer | | | | | | | | |
| Primer | | | | | | | | |
| First | | | | | | | | |
| 2$^1$ | | 1/112 | 10 | 90 | 10 | 90 | 25 | 75 |
| 2$^2$ | | 1/131 | 25 | 75 | 25 | 75 | 40 | 60 |
| 3$^1$ | 0 | 2/151 | 40 | 60 | 50 | 50 | 50 | 50 |
| 3$^2$ | 0 | 2/171 | 50 | 50 | 50 | 50 | | |
| 4 | 0 | 2/187 | 60 | 40 | 60 | 40 | | |
| 5 | 0 | 2/208 | 60 | 40 | 60 | 40 | | |
| 6 | 4 | 9/252 | | | | | | |
| 7 | | | | | | | | |
| 8 | | | | | | | | |

[*] For use with the IRI in Appendix B.

[†] Percentages can be easily calculated using the word recognition formula on page 156, or see the IRI in Appendix B for corresponding reading levels, that is, independent, instructional, or frustration levels.

| | |
|---|---|
| Level at which WRI was begun | 3$^1$ |
| Level at which oral reading was begun | 5 |
| Oral reading—word recognition | |
|     Independent level | 5 |
|     Instructional level | 6 |
|     Frustration level | |

*(continued)*

**FIGURE 8.3** *(continued)*

Oral reading—comprehension

| | |
|---|---|
| Independent level | $2^1$ |
| Instructional level | $2^2$ |
| Frustration level | $3^2$ |

Silent reading—comprehension

| | |
|---|---|
| Independent level | $2^1$ |
| Instructional level | $2^2$ |
| Frustration level | $3^1$ |
| Listening capacity level | $2^1$ |

Word analysis

Consonants—single

initial _____

medial _____

final _____

Consonants—double

blends _____

digraphs _____

Consonants—silent _____

Vowels—single

short _____

long _____

Vowels—double

digraphs _____

diphthongs _____

Effect of final *e* on vowel _____

Vowel controlled by *r* _____

Structural analysis

prefixes _____

suffixes _____

combining forms _____

inflectional endings _____

Compound words _____

Accent _____

**FIGURE 8.3**

Special Notes on Strengths and Needs

*Susan has excellent word identification skills. She was able to answer literal comprehension questions. She appears to need some additional help with understanding word meanings and higher-level comprehension, including main ideas and inference.*

Comments on Behavior During the Testing

*She enjoyed reading aloud. She started squirming in her chair whenever comprehension questions were asked. She also squirmed in her chair when I was reading aloud to her.*

Recommendations

*Help Susan expand her vocabulary. Work on literal and interpretive comprehension skills. Give her a cloze test to further check her use of syntactic and semantic clues to figure out word meanings.*

## AN OVERVIEW OF MISCUE ANALYSIS

### WHAT IS MISCUE ANALYSIS AND WHAT IS ITS PURPOSE?

**Miscue analysis**
A process that helps teachers learn how readers use language cues to construct meaning.

**Miscue**
Unexpected response to print.

Kenneth Goodman feels that *miscue analysis* goes beyond the "superficial behavior of readers" to learn how readers get meaning from language.[12] He objects to the use of the term *errors* because he feels that nothing the reader does in reading is accidental, and *error* implies randomness.[13] When teachers understand how *miscues*, which are unexpected responses to print, relate to expected responses, they will better understand how readers are using the reading process. That is, the analysis helps them catalog what readers already know that enables them to read as they currently do.

[12]Kenneth S. Goodman, "Miscues: Windows on the Reading Process," in *Miscue Analysis,* ed. Kenneth S. Goodman (Urbana, IL: National Council of Teachers of English, 1973), p. 5.

[13]The National Assessment of Educational Progress in its Reading Report Cards uses *deviation from text* in place of the term *error.*

## HOW CAN MISCUE ANALYSIS BE USED?

To analyze readers' miscues, Goodman developed an analytic taxonomy that considers the relationship between the expected response (ER) and the observed response (OR). Teachers who use this taxonomy can analyze the causes of a reader's miscues from a number of angles. However, the original taxonomy is extremely time-consuming for classroom teachers. It contains nineteen questions, and each miscue is analyzed in terms of these nineteen questions. This instrument is extremely thorough and complex. Recognizing this, Ken's wife Yetta Goodman designed a more streamlined version, the Reading Miscue Inventory (RMI), to be more classroom-teacher friendly. She condensed the nineteen questions, which involved from four to fifteen possible responses for each, to nine questions with three choices each.

Miscue analysis, with its emphasis on reading as a meaning-making process, has greatly influenced how we assess children's reading. It has heightened the consciousness of those using the IRI. Many teachers are now concerned not only with the number of errors but also with the positive information those errors reveal about their students. Most would agree that constructing meaning is more important than absolute accuracy of word pronunciation.[14]

Even less complex than the RMI is the modified miscue analysis procedure shown below, which is easily applied in the classroom and can be used with nearly any text.

## MODIFIED MISCUE ANALYSIS[15]

*Preparing for the Modified Miscue Analysis*

1. Choose an appropriate text. A passage of 150 words is acceptable for this assessment. The passage should be long enough to help you see if and how the reader uses reading strategies. You might want to use a passage from a book the child is reading.
2. Make a copy of the passage for the reader as well as for yourself. You can write on your copy while the reader reads from his or hers.
3. Make enough copies of the Modified Miscue Analysis Forms shown in Figure 8.4.

*Administering the Modified Miscue Analysis*

1. As with administering the IRI, you want to establish rapport with the child who will be reading.
2. Explain the procedure, saying something like, "I would like to listen to you read so that I can hear what you do when you read. I am going to take notes while you read."
3. Ask the child to begin reading from his or her copy.
4. Watch the reader. Do his or her body language or facial expressions note comfort or anxiety? Does the child hold the book too close or too far away?
5. As the child reads, make notes on your copy of the passage using the same notations as stated for coding the IRI (see Table 8.2 on page 150).
6. After the reading, ask the child to retell what he or she remembers from the reading. Note how well the child recalls the main events from the passage and rank it as outstanding, adequate, or inadequate.

*Scoring the Modified Miscue Analysis*

Remember that the premise behind miscue analysis is that there is a logical reason for what the reader is doing when reading. The purpose of the analysis is to get a glimpse of this logic and to see which specific language cues the child uses when reading. The procedures listed here can help in this analysis.

---

[14]S. Kucer, *Dimensions of Literacy,* 3rd ed. (New York: Taylor & Francis, 2009). P. Johnson, *Assessment in Reading* (Newark, Delaware: International Reading Association, 2008).

[15]M. Opitz and T. Rasinski, *Good-bye Round Robin,* Rev. ed. (Portsmouth, NH: Heinemann, 2008).

**FIGURE 8.4** **Modified Miscue Analysis Form**

Reader's Name: _____ Grade: _____

Title and pages: _____ Date: _____

Three important questions to ask for each miscue:
  M = meaning: Does the miscue make sense?
  S = structure: Does the sentence sound right?
  V = visual: Does the miscue resemble the printed word?

| *Student* | *Text* | *Cues Used* | | |
|---|---|---|---|---|
| | | M | S | V |
| | | M | S | V |
| | | M | S | V |
| | | M | S | V |
| | | M | S | V |
| | | M | S | V |
| | | M | S | V |
| | | M | S | V |
| | | M | S | V |
| | | M | S | V |
| | | M | S | V |
| | | M | S | V |
| | | M | S | V |
| | | M | S | V |
| | | M | S | V |
| | | M | S | V |
| | | M | S | V |
| | | M | S | V |

1. Using the Miscue Analysis Form in Figure 8.4, write every word the child miscued and the actual word as it appears in the text.
2. As you attempt to figure out which cues the child used to miscue, you will need to look at the passage on which you recorded the child's reading behaviors.
3. Ask yourself the three questions shown on the form *for every miscue*. If the answer is "yes," circle the appropriate letter(s): M, S, V.
4. Answer all questions and record any other observations on the Summary of Observations form shown in Figure 8.5.
5. Based on your analysis, make a decision about what you think the child knows and what he or she needs to learn and design instruction accordingly.

# AN OVERVIEW OF THE RUNNING RECORD

## WHAT IS A RUNNING RECORD?

**Running record**
Documentation of a child's reading.

Go to the Assignments and Activities section of Topic 2: Reading Assessment in the MyEducationLab for your course and complete the activity entitled "Definition and Demonstration of a Running Record." As you watch the video and answer the accompanying questions, pay close attention to the marking conventions the teacher uses. Think about how these markings can be helpful when interpreting the child's reading performance.

A running record is a documentation of a child's reading. Like the IRI, it is a systematic way of observing and chronicling a child's oral reading behavior. Introduced in the United States by Marie Clay, the running record was originally designed so that teachers could observe the reading behaviors children were using as they read a text in a naturally occurring context. With a blank piece of paper, a teacher could sit down next to a child and use a specific coding system to note what the child did when reading aloud to the teacher. The teacher could take these records "on the run" as he or she moved from student to student. The notes could then be further analyzed to assess what specific children were doing when reading.[16]

## WHAT ARE THE PURPOSES OF A RUNNING RECORD?

Clay lists and explains several reasons for running records. The one that most teachers are concerned with focuses on using the results of running records to inform instruction.[17] As such, teachers can interpret children's performances and use their interpretations in several ways: to evaluate text difficulty; to group children; to adjust instruction, which might entail having children progress through texts at different rates; to note the progress of individual children in a variety of reading-related behaviors such as use of different language cues; and to note specific difficulties that children may be having with reading.

## HOW ARE RUNNING RECORDS AND IRIs SIMILAR?

Running records and IRIs have several common aspects. Three of the most important are listed below.

First, they are based on similar beliefs about the value of having students read aloud as a way of showing what they are able to do as readers. Both require students to read orally so that the teacher can get a glimpse of how students are reading, the strategies they use in reading, and whether they self-correct any miscues. Both help the teacher to determine children's functional reading levels (i.e., independent, instructional, and frustrational) so that appropriate texts can be provided for both independent and instructional reading experiences.

Second, running records and IRIs use similar coding systems to mark the types of miscues that children make when reading. Consistency is important so that teachers can better interpret their markings when analyzing reading behaviors.

[16]M. Clay, *The Early Detection of Reading Difficulties* (Portsmouth, NH: Heinemann, 1995).
[17]Ibid.

---

**FIGURE 8.5   Modified Miscue Analysis: Summary of Observations**

1. What did the reader do when unknown words were encountered? (Check all that apply.)

_____ made an attempt in these ways:

     _____ used meaning cues     _____ used structure cues     _____ used letter/sound cues

     _____ made repeated tries     _____ used pictures     _____ skipped it and read on

     _____ used memory     _____ looked at another source

     _____ other: _____

_____ made no attempt     _____ asked for help     _____ waited for teacher help

2. Which cues did the reader use most often? _____

_____

3. How often did the reader attempt to self-correct when meaning was not maintained?

     (Circle one)     always     sometimes     seldom     never

     Comments: _____

4. How often did the reader make repetitions?

     (Circle one)     always     sometimes     seldom     never

     Comments: _____

5. Did the reader attend to punctuation?     _____ mostly     _____ somewhat     _____ little

     Comments: _____

***Comprehension***

Retelling was (Circle one):     outstanding     adequate     inadequate

Comments: _____

_____

Other observations: _____

_____

Third, both use connected text when assessing reading. That is, both are based on the philosophical premise that having children reading "real" text is reflective of what they actually do when reading. Therefore, connected text must be used to assess reading if we want to see what strategies children apply when they approach texts.

## HOW ARE RUNNING RECORDS AND IRIs DIFFERENT?

Although running records and IRIs have much in common, they also have some differences. The most notable difference is that, as originally conceived, running records had no comprehension measure because more attention was paid to word accuracy and the way the child actually read the text. Self-corrections were viewed as evidence of comprehension. However, most teachers and reading specialists who use running records also recognize the importance of a separate comprehension measure and they have children do some sort of retelling or answering of questions, which brings the running record more in line with the IRI comprehension measures.

Another major difference between the two is that a running record can be completed with any text, whereas an IRI uses a set of graded passages. However, most teachers use a leveled set of books when using running records and chart children's progress relative to these levels. The text that is used resembles natural language patterns and is therefore seen as more authentic than the passages in an IRI. Depending on how passages are selected for an IRI, this may or may not be the case.

Yet another difference has to do with access. Although most IRI authors provide passages that are aimed at assessing first-grade children's reading, they rarely accomplish this task. Most often, the passages are too difficult, especially at the beginning of the year. The running record resolves this issue because teachers can use commercially prepared, leveled texts that children are able to read. The *Developmental Reading Assessment* (DRA)[18] is often used by primary grade teachers because it offers leveled texts and accompanying materials that are easy to use.

A fourth major difference is that IRIs are most often used to get an estimate of a child's functional reading levels for placement purposes. This is not the case with running records. Running records are given to inform instruction, and many teachers frequently administer them to determine which texts children should be reading. Although there are some concerns about too much focus on the word accuracy score to select texts to the neglect of considering other factors such as the reader's background and the type of text to be read, the main point here is that running records are used much more frequently than IRIs.

## ADMINISTERING A RUNNING RECORD

Although running record administration and scoring procedures are similar to those used for IRIs, there are a few differences. You might want to take a look at the completed example on pages 177 and 179 before reading the following administration and scoring procedures.

1. Choose a text.
2. Make copies of both the Running Record form (Figure 8.6) and the Running Record Summary (Figure 8.7). You might want to use the Running Record form as is or you might want to write the words from the text you will be using on each line like the one shown in the example in Figure 8.9 on page 177.
3. Assess children individually and begin by saying something like this: "I would like to listen to you read this book. While you are reading, I am going to take some notes so that I can remember how well you read." Sit next to the child so that you can watch his or her behavior rather than the reverse!

---

[18]J. Beaver, *The Developmental Reading Assessment* (New York: Scott Foresman, 2001).

# FIGURE 8.6 Running Record

Name: _____ Date: _____

Title of Book: _____ Author: _____

| Page | Reading Performance | Miscues M S V | Self-Corrects M S V |
|------|---------------------|---------------|---------------------|
|  |  |  |  |
|  |  |  |  |
|  |  |  |  |
|  |  |  |  |
|  |  |  |  |
|  |  |  |  |
|  |  |  |  |
|  |  |  |  |
|  |  |  |  |
|  |  |  |  |
|  |  |  |  |
|  |  |  |  |
|  |  |  |  |
|  |  |  |  |
|  |  |  |  |
|  |  |  |  |
|  |  |  |  |
|  |  |  |  |
|  |  |  |  |
|  |  |  |  |
|  |  |  |  |
|  |  |  |  |
|  |  |  |  |
|  |  |  |  |
|  |  |  |  |
|  |  |  |  |
|  |  |  |  |
|  |  | **Totals** | |

M = Meaning Cue    S = Structure Cue    V = Visual Cue

Source: From *Reaching Readers* by M. Opitz and M. Ford, 2001. Portsmouth, NH: Heineman.

---

## FIGURE 8.7   Running Record Summary

---

Name: _____   Date: _____

Title of Book: _____   Author: _____

### Summary of Reading Performance

Total # of Words _____   Total # of Miscues _____   % of Accuracy _____

### Reading Level (Circle the one that matches the % of accuracy.)

95% – 100% = Independent   90% – 94% = Instructional   89% or lower = Frustration

Total # of Self-Corrections _____   Self-Correction rate 1: _____

Note: Self-correction rates of 1:3, 1:4, or 1:5 are good. Each ratio shows that the reader is attending to discrepancies when reading.

---

### Summary of Observation

1. What did the reader do when unknown words were encountered?

   _____ made an attempt

   The reader made an attempt in these ways:

   _____ asked for help                 _____ looked at pictures

   _____ used letter/sound knowledge    _____ used meaning

   _____ used structure (syntax)        _____ tried again

   _____ skipped it and continued reading   _____ looked at another source

2. How often did the reader attempt to self-correct when meaning was not maintained?

   (Circle one)   always   frequently   sometimes   seldom   never

3. When the reader did self-correct, which cues were used? (✔ all that apply.)

   _____ letter/sound knowledge (visual)   _____ meaning   _____ syntax (structure)

### Calculating Accuracy Rate

1. Subtract the total number of miscues from the total number of words in the text to determine the number of words that were correctly read.

2. Divide the number of words correctly read by the number of words in the passage to determine % of accuracy.

   Example:  58 total words – 12 miscues = 46 words read correctly
   46 words read correctly ÷ 58 total words = 79% accuracy

### Calculating Self-Correction Rate

Use this formula:  $\dfrac{\text{self-correction} + \text{miscues}}{\text{self-corrections}} = 1:$ _____

---

**FIGURE 8.8   Retelling**

Name: _____

**Directions:** Indicate with a check the extent to which the reader's retelling includes or provides evidence of the following information.

| Retelling | None | Low | Moderate | High |
|---|---|---|---|---|
| 1. Includes information directly stated in text. | | | | |
| 2. Includes information inferred directly or indirectly from text. | | | | |
| 3. Includes what is important to remember from text. | | | | |
| 4. Provides relevant content and concepts. | | | | |
| 5. Indicates attempt to connect background knowledge to text information. | | | | |
| 6. Indicated attempt to make summary statements or generalizations based on text that can be applied to the real world. | | | | |
| 7. Indicated highly individualistic and creative impressions of or reactions to the real world. | | | | |
| 8. Indicates effective involvement with the text. | | | | |
| 9. Demonstrates appropriate use of language (vocabulary, sentence structure, language conventions). | | | | |
| 10. Indicates ability to organize or compose the retelling. | | | | |
| 11. Demonstrates sense of audience or purpose. | | | | |
| 12. Indicates control of the mechanics of speaking or writing. | | | | |

**Interpretation:** Items 1–4 indicate the reader's comprehension of textual information; items 5–8 indicate metacognitive awareness, strategy use, and involvement with text; items 9–12 indicate facility with language and language development.

*Source:* From *Flexible Grouping in Reading* by Michael Opitz. Published by Scholastic Teaching Resources/ Scholastic, Inc. Copyright © 1998 by Michael Opitz. Reprinted by permission.

4. Have the child read the book while you record the reading on the Running Record form. If you are using a form with no text, use the following notations:
   - Make a check for each word read as shown in the book.
   - Write and circle any word that is omitted.
   - Add a caret for any word that the child inserts and write the word.
   - Write and draw a line through any word that is substituted and write what the child said in its place.
   - If the child repeats, draw an arrow to indicate where the child went back to reread.
   - Write SC when the child self-corrects.
   - If the child stops for more than 5 seconds, tell the student the word. Put a "T" for the stated word.
   - If the child loses his or her place or if the child begins reading something that is far different from the text, stop the child, point to where you want the child to start reading again, and say something like, "Try reading this again." Put brackets to indicate the problem section and write TTA inside the brackets.

   If you are using a form that includes the text the child is reading, use the following notations:
   - Place a check above each word as shown in the book.
   - Circle any word that is omitted.
   - If a child inserts a word, add a caret where the child inserts the word and write the word.
   - If the child substitutes a word, draw a line through the word and write the word the child stated above it.
   - If the child repeats, draw an arrow to indicate where the child went back to reread.
   - Write SC on or above the word when the child self-corrects.
   - If the child stops for more than 5 seconds, tell the student the word. Put a "T" for the stated word on or above the word.
   - If the child loses his or her place or if the child begins reading something that is far different from the text, stop the child, point to where you want the child to start reading again, and say something like, "Try reading this again." Put brackets around the problem section and write TTA above the section.

5. To check comprehension, have the child do a retelling and note the degree to which the child was able to retell using a form similar to Figure 8.8.

## SCORING A RUNNING RECORD

The following are counted as errors:

- omissions
- insertions
- substitutions
- told words or told to try that again

### Special Note

All repeated errors are recorded. For example, if the child substitutes the word "a" for "the" two times, each time, this substitution would count as an error. Clay comments, "It is only when you go to the trouble of analyzing *all the errors* that you get quality information about the way the reader is working on print."[19] ■

[19]Clay (1985/1995).

---

### FIGURE 8.9   A Running Record of Your Reading

Name: _Jesse_                                                                  Date: _Today_

Title of Book: _Summertime_            Author: _MacLeod, Skelton, & Strong_

| Page | The reading performance | Errors<br>M S V | Self-Corrects<br>M S V |
|---|---|---|---|
| 1 | ✓ ✓  ✓   spring<br>I like the ~~summer~~. | (M)(S) V | |
| 1 | ✓    ✓   woke ✓  ✓<br>The birds ~~wake~~ me up. | (M)(S)(V) | |
| 2 | ✓✓   ✓    ✓   ✓ ✓   ✓<br>I like wearing shorts and a T-shirt. | | |
| 3 | ✓✓ to wear   ✓    ✓    ✓<br>I like ˄ ~~wearing~~ sandals without socks. | (M)(S) V<br>(M)(S)(V) | |
| 4 | ✓ ✓   ✓    ✓   ✓ ✓  ✓<br>I like playing outside in the sun. | | |
| 5 | ✓have sc ⌐R    ✓  ✓ ✓    ✓<br>⌐I ~~like~~ helping Mom in the garden | | (M)(S)(V) |
| 6 | ✓✓    ✓    ✓       ✓<br>I like climbing the (apple) tree. | (M)(S)(V) | |
| 7 | ✓✓   ✓  ✓ ✓     ✓<br>I like eating in the backyard. | | |
| 8 | ✓  ✓  ✓   ✓   ✓   ✓ ✓ ⌐when sc ✓   ✓<br>But, I don't like going to bed ~~before~~ it's dark! | | M S (V) |
| | | M S V<br>5 5 2 | M S V<br>1 1 2 |
| | **Totals** | 5 | 2 |

As with miscue analysis, the running record can shed some light on the language cues the child may have used to read the text as he or she did. To get the most out of the running record, we need to go beyond simply counting the number of errors the child makes and look at why the child might have performed the way he or she did. In the short term, this analysis can help teachers to see which language cues the child uses as well as those that may need additional work. In the long term, the analysis of miscues over time can yield a pattern of behavior. Here are some suggestions for going beyond accuracy to look more closely at what the child did when reading:

1. Write M, S, and V for each error and self-correction. Remember that a self-correction is not counted as an error, nor is a repetition.
2. Read the sentence up to where each error was made and ask yourself these questions:
   • Does it make sense? If so, circle the M. This indicates that the child was attending to meaning when reading.

- Does it sound right? If so, circle the S. This indicates that the child was attending to the grammatical structure.
- Does it look like the actual word in the text? If so, circle the V. This indicates that the child was attending to the printed text.
3. For each self-correction, ask yourself what made the reader go back to self-correct. Ask yourself these questions:
   - Did the child self-correct because meaning was disrupted? If so, circle the M.
   - Did the child self-correct because it didn't sound right? If so, circle the S.
   - Did the child self-correct because the word didn't look like the one shown in the text? If so, circle the V.
4. Calculate the accuracy rate and the self-correction rate using the formula shown on the Running Record Summary form in Figure 8.7.
5. Record additional observations on the Running Record Summary form (Figure 8.7).
6. Take a look at the comprehension measure to determine how well the child appeared to comprehend the selection.
7. Use the results to design appropriate instruction.

## INTERPRETING A RUNNING RECORD

Taking a look at the summary (Figure 8.10), we are now in a position to interpret Jesse's reading behavior and make some inferences about what we need to do next. Let's first take a look at what Jesse appears to be doing well (his strengths). We'll then consider what he might need to learn (his needs) to advance as a reader.

*Strengths*

- Monitors self as evidenced by his self-corrections.
- Uses all three language cues: letter/sound knowledge, syntax, meaning.
- Attempts a word more than once when he senses that there is a problem.
- Uses all three language cues to self-correct.

In terms of comprehension, Jesse was able to retell the story with ease and also talked about what he likes to do in the spring. Neither literal nor inferential comprehension appeared to pose any problems with this particular text.

*Needs*

- Expand strategies to include cross-checking with pictures or looking back to see where he has seen a word before as ways of figuring out unknown words.
- Increase sight word vocabulary. This might enable him to advance to a more sophisticated instructional level.
- Give additional attention to visual cues. Jesse uses all three language cues; however, according to the results of this running record, he relies most heavily on meaning and syntax.

## REVISITING THE OPENING SCENARIO

Based on Ms. Mills' analysis of Vicki's reading performance on the IRI, how can she use Vicki's strengths as a reader to inform instruction focused on her needs? Develop a plan to present to Ms. Mills.

**FIGURE 8.10   Running Record Summary**

Title of Book: *Summertime*                                    Author: _____

**Summary of Reading Performance**

Total # of Words _58_     Total # of Errors _5_     % of accuracy _91%_

**Reading Level**  (Circle the one that matches the % of accuracy.)

95% – 100% = Independent     (90% – 94% = Instructional)     89% or lower = Frustration

Total # of Self-Corrections _2_     Self-Correction Rate 1: _3.5_

Note: Self-correction rates of 1:3, 1:4, or 1:5 are good. Each ratio shows that the reader is attending to discrepancies when reading.

**Summary of Observations**

1. What did the reader do when unknown words were encountered? (✔ all that apply)

   _____ made no attempt

   The reader made an attempt in these ways:

   _____ asked for help                          _____ looked at pictures

   ✓ used letter/sound knowledge       ✓ used meaning

   ✓ used structure (syntax)               ✓ tried again

   _____ skipped it and continued reading     _____ looked at another source

2. How often did the reader attempt to self-correct when meaning was not maintained?

   (Circle one)     always     frequently     (sometimes)     seldom     never

3. When the reader did self-correct, which cues were used? (✔ all that apply)

   ✓ letter/sound knowledge (visual)     ✓ meaning     ✓ syntax (structure)

**Calculating Accuracy Rate**

1. Subtract the total # of errors from the total # of words in the text to determine the number of words that were correctly read.

2. Divide the number of words correctly read by the number of words in the passage to determine % of accuracy.

   Example:  58 total words – 12 errors = 46 words read correctly
   46 words read correctly ÷ 58 total words = 79% accuracy

**Calculating Self-Correction Rate**

Use this formula:  $\dfrac{\text{self-corrections} + \text{errors}}{\text{self-corrections}} = 1:\underline{\quad}$

# AUTHORS' SUMMARY

In Chapter 8, we discussed oral reading for assessing students' reading. An Informal Reading Inventory (IRI) is a valuable assessment instrument because it can provide information about a student's reading levels and provide opportunity for a teacher to gain insight into a child's reading strengths and needs. We provided information on the IRI, its purposes, the criteria for estimating reading levels, how to administer one, how to mark oral reading errors, and how to score them. We also presented miscue analysis and explained how research in this area has heightened the consciousness of teachers using the IRI so that many are now concerned not only with the number of errors students make but also with what the errors tell them about readers' process of making meaning. Finally, we examined the running record, explaining it and discussing how it is similar to and different from an IRI.

# SUGGESTIONS FOR THOUGHT QUESTIONS AND ACTIVITIES

1. Administer an IRI, a modified miscue, or a running record to a child who has a reading problem.
2. Practice coding errors on an oral reading passage by listening to a tape of a child reading a passage.
3. Practice analyzing miscues using a child's taped reading and the forms shown in Figures 8.4 and 8.5.
4. Explain when you might choose to do a running record instead of an IRI.
5. Choose a story from a reading program and make up comprehension questions for it, including literal, interpretive, and critical reading questions.

# WEB SITES

http://ww2.chandler.k12.az.us/tarwater-elementary/teacherresource/Running%20Records.htm

After supplying a definition of running records, this site explains the various miscues (i.e., semantic, syntactic, and graphophonic) and then describes the processes of conducting a running record. The site also gives common teacher notations and the reasoning for each.

http://www.pampetty.com/420iriadminister.htm

This site explains how to administer an Informal Reading Inventory (IRI).

# SELECTED BIBLIOGRAPHY

Adams, Marilyn J. *Beginning to Read: Thinking and Learning about Print.* Cambridge, MA: MIT Press, 1990.

Beaver, J. *The Developmental Reading Assessment.* New York: Scott Foresman, 2001.

Betts, Emmett A. *Foundations of Reading Instruction.* New York: American Book Company, 1946.

Burns, Paul C., and Betty D. Roe. *Informal Reading Inventory: Preprimer to Twelfth Grade,* 5th ed. Boston: Houghton Mifflin, 1999.

Clay, M. *The Early Detection of Reading Difficulties.* Portsmouth, NH: Heinemann, 1995.

Duffelmeyer, Frederick, and Barbara Blakely Duffelmeyer. "Are IRI Passages Suitable for Assessing Main Idea Comprehension?" *The Reading Teacher* 42 (February, 1989): 358–363.

Duffelmeyer, Frederick, Susan R. Robinson, and Susan E. Squier. "Vocabulary Questions on Informal Reading Inventories." *The Reading Teacher* 43 (November, 1989): 142–148.

Forell, Elizabeth. "The Case for Conservative Reader Placement." *The Reading Teacher* 38 (May, 1985): 857–862.

Gillis, M. K., and Mary W. Olson. "Elementary IRIs: Do They Reflect What We Know about Text Type Structure and Comprehension?" *Reading Research and Instruction* 27 (Fall, 1987): 36–44.

Johnson, Marjorie S., Roy A. Kress, and John J. Pikulski. *Informal Reading Inventories,* 2nd ed. Newark, DE: International Reading Association, 1987.

Martin-Lara, Susan G. "Reading Placement for Code Switchers." *The Reading Teacher* 42 (January, 1989): 278–282.

Morris, Darrell, Criss Ervin, and Kim Conrad. "A Case Study of Middle School Reading Disability." *The Reading Teacher* 49 (February, 1996): 368–377.

Opitz, M., and M. Ford. *Reaching Readers.* Portsmouth, NH: Heinemann, 2001.

Opitz, M., and T. Rasinski. *Good-bye Round Robin.* Portsmouth, NH: Heinemann, 1998.

Pikulski, John J. "Informal Reading Inventory," in Assessment Section. *The Reading Teacher* 43 (March, 1990): 514–516.

Silvaroli, J. Nicholas, and Warren H. Wheelock. *Classroom Reading Inventory,* 9th ed. New York: McGraw-Hill, 2001.

Now go to Topic 2: "Reading Assessment" in MyEducationLab (www.myeducationlab.com) for your course, where you can:

- Find learning outcomes for "Reading Assessment" along with national standards that connect to these outcomes.
- Complete Assignments and Activities that can help you more deeply understand the chapter content.
- Examine challenging situations and cases presented in the IRIS Center Resources.
- Access video clips of CCSSO National Teacher of the Year award winners responding to the question, "Why Do I Teach?" in the Teacher Talk section.
- Apply and practice your understanding of the core teaching skills identified in the chapter with Building Teaching Skills and Dispositions learning units.

**9**

**CHAPTER** OUTLINE

- Scenario: Mr. Hall's Text-Packed Classroom
- Reasons for using a Variety of Texts
- Text Types
- Revisiting the Opening Scenario

**PART 3**
Reading Content and Instruction

# Using Texts to Help Children Advance as Readers

**SCENARIO:** MR. HALL'S TEXT-PACKED CLASSROOM

> When parents walk into Mr. Hall's room, they are immediately impressed with the huge variety of text. They see shelves, crates, tubs, cabinets, bulletin boards, and walls all filled or covered with different kinds of texts. They are also surprised to see children out of their seats and going to different places in the room, instead of reading quietly at their desks. Some are reading from *Sports Illustrated* magazine in a small group with Mr. Hall. Others are across the room looking at weather report charts from today's newspaper. In yet another area, students are reading self-selected books independently. At another station, students are looking at a Web site about whaling in Greenland. During the next break, parents ask why he has students reading so many different kinds of texts. How might he respond?

## CHAPTER OBJECTIVES

After reading this chapter, you should be able to:

- Discuss the importance of providing students with time to read in school.
- Discuss reasons for using different types of texts.
- Explain how to use different types of texts for instruction.

Reading helps reading! Not only is the amount of time spent in reading essential for success in reading but also the amount of actual reading accomplished is vital to reading achievement.[1] Researchers have found that children who excel in reading read significantly more text than those who find reading difficult. This is true both in and out of the classroom. Historically, children who need the most practice reading connected text have instead spent their time learning isolated skills. They spend little or no time actually reading. In particular, struggling readers have few opportunities to practice silent reading behaviors.[2] Even though a teacher may spend equal amounts of time with both types of students, what happens during that time is qualitatively different. Teachers appear to have less proficient readers spend more time on oral reading; they spend more time correcting oral reading errors and working on individual words.[3]

In the Nation's Report Cards, findings consistently show a positive relationship between achievement and exposure to intensive reading experiences.[4] In other words, those students who stated they read more frequently for fun on their own time, on the average, achieved better scores in reading than those who reported reading less frequently. Students who were involved in frequent discussions about their studies with friends or family had higher average reading proficiency than students who reported little or no discussion.[5]

As struggling readers finish elementary school, many have internalized the misconception that only picture books, novels, and textbooks count as "reading."

---

[1]Richard L. Allington, *What Really Matters for Struggling Readers,* 2nd ed. (Boston: Allyn & Bacon, 2005).

[2]Richard L. Allington, "Poor Readers Don't Get to Read Much in Reading Groups," *Language Arts* 57 (November/December, 1980): 874.

[3]Ibid., pp. 872–876.

[4]Patricia L. Donahue et al., *NAEP 1998 Reading Report Card for the Nation and the States,* National Assessment of Educational Progress (Washington, DC: Office of Educational Research and Improvement, U.S. Department of Education, 1999), p. 109.

[5]Ibid., p. 103.

Clearly this is unfortunate, and it may happen for a variety of reasons. If many students do not find a print-rich environment at home, they need to enter classrooms where teachers provide ample opportunities for wide reading using a variety of text types. In this chapter, we describe many types of texts teachers can use to teach reading.

# REASONS FOR USING A VARIETY OF TEXTS

In everyday life, we read several different types of texts. What we read depends on several factors, including interest and purpose. Using a variety of texts, then, is necessary to help students learn what it means to be a reader. Remember that we are teaching children to be readers rather than merely teaching them to read. Right from the start, children need to be reading books and other works written and illustrated by a variety of authors and illustrators. Here are seven additional reasons for using many different kinds of texts:

1. *To motivate all children to be readers.* When students read from a wide variety of texts, they are likely to connect print in the classroom to the "real world" print they encounter outside of school. Teachers who use a variety of text types honor the fact that what students see and do outside the classroom has value for school learning, too.[6] We want students to value reading.

2. *To capitalize on student interest.* Some students would rather read information texts than stories. They like learning about specific details related to given topics. Providing these children with texts they enjoy motivates them to read.[7]

3. *To address reading attitudes.* Attitudes have a directive and dynamic influence on all our lives, and once they are set, they are difficult to change. Concomitant learnings such as reading attitudes often remain with students more than the subject matter itself. Therefore, using many different texts can help children develop a love of reading.

4. *To help students understand that different texts are written in different ways.* Stories are written using a story grammar that includes setting, characters, problem, attempts to solve the problem, and resolution. Expository text (i.e., text written to inform) may encompass sequence of events, compare/contrast, or use other text structures. Knowing about these different formats or structures that are used to write texts better ensures that students will better comprehend them.[8]

5. *To expose children to content-specific vocabulary and new concepts.* As a result of reading a variety of texts, students acquire larger vocabularies. For example, when reading an informational article about spiders, students learn words associated with spiders. An increase in knowledge assures that better reading comprehension will occur.[9]

[6]M. Opitz and M. Ford, *Books and Beyond: New Ways to Reach Readers* (Portsmouth, NH: Heinemann, 2006).

[7]J. H. Reed and D. L. Schallert, "The Nature of Involvement in Academic Discourse," *Journal of Educational Psychology* 85 (1993): 253–266.

[8]K. D. Muth, ed., *Children's Comprehension of Text* (Newark, DE: International Reading Association, 1989).

[9]P. A. Alexander, "The Past, Present, and Future of Knowledge Research: A Re-examination of the Role of Knowledge in Learning and Instructing," *Educational Psychologist* 31 (1996): 89–92.

6. *To serve as a scaffold.* Because stories are generally easier for students to read than nonfiction, fiction and nonfiction can be paired so that when students are finished reading one book, they have a better understanding of the content.[10] For example, as a way of helping children understand something about apples, children could first take a look at *Dappled Apples* (Carr, 2001) or *The Apple Pie Tree* (Hall, 1996) before they look at *Apples* (Robbins, 2002), which is a nonfiction selection. Having acquired an understanding of the material presented in these texts, the reader is more likely to comprehend information presented in other books such as textbooks. Reading texts that relate to a specific topic is another way to provide this scaffolding.

7. *To broaden students' knowledge base.* Good comprehension is dependent on knowledge. If we know something about the topic we are reading, we are more apt to understand what we have read and to remember it longer. The reverse is also true. Exposing children to different ideas presented in different texts is a way of broadening a student's knowledge base.[11]

## TEXT TYPES

There are many ways to use texts to help children learn to read better. Because there are so many different types of texts, we have divided them into three broad categories to better explain and describe them: commercial, trade, and other. *Commercial books* are texts that have been written for a given program. Three types of commercial books exist: little books, basal readers, and textbooks. *Little books* are small books that can be easily held by young children. The books are usually the same size, have a paperback cover, and have few pages. *Basal readers* are grade-level anthologies accompanied by additional materials such as teacher guides, workbooks, and commercially created tests. *Textbooks* are written for specific content areas and are used primarily for instructional purposes. Most often these commercial texts have to be ordered directly from the publisher; they are not available in bookstores or public libraries.

*Trade books* can be found in bookstores and libraries. They are sometimes called *authentic literature* because they are primarily written to communicate a message to the reader. They are not created for a specific program. Authors who write these books are most interested in conveying their ideas, and they do so using a variety of words and illustrations. For the purposes of this book, children's literature, authentic literature, and trade books have the same meaning.

*Other* encompasses texts that don't fit neatly into either of the previous two categories. Magazines, newspapers, real-life texts, and electronic texts are in this category.

Two points of confusion can surface when we talk about using different texts to teach children. One involves the way trade books are used in other programs. Sometimes the best of these trade books are selected for grade-level anthologies which, when taken together, comprise a reading program (i.e., a basal reader). Another point of confusion involves the idea of "leveled" books. Basically, these are collections of books from two categories—commercial *and* trade—that are leveled

---

[10]D. Camp, "It Takes Two: Teaching with Twin Texts of Fact and Fiction," *The Reading Teacher* 53 (2000): 400–408.

[11]Alexander (1996). See also R. H. Yopp and H. K. Yopp, "Sharing Informational Text with Young Children," *The Reading Teacher* 53 (2000): 410–423.

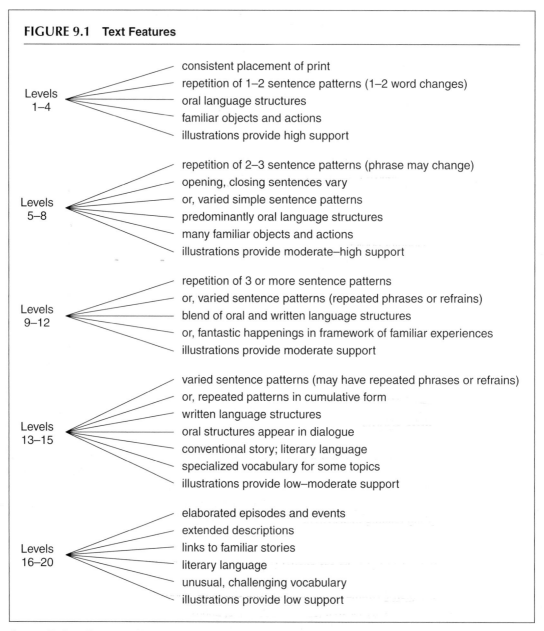

**FIGURE 9.1** **Text Features**

Levels 1–4
- consistent placement of print
- repetition of 1–2 sentence patterns (1–2 word changes)
- oral language structures
- familiar objects and actions
- illustrations provide high support

Levels 5–8
- repetition of 2–3 sentence patterns (phrase may change)
- opening, closing sentences vary
- or, varied simple sentence patterns
- predominantly oral language structures
- many familiar objects and actions
- illustrations provide moderate–high support

Levels 9–12
- repetition of 3 or more sentence patterns
- or, varied sentence patterns (repeated phrases or refrains)
- blend of oral and written language structures
- or, fantastic happenings in framework of familiar experiences
- illustrations provide moderate support

Levels 13–15
- varied sentence patterns (may have repeated phrases or refrains)
- or, repeated patterns in cumulative form
- written language structures
- oral structures appear in dialogue
- conventional story; literary language
- specialized vocabulary for some topics
- illustrations provide low–moderate support

Levels 16–20
- elaborated episodes and events
- extended descriptions
- links to familiar stories
- literary language
- unusual, challenging vocabulary
- illustrations provide low support

*Source:* Barbara Peterson. *Characteristics of Text That Support Beginning Readers.* The Ohio State University. 1998.

according to difficulty.[12] As Figure 9.1 shows, specific features are used to determine the book's level of difficulty.

Table 9.1 illustrates the different texts that can be used for independent and small group reading instruction and shows the most appropriate grade levels in which the texts are used. Additional information for each type of text, including a description, examples, reasons for using the text, and teaching suggestions, appears on the pages that follow.

[12]Ibid.

**TABLE 9.1   Texts for Independent and Small Group Reading Instruction**

| Text Type/Grade Level | 1 | 2 | 3 | 4 | 5 | 6 |
|---|---|---|---|---|---|---|
| *Commercial books* | | | | | | |
| Little books | • | • | | | | |
| Basal readers | • | • | • | • | • | • |
| Textbooks | • | • | • | • | • | • |
| *Children's literature* | | | | | | |
| Predictable books | • | • | | | | |
| Information (nonfiction) | • | • | • | • | • | • |
| Multilevel literature | • | • | • | • | • | • |
| Series books | • | • | • | • | • | • |
| Poetry | • | • | • | • | • | • |
| Chapter books | | • | • | • | • | • |
| Multicultural literature | • | • | • | • | • | • |
| *Other* | | | | | | |
| Magazines | • | • | • | • | • | • |
| Newspapers | • | • | • | • | • | • |
| Real-Life Texts | • | • | • | • | • | • |
| Electronic Texts | • | • | • | • | • | • |

## COMMERCIAL BOOKS

### *Little Books*

**Description**

Little books are small books that are easily held by young children. They are usually the same size, have a paperback cover, and contain just a few pages. Many times, these books are written by different authors, yet all titles are leveled by the company that produces them. They are then assembled to create sets of readers that can be used for small group reading instruction.

**Examples**

Sets of little books are available from a number of publishers including the following:

- Pair-It Extreme (Houghton Mifflin Harcourt, 2009)
- Literacy by Design (Harcourt Archive, 2008)

**Why Use Them?**

Little books are especially designed for use with beginning readers starting in kindergarten and continuing through first grade. They are sometimes used with children in second grade as well. As leveled texts are packaged in multiple sets, the books can be used for demonstrations and interventions with young readers in small group settings. Likewise, the increasingly challenging texts facilitate the scaffolded instruction discussed earlier. They have the look and feel of real books, and their use more closely parallels reading experiences in which children's literature is used. They have a strong appeal to young readers because they convey a sense of reading whole books. Generally inexpensive, they can be used to create a classroom library of accessible books for use during independent reading time as well as guided reading.

### Teaching Suggestions

- Select an appropriate title for a group of children who are reading at a similar general achievement level. After providing an introduction to the text, invite children to read it to themselves. After they have read the book, engage the children in one or more ways. They may first discuss the text and read aloud a part they liked the best. If you are focusing on teaching different ways to figure out unknown words, select a word from the text that posed difficulty, write it and the sentence in which it appears on the board, and ask children how they can go about figuring out this unknown word.
- Using some common element such as story setting, select texts at different levels to represent the readers in the group. After children have had time to read their assigned books, teach them about story setting. Allow students time to share details about where their stories took place.

## *Basal Readers*

### Description

Basal readers are the central components of commercially developed reading programs. They are often structured as anthologies of grade-leveled texts with additional supportive materials such as teacher guides and student workbooks available. Basal readers are most often selected and purchased to provide a cohesive, consistent, continuous reading curricula across and between grade levels throughout a school district or within individual schools. In most classrooms, each child is provided a copy of the anthology (i.e., reader) to use during guided reading.

### Examples

- Houghton Mifflin Reading (2008)
- Reading Street (Scott Foresman, 2008)

### Why Use Them?

The use of basal readers is strongly encouraged and expected in many school districts. In fact, after these materials are purchased, little if any money is left over to purchase other materials that can be used to teach reading. One reason for using basal readers, then, has to do with district administrators' level of expectations. Another has to do with access. All students are provided with reading materials and teachers are provided with ample materials for instructional support. The selections are somewhat organized by increasingly sophisticated vocabulary, concepts, and text structures so that the selections within the anthologies can be used to scaffold instruction in much the same way as the "little books" discussed above.

### Teaching Suggestions

- Choose individual selections within the basal anthology to use for a demonstration or intervention lesson.
- Newer basal reading anthologies have the added advantage of having selections organized by theme. Using these themed stories for common and shared-response activities with small groups of students is a natural. Assign all students within a group the same selection within a theme and then ask them to share something of interest. Another way to capitalize on the use of these themed stories is to have different students read different stories within the theme. Once finished, students can compare and contrast their stories and tell how their stories relate to the overall theme.

Go to the Assignments and Activities section of Topic 11: Reading Difficulties and Intervention Strategies in the MyEducationLab for your course and complete the activity entitled "Intervention Strategies for Nonfiction Reading." As you watch the video and answer the accompanying questions, think about your own reading of textbooks. Do you pay attention to diagrams and figures to help determine the most important information?

Go to the Assignments and Activities section of Topic 9: Reading Comprehension in the MyEducationLab for your course and complete the activity entitled "Content Area Text Structure and Comprehension." As you watch the video and answer the accompanying questions, reflect on how you might teach younger children about text structure. Which text features would you teach them? Why?

## *Textbooks*

### Description

Besides the materials purchased for and used in the classroom reading/language arts program, a number of other commercially prepared texts are written for specific content areas such as science, social studies, and mathematics. Often, one series is selected for a school or school district. A series is most often composed of a set of common core texts, each containing grade-level appropriate presentations of increasingly sophisticated subject area content. Each student is provided a copy of the grade-level text.

### Examples of Companies That Publish Textbook Series

- Scholastic
- Prentice-Hall
- Silver/Burdett/Ginn

### Why Use Them?

As is the case with basal readers, both teachers and students usually have easy access to textbooks. They are often selected, purchased, and distributed by school district person-nel as a foundation for content area curricula. As with basal readers, the use of textbooks is often strongly encouraged because significant resources have been used to purchase them. Therefore, one reason to use textbooks is to meet externally mandated expectations. Another, perhaps more essential reason for using textbooks focuses on student success. As we all know, students will encounter textbook-based instruction in specific content areas. Students' success depends on their ability to handle the reading demands of these texts. The goal is to improve students' ability to negotiate their way through these texts with maximum comprehension. See Chapter 13 for additional suggestions on helping children read textbooks in content areas.

### Teaching Suggestions

- Choose a specific section of the textbook to show students how to do a preview as a warm-up for successful reading. After students have previewed the section, allow time for them to read the text to themselves. Once they have finished reading, have students relate information that they discovered.
- Most textbook chapters are divided by subheadings. Either assign or invite students to choose the section they would like to read; then, ask them to look for three specific ideas they can share with others in the group. Once they have finished reading, have students in the group create a note-taking guide to record information about the other sections of the chapter that they did not read.

## CHILDREN'S LITERATURE

## *Predictable Books*

### Description

Predictable books are written with specific features that enable children to read with ease. They share the following characteristics:

- *Pictures that support the text.* These pictures illustrate what the text says, so the child can use them to help read the text.
- *Repeated sentence or phrase.* The same sentence or phrase is repeated on nearly every page. The repetition helps the young reader use memory to read the sentence or phrase.

- *Rhyme and rhythm.* The use of both rhyme and rhythm cues the reader with oral language features that facilitate reading.
- *Cumulative pattern.* As the story progresses, new lines are added, but previous lines are repeated, thus providing the reader with practice.
- *Familiar sequence.* Days of the week or counting are two examples of this feature. Students use what they know about both to successfully read the text at hand.

### Examples

- *The Napping House* (Wood, 2009)
- *Everywhere the Cow Says Moo* (Weinstein, 2008)
- *Hug* (Alborough, 2009)
- *The Deep Blue Sea: A Book of Colors* (Wood, 2005)
- *Good Morning, Digger* (Rockwell, 2005)
- *Mommies Say Shhh!* (Polacco, 2005)
- *Why Not?* (Wormell, 2000)
- *One Red Dot* (Carter, 2005)

### Why Use Them?

Predictable books are advantageous for several reasons.[13] First, these books employ the language features listed above that enable children to read with greater ease. Second, they enable children to read authentic literature from the very beginning, thus helping children to see that they can read "real" books. Third, although they are most often used with beginning readers, predictable books provide a tremendous amount of support and success for English language learners and for older children who struggle with reading. Fourth, many predictable books are published as "big books," oversized versions of a book. They lend themselves to interactive sessions with a large group, which helps all students to see that they are a part of the classroom community.

### Teaching Suggestions

- Select an appropriate title for a group of children who are reading at a similar general achievement level. Introduce the text and then invite children to read it to themselves. After they have read the book, engage the children in one or more ways. They may first discuss the text and read aloud a part they liked the best. If you are focusing on teaching different ways to figure out unknown words, select a word from the text that posed difficulty, write it and the sentence in which it appears on the board, and ask children how they can go about figuring out this unknown word.
- Using some common element such as story setting, select texts at different levels to represent the readers in the group. After children have had time to read their assigned books, teach them about story setting. Allow students time to share details about where their stories took place.
- When using a big book that contains a repetitive passage, think about pausing during the reading as you come to the passage to give children an opportunity to chime in. To help children develop a speech-to-print match, point to the words as they are read.

## *Information Books (Nonfiction)*

### Description

Nonfiction books present factual information about a given topic. They are usually accompanied by photographs and illustrations to help students better understand the content.

---

[13]M. B. Thogmartin, *Teach a Child to Read with Children's Books,* 2nd ed. (Bloomington, IN: Educational Resource Center, 1998).

**Examples**

- *Faces of the Moon* (Crelin, 2009)
- *Bird, Butterfly, Eel* (Prosek, 2009)
- *River of Dreams—Story of the Hudson River* (Talbott, 2009)
- *Panda Kindergarten* (Ryder, 2009)
- *Baby Sea Otter* (Tatham, 2005)
- *Into the Ice: The Story of the Arctic Exploration* (Curlee, 1998)
- *Liberty Rising: The Story of the Statue of Liberty* (Shea, 2005)
- *On Earth* (Karas, 2005)
- *Show Off: How to Do Absolutely Everything One Step at a Time* (Stephens & Mann, 2009)
- *In 1776* (Marzollo, 1994)
- *Moon: Science, History, and Mystery* (Ross, 2009)

**Why Use Them?**
There are two sound reasons for using information texts. First, they present facts about the world around us. Because many children are curious about their surroundings, these texts provide motivating and interesting reading material. Second, the text structures used to write information texts differ from those used to write fiction. Students need to learn how to navigate all of these different types of texts in order to become competent readers. Informational text structures include comparison/contrast, description, sequence, and problem/solution.

**Teaching Suggestions**

- Select a text with specific features that you want to teach students. For example, you might want to show them how to read a diagram and the way it relates to the written text. After providing instruction, have children read the text and follow up with a discussion in which children talk about how the diagram helped them read the text.
- Use a specific nonfiction selection to show students how to process the information presented: picture captions, subheadings, bold print, and other features. After providing this introduction, have students read the text. They can then report one or two ideas they learned from the text.

## *Multilevel Books*
**Description**
Multilevel books are written with multiple story lines. Books that have simple story lines and contain more information about specific features in the text at the end of the book are also considered multilevel. Although some of these books are fiction, the majority are nonfiction (informational). Still others combine fiction and nonfiction.

**Examples**

- *Heart of Texas* (Melmed, 2009) is a nonfiction alphabet text that celebrates Texas with three levels of reading on each page.
- *A Subway for New York* (Weitzman, 2005) is a nonfiction selection containing two story lines. *Elephants Can Paint, Too* (Arnold, 2005) is another example.
- *This Rocket* (Collicut, 2005) is a nonfiction text that has a simple story line with accompanying information in the front and back of the text that gives a brief history of rockets (front) and tells about the Apollo 11 mission (back).

- *Sharks and Other Dangers of the Deep* (Mugford, 2005) is an example that contains three story lines.
- *Wise Guy: The Life and Philosophy of Socrates* (Usher, 2005) is an example that contains two story lines and information at the end of the text.
- *Lucille Lost* (George and Murphy, 2006) is an example that has a story line about a turtle's adventure and then corresponding nonfiction facts about turtles at the bottom of each page.

**Why Use Them?**

Regardless of reading level or background, all children can read all or some portions of these texts. Using these texts, then, is one way of showing students that they can all read a similar text and get something out of the experience, that they are part of one community of learners.

The books are also rich in content; they contain much information about objects or situations that interest children. These texts also provide a scaffold for meaningful repeated reading. That is, once children hear other parts of the story from either the teacher or classmates, they are more likely to be able to read the text themselves. Finally, in terms of resources, schools can get a great deal of use out of these books with fewer dollars spent.

**Teaching Suggestions**

- If students are grouped by similar level or background, different groups can read different parts of the text. For example, those who are just getting a handle on how print functions or those who have little background about the topic at hand could be invited to follow along as the teacher reads part of text. Next, the teacher may have students choral read their part while he or she reads the additional text shown on the page, thus building children's background and knowledge base.
- After each group member has read through the text pertaining to the parts most appropriate for the given group, children can be grouped by twos (if the book has two story lines or parts) and threes (if the book has three story lines or parts). In turn, each person can read his or her part of the text while others listen. To emphasize listening comprehension, each group could be given one text that is passed from one person to the next as each part is read.
- In pair work, if the focus is on helping the less experienced reader attain a larger reading vocabulary and hear an example of fluent reading, each child could be provided a copy of the text and the less experienced reader could follow along as the partner reads aloud. This particular way of reading provides the less experienced reader or the child with a limited background with a scaffold, enabling him or her to read a good portion of the text at a later time.

## Series Books

### Description

Series books share common elements such as characters, author's style, words, and format. Children can often follow the development of story characters and share in their adventures in each succeeding book in the series.

### Examples

- Mills, Claudia, *Gus and Grandpa* (grades 1–2)
- Willems, Mo, *Elephant and Piggie* (grades 1–2)
- Reilly-Giff, Patricia, *Polk Street Kids* (grades 2–3)

- Adler, David, *Cam Jansen* (grades 2–3)
- West, Tracey, *Planet Earth* (grades 2–4)
- Greenburg, Dan, *Zack Files* (grades 2–5)
- Kinney, Jeff, *Diary of a Wimpy Kid* (grades 2–4)
- Erickson, John, *Hank, the Cowdog* (grades 3–4)
- Stilton, Geronimo, *Geronimo Stilton* (grades 3–4)
- Hirschmann, Kris, *Planet Earth* (grades 4–6)
- Rowling, J.K., *Harry Potter* (grades 4–6)
- Lupica, Mike, *Comeback Kids* (grades 4–6)

### Why Use Them?

Series books can be very effective as a source of reading material for three reasons. First, they provide meaningful reading practice. Once children get hooked on a series, they have a desire to read additional books in the series. Because characters, plot structure, and words are common to all books in the series, students get a lot of meaningful practice. In other words, the natural redundancy of these features provides support for even the most novice readers, enabling many children to read the texts and to gain confidence.

Second, series books provide opportunities for children to discuss and interpret events in the series. Students reading different titles in the series will make their own interpretations based on their own backgrounds. Talking with others broadens understanding.

Third, series books provide children with opportunities to make inferences. When reading the books out of order, especially, children must infer what has come before and how their book fits into the series. In effect, they get to solve a reading puzzle as they read different books in the series. Solving this puzzle can be very engaging for children and is even more challenging when the books in the series are numbered, but read out of order.

### Teaching Suggestions

- Group students according to who is reading the same series. Children can then discuss their books with teacher guidance. Several different teaching points could emerge, such as what all of the books have in common or how reading series books can increase comprehension.
- To help children experience being a part of a larger community of readers, provide each child in the class with a different book in the series. Children can then be grouped in a variety of ways for small group reading instruction. For example, those children who need to learn how to better use words to create visual images can be grouped together to learn this task. Those children who need to learn how to pay attention to meaning as well as visual cues can be grouped together. After they have been taught the given strategy, they can then practice it using their series book as the teacher provides guidance.

## *Poetry*

### Description

Poetry is writing in which rhythm, sound, and language are used to create images, thoughts, and emotional responses. Usually concise, poetry takes on many forms such as *narrative poetry,* which tells a story; *lyric poetry,* in which much rhythm is used; *humorous poetry,* in which everyday objects or events are portrayed in absurd ways; and *nonsense poetry,* which uses meaningless words and much exaggeration.[14]

---

[14]F. Goforth, *Literature and the Learner* (Belmont, CA: Wadsworth, 1998).

**Examples**

- *Flying Eagle* (Bardhan-Quallen, 2009)
- *Sky Magic* (Hopkins, 2009)
- *The Scarecrow's Dance* (Yolen, 2009)
- *Dinothesaurus* (Florian, 2009)
- *A Foot in the Mouth: Poems to Speak, Sing, & Shout* (Janeczco, 2009)
- *In the Swim* (Florian, 1997)
- *School Supplies: A Book of Poems* (Hopkins, 1996)
- *Block City* (Stevenson, 2005)
- *Down to the Sea in Ships* (Sturges, 2005)
- *When I Heard the Learn'd Astronomer* (Whitman, 2004)

**Why Use It?**

Poetry uses different forms than other kinds of writing. Exposing children to poetry opens up this style of writing to them, increasing their comprehension of it. Because many poems are succinct and use words that convey images, poems are excellent selections to help children learn to visualize. And because they are short, poems tend to be less intimidating for even the most novice reader. Finally, poetry helps students develop numerous reading skills such as phrasing, fluency, and comprehension.

**Teaching Suggestions**

- Select a poem to help students learn how to use words to create visual images. After modeling the process, provide students with another poem, giving them time to read it. Once they have read the poem, ask students to discuss specific lines and the images they saw when they read them.
- To model fluency and reading poetry for enjoyment, select a poem and read it to the students. Point out how the phrases helped you know how to read the poem. Next, provide students with several poetry books. Invite them to choose and read a poem. Once they have read silently, have students read their poems aloud to the group.
- Students can also create materials to use during guided reading experiences once they become familiar with common core poems introduced during shared reading. Lines or stanzas from the poems can be printed on one side of a blank page. During independent work time, students can add illustrations to these pages, bind the pages, and create their own copy of a text. Then the teacher can invite students to bring their books to the guided reading table to use in demonstration and intervention lessons.

## *Chapter Books*

**Description**

Chapter books are divided into different segments or chapters. They range in sophistication beginning with the very easiest in first grade and increasing in difficulty throughout the grades.

**Examples**

- Chapter books for novice readers
  *Henry and Mudge* series (Cynthia Rylant)
  *Frog and Toad* series (Arnold Lobel)
  *Little Bear* series (Else Minarik)

- Chapter books for older readers
  Recent Newbery award and honor books
  *The Graveyard Book* (Gaiman, 2008)
  *Holes* (Sachar, 2008)
  *Bud, Not Buddy* (Curtis, 2004)
  *Missing May* (Rylant, 2003)
  *The Giver* (Lowry, 2002)
  *Walk Two Moons* (Creech, 1996)
  *Shiloh* (Naylor, 2000)

**Why Use Them?**
Chapter books afford children with an opportunity to extend themselves into books that they will be reading in their everyday lives. Chapter books help students learn how a story is connected by individual sections. Reading these books is also a signal to children that they are becoming more competent readers. Chapter books also provide logical stopping points for instructional purposes.

**Teaching Suggestions**

- Provide all students in the group with the same chapter book and give a structure for reading the book.
- Use chapter books to engage children in an author study. Different groups of children can read different chapter books by the same author. Author style across texts can become a focal point for instruction. Certain authors, such as Cynthia Rylant, Patricia Reilly Giff, Gary Paulsen, and William Steig, have written at all levels—picture books, simple chapter books, complex young adult novels, and adult fiction and nonfiction. Studies of these authors allow teachers who work with a wide range of readers to match appropriate texts to their students' levels, while still engaging all students in a cohesive classroom conversation about the author.

## *Multicultural Books*

**Description**
Multicultural literature refers to all genres that portray the likenesses and differences among social, cultural, and ethnic groups. They are written to reflect our diverse society.

**Examples**

- *Hansel and Gretel* (Isadora, 2009)
- *Babu's Song* (Stuve-Bodeen, 2003)
- *Rent Part Jazz* (Miller, 2001)
- *Most Loved in All the World* (Hegamin and Cabrera, 2009)
- *Erika-San* (Say, 2009)
- *Muktar and the Camels* (Graber and Mack, 2009)
- *The Beckoning Cat* (Nishizuka, 2009)
- *Celia Cruz, Queen of Salsa* (Chambers, 2005)
- *Rosa* (Giovanni, 2005)
- *My Nana and Me* (Smalls, 2005)
- *Meow: Cat Stories from Around the World* (Yolen, 2005)
- *Beyond the Great Mountains* (Young, 2005)

**Why Use It?**
All children need books that represent their cultural heritage. Reading multicultural books gives all children characters with whom they can identify. Multicultural literature

also provides children with opportunities to learn about similarities and differences among people and to consider different points of view.

The importance of learning about other groups of people through literature is aptly expressed in the following:

> I never felt the world-wide importance of the children's heritage in literature more than on a day when I stood with Mrs. Ben Zvi, wife of the [then] President of Israel, in the midst of the book boxes she had filled for the centers in Jerusalem where refugee boys and girls were gathered for storytelling and reading of the world's great classics for children. "We want our boys and girls to be at home with the other children of the world," she said, "and I know of no better way than through mutual enjoyment of the world's great stories."[15]

As Diakiw states, "Young children find it easier to assimilate new information when this information is presented within the structure of a story."[16] The story acts as a bridge to help children "link their growing understanding of other cultures to their personal experience and background knowledge."[17]

The characteristics of "good" books are operative for all children regardless of background. Any book they read must help them to feel good about themselves. It must help them to view themselves in a positive light, to achieve a better self-concept, and to gain a feeling of worth.

A book that hinders a child from finding his or her identity or that portrays the child in a stereotyped role is a book that would be considered poor reading for all children.

When selecting books for a class library, teachers should try to put themselves in the position of their students and ask these questions: How would I feel if I read this book? Would this book make me come back for another one? Will this book interest me? Are these books written on many readability levels? Does the book portray the black child or any other minority child as an individual? Are the adults portrayed in a nonchildlike manner? Are the characters supplied with traits and personalities that are positive? Would all children want to read the book?

If the answers are "yes," the teacher should choose the book, but even one "no" answer should disqualify it.

The importance of providing children with books that convey hope, and with which children can identify because the books mirror their lives, cannot be overemphasized. Another factor, which is as important, concerns the images that children obtain when they read a book about people with different racial or ethnic backgrounds. Since children are greatly influenced by what they read, the way that people are portrayed in books will have a profound effect on children's perceptions of them.

### Teaching Suggestions

- Select a topic or theme that will encourage students to select multicultural books during reading instruction. For example, if the focus is on the effects of prejudice and discrimination, students can explore nonfiction and fiction titles at many different levels. Some might be reading picture books such as Robert Coles's *Ruby Bridges* and others might be reading novellas such as Mildred Taylor's *The Gold Cadillac*.

[15]Dora V. Smith, "Children's Literature Today," *Elementary English* 47 (October, 1970): 778.

[16]Jerry Y. Diakiw, "Children's Literature and Global Education: Understanding the Developing World," *The Reading Teacher* 43 (January, 1990): 297.

[17]Ibid.

The teacher brings small groups of students together to discuss the issues and ideas in their books related to the topic.

• Encourage critical literacy by selecting certain texts and then guiding students to look at those texts from perspectives other than their own. A teacher working on a frontier/pioneer theme may have small groups of students reading different trade books such as Laura Ingalls Wilder's *Little House in the Big Woods* and Carol Ryrie Brink's *Caddie Woodlawn*. Discussions can be structured by the teacher to ask students to respond to what was written by assuming various roles (Native Americans, pioneer children, modern women, etc.) to show how taking different perspectives helps readers to critically analyze texts. Introducing contrasting texts such as Michael Dorris's *Sees Behind Trees,* which focuses on a Native American perspective, allows the teacher to guide students through additional comparisons and contrasts as they look critically at historical events.

## OTHER TEXTS

### *Magazines*

**Description**

Magazines are compilations of articles and stories designed to inform readers about many different topics. Columns of text, pictures with captions, short tidbits about different topics, diagrams, and advertisements are often used to create a magazine. Most magazines focus on a specific audience and feature articles that would appeal to this audience.

**Examples**

• *Sesame Street Magazine* (ages 0–6)
• *Ladybug Magazine* (ages 2–6)
• *Zoobooks* (ages 6–14)
• *American Girl* (ages 8–12)
• *Cricket Magazine* (ages 8–14)
• *Faces Magazine* (ages 8–14)
• *National Geographic Kids* (ages 8–14)
• *Sports Illustrated for Kids* (ages 8–14)

**Why Use Them?**

Reading a magazine requires the reader to be "magazine literate." According to Stoll, being magazine literate means that the reader knows how the publication works—how it is organized, where to locate specific information, and how to maximize the magazine's potential.[18] Using magazines for guided reading, then, is an excellent way to help students become magazine literate. Time can be devoted to teaching children how to read magazines and to explaining that magazines reflect many different personalities. Because some magazines include articles written by children and contain high-interest articles, they provide very motivating reading material. They can also serve as a catalyst for meaningful writing experiences; students can be encouraged to write their own articles for publication and to write letters to the editor. Finally, because columns of text, pictures with short captions, short blurbs about given topics, and diagrams are used in magazines, they provide a wide range of information that can be accessed by all readers.

---

[18]D. Stoll, ed., *Magazines for Kids and Teens,* Rev. ed. (Glassboro, NJ: Educational Press of America and Newark, DE: International Reading Association, 1997).

**Teaching Suggestions**

- Choose a specific magazine and devise a guided reading experience designed to show students the features of the magazine: how it is organized, the table of contents, the variety of articles, and so on. Students can then choose an article to read and share what they discovered with the rest of the group.
- Some magazines, such as *Zoobooks,* devote an entire issue to a given topic such as elephants. Provide a copy of the magazine for each student in the group. Show them how to skim the text, looking for facts about elephants. Then have students do the same, searching for three facts about elephants that they want to share with others in the group. As they report their findings, make a chart that shows their ideas.

## *Newspapers*

### Description

Newspapers are collections of informational articles, advertisements, comics, and features that are written to inform the public about current events. Most are published daily, although some specifically written for classroom use are published weekly.

### Examples

- *Weekly Reader* (preschool–grade 6)
- *Scholastic News* (grades 1–6)
- Kids page or mini-page from local newspaper (grades 1–3)
- Local newspaper (grades 3–6)

### Why Use Them?

Newspapers provide a wealth of reading material in everyday life. They supply information about current events at several levels. Like other reading materials, however, they are written with a specific format. Readers must learn how a newspaper is written so that they can find the information they need and successfully negotiate their way through it without feeling overwhelmed. Small group reading instruction is a perfect fit for this. Specific newspapers and articles can be used to show students the variety of texts that are found in newspapers and how to read each one. Students can also learn how to read articles looking for the questions that most articles address: who, what, when, where, why, and how. Reading newspapers also helps students increase their world knowledge of given topics—thus enhancing their reading comprehension of these same topics when they are encountered in other texts. Finally, using newspapers helps students to see themselves as "real-life" readers. They see others reading newspapers outside of school and begin to recognize that they can too.

### Teaching Suggestions

- Use the mini-page of the local newspaper to show students how it is organized. If the purpose of using the newspaper is to show students that articles focus on specific questions (who, what, when, where, why, how), list these key words on the board and then direct students to read a specific article searching for answers to these questions.
- As with other texts, news stories can present some challenging words for students to decipher. You may want to show students how to use context clues to

determine the meaning of an unknown word. Once you have modeled this, have students apply the strategy to an article they choose to read or one that you have chosen for them.

- Once students are familiar with the various parts of the paper, use it to teach critical thinking skills. For example, bring in different newspapers and have students read the same story as presented in the different papers. Students can discuss the headlines for the story and make up their own headlines using different voices—neutral, positive, or negative. You can also talk about how the tone of the headline influences readers.

- Discuss with students the differences between editorials and regular news stories. Then have them compare different editorials with news stories on the same topic. Next, invite students to discuss whether the news was adequately explained and whether the editor expressed his or her views. Finally, have students write their own editorials about a story they have been following for a number of days.

- Encourage children to be reporters and to cover school or community events. They can write about the events as both news stories and editorials.

## *Real-Life Texts*

### Description

There are texts all around us in real life.[19] These include all print that children find in the world around them: packaging, advertising, corporate logos, notices, and other types of text. While all the types of text in previous sections of this chapter are certainly found in the real world, teachers should also make sure their rooms are well-stocked with all types of print students find around them in the world. These types of materials are not intentionally designed for classroom purposes, but they can certainly be used for instruction nonetheless. We classify real-life texts into the following categories: labels, games and entertainment, music, advertisements, signs, financial transactions, manuals, official documents, books (beyond those already discussed), correspondence, tables, schedules, calendars, maps, diagrams, charts, and lists.

### Examples[20]

*Labels*

1. Product name
2. Ingredients
3. Safety cautions
4. Directions for use
5. Company information
6. Approvals
7. Nutritional information
8. Medical

*Entertainment*

9. Board games and card games (traditional)
10. Instructions (see Rules and Procedures in manuals)

11. Trading-card games (*Pokemon, YuGiOh, Magic*)
12. Sports cards
13. Restaurant menus

*Music*

14. Lyrics from songs
15. CD inserts
16. List of song titles (from CDs, etc.)
17. Sheet music, with and without lyrics

*Advertisements*

18. Magazine and newspaper advertisements
19. Want ads

(*continued*)

---

[19]M. Opitz and M. Ford, *Books and Beyond: New Ways to Reach Readers* (Portsmouth, NH: Heinemann, 2006). J. Erekson, "What counts as reading?" Unpublished document (2009).

[20]Ibid.

(continued)

20. Billboards
21. Pull-out ad sections in newspapers and magazines
22. Catalogs
23. Brochures
24. Dot com web sites (commercial ads)
25. Web banners
26. Posters
27. Flyers
28. Announcement/invitation
29. Bumper stickers
30. Logos
31. Slogans
32. Banners
33. Buttons
34. T-shirts, sweatshirts, hats
35. Balloons

*Signs*

36. Words only
37. Picture plus words
38. Picture only

*Financial Transactions*

39. Receipts
40. Checks
41. Bills
42. Charge card slips
43. Online receipts
44. Shipping and handling charts
45. Coupons

*Manuals*

46. How-to books or sheets
    a. Assemble or install
    b. Diagnostics or schematics
    c. Repair and maintenance
    d. Make something work
47. Rules and procedures
48. Recipes
49. Handbook (for car, stereo, camera, appliances, video games)

*Official Documents*

50. Legal documents
51. Property documents (titles, deeds, permits)

52. Certificates of birth, death, marriage
53. Church records (such as baptisms, marriages)
54. Application forms
55. Grave stones

*Books*

56. Comic books
57. Comic strip collections
58. Photojournalism
59. Coffee table books

*Correspondence*

60. Informal personal letters
61. Formal business letters
62. Postcards
63. E-mail
64. Text messaging/instant messaging
65. Informal notes
66. Formal notes and messages
67. Giving directions

*Tables, Schedules, Calendars*

68. Date books and planners (daily, weekly, monthly, yearly formats)
69. Schedules of events
70. Regular schedules (such as air, train, bus)
71. Score sheets
72. Tally sheets
73. Weather reports
74. Stock tables

*Visuals*

75. Maps (e.g., distribution, topographical, globe)
76. Diagrams (e.g., flow chart, mind web, labeled parts)
77. Charts (e.g., raw data, bar graph, scatter plot)
78. Lists (e.g., grocery list, to do list)

**Why Use Them?**

Real-life texts are helpful for reaching students who need a motivation boost. Many struggling readers have developed attitudes about typical classroom types of texts that create a wall, blocking their success. Certain real-life texts will enable readers to make better use of their subject knowledge, background experiences, and technical vocabulary, leading to greater success with reading. They may not view these texts as "reading" and so past habits of thought may not get in the way as much. Since these types of texts are well outside the realm of textbooks, tests, and text leveling systems, when students read real-life texts, they are likely to perceive the reading as authentic. Also, each type of text above is written with a different structure and format. This helps students apply skills and strategies in flexible ways, encouraging transfer of school knowledge to the world outside the classroom. Using these types of text will help children expand their definition of what it means to be a reader, and makes these types of texts both acceptable and accessible during the school day.

### Teaching Suggestions[21]

1. Add real-life texts to existing literacy centers. For example, adding catalogs and ads to a math corner or applications and forms to a writing center often leads to additional reading and writing opportunities.
2. Entire portable learning stations can be developed around real-life materials. Collections can be placed in tubs that students can take back to their desks to engage in explorations. Using one tub, students might sort and plan a shopping trip using coupons and grocery store ads. Using another, students might plan out a vacation using travel brochures and other travel information in the tub.

### *Electronic Texts*

#### Description
Electronic texts are any texts that exist in electronic digital environments. These texts are primarily accessible through computers and available on the Internet. Kamil, Kim, and Lane[22] classify electronic text in two primary categories. First is any text found on the computer screen (e-mail messages, help screens, instructions). They point out that this text exists digitally and can be transmitted from one computer to another. Except for navigational differences, readers often approach this text in much the same way as they do print formats. The second category is any electronic text augmented by hyperlinks, hypertext, or hypermedia. These more complicated augmented texts are most often found on the Internet.

#### Examples
In addition to the web sites cited at the end of this chapter, we recommend the following five sites that are primarily designed for children:

Yahooligans!, http://yahooligans.yahoo.com/, is a web guide for children. As a search engine, it searches for specific information that students request.

Children's Reading Room, http://unmuseum.mus.pa.us/crr/, provides a selection of stories that children can download and print. Stories vary in length.

PBS Kids, http://pbskids.org/. Arthur, Barney, and Clifford are but a few of the PBS Kids shows this site features. *Martha Speaks, Wordworld,* and *Between the*

---

[21]M. Opitz and M. Ford, *Books and Beyond: New Ways to Reach Readers* (Portsmouth, NH: Heinemann, 2006).

[22]M. L. Kamil, H. S. Kim, and D. Lane, "Electronic Text in the Classroom," in *The Texts in Elementary Classrooms,* eds. J. V. Hoffman and D. L. Schallert (Mahwah, NJ: Lawrence Erlbaum Associates, 2004), pp. 157–193.

*Lions* are programs tightly focused on reading and writing. Children can access stories, games, music, video, and even coloring forms related to different story characters.

Children's Storybooks Online: Stories for Kids of All Ages, http://www.magickeys .com/books, offers free storybooks for young and older children Many of the books are illustrated. The site also features riddles, puzzles, and information about how to publish a book.

RIF Reading Planet, http://rif.org/readingplanet/, features, among other activities, story maker which enables children to personalize stories by using their own words to add to the story. Children can also replace some words in the story and can write their own endings.

### Why Use Them?

As with the other types of texts we showcase in this chapter, there are several reasons for using electronic texts with all readers, but especially with those who find reading challenging and therefore uninteresting. First, electronic texts are often perceived as something totally removed from the school reading materials (e.g., textbooks, novels, anthologies) with which these children have not had much success. Electronic texts are seen as attractive, as something new and different. Second, electronic texts have features that can make reading easier. Text is easily searchable—the computer will scan and skim more effectively than a reader can. It is easily modified. Software exists to reformat cybertexts into more viewer friendly texts for different purposes.[23]

Electronic texts with hypermedia links can actually provide support for comprehension.[24] Imagine not understanding a word, concept, or idea you are reading about and then being able to click on the screen. The photo or video that comes up will provide the clarification you need to better understand the passage. Audio recordings found in many electronic texts allow children who rely on their auditory processes to receive this support. One site that provides several texts for students to read with auditory and visual support is http://starfall.com.

Third, electronic texts exist on an endless number of topics.[25] Teachers can easily find more than one topic they can use to entice their most difficult-to-reach readers.

### Teaching Suggestions

1. Students can independently (or with a partner) locate information related to a specific topic with the expectation that they will then share their findings with others.
2. Students can visit preapproved web sites of their choosing and read about topics of interest. With an instructional focus, cybertexts can be the resources independently

---

[23]D. J. Leu, C. K. Kinzer, J. Coiro, and D. Cammack, "Toward a Theory of New Literacies Emerging from the Internet and Other Information and Communication Technology," in *Theoretical Models and Processes of Reading,* 5th ed., eds. R. Rudell and N. Unrau (Newark, DE: International Reading Association, 2004). M. McKenna, L. Labbo, and D. Reinking, "Effective Use of Technology in Literacy Instruction," in *Best Practices in Literacy Instruction,* 2nd ed., eds. L. Morrow, L. Gambrell, and M. Pressley (New York: Guilford, 2003), pp. 307–331.

[24]J. Coiro, J., "Reading Comprehension on the Internet: Expanding Our Understanding of Reading Comprehension to Encompass New Literacies," *The Reading Teacher* 56 (2003): 458–464.

[25]Leu, D. Jr., "Internet Workshop: Making Time for Literacy," *Reading Online,* 2002, www.readingonline .org (accessed February 17, 2006).

consulted as students work on research and inquiry projects. The Internet Workshop is a fitting example.[26] Leu offers these four procedures:

a.  Locate an appropriate site and set a bookmark for the location. You might consider visiting *Ask Jeeves for Kids,* a directory and a search engine. Type in your question and it will find the site that best answers the question.

b.  Design the activity, making sure students need to use the site in order to complete it.

c.  Provide students with time to complete the activity.

d.  Provide time for students to share their discoveries.

Leu notes that once students are familiar with this format, they can then conduct their own inquiry projects.

## REVISITING THE OPENING SCENARIO

Now that you have read the chapter, how would you respond to parents about why Mr. Hall has students read from so many different kinds of texts? What are they learning from reading a variety of texts that they might not get from reading just a single type?

## AUTHORS' SUMMARY

In this chapter, we discussed the value of providing children with many opportunities to read. We also provided several reasons for teaching children to read a variety of texts and emphasized that children need to develop a love of reading from a very young age. We explained many different types of texts that can be used to help children develop this love of reading and to help children who are struggling with learning to read. Our explanation included the type of text, reasons for using the given type of text, examples, and teaching suggestions. The major point of the chapter is that knowledgeable teachers are aware of many different kinds of printed material, including books but going well beyond them, too, when planning effective instruction for reading improvement.

## SUGGESTIONS FOR THOUGHT QUESTIONS AND ACTIVITIES

1.  You are thinking about the open house that is about to take place at your school and want to make sure that your students' parents fully understand the importance of reading both in and out of school. To help get this point across, you have decided to provide parents with some suggested children's literature titles that they can use at home. Construct the list.

2.  Your principal just discovered that you are a believer in using many different texts to help children read. Although the idea makes sense to her, she doesn't fully understand how first-graders can read informational texts because she thinks they are way too hard for them. Besides, she thinks that children in first grade "learn to read" and it is only after doing so that they can "read to learn." What will you say to her?

3.  Explain how you would use one of the web sites mentioned in the chapter as a part of your reading diagnosis and improvement program.

4.  Construct a text set based on one topic you will be teaching. Include five or more different types of text. Keep your students in mind as you construct this text set. Which students will read which texts? How will the texts be assigned? Will you allow for student choice?

[26]Ibid.

# WEB SITES

http://www.literacymatters.org/content/text/intro.htm

This site provides information for teachers, parents, and students about text features and the importance of attending to the various text structures when reading. To aid teachers, the authors discuss explicit instruction, scaffolding instruction, modeling, think aloud strategies, questioning, and so on.

http://readingrockets.org/articles/16310

This link goes directly to an article addressing how teachers can make textbooks accessible and usable for students with learning disabilities. Perfect for new teachers and parents who are new to the disability arena or those searching for valuable resources, this article describes available software, e-text web sites and a critique of these sources, school system resources, the National Instructional Materials Accessibility Standard (NIMAS), and the IEP process.

# SELECTED BIBLIOGRAPHY

Allen, Vernon L. *Children as Teachers: Theory and Research on Tutoring.* New York: Academic Press, 1976.

Allington, Richard. *What Really Matters for Struggling Readers,* 2nd ed. Boston: Allyn and Bacon, 2005.

Almasi, J. F., M. G. McKeown, and I. L. Beck. "The Return of Engaged Reading in Classroom Discussions of Literature." *Journal of Literary Research* 28 (1996): 107–146.

Burgstahler, S., and L. Utterback. *New Kids on the Net: Internet Activities in Elementary Language Arts.* Boston: Allyn and Bacon, 2000.

Chandler-Olcott, K., and D. Mahar. "Considering Genre in the Digital Literacy Classroom." *Reading Online.* 2001. www.readingonline.org (accessed February 17, 2006).

Charles, C. M. *Individualizing Instruction,* 2nd ed. St Louis: C.V. Mosby, 1980.

Cohen, E. *Designing Groupwork: Strategies for the Heterogeneous Classroom.* New York: Teachers College Press, 1994.

Coiro, J. "Reading Comprehension on the Internet: Expanding Our Understanding of Reading Comprehension to Encompass New Literacies." *The Reading Teacher* 56 (2003): 458–464.

El-Hindi, A. "Beyond Classroom Boundaries: Constructivist Teaching with the Internet." *The Reading Teacher* 51(1998): 694–700.

Erekson, J. "What counts as reading?" Unpublished document, 2009.

Ford, M., and M. Opitz. "Using Centers to Engage Children During Guided Reading Time: Intensifying Learning Experiences Away from the Teacher." *The Reading Teacher* 55 (2002): 710–717.

Fresch, Mary Jo, and Peggy Harkins. *The Power of Picture Books.* Urbana, IL: National Council of Teachers of English, 2009.

Gates, Arthur I. *New Methods in Primary Reading.* New York: Teachers' College Press, 1928.

Geisert, Paul G., and Mynga K. Futrell. *Teachers, Computers, and Curriculum: Microcomputers in the Classroom,* 3rd ed. Boston: Allyn and Bacon, 2000.

Goldman, S. R., and J. A. Rakestraw Jr. "Structural Aspects of Constructing Meaning from Text." In *Handbook of Reading Research,* Volume III, edited by M. L. Kamil, P. B. Mosenthal, P. D. Pearson, and R. Barr, pp. 311–335. Mahwah, NJ: Erlbaum, 2000.

Harris, T., and R. Hodges, eds. *The Literacy Dictionary.* Newark, DE: International Reading Association, 1995.

Hiebert, Elfrieda H. *Reading More, Reading Better.* New York: Guilford Press, 2009.

Hiebert, Elfrienda H., and Misty Sailors. *Finding the Right Texts.* New York: Guilford Press, 2009.

International Reading Association. "Integrating Literacy and Technology in the Curriculum: A Position Statement." 2001. http://www.reading.org/positions/technology.html (accessed February 21, 2006).

Jackobson, Julie, et al. "Cross-Age Tutoring: A Literacy Improvement Approach for Struggling Adolescent Readers." *Journal of Adolescent & Adult Literacy* 44 (March, 2001): 528–536.

Kamil, M. L., H. S. Kim, and D. Lane. "Electronic Text in the Classroom." In *The Texts in Elementary Classrooms,* edited by J. V. Hoffman and D. L. Schallert, 157–193. Mahwah, NJ: Lawrence Erlbaum Associates, 2004.

Kreul, M. "Connecting Technology and Literacy: A Journey from 'How Do I Turn on This Computer?' to 'My Class Is Blogging Their Book Reviews for Literature Circles'." In *Innovative Approaches to Literacy Education: Using the Internet to Support New Literacies,* edited by R. A. Karchmer, M. H. Mallette, J. Kara-Soteriou, and

D. J. Leu, 138–156. Newark, DE: International Reading Association, 2005.

Leu, D. Jr. "Internet Workshop: Making Time for Literacy." *Reading Online* (2002). www.readingonline.org (accessed February 17, 2006).

Leu, D. Jr., C. K. Kinzer, J. Coiro, and D. Cammack. "Toward a Theory of New Literacies Emerging from the Internet and Other Information and Communication Technology." In *Theoretical Models and Processes of Reading,* 5th ed., edited by R. Rudell and N. Unrau. Newark, DE: International Reading Association, 2004.

Leu, D. Jr., M. H. Mallette, R. A. Karchmer, and J. Kara-Soteriou. "Contextualizing the New Literacies of Information and Communication Technologies in Theory, Research and Practice." In *Innovative Approaches to Literacy Education: Using the Internet to Support New Literacies,* edited by R. A. Karchmer, M. H. Mallette, J. Kara-Soteriou, and D. J. Leu, 1–10. Newark, DE: International Reading Association, 2005.

Malloy, J. A., and L. B. Gambrell. "Approaching the Unavoidable: Literacy Instruction and the Internet." *The Reading Teacher* 59 (2006): 482–484.

McKenna, M., D. Reinking, and L. Labbo. "Using Talking Books with Reading-Disabled Students." *Reading and Writing Quarterly* 13 (1997): 185–190.

McKenna, M., L. Labbo, and D. Reinking. "Effective Use of Technology in Literacy Instruction." In *Best Practices in Literacy Instruction,* 2nd ed., edited by L. Morrow, L. Gambrell, and M. Pressley, 307–331. New York: Guilford, 2003.

Mesmer, Heidi Anne E. *Tools for Matching Readers to Texts.* New York: The Guilford Press, 2008.

Opitz, Michael F. *Getting the Most from Predictable Books.* New York: Scholastic, 1995.

Opitz, Michael F. *Learning Centers: Getting Them Started, Keeping Them Going.* New York: Scholastic, 1994.

Opitz, Michael F., and Michael P. Ford. *Reaching Readers.* Portsmouth, NH: Heinemann, 2006.

Opitz, Michael F., and Michael P. Ford. *Books and Beyond: New Ways to Reach Readers.* Portsmouth, NH: Heinemann, 2007.

Peterson, Barbara. "Selecting Books for Beginning Readers." In *Bridges to Literacy,* edited by D. DeFord, C. Lyons, and G. Pinnel. Portsmouth, NH: Heinemann, 2001.

Reeves, Harriet Ramsey. "Individual Conferences—Diagnostic Tools." *The Reading Teacher* 24 (February, 1971): 411–415.

Solomon, G. "Digital Equity: It's Not Just About Access Anymore." *Technology and Learning* 22 (2002) : 18– 26.

Stead, Tony. *Good Choice! Supporting Independent Reading and Response K–6.* Portland, ME: Stenhouse, 2009.

Szymusiak, Karen, Franki Sibberson, and Lisa Koch. *Beyond Leveled Books: Supporting Early and Transitional Readers in Grades K–5.* Portland, ME: Stenhouse, 2008.

Wedwick, Linda, and Jessica Ann Wutz. *Bookmatch: How to Scaffold Student Book Selection for Independent Reading.* Newark, DE: International Reading Association, 2008.

Wooten, Deborah, and Bernice E. Cullinan. *Children's Literature in the Reading Program.* Newark, DE: International Reading Association, 2009.

## CHILDREN'S LITERATURE CITED

Adler, David. *Cam Jansen: The Catnapping Mystery.* New York: Putnam, 2005.

Alborough, Jez. *Hug.* Somerville, MA: Candlewick, 2009.

Arnold, Katya. *Elephants Can Paint, Too.* New York: Simon & Schuster, 2005.

Bardhan-Quallen, Sudipta. *Flying Eagle.* Watertown, MA: Charlesbridge, 2009.

Carr, Jan. *Dappled Apples.* New York: Holiday House, 2001.

Carter, David. *One Red Dot.* New York: Simon & Schuster, 2005.

Chambers, Veronica. *Celia Cruz, Queen of Salsa.* New York: Penguin, 2005.

Collicutt, Paul. *This Rocket.* New York: Farrar, Straus, & Giroux, 2005.

Creech, Sharon. *Walk Two Moons.* New York: HarperCollins, 1996.

Crelin, Bob. *Faces of the Moon.* Watertown, MA: Charlesbridge, 2009.

Curlee, Lynn. *Into the Ice: The Story of Arctic Exploration.* Boston, MA: Houghton Mifflin, 1998.

Curtis, Christopher Paul. *Bud, Not Buddy.* New York: Random House, 2004.

Erickson, John. *Hank, the Cowdog: The Secret Laundry Monster Files.* New York: Viking, 2002.

Florian, Douglas. *Dinothesaurus.* New York: Atheneum, 2009.

Florian, Douglas. *In the Swim.* San Diego: Harcourt, 1997.

Gaiman, Neil. *The Graveyard Book.* New York: HarperCollins, 2008.

George, Margaret, and Christopher Murphy. *Lucille Lost.* New York, Viking, 2006.

Giovanni, Nikki. *Rosa.* New York: Henry Holt, 2005.

Graber, Janet. *Muktar & the Camels.* New York: Henry Holt, 2009.

Greenburg, Dan. *The Boy Who Cried Big Foot (Zack Files).* New York: Grosset & Dunlap, 2000.

Hall, Zoe. *The Apple Pie Tree.* New York: Scholastic, 1996.

Hegamin, Cozbi. *Most Loved in All the World.* Boston: Houghton Mifflin, 2009.

Hirschmann, Kris. *Big World, Small World (Planet Earth series).* New York: Scholastic, 2009.

Hopkins, Lee Bennett. *School Supplies: A Book of Poems.* New York: Simon & Schuster, 1996.

Hopkins, Lee Bennett. *Sky Magic.* New York: Penguin, 2009.

Isadora, Rachel. *Hansel and Gretel.* New York: G. P. Putnam's Sons, 2009.

Janeczco, Paul. *A Foot in the Mouth: Poems to Speak, Sing, & Shout.* Somerville, MA: Candlewick, 2009.

Karas, G. Brian. *On Earth.* New York: Putnam, 2005.

Kinney, Jeff. *The Last Straw (Diary of a Wimpy Kid series).* New York: Abrams, 2009.

Lobel, Arnold. *Days with Frog and Toad.* New York: HarperCollins, 1984.

Lowry, Lois. *The Giver.* New York: Random House, 2002.

Lupica, Mike. *Two Minute Drill (Comeback Kids series).* New York: Puffin, 2007.

Marzollo, Jean. *In 1776.* New York: Scholastic, 1994.

Melmed, Laura. *Heart of Texas.* New York: HarperCollins, 2009.

Miller, William. *Rend Part Jazz.* New York: Lee & Low, 2001.

Mills, Claudia. *Gus and Grandpa.* New York: Farrar, Straus, & Giroux, 1997.

Minarak, Else. *Little Bear.* New York: HarperCollins, 1957.

Mugford, Simon. *Sharks and Other Dangers of the Deep.* New York: St. Martin's Press, 2005.

Naylor, Phyllis. *Shiloh.* New York: Aladdin, 2000.

Nishizuka, Koko. *The Beckoning Cat.* New York: Holiday House, 2009.

Polacco, Patricia. *Mommies Say Shhh!* New York: Philomel, 2005.

Prosek, James. *Bird, Butterfly, Eel.* New York: Simon & Schuster, 2009.

Reilly-Giff, Patricia. *Meet the Polk Street Kids.* New York: Doubleday, 1988.

Robbins, Ken. *Apples.* New York: Simon & Schuster, 2002.

Rockwell, Anne. *Good Morning, Digger.* New York: Viking, 2005.

Ross, Stewart. *Moon: Science, History, and Mystery.* New York: Scholastic, 2009.

Rowling, J.K. *Harry Potter and the Sorcerer's Stone.* New York: Scholastic, 1996.

Ryder, Joanne. *Panda Kindergarten.* New York: HarperCollins, 2009.

Rylant, Cynthia. *Henry and Mudge (series).* New York: Aladdin, 1996.

Rylant, Cynthia. *Missing May.* New York: Yearling, 2003.

Sachar, Louis. *Holes.* New York: Farrar, Straus, & Giroux, 2008.

Say, Allen. *Erika-San.* Boston: Houghton Mifflin Harcourt, 2009.

Shea, Pegi Deitz. *Liberty Rising: The Story of the Statue of Liberty.* New York: Henry Holt, 2005.

Smalls, Irene. *My Nana and Me.* New York: Little, Brown, 2005.

Stephens, Sarah Hines and Bethany Mann. *Show Off: How to Do Absolutely Everything One Step at a Time.* San Francisco, CA: Candlewick, 2009.

Stevenson, Robert Louis. *Block City.* New York: Simon & Schuster, 2005.

Stilton, Geronimo. *Geronimo Stilton.* New York: Scholastic, 2004.

Sturges, Philemon. *Down to the Sea in Ships.* New York: Putnam, 2005.

Stuve-Bodeen, Stephanie. *Babu's Song.* New York: Lee & Low, 2003.

Talbott, Hudson. *River of Dreams—Story of the Hudson River.* New York: G. P. Putnam's Sons, 2009.

Tatham, Betty. *Baby Sea Otters.* New York: Henry Holt, 2005.

Usher, M. D. *Wise Guy: The Life and Philosophy of Socrates.* New York: Farrar, Straus, & Giroux, 2005.

Weinstein, Ellen. *Everywhere the Cow Says Moo.* Honesdale, PA: Boyds Mills, 2008.

Weitzman, David. *A Subway for New York.* New York: Farrar, Straus, & Giroux, 2005.

West, Tracey. *Incredible Reptiles (Planet Earth series).* New York: Scholastic, 2009.

Whitman, Walt. *When I Heard the Learn'd Astronomer.* New York: Simon & Schuster, 2004.

Willems, Mo. *There Is a Bird on Your Head (Elephant & Piggie series).* New York: Hyperion, 2007.

Wood, Audrey. *The Deep Blue Sea: A Book of Colors.* New York: Scholastic, 2005.

Wood, Audrey. *The Napping House.* Boston: Houghton Mifflin Harcourt, 2009.

Wormell, Mary. *Why Not?* New York: Farrar, Straus, & Giroux, 2000.

Yolen, Jane. *Meow: Cat Stories from Around the World.* New York: HarperCollins, 2005.

Yolen, Jane. *The Scarecrow's Dance.* New York: Simon & Schuster, 2009.

Young, Ed. *Beyond the Great Mountains: A Visual Poem About China.* San Francisco: Chronicle, 2005.

PEARSON
# myeducationlab

Now go to Topic 11: "Reading Difficulties and Intervention Strategies" and Topic 9: "Reading Comprehension" in MyEducationLab (www.myeducationlab.com) for your course, where you can:

- Find learning outcomes for "Reading Difficulties and Intervention Strategies" and "Reading Comprehension" along with national standards that connect to these outcomes.
- Complete Assignments and Activities that can help you more deeply understand the chapter content.
- Examine challenging situations and cases presented in the IRIS Center Resources.
- Access video clips of CCSSO National Teacher of the Year award winners responding to the question, "Why Do I Teach?" in the Teacher Talk section.
- Apply and practice your understanding of the core teaching skills identified in the chapter with Building Teaching Skills and Dispositions learning units.

# 10

## Helping Children Comprehend

**CHAPTER OUTLINE**

- Scenario: Alan's Comprehension
- Building Background about Comprehension
- Oral Reading, Fluency, and Reading Comprehension
- Comprehension Skills
- Comprehension Strategies
- Assessing Comprehension
- Teaching Comprehension
- Revisiting the Opening Scenario

# SCENARIO: ALAN'S COMPREHENSION

*Thinking about it*

Alan is a fifth-grader who scored at a 4.2 level on the reading comprehension subtest of the *California Achievement Tests* in the fall of this school year. Observing Alan when he is reading many different kinds of texts in many different contexts, Ms. Mills sees that Alan appears able to comprehend and recall information that is mentioned in the texts. She also notices that he appears to need help with higher-level comprehension skills such as making inferences. She decides to review the specific items on the reading comprehension subtest to see if Alan's comprehension performance coincides with her observations and discovers that it does. Her analysis shows that Alan answered all literal-level questions accurately but answered higher-level comprehension questions incorrectly. Using the results of her observations and test item analysis, Ms. Mills concludes that literal-level comprehension is Alan's strength. What he needs is help in learning how to use higher-order thinking skills such as inferring to comprehend beyond the literal level.

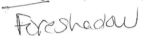

*Foreshadow*

## CHAPTER OBJECTIVES

*good writer makes details meaningful*

After reading the chapter, you should be able to:

- Discuss how listening comprehension relates to reading comprehension.
- Explain what is meant by explicit instruction in comprehension.
- Explain the difference between comprehension skills and comprehension strategies.
- Explain how teachers can help students to develop various comprehension skills and strategies.
- Discuss different ways to assess comprehension.

In this chapter we provide teachers with background information about reading comprehension. We then offer specific ways to assess reading comprehension. Finally, we provide teaching strategies that will enable teachers to design suitable instruction to enhance students' reading comprehension.

## BUILDING BACKGROUND ABOUT COMPREHENSION

### COMPREHENSION

**Comprehension**
Understanding; the effort and process used to get the meaning of something.

Comprehension happens in a reader's mind, which means it cannot be observed or measured directly. We can only infer from overt behavior that someone "understands." *Webster's Third New International Dictionary* defines *comprehension* as "the act or action of grasping (as an act or process) with the intellect," and *intellect* is defined as "the capacity for rational or intelligent thought especially when highly developed." The more intelligent an individual is, the more able he or she is to comprehend. What may not be so obvious is that people who have difficulty understanding may have this difficulty because they have not had experiences that require a variety of levels of thinking; thus, they may not have learned how to comprehend.

### LISTENING COMPREHENSION

To be able to recognize expressions in print, students must have heard these phrases in the past; they must be in the students' listening vocabulary. Reading comprehension depends on comprehension of spoken language. Students who are sensitive to the

Go to the Assignments and Activities section of Topic 9: Reading Comprehension in the MyEducationLab for your course and complete the activity entitled "What is Reading Comprehension?" As you watch the video and answer the accompanying questions, consider the differences between word identification and comprehension, and consider how much time is spent on each.

**Listening vocabulary**
The words one knows the meaning of when they are said aloud.

arrangement of words in oral language are more sensitive to the same idea in written language. Strong listening comprehension also involves speaking, since children figure oral language out not by mimicry, but rather by testing out their ideas in speech situations (Kucer, 2009). Through listening and speaking, children learn many expressions they will eventually see in print. Listening and speaking take place all the time. Teachers orally explain word meanings and discuss what the text says. Students listen to other children read orally, talk about books, and explain their contents. Participation in any language-rich activities, such as conversation or viewing media with dialog, will enhance children's listening comprehension.

Many students prefer to listen to read-alouds rather than to read independently. These children gain more comprehension and retention from listening because of the important added cues they receive from the speaker, such as stress given to words or phrases and facial expressions.[1] Other children prefer to read independently because they can set their own rate of reading for maximum comprehension and retention. Both listening and reading are important and the teacher's goal should be to get students to feel comfortable in both situations.

Sometimes, a student can understand a passage when it is read orally, but cannot understand it when reading it alone. This indicates that the words are in the student's *listening vocabulary* but that the student may not have gained the skills necessary for understanding their written forms.

A person who does not do well in listening comprehension skills will usually not do well in reading comprehension skills. Help in one area usually enhances the other because both listening and reading contain some important similar skills,[2] as researchers going as far back as the 1930s have noted. For example, an investigation made in 1936 found that children who did poorly in comprehension through listening also did poorly in reading comprehension.[3] Research in 1955 on the relationship between reading and listening found that practice in listening for detail will produce a significant gain in reading for the same purpose.[4] Others have also found that training in listening comprehension skills will produce significant gains in reading comprehension[5] and that reading and listening involve similar thinking skills.[6]

Findings from a number of other studies strongly support the link between reading and listening comprehension. In one such study, a researcher asked whether some good decoders in reading are poor comprehenders because of an overemphasis on word accuracy when decoding or because of a lack of listening comprehension; that is, the decoders are "word callers" who do not have the words in their listening vocabulary. The results of the study suggest that the students' "listening vocabulary was not better than their reading comprehension. So, decoding does not seem to distract or otherwise interfere with comprehension among children whose decoding skills are well developed.

[1]Robert Ruddell, "Oral Language and the Development of Other Language Skills," *Elementary English* 43 (May, 1966): 489–498.

[2]Thomas Jolly, "Listen My Children and You Shall Read," *Language Arts* 57 (February, 1980): 214–217.

[3]William E. Young, "The Relation of Reading Comprehension and Retention to Hearing Comprehension and Retention," *Journal of Experimental Education* 5 (September, 1936): 30–39.

[4]Annette P. Kelty, "An Experimental Study to Determine the Effect of Listening for Certain Purposes upon Achievement in Reading for Those Purposes," *Abstracts of Field Studies for the Degree of Doctor of Education* 15 (Greeley: Colorado State College of Education, 1955): 82–95.

[5]Sybil M. Hoffman, "The Effect of a Listening Skills Program on the Reading Comprehension of Fourth Grade Students," Ph.D. dissertation, Walden University, 1978. Janice A. Dole and Virginia Simon Feldman, "The Development and Validation of a Listening Comprehension Test as a Predictor of Reading Comprehension: Preliminary Results," *Educational Research Quarterly* 9 (1984–1985): 40–46.

[6]Thomas Sticht et al., *Auding and Reading: A Developmental Model* (Alexandria, VA.: Human Resources Research Organization, 1974). Walter Kintsch and Ely Kozminsky, "Summarizing Stories After Reading and Listening," *Journal of Educational Psychology* 69 (1977): 491–499.

Go to the Assignments and Activities section of Topic 9: Reading Comprehension in the MyEducationLab for your course and complete the activity entitled "Dimensions of Comprehension." As you watch the video and answer the accompanying questions, consider how teachers can use knowledge about these dimensions to help students succeed.

[Instead, according to the investigator] once a child has become a good decoder, differences in reading ability will reflect differences in listening ability."[7]

Although there are many common factors involved in the decoding of reading and listening—which would account for the relationship between the two areas—listening and reading are, nonetheless, separated by unique factors. The most obvious is that listening calls for *hearing,* whereas reading calls for *seeing.* As previously stated, in the area of listening, the speakers are doing much of the interpretation for the listeners by their expressions, inflections, stresses, and pauses. Similarly, the listeners do not have to make the proper *grapheme (letter)–phoneme (sound) correspondences* because these have already been done for them by the speakers. It is possible for students to achieve excellent listening comprehension but not to do as well in reading comprehension.

Readers must identify words and organize them into phrases and sentences to build basic meaning. Readers must also be able to build a larger meaning for a whole text, to determine the shades of meaning implied by the words, to recognize any special figures of speech, and to synthesize the ideas expressed in a text.

In Table 10.1 we show some of the similarities between listening comprehension skills and reading comprehension skills. We also show the different levels of listening and offer a brief definition of each level.

## READING COMPREHENSION

*Reading comprehension* is a complex intellectual process involving a number of abilities. The two major abilities involve knowing word meanings and using verbal reasoning. Without word meanings and verbal reasoning, there would be no reading comprehension; and without reading comprehension, there is no reading. Most people would agree with these statements; however, disagreement surfaces when we ask, "How does an individual achieve comprehension while reading?" In 1917, Edward Thorndike put forth his statement that "reading is a very elaborate procedure, involving a weighing of each of many elements in a sentence, their organization in the proper relations to one another, and the cooperation of many forces to determine final response."[8] He stated further that even the act of answering simple questions includes all the features characteristic of typical reasoning. Today investigators are still exploring reading comprehension in attempts to understand it better, and through the years many have expounded and expanded on Thorndike's theories.[9]

For more than a quarter of a century, research into the process of understanding has been influenced by the fields of psycholinguistics and cognitive psychology. As a result, terms such as *surface structure, deep structure, microstructure, macrostructure, semantic networks, schemata, story grammar, story structure,* and *metacognition* are used by authors who provide explanations about comprehension.

Although it is difficult to state definitively how people achieve comprehension while reading, researchers report that good comprehenders appear to have certain characteristics.[10] Good comprehenders are able to do inferential reasoning; they can state the main or central ideas of information; they can assimilate, categorize, compare, see

> **Reading comprehension**
>
> A complex intellectual process involving a number of abilities. The two major abilities involve knowing word meanings and reasoning with verbal concepts.

[7]Susan Dymock, "Reading But Not Understanding," *Journal of Reading* 37 (October, 1993): 90.

[8]Edward L. Thorndike, "Reading as Reasoning: A Study of Mistakes in Paragraph Reading," *Journal of Educational Psychology* 8, no. 6 (June, 1917): 323.

[9]Cathy Collins Black and Michael Pressley, eds., *Comprehension Instruction: Research-Based Best Practices* (New York: Guilford, 2002).

[10]Barbara M. Taylor, "Children's Memory for Expository Text After Reading," *Reading Research Quarterly* 15, no. 3 (1980): 399–411. B. J. Bartlett, "Top-Level Structure as an Organizational Strategy for Recall of Classroom Text," unpublished doctoral dissertation, Arizona State University, 1978. John P. Richards and Catherine W. Hatcher, "Interspersed Meaningful Learning Questions as Semantic Cues for Poor Comprehenders," *Reading Research Quarterly* 13, no. 4 (1977–1978): 551–552.

**TABLE 10.1    Comparison of Listening Comprehension and Reading Comprehension**

| Listening Levels | Listening Comprehension Skills | Reading Comprehension Skills |
|---|:---:|:---:|
| **Discriminative Listening:** Knowing which sounds to attend to and which to ignore; distinguishing verbal and nonverbal cues | | |
| • Phonological awareness | X | |
| • Vocal expression | X | |
| • Onomatopoeia | X | |
| **Precise Listening:** Paying attention and ascertaining details | | |
| • Associating words with meanings | X | X |
| • Deducing meaning of words from context | X | X |
| • Recalling details and sequences | X | X |
| • Following directions | X | X |
| • Recognizing multiple characters | X | X |
| **Strategic Listening:** Listening to gain understanding of the intended meaning of the message | | |
| • Connecting prior knowledge | X | X |
| • Summarizing | X | X |
| • Predicting | X | X |
| • Asking questions | X | X |
| • Inferencing | X | X |
| • Identifying main ideas | X | X |
| **Critical Listening:** Analyzing the message and evaluating it | | |
| • Recognizing emotive language | X | X |
| • Recognizing bias | X | X |
| • Distinguishing between fact and opinion | X | X |
| • Evaluating sources | X | X |
| • Detecting propaganda devices | X | X |
| **Appreciative Listening:** Listening to appreciate oral style | | |
| • Recognizing the power of language | X | X |
| • Appreciating oral interpretations | X | |
| • Understanding the power of imagination | X | X |

*Source:* Opitz, M., and M. Zbaracki. *Listen Hear! 25 Effective Listening Comprehension Strategies.* Portsmouth, NH: Heinemann, 2004.

relationships, analyze, synthesize, and evaluate information. They engage in meaningful learning by assimilating new material into concepts already existing in their cognitive structures;[11] that is, good comprehenders relate their new learning to what they already know. Also, good comprehenders are able to think beyond the information given; they are able to come up with new or alternate solutions. In addition, they seem to know what information to attend to and what to ignore. Clearly, people who have good strategies for processing information are able to bring more to and gain more from what they are reading or listening to than those who do not have these strategies. As we explain in Chapter 1, good comprehenders are active, purposeful, evaluative, thoughtful, strategic, persistent, and productive.

**Schema theory**
Deals with relations between prior knowledge and comprehension.

*Schema theory* deals with the relations between prior knowledge and comprehension. "According to schema theory, the reader's background knowledge serves as scaffolding to

[11]Richards and Hatcher, p. 552.

aid in encoding information from the text."[12] A person with more background knowledge for a given text will comprehend better than one with less background. Preparing readers for what they will be reading "by actively building topic knowledge prior to reading will facilitate learning from text."[13]

## READING COMPREHENSION TAXONOMIES

**Reading comprehension taxonomy**
A hierarchy of reading comprehension skills ranging from the more simplistic to the more complex ones; a classification of these skills.

A number of *reading comprehension taxonomies* exist, and many appear similar to one another. This similarity is not surprising. Usually, the individuals who develop a new taxonomy do so because they are unhappy with an existing one for some reason and want to improve on it. As a result, they may change category headings, but keep similar descriptions of the categories, or they may change the order of the hierarchy. Most of the existing taxonomies are adaptations in one way or another of Bloom's taxonomy of educational objectives in the cognitive domain, which is concerned with the thinking that students should achieve in any discipline. Bloom's taxonomy is based on an ordered set of objectives ranging from the more simplistic skills to the more complex ones. Bloom's objectives are cumulative in that each one includes the one preceding it.[14] And most taxonomies that have been evolved since are also cumulative.

In this text, we use an adaptation of Nila Banton Smith's model.[15] In her original model, she presented literal-level reading skills as requiring no thinking. We believe that literal-type questions do require thinking, even though it is a low-level type of thinking. In our model, we divide the comprehension skills into four categories. Each category is cumulative in building on the others. The four comprehension categories are (1) literal comprehension, (2) interpretation, (3) critical reading, and (4) creative reading.

Two cautions are in order here. Grade level and age have little to do with the taxonomy. That is, children of all ages can engage at all levels of the taxonomy. Second, we need to guard against a strict linear type of thinking. Our own teaching experiences have shown us that there are some children who are able to answer higher-level comprehension questions, yet have difficulty answering literal questions. We offer the taxonomy as a way of helping you to think about the variety of questions that need to be used to better ensure thoughtful learners.

### *Literal Comprehension*

**Literal comprehension**
The ability to obtain a low-level type of understanding by using only information that is explicitly stated.

*Literal comprehension* represents the ability to obtain a low-level type of understanding by using only explicitly stated information. This category requires a lower level of thinking skills than the other three categories. Answers to literal questions simply demand that the student recall from memory what the book says.

Although the ability to answer literal-type questions is considered a low-level type of thinking, it should *not* be construed that reading for details to gain facts that are explicitly stated is unimportant. A fund of knowledge is important and necessary in order to read texts in many different content areas. It is also the foundation for high-level thinking. If we want students to graduate to higher levels of thinking, we need to make sure that we ask more than just literal questions.

[12]Steven Stahl, Michael G. Jacobson, Charlotte E. Davis, and Robin L. Davis, "Prior Knowledge and Difficult Vocabulary in the Comprehension of Unfamiliar Text," *Reading Research Quarterly* 24 (Winter, 1989): 29.

[13]Ibid., p. 30.

[14]Benjamin Bloom, *Taxonomy of Educational Objectives Handbook 1: The Cognitive Domain* (New York: David McKay Co., 1956).

[15]Nila Banton Smith, "The Many Faces of Reading Comprehension," *The Reading Teacher* 23 (December, 1969): 249–259, 291.

### Interpretation

**Interpretation**
A reading level that demands a higher level of thinking ability because the material it involves is not directly stated in the text but only suggested or implied.

*Interpretation* is the next step in the hierarchy. This category demands a higher level of thinking because the questions require answers that are suggested or implied by the text, but are not directly stated. To answer questions at the interpretive level, readers must have problem-solving ability and be able to work at various levels of abstraction. Obviously, children with learning difficulties will have trouble working at this level, as well as in the next two categories.

The interpretive level is the one at which the most confusion exists when it comes to categorizing skills. The confusion concerns the term *inference. Inference* can be defined as something derived by reasoning; something that is not directly stated but suggested in the statement; a logical conclusion that is drawn from statements; a deduction; or an induction. From the definitions, we can see that inference is a broad reasoning skill and that there are many different kinds of inferences. All the reading skills in interpretation rely on the reader's ability to "infer" the answer in one way or another. However, by grouping all the interpretive reading skills under inference, "Some of the most distinctive and desirable skills would become smothered and obscured."[16]

Some of the reading skills that are usually grouped under interpretation are as follows:

- Determining word meanings from context.
- Finding main ideas.
- "Reading between the lines" or drawing inferences.[17]
- Drawing conclusions.
- Making generalizations.
- Recognizing cause-and-effect reasoning.
- Recognizing analogies.

### Critical Reading

**Critical reading**
A high-level reading skill that involves evaluation—making a personal judgment on the accuracy, value, and truthfulness of what is read.

*Critical reading* is at a higher level than the first two categories because it involves evaluation—the making of a personal judgment on the accuracy, value, and truthfulness of what is read. To be able to make judgments, a reader must be able to collect, interpret, apply, analyze, and synthesize the information. Critical reading includes skills such as the ability to differentiate between fact and opinion and between fantasy and reality, as well as the ability to discern propaganda techniques. Critical reading is related to critical listening because they both require critical thinking.

### Creative Reading

**Creative reading**
Uses divergent thinking skills to go beyond the literal comprehension, interpretation, and critical reading levels.

*Creative reading* uses divergent thinking skills to go beyond the literal comprehension, interpretation, and critical reading levels. In creative reading, the reader tries to come up with new or alternate solutions to those presented by the writer.

# ORAL READING, FLUENCY, AND READING COMPREHENSION

Oral reading is another consideration related to reading comprehension. Although it is true that we most often read silently, oral reading is necessary as well, especially as it relates to reading comprehension. Through oral reading, students can further develop

[16]Ibid., pp. 255–256.

[17]Although, as already stated, all the interpretive skills depend on the reader's ability to infer meanings, the specific skill of "reading between the lines" is the one that teachers usually refer to when they say they are teaching *inference.*

Go to the Assignments and Activities section of Topic 7: Fluency in the MyEducationLab for your course and complete the activity entitled "Fluency and Comprehension." As you watch the video and answer the accompanying questions, consider how you can tell when fluency is actually a demonstration of comprehension rather than just quick word reading.

reading comprehension strategies such as making connections, predicting, visualizing, questioning, using prior knowledge, monitoring while reading, summarizing, and making inferences. Some students may need to learn how to visualize when reading, whereas others may need to learn how to use signals provided by the author to convey an idea (i.e., typographical signals).

Another reason for using oral reading is to teach children how to read with fluency, which appears to be associated with competent reading. That is, according to the reported results of the 2002 National Assessment of Educational Progress (NAEP), "Students who can read text passages aloud accurately and fluently at an appropriate pace are more likely to understand what they are reading, both silently and orally."[18] However, evidence from the same study appears to indicate that many of those tested need additional instruction to enhance their ability to comprehend. Put another way, beautiful oral reading is not a guarantee of reading comprehension. So, although reading fluency (i.e., "an effortless, smooth, and coherent oral production of a given passage . . . in terms of phrasing, adherence to the author's syntax, and expressiveness"[19]) is something many competent readers display, we have to guard against thinking of it as the missing link that will help all students better comprehend. Instead, we need to focus on explicitly teaching reading comprehension and look for fluency as a sign that our instruction is working.

## GUIDING PRINCIPLES

At least three guiding principles must be adhered to for effective use of these and other oral reading strategies that are meant to enhance comprehension. First, the specific strategy must be identified. Do students need to learn to visualize? If so, induced imagery would be a good choice. Do students need to learn to attend to features such as enlarged print to see how doing so helps with understanding text? If so, then using a strategy such as "look for the signals"[20] would be a good choice.

Second, specific examples from children's literature selections should be provided. Using authentic examples is essential, for it shows children how authors actually use words and other typographic symbols to convey their ideas. Using children's literature also helps students connect the exercise with actual reading experiences. In other words, they can see the connection between the lesson and everyday reading.

Third, students need to be provided with meaningful practice. Students need time to actually use the skill that has just been taught as they read, making their internalization of it more likely. Novels such as *Maniac Magee* (Spinelli, 1990), *Dear Mr. Henshaw* (Cleary, 1983) and picture books such as *Alligator Baby* (Munsch, 1997) and *When Papa Snores* (Long, 2000) are just a few examples that teachers can use to provide students with meaningful practice. Students can be reminded to use visualizing or attend to typographical cues as they read throughout the day. Students might also be encouraged to share examples of what they discovered.

## COMPREHENSION SKILLS

The comprehension taxonomy presented on pages 213–214 contains several comprehension skills for each level. Identifying the main idea of a paragraph, identifying the central idea of a passage, using visuals, and making inferences are just four skills. All

---

[18]K. Manzo, "More Focus on Reading Fluency Needed, Study Suggests," *Education Week* 25 (2005): 11.

[19]Ibid.

[20]M. Opitz and T. Raskinski. *Good-bye Round Robin,* Rev. ed. (Portsmouth, NH: Heinemann, 2008).

of these are interpretive level reading skills and we present them here for both primary and intermediate grade children as examples of how skills can be assessed and taught.

## MAIN IDEA OF A PARAGRAPH

### Background

The main idea is probably the skill with which teachers and students spend the most time; this is good because it seems to pose difficulty for some students. Students have more difficulty coming up with the main idea themselves than choosing one from a given list. In fact, identifying the main idea is much more difficult for many students, even if it is directly stated.[21]

Because of the difficulty of the main idea construction (identification) task, sufficient time must be allotted to provide the needed "think time." In addition, researchers have reported "that if readers' prior knowledge for the text topic is not sufficient, the difficulty of main idea construction is compounded."[22] Also, if the paragraph is not well constructed and cohesive, it becomes more difficult to discern its main idea.

Confusion in finding the main idea may exist because the very concept of a "main idea" seems to mean different things to different people. One researcher investigating the literature found that "educators have increasingly given attention to main idea comprehension, but with no concomitant increase in the clarity of what is meant by main or important ideas. The exact nature of main ideas and the teaching practices intended to help students grasp main ideas vary considerably."[23]

Even though the concept of main idea is nebulous to some researchers and the "notion that different readers can (and should) construct identical main ideas for the same text has been questioned,"[24] the the ability to find the main idea in a text is a very important skill for reading, writing, and studying that can and should be taught. It is possible that the skepticism concerning the ability to teach main idea comprehension may result from "the failure to teach students to transfer their main idea skills to texts other than those found in their readers."[25] Some studies have found that "students who have been taught to identify main ideas using only contrived texts such as those found in basal reader skills lessons will have difficulty transferring their main idea skills to naturally occurring texts."[26] (The majority of reading programs in the recent past and present time have been literature-based, using whole pieces of literature rather than "contrived texts," which should counter the former criticism.)

In reading and writing, finding the main idea is very useful. In reading, the main idea helps readers to remember and understand what they have read. In writing, the main idea gives unity and order to a paragraph.

The *main idea* of a paragraph is the central thought of the paragraph. It is what the paragraph is about. Without a main idea, the paragraph would just be a confusion of sentences. All the sentences in the paragraph should develop the main idea.

### Finding the Main Idea of a Paragraph

To find the main idea of a paragraph, readers must find what common element the sentences share. Some textbook writers place the main idea at the beginning of a paragraph

> **Main idea**
> The central thought of a paragraph. All the sentences in the paragraph develop the main idea.

[21]Peter P. Afflerbach, "The Influence of Prior Knowledge on Expert Readers' Main Idea Construction Strategies," *Reading Research Quarterly* 25 (Winter, 1990): 44.

[22]Ibid.

[23]James W. Cunningham and David W. Moore, "The Confused World of Main Idea," in *Teaching Main Idea Comprehension,* ed. James Baumann (Newark, DE: International Reading Association, 1986), p. 2.

[24]Afflerbach, p. 45.

[25]Victoria Chou Hare, Mitchell Rabinowitz, and Karen Magnus Schieble, "Text Effects on Main Idea Comprehension," *Reading Research Quarterly* 24 (Winter, 1989): 72.

[26]Ibid.

and may actually put the topic of the paragraph in bold print in order to emphasize it. However, in literature, this is not a common practice. In some paragraphs the main idea is indirectly stated, or implied, and you have to find it from the clues given by the author.

Although there is no foolproof method for finding the main idea, there is a widely used procedure that has proved to be helpful. In order to use this procedure, you should know that a paragraph is always written about something or someone. The something or someone is the topic of the paragraph. The writer is interested in telling his or her readers something about the topic of the paragraph. To find the main idea of a paragraph, you must determine what the topic of the paragraph is and what the author is trying to say about the topic that is special or unique. Once you have found these two things, you should have the main idea. This procedure is useful in finding the main idea of various types of paragraphs.

Reread the preceding paragraph and state its main idea. *Answer:* A procedure helpful in finding the main idea of a paragraph is described.

Now read the following paragraph. After you have read the passage, choose the statement that *best* states the main idea.

Frank Yano looked like an old man, but he was only thirty. Born to parents who were alcoholics, Frank himself started drinking when he was only eight. He actually had tasted alcohol earlier, but it wasn't until he was eight or nine that he became a habitual drinker. His whole life since then has been dedicated to seeking the bottle.

1. Frank Yano looks old, but he's not.
2. Frank Yano enjoys being an alcoholic.
3. Frank Yano was a child alcoholic.
4. Frank Yano has been an alcoholic since childhood.
5. Frank Yano would like to change his life of drinking, but he can't.
6. Frank Yano's parents helped him become an alcoholic.

Answer: #4

Numbers 1 and 3 are too specific because they each relate to only one detail in the paragraph. Numbers 2 and 5 are not found in the paragraph; that is, no clues are given about Frank Yano's wanting to change his life or about his enjoying his life as an alcoholic. Number 6 is also too specific to be the main idea because it relates to only one detail. Number 4 is the answer because what is unique about Frank Yano is that he has been an alcoholic since early childhood. All the details in the paragraph support this main idea.

The main idea of a paragraph is a general statement of the content of a paragraph. You must be careful, however, that your main idea statement is not so general that it suggests information that is not given in the paragraph.

Textbook authors usually see to it that their paragraphs have clear-cut main ideas. The main ideas of paragraphs in other books may be less obvious. The literary author is usually more concerned with writing expressively than with explicitly stating the main ideas. The main idea may be indirectly given. If this is the case, the steps presented earlier are especially helpful. Let's look again at the steps involved in finding the main idea.

1. Find the topic of the paragraph.
2. Find what is special about the topic. To do this, gather clues from the paragraph, find out what all the clues have in common, and make a general statement about the clues.

*Guidelines on Topic Sentences and Main Ideas*

1. The topic sentence is usually the first sentence in a paragraph, and it states what the paragraph will be about by naming the topic. From the topic sentence you can

**Supporting details**

Additional information that supports, explains, or illustrates the main idea. Some of the ways that supporting details may be arranged are as cause and effect, examples, sequence of events, descriptions, definitions, comparisons, or contrasts.

usually anticipate certain events. You can usually determine that the following sentences will supply *supporting details* as examples, contrasts, similarities, sequence of events, cause-and-effect situations, and so on to support the main idea.

2. The main idea can be developed in many different ways. Whatever technique is used to develop the main idea, it must support and add meaning to the main idea.
3. A topic sentence may or may not contain the main idea.
4. It is possible for any sentence in the paragraph to be the topic sentence.
5. Some paragraphs may not have a topic sentence.
6. Do not confuse the topic sentence with the main idea. The topic sentence usually anticipates both the main idea and the development of the main idea.
7. Even though the topic sentence is stated explicitly (fully and clearly) in a paragraph, the main idea may not be stated explicitly.

Some students may already know how to identify main ideas and others may not. In Figure 10.1, we provide a sample informal assessment for teachers to use to determine who can and cannot identify main ideas.

### *Instructional Suggestions: Primary Grades*

Here are some instructional techniques and materials to use with your students who need some additional explicit instruction.

1. Present the following paragraph to your students:

Sharon was sad. She felt like crying. She still couldn't believe it. Her best friend, Jane, had moved away. Her best friend had left her. What would she do?

Ask your students what the topic of the paragraph is or about whom or what the paragraph is written.

*Answer:* Sharon

---

**FIGURE 10.1  Informal Assessment of Main Idea**

PRIMARY-GRADE LEVEL

*ASSESSING FOR MAIN IDEA*

Objective 1: The students will choose a statement that best states the main idea of a short one-paragraph story.
Objective 2: The students will state a title for a story that gives an idea of what the story is about.

**Directions: Read the short story. Then read the statements that follow the story. Choose the one that *best* states the main idea of the story. Also, state a title for the story.**

Tom and Jim are not feeling very happy. They have just had their first fight. Tom and Jim have never had a fight before. Tom thought about the fight. Jim thought about the fight. They both felt sad.

1. Tom and Jim are sad.
2. Tom and Jim have never fought before.
3. Tom and Jim's first fight makes them feel sad.
4. Tom and Jim fight.
5. Tom and Jim feel ill.

Answers: Number 3. *Sample title:* Tom and Jim's First Fight
Tell students the results.

Ask your students what the writer is saying that is special about Sharon.

*Answer:* Sharon is sad because her best friend moved away.

Tell your students that to find the main idea of the story, they need to figure out who or what the story is about and what is special about the who or what of the story.

2. Present your students with exercises such as the following. Ask your students to read the short story below. Ask them also to read the statements that follow the short story, and choose the one that best states the main idea of the story. Then ask your students to write a title for the story that gives readers an idea of what the story is about.

Tom and Jim live on the moon. They spend a lot of time in their house. They have to because it is very hot when the sun is out. It is also very cold when the sun is not out. On the moon, daylight lasts for fourteen earth days. Darkness or nighttime lasts for fourteen earth days, too.

1. It's cold on the moon.
2. Tom and Jim stay in their house a lot.
3. The moon's weather.
4. Tom and Jim's house.
5. The moon's weather forces Tom and Jim to stay in their house.
6. Tom and Jim like to stay in their house.

Answers: Number 5. Sample title: The Moon's Weather

3. Discuss with your students the difference between the title and the main idea. Help them to see that the title and the main idea are not necessarily the same, and that the main idea is usually more fully stated than the title.

4. Another way of teaching main ideas is to use your hand. Trace a figure of your hand on an overhead transparency. Provide children with a statement (the main idea), which you write in the palm of the hand. For example, write the sentence, "We are having fun at school today." Next, ask children to volunteer some ideas that prove they are having fun at school. As they volunteer their ideas, write each one in a finger. These are actually the supporting details, but students do not need to know this at this point in the lesson. Now invite the class to read the entire "hand" with you. Once finished, tell students that they have just learned about main idea and supporting details. Just like the palm of your hand holds your fingers together, so too, the main idea holds the details together. You may also want to show them how to rewrite the statements on the hand into paragraph form. See Figure 10.2 for a sample completed hand.

As with primary students, some intermediate students may already know how to identify the main idea and others may not. In Figure 10.3, we provide a sample informal assessment for the intermediate-grade level.

### *Instructional Suggestions for Intermediate Grades*
Here are some instructional techniques and materials that you can use with your students who need additional explicit instruction:

1. Have your students read the following two paragraphs. After they read them, try to elicit from them which is a better paragraph and why. You should tell them that the first one makes sense because it is well organized. Readers can tell what the author is trying to say because there is only one main idea and all the sentences in the paragraph expand on the main idea. Point out how disorganized the second paragraph is and how difficult it is to discover what the main idea is because each sentence seems to be about a different topic.

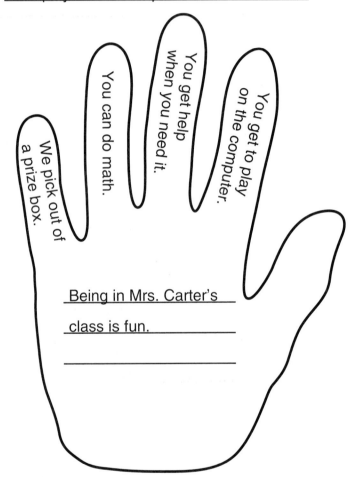

Being in Mrs. Carter's class is
fun. We pick out of a prize box for
most stars. You can do math. She helps
people when they need help. She lets
us play on the computer.

We pick out of a prize box.

You can do math.

You get help when you need it.

You get to play on the computer.

Being in Mrs. Carter's class is fun.

**FIGURE 10.2** Main Idea/Supporting Details Hand.

**Organized Paragraph**

All through school, John's one goal was athletic success so that he could be in the Olympics. John's goal to be in the Olympics became such an obsession that he could not do anything that did not directly or indirectly relate to achieving his goal. He practiced for hours every day. He exercised, ate well, and slept at least eight hours every night. Throughout school, John allowed nothing and no one to deter him from his goal.

---

**FIGURE 10.3**  **Informal Assessment of Main Idea**

---

INTERMEDIATE-GRADE LEVEL

*SKILL: MAIN IDEA OF A PARAGRAPH*

Objective: The students will state the main idea of a paragraph.

**Directions: Read the paragraph carefully. Write the main idea of it in the space below.**

Jim and his friends planned to go on a camping trip. For weeks, he and his friends talked about nothing else. They planned every detail of the trip. They studied maps and read books on camping. Everything was set. Everything, that is, except for asking their parents to let them go. Jim and his friends had planned everything. They had not planned on their parents not letting them go. However, that is what happened. Jim's and his friends' parents did not allow them to go.

Answer: Jim and his friends' plans to go camping are blocked by their parents.
Tell students the results.

---

### Disorganized Paragraph

All through school, John's one goal was to be the best so that he could be in the Olympics. He practiced for hours every day. John's family was unhappy about John's obsession to be in the Olympics. John's social life was more like a monk's than that of a star athlete. John's coach was a difficult man to please.

2. Have your students reread the organized paragraph. After they read the paragraph, have them choose the word or words that *best* answer the two questions that follow.

  a. What is the topic of the paragraph?
  (1) exercise and practice
  (2) work
  (3) Olympics
  (4) John's goal
  (5) athletic success
  (6) attempts

Answer: 4

  b. What is the author saying about John's goal to be in the Olympics (the topic) that is special and that helps tie the details together?
  (1) That it needed time and patience.
  (2) That it was a good one.
  (3) That it was not a reasonable one.
  (4) That it was the most important thing in John's life.
  (5) That it required good health.
  (6) That it was too much for John.

Answer: 4

Tell your students that if they put the two answers together, they should have the main idea of the paragraph. Main idea: The goal, being in the Olympics, was the most important thing in John's life.

3. Choose a number of paragraphs from the students' social studies or science books. First have them find the topic of each paragraph and then have them state the main idea of each paragraph. Go over the procedure for finding the main idea with them.

## FINDING THE CENTRAL IDEA OF A GROUP OF PARAGRAPHS

### *Background*

**Central idea**
The main idea of a larger chunk of text.

We generally use the term *central idea* rather than *main idea* when we refer to a *group* of paragraphs, a story, or an article. However, the procedure for finding the main idea and for finding the central idea is the same.

The central idea of a story is the central thought of the story. All the paragraphs of the story should develop the central idea. To find the central idea of a story, students must find what common element the paragraphs in the story share. The introductory paragraph is usually helpful because it either contains or anticipates what the central idea is and how it will be developed. The procedure for finding the central idea of a story is similar to that for finding the main idea of a paragraph.

It is important to help your students recognize that the title of a story and the central idea are not necessarily the same. The ability to state the title of a story is related to the skill of finding the central idea; however, many times the title merely gives the topic of the story. The central idea is usually more fully stated than the title.

You may wish to use the informal assessment for central idea that we show in Figure 10.4 to determine those students who might need some instruction. The informal assessment in Figure 10.5 is intended for intermediate grade students.

---

**FIGURE 10.4    Informal Assessment: Central Idea**

---

UPPER PRIMARY-GRADE LEVEL

*SKILL: CENTRAL IDEA OF A SHORT STORY*

Objective 1: The students will state the central idea of a short story.

Objective 2: The students will state a title for a story.

**Directions: Read the story. Write the central idea of the story. Then write a title for the story that gives readers an idea of what the story is about.**

Once upon a time in the deep green jungle of Africa, there lived a cruel lion. This lion frightened all the animals in the jungle. No animal was safe from this lion. One day the animals met and came up with a plan. The plan was not a very good one, but it was the best they could think of. Each day one animal would go to the lion to be eaten by him. That way the other animals would know that they were safe for a little while. The lion agreed to the plan and that is how they lived for a time.

One day it was the sly fox's turn to be eaten by the lion. Mr. Fox, however, had other plans. Mr. Fox went to the lion's cave an hour late. The lion was very angry. "Why are you so late? I am hungry," he said. Mr. Fox answered, "Oh, I am so sorry to be late, but another very, very big lion tried to catch me. I ran away from him so that you could eat me." When the lion heard about the other lion, he became more angry. "Another lion?" he asked. "I want to see him." The fox told the lion that he would take him to see the other lion. The fox led the lion through the jungle. When they came to a well, the fox stopped. "Look in there," said the fox. "The other lion is in there." The lion looked in the well, and he did indeed see a lion. He got so angry that he jumped in the well to fight the lion. That was, of course, the end of the lion.

Answers: *Central idea:* A clever fox outsmarts a cruel lion.

*Sample title:* The Clever Fox and the Cruel Lion or A Fox Outsmarts a Lion.

Tell students the results.

---

**FIGURE 10.5   Informal Assessment: Central Idea**

---

INTERMEDIATE-GRADE LEVEL

*SKILL: CENTRAL IDEA OF A SHORT STORY*

Objective 1: The students will state the central idea of a short story.

Objective 2: The students will be able to state a title for a story.

> **Directions: Read carefully the following short story to determine the central idea of the story. After you have found the central idea of the story, choose a title for the story that gives readers an idea of what the story is about.**

A man and his son went to the market one morning. They took along a donkey to bring back whatever they would buy.

As they walked down the road, they met a woman who looked at them with a sour face. "Are you not ashamed," she called to the father, "to let your little boy walk in the hot sun, when he should be riding on the donkey?"

The father stopped and lifted his boy to the donkey's back. So they went on.

After a little while they met an old man. He began at once to scold the boy. "You ungrateful son!" he shouted. "You let your poor old father walk while you sit there on the donkey like a lazy good-for-nothing!"

When the old man had passed, the father took his frightened son from the donkey and got onto the animal himself.

Further on they met another man who looked at them angrily. "How can you let your child walk in the dusty road?" he asked. "And you sit up there by yourself!"

The father was troubled, but he reached down and lifted his son up where he could sit on the donkey in front of him.

A little later they met a man and his wife, each of them riding a donkey. The husband called out, "You cruel man! How can you let the poor donkey carry such a heavy load? Get off at once! You are big enough and strong enough to carry the little animal instead of making it carry two of you."

The poor man was now really perplexed. He got off the donkey and took his son off, too.

Then he cut down a young tree for a pole and trimmed it. He tied the donkey's four feet to the pole. Then he and his son lifted the pole. They trudged along, carrying the donkey between them.

As they were crossing a bridge over a stream, they met with a crowd of young men. Seeing the donkey being carried on a pole, they started to laugh and shout. Their noise startled the poor donkey who started to kick violently and broke the ropes holding his feet. As he frisked about, he tumbled off the bridge and was drowned.

The man looked sadly into the stream and shook his head.

"My son," he said to the boy, "you cannot please everybody."

Answers: *Central idea:* A man and his son learn that you cannot please everyone.

*Sample title:* You Can't Please Everyone

Tell students the results.

---

*Instructional Suggestions for Upper Primary Grades*

Here are some instructional techniques you can use with your students who need additional explicit instruction.

1. Choose a short story the children know and enjoy reading. Have them state what the topic of the story is. Then have them go over the story and try to state what is the most important thing about the topic. Have them put the two together.

2. Have the children write their own short stories. Have them state the central idea of their short stories. Have them go over each of their paragraphs to see if each one helps develop their central idea. Have them write a title for their stories.

### Instructional Suggestions for Intermediate-Grade Level

Here are some instructional techniques you can use with your students who need additional explicit instruction.

1. Choose a story the students have read. Ask them to state the topic of the story. Then have them reread the story to state what is the most important thing about the topic. Ask them to put these together. Then have them review the story to determine whether everything in the story is related to their central idea.

2. Ask students to write their own stories. Have them state the central idea and write a title for their stories.

3. Choose some short stories and follow the same procedure for finding the central idea. Present the short stories without the titles. Ask the students to make up a title for each short story. Discuss the fact that the title and the central idea are not necessarily the same, and explore what the differences are.

### Visual Representations and Main Idea

It is difficult to read a textbook, magazine, or newspaper without finding a variety of visual representations in the form of graphs, diagrams, and charts. Visuals provide relief from print, and a graphic representation is often worth a thousand words. Graphs, diagrams, and charts grab readers' attention, and pack a great amount of information into a small space. *USA Today* uses pictorial representations every day in each section of the newspaper for these reasons.

Writers use graphs, diagrams, and charts to convey information, and each one, like a paragraph, has a main idea. To understand the charts, diagrams, and graphs, you must be able to get the main idea of them. Not surprisingly, the technique readers use to do this is similar to that for finding the main idea of a paragraph.

Figure 10.6 is a graph from *Health Behaviors* by Rosalind Reed and Thomas A. Lang.[27] Let's go through the various steps to get the main idea of it. Remember, to find the main idea, we must first find the topic of the chart, diagram, or graph and then note what is special or unique about it. All the details should develop the main idea. (Note that writers also usually give clues to the topic of their graphs, diagrams, and charts.) Here are the steps readers would go through:

1. Look carefully at the graph to determine its topic. Notice that it deals with smokers and nonsmokers and their mortality rates for selected diseases. Therefore, the topic is:

> The mortality rates of smokers and nonsmokers for selected diseases.

2. Next, find what is special about the topic. In looking at the graph again, note that the writer is obviously making a comparison between smokers and nonsmokers. The comparison is about various types of diseases. In addition and what is most crucial is that the smokers have consistently higher mortality rates for all presented diseases. Therefore, the main idea must be:

> The mortality rates for smokers are consistently higher than for nonsmokers for all selected diseases.

---

[27]Rosalind Reed and Thomas A. Lang, *Health Behaviors* (St. Paul, MN: West Publications, 1988), p. 328.

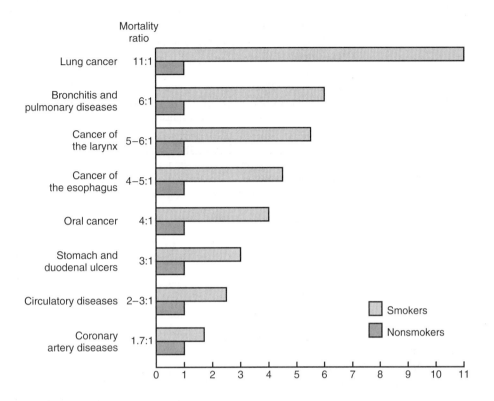

**FIGURE 10.6** Mortality Rates for Smokers and Nonsmokers for Selected Diseases. *Source:* From *Health Behaviors* by Rosalind Reed and Thomas A. Lang. St. Paul, MN: West Publications, 1988, p. 328.

## DRAWING INFERENCES

Many times writers do not directly state what they mean, but present ideas in a more indirect, roundabout way. That is why inference is called the ability to "read between the lines." *Inference* is defined as *understanding that is not derived from a direct statement but from an indirect suggestion in what is stated.* Readers draw inferences from writings; authors make implications or imply meanings.

The ability to draw inferences is especially important in reading fiction, but it is necessary for nonfiction, also. Authors rely on inferences to make their stories more interesting and enjoyable. Mystery writers find inference essential to maintaining suspense. For example, Sherlock Holmes and Encyclopedia Brown mysteries are based on the sleuth's ability to uncover evidence in the form of clues that are not obvious to others around them.

Inference is an important process that authors rely on. Good readers must be alert to the various ways that authors encourage inference.

**Inference**
Understanding that is not derived from a direct statement but from an indirect suggestion in what is stated; understanding of what is implied.

### *Implied Statements*

As noted, writers count on inference to make their writing more interesting and enjoyable. Rather than directly stating something, they present it indirectly. To understand the writing, the reader must be alert and be able to detect the clues that the author gives. For example, in the sentence *Things are always popping and alive when the twins Herb and Jack are around,* you are given some clues to Herb's and Jack's personalities, even though the author has not directly said anything about them. From the statement, you could make the inference that the twins are lively and lots of fun to be around.

You must be careful, however, that you *do not read more* into some statements than is intended. For example, read the following statements and put a circle around the correct answer. *Example:* Mary got out of bed and looked out of the window. She saw that the ground had something white on it. What season of the year was it? (a) winter, (b) summer, (c) spring, (d) fall, (e) can't tell.

The answer is "(e) can't tell." Many people choose "(a) winter" for the answer. However, the answer is (e) because the "something white" could be anything; there isn't enough evidence to choose (a). Even if the something white was snow, in some parts of the world, including the United States, it can snow in the spring or fall.

Good readers, while reading, try to gather clues to draw inferences about what they read. Although effective readers do this, they are not usually aware of it. As Sherlock Holmes says in *A Study in Scarlet,* "From long habit the train of thought ran so swiftly through my mind that I arrived at the conclusions without being conscious of intermediate steps."

In Figures 10.7 and 10.8 we provide an informal assessment procedure that you can use to assess inference at the primary-grade level and intermediate-grade level.

### Instructional Suggestions for Primary-Grade Level

Here are some instructional procedures and materials to use with your students who need additional explicit instruction.

1. Present the following short selection to your students:

Sharon and Carol are going out to play. They are dressed very warmly.

Ask your students what they can say about the weather outside. They should say that it must be cold outside because the children are dressed very warmly. Even though the writer didn't say that it was cold outside, there was enough evidence to make this inference.

Now ask the children to tell you what season of the year it is. They should say that they can't tell because there is not enough evidence. It could be cold in the fall and spring. Some children might be able to state that they can't tell because different parts of the country and the world have different climates.

2. Give your students a number of opportunities to make inferences from stories they are reading if enough evidence exists.

### Instructional Suggestions for Intermediate-Grade Level

Here are some instructional procedures and materials that you can use with your students who need additional explicit instruction.

1. Present your students with the following statements:

Jack looks out of the train window. All he sees are miles and miles of leafless trees.

Ask them whether Jack just began to look out of the window. The students should answer "no." Ask them how they know this. They should say because the text says that he saw miles and miles of trees. He couldn't see "miles and miles of trees" unless he had been looking out the window for a while.

Ask them whether Jack is traveling through a densely populated or sparsely populated area. They should say that Jack is traveling through a sparsely populated area. Ask them how they know this. They should say because the area has so many trees. Ask them what kind of area it is. The students should say that it could be a forest or a park or a preserve. Not enough evidence is given to determine this. Ask them if they can determine what season of the year it is since there are leafless trees. They should say

**FIGURE 10.7   Informal Assessment: Inference**

PRIMARY-GRADE LEVEL

*SKILL: INFERENCE OR "READING BETWEEN THE LINES"*

Objective: The students will read a short story and answer inference questions about it.

**Directions: Read the short story. Then answer the questions.**

Cleo and Scabbers are a cat and rat. They are good friends. They live on the moon. Cleo and Scabbers love to ride in space. Their school goes on a space trip every month. Cleo and Scabbers must wear their space clothes and their air masks in the spaceship. All the other moon cats and rats must wear them, too. Cleo and Scabbers want to be space-ship pilots. This is the same spaceship that brought Cleo and Scabbers to the moon. The spaceship has its own landing place. It is well taken care of. Special cats and rats take care of the spaceship. Cleo and Scabbers are happy that they can ride in the spaceship.

1. Is there air in the spaceship? Explain.

2. Were Cleo and Scabbers born on the moon? Explain.

3. Is the spaceship important to the moon cats and rats? Explain.

4. Is travel an important part of school learning? Explain.

5. Do Cleo and Scabbers know what they want to do when they grow up? Explain.

Answers:
1. No. Cleo and Scabbers wear their space clothes and their air masks in the spaceship.
2. No. It is stated that the spaceship is the same one that brought Cleo and Scabbers to the moon.
3. Yes. It is their means of travel. It is stated that there are special cats and rats who take care of the spaceship and that the spaceship is well taken care of.
4. Yes. Every month the school goes on a space trip.
5. Yes. It is stated that they want to be spaceship pilots.

Tell students the results.

**FIGURE 10.8** **Informal Assessment: Inference**

INTERMEDIATE-GRADE LEVEL

*SKILL: INFERENCE OR "READING BETWEEN THE LINES"*

Objective: The students will make inferences about short selections if enough evidence exists for the inferences.

> **Directions: Read the following selection *very carefully.* Without looking back at the selection, try to answer the questions.**
>
> The two men looked at each other. They would have to make the decision that might cost many lives. They kept rubbing their hands together to keep warm. Although they were dressed in furs and every part of them was covered except for their faces, they could still feel the cold. The fire that had been made for them from pine trees was subsiding. It was getting light. They had promised their men a decision at dawn. Should they go forward or should they retreat? So many lives had already been lost.

a. Did this take place at the North Pole or South Pole? _____

   How do you know? _____

   _____

   _____

   _____

b. Circle the word that best fits the two men. The two men were: (1) trappers (2) officers (3) soldiers (4) guides. Explain why you made your choice.

**Explain:** _____

   _____

   _____

c. What inference can you draw from this short passage? Circle the answer.
   (1) The men were on a hunting trip.
   (2) The men were at war with a foreign nation.
   (3) The decision that the two men had to make concerned whether to take an offensive or defensive position in some kind of battle.
   (4) The men were on a hunting trip, but they got caught in a bad storm.

**Explain:** _____

   _____

   _____

Answers:

(a) No. There are no pine trees at the North or South Pole. (b) Officers. Guides would not talk about *their* men. Guides usually act as advisers. They do not make decisions. Trappers trap animals for fur. Also, it is stated that the fire had been made for them. Officers do not usually prepare the camp. (c) The term *retreat* would be a commander's term. Nothing was stated about a storm nor was anything stated or suggested about a foreign nation. Hunters would not usually hunt under such adverse conditions. It was too cold to hunt big game, and hunters would very rarely lose so many lives.

Tell students the results.

"no." It could be any season of the year. It is not stated in what part of the country or world Jack is traveling. The trees could be leafless as a result of a forest fire, disease, drought, or some other cause.

2. Have students read a number of stories and see what inferences they can draw from them. Help them to recognize that enough evidence should exist to make an inference. Tell them that many times people "jump to conclusions" before they have enough evidence. This can cause problems. Taking an educated guess is helpful in scientific activities and in searching for the answers to difficult questions. Students should be encouraged to make educated guesses, but they need to recognize when they do not have enough evidence to do so.

## COMPREHENSION STRATEGIES

In addition to specific comprehension skills, there are comprehension strategies (i.e., mental processes) that may require some explicit instruction. As with the skills noted above, remember that students need plenty of time to read in order to actually apply these skills and strategies. The six strategies shown in Figure 10.13A–F on pages 244–250—making connections, making predictions, monitoring understanding, visualizing, questioning, and retelling/summarizing—are research-based. Each sample lesson includes a brief overview of the particular strategy, some teaching suggestions, and some ideas for providing students with meaningful practice. This figure also provides a list of children's literature selections that can be used to teach each strategy. Our goal with strategic thinking is that students will learn to use it as a problem-solving strategy when text is difficult. As students become more proficient with various types of text, we expect that the thinking they use for comprehension will become more automatic—that is, strategies become skills.[28]

## ASSESSING COMPREHENSION

As we emphasize throughout this text, assessment drives instruction. This is true for comprehension instruction as well as any other aspect of reading. The three questions cited in previous chapters also apply when we think about comprehension assessment: What do I want to know? Why do I want to know? How can I best discover it? (See Table 10.2 on p. 230.) There are four ways we can answer these questions.

First, some of the assessment techniques mentioned in earlier chapters are excellent tools for answering the questions. These include retelling, asking questions representative of the different comprehension levels (such as those used in the informal reading inventory), observation, and interviewing students. Additional ways to use questioning are shown in the next section.

Second, teachers can use teacher-created informal assessments such as those shown throughout this chapter. Use students' performance on these assessments to determine whether they need additional explicit comprehension instruction.

Third, teachers can look at how students perform on comprehension-related tasks in content reading. That is, we want students to see that teachers expect them to use comprehension skills and strategies any time they read. For example, if teachers expect students to summarize, they can provide a summarizing activity during social studies reading and note whether students use what they know about summarizing in this context.

Fourth, teachers can use cloze or maze procedures, which require teachers to prepare the text in special ways.

[28]P. Afflerbach, P. D. Pearson, and S. G. Paris, "Clarifying Differences Between Reading Skills and Reading Strategies." *The Reading Teacher* 61, no. 5 (2008): 364–373.

**TABLE 10.2   Selecting Appropriate Comprehension Measures**

| *What Do I Want to Know?* | *Why Do I Want to Know?* | *How Can I Best Discover It?* |
|---|---|---|
| Are students acquiring and applying specific comprehension skills and strategies when reading? | Good readers have many skills and strategies at their disposal and they use those they find most appropriate when reading given texts. I want to make sure that all students are acquiring and applying comprehension skills and strategies because both will help them become able readers. | • Observation<br>• Performance on daily comprehension tasks<br>• Cloze<br>• Maze |
| Are students able to comprehend at different levels? | Many different levels of comprehension are necessary for excellent comprehension. I want to make sure that students are using higher-level comprehension as well as literal comprehension. | • Retelling<br>• Comprehension test from IRI<br>• Talking with students<br>• Questioning |
| Are students aware of the strategies they use to comprehend text? | Metacognition is an important part of comprehension. If students are aware of the strategies they use in reading, they are more likely to use them. I can also help students to expand their repertoire of strategies if necessary. | • Student interview<br>• Student self-assessment |

## QUESTIONING AS A DIAGNOSTIC TECHNIQUE

Asking questions is not only an important part of teaching and learning, it is also very useful in diagnosis. Teachers' questions, which can stimulate students to use literal- or higher-level thinking, give insight into students' comprehension. Student responses can help a teacher to see whether students are organizing information for memory; whether they are able to see relationships and make comparisons; and whether the materials the students are reading or listening to are too difficult or too easy.

Students' questions are an important part of their learning, and they are essential diagnostic aids in giving teachers feedback on the students' ability to understand information. In order to ask good questions, students must know their material. As a result, those students who ask the best questions are usually those who know the material best. Confusing questions are a signal that the teacher needs to slow down or reteach certain material.

Teachers can use questioning as a diagnostic technique to learn about their students' thinking ability. Here are some examples.

The teacher has the children read a short story. The story is about a boy who wants to go to school, but he can't because he is too young. The teacher tells the children that she is going to make up some questions about the story, and the children have to tell her whether the questions that she makes up can actually be answered. If a question can be answered, the student should answer it; if a question cannot be answered, the student must tell why. The teacher makes up the following questions:

1. What are the names of Ben's sister and brother who go to school?
2. Why does Ben want to go to school?
3. Make up an adventure for Ben.
4. Why can't Ben go to school?

5. What are the names of the bus driver's children?
6. What does Ben do in the summer?

This technique can help the teacher learn which children are able to concentrate, as well as which children are able to do different kinds of thinking. Questions 1 and 4 are literal questions; question 2 is an inferential question; question 3 is a creative question; and questions 5 and 6 are not able to be answered because no such information was given in the story, either directly or indirectly.

A more difficult questioning technique that the teacher could use with children is to have them make up questions for a selection that they have read.

After students have read a selection, the teacher can ask them to make up three different questions. The first question should be one for which the answer is directly stated in the passage. The second question should be one for which the answer is not directly stated in the passage. The third question should be one that requires an answer that goes beyond the text.

In early primary grades, the teacher can use pictures as the stimuli for questions, or the teacher can relate a short story to the children and have them devise questions for it.

Here are some questions that a group of fourth-grade children made up after reading a story about Melissa and her friend Fred, who were always getting into trouble.

1. Who is Melissa's best friend? (literal)
2. What is the main idea of the story? (inferential)
3. From the story, what can we say about the main character's personality? (inferential)
4. Relate an event that you think Melissa could get into. (creative)

The children who made up the questions challenged their classmates to answer them and then they were responsible for determining whether their classmates had answered them correctly.

## CLOZE PROCEDURE

Can you supply the _____ that fits this sentence? When you came to the missing word in this sentence, did you try to gain closure by supplying a term such as *word* to complete the incomplete sentence? If you did, you were engaged in the process of *closure,* which involves the ability of the reader to use context clues to determine the needed word.

The *cloze procedure* was primarily developed by Wilson Taylor in 1953 as a measure of readability, that is, to test the difficulty of instructional materials and to evaluate their suitability for students. It has since been used for a number of other purposes, especially as a measure of a student's comprehension.

Cloze procedure is not a comprehension skill; it is a technique that helps teachers gain information about a variety of language facility and comprehension skills. A *cloze test* or exercise is one in which the reader must supply words that have been systematically deleted from a text at a particular grade level.

There is no set procedure for determining the length of the passage or the number of deletions that a passage should have. However, if you wish to apply the criteria for reading levels that have been used in research with the traditional cloze procedure, you should follow these rules. First, only words must be deleted, and the replacements for each word must be the *exact* word, not a synonym. Second, the words must be deleted in a systematic manner. The researchers who have developed the criteria for scoring cloze tests state that "any departure from these rules leaves the teacher with uninterpretable results."[29]

**Cloze procedure**
A technique that helps teachers gain information about a variety of language facility and comprehension ability skills.

**Cloze test**
Reader must supply words which have been systematically deleted from a passage.

[29]John R. Bormuth, "The Cloze Procedure: Literacy in the Classroom," in *Help for the Reading Teacher: New Directions in Research,* ed. William D. Page (Urbana, IL: National Conference on Research in English, 1975), p. 67.

The traditional cloze procedure consists of deleting every fifth word of a passage that is representative of the material being tested. The passage that is chosen should be able to stand alone. Usually the first and last sentences of the passage remain intact. Then, beginning with either the first, second, third, fourth, or fifth word of the second sentence, every fifth word of a 250–260 word passage should be deleted.

At the intermediate-grade levels and higher, the passage is usually 250 words, and every fifth word is deleted. For maximum reliability, a passage should have at least fifty deletions. At the primary-grade level, the passage is usually shorter, and every eighth or tenth word is deleted. A cloze technique would not yield as reliable a score for the primary-grade level as for the intermediate-grade level because passages for the former are shorter and have fewer deletions.

Teachers can use cloze exercises for diagnosis, review, instruction, and testing. In constructing the exercise, the main point to remember is its *purpose*. If the purpose is to test a student's retention of some concepts in a specific area, the exact term is usually necessary; however, if the purpose is to gain information about a student's language facility, ability to use context clues, vocabulary development, or comprehension, the exact term is not as important because often many words will make sense in a passage.

### Scoring the Cloze Test

If you have deleted fifty words, the procedure for scoring the cloze test is very easy. All you have to do is multiply the number of correct insertions by two and add a percentage symbol. For example, twenty-five correct insertions would be equal to 50 percent. If you have not deleted exactly fifty words, use the following formula, in which the number of correct insertions is divided by the number of blanks and multiplied by 100 percent.

$$\frac{40}{60} \times 100\% = (40 \div 60) \times 100\%$$

$$= 67\% \text{ (rounded to nearest digit)}$$

For a traditional cloze test in which only exact words are counted as correct and every fifth word has been deleted, a score below 44 percent would indicate a frustration level. A score between 44 and 57 percent would indicate the instructional level, and scores above 57 percent would indicate the independent level. It is important to note that these criteria should be used only if the exact words are used and if every fifth word has been deleted from the passage. These levels are indicative of the text that was used to design the test. In other words, they tell how the student matches up to the text to be used for instruction.

*Reading Levels Scale for Cloze Procedure*

| | |
|---|---|
| Independent level | 58% and above |
| Instructional level | 44% through 57% |
| Frustration level | 43% and below |

### Variations of the Traditional Cloze Procedure: An Emphasis on Diagnosis

Variations of the cloze technique are sometimes used. For example, rather than deleting every fifth or tenth word, every noun or verb is deleted, or every function or structure word (definite and indefinite articles, conjunctions, prepositions, and so on) is deleted.

This technique is used when the teacher wishes to gain information about a student's sentence sense. For example:

Jane threw _____ ball _____ Mary. (the, to)

Another variation of the cloze technique is to delete key words in the passage. This technique is useful for determining whether students have retained certain information. For example:

A technique in which the reader must supply words is called the _____ procedure. (cloze)

Cloze technique can also be adapted for other uses. Students can be presented with a passage in which they must complete the incomplete words. For example:

Dick r _____ his bike every day. (rides)

Another adaptation is to present students with a passage in which every nth word is deleted. They must then choose words from a given word list that *best* fit the blanks.

Here is an example of an exercise using the cloze technique for an upper primary grade. Notice how explicitly the instructions are stated for the students, and also notice that the first and last sentences of the passage are given intact.

In addition, note that the deletion pattern is not the same throughout the passage.

*Directions: Read the first and last sentences that have no missing words in them to get a clue as to what the story is about. Then read very carefully each sentence that has a missing word or words in it. Using context clues, figure out a word that would make sense in the story and put it in the blank.*

In the forest live a kind old man and woman. (1) _____ have been living in (2) _____ forest for almost ten (3) _____. They had decided to (4) _____ to the forest because they (5) _____nature.

The kind old (6) _____ and woman make their (7) _____ by baking breads and cakes and (8) _____ them to the people who (9) _____ the forest. Everyone who (10) _____ the forest usually buys (11) _____ bread or cake from the old (12) _____. The kind old man and woman are happy in the forest.

Answers: 1. They, 2. the, 3. years, 4. move, 5. love, like, 6. man, 7. living, 8. selling, 9. visit, 10. visits, 11. some, 12. couple.

Here is an example of an exercise using cloze technique for an intermediate grade.

*Directions: Read the first and last sentences of the story to get a clue as to what the story is about. Then read each sentence that has a missing word or words very carefully. Using context clues, insert a word in each blank so that the story makes sense.*

Everyone was looking forward to Friday night because that was the night of the big basketball game. This (1) _____ would determine the championship (2) _____ Deerville High and Yorktown (3) _____. For years Deerville High and (4) _____ High have been rivals. This (5) _____ was very

(6) _____ because so far (7) _____ school had won
(8) _____ equal number of games. (9) _____ game on
Friday night would break the (10) _____.

Friday night finally arrived. The game (11) _____ the championship title (12) _____ being played in the Deerville High
(13) _____ because the game (14) _____ year had
been played (15) _____ the Yorktown High gym.
(16) _____ gym was so (17) _____ that many
spectators were without (18) _____. When the two teams
(19) _____ the gym from the dressing areas,
(20) _____ were thunderous (21) _____ and
whistles from the (22) _____. Each team went through
(23) _____ warm-up drills of (24) _____ baskets and
passing. Then the buzzer (25) _____. The game would begin
(26) _____ a moment. Just as the referee (27) _____
the ball in the (28) _____ for the starting jumpball, the lights
(29) _____ the gym went (30) _____.
There was complete darkness. Everyone (31) _____ taken by
surprise. Almost immediately a (32) _____ on the loudspeaker
(33) _____ that the game would have (34) _____ be
postponed because of a (35) _____ failure. The game would take
(36) _____ next Friday. All were (37) _____ to remain
where they (38) _____ until someone with a flashlight came to help
them. Everyone was disappointed that the game had to be cancelled.

Answers: (1) game, (2) between, (3) High, (4) Yorktown, (5) game, (6) important,
(7) each, (8) an, (9) The, (10) tie, (11) for, (12) was, (13) gym, (14) last, (15) in,
(16) The, (17) crowded, (18) seats, (19) entered, (20) there, (21) cheers, (22) spectators, audience, *or* crowd, (23) its, (24) shooting, (25) sounded *or* rang, (26) in,
(27) threw, (28) air, (29) in, (30) out, (31) was, (32) voice, (33) announced, (34) to,
(35) power, (36) place, (37) told, (38) were

## MAZE PROCEDURE

Some teachers prefer to use a maze instead of a cloze procedure because they find it
easier for students to use. Because words are added rather than deleted every fifth word,
they believe that it gives students more support. To compensate for this ease, the
scoring is a little different. That is, students have to achieve at higher levels to reach
independent, instructional, and frustrational levels.

Basically, the maze is the same as the cloze with the exception of adding words
and establishing cut-off scores. The Venn diagram shown in Figure 10.9 shows how the
two are alike and different.

The checklists shown in Figure 10.10 and Figure 10.11 can provide a means of documenting observations, which need to take place in a variety of contexts. As stated in
this chapter and throughout this text, students need to read a great deal, and they need to
read many different kinds of texts if they are to become accomplished readers. Note that
one of the checklists focuses on documenting students' listening comprehension.

## META-COMPREHENSION STRATEGY INDEX

The *Meta-Comprehension Strategy Index* is another meaningful way to assess students'
awareness of the strategies they use in reading. Complete information including the test,
administration and scoring procedures, and suggested instructional techniques can be
found in *The Reading Teacher* (Schmitt, March, 1990): 454–461.

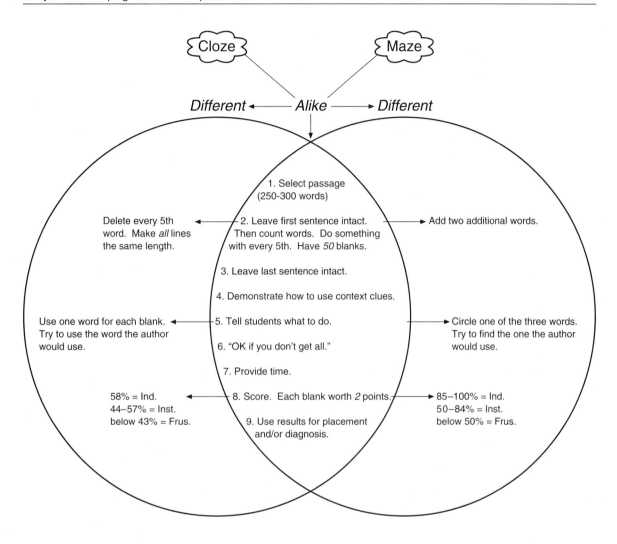

**FIGURE 10.9**    Comparison of Cloze and Maze Testing Procedure.

## TEACHING COMPREHENSION

Time spent in reading seems to be an important variable for success in reading, whether it is direct instructional time or time spent reading independently. However, we cannot count on students reading outside school because of the many other enjoyable activities, as well as responsibilities, that compete for their time and attention. Therefore, we must plan for students to have time to read in school, as well as time for explicit instruction in reading comprehension.

There are various teaching strategies that can be used with explicit instruction; some are less structured than others. Explicit instruction requires teachers to present strategies to help their students comprehend the material being read; this is done in addition to asking children questions before, during, and after they read. "Direct [explicit] instruction in comprehension means explaining the steps in a thought process

---

**FIGURE 10.10 Diagnostic Checklist for Listening Comprehension***

Student's Name: _____

Grade: _____

Teacher: _____

|  | Yes | No |
|---|---|---|
| 1. Precise listening. The child, after listening to a passage, can answer questions that relate to information explicitly stated in the passage. |  |  |
| 2. Strategic listening. The child, after listening to a passage, can answer questions dealing with |  |  |
| a. finding the main idea. |  |  |
| b. generalization. |  |  |
| c. "reading between the lines." |  |  |
| d. conclusions. |  |  |
| e. cause-effect relationships. |  |  |
| f. multiple meanings. |  |  |
| 3. Critical listening. The child, after listening to a passage, can answer questions dealing with |  |  |
| a. propaganda. |  |  |
| b. fact or opinion. |  |  |
| c. bias. |  |  |
| d. emotive language. |  |  |
| 4. Appreciative listening. The child voluntarily chooses to listen to various tapes. |  |  |

*The length and difficulty of the selection used are determined by the grade level and the developmental level of the individual child. Also, this is not an inclusive list of listening comprehension skills.

---

that gives birth to comprehension."[30] The instructional pattern that teachers use to help students gain comprehension will vary based on the concept being learned, the composition of the class, and the ability of the teacher.

Providing instruction before, during, and after the reading activity is a way to design supportive instruction. Before reading, prepare the students for the reading activity by doing some of the following: previewing the reading selection, going over new vocabulary or difficult words, teaching any strategies that students will need to read the material, as well as actively building topic knowledge.

During reading, give students a number of questions to think about as they read or encourage students to ask questions about the text material. Challenge students to act as investigative reporters while they are reading.

After reading, students can answer their own questions or the teacher's questions, state the main idea of the selection, summarize it, discuss their feelings toward the material, or tell how they used a specific comprehension strategy such as visualizing. There are numerous comprehension teaching strategies that can be used as a part of an explicit reading

[30]Richard C. Anderson et al., *Becoming a Nation of Readers: The Report of the Commission on Reading* (Washington, DC: National Institute of Education, 1985), p. 72.

**FIGURE 10.11** **Diagnostic Checklist for Selected Reading Comprehension Skills**

Student's Name: _____

Grade: _____

Teacher: _____

| | Yes | No |
|---|---|---|
| 1. The student is able to state the meaning of a word in context. | | |
| 2. The student is able to give the meaning of a phrase or a clause in a sentence. | | |
| 3. The student is able to give variations of meanings for homographs (words spelled the same but with more than one meaning, for example, *train, mean, saw, sole,* and so on). | | |
| 4. The student is able to give the meaning of a sentence in a paragraph. | | |
| 5. The student is able to recall information that is explicitly stated in the passage (literal questions). | | |
| 6. The student is able to state the main idea of a paragraph. | | |
| 7. The student is able to state details to support the main idea of a paragraph. | | |
| 8. The student is able to summarize a paragraph. | | |
| 9. The student is able to answer a question that requires reading between the lines. | | |
| 10. The student is able to draw a conclusion from what is read. | | |
| 11. The student can hypothesize the author's purpose for writing the selection. | | |
| 12. The student can differentiate between fact and opinion. | | |
| 13. The student can differentiate between fantasy and reality. | | |
| 14. The student can detect bias in a story. | | |
| 15. The student can detect various propaganda tactics that are used in a story. | | |
| 16. The student can go beyond the text to come up with alternate solutions or ways to end a story or solve a problem in the selection. | | |
| 17. The student shows that he or she enjoys reading by voluntarily choosing to read. | | |
| 18. The student shows the ability to use a variety of comprehension strategies when reading (e.g., visualizing, predicting, monitoring, asking questions). | | |

lesson. Purpose is what guides the selection of the specific teaching strategy chosen for any given lesson. The following sections provide eight suggestions for teaching strategies.

When teaching comprehension, focus first on *listening comprehension* so the students can learn the strategy or skill without the demands of word identification. Then teach the same skill, but have students do the reading, which places emphasis on reading comprehension (transfer of learning).

## THE DIRECTED READING–THINKING ACTIVITY

The *Directed Reading–Thinking Activity* (DRTA) can be an especially effective approach in the hands of good teachers, whether they use a basal reader series or trade books.

DRTA requires that students be active participants. "The reading–thinking process must begin in the mind of the reader. He must raise the questions and to him belongs the challenge and the responsibility of a judgment. The teacher keeps the process active and changes the amount of data to be processed."[31] Here is an outline of the process:[32]

> I.  Pupil actions
>     A.  Predict (set purposes)
>     B.  Read (process ideas)
>     C.  Prove (test answers)
> II.  Teacher actions
>     A.  What do you think? (activate thought)
>     B.  Why do you think so? (agitate thought)
>     C.  Prove it. (require evidence)

In order to use DRTA effectively, teachers must know how to encourage students to ask questions that stimulate higher-level thinking; teachers must be well-versed in facilitating the inquiry process.

## THINK ALOUD

Many good teachers have probably used this approach, but may not have been aware of it. Often when a teacher has students who have difficulty understanding something that is being explained, the teacher may "model" the skill for them. That is, the teacher "thinks aloud" or verbalizes thoughts to give students insight into the process. The teacher literally states out loud exactly the steps that he or she goes through to solve the problem or gain an understanding of a concept. Many reading program authors are including modeling as part of their instructional plans.

Here are some suggested teaching procedures:[33]

1.  Choose a passage to read aloud. The passage should have some areas that will pose some difficulties such as unknown words. It could also contain an excellent description that would be perfect if you want to teach students something about visualizing.
2.  Begin reading the passage orally while students follow. When you come to a trouble spot, stop and think through it aloud while students listen to what you say.
3.  When you have finished reading, invite students to add any thoughts to yours.
4.  Partner the students up and have them practice.
5.  Remind students to use the strategy when they are reading silently. A self-evaluation form such as the one shown in Figure 10.12 might help students evaluate how well they read.

**Directed Reading–Thinking Activity**
(DRTA) Requires teachers to nurture the inquiry process and students to be active participants and questioners; includes prediction and verification.

Go to the Assignments and Activities section of Topic 9: Reading Comprehension in the MyEducationLab for your course and complete the activity entitled "Modeling a Think Aloud." As you watch the video and answer the accompanying questions, consider how thinking skills are invisible to students.

---

[31]Russell G. Stauffer, *Directing the Reading—Thinking Process* (New York: Harper & Row, 1975), p. 37.

[32]Ibid.

[33]B. Davey, "Think Aloud: Modeling the Cognitive Processes of Reading Comprehension," *Journal of Reading* 27 (1983): 44–47.

---

**FIGURE 10.12　Analyzing My Reading**

Name _____ Date _____

What I read: _____

Here's what I did and how well I think I did it:

|  | *Little* | *Some* | *Much* |
|---|---|---|---|
| 1. I formed questions before reading. |  |  |  |
| 2. I tried to make pictures using the author's words. |  |  |  |
| 3. I made some connections with other books. |  |  |  |
| 4. I knew when I was having a problem and I did something to fix the problem so that I could continue reading with understanding. |  |  |  |
| 5. I was able to comprehend this text. |  |  |  |

## REPEATED READING

**Repeated reading**
Similar to paired reading; child reads along (assisted reading with model or tape) until he or she gains confidence to read alone.

*Repeated reading* is a technique that has gained favor among a number of teachers to help students who have poor oral reading skills to achieve fluency in reading. A suggested procedure for repeated readings follows:[34]

> *Passage length:* Short; about 50 to 100 words
> *Types of passages:* Any reading materials that will be of interest to the child
> *Readability level of passage:* Start at independent level; proceed to more difficult passages as the child gains confidence in oral reading; controlled vocabulary is not imperative.
> *Assisted reading:* Use the read-along approach (assisted reading with a model or tape) to help with phrasing and speed; use when speed is below 45 words per minute (WPM), even though the child makes few errors.
> *Unassisted reading:* Use when the child reaches 60 WPM.

## RECIPROCAL READING INSTRUCTION

**Reciprocal reading instruction**
A teacher-directed technique consisting of four steps: summarizing, questioning, clarifying, and predicting.

*Reciprocal reading instruction*, which is used in a group setting to help students gain comprehension skills,[35] is a teacher-directed technique because it requires the teacher to first model the four steps for students before having them perform the task. Also, like all techniques, reciprocal reading instruction is only as good as the teacher presenting it.

---

[34]Adapted from Sarah L. Dowhower, "Repeated Reading: Research into Practice," *The Reading Teacher* 42 (March, 1989): 504–506.

[35]*See* Ann L. Brown, Annemarie Sullivan Palincsar, and Bonnie B. Armbruster, "Instructing Comprehension-Fostering Activities in Interactive Learning Situations," in *Learning and Comprehension of Text,* eds. Heinz Mandl et al. (Hillsdale, NJ: Lawrence Erlbaum, 1984).

The four steps involved in this technique are summarizing, questioning, clarifying, and predicting. When the students in the group have all read a specified passage, the teacher models the four steps for them. After the teacher has modeled the passage using all four steps, he or she has the students do the same. The amount of help given and the number of times that the teacher will model how to use the procedure for the children will vary depending on the individual needs of the children.

## LITERATURE WEBBING

**Literature webbing**
A story map technique to help guide children in using predictable trade books.

Success breeds success! If children have good experiences in reading at an early age, these experiences will help instill good attitudes about reading in them. Predictable books appear to be one way to provide these experiences.[36] *Literature webbing* is a story map or graphic illustration that teachers can use as one approach to guide them in using predictable trade books with their children.

The literature webbing strategy lesson (LWSL), which is an adaptation by Reutzel and Fawson of Watson and Crowley's Story Schema Lessons to "provide support for early readers,"[37] includes a six-step process. The preliminary preparation includes the teacher's reading of the text and excerpting a number of samples from it that are large enough that children can make predictions about them. (The excerpts can be accompanied by enlarged illustrations if this procedure is used early in the year.) After the excerpts are chosen, the title of the book is placed in the center of the board with various web strands projecting from the title. (There are three more strands than needed for the number of excerpts. These strands, which are used for discussion purposes, are personal responses to the book, other books we've read like this one, and language extension activities.) Then the children follow these six steps:[38]

1. Sample the book by reading the randomly ordered illustrations and text excerpts that are placed on the chalk tray below the literature web.
2. Predict the pattern or order of the book by placing the excerpts in clockwise order around the literature web.
3. Read the predictable book straight through. (It may be a big book or a number of copies of the normal-sized text.)
4. Confirm or correct their predictions.
5. Discuss the remaining three strands that are on the board (see above).
6. Participate in independent or supported reading activities.

## QUESTIONING STRATEGIES

Some children need help in developing higher-level reading comprehension skills. Asking many types of questions that demand higher-level skills will better ensure that students become thoughtful and insightful readers.

The kinds of questions the teacher asks will determine the kinds of answers he or she receives. In addition to asking a question that calls for a literal response, use questions that call for higher levels of thinking. This process can begin as early as kindergarten and first grade. For example, suppose the children are looking at a picture in which a few children are dressed in hats, snow pants, jackets, and scarves. After asking the children what kind of clothes the children in the picture are wearing, try to

---

[36]D. Ray Reutzel and Parker C. Fawson, "Using a Literature Webbing Strategy Lesson with Predictable Books," *The Reading Teacher* 43 (December, 1989): 208.

[37]Ibid., p. 209.

[38]Ibid.

elicit from students the answers to the following questions: "What kind of day do you think it is?" "What do you think the children are going to do?"

This type of inference question is very simple because it is geared to the cognitive development level of the children. As the children progress to higher levels of thinking, they should be confronted with more complex interpretation or inference problems. Work with children according to their individual levels. Expect all the children to be able to perform, but avoid putting students in situations that frustrate rather than stimulate them.

Critical reading skills are essential for good readers. Use primary graders' love of folktales to begin to develop some critical reading skills. For example, after the children have read "The Little Red Hen," ask questions such as the following:

1. Should the Little Red Hen have shared the bread with the other animals? Explain.
2. Would you have shared the bread with the other animals? Explain.
3. Do you think animals can talk? Explain.
4. Do you feel sorry for the other animals? Explain.
5. Do you think this story is true? Explain.

Creative reading questions are probably the most ignored. To help children in this area, learn how to ask questions that require divergent rather than convergent answers. Some questions that should stimulate *divergent thinking* on the part of the reader would be the following:

**Divergent thinking**
The many different ways to solve problems or to look at things.

1. After reading "The Little Red Hen," try to come up with another ending for the story.
2. Try to add another animal to the story of "The Little Red Hen."
3. Try to add another part to the story of "The Little Red Hen."

Divergent answers require more time than convergent answers. Also, there is no one correct answer.

Following are a short reading selection and examples of four different types of comprehension questions. Read both as practice in recognizing the different types of questions at the four levels.

One day in the summer, some of my friends and I decided to go on an overnight hiking trip. We all started out fresh and full of energy. About halfway to our destination, when the sun was almost directly overhead, one-third of my friends decided to return home. The remaining four of us, however, continued on our hike. Our plan was to reach our destination by sunset. About six hours later as the four of us, exhausted and famished, were slowly edging ourselves in the direction of the setting sun, we saw a sight that astonished us. There, at the camping site, were our friends who had claimed that they were returning home. It seems that they did indeed go home, but only to pick up a car and drive out to the campsite.

The following are the four different types of comprehension questions:

*Literal comprehension:* What season of the year was it in the story? What kind of trip were the people going on?

*Interpretation:* About what time of day was it when some of the people decided to return home? How many people were there when they first started out on the trip? In what direction were the hikers heading when they saw a sight that astonished them? At about what time did the sun set?

*Critical reading:* How do you think the hikers felt when they reached their destination? Do you feel that the people who went home did the right thing by driving back to the site rather than hiking? Explain.

*Creative reading:* What do you think the exhausted hikers did and said when they saw the two who had supposedly gone home?

**Question–Answer Relationships (QARs)**
Helps students distinguish between "what they have in their heads" and information that is in the text.

# QUESTION–ANSWER RELATIONSHIPS (QARS)

The more children understand what they do when they are in the act of answering questions, the better question solvers they can be. Raphael has designed an instructional strategy, Question–Answer Relationships (QARs), that teachers can use to help their students gain insights into how they go about reading text and answering questions. It helps students "realize the need to consider both information in the text and information from their own knowledge background."[39]

In the QAR technique, students learn to distinguish between information that "they have in their heads" and information that is in the text. The following steps can help children gain facility in QAR. Note that the amount of time children spend at each step is determined by the individual differences of the students.

*Step 1.* Students gain help in understanding differences between what is in their heads and what is in the text. Ask children to read a passage, and then present questions that guide them to gain the needed understandings. Here is a short sample:

> Mike and his father went to the ball game.
> They were lucky to get tickets for the game.
> They saw many people they knew.
> At the game Mike and his father ate hot dogs.
> They also drank soda.

Ask the students the following questions:

1. Where did Mike and his father go? (To the ball game)
2. Where did they see the people? (At the ball game)

Point out to the children that the first answer is directly stated, whereas the second is not; it is "in their heads."

*Step 2.* The "In the Book" category is divided into two parts. The first deals with information that is directly stated in a single sentence in the passage, and the second deals with piecing together the answer from different parts of the passage. (Raphael calls this step "Think and Search" or "Putting It Together.")[40]

Give the children practice in doing this.

*Step 3.* This is similar to Step 2 except that now the "In My Head" category is divided into two parts: "Author and You" and "On My Own."[41] Help students recognize whether the question is text-dependent or independent. For example, answering the first question below would require the student to read the text, even though the answer would come from the student's background of experiences. However, the student can answer the second without reading the passage.

1. How else do you think the cat could have escaped?
2. How would you feel if you were lost?

[39]Taffy E. Raphael, "Teaching Question–Answer Relationships, Revisited," *The Reading Teacher* 39 (February, 1986): 517.

[40]Ibid., p. 518.

[41]Ibid.

The QAR approach can be very useful in introducing children to inferential reasoning; it helps them to better understand what information is directly stated and what is implied. Teachers can modify the QAR approach to suit their students' needs.

## RE-QUEST

Re-Quest stands for reciprocal questioning. It is different from reciprocal teaching, and was developed to increase students' comprehension.[42] But it is also tied to engagement and motivation. Students get used to being "quizzed" about things they have read. This is not authentic communication, and they know it. In Re-Quest, students get a turn to think of questions and get answers from someone else. This reverses the typical power structure of questioning. When paired with Question–Answer Relationships, Re-Quest becomes a tool for higher-level thinking. Coach students to ask questions that can be answered in two ways: (1) By looking at or remembering what was in the text, and (2) by problem-solving, putting clues together, or using outside knowledge and opinion.

Decide with the students on a length of passage to read before stopping. In the original method, Manzo & Manzo stopped after every sentence for students who were losing comprehension at that level. You may stop after paragraphs, pages, or even chapters. Decide on an appropriate turn-taking strategy that involves both the teacher and the students reading. Decide whether you will read silently or orally. If reading orally, take turns reading and listening.

- Teacher reads.
- Stop at the determined place.
- Students ask questions for teacher (or other students) to answer.
- Student reads.
- Teacher gets to ask questions for students to answer.
- Continue taking turns.
- Use QAR procedure to reinforce higher-order thinking in questions.

---

[42]A. V. Manzo, "The Re-Quest Procedure," *Journal of Reading* 13 (1969): 123–126.

**FIGURE 10.13A　Comprehension Strategy: Making Connections**

*What is Making Connections?*

This strategy has readers (a) connect their knowledge to a selection, (b) connect other texts to a selection, and (c) connect their responses to a selection.

*How do I teach Making Connections?*

1. **Introduction:** Present a short selection to students and have them tell what they **know** about the topic, if the selection makes them think of other **stories**, and how they might **respond** to the selection. State that these are different kinds of **connections** a reader can make to a selection. Explain that making connections helps readers understand stories better and enjoy them more.

2. **Instruction:** Write on the board, a chart, or a transparency three different kinds of connections a reader can make to a selection:

   - Connections to what a reader **knows**.
   - Connections to other **stories**.
   - Connections to story **responses**.

   Model how to make connections by using a poster selection, a selection from a read-aloud book, or a magazine. Model connecting by reading a part of the story and then thinking aloud as you make connections for students by asking and answering questions such as the following: (1) Connections to what a reader **knows**. "What do I know about this topic? Can I say or write down those ideas?" (2) Connections to other **stories**. "Does this story remind me of another story? Do I know other stories by this same author or illustrator? How are they alike and different?" (3) Connections to story **responses**. "Did I enjoy this story? Was it interesting or funny? What do I think about the characters or what happened?"

3. **Guided Practice:** Have students practice making connections by reading the next section of the selection and asking themselves **know**, **story**, and **response** connection questions like those above. Provide support and extra modeling as necessary to guide students through the process of making connections.

*How can students practice Making Connections?*

Have students complete a connection chart as a group, with a partner, or individually. Have students discuss and write **know**, **story**, and **response** connections before, during, and after reading the selection.

| *Making connections to . . .* | | |
|---|---|---|
| what I **know**. | other **stories**. | story **responses**. |
|  |  |  |

**FIGURE 10.13B   Comprehension Strategy: Making Predictions**

*What is Making Predictions?*

This strategy requires students to (a) use prior knowledge and information in a selection to make logical guesses or predictions about events in the selection, (b) read on to check (verify) their predictions, and (c) change or make new predictions from the new information in the selection.

*How do I teach Making Predictions?*

1. **Introduction:** Present a picture or read a short selection to students and have them guess what might happen next. Tell them that these guesses are ***predictions***. Explain that making predictions helps readers think about the story and look for ideas the writer might tell them later. State also that making and checking predictions gives readers a purpose for reading and helps them understand what they read.

2. **Instruction:** Write the four steps for making predictions on the board, a chart, or a transparency:

   Step 1. ***Read*** a part of the story.
   Step 2. ***Predict*** what will happen next.
   Step 3. Read on and ***Check*** predictions (**T** = True, **F** = False, **CT** = Can't Tell Yet.)
   Step 4. ***Change*** or make new predictions.

   Model how to follow these steps using a poster selection, a selection from a read-aloud book, or a magazine: (1) ***Read*** aloud part of the selection. (2) Think aloud as you make several ***predictions*** and write them down. (3) Read more of the selection and think aloud as you ***check*** the predictions by writing **T** (**T**rue), **F** (**F**alse), or **CT** (**C**an't **T**ell Yet) after each. (4) ***Change*** the predictions or make new ones from new ideas in the selection.

3. **Guided Practice:** Have students follow the four steps on the next portion of the selection by having them ***read***, ***predict***, ***check*** predictions, and ***change*** or make new ones. Provide support and reteaching as necessary to guide students through the prediction process.

*How can students practice Making Predictions?*

Have students complete a prediction equation as a group, with a partner, or individually. Ask students to write ***clues*** from the story and ideas they ***know*** that lead them to a ***prediction***. Then have students ***check*** their predictions and either change them or make new ones.

$$\boxed{\textbf{Clues from the story}} \quad \textbf{+} \quad \boxed{\textbf{What I know}} \quad \textbf{=} \quad \boxed{\textbf{Prediction}}$$

Check your prediction. Was it (circle one)   **T   F   CT** ?

Change your prediction or make a new one: _____

_____

*(continued)*

**FIGURE 10.13C   Comprehension Strategy: Monitoring Understanding**   *(continued)*

*What is Monitoring Understanding?*

This strategy has readers (a) develop the ability to recognize comprehension breakdowns when they occur, and (b) apply fix-up strategies to correct comprehension difficulties.

*How do I teach Monitoring Understanding?*

1. **Introduction:** Read aloud a short selection to students, but insert several words or short sentences that do not make sense within the overall passage. Ask students "Did that story make sense? Why not?" State that what they did was to check or *monitor* their reading comprehension. Explain that *monitoring* reading comprehension is important so that readers can tell when a selection is not making sense. They can then correct, or fix up, their understanding.

2. **Instruction:** Write on the board, a chart, or a transparency the two steps for monitoring comprehension:

   Step 1.  Read part of a selection, stop, and ask "Is this selection making sense?"
   Step 2.  If you answer "No," then try one or more of these fix-up strategies:
   • Read the sentence or paragraph again.
   • Retell the sentence or paragraph in your own words.
   • Ask a question or make a prediction.
   • Read on and see if the selection makes sense.

Model how to monitor comprehension by selecting a challenging selection from a poster, a read-aloud book, or a magazine. Model monitoring by reading a paragraph, stopping, and asking "Is this making sense?" Answer "No," and indicate what has you confused, such as a main idea, a character's motive, a cause/effect relationship, or a word referent that is not clear. Then select one or more of the "fix-up" strategies and model how to apply each by thinking aloud as you clarify the confusing part of the selection.

3. **Guided Practice:** Have students practice monitoring by inviting volunteers to read the next section of the selection, asking "Is this making sense?", and then applying one or more of the fix-up strategies to help them comprehend. Provide support and extra modeling as necessary to guide students through the process of monitoring.

*How can students practice Monitoring Understanding?*

Make comprehension monitoring "Stop Signs" as below. Have students use them as they read, stopping at the end of each paragraph or page, putting down the stop sign with Side 1 up, and asking "Is this making sense?" If they answer "No," then have them turn the sign to Side 2 and try one or more of the fix-up strategies.

Stop!
Is this making
sense?

To Fix Up
reread, retell,
question, predict,
or read on.

---

FIGURE 10.13D   **Comprehension Strategy: Visualizing**

*What is Visualizing?*

This strategy has readers create pictures in their minds to promote their understanding, recall, and appreciation of a selection.

*How do I teach Visualizing?*

1. **Introduction:** Ask students to close their eyes and listen carefully while you read aloud a short, descriptive selection. When you have finished, have students open their eyes, and ask "What was the selection about? Did anyone see a picture of what you heard? Can you tell us about the picture you drew in your mind?" Explain that making a mental picture, or *visualizing*, is a powerful way to help listeners and readers understand, remember, and enjoy a selection.

2. **Instruction:** Write on the board, a chart, or a transparency the following ideas to help students visualize as they are reading:

   - Read a selection carefully.
   - Look for words that tell about *settings*, *actions*, *colors*, *characters*, or *sounds*.
   - Use the writer's words to *visualize*, or make a mental picture of, the selection.

Model how to visualize by using a selection from a poster, a read-aloud book, or a magazine. Think aloud as you (1) read part of the story and look for words to help you visualize; (2) comment on words that tell about actions, colors, characters, sounds, or settings; and (3) use the writer's words to paint a verbal picture of the scene or events in the selection.

3. **Guided Practice:** Practice visualizing by inviting volunteers to read the next portion of the selection and talk about the words that help them form mental pictures. Then have them describe the pictures they drew in their minds as they read. Invite students to compare how their visualizations were alike and different, noting how readers paint different pictures for the same selection. Discuss how visualizing might help them understand, remember, or enjoy a selection.

*How can students practice Visualizing?*

Complete a visualizing chart as students read a selection. Have them write words the author uses to help them visualize. Then have them draw pictures that show their visualizations.

| *To visualize while I read, I can . . .* | |
| --- | --- |
| write words that help me make mental pictures. | draw a picture of what I saw in my mind. |
|  |  |

*(continued)*

**FIGURE 10.13E Comprehension Strategy: Questioning** *(continued)*

### *What is Questioning?*

With this strategy, readers learn to generate questions as they read. Self-questioning promotes active, engaged reading and enhances students' literal, inferential, and critical comprehension.

### *How do I teach Questioning?*

1. **Introduction:** Read aloud a short selection that requires some interpretation. Stop occasionally and ask questions like "Who is the main character? I wonder when this story takes place? What's the writer's main point here? What will happen next?" Ask the students what you were doing. State that you were asking yourself questions about the selection as you read. Explain that *questioning*—readers asking themselves about the selection—is a useful way to better understand, remember, and enjoy what one reads.

2. **Instruction:** Write on the board, a chart, or a transparency different categories and examples of questions readers might ask themselves as they try to understand a selection:

   - *Setting:* Who are the characters? When and where is this taking place?
   - *Events:* What happened? What caused it to happen? What did the author leave out and expect me to figure out? What was the result of these events?
   - *Content:* What do I know about this topic? What's the main idea here? How does one event lead to another? What conclusion can I draw?
   - *Response:* What would I do? Do I agree with the character's actions? What was funny, sad, or interesting? Does this remind me of something else I have read?

Model how to self-question when reading a selection from a poster, read-aloud book, or a magazine. Think aloud by asking setting, event, content, and response questions. Help students realize that there are no "right" questions but only those that help them understand and appreciate what they are reading.

3. **Guided Practice:** Invite students to engage in self-questioning as they read subsequent sections of the selection. Encourage them to ask a variety of setting, event, content, and response questions. Help students realize that there are no "right" questions but only those that help them understand and appreciate what they are reading.

### *How can students practice Questioning?*

Create a self-questioning map. Use the map to help students self-question as they read fiction, nonfiction, and other genres. Write setting, event, content, and response questions on the map.

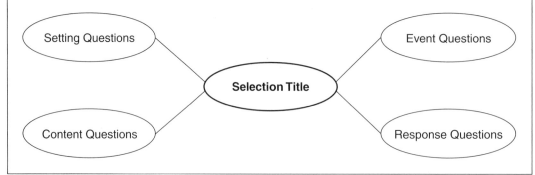

**FIGURE 10.13F   Comprehension Strategy: Retelling/Summarizing**

*What is Retelling/Summarizing?*

These strategies have readers identify and work with the main ideas and supporting details of a selection. Retelling requires students to restate the major events and supporting details in a selection. Summarizing requires students to extract only the main ideas from a selection.

*How do I teach Retelling/Summarizing?*

1. **Introduction:** Read aloud a short selection. Then retell the selection by restating the main events in order, and summarize the selection by constructing a statement that tells the main ideas of the selection. Ask students whether they can describe the two things you just did and how they were alike and different. Explain that the first was a *retelling* (saying the events in a selection in the order in which they happened) and the second was a *summary* (saying just the main ideas of a selection).

2. **Instruction:** Write on the board, a chart, or a transparency the following descriptions:

| *To retell a selection . . .* | *To summarize a selection . . .* |
|---|---|
| • say or write the main events and important details. <br> • say or write them in the order in which they happened. | • figure out the most important ideas or events in the selection. <br> • say or write them in a brief statement. |

Model how to retell and summarize by selecting a short item from a poster, read-aloud book, or magazine. Read the selection and then retell it, including the main events and important details in the order in which they happened. Next, summarize the selection, thinking aloud to show how you figured out the main ideas and then constructed a short statement to express them. Invite students to explain how your retelling differed from your summary (for example, retelling is longer, includes more detail, uses many words from the selection; summary is shorter and includes only the main ideas from the selection).

3. **Guided Practice:** Select and read another short passage and invite students to offer first a retelling of it and then a summary of it. Refer them to the chart as needed. Ask students to compare and contrast the retelling and summary for similarities and differences.

*How can students practice Retelling/Summarizing?*

Select a short passage and have students generate both a retelling and a summary and write them on a chart. Have them consider how their retelling and summary are alike and different. Ask how they both are helpful for understanding and remembering important ideas in selections.

| Retelling of _____ | Summary of _____ |
|---|---|

*(continued)*

**FIGURE 10.13G    Comprehension Strategy: Additional Titles for Comprehension Strategy Development**

### Making Connections

Dewdney, Anna. *Llama Llama Mad at Mama*. New York: Penguin, 2007.
Hall, Donald. *Ox-Cart Man*. New York: Puffin, 1983.
Viorst, Judith. *Alexander and the Terrible, Horrible, No Good, Very Bad Day*. New York: Aladdin, 1987.

### Making Predictions

George, Lindsay Barrett. *In the Garden: Who's Been Here?* New York: HarperCollins, 2006.
Lewis, J. Patrick. *Spot the Plot: A Riddle Book of Book Riddles*. San Francisco, CA: Chronicle, 2009.
Macdonald, Suse. *Shape by Shape*. New York: Simon & Schuster, 2009.
Parish, Herman. *Amelia Bedelia's First Day of School*. New York: HarperCollins, 2009.
Schaefer, Lola M. *An Island Grows*. New York: HarperCollins, 2006.

### Monitoring Understanding

Adler, David. *Don't Talk to Me About the War*. New York: Penguin, 2008.
Parry, Florence. *The Day of Ahmed's Secret*. New York: HarperCollins, 2005.
Snicket, Lemony. *The Composer Is Dead*. New York: HarperCollins, 2009.

### Visualizing

Brown, Ruth. *Toad*. New York: Penguin, 1997.
Yolen, Jane. *Color Me a Rhyme*. Honesdale, PA: Boyds Mills, 2003.

### Questioning

Bunting, Eve. *How Many Days to America*. New York: Clarion, 1988.
Gerstein, Mordicai. *Leaving the Nest*. New York: Farrar, Straus, & Giroux, 2007.
Van Allsburg, Chris. *The Widow's Broom*. New York: Houghton Mifflin, 1992.

### Retelling/Summarizing

Auch, Mary Jane & Herm. *The Plot Chickens*. New York: Holiday House, 2009.
Martin, Jacqueline Briggs. *Snowflake Bentley*. New York: Houghton Mifflin, 1998.
Swinburne, Stephen. *A Butterfly Grows*. Boston: Houghton Mifflin Harcourt, 2009.

*Source:* From *Summer Success Reading* by James F. Baumann, Michael F. Opitz, Laura Robb. Text copyright © 2001 Great Source Education Group, a division of Houghton Mifflin Company. Reprinted by permission. All rights reserved.

## REVISITING THE OPENING SCENARIO

After reviewing and thinking about the teaching strategies presented in this chapter, provide Ms. Mills with some specific suggestions on ways she can help Alan learn to use higher-order thinking skills during reading.

## AUTHORS' SUMMARY

In this chapter, we provided background information about comprehension. We emphasized that comprehension involves thinking and that just as there are various levels of thinking, so too are there various levels of comprehension. We then discussed comprehension skills and strategies that are important for readers to know and use in order to comprehend. Assessment is essential and we offered numerous suggestions for how to assess what students know and need to know. Finally, we offered instructional strategies teachers can use to enhance students' comprehension.

## SUGGESTIONS FOR THOUGHT QUESTIONS AND ACTIVITIES

1. Generate reading comprehension questions for a selection that would elicit higher-level reading/thinking responses.
2. Present a reading comprehension lesson and record it. Note the kinds of questions you ask. Critique your lesson and state some ways in which you can improve it.
3. Use one of the strategies presented in this chapter to teach a reading lesson.
4. You have a student in your class who has difficulty answering comprehension questions. How would you go about determining what his or her problems are? What can you do to help this student?
5. How would you develop a recreational reading program in your classroom? What techniques and procedures would you use? Suggest three ways to encourage students to read voluntarily.

## WEBSITES

http://www.textmapping.org/

This site provides lesson guides and opportunities to network with others, including teachers and education researchers. The site also contains links to research on reading comprehension skills instruction, and free resources for teacher-trainers, presenters, and schools of education.

http://teachersfirst.com/getsource.cfm?id=6812

This site provides before, during, and after reading strategies for teachers to imbed in their lesson plans. It contains a description of each strategy and its purpose(s) and then links to a full lesson containing the strategy in which examples and differentiation possibilities are provided.

http://www.world-english.org/listening_exercises.htm

The World-English site provides a variety of listening comprehension exercises. Choose from a variety of topics and focus areas, including but not limited to family histories, news stories, and cars. The site also covers ESL listening comprehension.

http://www.lessonplans4teachers.com/listening.php

This site from Nova Southeastern University offers lessons on listening skills and listening rubrics. The site also provides thematic units, worksheets, lesson templates, and ESL materials. Once a link is chosen, the site provides access to other web sites and links.

## SELECTED BIBLIOGRAPHY

Blachowicz, C., and D. Ogle. *Reading Comprehension: Strategies for Independent Learners.* New York: Guilford, 2001.

Block, C. C., L. L. Rodgers, and R. B. Johnson. *Comprehension Process Instruction.* New York: Guilford, 2004.

Boyles, N. N. *Constructing Meaning Through Kid-Friendly Comprehension Strategy Instruction.* Gainesville, FL: Maupin House, 2004.

Buss, Kathleen, and Leslie McClain-Ruelle, eds. *Creating a Classroom Newspaper.* Newark, DE: International Reading Association, 2000.

Cianciolo, Patricia J. *Informational Picture Books for Children.* Chicago: American Library Association, 2000.

Cole, A. *Knee to Knee, Eye to Eye: Circling in on Comprehension.* Portsmouth, NH: Heinemann, 2003.

Cramer, Eugene H., and Marrietta Castle, eds. *Fostering the Love of Reading: The Affective Domain in Reading Education.* Newark, DE: International Reading Association, 1994.

Dorn, L. J., and C. Soffos. *Teaching for Deep Comprehension: A Reading Workshop Approach.* Portland, ME: Stenhouse, 2005.

Galda, Lee, et al. "Children's Literature." In *Handbook of Reading Research,* Vol. III, edited by Michael L. Kamil et al., 361–380. Mahwah, NJ: Lawrence Erlbaum, 2000.

Hoyt, L., et al. *Spotlight on Comprehension: Building a Literacy of Thoughtfulness.* Portsmouth, NH: Heinemann, 2005.

Kucer, S. *Dimensions of Literacy,* 2nd ed. Mahwah, NJ: Erlbaum.

Mantione, R., and S. Smead. *Weaving Through Words: Using the Arts to Teach Reading Comprehension Strategies.* Newark, DE: International Reading Association, 2003.

Marriott, D. *Comprehension Right from the Start.* Portsmouth, NH: Heinemann, 2003.

Oczkus, L. *Reciprocal Teaching at Work: Strategies for Improving Reading Comprehension.* Newark, DE: International Reading Association, 2003.

Outsen, N., and S. Yulga. *Teaching Comprehension Strategies All Readers Need.* New York: Scholastic, 2002.

Owocki, G. *Comprehension: Strategic Instruction for K–3 Students.* Portsmouth, NH: Heinemann, 2003.

Pierce, Cathryn M., ed. *Adventuring with Books: A Booklet for PreK–Grade 6,* 12th ed. Urbana, IL: National Council of Teachers of English, 2000.

Post, Arden Ruth, et al. *Celebrating Children's Choices: 25 Years of Children's Favorite Books.* Newark, DE: International Reading Association, 2000.

Pressley, Michael. "What Should Comprehension Instruction Be the Instruction Of?" In *Handbook of Reading Research,* Vol. III, edited by Michael L. Kamil et al., 545–62. Mahwah, NJ: Lawrence Erlbaum, 2000.

Rubin, Dorothy. *Comprehension Skills and Strategies in a Balanced Reading Program.* Torrance, CA: Fearon Teacher Aids, 1998.

———. *Elementary Language Arts,* 6th ed. Boston: Allyn and Bacon, 2000.

———. *Word Meaning & Reasoning Strategies* (a three-book series). Torrance, CA: Good Apple, 1996.

Sadler, C. *Comprehension Strategies for Middle Grade Learners: A Handbook for Content Area Teachers.* Newark, DE: International Reading Association, 2001.

Shaw, D. *Retelling Strategies to Improve Reading Comprehension.* New York: Scholastic, 2005.

Spiegel, D. *Classroom Discussion.* New York: Scholastic, 2005.

Sweet, A., and C. Snow, eds. *Rethinking Reading Comprehension.* New York: Guilford, 2003.

Wilhelm, J. *Action Strategies for Deepening Comprehension.* New York: Scholastic, 2002.

# CHILDREN'S LITERATURE CITED

Adler, David. *Don't Talk to Me About the War.* New York: Penguin, 2008.

Auch, Mary Jane, & Herm Auch. *The Plot Chickens.* New York: Holiday House, 2009.

Brown, Ruth. *Toad.* New York: Penguin, 1997.

Bunting, Eve. *How Many Days to America.* New York: Clarion, 1988.

Cleary, Beverly. *Dear Mr. Henshaw.* New York: Dell, 1983.

Dewdney, Anna. *Llama Llama Mad at Mama.* New York: Penguin, 2007.

Floca, Brian. *Lightship.* New York: Atheneum, 2007.

George, Lindsay Barrett. *In the Garden: Who's Been Here?* New York: HarperCollins, 2006.

Gerstein, Mordicai. *Leaving the Nest.* New York: Farrar, Straus, & Giroux, 2007.

Hall, Donald. *Ox-Cart Man.* New York: Puffin, 1983.

Lewis, J. Patrick. *Spot the Plot: A Riddle Book of Book Riddles.* San Francisco, CA: Chronicle, 2009.

Long, Melinda. *When Papa Snores.* New York: Simon & Schuster, 2000.

Macdonald, Suse. *Shape by Shape.* New York: Simon & Schuster, 2009.

Martin, Jacqueline Briggs. *Snowflake Bentley.* New York: Houghton Mifflin, 1998.

Munsch, Robert. *Alligator Baby.* New York: Scholastic, 1997.

Parish, Herman. *Amelia Bedelia's First Day of School.* New York: HarperCollins, 2009.

Parry, Florence. *The Day of Ahmed's Secret.* New York: HarperCollins, 2005.

Schaefer, Lola. *An Island Grows.* New York: HarperCollins, 2006.

Snicket, Lemony. *The Composer Is Dead.* New York: HarperCollins, 2009.

Spinelli, Jerry. *Maniac Magee.* New York: Little, Brown, 1990.

Swinburne, Stephen. *A Butterfly Grows.* Boston: Houghton Mifflin Harcourt, 2009.

Van Allsburg, Chris. *The Widow's Broom.* New York: Houghton Mifflin, 1992.

Viorst, Judith. *Alexander and the Terrible, Horrible, No Good, Very Bad Day.* New York: Aladdin, 1987.

Yolen, Jane. *Color Me a Rhyme.* Honesdale, PA: Boyds Mills, 2003.

**myeducationlab**

Now go to Topic 9: "Reading Comprehension" and Topic 7: "Fluency" in MyEducationLab (www.myeducationlab.com) for your course, where you can:

- Find learning outcomes for "Reading Comprehension" and "Fluency" along with national standards that connect to these outcomes.
- Complete Assignments and Activities that can help you more deeply understand the chapter content.
- Examine challenging situations and cases presented in the IRIS Center Resources.
- Access video clips of CCSSO National Teacher of the Year award winners responding to the question, "Why Do I Teach?" in the Teacher Talk section.
- Apply and practice your understanding of the core teaching skills identified in the chapter with Building Teaching Skills and Dispositions learning units.

# 11

**CHAPTER OUTLINE**

- Scenario: Mr. Jackson
  and Vocabulary Expansion
- Vocabulary Development
- Assessing Vocabulary
- Teaching Vocabulary
- Revisiting the Opening Scenario

# Helping Children Acquire and Apply Vocabulary

# SCENARIO: MR. JACKSON AND VOCABULARY EXPANSION

> Mr. Jackson was feeling dismayed when one student in his sixth-grade reading class said to him, "Mr. Jackson, I have a great amount of animosity toward you."
>
> Mr. Jackson was upset because he thought that he had very good rapport with the student, and thought the student enjoyed being in his class. Because the student's statement did not ring true, Mr. Jackson decided to question him.
>
> "Craig," Mr. Jackson said, "Is anything wrong? Have I done anything to offend you in any way?"
>
> Craig appeared perplexed. He looked Mr. Jackson straight in the eye and said, "No, I like your class. I look forward to coming to it."
>
> "If that is true," said Mr. Jackson, "then why did you say you disliked me?"
>
> "I didn't," said Craig. "I said that I like you a lot. I said just the opposite."
>
> What became clear to Mr. Jackson was that Craig apparently did not know the meaning of *animosity*. When Mr. Jackson asked Craig why he used the word *animosity*, Craig replied, "I like the way it looks and sounds, so I use it a lot." This encounter reminded Mr. Jackson that many students use words they can pronounce yet may not fully understand.

As the scenario helps to illustrate, good vocabulary and good reading go hand in hand. Readers must know the meanings of words if they are to understand what they are reading. Readers need to know how word meanings function in sentences and paragraphs to comprehend texts.

As children advance in concept development, their vocabulary development advances because the two are interrelated (see Chapter 7). Years ago, MacGinitie noted that "vocabulary is a key variable in reading comprehension and is a major feature of most tests of academic aptitude."[1] Investigators continue to confirm this earlier finding. For example, Daneman (1991) remarks: "Numerous researchers have noted that poor readers have smaller vocabularies than good readers. Indeed, vocabulary knowledge is one of the best single predictors of reading comprehension."[2] Current researchers all point to the need for readers to have a wide reading vocabulary in order to best comprehend a variety of texts.[3]

Given these findings, how can we help children to expand their vocabulary knowledge? The answers to this question provide the focus for this chapter. Our purpose is to provide teachers with some background related to reading vocabulary development, ways to assess reading vocabulary, and some specific suggestions for helping students to acquire a large reading vocabulary.

## CHAPTER OBJECTIVES

By the end of this chapter, you should be able to:

- Discuss what is involved in acquiring a reading vocabulary.
- Explain what is meant by *vocabulary consciousness.*

---

[1] Walter M. MacGinitie, "Language Development," in *Encyclopedia of Educational Research,* 4th ed. (London: Collier-Macmillan, 1969), p. 693.

[2] Meredyth Daneman, "Individual Differences in Reading Skills," in *Handbook of Reading Research,* Vol. II, eds. Rebecca Barr, Michael L. Kamil, Peter Mosenthal, and P. David Pearson (New York: Longman, 1991), p. 524.

[3] C. Blachowicz and P. Fisher, *Teaching vocabulary in all classrooms,* 2nd ed. (Columbus, OH: Merrill/Prentice-Hall, 2001). I. L. Beck, M. G. McKeown, and L. Kucan, *Bringing Words to Life: Robust Vocabulary Instruction* (New York: Guilford Press, 2002). M. Graves, *The Vocabulary Book: Learning and Instruction* (Newark, DE: International Reading Association, 2006).

- Define terms associated with word parts, and provide examples of types of words.
- Explain guidelines for effective vocabulary instruction.
- Explain how to document student progress in attaining a reading vocabulary.

## VOCABULARY DEVELOPMENT

### ACQUIRING VOCABULARY

Just how is it that readers acquire a reading vocabulary? Certainly, explicit instruction is one way. In fact, the development of vocabulary is too important to children's success in school to be left to chance. Teachers need to provide children with a planned vocabulary expansion program when they first enter school. "Direct vocabulary instruction is generally shown to result in an increase in both word knowledge and reading comprehension."[4]

For a vocabulary program to be successful, the teacher must recognize that individual differences exist between the amount and kinds of words that kindergarten and first-grade children have in their listening vocabulary (i.e., their ability to understand a word when it is spoken). Some children come to school with a rich and varied vocabulary, whereas others have a more limited and narrow vocabulary.[5]

Young children's listening vocabulary is larger than their speaking vocabulary and much larger than their reading and writing vocabularies (see Figure 11.1). All four areas of vocabulary need to be developed. However, since children first learn language through the aural–oral approach, continuing to expand their listening and speaking vocabularies is necessary.

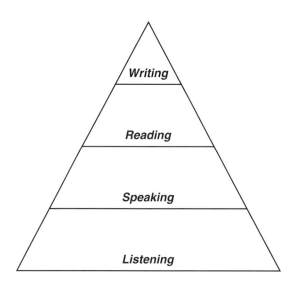

**FIGURE 11.1** Children's Vocabularies.

[4]M. J. Adams, *Beginning to Read: Thinking and Learning about Print.* (Cambridge, MA: MIT Press, 1990), p. 29. P. Hickman, S. Pollard-Durodola, and S. Vaughn, 2004. "Storybook Reading: Improving Vocabulary and Comprehension for English Language Learners," *The Reading Teacher,* 57 (2004): 720–730. National Reading Panel, 2000; see p. 464.

[5]B. Hart and T. R. Risley, *Meaningful Differences in the Everyday Experience of Young American Children* (Baltimore: Brookes, 1995).

There are three basic ways teachers can help children to acquire words: (1) Create a word-rich environment; (2) create independent word learners; and (3) model good word learning.[6] Taken together, all of these routes to vocabulary acquisition help children to develop a vocabulary consciousness, one goal of a vocabulary program.

## VOCABULARY CONSCIOUSNESS

In the primary grades, children are beginning to encounter words that are spelled the same but have different meanings, based on their context in the sentence. Students learn that the word *saw* in "I saw Jennifer" carries a different meaning than *saw* in the sentence, "Andrew will help his uncle saw the tree." When children recognize that *saw, train, coat,* and many other words have different meanings based on surrounding words, this is a sign that they are building a *vocabulary consciousness.* Another sign is when they begin to ask about and look up the meanings of new words they come across in their everyday activities. When teachers see these signs, they can be certain that students are developing vocabulary consciousness.

> **Vocabulary consciousness**
> An awareness that words may have different meanings based on their context and a desire to increase one's vocabulary.

## LEVELS OF KNOWING A WORD

Some words are more difficult to acquire than others. Learners appear to go through several levels of knowing a word. We illustrate these levels as a ladder in Figure 11.2. The figure also shows that to move up the ladder, children need much meaningful practice and repeated exposure. The first level is where they display no awareness of the word, neither recognizing it visually nor understanding it. Assuming that learners continue to work to acquire the word, they then move into the second level, which is where they begin to be somewhat acquainted with the word. Learners recognize it with some help. This is similar to being introduced to an individual and then seeing the person in another situation. If we are fortunate to be with someone who can give us a clue about who the person is, we can call the person by name and perhaps engage in a conversation. We *recognize* the person because we were prompted. The third level, the one learners strive to reach with words they feel are important, is the identification stage. At this level, they can identify a word instantaneously, have a better understanding of it,

## Levels of Knowing a Word

**Practice ~ Repeated exposure**

- can identify
- attain deeper, richer knowledge of the word

- can recognize
- somewhat acquainted

- not known

**FIGURE 11.2**   Levels of Knowing a Word

[6]C. L. Blachowicz and P. J. Fisher, (2000). "Vocabulary Instruction," in *Handbook of Reading Research,* Vol. III, eds. M. L. Kamil, P. B. Mosenthal, P. D. Pearson, and R. Barr (Mahwah, NJ: Erlbaum, 2000), pp. 503–523.

and develop deeper meanings for the word. Once learners are at this third stage, they continue to deepen their understanding of a word. Vocabulary acquisition is never truly "complete" for any word.[7] Take the word *catastrophe,* for example. While many are familiar with the word and can identify it without difficulty, 9/11 certainly helped many readers develop a deeper meaning of the word.

## TYPES OF WORDS

When thinking of teaching reading vocabulary, teachers need to remember that not all words are created equal. Try this exercise and see if you can determine which word in each group is the easiest for a reader to learn:

| *Group 1* | *Group 2* |
| --- | --- |
| ant | of |
| and | said |
| are | elephant |

Go to the Assignments and Activities section of Topic 6: Vocabulary in the MyEducationLab for your course and complete the activity entitled "Word Parts." As you watch the video and answer the accompanying questions, consider the emphasis on *meaning* in word parts.

Did you select *ant* from the first group and *elephant* from the second group? If so, you are correct because both are nouns. Nouns are easier to learn to read than other words because you can put an image with them. Even though elephant is a much longer word, it is much easier to picture than "of"! One reason so many young children can identify just about any name of any dinosaur, then, is that they are interested in knowing the dinosaur names and each name has a distinct image associated with it. Concrete words, such as action verbs, nouns, and adjectives are easy for students to learn and do not make high demands for context. They can stand alone. Abstract words, including words with grammatical and linguistic functions, and homophones, homonyms, and homographs may be more difficult. While the words may contain fewer letters, they make high demands for context in order to be understood. Many times these words are "glue" words—they serve to hold the concrete elements of the sentence together.

## SIGHT VOCABULARY

**Sight words**
Words readers can identify instantaneously.

*Sight words* are those words that readers can identify without conscious decoding; they know them instantaneously. All readers have their own personalized sight vocabulary because they have varied interests, which lead them to read texts associated with those interests. For example, an individual who is interested in sports would have a different personalized sight vocabulary than a person interested in music. This being said, when teachers talk of helping children to develop sight vocabulary, they are often really referring to *high-frequency* words. These are words that occur most often in children's books; hence, the label high-frequency. Different researchers have compiled high-frequency lists. Two of the most common lists are the Dolch list and the Fry Instant Word List. Because the Fry Instant Word List is more current, we provide a copy of the first 100 words in Figure 11.3. Teachers need to recognize that children may come to school with a huge store of sight words, yet few of these may come from the high-frequency lists.

**High-frequency words**
Words that appear most often in texts.

## DEFINING WORD PART TERMS

There are many words in our language that combine with other words to form new words, for example, *grandfather* and *boardwalk* (compound words). You can also combine a root (base) word with a letter or a group of letters either at the beginning (*prefix*)

**Prefix**
A letter or a sequence of letters added to the beginning of a root word.

[7]M. B. McVee, J. R. Gavelek, and K. L. Dunsmore. (2007). "Considerations of the Social, Individual, and Embodied: A Response to Comments on 'Schema Theory Revisited,'" *Review of Educational Research* 77, no. 2 (2007): 245–248.

---

### FIGURE 11.3   The Instant Words* First Hundred

These are the most common words in English, ranked in frequency order. The first 25 make up about a third of all printed material. The first 100 make up about half of all written material. Is it any wonder that all students must learn to identify these words instantly and to spell them correctly also?

| *Words 1–25* | *Words 26–50* | *Words 51–75* | *Words 76–100* |
|---|---|---|---|
| the | or | will | number |
| of | one | up | no |
| and | had | other | way |
| a | by | about | could |
| to | word | out | people |
| in | but | many | my |
| is | not | then | than |
| you | what | them | first |
| that | all | these | water |
| it | were | so | been |
| he | we | some | call |
| was | when | her | who |
| for | your | would | oil |
| on | can | make | now |
| are | said | like | find |
| as | there | him | long |
| with | use | into | down |
| his | an | time | day |
| they | each | has | did |
| I | which | look | get |
| at | she | two | come |
| be | do | more | made |
| this | how | write | may |
| have | their | go | part |
| from | if | see | over |

**Common suffixes:** *-s, -ing, -ed*

*For additional instant words, see *The Reading Teacher's Book of Lists* by E. Fry, D. Fountoukidis, and J. Polk. Englewood Cliffs NJ: Jossey-Bass, 2000. Reprinted with permission.

---

**Suffix**
A letter or a sequence of letters added to the end of a root word.

**Affixes**
Prefixes and suffixes.

or end (*suffix*) of the root word to form a new, related word, for example, *replay* and *played. Affix* is a term used to refer either to a prefix or a suffix.

In the words *replay* and *played, play* is a root or base, *re* is a prefix, and *ed* is a suffix. A *root* is the smallest unit of a word that can exist and retain its basic meaning. It cannot be subdivided any further. *Replay* is not a root word because it can be subdivided to *play. Play* is a root word because it cannot be divided further and still retain a meaning related to the root word.

*Derivatives* are combinations of root words with either prefixes or suffixes or both. *Combining forms* are usually defined as roots borrowed from another language that join together or that join with a prefix, a suffix, or both a prefix and a suffix to form a word. Many times the English combining forms are derived from Greek and Latin roots.

**Root**
Smallest unit of a word that can exist and retain its basic meaning.

**Derivatives**
Combinations of root words with prefixes or suffixes, or both.

**Context clue**
An item of information from the words surrounding a particular word in the form of a synonym, antonym, example, definition, description, explanation, and so on, that helps shed light on the meaning of that particular word.

Go to the Assignments and Activities section of Topic 6: Vocabulary in the MyEducationLab for your course and complete the activity entitled "Using Context Clues." As you watch the video and answer the accompanying questions, consider the questions and guidance needed to help students use context clues effectively.

In some vocabulary books, in which the major emphasis is on vocabulary expansion rather than on the naming of word parts, a *combining form* is defined in a more general sense to include any word part that can join with another word or word part to form a word or a new word.[8]

## CONTEXT CLUES

Students need to learn that words have multiple meanings and must understand how to determine the correct meanings from sentence context. Context clues are a vital aid in learning vocabulary and reading comprehension because there is such ambiguity in the English language. There are many different types of context clues. Each type needs to be taught to students so they have a variety of context-based strategies.[9]

### Definition, Explanation, and Description Context Clues

There are times when you can get the meaning of a word from context clues. By *context* we mean the words surrounding a word that can shed light on its meaning.

If the writer wants to make sure that you get the meaning of a word, he or she will define, explain, or describe the word in the sentence. The *context clue* in the form of definition, description, or explanation is the specific item of information that helps the reader to figure out the meaning of a particular word. For example, the word *context* has been defined because it is a key word in this section. The definition is the context clue. In the following examples, the writer actually gives the reader the definition of a word. (Sentences such as these are generally found in textbooks or technical journals.)

### Examples

1. An *axis* is a straight line, real or imaginary, that passes through the center of rotation in a revolving body at a right angle to the plane of rotation.
2. In geometry, a plane figure of six sides and six angles is called a *hexagon.*

In the next examples, notice how the writers *describe* the words they want readers to know.

1. Although my *diligent* friend works from morning to night, he never complains.
2. Interior paints no longer contain *toxic* materials that might endanger the health of infants and small children.
3. The *cryptic* message—which looks as mysterious and secretive as it is—is difficult to decode.

The word *or* may be used by the writer when he uses another word or words with a similar meaning. Example: John said that he felt ill after having eaten *rancid* or *spoiled* butter.

The words *that is* and its abbreviation *i.e.* usually signal that an explanation will follow. Example: "A human is a biped, that is, an animal having only two feet," or "A human is a biped (i.e., an animal having only two feet)."

### Example and Comparison/Contrast Context Clues

Many times an author helps readers get the meaning of a word by giving *examples* illustrating the use of the word. Notice how the examples that the writer gives in the following sentence help readers determine the meaning of the word *illuminated.*

[8]Dorothy Rubin, *Gaining Word Power*, 5th ed. (Boston: Allyn and Bacon, 2000).

[9]J. Allen, *Words, Words, Words: Teaching Vocabulary in Grades 4–12* (Portland, ME: Stenhouse, 1999).

**Example**
Something representative of a whole or a group.

**Comparison**
A demonstration of the similarities between persons, ideas, things, and so on.

**Contrast**
A demonstration of the differences between persons, ideas, things, and so on.

*Example* The lantern *illuminated* the cave so well that we were able to see the crystal formations and even spiders crawling on the rocks.

(From the sentence, you can determine that *illuminated* means "lit up.")

Another technique writers employ that can help readers gain the meaning of a word is *comparison*. Comparison usually shows the similarities between persons, ideas, and things. For example, in the following sentence, notice how readers can determine the meaning of *passive* through the writer's comparison of Paul to a bear in winter.

*Example* Paul is as *passive* as a bear sleeping away the winter.

(From the sentence, you can determine that *passive* means "inactive.")

*Contrast* is another method writers use that can help readers figure out word meanings. Contrast is usually used to show differences between persons, ideas, and things. In the following sentence, readers can determine the meaning of *optimist* because they know that *optimist* is somehow the opposite of *"one who is gloomy or one who expects the worst."*

*Example*

1. My sister Marie is an *optimist,* but her boyfriend is one who is always gloomy and expects the worst to happen.

(From the sentence, you can determine that optimist means "one who expects the best" or "one who is cheerful.")

The writer may use the words *for example* or the abbreviation *e.g.,* to signal that examples are to follow. Example: *Condiments,* for example, pepper, salt, and mustard, make food taste better. (From the examples of condiments, you can determine that condiments are seasonings.)

An example is something that is representative of a whole or a group. It can be a particular single item, incident, fact, or situation that typifies the whole.

Many times such words as *but, yet, although, however,* and *rather than* signal that a contrast is being used. Example: My father thought he owned an authentic antique chest, but he was told recently that it was a fake. (From the sentence, you can tell that authentic is the opposite of fake; therefore, authentic means "not false but genuine or real.")

### Synonym and Antonym Context Clues

Often a word can be defined by another, more familiar word having basically the same meaning. For example, *void* is defined as *empty* and *corpulent* is defined as *fat. Void* and *empty,* and *corpulent* and *fat* are synonyms. *Synonyms* are different words that have the same or nearly the same meaning. Writers use synonyms to make their writing clearer and more expressive.

**Synonyms**
Words similar in meaning.

### Examples

    a. (1) The frightened child *looked* at the man.
        (2) The frightened child *peered* at the man.
    b. (1) We *walked* through the park.
        (2) We *strolled* through the park.
    c. (1) The *noise* brought the police to the scene.
        (2) The *uproar* brought the police to the scene.

**Antonyms**
Words opposite in meaning.

*Antonyms* are words opposite in meaning to each other. Examples: tall—short; fat—thin; least—most; worst—best. Antonyms, which are used to show contrast, help to make sentences clearer and more informative.

### Examples

1. My biology professor gives *succinct* lectures, but his assistant is *verbose.*
2. My math professor claims that all the problems she gives us are *simple* ones, but we feel that they are *intricate* and hard to solve.

### Homonym Context Clues

**Homonyms**
Words that are spelled and sound the same but have different meanings.

Many words are spelled and sound the same but have different meanings, such as *will* and *orange.* These words are called *homonyms.* The meaning of a homonym is determined by the way it is used in a sentence. For example, see the multiple uses of the term *run* below. In the sentences here notice how the word's placement in the sentence and the surrounding words help readers to figure out the appropriate meaning.

### Examples

1. Walk, don't *run.*
2. I have a *run* in my stocking.
3. Senator Jones said that he would not *run* for another term.
4. The trucker finished his *run* to Detroit.
5. She is going to *run* in a ten-mile race.
6. The play had a *run* of two years.

In sentence 1, *run* means "go quickly by moving the legs more rapidly than at a walk."
In sentence 2, *run* means "a tear or to cause stitches to unravel."
In sentence 3, *run* means "be or campaign as a candidate for election."
In sentence 4, *run* means "route."
In sentence 5, *run* means "take part in a race."
In sentence 6, *run* means "continuous course of performances."

### Homograph Context Clues

Some words are spelled the same but do not sound the same. For example, *refuse* means "trash"; *refuse* means "to decline to accept." In the sentences below, *refuse* meaning "trash" is pronounced differently from *refuse* meaning "to decline to accept." Readers can determine the meaning of *refuse* from the way it is used in the sentence, that is, from context clues.

1. During the garbage strike, there were tons of uncollected *refuse* on the streets of the city.
2. I *refuse* to go along with you in that project because it seems unethical to me.

### Homophone Context Clues

*Homophones* are words that sound alike but have different spellings and meanings. Here are some examples of homonyms or homophones. In the example sentences below, notice how the pronunciation of the words is the same, but the meaning and spelling are different.

1. One *way* to stay healthy is to *weigh* oneself.
2. I ate *plain* yogurt while flying on a *plane.*

**Categorizing**
A thinking skill involving the ability to classify items into general and specific categories.

## CATEGORIZATION

The ability to divide items into categories is an important thinking skill. As children advance as readers, they should be able to differentiate and group items into increasingly more complex categories. Primary-grade children should be able to categorize a cat as distinct from a mouse or a rabbit. They should be able to group cat, dog, and cow together as animals. As these children develop their thinking skills, they should be able to proceed from more generalized classifications to more specialized classifications. We provide assessment and teaching strategies for categorization later in this chapter.

## ANALOGIES

Analogies represent inferential thinking because they transfer relationships from one subject to another. Instead of comparing words directly, an analogy gets readers focused on the reasons for the connections between words. Analogies actually help students focus on the nature of the connection—why things compare, not just whether they do or do not compare. In order to make analogies, students must have a good stock of vocabulary and the ability to see relationships. Students who are able to classify often still need help understanding how analogies work.

Teachers can begin to expose children to simple analogies based on familiar relationships.[10] To be able to make the best use of analogies or to complete an analogy statement (sometimes called a *proportion*), children must (a) know the meanings of the words and (b) know the relationships between words. For example: *Sad is to happy as good is to* _____. Students who know the meanings of *sad* and *happy* may also know that *sad* is the opposite of *happy;* consequently, we can help them learn to complete the analogy with words like *bad, evil, awful, naughty or rotten.* (See Figure 11.4.)

Some of the relationships that words may have to one another are similar meanings, opposite meanings, members of a class, going from particular to general, going from general to particular, degree of intensity, specialized labels, characteristics, cause and effect, function, whole to part, or ratio. There is almost no end to the ways we might compare relationships, so the relationships mentioned above do not have to be memorized. Tell your students that they will gain clues from the pairs making up the analogies; that is, the words express the relationship. For example: "*pretty* is to *beautiful*—the relationship is degree of intensity (the state of being stronger, greater, or more than); "*hot* is to *cold*"—the relationship is one of opposites; "*car* is to *vehicle*"—the relationship is classification.

To ensure students' success, review the word lists of the analogy exercises to determine whether students are familiar with the vocabulary. Encourage them to use dictionaries to look up any unfamiliar words. Analogy activities can be done in small groups or with the entire class as well as individually. If children work individually, review the answers together in a group so that interaction and discussion can further enhance vocabulary development. These activities can be done orally or with writing.

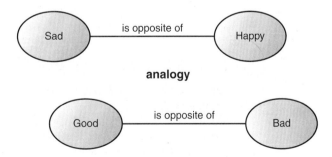

**FIGURE 11.4**   The analogy compares the *relationship* between words.

[10]See Sister Josephine, C.S.J., "An Analogy Test for Preschool Children," *Education* (December, 1965): 235–237.

## ASSESSING VOCABULARY

As we mention throughout this text, assessment drives instruction. This is true for vocabulary instruction as well as for any other aspect of reading. Three questions continually surface: What do I want to know? Why do I want to know? How can I best discover it? In terms of vocabulary, we want to know about several dimensions. We can approach these questions in two main ways.

First, some of the assessment techniques mentioned in earlier chapters are excellent tools for answering these questions. These include observation, talking with students, and using the word test of an informal reading inventory. Teachers can use checklists such as those shown in Figure 11.5 and 11.6 on pages 266–267 to document observations for primary and middle-grade readers' vocabulary development. We underscore that these observations need to occur in a variety of contexts while students are reading a variety of texts.

Second, teachers can use teacher-created informal assessments such as the ones shown later in this chapter. These can be used to help shed light on which students might need additional help learning a given aspect of vocabulary.

As we indicate in Table 11.1 teachers need to remember that purpose dictates the selection of the most appropriate assessment measure. Keep in mind that measuring the number of words in a person's vocabulary is nearly impossible. So what is essential is to know whether students have a store of words they can call on when reading, thereby enabling comprehension. Teachers must also find out about readers' vocabulary consciousness, which has to do with their desire to explore and add breadth (new words) and depth (added meanings) to their reading vocabulary.

## TEACHING VOCABULARY

Learning vocabulary can be a fun and rewarding experience. Remember that one goal of the vocabulary program is to help children develop a vocabulary consciousness. To do so, teachers need to integrate vocabulary instruction across all content areas so readers can see the meaningful use of words in different contexts. Teachers also need to provide readers with enough repetition so that they can learn to identify many words. Finally, instruction should be designed to use what students know to teach them something they need to learn. For example, students might know *car* and teachers can use that word to help them learn the word *vehicle,* a broader category to which a car belongs.

Drawing on the research of those who study vocabulary development, we provide some general guidelines for effective vocabulary instruction. Many of the teaching strategies that follow are ways to put these guidelines into action.

### GUIDELINES FOR EFFECTIVE VOCABULARY INSTRUCTION[11]

1: Create a word-rich environment.
   √ Promote wide reading.
   √ Provide time for discussion of new words and ideas.
   √ Intentionally focus on word learning in all content areas.
   √ Use time-effective strategies such as "word of the day."
   √ Be enthusiastic about acquiring new words.

[11]C. Blachowicz and P. Fisher, *Teaching Vocabulary in All Classrooms,* 2nd ed. (Englewood Cliffs, NJ: Merrill, 2002).

**TABLE 11.1   Three Important Questions for Assessing Vocabulary**

| *What Do I Want to Know?* | *Why Do I Want to Know?* | *How Can I Best Discover It?* |
|---|---|---|
| Do students have a store of sight words? | Having a sight vocabulary is essential for reading. If a student is limited in this area, I need to provide opportunities for the students to acquire and apply new words. | • Observation<br>• Word test from IRI |
| Are students developing a vocabulary consciousness? | Having a desire to learn words is a sure way for students to continue to expand their vocabularies, making comprehension of increasingly more complex texts possible. | • Self-selection strategy<br>• Talking with students<br>• Students' contributions to Word Wall |
| Are students able to apply what they know about word parts as one way to learn about new words? | The purpose for learning word parts is to use them when reading. I want to know if students are applying what they are learning and if not, why not. | • Talking with students<br>• Observation |
| How much time do students spend reading? | Wide reading is one way for students to acquire a large vocabulary. I need to ensure time in school for this reading, especially if students are not able to read after school for one reason or another. | • Independent Reading Record<br>• Observation |
| How do students use context clues? | Good readers use a variety of context clues to figure out word meanings. Teachers need to know which clues students use, and which ones they need to learn | • Observation |
| In what ways do students categorize words? | When students divide items into categories, it shows that they are organizing words into meaningful schemata, or mental maps. | • Chart for Categorizing Vocabulary Usage (Figure 11.7) |
| In what ways do students use relationships between and among words to better understand them? | Relationships are connections, and students who can see relationships between words and classifications of words show evidence of a meaningful schema, and also of higher-level thinking skills. | • Observation during oral analogies exercises |

2: Create independent word learners.
  √ Select and teach words that are central to the understanding of a topic.
  √ Show students how to use context clues.
  √ Show students how to use word parts.
  √ Allow for some self-selection.
3: Model good word learning.
  √ Show active involvement.
  √ Use graphic displays with discussion.
  √ Personalize words.
  √ Gather information from different sources.
  √ Play and experiment with words.

## TEACHING STRATEGIES

There are several ways to teach vocabulary. *Purpose* is what guides selection of any specific teaching strategy. Many of these strategies can be used when designing

**FIGURE 11.5 Diagnostic Checklist for Vocabulary Development (Primary Grades)**

Student's Name: _____

Grade: _____

Teacher: _____

| | Yes | No |
|---|---|---|
| 1. The child shows that he or she is developing a vocabulary consciousness by recognizing that some words have more than one meaning. | | |
| 2. The child uses context clues to figure out word meanings. | | |
| 3. The child can state the opposite of words such as *stop, tall, fat, long, happy, big.* | | |
| 4. The child can state the synonym of words such as *big, heavy, thin, mean, fast, hit.* | | |
| 5. The child can state different meanings for homographs (words that are spelled the same but have different meanings) based on their use in a sentence. Examples:<br> I did not *state* what *state* I live in.<br> Do not *roll* the *roll* on the floor.<br> *Train* your dog not to bark when he hears a *train.* | | |
| 6. The child is developing a vocabulary of the senses by being able to state words that describe various sounds, smells, sights, tastes, and touches. | | |
| 7. The child is expanding his or her vocabulary by combining two words to form compound words such as *grandfather, bedroom, cupcake, backyard, toothpick, buttercup, firefighter.* | | |
| 8. The child is expanding his or her vocabulary by combining roots of words with prefixes and suffixes. Examples: *return, friendly, unhappy, disagree, dirty, precook, unfriendly.* | | |
| 9. The child is able to give the answer to a number of word riddles. | | |
| 10. The child is able to make up a number of word riddles. | | |
| 11. The child is able to classify various objects such as fruits, animals, colors, pets, and so on. | | |
| 12. The child is able to give words that are associated with certain objects and ideas. Example: hospital—*nurse, doctor, beds, sick people, medicine,* and so on. | | |
| 13. The child is able to complete some analogy proportions such as *Happy is to sad as fat is to* _____ . | | |
| 14. The child shows that he or she is developing a vocabulary consciousness by using the dictionary to look up unknown words. | | |

**FIGURE 11.6 Diagnostic Checklist for Vocabulary Development (Intermediate Grades)**

Student's Name: _____

Grade: _____

Teacher: _____

| | Yes | No |
|---|---|---|
| 1. The student recognizes that many words have more than one meaning. | | |
| 2. The student uses context clues to figure out the meanings. | | |
| 3. The student can give synonyms for words such as *similar, secluded, passive, brief, old, cryptic, anxious.* | | |
| 4. The student can give antonyms for words such as *prior, most, less, best, optimist, rash, humble, content.* | | |
| 5. The student can state different meanings for homographs (words that are spelled the same but have different meanings) based on their use in a sentence, for example:<br>It is against the law to *litter* the streets.<br>The man was placed on the *litter* in the ambulance.<br>My dog gave birth to a *litter* of puppies. | | |
| 6. The student is able to use word parts to figure out word meanings. | | |
| 7. The student is able to use word parts to build words. | | |
| 8. The student is able to complete analogy statements or proportions. | | |
| 9. The student is able to give the connotative meaning of a number of words. | | |
| 10. The student is able to work with word categories. | | |
| 11. The student is able to answer a number of word riddles. | | |
| 12. The student is able to make up a number of word riddles. | | |
| 13. The student uses the dictionary to find word meanings. | | |

explicit vocabulary instruction focused on helping students understand key vocabulary. Remember, though, that we are teaching for independence; we want students to employ several of these strategies when they are on their own and come to unknown words. And remember the value of providing time for children to read books and other print sources in class. Wide reading is one sure way to help children acquire a large store of words. What follows are ten specific ways that teachers can help children toward this goal.

### 1. Use Explicit Teaching

When designing explicit instruction, you might find STAR[12] helpful. Here are the steps:

1. **S** (Select). Determine which words students need to know to better understand the text at hand. Keep the number limited to six words.
2. **T** (Teach). Select the appropriate strategy to help students learn the words. Some strategies work best before students read, whereas others work best during or after reading. For example, the *Knowledge Rating* (see page 281) is excellent to use before students actually begin reading. *Word Chain* (see page 281) is a perfect fit for review that takes place after reading. The *Context-Use* lesson (see page 269) is a natural strategy to use both before and during reading.
3. **A** (Activate). Connect the words with students' writing. Think about creating a set of words that contain some of the words they are learning. In other words, give them many exposures to the words in different contexts to provide them with meaningful repetition that will better ensure their understanding of the word(s).
4. **R** (Revisit). Use review activities such as *Word Chain* to help students revisit words. You might also ask students to use their words to create games such as crossword puzzles.

### 2. Teach Students How to Use Context Clues

Below are two specific lesson structures that can be used across grade levels to help students learn to use context clues. Following these lessons, we provide an extensive list of stand-alone techniques you can use for vocabulary instruction at any time.

*Three-Day Lesson for Teaching Students to Use Context Clues[13]*

### Day 1:

1. Read a riddle aloud and ask students to guess the answer:
   "I am a color which symbolizes wealth. I am often seen on the robes of queens and kings. I am also on petals of flowers. What am I?" (Answer: purple)
2. Have students point out any clues or cues that gave away the answer.
3. Have students create a riddle to share with others.

### Day 2:

1. Provide time for students to share their riddles. As each is solved, ask students how the clues in each helped them find the answer.
2. Tell students that context clues, like clues in a riddle, are the clues in the text that can help them understand a word they might not know.
3. Provide students with a short passage that contains an unknown word.

   ***Example:*** The *werbert* Sam brought for lunch looked delicious. It had layers of roast beef, cheese, lettuce, and tomato piled between two slices of bread.

4. Ask students to read the passage and underline the unknown word.
5. Ask students to look for clues in the text that help reveal the meaning of the word.

[12]C. Blachowicz and P. Fisher, "Vocabulary Lessons," *Educational Leadership* (March, 2004): 66–69.

[13]L. Nickerson, *Quick Activities to Build a Very Voluminous Vocabulary* (New York, NY: Scholastic, 1998).

6. Using these clues, have students predict the meaning of the word.
7. Repeat the procedure with other passages.

**Day 3:**

1. Review the steps that can be used to find context clues in a passage.
2. Have students find an unknown word in the dictionary and write a short passage using it. Make sure they add clues to the meaning.
3. Have students exchange passages with others and use the process described on Day 2 to figure out unknown words.

*Context-Use Lesson*[14]

1. Write a passage on a chart or on an overhead transparency and omit a contextually explained word.
2. Show students how they can use context using the following steps. Actually go through the process yourself and think aloud so that they can better understand how to use the process:

   a. LOOK. Before, at, and after the word.
   b. REASON. Connect what you know with what the author has written.
   c. PREDICT a possible meaning.
   d. RESOLVE OR REDO. Decide if you know enough or should keep going.

3. Insert the omitted word.
4. Display another passage and have the students go through the process with your guidance.
5. Allow for discussion.
6. Reveal the author's word choice.

**Additional Techniques for Teaching Context Clues**

1. Present to your students the following sentence, which should have an unfamiliar word in it.

   Mary is usually a prudent person. However, yesterday she was very foolish.

   Ask students how they can use the second sentence to figure out the meaning of *prudent*.

   Discuss how the second sentence gives a clue to the word *prudent*. From the second sentence, we want readers to realize that *prudent* means the opposite of *foolish*.

2. Put the following sentences on the chalkboard, and have the students use the context clues to help them figure out the meanings of each underlined word. Tell them that sometimes the clue that will help them figure out the word meaning is in the next sentence. Review each sentence with the students.

   - My kitten is very <u>tame.</u> She will not hurt anyone.
   - Everyone seems to know her. She must be a <u>famous</u> writer.
   - That is such an <u>enormous</u> ice-cream cone. You will have to get lots of people to help you eat some of it.
   - That street is so <u>broad</u> that we can all walk side by side.
   - The lion is a <u>fierce</u> animal that devours its prey.

[14]Blachowicz and Fisher (2002).

3. Hold up two pictures. The first picture is of a train, and the second shows a boy trying to train his dog. Ask what the two pictures have in common. Try to get students to make up sentences about what is taking place. Write the sentences about the two pictures on the board. Ask students to use the word *train* for both pictures.

4. Ask students to construct sentences using a homograph, homophone, or homonym. Ask them to make an illustration to coincide with the sentence. Collected sentences can be made into a class book demonstrating how all three types of context clues are used by authors.

5. Give students a sentence that uses comparison and ask them to see if they can figure out the meaning of an unfamiliar word.

Fred is as *obstinate* as a mule.

Ask the students to give you the meaning of *obstinate.* Since a mule is an animal that is considered stubborn, your students should get an idea of *obstinate* as meaning "stubborn."

6. Present students with a number of phrases. Tell them that the same word can fit in each set of phrases. The meaning of the word changes based on the words surrounding it (context). For example: a *brush* with the law; *brush* your teeth; a *brush* for your hair.

7. State a word such as *run.* Present sentences to your students and ask them to give the meaning of *run* in each sentence. Have them note that the meaning is different for each. Have them write four other sentences using *run* in different ways. Show them multiple definitions for *run* in the dictionary.

### 3. Teach Students to Use Word Part Clues

**Combining forms**
Roots borrowed from another language combine with each other or with affixes to form a word.

Vocabulary expansion depends on students' past reading, past experiences, and interests. If students are curious about sea life and you have an aquarium in the classroom, *combining forms* such as *aqua,* meaning "water," or *mare* meaning "sea" could help them develop meaningful associations. A reader could combine the form *aqua* to generate such terms as *aquaplane, aqueduct,* and *aquanaut.* Since *mare* means "sea," students could be given the term *marine* for discussion. Students also need to be aware of how they can break words apart using affixes and root words. For example, when coming to the word *discontinued* students can be taught how to break the prefix "dis" away from the word "continue," and to understand the meaning of the prefix.

We might present combining forms in a chart or diagram. Below, the forms *cardio, tele, graph,* and *gram,* are organized together:

cardiograph          telegraph
cardiogram          telegram

After students know that *cardio* means "heart" and *tele* means "from a distance," ask them to try to determine the meaning of *graph,* as used in *cardiograph* and *telegraph.* Have them try to figure out the meaning of *gram,* as used in *telegram* and *cardiogram.*

These types of word-combining activities are designed to help students increase their vocabulary consciousness. They come to realize that words are human-made, that language is living and changing, and that as people develop new concepts, they create new words to identify them. *Astronaut* and *aquanaut* are good examples of words that came into being because of space and undersea exploration.

Next we present information and sample lessons for combining forms, and for breaking forms apart.

*Combining Forms Lesson*

1. State and write the combining form *bi* on the board.
2. Challenge the students to generate any words that they can think of that have this combining form, for example, *bicycle, bimonthly, biweekly.*
3. Since the most common word is *bicycle,* ask the students if they can figure out the meaning of *bi* from *bicycle.* Someone will probably volunteer *two* because a bicycle is a *two* wheeler.
4. Ask for volunteers to state other *bi* words and write them on the board. For example, *biped:* say, "We know that *bi* means *two*; let's see if we can figure out what *biped* means."
5. State two sentences using *biped*: *All humans are bipeds. However, not all animals are bipeds.* Ask, "Can anyone guess what *biped* means? Remember, you know what *bi* means."
6. To encourage and help students more, say, "Let me give you another word containing the combining form *ped.* Perhaps that will help you to get the meaning of *biped.*"
7. State and write *pedestrian* on the board and write the following sentence on the board: *Motorists must look out for pedestrians.* If the students still need help with the analysis, ask the students to state what they do when they ride a bicycle. Ideally, someone will say "pedal." If not, suggest "pedal" and write the following sentence on the board: *People pedal hard when they want to go fast.* At this point, students should be able to give the meaning of *ped* as "foot." *Biped* should be defined as "two-footed," and *pedestrian* as someone "who is on foot or walking."
8. Tell students about how useful combining forms can be in expanding vocabulary and in helping them figure out unknown words when reading.

*Breaking Apart Affixes*[15]

1. Lay aside the prefix.
2. Lay aside each suffix, one at a time.
3. If the root is unfamiliar, decode it.
4. Put back the suffix closest to the root.
5. If there is a second suffix, add it next.
6. Put back the prefix.
7. Read the word in the sentence to check meaning.

*Teaching Prefixes*[16]

1. Present a prefix in isolation and attached to four words.

   ***Example:*** *con-construct, converge, conference, connect*

2. Define the prefix.

   ***Example:*** *Con-* means "to put together"

3. Use the whole words in sentences:

   ***Example:*** Builders *construct* houses.

---

[15]D. Durkin, *Teaching Them to Read.* (Boston: Allyn and Bacon, 1989).

[16]M. Graves and H. Hammond, "A Validated Procedure for Teaching Prefixes and Its Effect on Students' Ability to Assign Meanings to Novel Words," in *Perspectives on Reading Research & Instruction*, eds. M. Kamil & A. Moe (Washington, DC: National Reading Conference, 1980), pp. 184–188.

4. Define the whole words.

**Example:** To *construct* means to put or fit together.

5. After completing the above four steps with several prefixes, have students practice matching different prefixes to their meanings and root words to prefixes.
6. Have students identify the meanings of new words with familiar prefixes.

Here is a list of some often-used word parts and vocabulary words derived from them:

| *Word Parts* | *Vocabulary Words* |
|---|---|
| anthropo—man | anthropology |
| astro—star | astronomy, astrology |
| audio—hearing | audiology, auditory, audition, audible |
| auto—self | automatic, autocracy |
| bene—good | benefit, beneficiary |
| bio—life | biology, biography, autobiography |
| chrono—time | chronological, chronometer |
| cosmo—world | microcosm, cosmology, cosmopolitan |
| gamy—marriage | monogamy, bigamy, polygamy |
| geo—earth | geography, geology |
| gram—written or drawn | telegram, monogram |
| graph—written or drawn, instrument | telegraph, graphic |

**Categorizing**
A thinking skill involving the ability to classify items into general and specific categories.

### 4. Teach Students to Categorize Words

When readers *categorize* words, they are working on incorporating the words into a larger structure of meaning. Categorized words have connections based on word meaning, usage, and the function of the words. We want to teach students to talk about the categories words fit into and do not fit into. This will help them make places for the words to "live" in their minds.

Learning to see the difference between everyday social language and academic language is one key way to categorize vocabulary. The vocabulary students encounter in text and in the classroom is not the same as the vocabulary they learn with friends and family. For example, when children first encounter a word like *difficult* they may not have much experience with this academic synonym for *hard*.

Another key category for vocabulary is a continuum of general to specific usage. For example, the word *stop* is used fairly generally, and yet the word *freeze* means "to stop" in highly specific situations, such as for police or for financial institutions. Figure 11.7 shows these categories in grid form.

By the time children come to school, they are able to make many discriminations and are beginning to classify. Here are some suggested activities appropriate for children in different grade levels.

1. Five-year-olds can put things together that belong together—blocks of the same size in the same place; clothes for each doll in the right suitcase; parts of a puzzle in the right box; scissors, brushes, and paints in the spaces designated for these materials.
2. First-graders may separate things that magnets can pick up from things they do not pick up by using two boxes—one marked "yes" and the other marked "no."

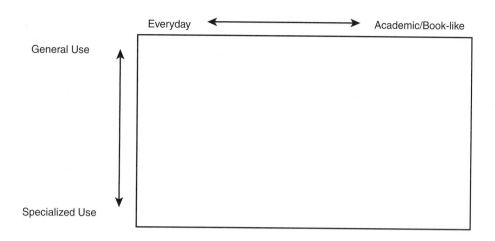

Try placing these words and phrases in the grid above:

- Stay, remain, linger
- In back, behind, posterior
- Soap, detergent, amphiphilic surfactant
- Church, religion, belief system, mysticism
- Act, behave, act out, behavior, drama, dramatize, histrionics
- Find, locate, pinpoint
- See, notice, perceive
- Good at, proficient
- Good for, healthy
- Snacks, hors d'oeuvres, nutrients
- Sick, under the weather, disease

**FIGURE 11.7** Chart for Categorizing Vocabulary Usage

*Source:* From J. Erekson, in *Comprehension and English Language Learners: 25 Oral Reading Strategies That Cross Proficiency Levels,* eds. M. Opitz and L. Guccione (Portsmouth, NH: Heinemann, 2009).

They can think of two kinds of stories—true and make-believe stories. They can make booklets representing homes, dividing the pictures they have cut from magazines into several categories—living rooms, dining rooms, bedrooms, and so on. They can make two piles of magazines labeled "To Cut" and "To Read."[17]

3. Second-grade pupils continue to put things together that belong together—such as outdoor temperature readings and indoor temperature readings, valentines in individual mail boxes in the play post office, and flannel graph figures made to use in telling a story in the envelope with the title of the story. In addition, seven-year-olds begin to understand finer classifications under large headings; for example, in a study of the job of a florist, plants may be classified as "plants that grow indoors" and "plants that grow outdoors." Indoor plants may be further subdivided into "plants that grow from seeds," "plants that grow from cuttings," and "plants that grow from bulbs." After visiting the local bakery, second graders who are writing stories and drawing pictures of their trip can list the details in two columns—in one, "things we saw in the store," in the other, "things we saw in the kitchen."

4. Third-grade students have many opportunities to classify their ideas and arrange them in organized form. During a study of food in their community, one group put up a bulletin board to answer the question "What parts of plants do

---

[17]Although grade designations are given, teachers must take the individual differences of students into account. Some first-graders may be at a third-grade level; others may be at a first-grade or lower skill developmental level.

we eat?" The pictures and captions followed this tabulation formulated by the third-graders:

| Leaves | Seeds | Fruits | Roots |
|--------|-------|--------|-------|
| cabbage | peas | apples | carrots |
| lettuce | beans | oranges | radishes |
| spinach | corn | plums | |

The file of "Games We Know" in one third-grade class was divided into two parts by the students—"indoor games" and "outdoor games." Each of these categories was further subdivided into "games with equipment" and "games without equipment."

After a visit to the supermarket, a third-grade class made a book containing stories and pictures of the trip. The organization of the booklet with its numbered pages was shown in the Table of Contents:

### OUR VISIT TO THE FOOD MARKET

1. The Fruit and Vegetable Department .......................... 1
    Kinds of Fruits ........................................................ 3
    Kinds of Vegetables ................................................ 4
    Where the Fruits and Vegetables Come From .......... 6
    Making the Packages .............................................. 8
    Finding the Prices .................................................. 9
    Storing the Fruits and Vegetables ........................ 11

2. The Meat Department .......................................... 14
    Kinds of Meat ........................................................ 16
    Where Different Kinds of Meat Come From .......... 18
    Keeping Meat ........................................................ 21
    Storing Meat .......................................................... 22
    Packaging Meat ...................................................... 24

### Sample Exercises

- Group these words into categories: apple, peach, potato, rice, oats, cucumber, barley, peanuts, acorn, pecans, almonds, pear. (A possible outcome is given below.)

| Nuts | Fruits | Vegetables | Grains |
|------|--------|------------|--------|
| peanuts | apple | potato | rice |
| acorn | peach | cucumber | oats |
| pecans | pear | | barley |
| almonds | | | |

- Circle the word that does not belong.

    Airedale    Persian    Angora    Siamese

Discuss why you circled the word you did.

1. Present students with the following list of words and have them group them in as many ways as they can think of:

| | |
|------|------|
| chalk | book |
| checkers | library |
| pencil | auditorium |

| | |
|---|---|
| paper | science books |
| student | baseball |
| teacher | nurse |
| chalkboard | jump rope |
| desk | basketball |
| classroom | pen |
| principal | chess |
| history books | spelling books |

2. Present the following exercise to your students. Tell them, "Here is a group of words. Put the words into five groups according to a common feature and state the common feature for each group." This activity is a more difficult one because students have to state the common feature. Partner or group discussion during an exercise like this is appropriate—it gives students a chance to see how others think and categorize, and gives them many opportunities to use target vocabulary words. After students have finished the exercise, lead some whole-class discussion about their decisions.

wood, brass, round, silk, oil, wheat, tin, wool, satin, coal, nylon, iron, barley, oats, oval, cylindrical

1. _____

_____

_____ Common feature _____

2. _____

_____

_____ Common feature _____

3. _____

_____

_____ Common feature _____

4. _____

_____

_____ Common feature _____

5. _____

_____

_____ Common feature _____

Answers: 1. wood, oil, coal—fuels 2. brass, tin, iron—metals 3. silk, wool, satin, nylon—fabrics 4. round, cylindrical, oval—shapes 5. wheat, barley, oats—grains

The Frayer Model and List-Group-Label are two additional ways to teach categorizing.

**Frayer Model[18]**

| Step | Example Using the Word "Treasurer" |
|---|---|
| 1. Define the new concept, discriminating the attributes relevant to all instances of the concept. | The discriminating attributes of *treasurer* are membership in an organization and responsibility for the accounts. |
| 2. Discriminate the relevant from the irrelevant properties of the concept. | The amount of money the treasurer is responsible for is an irrelevant attribute. |
| 3. Provide an example of the concept. | The "treasurer of the school board" and the "treasurer of the school book club" |
| 4. Provide a nonexample of the concept. | The "chairman or secretary of the board" and a "banker" are nonexamples. |
| 5. Relate the concept to a subordinate concept. | Generic instances of a treasurer such as the treasurer of a country club or another club |
| 6. Relate the concept to a superordinate concept. | People who deal with money |
| 7. Relate the concept to a coordinate term. | Bookkeeper |

*List-Group-Label[19]*

1. Provide students with a list of words related to a given subject. Keep the list to no more than 25 words.
2. Provide students with time to group them.
3. Ask students to label each group of words.
4. If you want, collect different categories of words and display them for the whole class. If some words do not fit, have a miscellaneous category or ask students to brainstorm additional words to go with them to form another category.

**Analogy**
A comparison of relationships between words or ideas.

### 5. Teach Students to Make Analogies

Here are some instructional procedures and materials that you can use to help students understand *analogies:*

1. Present students with the words *hot* and *cold.* Ask them what the relationship between the two words is. Help them to recognize that *hot* and *cold* are opposites. Present students with the words *tall* and *short.* Ask them what the relationship between the words is. Again, help them to recognize that they are opposites. Tell them that they are going to work with word relationships. The first relationship will be opposites. Put the following on the chalkboard:

*Thin* is to *fat* as *little* is to _____.

Ask them to give you a word that would fit the blank. Present a number of opposite relationships to your students.

2. Present students with the words *little* and *small.* Ask them what the relationship between the words is. Help them to recognize that these words have the same meaning; they are synonyms. Present students with the words *big* and *large.* Ask them what the

---

[18]D. Frayer, W. Frederick, and H. Klausmeier, *A Scheme for Testing the Level of Concept Mastery* (Working Paper no. 16), (Madison: University of Wisconsin, 1969).

[19]J. Readence and L. Searfoss, "Teaching Strategies for Vocabulary Development," *English Journal* 69 (1980): 43–46.

relationship between the words is. Again, help them to recognize that the words are similar in meaning. Tell the students that they are going to work with word relationships. This time the word relationship is synonyms. Put the following on the chalkboard:

*Sad* is to *gloomy* as *happy* is to _____.

Ask them to give you a word that would fit the blank. Present a number of such relationships to your students.

3. Do the same as above for different kinds of relationships.

Go over each analogy with the students. Have them explain why they chose the word that they did.

4. Discuss the various relationships that words can have to one another and ask the students to give examples. Put the examples on large newsprint so that students can refer to them. As students learn new relationships, have them add to the list.

For example:

Opposites: *hot* is to *cold*
Similarities: *thin* is to *lean*
Degree of intensity: *pretty* is to *beautiful*
Classification: *boat* is to *vehicle*
Ratio: *5* is to *10*
Part is to whole: *finger* is to *hand*
Whole is to part: *foot* is to *toe*
Parent is to child: *bear* is to *cub*

5. Have students construct their own analogies.

### 6. Teach Vocabulary with Children's Literature

Reading literature aloud to children is a viable means of increasing vocabulary and reading achievement.[20] Be sure to choose books that appeal to children. The authors of these books must be aware of what is important to a child and what is likely to be confusing so that they can build meaning out of words through the kind of imagery that makes sense to a child. For example, in *Mike Mulligan and His Steam Shovel,* the meaning of *steam shovel* is clarified by giving numerous examples in which a steam shovel is used. In Margaret Wise Brown's book *The Dead Bird,* the meaning of *dead* is given by a description of the bird's state.[21]

Here are some additional titles sure to assist vocabulary development:

Adler, David. *How Tall, How Short, How Far Away?* New York: Holiday House, 1999.
Adoff, Arnold. *Outside, Inside.* San Diego, CA: Harcourt, 1981.
Agee, Jon. *Palindromania.* New York: Farrar, Straus, & Giroux, 2002.
———. *Elvis Lives! And Other Anagrams.* New York: Farrar, Straus, & Giroux, 2000.
———. *Who Ordered the Jumbo Shrimp? And Other Oxymorons.* New York: Farrar, Straus, & Giroux, 1998.
Appelt, Kathi. *Piggies in a Polka.* San Diego, CA: Harcourt, 2003.
Arnold, Tedd. *More Parts.* New York: Dial, 2001.
Ballard, Robin. *Carnival.* New York; Greenwillow, 1995.
Bass, Hester. *The Secret World of Walter Anderson.* Somerville, MA: Candlewick, 2009.

---

[20]Dorothy H. Cohen, "The Effect of Literature on Vocabulary and Reading Achievement," *Elementary English* 45 (February, 1968): 209–213, 217.

[21]D. Cohen, "Word Meaning and the Literary Experience in Early Childhood," *Elementary English* 46 (November, 1969): 914–925.

Bee, William. *Whatever.* Cambridge, MA: Candlewick, 1995.

Coffelt, Nancy. *Big, Bigger, Biggest.* New York: Holt, 2009.

Cohen, Peter. *Boris's Glasses.* New York: Farrar, Straus, & Giroux, 2003.

Crimi, Carolyn. *Outside, Inside.* New York: Simon & Schuster, 1995.

Crowther, Robert. *Colors.* Cambridge, MA: Candlewick, 2001.

DeGross, Monalisa. *Donovan's Word Jar.* New York: HarperCollins, 1998.

Dunphy, Madeline. *Here Is the Southwestern Desert.* New York: Hyperion, 1995.

———. *Here Is the Tropical Rain Forest.* New York: Hyperion, 1994.

———. *Here Is the Artic Winter.* New York: Hyperion, 1993.

Elya, Susan. *Oh No, Gotta Go!* New York: Putnam, 2003.

Emberly, Ed. *Glad Monster, Sad Monster: A Book about Feelings.* New York; Little, Brown, 1997.

Frasier, Debra. *Miss Alaineus: A Vocabulary Disaster.* San Diego, CA: Harcourt, 2000.

Glassman, Peter. *My Dad's Job.* New York: Simon & Schuster, 2003.

Grover, Max. *Max's Wacky Taxi Day.* San Diego, CA: Harcourt, 1997.

Harley, Avis. *African Acrostics.* Somerville, MA: Candlewick, 2009.

Hirschi, Ron. *Faces in the Forest.* New York: Cobblehill/Dutton, 1997.

Hoban, Tana. *So Many Circles, So Many Squares.* New York: Greenwillow, 1998.

———. *All About Where.* New York: Greenwillow, 1991.

———. *Shapes, Shapes, Shapes.* New York; Greenwillow, 1986.

———. *Is it Larger? Is it Smaller?* New York: Greenwillow, 1985.

Jeppson, Ann-Sofie. *Here Comes Pontus!* New York: Farrar, Straus, & Giroux, 2000.

Kalman, Maira. *What Pete Ate from A to Z.* New York: Putnam, 2001.

Kirk, Daniel. *Trash Trucks!* New York: Putnam, 1997.

Kiss, Andrew. *A Mountain Alphabet.* Toronto, Canada: Tundra, 1996.

Lasky, Kathryn. *Pond Year.* Cambridge, MA: Candlewick, 1995.

Leedy, Loreen. *Crazy Like a Fox – A Simile Story.* New York: Holiday House, 2008.

Levitt, Paul, Douglas Burger, and Elissa Guralnick. *The Weighty Word Book.* Boulder, CO: Manuscripts Ltd, 1985.

Lewin, Ted. *Fair!* New York: Lothrop, 1997.

Mitchell, Joyce Slayton. *Tractor-Trailer Trucker: A Powerful Truck Book.* Berkeley, CA: Tricycle Press, 2000.

Morris, Ann. *Shoes, Shoes, Shoes.* New York: Lothrop, 1995.

Reinhart, Matthew. *Animal Opposites: A Pop-Up Book of Opposites.* New York: Little Simon, 2002.

Rotner, Shelly, and Richard Olivo. *Close, Closer, Closest.* New York: Atheneum, 1997.

Samoyault, Tiphanie. *Alphabetical Order: How the Alphabet Began.* New York: Viking, 1998.

Siebert, Diane. *Truck Song.* New York: Harper Trophy, 1984.

Silverstein, Shel. *Runny Babbit: A Billy Sook.* New York: HarperCollins, 2005.

Smith, Charles R. Jr. *Short Takes.* New York: Dutton, 2001.

Sobel, June. *B Is for Bulldozer: A Construction ABC.* San Diego: Harcourt, 2003.

Spires, Elizabeth. *Riddle Road: Puzzles in Poems and Pictures.* New York: McElderry, 1999.

Stojic, Manya. *Hello World! Greetings in 42 Languages Around the Globe!* New York: Scholastic, 2002.

Tobias, Tobi. *A World of Words: An ABC of Quotations.* New York: Lothrop, 1998.

Yoe, Craig. *Mighty Book of Jokes.* New York: Price, Stern, Sloan, 2001.

Yoe, Craig. *Mighty Book of Riddles.* New York: Price, Stern, Sloan, 2001.

### 7. Teach Vocabulary Using Web Sites

Web sites provide a vehicle that can help students get excited about vocabulary study. Technology can be integrated into explicit teaching before, during, or after a reading experience. Likewise, students can use web sites independently for meaningful vocabulary activities. Here are some they might want to visit:

www.vocabulary.com can be used by middle and high school students and teachers. It contains several kinds of puzzles written at different levels. Emphasis is placed on definitions and root words. This is also a good site for those trying to improve their vocabularies in preparation for the SAT.

http://rhymezone.com contains a rhyming dictionary and thesaurus. Visitors can type in a word and locate several words associated with it such as rhymes, synonyms, definitions, quotations, pictures, and words with similar spellings.

www.wordsmith.org/awad contains a word a day. Visitors can subscribe to it so that they receive a word each day through e-mail. They can also find additional words by searching the archives. An explanation of origin, a definition, a pronunciation guide, and at least one quote using the word are provided.

http://www.englishclub.net provides grammar and vocabulary activities, word games, and other activities. It also offers free handouts for ESL teachers.

www.m-w.com is a site from Merriam-Webster that offers several resources including an online dictionary and daily word games.

### 8. Use a Word Wall

Most teachers recognize that children need direct instruction in vocabulary and that students enjoy various fun word activities that help them to develop needed skills. A Word Wall is a display of words on cards. It is most meaningful when it is created by students and their teacher. It is versatile and its use is limited only by the teacher's creativity. A word wall can be used for review, reinforcement, skill enhancement purposes, teaching a new skill, or as a writing reference.

Teachers can work with one specific category, such as contractions, or with a number of categories. What the teacher does is based on his or her objectives. The teacher can have the whole class involved or children can work in groups or teams.

World Walls are most often seen in the primary grades, but they can be used at any grade level. In the upper grades, teachers generally use Word Walls to expand students' vocabulary.

In preparing to use a Word Wall, teachers must be clear about their purposes. For example, a teacher who is reviewing homophones, homographs, word families, and contractions can have available a box of representative word cards of similar size. At the top of the Wall Board, the four categories being reviewed are listed. In turn, children draw two cards from the box and place the words under the correct category. If one word is a contraction, the other card must have the two words that make up the contraction. If the two words are *red* and *read,* the words are placed under homophones. If the two words are *cake* and *bake,* the words would be listed under word families.

### 9. Use a Variety of Other Vocabulary-Oriented Activities to Engage All Students
### Self-Selection Strategy[22]

1. Invite students to bring two words to class that they have found in reading or listening.
2. Allow students to present their words to the group.
3. Ask the group to vote on five to eight words to be learned for the week.
4. Lead a class discussion to clarify, elaborate, and extend word meanings.

[22]M. Haggard, "The Vocabulary Self-Selection Strategy: An Active Approach to Word Learning" *Journal of Reading* 26 (1982): 203–207.

5. Have students enter their words into personal word logs and ask them to create some sort of memory and meaning device (e.g., chart, diagram, picture, word map).
6. Ask students to use the words in various ways to provide practice with them.

### Yea/Nay[23]

1. Provide students with two different cards, one that says "Yea" and one that says "Nay."
2. Read a question with one or two words that students might or might not understand. *Example:* Would a *corpse* be a good *conversationalist?*
3. After reading the question, give students 5–10 seconds to think and then ask, "Yea or Nay? 1, 2, 3."
4. On the count of 3, students hold up their choices while you call on individuals to explain their choices.

### Create Word Riddles[24]

1. Pick a subject (e.g., *pig*).
2. Generate a list of related words (e.g., *ham, pen, hog*).
3. Pick a word (e.g., *ham*), drop the first letter(s) to get a shortened version (e.g., *am*), and find a list of words that begin the way the shortened version begins (e.g., *ambulance, amnesia*).
4. Put back the missing letter to create a new word (e.g., *hambulance*).
5. Make up a riddle for which this word is the answer (e.g., *What do you use to take a pig to the hospital?*).

### Semantic Feature Analysis[25]

1. Select a category.
2. List words in the category on the left-hand column of a grid.
3. List and add features across the top row of the grid.
4. Determine feature possession. Which words have which features? Place an "X" in the corresponding cell.
5. Add more words and features.
6. Continue completing the grid.
7. Examine and discuss the grid.

### Word Map[26]

1. Divide a piece of paper into four parts.
2. Write a word in the center of the paper.
3. Label each square with the following labels: synonym, antonym, example, nonexample.
4. Have students write the distinguishing features for the word in the center.

Go to the Assignments and Activities section of Topic 3: Reading Diagnosis in the MyEducationLab for your course and complete the activity entitled "Vocabulary Word Study." As you watch the video and answer the accompanying questions, consider how both synonyms and antonyms are ways to categorize words.

---

[23]I. Beck and M. McKeown, "Learning Words Well: A Program to Enhance Vocabulary and Comprehension," *The Reading Teacher* 36 (1983): 622–625.

[24]M. Thaler, "Reading, Writing, and Riddling" *Learning* (1988): 58–59.

[25]S. Pittelman, J. Heimlich, R. Berglund, and M. French, *Semantic Feature Analysis: Classroom Applications* (Newark, DE: International Reading Association, 1991).

[26]R. Schwartz and T. Raphael, "Concept of Definition: A Key to Improving Students' Vocabulary," *The Reading Teacher* 39 (1985): 198–205.

| Synonym: Mad | Antonym: Happy |
|---|---|
| *Angry* | |
| Example: My Dad when I do something wrong | Nonexample: When I score a home run |

### Word Chain[27]

1. Identify a word associated with what you have been studying.
2. Write the word for all to see.
3. Tell students that they need to think of a second word that begins with the last letter of the displayed word. The word also has to relate to the displayed word in some way.
4. Continue building the chain until all possibilities have been exhausted.

*Note:* I have been very successful using this as a small group activity in college classes.

### Knowledge Rating[28]

1. Present students with a list of words in grid form as shown below.

| Word | Know Well | Seen/Heard It | Don't Know It |
|---|---|---|---|
| Apartment | √ | | |
| Villa | | √ | |
| Geodesic dome | | √ | |
| Yurt | | | √ |

2. Ask students to rate their understanding of each term by placing a √ in the appropriate column on the grid.
3. After students have rated themselves, invite them to share their ideas about the words and highlight the words that you feel need to be addressed.
4. Have students make predictions about what they will be reading based on these words. For example, you might say something like, "What do you think the topic of this chapter will be, based on our discussion of these words?"

### Book Aids[29]

Experienced readers know that authors use aids to signal important words, which helps the reader to comprehend. Most often, these aids and their functions have to be taught to students. Here are some examples:

1. *The use of boldface type and italics*
2. *Glossaries*
3. *Pronunciation guides*

---

[27]A. Trussell-Cullen, *50 Wonderful Word Games* (New York, NY: Scholastic, 1998).

[28]C. Blachowicz. "Problem-Solving Strategies for Academic Success" in *Language Learning Disabilities in School-Aged Children and Adolescents: Some Principles and Applications,* eds. G. P. Wallach and K. G. Butter (Englewood Cliffs, NJ: Merrill/Prentice Hall, 1994), pp. 304–322.

[29]C. Blachowicz and P. Fisher, *Teaching Vocabulary in all Classrooms,* 2nd ed. (Upper Saddle River, NJ: Merrill/Prentice Hall, 2002).

4. *Words defined contextually* (e.g., "Pollution, the soiling of the air and water, is an increasing threat to wildlife in the Gulf region.")
5. *End of unit exercises.* (Emphasize how important it is to look at these BEFORE reading to see what will be highlighted.)

## REVISITING THE OPENING SCENARIO

Craig already has an "opening" in his mind for the word animosity. Craig's desire to use a new word shows vocabulary consciousness. So while his "incorrect" use of the words may seem like an error at first, it is actually a strength to build on. Using context, categorization, analogies, literature, and other tools, how can Mr. Jackson use what Craig knows to help him learn what he does not yet know about the word?

## AUTHORS' SUMMARY

In this chapter, we presented information about helping children acquire an ever-expanding reading vocabulary. To this end, we provided an explanation about how vocabulary develops, including vocabulary acquisition, vocabulary consciousness, levels of knowing a word, types of words, sight words, and word part terminology. As with other aspects of reading, assessing vocabulary is necessary and we offered some assessment suggestions, reminding you that three questions need to be asked and answered in order to select the most appropriate assessment technique: What do I want to know? Why do I want to know? How can I best discover it? We then provided some guidelines for teaching vocabulary effectively, along with several teaching suggestions. We continually stressed that good vocabulary and good reading go hand in hand and that children who have a large vocabulary are more likely to be successful readers because they have an understanding of many words. Finally, we underscored the importance of having students do a lot of reading to increase their vocabularies.

## SUGGESTIONS FOR THOUGHT QUESTIONS AND ACTIVITIES

1. You are interested in developing a vocabulary expansion program using combining forms. How would you go about doing it? What kinds of activities would you develop for students who are weak in vocabulary?
2. Explain how you can assess students' vocabulary strengths and needs in content areas.
3. Construct a pretest to determine whether your intermediate-grade students have knowledge of some often-used combining forms.
4. You have been asked to generate a number of diagnostic tests for intermediate-grade students in vocabulary development. What kind of diagnostic tests would you develop?
5. Develop a Word Wall activity to help your children learn to read and spell.

## WEB SITES

http://www.vocabulary.com/

This vocabulary web site offers lessons and materials on root words, thematic puzzles, word lists, test preparation, and various topical vocabulary-related links.

http://teachersfirst.com/vocabulary.cfm

This site provides access to various web sites and resources centered on the various issues associated with teaching vocabulary. With in-depth annotations on this main page, teachers can pick and choose relevant sites in a matter of minutes.

http://freereading.net/index.php?title=Vocabulary_Activities

As a whole, *FreeReading* is a "high-quality, open-source, free reading intervention program for grades

K–3." This particular link offers various vocabulary activities including printable graphic organizers and other types of templates.

http://www.superkids.com/aweb/tools/words/

The SuperKids web site provides a variety of word games, puzzles, scrambles, and more. The site is organized in such a way that teachers could project the activities on a screen for whole class interaction or set up individual work.

http://www.studyspanish.com/vocab/select.htm

Offering numerous opportunities and free memberships for teachers, the StudySpanish web site provides vocabulary, pronunciation, and grammar-building in Spanish. Though no English connections are made, teachers could provide Spanish-speaking students with ways to connect the English words to Spanish words.

## SELECTED BIBLIOGRAPHY

Allen, J. *Words, Words, Words: Teaching Vocabulary in Grades 4–12.* York, ME: Stenhouse Publishers, 1999.

Baumann, J. F., and E. Kame'Enui, eds. *Vocabulary Instruction: Research to Practice.* New York: Guildford, 2004.

Blachowicz, C., and C. Obrochta. "Vocabulary Visits: Virtual Field Trips for Content Vocabulary Development." *The Reading Teacher, 59* (2005): 262–268.

Blachowicz, Camille L. Z., and Peter Fisher. "Vocabulary Instruction." In, *Handbook of Reading Research,* Vol. III, edited by Michael L. Kamil et al. Mahwah, NJ: Lawrence Erlbaum, 2000.

Chall, Jeanne S. *Learning to Read: The Great Debate,* 2nd ed. New York: McGraw-Hill, 1983.

———. "Two Vocabularies for Reading: Recognition and Reading." In *The Nature of Vocabulary Acquisition,* edited by M. G. McKeown and M. E. Curtis, 7–17. Hillsdale, NJ: Erlbaum, 1987.

Hartill, M. *Fab Vocab!* New York, NY: Scholastic, 1998.

Johnson, B. *Wordworks: Exploring Language Play.* Golden, CO: Fulcrum, 1999.

Johnson, Dale D. *Vocabulary in the Elementary and Middle Grades.* Boston: Allyn and Bacon, 2001.

Mazano, R., and D. Pickering. *Building Academic Vocabulary.* Alexandria, VA: Association for Supervision and Curriculum Development, 2005.

Nagy, W. *Teaching Vocabulary to Improve Reading Comprehension.* Newark, DE: International Reading Association, 1988.

Nagy, William E., and Judith A. Scott. "Vocabulary Processes." In, *Handbook of Reading Research,* Vol. III, edited by Michael L. Kamil et al. Mahwah, NJ: Lawrence Erlbaum, 2000.

Ohanian, S. *The Great Word Catalogue: Fundamental Activities for Building Vocabulary.* Portsmouth, NH: Heinemann, 2002.

Robb, L. *Easy Mini-Lessons for Building Vocabulary.* New York: Scholastic, 1999.

Rubin, Dorothy. *Gaining Word Power,* 6th ed. Boston: Allyn and Bacon, 2000.

———. *Phonics Skills and Strategies in a Balanced Reading Program* (Levels 1–4 series). Torrance, CA: Fearon Teacher Aids, 1998.

———. "Vocabulary Development in the Language Arts Program," in *Elementary Language Arts,* 6th ed. Boston: Allyn and Bacon, 2000.

———. *Vocabulary Skills and Strategies in a Balanced Reading Program.* Torrance, CA: Fearon Teacher Aids, 1998.

Schwartz, R., and T. Raphael, "Concept of Definition: A Key to Improving Students' Vocabulary." *The Reading Teacher* (1985): 198–203.

Tompkins, G. E., and C. Blanchfield. *Teaching Vocabulary: 50 Creative Strategies, Grades K-12.* New York: Prentice-Hall, 2004.

## CHILDREN'S LITERATURE CITED

Adler, David. *How Tall, How Short, How Far Away?* New York: Holiday House, 1999.

Adoff, Arnold. *Outside, Inside.* San Diego, CA: Harcourt, 1981.

Agee, Jon. *Palindromania.* New York: Farrar, Straus, & Giroux, 2002.

———. *Elvis Lives! And Other Anagrams.* New York: Farrar, Straus, & Giroux, 2000.

———. *Who Ordered the Jumbo Shrimp? And Other Oxymorons.* New York: Farrar, Straus, & Giroux, 1998.

Appelt, Kathi. *Piggies in a Polka.* San Diego, CA: Harcourt, 2003.

Arnold, Tedd. *More Parts.* New York: Dial, 2001.

Ballard, Robin. *Carnival.* New York; Greenwillow, 1995.

Bass, Hester. *The Secret World of Walter Anderson.* Somerville, MA: Candlewick, 2009.

Bee, William. *Whatever*. Cambridge, MA: Candlewick, 2005.

Coffelt, Nancy. *Big, Bigger, Biggest*. New York: Holt, 2009.

Cohen, Peter. *Boris's Glasses*. New York: Farrar, Straus, & Giroux, 2003.

Crimi, Carolyn. *Outside, Inside*. New York: Simon & Schuster, 1995.

Crowther, Robert. *Colors*. Cambridge, MA: Candlewick, 2001.

DeGross, Monalisa. *Donovan's Word Jar*. New York: HarperCollins, 1998.

Dunphy, Madeline. *Here Is the Southwestern Desert*. New York: Hyperion, 1995.

———. *Here Is the Tropical Rain Forest*. New York: Hyperion, 1994.

———. *Here Is the Arctic Winter*. New York: Hyperion, 1993.

Elya, Susan. *Oh no, Gotta Go!* New York: Putnam, 2003.

Emberly, Ed. *Glad Monster, Sad Monster: A Book about Feelings*. New York: Little, Brown, 1997.

Frasier, Debra. *Miss Alaineus: A Vocabulary Disaster*. San Diego, CA: Harcourt, 2000.

Glassman, Peter. *My Dad's Job*. New York: Simon & Schuster, 2003.

Grover, Max. *Max's Wacky Taxi Day*. San Diego, CA: Harcourt, 1997.

Harley, Avis. *African Acrostics*. Somerville, MA: Candlewick, 2009.

Hirschi, Ron. *Faces in the Forest*. New York; Cobblehill/Dutton, 1997.

Hoban, Tana. *So Many Circles, So Many Squares*. New York: Greenwillow, 1998.

———. *All About Where*. New York: Greenwillow, 1991.

———. *Shapes, Shapes, Shapes*. New York; Greenwillow, 1986.

———. *Is It Larger? Is It Smaller?* New York: Greenwillow, 1985.

Jeppson, Ann-Sofie. *Here Comes Pontus!* New York: Farrar, Straus, & Giroux, 2000.

Kalman, Maira. *What Pete Ate from A to Z*. New York: Putnam, 2001.

Kirk, Daniel. *Trash Trucks!* New York: Putnam, 1997.

Kiss, Andrew. *A Mountain Alphabet*. Toronto, Canada: Tundra, 1996.

Lasky, Kathryn. *Pond Year*. Cambridge, MA: Candlewick, 1995.

Leedy, Loreen. *Crazy Like a Fox—A Simile Story*. New York: Holiday House, 2008.

Levitt, Paul, Douglas Burger, and Elissa Guralnick. *The Weighty Word Book*. Boulder, CO: Manuscripts Ltd., 1985.

Lewin, Ted. *Fair!* New York: Lothrop, 1997.

Mitchell, Joyce Slayton. *Tractor-Trailer Trucker: A Powerful Truck Book*. Berkeley, CA: Tricycle Press, 2000.

Morris, Ann. *Shoes, Shoes, Shoes*. New York: Lothrop, 1995.

Reinhart, Matthew. *Animal Opposites: A Pop-Up Book of Opposites*. New York: Little Simon, 2002.

Rotner, Shelly, and Richard Olivo. *Close, Closer, Closest*. New York: Atheneum, 1997.

Samoyault, Tiphanie. *Alphabetical Order: How the Alphabet Began*. New York: Viking, 1998.

Siebert, Diane. *Truck Song*. New York: Harper Trophy, 1984.

Silverstein, Shel. *Runny Babbit: A Billy Sook*. New York: HarperCollins, 2005.

Smith, Charles R. Jr. *Short Takes*. New York: Dutton, 2001.

Sobel, June. *B Is for Bulldozer: A Construction ABC*. San Diego: Harcourt, 2003.

Spires, Elizabeth. *Riddle Road: Puzzles in Poems and Pictures*. New York: McElderry, 1999.

Stojic, Manya. *Hello World! Greetings in 42 Languages Around the Globe!* New York: Scholastic, 2002.

Tobias, Tobi. *A World of Words: An ABC of Quotations*. New York: Lothrop, 1998.

Yoe, Craig. *Mighty Book of Jokes*. New York: Price, Stern, Sloan, 2001.

Yoe, Craig. *Mighty Book of Riddles*. New York: Price, Stern, Sloan, 2001.

PEARSON
**myeducationlab**

Now go to Topic 6: "Vocabulary" and Topic 3: "Reading Diagnosis" in MyEducationLab (www.myeducationlab.com) for your course, where you can:

- Find learning outcomes for "Vocabulary" and "Reading Diagnosis" along with national standards that connect to these outcomes.
- Complete Assignments and Activities that can help you more deeply understand the chapter content.
- Examine challenging situations and cases presented in the IRIS Center Resources.
- Access video clips of CCSSO National Teacher of the Year award winners responding to the question, "Why Do I Teach?" in the Teacher Talk section.
- Apply and practice your understanding of the core teaching skills identified in the chapter with Building Teaching Skills and Dispositions learning units.

# Helping Children
# Apply Phonics

## CHAPTER OUTLINE

- Scenario: Understanding Jorge
- Phonics Content Knowledge
- A Developmental Sequence
  of Phonics
- Assessing Phonics
- Teaching Phonics
- Revisiting the Opening Scenario

12

**SCENARIO:** UNDERSTANDING JORGE

Jorge is a student in Ms. Mills's third-grade class. He scored at a 1.2 level on the reading comprehension subtest of the *California Achievement Tests.*[*] Ms. Mills is confused about this score because Jorge is quite verbal; he always has a lot of information to contribute on many topics; and he is able to answer comprehension questions with ease. To better understand Jorge's reading ability, Ms. Mills decides to give him an Informal Reading Inventory.

To encourage feelings of success from the beginning of the assessment, Ms. Mills starts Jorge two grade levels below his current grade level. She discovers that Jorge is able to answer all the comprehension questions for the oral and silent reading passages through the third level, even with numerous word errors in the oral reading passages. At the third-grade level, the number of word recognition errors increase to a frustration level. Consequently, she decides to continue the passages as a listening capacity test. She reads aloud one passage from each level and asks Jorge the questions. Jorge is able to answer all questions correctly up to the eighth level.

In talking to Jorge, Ms. Mills learns that Jorge's parents are both professionals and well known in their fields, that Jorge is an only child, that he goes everywhere with his parents, and that he is included in their interesting conversations. Jorge's background information certainly matches his propensity to engage in conversations and answer questions, but it tells her little about his decoding ability. She wonders if the mismatch between phonics skill and comprehension could explain his achievement test score. Ms. Mills realizes from the types of errors he made reading aloud that Jorge probably used context clues to gain information from the text. Ms. Mills wonders how she can gain a greater insight into Jorge's decoding abilities, and how to decide what to teach.

## CHAPTER OBJECTIVES

After reading the chapter, you should be able to:

- Discuss the place of phonics in the reading program.
- Discuss the various word recognition strategies.
- Explain a variety of phonics terms, including *consonant, digraph, diphthong, blend, open and closed syllable, rime,* and *onset.*
- Explain what is meant by *explicit, systematic phonics instruction.*
- Explain what is meant by *implicit, systematic phonics instruction.*

In this chapter, we focus on helping teachers better understand phonics, including a suggested sequence of phonics skills. Teachers are in a better position to help students improve as readers when they understand the content of phonics, when they know how to assess students' ability to use phonics as a reading strategy, and when they teach students meaningful application of phonics.

When we explain the phonics system, we use the word *generalization* rather than *rule. Generalization* implies that the pattern sometimes applies and that the reader needs to give it a try, with the understanding that English words may have various spellings for one sound. *Rule,* on the other hand, implies consistency. We deliberately use the term *generalization* because it implies more flexibility. We also use the term because of our work with children, who believe breaking rules is wrong. They may have great difficulty being flexible phonics users when they need to break a rule to read or spell real English words.

Generalizations should only be taught if enough cases warrant their teaching. Research on phoneme-grapheme relationships has been done with specific rule generalizations

[*]Now called *TerraNovaCAT.*

and the percentage of instances where words followed the rule. Some investigators have claimed that a rule should not be taught unless it holds true at least 75 percent of the time.[1] However, the decision to teach a generalization depends on its usefulness. For example, even though the "silent e" generalization for long vowel sounds has 63 percent applicability, it is highly represented among the most frequent words (such as *like, make, joke*). We teach it as a generalization because it can be useful for beginning readers.

## PHONICS CONTENT KNOWLEDGE

*Phonics* is the study of relationships between the sounds (phonemes) of a language and the letter symbols (graphemes) of a written language. Readers combine their knowledge of phonics with other strategies to read words and comprehend text.

## A DEVELOPMENTAL SEQUENCE OF PHONICS

**Phonics**
The study of the relationships between sounds and letters in a language.

Although the teaching of phonics will vary according to the strengths and needs of students, certain skills are often achieved before others. As students acquire skills, we want to build systematically on their successes. Surprisingly, although research on phonics programs all points to the fact that a sequence should be followed, no specific sequence has been identified as better than another (Snow, Burns, & Griffin, 1998)[2]. What we offer here, then, is one possible sequence. Developmentally, in early reading children usually have memorized a personalized bank of sight words. When children learn that some of these words look like and/or sound like other words, they are showing an awareness of phonics. Although children may identify words by sight, this doesn't necessarily mean that they can use the sound–letter relationships that form these words. A good place to begin, then, is to use words they *can* identify to teach them specific phonics skills. Using the known to teach the unknown is always a good strategy.

Following is an outline of the content typically addressed in phonics programs. In the text that follows the outline, for each element we provide a definition, examples, and exercises to help teachers better internalize phonics content that they need to help their students grow as readers.

1. Auditory discrimination.
2. Visual discrimination.
3. Consonants.
   a. Initial consonants.
   b. Final consonants.
   c. Initial consonant blends (clusters) (*bl, st, str*).
   d. Final consonant blends (clusters). (*nd, nt, sk*).
   e. Initial consonant digraphs (*th, ch, sh*).
   f. Final consonant digraphs (*ng, gh*).
   g. Silent consonant digraphs (*kn, pn, wr*).
4. Phonograms.

[1]Theodore Clymer, "The Utility of Phonic Generalizations in the Primary Grades," *The Reading Teacher* 16 (January, 1963): 252–258. Lillie Smith Davis, "The Applicability of Phonic Generalizations to Selected Spelling Programs," *Elementary English* 49 (May, 1972): 706–712.

[2]Catherine E. Snow, M. Susan Burns, and Peg Griffin, eds. *Preventing Reading Difficulties in Young Children* (Washington D.C.: National Academy Press, 1998).

5. Vowels.
   a. Long vowel sounds.
   b. Short vowel sounds.
   c. Effect of final *e* on vowel.
   d. Double vowels.
      (1) Digraphs.
      (2) Diphthongs.
   e. Vowel controlled by *r*.
6. Special letters and sounds.
7. Syllabication.
   a. Meaning of syllable.
   b. Generalizations.
      (1) Double consonant vc/cv.
      (2) Vowel-consonant-vowel v/cv.
      (3) Consonant with special *le* c/cle or v/cle.
   c. Syllable phonics.
   d. Stress/unstress.[3]

## AUDITORY AND VISUAL DISCRIMINATION

In order to connect sounds with letters, children need to be able to both hear and visually discriminate among them. This section includes samples of exercises that should help teachers understand these two types of discrimination.

### Auditory Discrimination

*Auditory discrimination* is the ability to detect differences and similarities in sounds. Auditory processing is totally dependent on hearing and auditory areas of the brain, not on letter identification. Children can have strong auditory awareness, and yet still be unable to identify or use alphabet letters. Early in reading, these are separate skill sets.

**Auditory discrimination**
Ability to detect differences and similarities in sounds.

## SAMPLE EXERCISE

**Directions: Partner up. Have one person take on the role of teacher, and the other the role of student. The teacher says: "Listen carefully. See if you can tell me which pair of words is the same." Be careful not to show the student the printed words.**

| | | | |
|---|---|---|---|
| sat | set | ball | bell |
| cap | cap | sing | singe |
| hand | hand | pan | pan |
| sail | sell | burn | but |

**Directions: Listen carefully. Give me another word that rhymes with**

can _____          fat _____

sail _____          day _____

**Directions: Listen carefully. Give me another word that begins like**

baby _____          can _____

door _____          fat _____

---

[3]It is conventional to use slashes to convey phonemic symbols, such as /b/ as in "ball" or /a/ as in "all." This differentiates between sounds and letters.

**Visual discrimination**
Ability to detect similarities and differences among written symbols.

### Visual Discrimination

*Visual discrimination* is the ability to detect similarities and differences among written symbols. As with auditory discrimination, children can know and recognize letters without auditory discrimination. Remember, the two are separate skill sets, especially for early readers.

## SAMPLE EXERCISE

**Directions: Draw a circle around the letter in each row that looks the same as the first letter in the row.**

| | | | | | |
|---|---|---|---|---|---|
| **s** | c | p | c | e | s |
| **p** | d | p | b | r | q |
| **l** | t | k | h | l | d |
| **b** | p | d | b | o | u |
| **d** | s | b | p | d | q |
| **m** | n | m | s | h | w |

**Directions: Draw a circle around the word in each row that looks the same as the first word in the row.**

| | | | | | |
|---|---|---|---|---|---|
| **car** | far | can | cap | car | fan |
| **dear** | bear | dark | deal | dear | bean |
| **pail** | sail | pail | bail | pain | pear |

**Initial consonant**
One stopped speech sound represented by one letter at the beginning of a word.

## CONSONANTS

### Initial Consonants

*Initial consonants* are consonants at the beginning of a word (one speech sound represented by one letter). For example: /b/ (bath), /d/ (damp), /f/ (fat), /g/ (girl).

## SAMPLE EXERCISE

**Directions: Partner up. Have one person take on the role of teacher, and the other the role of student. The teacher says: "Listen carefully. What is the letter that stands for the first sound you hear in the following words?"**

dog, mother, father, girl, boy, hat, cat, family

### Final Consonants

Final consonants are similar to the list given for the initial consonants, except that they appear at the end of the word. Examples of single consonants are /b/ (rob), /d/ (road), /g/ (pig).

## SAMPLE EXERCISE

**Directions: partner up. Have one person take on the role of teacher, and the other the role of student. The teacher says: "Listen carefully. What is the letter that stands for the last sound you hear in the following words?**

cab, dog, man, hat, tap, drop

**Consonant blends**
A combination of consonant sounds blended together so that the identity of each sound is retained.

# CONSONANT BLENDS

*Consonant blends* are two or more consonants, one after the other, that are blended together. In some reading programs, the term *consonant cluster* has replaced the term *consonant blend.*

### Initial Consonant Blends

Initial consonant blends appear at the beginning of a word. For example: */bl/* (black), */br/* (brown), *fr* (frame), */sk/* (skip).

## SAMPLE EXERCISE

**Directions: Partner up. Have one person take on the role of teacher, and the other the role of student. The teacher says: "Listen carefully. What are the two letters that stand for the first two sounds you hear in the following words?"**

blame, prune, flag, glove, glass, frog, snow, clear, break, crow

### Final Consonant Blends

Final consonant blends appear at the end of the word. While some final blends are also initial blends (such as */sk/* in "ask" and "skate"), many appear only at the ends of words. For example: */nd/* (kind), */mp/* (stamp).

## SAMPLE EXERCISE

**Directions: Partner up. Have one person take on the role of teacher, and the other the role of student. The teacher says: "Listen carefully. What are the last two letters that stand for the last two sounds you hear in the following words?"**

bump, fist, ask, slant, sink, find

**Consonant digraph**
Two consonant letters that represent one sound.

### Initial Consonant Digraphs

*Initial consonant digraphs* consist of two consonant letters that represent one speech sound at the beginning of a word. For example: *ch* (chair), *sh* (show), *th* (thank), *ph* (phone). Note that the sound normally associated with the consonant is replaced with a new speech sound.

## SAMPLE EXERCISE

**Directions: Partner up. Have one person take on the role of teacher, and the other the role of student. The teacher says: "Listen carefully. What are the two letters that stand for the first sound you hear in the following words?"**

chain, thumb, that, shall, phone, who, where

### Final Consonant Digraphs

These digraphs also represent only one sound, and appear at the end of a word. Examples of final consonant digraphs include *th* (booth), *ng* (sing), *sh* (mash), *ch* (bench), *gh* (rough). Note: It is possible to have a digraph represent one of the sounds in a cluster. In the word *bench, nch* represents a cluster (blend) because it is a blend of *two* sounds. The letter *n* represents one sound, and the digraph *ch* represents another sound.

## SAMPLE EXERCISE

**Silent consonant digraphs**
Two adjacent consonant letters, one of which is silent, for example, *kn* (know), *pn* (pneumonia).

**Directions: Partner up. Have one person take on the role of teacher, and the other the role of student. The teacher says: "Listen carefully. What are the two letters that stand for the last sound you hear in the following words?"**

flash, pinch, moth, ring, rough

### *Silent Consonant Digraphs*

*Silent consonant digraphs* consist of two consonant letters where one is silent and the other represents its usual speech sound. Examples are *kn* (know), *gh* (ghost), *wr* (wreck), *gn* (sign, gnome).

## SAMPLE EXERCISE

**Directions: Partner up. Have one person take on the role of teacher, and the other the role of student. The teacher says: "Listen carefully. What are the two letters that stand for the first sound you hear in the following words?"**

knife, ghastly, wren, pneumatic

### C *and* G

The letters *c* and *g* each have two sounds. For example, letter *c* has a soft sound in *cease, center, cent,* and *cite* and a hard sound in *cat, came, cook, call,* and *carry.* The letter *g* has a soft sound in *gym, George, gentle,* and *generation* and a hard sound in *go, get, game, gone,* and *garden.*

### Q

The letter *q* is always followed by the letter *u* in English words. At the beginning of a word, *qu* almost always represents a blend of two sounds, */kw/.* Examples are *queen, quilt, quiet, quack.* When *qu* appears at the end of a word in the *que* combination, it represents one sound, */k/.* Examples are *unique, antique, clique.*

## VOWEL SOUNDS

The vowel letters are *a, e, i, o,* and *u.* Sometimes *y* and *w* function as vowels (as in "day" and "low"). There are about 15 vowel sounds in English (Kucer, 2009)[4]. Listen to the vowel sounds as you read the following words: n*o*t, g*e*t, m*a*n, c*u*t, t*i*n, s*ee*, h*i*, d*ay*, d*o*, s*o*, *a*ll, c*a*r, n*ow*, t*oy*, sof*a*. Do you hear the fifteen different sounds? As you can see, there are more sounds than letters. This helps to explain why some children have more difficulty with learning and using vowels than they do with learning and using consonants. Consonants tend to be consistent and predictable, whereas vowels are neither.

---

[4]Steven Kucer, *Dimensions of Literacy* 3rd ed. (Mahwah, NJ: Erlbaum. 2009).

SAMPLE EXERCISE

**Directions: Partner up. Have one person take on the role of teacher, and the other the role of student. The teacher says: "Listen carefully. I will say a word. Tell me the vowel sound you hear in the word. Also tell me if you hear a long or short vowel sound."**

cat, note, make, mice, not, pet, but, cute

*Long Vowel Sounds*—a e i o u *and* y

The "long" vowel sounds are the five that correspond to vowel letter names. *Y* represents a long vowel sound when it occurs at the end of a word or syllable and when all the other letters in the word or syllable are consonants. For example: *by, cry, baby, deny*. Note that *y* in these words represents different vowel sounds. It stands for a long *i* sound in one-syllable words containing no other vowels. To familiarize your students with these sounds, use the exercise below.

SAMPLE EXERCISE

**Directions: Partner up. Have one person take on the role of teacher, and the other the role of student. The teacher shows the list of words to the student, then says: "Listen carefully. I will say a word. Tell me the vowel sound you hear in the word. Now point to the letter(s) that indicate the long vowel sound."**

| ape | beet | goal | try | use |
| sail | sea | slow | high | too |
| April | even | no | bike | sue |
| ate | any | toe | lie | few |

*Short Vowel Sounds*

Short vowel sounds in phonics are in opposing pairs with the long vowel sounds and letters. So there is a short sound to match each letter: *a, e, i, o,* and *u*. Likewise, the letter *y* also functions as a short *i* vowel sound in the middle of a word or in a syllable with no other vowel letters (e.g., *hymn, gym, synonym, bicycle*). The letter names do not tell you the short vowel sounds. You remember them because they are paired with a long vowel.

In the sample exercises below, notice the vowel generalization—*a single vowel letter in the middle of a word (or syllable) is usually representing the short vowel sound.*

SAMPLE EXERCISE

**Directions: Partner up. Have one person take on the role of teacher, and the other the role of student. The teacher shows the list of words to the student, then says: "Listen carefully. I will say a word. Tell me the vowel sound you hear in the word. Now point to the letter that indicates the short vowel sound."**

| not | get | man |
| got | let | can |
| pin | put | mad |
| tin | cut | cap |
| met | hat | had |

**Vowel digraph**
Two vowel letters that represent one speech sound.

## Vowel Digraphs

*Vowel digraphs* are two vowel letters next to each other in a word (or syllable) that stand for a single vowel sound; for example, *ea, oa, ai, ei, ie* in words like *beat, boat, hail, receive, believe.*

### SAMPLE EXERCISE

**Directions: Partner up. Have one person take on the role of teacher, and the other the role of student. The teacher shows the list of words to the student, then says: "Listen carefully. I will say a word. Tell me the vowel sound you hear in the word. Now point to the letters that indicate the vowel digraph."**

boat, keep, pail, way, bean

**Diphthongs**
Blends of vowel sounds written with two letters.

## Diphthongs

*Diphthongs* are blends of vowel sounds written with two letters. Examples include the vowels in words like *shout, foil, toy, cow.* In English, diphthongs are often treated as one vowel sound.

### SAMPLE EXERCISE

**Directions: Partner up. Have one person take on the role of teacher, and the other the role of student. The teacher shows the list of words to the student, then says: "Listen carefully. I will say a word. Tell me the vowel sound you hear in the word. Now point to the letters that indicate the diphthong (or vowel blend)."**

boy, boil, how, cow, out

## Vowel Controlled by r

A vowel sound that is followed by the consonant *r* is called an "*r*-controlled" vowel. Examples are *ar, ir, er, or, ur* in words like *car, fir, perch, or, hurt.*

### SAMPLE EXERCISE

**Directions: Partner up. Have one person take on the role of teacher, and the other the role of student. The teacher shows the list of words to the student, then says: "Listen carefully. I will say a word. Tell me the vowel sound you hear in the word. Now point to the letters that indicate the *r*-controlled vowel."**

her, far, stir, for, turn

**Schwa**
The unstressed vowel sound, which does not have a common letter.

## The Schwa

The *schwa* sound is the unstressed vowel sound. It does not have its own letter in the English alphabet, even though it can account for as much as 50 percent of all vowel sounds in speech. It is represented by an upside down *e* (ə) in the phonetic (speech) alphabet. The schwa sounds similar to the short *u* sound in the word *cut.* Any vowel letter can take on this sound when we pronounce the syllable without stress. Examples include b*e*lieve, p*o*lice, d*i*vide, Rom*a*n, penc*i*l, th*e*, w*a*s. In the examples, the italicized vowel letters represent the schwa sound. We find the schwa sound regularly in multiple syllable words, but also in single syllable words when they are unstressed (such as th*e*, and *a*).

**FIGURE 12.1**   **Most Common Phonograms in Rank Order Based on Frequency (Number of Uses in Monosyllabic Words)**

| Frequency | Rime | Example words |
|-----------|------|---------------|
| 26 | -ay | jay say pay day play |
| 26 | -ill | hill Bill will fill spill |
| 22 | -ip | ship dip tip skip trip |
| 19 | -at | cat fat bat rat sat |
| 19 | -am | ham jam dam ram Sam |
| 19 | -ag | bag rag tag wag sag |
| 19 | -ack | back sack Jack black track |
| 19 | -ank | bank sank tank blank drank |
| 19 | -ick | sick Dick pick quick chick |
| 18 | -ell | bell sell fell tell yell |
| 18 | -ot | pot not hot dot got |
| 18 | -ing | ring sing king wing thing |
| 18 | -ap | cap map tap clap trap |
| 18 | -unk | sunk junk bunk flunk skunk |
| 17 | -ail | pail jail nail sail tail |
| 17 | -ain | rain pain main chain plain |
| 17 | -eed | feed seed weed need freed |
| 17 | -y | my by dry try fly |
| 17 | -out | pout trout scout shout spout |
| 17 | -ug | rug bug hug dug tug |
| 16 | -op | mop cop pop top hop |
| 16 | -in | pin tin win chin thin |
| 16 | -an | pan man ran tan Dan |
| 16 | -est | best nest pest rest test |
| 16 | -ink | pink sink rink link drink |
| 16 | -ow | low slow grow show snow |
| 16 | -ew | new few chew grew blew |
| 16 | -ore | more sore tore store score |
| 15 | -ed | bed red fed led Ted |
| 15 | -ab | cab dab jab lab crab |
| 15 | -ob | cob job rob Bob knob |
| 15 | -ock | sock rock lock dock block |
| 15 | -ake | cake lake make take brake |
| 15 | -ine | line nine pine fine shine |
| 14 | -ight | knight light right night fight |
| 14 | -im | swim him Kim rim brim |
| 14 | -uck | duck luck suck truck buck |
| 14 | -um | gum bum hum drum plum |

*Source:* From Fry, E. "The Most Common Phonograms." *The Reading Teacher* 51 (1998): 620–622.

## PHONOGRAMS

**Phonogram**
Sets of letters with the same phonetic value in a number of words, that is, word families.

*Phonograms* are sets of letters with the same phonetic value in a number of words, that is, word families. Some examples of phonograms are *ay, ore, ot, unk* in the words *day, more, shot,* and *junk.* Phonograms are useful because we can read and spell many words with one phonogram (e.g., *bake, cake, rake, lake, take, make, fake*).

Figure 12.1 shows the most common phonograms, how frequently they occur, and example words.

## SYLLABLES

**Syllable**
A vowel and the consonants around it.

A *syllable* is a vowel sound and the consonant sounds around it. In phonics, a syllable contains vowel letters and the surrounding consonant letters, (such as *can dy* and *bea gle*). Readers need to understand syllables so they can break unfamiliar words into manageable chunks when decoding. In decoding a multisyllabic word, readers must first identify the syllables, decode each syllable, and then blend them all into the whole word.

## ASSESSING PHONICS

Go to the Assignments and Activities section of Topic 5: Phonemic Awareness and Phonics in the MyEducationLab for your course and complete the activity entitled "Decoding Through Word Chunking." As you watch the video and answer the accompanying questions, consider why English word reading is often taught in chunks of more than one letter.

As emphasized throughout this text, assessment drives instruction. This is true for phonics as well as for any other aspect of reading. Teachers need to ask and answer three questions in order to conduct meaningful assessment: *What* do I want to know? *Why* do I want to know? *How* can I best discover this information?

Related to phonics, then, *what* we want to know is if students are acquiring phonics skills and if they are applying them in their everyday reading. *Why* we want to know this centers on students' application of phonics. That is, using phonics in everyday reading is a main reason for knowing phonics. Assessing children will help reveal the degree to which children are making the connection between instruction and their reading, seeing phonics as a tool to assist them as they construct meaning. Fortunately, there are some practical, meaningful, and yes, even standardized ways for *how* to discover students' facility with phonics.

## FIVE MEANINGFUL WAYS TO ASSESS PHONICS

1. *Observation.* As noted in Chapter 5, observation can reveal much about students' reading behaviors. Using a checklist such as the one shown in Figure 12.2, teachers can watch and listen to children read and see what they do when they come to unknown words. They can then document what they see and hear on the checklist.

2. *Names Test* (Cunningham, 1990; Duffelmeyer, Kruse, Merkley, and Fyfe, 1994)[5]. This test, developed by Cunningham and later validated by Duffelmeyer and colleagues, assesses students' ability to use what they know about phonics in a meaningful context. The test is most useful for assessing children in second through fifth grade. Directions for administering the test and the accompanying forms are as follows:

*Administration Procedures:*

1. Make enough copies of the Names Test Scoring Sheet and the Scoring Matrix (see Figure 12.3) so that you have enough for each student who will be assessed.
2. Write each name on cards or make a class roster that shows the names. Students will read the names from these cards or this class roster.

[5]Patricia Cunningham, "The Names Test: A Quick Assessment of Decoding Ability." *The Reading Teacher,* 44: 124–129. 1990. F. A. Dufflemeyer, A. E. Kruse, D. J. Merkley, and S. A. Fyfe. "Further Validation and Enhancement of The Names Test." *The Reading Teacher,* 48: 118–128. 1994.

---

### FIGURE 12.2  Diagnostic Checklist for Word Recognition Skills

Student's Name: _____

Grade: _____

Teacher: _____

|  | Yes | No |
|---|---|---|
| 1. The student uses | | |
|   a. context clues. | | |
|   b. picture clues (graphs, maps, charts). | | |
| 2. The student asks someone to state the word. | | |
| 3. The student uses the dictionary to try to unlock unknown words. | | |

4. The student uses phonic analysis by recognizing
   a. consonants.
      (1) single consonants: initial, final.
      (2) consonant blends (clusters) (*br, sl, cl, st,* and so on).
      (3) consonant digraphs (*th, sh, ph, ch,* and so on).
      (4) silent consonants (*kn, gn, pn*).
   b. vowels.
      (1) short vowels (*cot, can, get,* and so on).
      (2) long vowels (*go, we, no,* and so on).
      (3) final silent *e* (*bake, tale, role*).
      (4) vowel digraphs (*ea, oa, ee, ai,* and so on).
      (5) diphthongs (*oi, oy*).
   c. the effect of *r* on the preceding vowel.
   d. special letters and sounds (*y, c, g,* and *q*).
   e. known phonograms or graphemic bases (a succession of graphemes that occurs with the same phonetic value in a number of words [*ight, id, at, ad, ack*]).

---

3. Individually administer the test. Hand the name cards or the class roster to the child and say something like, "I want you to pretend that you are the classroom teacher and that you are calling out names to see who is in school today."
4. As the child reads the names, write exactly what the child says above each name on the Names Test Scoring Sheet.
5. Use the Scoring Matrix to analyze the child's performance:
   - Locate each name on the matrix.
   - Circle any phonic elements that were mispronounced.
   - Count the circled elements for each category.
   - Record the total number of errors next to the total possible on the Names Test Scoring sheet.

**FIGURE 12.3**  **Names Test Scoring Sheet and Scoring Matrix**

Name _____ Grade _____ Teacher _____ Date _____

| | | | |
|---|---|---|---|
| Jay Conway | Tim Cornell | Chuck Hoke | Yolanda Clark |
| Kimberly Blake | Roberta Slade | Homer Preston | Gus Quincy |
| Cindy Sampson | Chester Wright | Ginger Yale | Patrick Tweed |
| Stanley Shaw | Wendy Swain | Glen Spencer | Fred Sherwood |
| Flo Thornton | Dee Skidmore | Grace Brewster | Ned Westmoreland |
| Ron Smitherman | Troy Whitlock | Vance Middleton | Zane Anderson |
| Bernard Pendergraph | Shane Fletcher | Floyd Sheldon | Dean Bateman |
| Austin Shepherd | Bertha Dale | Neal Wade | Jake Murphy |
| Joan Brooks | Gene Loomis | Thelma Rinehart | |

| _Phonics category_ | _Errors_ |
|---|---|
| Initial consonants | /37 |
| Initial consonant blends | /19 |
| Consonant digraphs | /15 |
| Short vowels | /36 |
| Long vowel/VC-final _e_ | /23 |
| Vowel digraphs | /15 |
| Controlled vowels | /25 |
| Schwa | /15 |

*(continued)*

**FIGURE 12.3** *(continued)*

Table 4
**Scoring matrix for the Names Test**

Name _____    Date _____

| Name | InCon | InConBl | ConDgr | ShVow | LngVow/VC-e | VowDgr | CtrVow | Schwa |
|------|-------|---------|--------|-------|-------------|--------|--------|-------|
| Anderson |  |  |  | A |  |  | er | o |
| Austin |  |  |  |  |  | Au |  | i |
| Bateman | B |  |  |  | ate |  |  | a |
| Bernard | B |  |  |  |  |  | er, ar |  |
| Bertha | B |  | th |  |  |  | er | a |
| Blake |  | Bl |  |  | ake |  |  |  |
| Brewster |  | Br |  |  |  |  | ew, er |  |
| Brooks |  | Br |  |  |  | oo |  |  |
| Chester |  |  | Ch | e |  |  | er |  |
| Chuck |  |  | Ch | u |  |  |  |  |
| Cindy | C |  |  | i | y |  |  |  |
| Clark |  | Cl |  |  |  |  | ar |  |
| Conway | C |  |  | o |  | ay |  |  |
| Cornell | C |  |  | e |  |  | or |  |
| Dale | D |  |  |  | ale |  |  |  |
| Dean | D |  |  |  |  | ea |  |  |
| Dee | D |  |  |  |  | ee |  |  |
| Fletcher |  | Fl | ch | e |  |  | er |  |
| Flo |  | Fl |  |  | o |  |  |  |
| Floyd |  | Fl |  |  |  | oy |  |  |
| Fred |  | Fr |  | e |  |  |  |  |
| Gene | G |  |  |  | ene |  |  |  |
| Ginger | G |  |  | i |  |  | er |  |
| Glen |  | Gl |  | e |  |  |  |  |
| Grace |  | Gr |  |  | ace |  |  |  |
| Gus | G |  |  | u |  |  |  |  |
| Hoke | H |  |  |  | oke |  |  |  |
| Homer | H |  |  |  | o |  | er |  |
| Jake | J |  |  |  | ake |  |  |  |
| Jay | J |  |  |  |  | ay |  |  |
| Joan | J |  |  |  |  | oa |  |  |
| Kimberly | K |  |  | i | y |  | er |  |
| Loomis | L |  |  |  |  | oo |  | i |
| Middleton | M |  |  | i |  |  |  | o |
| Murphy | M |  | ph |  | y |  | ur |  |

**FIGURE 12.3**

### Table 4
### Scoring matrix for the Names Test (cont'd.)

Name _____   Date _____

| Name | InCon | InConBl | ConDgr | ShVow | LngVow/VC-e | VowDgr | CtrVow | Schwa |
|---|---|---|---|---|---|---|---|---|
| Neal | N | | | | | ea | | |
| Ned | N | | | e | | | | |
| Patrick | P | | | a, i | | | | |
| Pendergraph | P | | ph | e, a | | | er | |
| Preston | | Pr | | e | | | | o |
| Quincy | | | | i | y | | | |
| Rinehart | R | | | | ine | | ar | |
| Roberta | R | | | | o | | er | a |
| Ron | R | | | o | | | | |
| Sampson | S | | | a | | | | o |
| Shane | | | Sh | | ane | | | |
| Shaw | | | Sh | | | | aw | |
| Sheldon | | | Sh | e | | | | o |
| Shepherd | | | Sh | e | | | er | |
| Sherwood | | | Sh | | | oo | er | |
| Skidmore | | Sk | | i | | | or | |
| Slade | | Sl | | | ade | | | |
| Smitherman | | Sm | th | i | | | er | a |
| Spencer | | Sp | | e | | | er | |
| Stanley | | St | | a | | ey | | |
| Swain | | Sw | | | | ai | | |
| Thelma | | | Th | e | | | | a |
| Thornton | | | Th | | | | or | o |
| Tim | T | | | i | | | | |
| Troy | | Tr | | | | oy | | |
| Tweed | | Tw | | | | ee | | |
| Vance | V | | | a | | | | |
| Wade | W | | | | ade | | | |
| Wendy | W | | | e | y | | | |
| Westmoreland | W | | | e | | | or | a |
| Whitlock | | | Wh | i, o | | | | |
| Wright | | | | | i | | | |
| Yale | Y | | | | ale | | | |
| Yolanda | Y | | | a | o | | | a |
| Zane | Z | | | | ane | | | |

6. Make some decisions about which phonic elements the child needs to learn how to use.
7. Design instruction to address the needs.

3. *Early Names Test* (Mather, Sammons, and Schwartz, 2006)[6]. Based on the work of Cunningham and Dufflemeyer, Mather and colleagues adapted the Names Test so that it would be more appropriate to use with first-grade students and older, struggling readers. Directions for administering the test and the accompanying forms are as follows:

*Administration Procedures:*

1. Make enough copies of the Names Test Scoring Sheet and the Scoring Matrix (see Figure 12.4) so that you have enough for each student who will be assessed.
2. Write each name on cards or make a class roster that shows the names. Students will read the names from these cards or this class roster.
3. Individually administer the test. Hand the name cards or the class roster to the child and say, "I want you to pretend that you are a teacher and you are calling out your students' names to take attendance. You are trying to figure out who is at school and who is not. Some of these names may be hard, but just do the best you can."
4. As the child reads the names, follow the scoring procedures on the form: Record a "1" for every correct response and a "0" for an incorrect response. Score both first and last names. Write incorrect responses directly above the name.
5. Use the Scoring Matrix to analyze the child's performance:
   • Locate each name on the matrix.
   • Circle any phonic elements that were mispronounced.
   • Count the circled elements for each category.
   • Record the total number of errors next to the total possible on the Names Test Scoring Sheet.
6. Make some decisions about which phonic elements the child needs to learn how to use.
7. Design instruction to address the needs.

4. *Tile Test* (Norman and Calfee, 2004)[7]. This is a more comprehensive assessment of early readers' understanding of English orthography. Norman and Calfee explain that the test "provides a hands-on interactive experience with letters and sounds for teachers who want to delve more deeply into students' underlying thinking" (p. 42). Using tiles and specific prompts, the teacher asks individual children to perform a variety of activities, each designed to reveal the child's understanding of phonics and metalingusitic awareness. Directions for administrating each section of the test are shown on the Tile Test Recording Sheet (see Figure 12.5 on page 305). Make enough copies so that you have one for each student who will be assessed. And, as with other phonics assessments, use what you discover to design appropriate instruction.

5. *Running Record* (Clay, 1985)[8]. Perhaps one of the easiest ways for teachers to see how children apply phonics to decode unknown words is to watch students read an authentic text and make note of what they see (i.e., running record). All forms and administration procedures can be found in Chapter 8.

---

[6]Nancy Mather, Janice Sammons, and Jonathan Schwartz, "Adaptations of the Names Test: Easy-to-use phonics assessments." *The Reading Teacher,* 60: 114–122. 2006.

[7]Kimberly A. Norman and Robert C. Calfee. "Tile Test: A hands-on approach for assessing phonics in the early grades." *The Reading Teacher,* 58: 42–52. 2004.

[8]Marie Clay. *The Early Detection of Reading Difficulties* (Portsmouth, NH: Heinemann, 1979).

---

**FIGURE 12.4** **Early Names Test and Scoring Sheet**

---

**Administration Instructions and Scoring Sheet**

---

**Say:** "I want you to pretend that you are a teacher and you are calling out your students' names to take attendance. You are trying to figure out who is at school and who is not. Some of these names may be hard, but just do the best you can."

**Scoring:** Record a 1 for a correct response and a 0 for an incorrect response. Score both first and last names. Write incorrect responses directly above the name.

Student's Name _____     Grade _____     Date _____

| | | | |
|---|---|---|---|
| Rob___ Hap___ | Jud___ Lem___ | Ray___ San___ | Pat___ Ling___ |
| Tim___ Bop___ | Brad___ Tash___ | Pam___ Rack___ | Trish___ Mot___ |
| Fred___ Tig___ | Bab___ Fum___ | Kate___ Tide___ | Brent___ Lake___ |
| Flip___ Mar___ | Jet___ Mit___ | Rand___ Lun___ | Jen___ Dut___ |
| Jake___ Bin___ | Sid___ Gold___ | Frank___ Lug___ | Grace___ Nup___ |
| Beck___ Daw___ | Dell___ Smush___ | Gus___ Lang___ | Lex___ Yub___ |
| Ross___ Quest___ | Dane___ Wong___ | Tom___ Zall___ | Gail___ Vog___ |
| Rod___ Blade___ | Tag___ Shick___ | | TOTAL_____ |

---

| *Phonics category* | *# missed/# possible* |
|---|---|
| Initial Consonants | ___/48 |
| Ending Consonants | ___/40 |
| Consonant Blend | ___/11 |
| Consonant Digraph | ___/10 |
| Short Vowel | ___/46 |
| Long vowel/VC-final *e* | ___/7 |
| Vowel Digraph | ___/2 |
| Rime | ___/58 |

*(continued)*

FIGURE 12.4   *(continued)*

**Scoring matrix for the Early Names Test**

Name _____   Grade _____   Date _____

| Name | Initial consonant | Ending consonant | Consonant blend | Consonant digraph | Short vowel | Long vowel/ Vowel-consonant-final *e* | Vowel digraph | Rime |
|---|---|---|---|---|---|---|---|---|
| Bab | B | -b | | | a | | | -ab |
| Beck | B | | | -ck | e | | | -eck |
| Bin | B | -n | | | i | | | -in |
| Blade | | -d | Bl- | | | a-e | | -ade |
| Bop | B | -p | | | o | | | -op |
| Brad | | -d | Br- | | a | | | -ad |
| Brent | | | Br- -nt | | e | | | -ent |
| Dane | D | -n | | | | a-e | | -ane |
| Daw | D | | | | | | -aw | -aw |
| Dell | D | -ll | | | e | | | -ell |
| Dut | D | -t | | | u | | | -ut |
| Flip | | -p | Fl- | | i | | | -ip |
| Frank | | | Fr- -nk | | a | | | -ank |
| Fred | | -d | Fr- | | e | | | -ed |
| Gold | G | | -ld | | | | | -old |
| Grace | | | Gr- | | | a-e | | -ace |
| Gus | G | -s | | | u | | | -us |
| Hap | H | -p | | | a | | | -ap |
| Jake | J | -k | | | | a-e | | -ake |
| Jen | J | -n | | | e | | | -en |
| Jet | J | -t | | | e | | | -et |
| Jud | J | -d | | | u | | | -ud |
| Kate | K | -t | | | | a-e | | -ate |
| Lake | L | -k | | | | a-e | | -ake |
| Lang | L | | | -ng | a | | | -ang |
| Lem | L | -m | | | e | | | -em |
| Lex | L | -x | | | e | | | -ex |
| Ling | L | | | -ng | i | | | -ing |
| Lug | L | -g | | | u | | | -ug |
| Lun | L | -n | | | u | | | -un |
| Mar | M | | | | | | | -ar |
| Mit | M | -t | | | i | | | -it |

---

**FIGURE 12.4**

---

### Scoring matrix for the Early Names Test (cont'd.)

---

Name _____ Grade _____ Date _____

| Name | Initial consonant | Ending consonant | Consonant blend | Consonant digraph | Short vowel | Long vowel/ Vowel-consonant-final *e* | Vowel digraph | Rime |
|------|------|------|------|------|------|------|------|------|
| Mot | M | -t | | | o | | | -ot |
| Nup | N | -p | | | u | | | -up |
| Pam | P | -m | | | a | | | -am |
| Pat | P | -t | | | a | | | -at |
| Quest | (Qu)* | | -st | | e | | | -est |
| Rack | R | | | -ck | a | | | -ack |
| Rand | R | | -nd | | a | | | -and |
| Ray | R | | | | | | -ay | -ay |
| Rob | R | -b | | | o | | | -ob |
| Rod | R | -d | | | o | | | -od |
| Ross | R | -ss | | | o | | | -oss |
| San | S | -n | | | a | | | -an |
| Shick | | | | Sh-<br>-ck | i | | | -ick |
| Sid | S | -d | | | i | | | -id |
| Smush | | | Sm- | -sh | u | | | -ush |
| Tag | T | -g | | | a | | | -ag |
| Tash | T | | | -sh | a | | | -ash |
| Tide | T | -d | | | | i-e | | -ide |
| Tig | T | -g | | | i | | | -ig |
| Tim | T | -m | | | i | | | -im |
| Tom | T | -m | | | o | | | -om |
| Trish | T | | Tr- | -sh | i | | | -ish |
| Vog | V | -g | | | o | | | -og |
| Wong | W | | | -ng | o | | | -ong |
| Yub | Y | -b | | | u | | | -ub |
| Zall | Z | -ll | | | | | | -all |

*Note:* *Qu is sometimes referred to as a consonant oddity or a consonant blend.*

*Source:* Adapted from N. Mather et al., *The Reading Teacher, 60 (2):* 114–122. 2006.

## TEACHING PHONICS

### GUIDELINES FOR EXEMPLARY PHONICS INSTRUCTION

Phonics instruction needs to excite and stimulate language learning. Children need to understand the joy in being able to manipulate the sounds and letters of their language to create words. Phonics instruction that is going to be most useful to children requires careful thought and planning. The instruction need not use worksheets, nor should it be a chore or a bore. Authors of many different commercial programs aim to help teachers with this thoughtful planning by providing scripted teacher manuals with accompanying student materials. But how can we be sure that these materials are the best to use?

Fortunately, there are some research-based guidelines for exemplary phonics instruction. These guidelines can provide a framework for designing phonics programs. If teachers must use a commercial phonics program, these guidelines can be helpful when examining the materials that comprise the program.

Exemplary phonics instruction:

1. Builds on what children already know about reading such as how print functions, what stories are and how they work, and the purpose for reading.
2. Builds on a foundation of phonological awareness (see Chapter 7).
3. Is clear and direct. That is, the explanations make sense, and the teacher uses demonstrations to help children better understand how to apply what they are learning.
4. Is integrated into a total reading program. In terms of explicit, formal instruction, this means that no more than 15–20 minutes per day is allotted to it. Children are provided with many reading and writing opportunities to apply their phonics knowledge.
5. Focuses on reading words rather than learning rules. To help children see that the purpose of phonics is to acquire words, children need to be taught how to look for patterns in words rather than how to memorize "rules."
6. Leads to automatic word identification. The purpose of phonics is to help children acquire a large store of words so that they can read with greater ease. They need much meaningful practice so that they can use these words instantaneously while reading.[9]

## SYNTHETIC AND ANALYTIC PHONICS INSTRUCTION

**Synthetic phonics instruction**
Each sound associated with letters in a word is pronounced in isolation, and then the sounds are blended together.

There are many techniques for teaching phonics. All can be classified as either synthetic or analytic depending on how the teacher designs the overall instruction. In *synthetic phonics instruction,* each sound associated with letters in a word is pronounced in isolation and then blended together. What usually takes place in the classroom is the following: The teacher shows the children the word *cat,* points to the letter *c* and says that it stands for the sound */k/.* The teacher then points to the letter *a* in the word *cat* and says it stands for the sound */a/* and then points to the letter *t* and says it stands for the sound */t/.* The children are then told to blend all three sounds together to read the word *cat.* A problem with this method is that it is very difficult to produce many consonant sounds in isolation, especially sounds such as */k/* and */t/* that cannot be drawn out like other sounds such as */s/* and */f/.*

**Analytic phonics instruction**
The teacher presents students with a whole word and asks them to break it into its sounds and letters.

In *analytic phonics instruction,* on the other hand, the teacher presents students with a whole word and asks them to break it into its sounds and letters. What usually takes place in the classroom is the following: The teacher presents students with a list of words that all begin with the same initial consonant such as the following:

girl game get

The teacher then helps the children to recognize that all the words begin with the same letter, *g.* Then the children are asked to listen carefully to the beginning sound of each word. The teacher pronounces each word and tells the children that the letter *g*

---

[9]S. Stahl, "Saying the 'p' Word: Nine Guidelines for Exemplary Phonics Instruction," *The Reading Teacher* 45 (1992): 618–625. S. Stahl, A. Duffy-Hester, and K. Stahl, "Everything You Wanted to Know About Phonics (But Were Afraid to Ask)," *Reading Research Quarterly* 33 (1998): 338–355.

**FIGURE 12.5   Tile Test Recording Sheet**

Name _____     Date _____

**Letters and sounds:** Display letter tiles m, a, p, i, s, t, d, n.

"Here are some letters. I'll say the name of a letter and ask you to point to the letter. Point to the tile that has the letter *m*." (Record. Continue procedure with each letter.)

"Now, I'll point to a tile and you'll tell me two things about the letter. First, the *name* of the letter and, second, the *sound* that it makes." (Record.)

| Identification | Name | Sound | Identification | Name | Sound |
|---|---|---|---|---|---|
| m _____ | | | s _____ | | |
| a _____ | | | t _____ | | |
| p _____ | | | d _____ | | |
| i _____ | | | n _____ | | |

**Words:** Add letter tiles f, b.

*Decoding.* "Now let's put some letters together to make words. I'll go first and make a word, then I'll ask you to read it for me." (Manipulate only necessary letters. Stop after *sat* and ask the first metalinguistic question.)

| | | | |
|---|---|---|---|
| pat | _____ | fin | _____ |
| sat* | _____ | pit | _____ |
| sam | _____ | tab | _____ |
| fan | _____ | mid | _____ |

*Metalinguistic question: "How did you know to say *sat* (or other pronunciation) that way?" _____

_____

Metalinguistic question: Rebuild the word that the student had the most difficulty with but decoded correctly. "How did you know to say _____ that way?" _____

*Spelling.* "Now, I'll say a word, and you'll build it for me." (As you dictate, clearly articulate by "stretching and exaggerating." Example: tan = /ta:::n:::/. Stop after *tad* and ask the first metalinguistic question.)

| | | | |
|---|---|---|---|
| tan | _____ | sip | _____ |
| tad* | _____ | tin | _____ |
| mad | _____ | pad | _____ |
| sap | _____ | fit | _____ |

*Metalinguistic question: "How did you know to (spell) *tad* that way?" _____

Metalinguistic question: Rebuild the word that the student had the most difficulty with but built correctly. "How did you know to build _____ that way?" _____

_____

*Sight-word reading.* Lay out the collection of word tiles. "I'll show you some words, and you read each one." (Record.)

| | | | | | | | |
|---|---|---|---|---|---|---|---|
| I | _____ | me | _____ | the | _____ | a | _____ |
| is | _____ | at | _____ | look | _____ | dog | _____ |
| cat | _____ | big | _____ | map | _____ | can | _____ |
| sat | _____ | fat | _____ | sit | _____ | on | _____ |
| run | _____ | | | | | | |

stands for the sound at the beginning of the words *girl, game, get.* The children are then often asked to come up with other words that begin with the letter *g,* like *game.*

Many teachers use a combination of synthetic and analytic phonics instruction. The most important thing is to use methods that help children unlock words as quickly as possible. Phonics instruction must give children the power and independence they need to pronounce unfamiliar words. The key, of course, is for children to use phonics to make words part of their sight vocabulary. This enables them to move more quickly toward comprehension.

## SEVEN WAYS TO TEACH PHONICS

There are two basic approaches to teaching phonics: implicit instruction and explicit instruction. Implicit instruction leads children to discover parts of words, whereas in explicit instruction teachers tell students what the parts are. Regardless of whether teachers use one or both approaches, instruction needs to be coupled with demonstrations. Because teachers want children to actually transfer this knowledge to their reading, they need to model how they can use what they just acquired.

As with any good instruction, purpose is what guides the selection of a specific way to teach. Below we provide seven different methods for helping students gain and use phonics knowledge as a comprehension tool.

### 1. Teach Word Identification Strategies

*Word identification* is the ability to both pronounce and understand words. There are many strategies teachers can use to help students do both. Rather than seeing them as isolated and separate strategies, readers use any combination of strategies to comprehend a text.[10]

> **Word identification**
> A twofold process that includes both pronunciation and knowledge of word meaning.

Being able to pronounce a word is important, but it does not guarantee word meaning. If we read a word we have never heard before, it would not be in our listening vocabulary; therefore, the pronunciation would not trigger an association with a word stored in our listening vocabulary bank. Sometimes the process happens in the reverse. That is, we know the meaning of the word yet have difficulty pronouncing it. Sometimes a "close enough" pronunciation helps us trigger a word meaning in the listening vocabulary. Overemphasizing pronunciation at the expense of meaning sends students a message about the purpose of reading—they may think reading is all about calling words.

One way to ascertain the strategies children use for word identification is to conduct a brainstorming session with the entire class. To prepare for the session, display two sheets of chart paper for all to see. Say something like, "Good readers sometimes see words that they do not know. When this happens, they try different ideas to figure out the word. What are some strategies you use when you see words you don't know?" As students share their ideas, write those that relate to pronunciation on one piece of chart paper and those that relate to meaning on the other. Remember that as the teacher, you always reserve the right to add to the lists. Therefore, if there are some strategies that students fail to mention, add them to the list. Once the lists have been created, see if students can figure out why you put the various strategies on different pieces of chart paper by saying something like, "All of the ideas on each of these charts are alike in some way. I think you might be able to tell me. Any volunteers?" If students cannot tell you, tell them! Write "Strategies for Gaining Pronunciation" and "Strategies for Gaining Meaning" as headings on the appropriate charts. Close the lesson by saying something like, "These are excellent reading strategies! I knew you were good readers and these charts show me that I was correct. You may have learned some new strategies

[10]P. Afflerbach, P. D. Pearson, and S. G. Paris, "Clarifying Differences Between Reading Skills and Reading Strategies," *The Reading Teacher* 61, no. 5 (2008): 364–373.

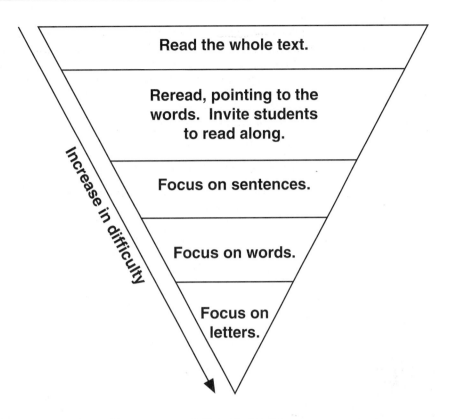

**FIGURE 12.6**   Whole-to-Part Phonics Instruction

to try when you come to a problem word. I am going to post these in our room as reminders. Make sure that when you are reading today, you take a look at the charts to help you figure out any words you don't know."

### 2. Teach from Whole to Part Using Nursery Rhymes and Children's Literature
Getting a sense of the whole is often a sure way to help children understand the parts.[11] Meaningful associations are made when students see how the parts relate to the overall text. There are a couple of ways to implement whole-to-part instruction.

### Whole-Part-Whole with Nursery Rhymes or Poems
The inverted triangle shown in Figure 12.6 is one way to think about whole-to-part instruction. Using this diagram, then, a teacher might begin with a nursery rhyme such as Humpty Dumpty that is displayed on a chart large enough for all to see. After reading the entire text a few times, the teacher invites the children to read along. The children need to know the rhyme well in order to complete the other parts of the triangle.

The second step involves writing each line of the rhyme on a sentence strip. Read the sentence strips to the children, placing them in a pocket holder for all to see. Ideally, the chart containing the nursery rhyme is next to the pocket chart. Point out (if no student tells you) that the two are the same. In turn, take each sentence strip out of the holder and place it on top of the sentence shown on the original chart. Reread the rhyme with the

[11]James Erekson, "Putting Humpty Dumpty Together Again: When Illustration Shuts Down Interpretation," *Journal of Visual Literacy,* 28: 145–162. 2009.

children, pointing to each word. Having modeled the process, ask the children to close their eyes while you take the sentence strips off the chart. Mix up the sentences and distribute them to some volunteers. In turn, each volunteer comes to the chart and places the sentence over the matching sentence on the chart. Reread the rhyme with the children.

The third step helps children to better understand "wordness" (i.e., word boundaries). Using a pair of scissors, cut each sentence strip apart and ask the children to count the number of words that fall on the floor. They can then reassemble the rhyme by placing the words over the matching words in the chart.

A fourth step involves helping children to understand that words are made of letters. Make word cards for some of the words shown in the rhyme, or use the words from the cut-apart sentences. Tell the children that you are going to cut apart a given word to show them how many letters make up that word. Then cut apart each word.

A fifth step involves phonic elements. Choose the words that focus on the phonic element you want them to notice and use these words to teach the skill. For example, if you want children to learn about the initial consonant *h,* select those words and use either explicit or implicit phonics instruction (described above) to teach them this initial consonant.

One important reminder is in order. Make sure that children reread the whole text every session. In this way, they will begin to see that all of the parts relate to the whole.

### Whole-Part-Whole with Children's Literature

Sometimes, using an entire children's literature selection to teach phonics is desirable. The procedures listed in Figure 12.7 will be helpful in this process. Although phonics is the major focus, you will notice that experiencing the book for enjoyment is the first step.

---

**FIGURE 12.7** **Whole-Part-Whole Phonics Instruction**

*Whole*

- Read aloud.
- Model expressive reading.
- Promote enjoyment.
- Provide extension activities:
  - dramatization
  - compare/contrast

*Part*

- Focus on phonic element.
- Use portion from text.
- Children participate.
- Provide visual reminder.
- Word slotter: build words.

*Whole*

- Present new book, same phonic element.
- Children read the story:
  - choral reading
  - partner reading
  - individual reading

*Source:* Based on Trachtenburg, 1990.

Of utmost importance is identifying the specific phonic element you want to teach and rounding up the children's books that contain enough examples so that children can apply what they have learned when reading a text. The following list identifies some books that can be used to teach both long and short vowels.

*Children's Literature for Whole-Part-Whole Phonics Instruction*

*Long a*: Cohen, C. L. *How Many Fish?* New York: HarperCollins, 1998.
*Long e:* Milgrim, D. *See Pip Point.* New York: Atheneum, 2003.
*Long i:* Ziefert, H. *A New House for Mole and Mouse.* New York: Puffin, 1987.
*Long o:* Bauer, M. D. *Rain.* New York: Aladdin, 2004.
*Long u:* Segal, L. *Tell Me a Trudy.* New York: Farrar, Straus, & Giroux, 1977.
*Short a:* Carle, E. *From Head to Toe.* New York: HarperCollins, 1997.
*Short e:* Ets, M. *Elephant in a Well.* New York: Viking, 1972.
*Short i:* Meister, C. *When Tiny Was Tiny.* New York: Puffin, 1999.
*Short o:* Foster, K., and G. Erickson, *A Mop for Pop.* New York: Barron's, 1991.
*Short u:* Lewison, W. C. *Buzz Said the Bee.* New York: Scholastic, 1992.

*Additional Children's Literature to Enhance Phonics Knowledge*

Baker, Keith. *Just How Long Can a Long String Be?!* New York: Scholastic, 2009.
—. *Cat Tricks.* San Diego, CA: Harcourt, 1997.
Ehlert, Lois. *Top Cat.* San Diego, CA: Harcourt, 1998.
Emberley, Rebecca, Adrian Emberley, and Ed Emberley. *There Was An Old Monster!* New York: Scholastic, 2009.
Enderle, Judith Ross, and Stephanie Gordon Tessler. *Six Creepy Sheep.* Honesdale, PA: Boyds Mills, 1992.
Hawkins, Colin, and Jacqui Hawkins. *Jen the Hen.* New York: G. P. Putnam's Sons, 2002.
Hepworth, Cathi. *Antics.* New York: G. P. Putnam's Sons, 1992.
—. *Bug Off!* New York: G. P. Putnam's Sons, 1998.
Johnston, Tony. *It's About Dogs.* San Diego, CA: Harcourt, 2000.
Le Guin, Ursula K. *Cat Dreams.* New York: Scholastic, 2009.
Mitton, Tony. *Farmer Joe and the Music Show.* New York: Scholastic, 2008.
Potter, Alicia. *Fritz Danced the Fandango.* New York: Scholastic, 2009.
Priceman, Marjorie. *Froggie Went A-Courting.* Boston: Little, Brown, and Company, 2000.
Pulver, Robin. *Silent Letters Loud and Clear.* New York: Holiday House, 2008.
Shaw, Nancy. *Sheep Take a Hike.* Boston: Houghton Mifflin, 1994.
Singer, Marilyn. *I'm Your Bus.* New York: Scholastic, 2009.
Wilbur, Richard. *The Pig in the Spigot.* San Diego, CA: Harcourt, 2000.
Wilhelm, Hans. *Come Rhyme with Me!* New York: Scholastic, 2008.
Yolen, Jane, and Mark Teague. *How Do Dinosaurs Say Good Night?* New York: Scholastic, 2000.
Zuckerman, Andrew. *Creature.* San Francisco, CA: Chronicle, 2009.

### 3. Use Word Sorts

Sorting is a way of categorizing pictures or words with similar sound features. Pictures or words can be sorted into several categories such as those that rhyme, beginning sounds, phonograms, and vowel sounds. Sorting activities help children form schema for phonics elements.

There are two basic ways to have children sort. In a *closed sort,* you give students the categories and ask them to sort a given number of cards. This type of sort

Go to the Assignments and Activities section of Topic 5: Phonemic Awareness and Phonics in the MyEducationLab for your course and complete the activity entitled "Onsets and Rimes in Phonics Instruction." As you watch the video and answer the accompanying questions, consider how reading authentic books can help children practice onset-rime phonics.

causes <u>convergent</u> thinking. In an *open sort,* you invite students to create and name the categories. This type of sort encourages <u>divergent</u> thinking. Both types of sorts are valuable and will help you to see what students know about words. However, open sorts lend even more insight into what students are noticing on their own—what they have internalized.

Here are some suggested steps for using word sorts:

1. Model what you expect students to do.
2. Give children several cards to sort into contrasting categories.
3. Provide practice with your guidance.
4. Have students work with one another to sort.

### 4. Teach Students How to Decode by Analogy

Basically, teaching students how to decode by analogy involves having them use a word they know to identify a word they do not know. For example, a child might know the word *cat,* yet not know the word *bat.* Assuming that both words are in the child's listening vocabulary, the teacher asks if *bat* looks like any other word that the child knows. If not, the teacher writes the word the child does know, *cat,* right above *bat.* He or she then has the child read *cat.* Most often, the child will see how the two words are the same and will read *bat* without additional help. Sometimes a prompt is provided such as, "If this word is *cat,* then this one has to be _____," to get the child to decode the word.

### 5. Use Writing

Perhaps one of the best ways for children to apply what they know about phonics and to learn more about it is for them to write. Regardless of what we *think* children know about phonics or what we *think* we taught them, their writing will show us what they have actually internalized to the point of being able to apply any given skill. For example, after learning about the "*ai*" spelling for long *a,* children may use it to spell all words having the long *a* sound. Just like when they are learning spoken language, they may overgeneralize.

We suggest giving each student a blank book and using class time for writing at least once a day. The books serve as evidence of the children's performance and growth over time.

### 6. Teach Students How to Make Words

Making words is a manipulative word-building activity designed by Cunningham.[12] This activity involves having children put letter cards together to form words and it can be used to either teach or reinforce building words with phonograms. Figure 12.8 provides an example.

### 7. Use Prompts When Reading with Students

As expert readers, we know that there are several strategies we can employ to figure out unknown words. We want to pass this expertise along to students so that they, too, can be independent readers. We want to help them develop what Clay calls a "self-extending system."[13] Prompting is one way to help them develop this system.

Knowing the type of prompt to provide depends on what we know about both the student and the word that is posing difficulty. Table 12.1 gives some guidance.

---

[12]P. Cunningham and J. Cunningham, "Making Words: Enhancing the Invented Spelling-Decoding Connection," *The Reading Teacher* 46: 106–115. 1992

[13]M. Clay, *The Early Detection of Reading Difficulties* (Portsmouth, NH: Heinemann, 1979).

**FIGURE 12.8   Make Words Lesson**

**Letters:**  a   d   n   s   t
**Words:**  at   an   and   Dan   tan   ant   sat   sad   sand   stand

**Name letters and their common sounds:** Before beginning to make words, have the students hold up each letter, name it, and say its common sound. Have the students show both the lower-case and capital letters.

**Make words:** Have the students make these words, then send one student to make each word using the big letters. DO NOT wait for everyone to make the word before sending someone up. Keep the lesson fast-paced and the students will pay better attention. When the word is made with the big letters, ask everyone to check their words and fix them if necessary.

1. Take 2 letters and make **at**. We are **at** school.
2. Take the **t** away and add a different letter to make **an**. I ate **an** apple.
3. Add a letter to **an** and you can spell **and**. I like apples **and** bananas.
4. Now we are going to do a trick with **and**. Move the letters in **and** around so that they spell **Dan**. Stretch out **Dan** and listen for where you hear the **D** and the **a** and the **n**. (Look for a student who has **Dan** spelled with a capital letter **D**, and send that student to make **Dan** with big letters.) My cousin's name is **Dan**.
5. Take the **D** away and add a letter to spell **tan**. I got a **tan** at the beach.
6. Now let's do the "move the letters around" trick with **tan** to spell **ant**. Stretch out **ant** with me and listen for where you hear the sounds. The **ant** is tiny.
7. Let's start over and make another 3-letter word, **sat**. The boy **sat** down.
8. Take the **t** away, add another letter, and you can spell **sad**. He was very **sad**.
9. Now we are going to spell a 4-letter word. Add 1 letter to **sad** and you can spell **sand**. Let's all say **sand** and listen for the letter we need to add. She digs in the **sand**.
10. The last word in every lesson is the secret word. Add 1 letter to **sand** and you can spell another word. I am going to look and see if anyone has figured out the secret word. (Give them no more than a minute to try to figure it out and then say a sentence with the secret word. Everyone **stand** up.) Have someone make **stand** with the big letters.

**Sort:** Collect the letters, then read with the students all the words in the pocket chart. Next, have them sort the words into columns according to their first letter.

| at | sat | Dan | tan |
|-----|------|-----|-----|
| an | sad | | |
| and | sand | | |
| ant | stand | | |

**Transfer:** Say some words in sentences and have the students repeat the words and decide what letter they begin with.

| dog   top   sun   add   apple   teacher   doctor   sister |
|---|

**TABLE 12.1 Word Analysis Prompts**

| Strategy | Use When | Example Prompt |
|---|---|---|
| Word part a student can pronounce | The unknown word has a part you know the student can pronounce | "There's a part of that word you can say. Find it and say it." |
| Analogy | The unknown word is similar to a word you know the student knows | "This word is like another one you know." |
| Each sound | The student has difficulty with chunking words, yet can figure out the word using each sound | "Say each sound in this word." |
| Context | The student is weak in using phonics clues | "Read to the end of the sentence and ask yourself what would make sense." |

*Source:* Based on Gunning, 2006.

## REVISITING THE OPENING SCENARIO

Ms. Mills was trying to decide how to best ascertain Jorge's decoding abilities, and how to teach the phonics he needed to learn. Now that you have read the chapter, you have an understanding of phonics content, assessment strategies, and teaching strategies. How would you recommend Ms. Mills proceed?

## AUTHORS' SUMMARY

In this chapter, we presented information about helping children to acquire and apply phonics knowledge. We provided an explanation of the importance of decoding in reading, along with a definition of phonics. Understanding terminology associated with phonics is important, which is why we discussed phonics terms and provided an exercise for each. We listed specific guidelines for teaching phonics as well as explaining explicit and implicit teaching. We listed and described seven teaching strategies for designing meaningful phonics lessons. As with other aspects of reading, assessing phonics is important and we offered some suggestions for how to do that. Throughout this chapter, we emphasized that phonics needs to be taught in conjunction with an emphasis on reading connected text and reading comprehension.

## SUGGESTIONS FOR THOUGHT QUESTIONS AND ACTIVITIES

1. You have been appointed to a special primary-grade reading committee. Your task is to help teachers better understand the role that phonics plays in the word recognition process. How would you go about doing this?
2. Design a workshop on meaningful ways to teach phonics. What will you present?
3. Present a lesson that would help a primary-grade student learn about a phonic element of your choice.
4. Your state legislators are proposing a bill to mandate the teaching of phonics in all schools. How do you feel about this? Prepare a talk expressing your views.

# WEB SITES

http://curry.edschool.virginia.edu/go/wil/home.html

This site gives access to a downloadable program designed for rural Head Start teachers. Included are instructional activities and materials designed to place young children on the track to success.

http://www1.ncte.org/library/files/Related_Groups/WLU/phonics.pdf

This link provides access to Constance Weaver's fact sheet on teaching phonics. In the article, Weaver explains the research behind integrating phonics instruction in a whole language curriculum. In addition to providing general information, the fact sheet includes an extensive bibliography.

http://teams.lacoe.edu/reading/assessments/inven.html

This site provides a focus on phonics, including a definition and assessments with teacher materials and step-by-step procedures.

http://db080.k12.sd.us/Reading%20Diagnosis.htm

This site provides definitions and examples of vowel and consonant "names" (e.g., *r*-controlled syllable) as well as student interest and background inventories and an inventory for parents. The site also presents before, during, and after reading strategies.

# SELECTED BIBLIOGRAPHY

Adams, Marilyn Jager. *Beginning to Read: Thinking and Learning about Print.* Cambridge, MA: MIT Press, 1990.

Beck, Isabel L. *Making Sense of Phonics: The Hows and Whys.* New York: Guilford, 2006.

Blachowicz, Camille L. Z., and Peter Fisher. "Vocabulary Instruction." In *Handbook of Reading Research,* Vol. III, edited by Michael L. Kamil et al., 503–525. Mahwah, NJ: Lawrence Erlbaum, 2000.

Chall, Jeanne S. *Learning to Read: The Great Debate,* 2nd ed. New York: McGraw-Hill, 1983.

———."Two Vocabularies for Reading: Recognition and Reading." In *The Nature of Vocabulary Acquisition,* edited by M. G. McKeown and M. E. Curtis, 7–17. Hillsdale, NJ: Lawrence Erlbaum, 1987.

Cunningham, Patricia M. *Phonics They Use.* Boston: Allyn and Bacon, 2009.

———. *Systematic Sequential Phonics They Use.* Greensboro, NC: Carson-Dellosa, 2000.

Dow, Roger S., and G. Thomas Baer. *Self-Paced Phonics.* Upper Saddle River, NJ: Merrill Prentice Hall, 2007.

Durkin, Delores. *Teaching Them to Read,* 6th ed. Boston: Allyn and Bacon, 1993.

———. *The Decoding Ability of Elementary School Students.* Reading Education Report No. 49. Champaign, IL: Center for the Study of Reading, University of Illinois, 1984.

Fox, Barbara J., and Marion A. Hull. *Phonics for the Teacher of Reading.* Upper Saddle River, NJ: Merrill Prentice Hall, 2002.

Fry, E. "The Most Common Phonograms." *The Reading Teacher* 51 (1998): 620–622.

Gruber, Barbara. "Boost Learning with Word Walls." *Teaching Pre K–8* (September, 1999): 64–66.

Gunning, T. *Assessing and Correcting Reading and Writing Difficulties,* 3rd ed. Boston: Allyn and Bacon, 2006.

Heilman, Arthur W. *Phonics in Proper Perspective.* Upper Saddle River, NJ: Merrill Prentice Hall 2002.

Johnson, Dale D. *Vocabulary in the Elementary and Middle Grades.* Boston: Allyn and Bacon, 2001.

Nagy, William E., and Judith A. Scott. "Vocabulary Processes." In *Handbook of Reading Research,* Vol. III, edited by Michael L. Kamil et al., 269–284. Mahwah, NJ: Lawrence Erlbaum, 2000.

Rubin, Dorothy. *Gaining Word Power,* 6th ed. Boston: Allyn and Bacon, 2000.

———. *Phonics Skills & Strategies in a Balanced Reading Program* (Levels 1-4 Series). Torrance, CA: Fearon Teacher Aids, 1998.

———. "Vocabulary Development in the Language Arts Program." *Elementary Language Arts,* 6th ed. Boston: Allyn and Bacon, 2000.

———. *Vocabulary Skills & Strategies in a Balanced Reading Program.* Torrance, CA. Fearon Teacher Aids, 1998.

Rycik, Mary T., and James A. Rycik. *Phonics and Word Identification.* Upper Saddle River, NJ: Merrill Prentice Hall, 2007.

Savage, John F. *Sound It Out!* Boston: McGraw-Hill, 2007.

Stahl, S. "Saying the 'p' Word: Nine Guidelines for Exemplary Phonics Instruction." *The Reading Teacher* 45 (1992): 618–625.

Stahl, S., A. Duffy-Hester, and K. Stahl. "Everything You Wanted to Know About Phonics (But Were Afraid to Ask). *Reading Research Quarterly* 33 (1998): 338–355.

Trachtenberg, P. "Using Children's Literature to Enhance Phonics Instruction." *The Reading Teacher* 43 (1990): 648–654.

# CHILDREN'S LITERATURE CITED

Baker, Keith. *Just How Long Can a Long String Be?!* New York: Scholastic, 2009.

———. *Cat Tricks.* San Diego, CA: Harcourt, 1997.

Bauer, M. D. *Rain.* New York: Alladin, 2004.

Carle, Eric. *From Head to Toe.* New York: HarperCollins, 1997.

Cohen, Caron Lee. *How Many Fish?* New York: HarperCollins, 1998.

Ehlert, Lois. *Top Cat.* San Diego, CA: Harcourt, 1998.

Emberley, Rebecca, Adrian Emberley, and Ed Emberley. *There Was an Old Monster!* New York: Scholastic, 2009.

Enderle, Judith Ross, and Stephanie Gordon Tessler. *Six Creepy Sheep.* Honesdale, PA: Boyds Mills, 1992.

Ets, Marie Hall. *Elephant in a Well.* New York: Viking, 1972.

Foster, Kelli, and Gina Erickson. *A Mop for Pop.* New York: Barron's, 1991.

Hawkins, Colin, and Jacqui Hawkins. *Jen the Hen.* New York: G. P. Putnam's Sons, 2002.

Hepworth, Cathi. *Antics.* New York: G. P. Putnam's Sons, 1992.

———. *Bug Off!* New York: G. P. Putnam's Sons, 1998.

Johnston, Tony. *It's About Dogs.* San Diego, CA: Harcourt, 2000.

Le Guin, Ursula K. *Cat Dreams.* New York: Scholastic, 2009.

Lewison, Wendy C. *Buzz Said the Bee.* New York: Scholastic, 1992.

Meister, Cari. *When Tiny Was Tiny.* New York: Puffin, 1999.

Milgrim, David. *See Pip Point.* New York: Atheneum, 2003.

Mitton, Tony. *Farmer Joe and the Music Show.* New York: Scholastic, 2008.

Potter, Alicia. *Fritz Danced the Fandango.* New York: Scholastic, 2009.

Priceman, Marjorie. *Froggie Went A-Courting.* Boston: Little, Brown, 2000.

Pulver, Robin. *Silent Letters Loud and Clear.* New York: Holiday House, 2008.

Segal, Lore. *Tell Me a Trudy.* New York: Farrar, Straus, & Giroux, 1977.

Shaw, Nancy. *Sheep Take a Hike.* Boston: Houghton Mifflin, 1994.

Singer, Marilyn. *I'm Your Bus.* New York: Scholastic, 2009.

Wilbur, Richard. *The Pig in the Spigot.* San Diego, CA: Harcourt, 2000.

Wilhelm, Hans. *Come Rhyme with Me!* New York: Scholastic, 2008.

Yolen, Jane, and Mark Teague. *How Do Dinosaurs Say Good Night?* New York: Scholastic, 2000.

Ziefert, Harriet. *A New House for Mole and Mouse.* New York: Puffin, 1987.

Zuckerman, Andrew. *Creature.* San Francisco, CA: Chronicle, 2009.

**PEARSON myeducationlab**

Now go to Topic 5: "Phonemic Awareness and Phonics" in MyEducationLab (www.myeducationlab.com) for your course, where you can:

- Find learning outcomes for "Phonemic Awareness and Phonics" along with national standards that connect to these outcomes.
- Complete Assignments and Activities that can help you more deeply understand the chapter content.
- Access video clips of CCSSO National Teacher of the Year award winners responding to the question, "Why Do I Teach?" in the Teacher Talk section.
- Apply and practice your understanding of the core teaching skills identified in the chapter with Building Teaching Skills and Dispositions learning units.

# Learning Strategies and Study Skills

## CHAPTER OUTLINE

- What Are Some Good Study Procedures?
- How to Study
- Scenario: Modeling the SQ3R Approach for Fourth-Grade Students
- Knowing the Textbook
- Concentration
- Following Directions
- Skimming
- Asking Questions
- Reading and Writing as Modes of Learning
- Scenario: Note Taking, Studying, and SQ3R
- Scenario: Semantic Mapping and Studying
- Test Taking
- The School Media Center and Media Literacy Skills

## CHAPTER OBJECTIVES

After reading the chapter, you should be able to:

- Describe what is involved in building good study habits.
- Explain how teachers can help students to combine SQ3R and note taking.
- Explain the role of skimming in studying.
- Explain how reading and writing assist learning.
- Explain how teachers can help students to be better note takers.

How many times have you heard students make the following statements?

"I spent all night studying, but I did very poorly on my exams."
"I reread the chapter ten times, but I still don't understand it."
"I always listen to music when I study."
"I like to be relaxed when I study."
"I don't need to study."
"I don't know how to study."

Many students do poorly in school because they have never learned how to study. Often, elementary school teachers spend little time helping children acquire study skills because they may lack the skills themselves,[1] or because they feel that this is the job of high school teachers. Many high school teachers spend little instructional time in this area because they assume that their students have already acquired the study skills they need. As a result, many students go through school without ever being taught how to study. Most children need help in acquiring good study habits and they need to understand that having good study habits will help them maximize their learning.

In this chapter, we offer some information and skills that are necessary for teachers to assist students in becoming better learners. Helping students to be better learners is important in a reading diagnosis and improvement program where the emphasis is on helping children acquire necessary skills from the onset of instruction.

## WHAT ARE SOME GOOD STUDY PROCEDURES?

**Study procedures**
(1) Build good habits, (2) devise a system that works for you, (3) keep at it, (4) maintain a certain degree of tension, and (5) concentrate.

Although there is no simple formula that will apply to all students, educational psychologists have found that some *study procedures* help all students. The key is in building good habits, devising a system that works for the individual student, and keeping at it.

Studying requires a certain amount of tension, concentration, and effort in a specific direction. The amount of tension varies with different individuals. The point is that studying takes a concerted effort and students who are prepared to make a proper effort can maximize their learning.

[1]Eunice N. Askov et al., "Study Skill Mastery Among Elementary Teachers," *The Reading Teacher* 30 (February, 1977): 485–488.

## BUILDING GOOD STUDY HABITS

There are three steps to consider when teaching students how to build good study habits.

1. **Teach students how to determine *when to study.*** Some students study just before an announced test. Some may even stay up until all hours and cram. Unfortunately, cramming does not bring about sustained learning. It can be justified only as a last resort. For sustained learning, a student must plan study time and spread it out over a period of time. Showing students how to plan an overall time schedule in which they allot time for studying along with social and physical activities and recreational reading will better ensure that they learn how to schedule their time independently. Students must recognize that regardless of whether they study in the evening, before or after dinner, or right after class during free periods, following a schedule is what's important. Consistency is important, too.

2. **Teach students how to determine *where to study*.** Some students are able to study well in a school or public library, but there are others who cannot. Most elementary school-aged students study at home. Regardless of where students study, they should choose a place that is comfortable and convenient, has enough light, and is *free from distractions.*

To help children establish a comfortable, convenient, and suitable place for study at home, the teacher and the children can design such a place in the classroom. A special area can be set aside as a study area. It should be as free from distractions as possible, comfortable, and well lighted. Students should be free to go to this area whenever they wish to study. If a student is in this area, other students should recognize that it is "off limits"; that is, other students should respect the student's desire to study and not interrupt or bother him or her.

Teachers must recognize that some students may not have a place at home to study for one reason or another. For example, they might live with several others in a small space with no room for a separate study area that is free of distractions. Discussing options with the students will help them to see that there are other places where they can study (e.g., after school in the school media center, the public library, or at a friend's house). Teachers must be sensitive to the fact that students who do not have a place to do homework or study at home are actually being penalized twice—once, because they do not have a place to study, and again for not doing the homework.

3. **Teach students how to determine the *amount of time* they need to spend studying.** Most students need to learn how to budget their study time so that they can get the most learning out of it. Children need to learn that the amount of time they allot for studying will vary and depends on the subject to be studied and how much background they bring to it. In some subjects, students may need to spend a lot of time studying because of their limited familiarity and background, whereas in other, more familiar subjects, students may only have to spend a short time studying. Regardless, students also need to understand the concept of *overlearning* because some students feel that if they know something, they do not have to study it at all. Overlearning helps people retain information over a long period of time. Overlearning happens when individuals continue to practice even after they think they have learned the material. One way to help students become aware of their own study habits is to provide them with a checklist such as the one shown in Figure 13.1. Students can also use this checklist to evaluate their own growth over a period of time. Teachers can use the diagnostic checklist shown in Figure 13.2 to document students' progress in attaining study skills.

Go to the Assignments and Activities section of Topic 9: Reading Comprehension in the MyEducationLab for your course and complete the activity entitled "Reading for Information." As you watch the video and answer the accompanying questions, consider how reading for information is different from reading for a literary experience.

**Overlearning**
Helps people retain information over a long period of time; occurs when individuals continue to practice even after they think they have learned the material.

---

**FIGURE 13.1 Student Checklist of Study Habits and Strategies**

|  | Always | Sometimes | Never |
|---|---|---|---|
| 1. I have a special study place. | | | |
| 2. My study place is quiet. | | | |
| 3. I set goals for myself. | | | |
| 4. I make good use of my time. | | | |
| 5. I first look over my reading assignment to get an overview of it. | | | |
| 6. I look for writers' aids such as words in italics or bold and words in margins. | | | |
| 7. I break up my reading assignment into manageable sections. | | | |
| 8. I set questions for my reading material. | | | |
| 9. After reading each section, I stop to answer my questions. | | | |
| 10. I also try to state the central idea of each passage. | | | |
| 11. I relate my present reading to past assignments. | | | |
| 12. I review my present reading assignment before going on to something else. | | | |
| 13. In reviewing, I state generalizations about what I have read. | | | |

*Survey – Question, Read, Recite, Review*

## HOW TO STUDY

**SQ3R**
A widely used study technique that involves five steps: survey, question, read, recite or recall, and review.

**Survey**
To gain an overview of the text material.

After teachers help students to acquire good study habits, they can teach students *how to study*. There are a number of study techniques and *SQ3R*[2] is one of them. It is a widely used technique that has proved helpful to many students. It is based on self-questioning, and is a great comprehension strategy to supplement the questioning techniques in Chapter 10. SQ3R works best for well-structured informational text with headers and clear topic sentences. Here are the five steps in this technique:

1. *Survey*—Students should get an overall sense of their learning task before proceeding to details. They should skim the whole text to obtain some idea(s) about the material and how it is organized.
2. *Question*—Students should check section headings and change these to questions to set their purposes for reading.

Many students can increase the effectiveness of their studying with only the *SQ* portion of this strategy. Students who have difficulty organizing or remembering can benefit just by increasing their sense of purpose through skimming and questioning. Others still need to figure out a fuller process for memory and understanding, and teachers can coach them to move on to the *3R* phase.

3. *Read*—Students should read to answer the questions that they have formulated for themselves. While reading, they should notice how the paragraphs are organized because this knowledge will help them remember the answer.

[2]Adapted from Francis P. Robinson, *Effective Study,* 4th ed. (New York: Harper & Row, 1970).

FIGURE 13.2  **Diagnostic Checklist for Reading and Study Skills**

Student's Name: _____

Grade: _____

Teacher: _____

| 1. Dictionary | Yes | No | Sometimes |
|---|---|---|---|

A. GRADES 1, 2

The student is able to

1. supply missing letters of the alphabet.
2. arrange words, none of which begin with the same letter, in alphabetical order.
3. list words, several of which begin with the same letter.
4. list words according to first and second letters.
5. list words according to the third letter.
6. find the meaning of a word.
7. find the correct spelling of a word.

B. GRADES 3, 4, 5, 6

The student is able to

1. locate words halfway in the dictionary.
2. open the dictionary by quarters and state the letters with which words begin.
3. open the dictionary by thirds and state the letters with which words begin.
4. open the dictionary at certain initial letters.
5. use key words at the head of each page as a guide to finding words.
6. use the dictionary to select meanings to fit the context (homographs).
7. use the dictionary to build up a vocabulary of synonyms.
8. use the dictionary to build up a vocabulary of antonyms.
9. answer questions about the derivation of a word.
10. use the dictionary to learn to pronounce a word.
11. use the dictionary to correctly syllabicate a word.
12. use the dictionary to get the correct usage of a word.
13. use the dictionary to determine the part(s) of speech of the word.
14. use the dictionary to gain the meanings of idiomatic phrases.

*(continued)*

FIGURE 13.2   *(continued)*

Student's Name: _____

Grade: _____

Teacher: _____

| 2. Library Skills | Yes | No | Sometimes |
|---|---|---|---|

A. PRIMARY GRADES

The student is able to

1. find books in the library.
2. state the kinds of books that are found in the library.

B. INTERMEDIATE GRADES

The student is able to

1. state the kinds of reference materials that are found in the library.
2. use the encyclopedia as an aid to gaining needed information.
3. find books in the school library.

| 3. Building Good Study Habits | Yes | No | Sometimes |
|---|---|---|---|

INTERMEDIATE GRADES

The student is able to

1. plan his or her studying time.
2. choose a place to study that is free from distractions.
3. recognize that he or she needs to study.

| 4. Study Procedures | Yes | No | Sometimes |
|---|---|---|---|

INTERMEDIATE GRADES

The student is able to

1. use the SQ3R technique when studying.
2. apply the SQ3R technique when studying a chapter in a textbook.

| 5. Concentration and Following Directions | Yes | No | Sometimes |
|---|---|---|---|

A. PRIMARY GRADES

The student is able to

1. listen carefully and follow directions.
2. read directions and follow them carefully.
3. show that concentration is increasing by being able to pay attention for longer periods of time.

**FIGURE 13.2**

| 5. Concentration and Following Directions | Yes | No | Sometimes |
|---|---|---|---|

**B. INTERMEDIATE GRADES**

The student is able to

| | Yes | No | Sometimes |
|---|---|---|---|
| 1. listen carefully and follow directions. | | | |
| 2. read directions and follow them correctly. | | | |
| 3. fill out some application forms. | | | |

| 6. Skimming | Yes | No | Sometimes |
|---|---|---|---|

**A. PRIMARY GRADES**

The student is able to

| | Yes | No | Sometimes |
|---|---|---|---|
| 1. find some information quickly by skimming. | | | |
| 2. skim a paragraph and state its topic. | | | |

**B. INTERMEDIATE GRADES**

The student is able to

| | Yes | No | Sometimes |
|---|---|---|---|
| 1. differentiate between skimming and studying. | | | |
| 2. recognize the role that skimming plays in studying. | | | |
| 3. locate information such as the departure time of trains by skimming train schedules. | | | |

| 7. Knowing the Textbook | Yes | No | Sometimes |
|---|---|---|---|

**A. PRIMARY GRADES**

The student is able to

| | Yes | No | Sometimes |
|---|---|---|---|
| 1. use the table of contents to find chapter headings. | | | |
| 2. use the glossary to gain the meaning of a word. | | | |
| 3. list the parts of a textbook. | | | |

**B. INTERMEDIATE GRADES**

The student is able to

| | Yes | No | Sometimes |
|---|---|---|---|
| 1. read the preface to learn about the author's purpose in writing the book. | | | |
| 2. skim the index to learn about the material that will be found in the book. | | | |
| 3. skim the index to find the page on which a specific topic is found. | | | |

| 8. Asking Questions | Yes | No | Sometimes |
|---|---|---|---|

**A. PRIMARY GRADES**

The student is able to

| | Yes | No | Sometimes |
|---|---|---|---|
| 1. formulate questions that will obtain the wanted information. | | | |
| 2. ask questions that are pertinent to the topic under discussion. | | | |

*(continued)*

**FIGURE 13.2** *(continued)*

| 8. Asking Questions | Yes | No | Sometimes |
|---|---|---|---|

**B. INTERMEDIATE GRADES**

The student will be able to

| | Yes | No | Sometimes |
|---|---|---|---|
| 1. ask questions that will help in studying for a test. | | | |
| 2. ask questions that will help in learning about what to study. | | | |

| 9. Test Taking | Yes | No | Sometimes |
|---|---|---|---|

**A. PRIMARY GRADES**

The student is able to

| | Yes | No | Sometimes |
|---|---|---|---|
| 1. read questions very carefully so that they are answered correctly. | | | |
| 2. follow directions in taking a test. | | | |

**B. INTERMEDIATE GRADES**

The student is able to

| | Yes | No | Sometimes |
|---|---|---|---|
| 1. recognize that he or she studies differently for objective and essay tests. | | | |
| 2. take objective tests. | | | |
| 3. take essay tests. | | | |
| 4. go over the test to learn why he or she did or did not do well. | | | |
| 5. ask questions about a test to learn from the mistakes. | | | |

| 10. Summaries | Yes | No | Sometimes |
|---|---|---|---|

**INTERMEDIATE GRADES**

The student is able to

| | Yes | No | Sometimes |
|---|---|---|---|
| 1. summarize a passage. | | | |
| 2. use a summary for study. | | | |

| 11. Note Taking | Yes | No | Sometimes |
|---|---|---|---|

**INTERMEDIATE GRADES**

The student is able to

| | Yes | No | Sometimes |
|---|---|---|---|
| 1. explain why note taking is a useful study tool. | | | |
| 2. explain why note taking is helpful in writing long papers. | | | |
| 3. take notes while listening to a talk. | | | |
| 4. take notes while reading to help remember important information. | | | |

**Recite or recall**
The process of answering a question from memory, without rereading the text or notes.

4. *Recite or recall—This step is very important.* Without referring to their books, students should try to answer the questions that they have formulated for themselves. (Writing down key ideas will provide necessary notes for future review. See the section on note taking.)

5. *Review*—Students should take a few moments to review the major headings and subheadings of the material they have just finished studying. You should recommend to your students that it's also a good idea to try to relate what they have just finished studying to the previous assignment on the same topic. (Their ability to relate their new learning to previous learning will determine how well they will remember the new material.)

Teachers need to make sure students understand that surveying an assignment will enable them to determine its organization and to obtain some ideas about it. However, to truly study, they need to recognize that one of the key factors in remembering information is recall or recitation rather than the immediate rereading of their assignment. The time they spend answering the questions is crucial to their learning.

The following scenario provides an example of how teachers can help their students adapt the SQ3R technique to suit their personal needs.

## SCENARIO: MODELING THE SQ3R APPROACH FOR FOURTH-GRADE STUDENTS

Ms. Mills tells her fourth-grade students that she is taking courses at the local college, and that they require a lot of reading. She also tells them that she can only get all of her reading accomplished because she knows how to study, thanks to a teacher who taught her how. Ms. Mills mentions that she wants to do the same for her students and she will show them what she does when she has to study something. She then takes students through the following steps:

*Step 1:* Ms. Mills chooses a chapter from the students' history textbook and has her students turn to the chapter. She then says, "I always quickly skim through an assignment first to get an idea of what it's about. So that's what I'm going to do. I want you to do the same."

Ms. Mills then says, "As I skim through the chapter, I look at some of the section headings to see if I should break the chapter up into parts to study. I do this if it's an area I don't know anything about. You give it a try, too."

*Step 2:* Ms. Mills says, "I try to be honest with myself. If the chapter has a great amount of new material, I know I should break it up into parts. Also, I know my concentration ability. If I don't feel I can study the whole chapter all at once, I will break this chapter into parts for study purposes and choose a few sections to study at a time. You can do the same."

*Step 3:* Ms. Mills says, "I look over the first part of the chapter I have decided to study. I check the section headings and use them to make up questions. If there are no section headings, I look for other clues such as words in margins, words in bold print, or words in italics. If the material doesn't have any of these, then I survey or skim it more slowly and also read the first sentence to get an idea of what the selection is about.

*Step 4:* "Now, I read the part I chose to study and try to answer my questions. As I do this, I try to determine how the writer has organized his paragraphs because that will help me remember the material," says Ms. Mills. She also tells her students that she makes sure she studies in an area where she will not have any distractions. When she studies, she really tries to concentrate.

*Step 5:* "This step is the most important for me. I stop to think about what I have read and answer my questions. If I can't answer my questions without looking at the book or using my notes, then I go back and reread that part."

*Step 6:* "Since I divided the chapter into parts, I take a few moments to go over the main points of the part I just finished studying before going on to a new part," says Ms. Mills.

*Step 7:* Ms. Mills tells her students that she then goes through the same steps in the next part. When she has completed the whole assignment, she reviews everything she has studied by going back to the beginning, looking at each section heading, and trying to state the main idea of each paragraph or the central idea of each section. She emphasizes to her students that they should always try to relate their new learning to their past learning because doing so will help them remember the information.

## TEACHING SQ3R

Here are some sample activities to give your students practice in using the SQ3R technique:

1. Like Ms. Mills, model the strategy.
2. Choose a selection your students have not read before, and have them do the following:
   a. Survey the selection to determine what it's about.
   b. Prepare six questions that can be used to set purposes for reading and that students can answer.
   c. Read the selection carefully.
   d. Without looking back at the selection, try to answer the six questions.
3. Choose a selection that your students have not read before, and have them formulate questions that could help them in studying.

PQ4R, which is similar to SQ3R and is a modification of it, is also widely used. PQ4R stands for Preview, Question, Read, Reflect, Recite, Review. In SQ3R, "reflect" is implied in the recall stage. However, the "mulling" of material (reflecting) is certainly important in studying. PQ4R is more explicit in designating this as a separate stage.

## KNOWING THE TEXTBOOK

Helping children to learn about the various parts of their textbooks is an important study skill that can save valuable time and effort. Here are some reading activities that students can do after they have acquired their textbooks:

1. *Survey the textbook.* Surveying helps students see how the author presents the material. Students should observe whether the author presents topic headings in bold print or in the margins. Students should also notice if there are diagrams, charts, cartoons, pictures, and other features.
2. *Read the preface.* In the preface or foreword, the author presents the purpose and plan for writing the book. Here the author usually describes the organization of the book and explains how the book either is different from others in the field or is a further contribution to the field of knowledge.
3. *Read the table of contents.* The table of contents provides a good idea of what to expect from the book. After reviewing the table of contents, students will know how each section they are reading relates to the rest of the book as they begin to study.

4. *Skim the index.* The index indicates in detail what material students will find in the book. It is an invaluable aid because it helps students find specific information that they need by giving them the page on which it appears.
5. *Check for a glossary.* Not all books have a glossary; however, a glossary is helpful because it gives students the meanings of specialized words or phrases used in the book.

## CONCENTRATION

**Concentration**
Sustained attention. It is essential for both studying and listening to lectures.

*Concentration* is sustained attention and it is necessary not only for studying but also for listening. *Concentration* demands a mental set or attitude, a determination that you will block everything out except what you are reading or listening to. It requires active involvement from wide awake and alert individuals. It also demands a positive frame of mind toward the task at hand. Establishing a nurturing classroom environment and encouraging students will greatly influence their concentration. Designing and delivering instruction that meaningfully engages students will better ensure concentration. The following activities will help students develop their concentration.

### Concentration Activities

### Activity 1: Word Concentration (Listening)

In playing this game, just two people are needed—a speaker and a listener. It can also be played with teams. In this game, the words that are presented are not related to one another, so that the listener must concentrate in order to be able to repeat them immediately. Children enjoy playing this game and are delighted when they find that they are able to pay attention for longer periods of time and are, therefore, able to repeat more and more of the words. The speaker says, "Listen carefully. I am going to say some words and when I am through, I want you to repeat them. I will state the words only once. Remember. Listen carefully and wait until I am finished to say them. I'll start with two words and then I'll keep adding one word. Let's do one together."

> *Example:* Speaker says, "Train, nail." The listener repeats, "Train, nail."

Set 1: can/dog . . . red/map . . .
Set 2: mail/milk/book . . . cake/pen/sad . . .
Set 3: sad/none/in/may . . . chair/help/two/six . . .
Set 4: name/sail/bike/pen/man . . .worm/boat/sick/has/more . . .
Set 5: chair/name/key/same/hop/note . . . leg/rope/teach/dance/dog/name . . .
Set 6: witch/rob/sleep/some/read/check/nuts . . . ball/ape/mind/sleep/dog/king/hair . . .
Set 7: spoon/mate/can/man/all/book/sad/show . . . love/rode/room/all/door/can/girl/pad . . .
Set 8: boat/lamp/paint/long/dock/teach/knife/win/chair . . . draw/food/pat/car/sand/pan/size/spring/farm . . .

### Activity 2: Adding Word Concentration (Listening)

The teacher says, "I'm going to say two sets of words. The second set has all the words from Set 1, but it also has a new word. You listen for and write the new word." Example: *Set 1:* pen, dog, tall. *Set 2:* tall, dog, pen, snow. (The new word is *snow.*)

*Set 1:* stamp, week, red
*Set 2:* week, stamp, red, (smoke)

*Set 1:* child, help, dark, nice
*Set 2:* child, (grow), help, nice, dark
*Set 1:* sun, spoon, mouth, five, bet
*Set 2:* spoon, mouth, five, (game), bet, sun
*Set 1:* wild, rose, bread, couch, pill, cup
*Set 2:* rose, bread, couch, pill, (crumb), cup, wild
*Set 1:* pin, fat, net, pine, wind, swing, dog
*Set 2:* fat, net, pine, wind, (damp), swing, pin, dog

## FOLLOWING DIRECTIONS

Being able to follow directions is an important skill that we use all our lives. Scarcely a day goes by without the need to follow directions. Cooking, baking, taking medication, driving, traveling, repairing, building, planning, taking examinations, doing assignments, filling out applications, and many other common activities require the ability to follow directions.

Teachers can provide students with the following pointers to help them understand how to follow directions. Consider displaying all of these pointers on a chart large enough for all to see so that children know where to look when they need to remember what to do when following directions.

1. Read the directions *carefully*. Read all words.
2. If you do not understand any directions, ask for help.
3. Concentrate!
4. Follow the directions that *are* given, not the ones you think ought to be given.
5. Reread the directions if you need to, and refer to them as you follow them.
6. Remember that some directions have steps. Follow each step.

Once students have been exposed to these pointers, give them some practice with applying them. Here are two activities you can use.

### Activity #1: Following Printed Instructions
*Directions:* Read carefully the entire list of directions that follows before doing anything. You have four minutes to complete this activity.

1. Put your name in the upper right-hand corner of this paper.
2. Put your address under your name.
3. Put your telephone number in the upper left-hand corner of this paper.
4. Add 9370 and 5641.
5. Subtract 453 from 671.
6. Raise your hand and say, "I'm the first."
7. Draw two squares, one triangle, and three circles.
8. Write the opposite of *hot*.
9. Stand up and stamp your feet.
10. Give three meanings for *spring*.
11. Write the numbers from one to ten backward.
12. Write the even numbers from two to twenty.
13. Write the odd numbers from one to twenty-one.
14. Write seven words that rhyme with *fat*.
15. Call out, "I have followed directions."
16. If you have read the directions carefully, you should have done nothing until now. Do only directions 1 and 2.

*Answer:* The directions stated that you should read the entire list of directions carefully *before doing anything.* You should have done only directions 1 and 2. When you take timed tests, you usually do *not* read the directions as carefully as you should.

### Activity #2: Following Printed Instructions to Read a Table

*Directions:* Read each numbered instruction only once, and then use the table to follow them.

| 1 | 7 | 3 | 4 | play | dog | man | M | N | O |
|---|---|---|---|------|-----|-----|---|---|---|
| P | Q | 35 | 32 | 63 | 15 | 10 | stop | under | big |

*Instructions*

1. If there are two numbers that added together equal 7 and a word that rhymes with *may,* put a line under the rhyming word.
2. If there is a word that means the same as *large,* a word opposite to *go,* and a word that rhymes with *fan,* put a circle around the three words.
3. If there are two numbers that added together equal 8, two numbers that added together equal 67, and a word the opposite of *over,* underline the two numbers that added together equal 8.
4. If there are five consecutive letters, four words that each contain a different vowel, and at least four odd numbers, put a cross on the five consecutive letters.
5. If there are six words, three even numbers, and two numbers that added together equal 45, circle the word *dog.*
6. If there are two numbers that added together equal 25, two numbers that added together equal 95, and three numbers that added together equal 79, put a circle around the three numbers that added together equal 79.

# SKIMMING

**Skimming**
Reading rapidly to find or locate information.

Setting purposes for reading is crucial for reading comprehension. Students need to learn that readers read for different purposes and that they adjust their rate of reading to their purpose. If they are reading for pleasure, they can read either quickly or slowly, based on the way they feel. If they are studying or reading information that is new to them, they will probably read very slowly. If, however, they are looking up a telephone number, a name, a date, or looking over a paragraph for its topic, they will read much more rapidly. Reading rapidly to find or locate information is called *skimming.* All skimming involves fast reading; however, there are different kinds of skimming. Skimming for a number, a date, or a name can usually be done much more quickly than skimming for the topic of a paragraph or to answer specific questions. (Some people call the most rapid reading *scanning* and the less rapid reading skimming.) Teachers can also help students to recognize that while they may read rapidly to locate some specific information, they most often read the surrounding information more slowly once they have located what they want.

Students also need to understand the difference between skimming and studying. Although skimming is used as part of the SQ3R technique when students survey a passage, skimming material is not the same as studying. Studying requires much slower and more concentrated reading. Skimming is an important skill because we use it so often throughout our lives, and many times it is the only way to get a job done in a reasonable amount of time.

Here are a few prompts teachers can give to students to provide them with some skimming practice:

*Skimming Prompts*

1. Skim newspaper headlines for a particular news item.
2. Skim movie ads for a particular movie.
3. Skim a web site for a particular book title or song.
4. Skim the Yellow Pages of the phone book for a designated topic.
5. Skim the television guide to find a particular show.

# ASKING QUESTIONS

Asking questions is an important part of learning. We have addressed asking questions for comprehension already in Chapter 10. Here, we focus on asking questions about the expectations for assignments, tests, and readings. Some students are afraid to ask clarifying questions for one reason or another. Students may not know how to formulate the question or may be "afraid of looking like a fool." Also, many students learn to "do school" and get by with as little personal interaction with teachers as possible. Clearly, in order for students to ask questions, they must feel comfortable enough to do so. A nonthreatening environment is important, and your invitations are essential. One way to help students feel more comfortable is to provide them with these three pointers:

1. Students who ask the best questions are usually those who know the material best.
2. Questions help students to better understand.
3. The questions students ask will probably help a number of other students.

**Questions**
A good way for students to gain better insight into a subject; questioning also gives the teacher feedback.

Knowing how and when to ask *questions* helps students to gain better insight into a subject and gives the teacher feedback. Student questions also help the teacher monitor the pace of a lesson. Teachers can also provide students with some help in learning how to ask questions of specific content. Here are some suggestions:

*Asking Questions about Tests*

1. What kind of test will it be? Will it be an objective or a subjective test? What kinds of questions will it have?
2. How long will the test be? (This will help the students to know whether it's a quiz (a minor exam) or a test (one that usually counts more than a quiz.)
3. Will dates, names, formulas, and other such specifics be stressed? (Whether these things are stressed is important for the student to know because it will influence the type of studying that he or she will do.)
4. Will it be an open-book or closed-book exam? (This option is important because it will influence the type of studying a student will do.)
5. What chapters will be addressed?

We suggest that teachers actually spend time working with students on how to talk to them about assignments and tests, as well as about the reading material. Your assignment sheets, handouts, and tests are actually reading material, and you want students to have a strong sense of purpose before they begin to work with them.

*Other Tips for Asking Questions*

1. Make the question specific.
2. State the question clearly.
3. Make sure that the question is related to the material.

Questions help give direction and organization to reading and guide students to be actively involved while reading. Good readers usually ask questions before, during, and after reading. The questions they ask are triggered in a number of ways. For example, they may have found some inconsistency in their reading or feel that the writer is being biased, or they may feel that what they are reading is confusing. Students who are good critical readers ask many questions of the text they are reading.

# READING AND WRITING AS MODES OF LEARNING

There are several reading and writing strategies that can help students learn better. Note taking, graphic organizers, and summaries are three strategies. Each calls for explicit instruction.

## NOTE TAKING FOR STUDYING

**Note taking**
A useful tool for studying and writing papers.

*Note taking* is a very important tool; it is useful not only in writing long papers, but also in studying. Students are usually concerned with note taking when they begin writing long reports or papers.

Students need to understand that notes consist of words and phrases that help people to remember important material. Notes do not have to be complete sentences; however, unless they are clear and organized, the notes will be difficult to study from later.

In the following scenario, Ms. Mills helps students develop these understandings.

##  SCENARIO: NOTE TAKING, STUDYING, AND SQ3R

Ms. Mills presents the following notes to her students on a transparency. (She tells the students that the notes do not belong to anyone in the class. Nevertheless, the notes are on a topic they have been studying.) She asks her students to examine the notes carefully.

Go to the Assignments and Activities section of Topic 9: Reading Comprehension in the MyEducationLab for your course and complete the activity entitled "Cornell Notes." As you watch the video and answer the accompanying questions, consider the merits of each type of note-taking system.

*Notes*

1. influenced by age
2. influenced by gender
3. skin
4. thin
5. outer layer
6. several layers
7. epidermis
8. dermis
9. tough
10. stores fat
11. thicker than epidermis

*List of Main Topics*

I. Age of skin
II. Layers of skin
III. Skin

She asks her students what they think about the notes. Are the notes "jogging their memories" about what they had studied? Refreshing memories is the main purpose of notes for studying. She then discusses with her students why the notes were not very helpful. Here are the things they stated:

It is difficult to make sense of these notes because the main topics are either vaguely stated, too general, or too specific.

The items in the list of notes can fit under more than one main topic; they are not precise enough; that is, they do not contain enough information to unmistakably identify or distinguish them.

Ms. Mills then tells her students that note taking for study can be incorporated in the SQ3R study technique. She presents the following suggested procedure for combining SQ3R and note taking to her students:

1. Read the whole selection to get an overview of what you have to study. A preliminary reading provides an overview of the organization of the material.
2. Choose a part of the selection to study, basing the choice on ability to concentrate.
3. Survey the part chosen and note the topic of the individual paragraph or group of paragraphs. Instead of the questions you would write in a normal SQ3R procedure, write the topic(s) in your notebook.
4. Read the part.
5. After finishing each paragraph, state its main idea. Put down *only* important supporting details under the main idea.

   a. Although a formal outline for notes is not necessary, *indent* the listing so that the relationship of supporting material to main ideas is clear.
   b. Try not to take any notes until after reading the whole paragraph. Remember that *recall* is the essential step in the SQ3R technique. By not taking notes until you have finished reading, you are more actively involved in thinking about the material while constructing notes.

**Semantic mapping (graphic organizer)**
A graphic representation used to illustrate concepts and relationships among concepts such as classes, properties, and examples.

Good notes are very helpful for review, and they can save students a great amount of time. Remind students that for study, if the material is new to them, it is usually a good idea to write the topic for each paragraph unless the paragraph is a transitional one. Also tell your students that textbook writers sometimes list the topics of their paragraphs in the margins and the students should be on the lookout for these helpful clues.

Some students find that a visual representation of the material helps them to remember information they have studied. The following scenario presents the *semantic mapping* technique Ms. Mills uses to help her students.

## SCENARIO: SEMANTIC MAPPING AND STUDYING

Ms. Mills tells her students that rather than taking notes using an informal outline, they could make a graphic illustration of what they are studying. She then enumerates these steps for her students:

*Step 1:* Again, as in SQ3R, choose the amount of information you will be studying. (This is usually more than a paragraph.)
*Step 2:* Set purposes for reading.
*Step 3:* Read the material.
*Step 4:* Determine the central idea of what you have read and place it in the center of a blank sheet of paper.
*Step 5:* Reread each paragraph, state the main topic of each, and draw a line or an arrow connecting it to the central idea.
*Step 6:* Review the material once again and write down the important supporting details, connecting each to its main topic. (Figure 13.3 is an example of a semantic map that Ms. Mills did with her class.)

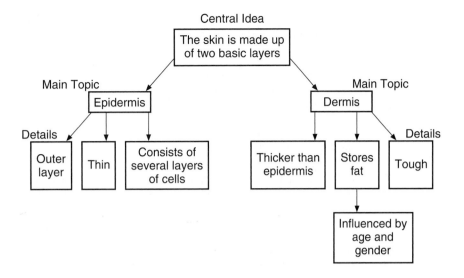

**FIGURE 13.3**    Graphic Organizer as an Aid to Studying

## SUMMARIES AS A MODE OF LEARNING

Many teachers help students learn how to summarize passages because they recognize summaries as a viable means of gaining the essential information. Summarizing material helps students retain the most important facts in a long passage, and if the summary is a written summary, it helps to integrate the reading and writing processes.

Beginning with paragraphs and working up to longer passages is one way to help students learn how to summarize. Children need to see and understand that a good *summary* is brief and includes only essential information. The main idea of the paragraph (if only a paragraph is being summarized) or the central idea of an article and the important facts should be stated, but not necessarily in the sequence presented in the article. Students also need to know that a summary can only include the information stated in the paragraph or article.

Many times, students confuse retelling with summarizing. Although the two are related, retelling involves more details than summarizing. We suggest using a lesson similar to the one shown in Figure 13.4 to help students better understand both retelling and summarizing.

**Summary**
A brief statement of the essential information in a longer piece.

## TEST TAKING

The term *test* can make some students shudder. However, tests are a part of life and students need to learn how to use them to their best advantage.

The more students know about tests, the better they can do on them. Teachers can teach general test-taking principles such as those listed below and post them in the classroom on a chart so that children have a visual reminder. The principles teachers present to their students will depend on the grade level they are teaching as well as the students with whom they are working. Explicitly teaching students test-taking principles will increase their likelihood of success. In fact, research has shown that people do better on tests if they know certain test-taking techniques and are familiar with the various types of tests.

---

### FIGURE 13.4 Retelling/Summarizing Lesson

*What is Retelling/Summarizing?*

These strategies have readers identify and work with the main ideas and supporting details of a selection. Retelling requires students to restate the major events and supporting details in a selection. Summarizing requires students to extract only the main ideas from a selection.

*How do I teach Retelling/Summarizing?*

1. **Introduction:** Read aloud a short selection. Then retell the selection by restating the main events in order, and summarize the selection by constructing a statement that tells the main ideas of the selection. Ask students whether they can describe the two things you just did and how they were alike and different. Explain that the first was a *retelling* (saying the events in a selection in the order in which they happened) and the second was a *summary* (saying just the main ideas of a selection).

2. **Instruction:** Write on the board, a chart, or a transparency the following descriptions:

| *To retell a selection . . .* | *To summarize a selection . . .* |
|---|---|
| • say or write the main events and important details.<br>• say or write them in the order in which they happened. | • figure out the most important ideas or events in the selection.<br>• say or write them in a brief statement. |

Model how to retell and summarize by selecting a short item from a poster, read-aloud book, or magazine. Read the selection and then retell it, including the main events and important details in the order in which they happened. Next, summarize the selection, thinking aloud to show how you figured out the main ideas and then constructed a short statement to express them. Invite students to explain how your retelling differed from your summary (for example, retelling is longer, includes more detail, uses many words from the selection; summary is shorter and includes only the main ideas from the selection).

3. **Guided Practice:** Select and read another short passage and invite students to offer first a retelling of it and then a summary of it. Refer them to the chart as needed. Ask students to compare and contrast the retelling and summary for similarities and differences.

*How can students practice Retelling/Summarizing?*

Select a short passage and have students generate both a retelling and a summary and write them on a chart. Have them consider how their retelling and summary are alike and different. Ask how they both are helpful for understanding and remembering important ideas in selections.

| Retelling of _____ | Summary of _____ |
|---|---|

*Source:* From *Summer Success Reading* by James F. Baumann, Michael F. Opitz, and Laura Robb. Text copyright © Great Source Education Group, a division of Houghton Mifflin Company. Reprinted by permission. All rights reserved.

## TEST-TAKING PRINCIPLES

*Before*

1. Plan to do well. Have a positive attitude.
2. Be well rested.
3. Be prepared. The better prepared you are, the less nervous and anxious you will be.
4. See tests as learning experiences.
5. Look over the whole test before you begin. Notice the types of questions asked and the points allotted for each question. (Students have to learn not to spend a long time on a one- to five-point question that they know a lot about. They should answer it and go on.)
6. Allot your time wisely and check the time.
7. Concentrate!

*During*

8. Read instructions very carefully. (Some students need to be taught to answer each question appropriately. For example, if a question asks for a description and *examples,* be sure to give examples.) If you do not understand the instructions, you should ask the teacher to clarify them.
9. Begin with the questions you know you can successfully answer. This will give you a feeling of confidence and success.
10. If you do not know an answer, make an intelligent guess. As long as the penalty for a wrong answer is the same as for no answer, it pays to take a calculated guess.
11. Work on the questions that are worth the greatest number of points.
12. Allow for time to review your test responses. Check to see that you have answered all the questions. Be leery about changing a response unless you have found a particular reason to do so while reviewing the test. For example, you may have misread the question, you may have misinterpreted the question, or you may not have realized that it was a "tricky" question. If the question is straightforward, it's probably better to leave your first response.

*After*

13. After the test has been graded and returned, review it with your teacher. Doing so will help you to learn from the testing experience. You want to understand why your responses were graded as correct or incorrect.
14. Examine the test after you get it back to determine what your teacher emphasizes.

# THE SCHOOL MEDIA CENTER AND MEDIA LITERACY SKILLS

The school media center needs to be an integral part of students' learning experiences. A number of school architects design schools so that the media center is literally in the center of the building, easily accessible to all classrooms. The media center becomes the students' storehouse of information and a reservoir of endless delight. It is the heart of the school.

The atmosphere in the media center should be one that makes children feel welcome, invited, and wanted. The media specialist is the one who is responsible for setting this tone. A friendly, warm person who loves children and books—and other forms of texts such as magazines and cybertext—will usually have a media center that has similar characteristics.

An enthusiastic and inventive media specialist will, by various means, act as an invitation to children to come to the media center during scheduled and unscheduled times. Some media specialists engage in weekly storytelling for all grade levels. Some media specialists also act as a resource person in helping the classroom teacher develop children's media literacy skills. Once students gain the "library habit," it is hard to break, and it will remain with them throughout their lives.

Following are some of the media literacy skills appropriate for elementary school children.

## PRIMARY GRADES

In the primary grades, children are ready to acquire some of the media literacy skills that will help them become independent library users. Teachers can help primary-grade children learn the kinds of books that are available in the media center, for example, fiction and nonfiction books. Providing the names of different types of books (e.g., fiction or nonfiction) with accompanying text examples will help children better understand the terms and how they relate to books. Using familiar books is a sure way to help students understand.

## INTERMEDIATE AND UPPER-ELEMENTARY GRADES

By the fourth grade, children can learn about other categories of books in the media center, such as reference books.

### *Reference Books*

Children in the elementary grades ask many questions about many different topics. Using some of these questions to help children learn about reference sources is extremely meaningful. Children need to understand that we live in an information age and that knowing how to access information is more important than trying to know everything, which is an impossible task anyway. Reference books can help all students in their attempts to learn about any given topic. For example, the *Readers' Guide to Periodical Literature* will help a student to find magazine articles written on almost any subject of interest. There are reference books on language and usage, such as Roget's *Thesaurus of English Words and Phrases,* which help upper-grade students find synonyms and less trite words to use in their writing.

The dictionary, which is a very important reference book, is probably the one with which the students are the most familiar. It is helpful in supplying the following information:

1. Spelling.
2. Correct usage.
3. Derivations and inflected forms.
4. Accents and other diacritical markings.
5. Antonyms.
6. Synonyms.
7. Syllabication.
8. Definitions.
9. Parts of speech.
10. Idiomatic phrases.

The most often used reference book in elementary school, besides the dictionary, is the encyclopedia. Children need to learn how to use the encyclopedia as a tool and as an aid, rather than as an end in itself. That is, children should be shown how to extract and paraphrase information from the encyclopedia rather than copying the article verbatim. The same is true when children use an online reference.

In the upper elementary grades, children should learn that there are many reference books available in the library which can supply information about a famous writer, baseball player, scientist, celebrity, and others. The key factor is being aware that these reference sources exist and knowing which book to go to for the needed information.

Providing thought-provoking assignments that call on children to seek out different reference books is one way to help them become familiar with the many different reference texts.

## AUTHORS' SUMMARY

In this chapter, we provided information and teaching procedures for helping students to learn necessary study skills. We explained the importance of building good study habits and teaching students how to study. We also offered teaching suggestions to help teachers design instruction that will help their students learn both. We also provided information and teaching suggestions about concentration, questioning, skimming, summarizing, and reading and writing strategies as modes of learning.

## SUGGESTIONS FOR THOUGHT QUESTIONS AND ACTIVITIES

1. You have been appointed to a special committee to help develop a study skills program for your elementary school. What suggestions would you make? What kinds of skills and activities would you recommend for the primary grades? For the intermediate grades?
2. Some teachers in your school system feel that elementary-grade children are too immature to learn study skill techniques. How would you convince these teachers that this is not so?
3. How can reading and writing be used as modes of learning?
4. Explain the role of graphic representations such as semantic maps in learning information. Then design a graphic organizer you would use to help your students learn a given topic.

## WEB SITES

http://www.greece.k12.ny.us/instruction/ela/6–12/Tools/Index.htm

This site provides tools teachers can model and then have students use to generate deeper levels of engagement with texts and content. The site contains PDF versions of activities and resources offering teachers easy access to materials. Materials include graphic organizers, note-taking strategies, questioning processes, and so on addressing both reading and writing.

http://teachersfirst.com/index.cfm

This web site is a comprehensive, free web site designed to provide teachers with thousands of web resources to search for specific content sources (lessons and units) or specific topic sources. TeachersFirst also contains resources geared for novice and experienced teachers, providing a non-threatening source of support.

http://www.storyplace.org/

The children's digital library is a Spanish and English interactive reading site with preschool and elementary libraries. The storyplace also enables children to use their own name in a story that the site provides. The story has comic-like features with talking characters and silent reading features. Offering various activities in which children could participate, the site includes online, take home, printable sources for parents or teachers (e.g., stories, connect the dots, etc.). The site also has parent activities.

# SELECTED BIBLIOGRAPHY

Irvin, Judith L., and Elaine D. Rose. *Starting Early with Study Skills: A Week by Week Guide for Elementary Students.* Boston: Allyn and Bacon, 1995.

Luckie, William R., and Wood Smethurst. *Study Power: Study Skills to Improve Your Learning and Your Grades.* Cambridge, MA: Brookline Books, 1997.

Rubin, Dorothy. *Comprehension Skills & Strategies in a Balanced Reading Program.* Torrance, CA: Fearon Teacher Aids, 1998.

———. *Gaining Word Power,* 5th ed. Boston: Allyn and Bacon, 2000.

———. *Word Meaning and Reasoning Strategies* (a three book series). Torrance, CA: Good Apple, 2001.

———. *Writing & Thinking Skills: Paragraphs and Composition.* Torrance, CA: Good Apple, 2000.

———. *Writing & Thinking Skills: Sentence Writing.* Torrance, CA: Good Apple, 2000.

———. *Writing & Thinking Skills: Fun with Writing.* Torrance, CA: Good Apple, 2001.

Now go to Topic 9: "Reading Comprehension" in MyEducationLab (www.myeducationlab.com) for your course, where you can:

- Find learning outcomes for "Reading Comprehension" along with national standards that connect to these outcomes.
- Complete Assignments and Activities that can help you more deeply understand the chapter content.
- Examine challenging situations and cases presented in the IRIS Center Resources.
- Access video clips of CCSSO National Teacher of the Year award winners responding to the question, "Why Do I Teach?" in the Teacher Talk section.
- Apply and practice your understanding of the core teaching skills identified in the chapter with Building Teaching Skills and Dispositions learning units.

# Partnering with Parents

**14**

## CHAPTER OUTLINE

- Scenario: David's Father Talks with Mr. Gonzalez
- Parental Involvement in the Schools
- Research on Parental Involvement in their Children's Education
- Parental Involvement in Regular School Reading Programs
- Television, Computers, Parents, Children, and Reading
- Revisiting the Opening Scenario

**SCENARIO:** DAVID'S FATHER TALKS WITH MR. GONZALEZ

"He seems so unmotivated to read these days," David's father comments to Mr. Gonzalez, David's third-grade teacher. "I mean," he continues, "I used to be able to get David to read just about anything I told him to read but now he has lost interest. He seems more interested in playing sports or goofing around with his friends."

Curious, Mr. Gonzalez probes to see how he might be able to help the situation. He comments, "I have noticed that David likes to read riddle books, comics, and stories about sports figures." David's father looks a little surprised. He asks, "Are these okay for David to read? Will they really help him to be a better reader?"

Mr. Gonzalez uses this question as an opener to talk with David's father about how having David read these and other types of self-selected books will indeed increase his reading skills. He explains that David's vocabulary only stands to increase as a result of doing much independent reading on topics of his choice. He also explains that David might need to understand that even though he likes to play sports and play games with friends, he can still make time for reading. He might need to be taught how to balance his time. Mr. Gonzalez ends his discussion by giving David's father a few books and magazines from the classroom library that he thinks David will enjoy at home. He reminds David's father to let David choose what to read and to set a time for David to read independently.

"I'll give it a try, Mr. Gonzalez. Thanks for taking some time to help us out." With that, David's father leaves. A firm believer in parental involvement, Mr. Gonzalez reflects on the exchange. He feels pleased that he has such a close relationship with his students' parents that they feel comfortable talking to him whenever the need arises. Mr. Gonzalez shows that he understands what many researchers report about parental involvement. It is essential in order for their children to maximize their reading potential.

## CHAPTER OBJECTIVES

After reading the chapter, you should be able to:

- Discuss the kinds of reading programs in which parents are involved.
- Discuss the success of parental involvement programs.
- Describe some ways parents can help their children.

In this chapter, we discuss parental involvement and suggest some ways that teachers can invite parents to contribute to their children's reading successes.

## PARENTAL INVOLVEMENT IN THE SCHOOLS

Parental involvement in the schools is ever present. Parents sit on the boards of education; they are involved in parent–teacher associations, parent councils, and parent clubs. Parents help formulate school policy, have a say in curriculum, and even help to choose textbooks. Parents definitely have a voice in school matters. In many school districts across the country, parents are seen as partners and potential resources.

While most agree that parental involvement helps students to achieve better, just how to best involve them is often the sticking point. For example, if teachers invite parents to come to evening meetings, several may not be able to show for one reason or another. After working all day, getting dinner prepared and served, tidying the kitchen, and making sure that the children are doing their chores and homework, parents may be

Go to the Assignments and Activities section of Topic 15: Parents and Families in the MyEducationLab for your course and complete the activity entitled "Parental Involvement." As you watch the video and answer the accompanying questions, consider how the school sets the tone and expectation for parent involvement.

too exhausted to go to an evening meeting. Finding a sitter may also be difficult, which is another reason parents may choose to stay home.

There are numerous other challenges, including working with parents who are challenged readers and writers themselves and those whose first language is not English. The good news is that recognizing the challenges puts teachers in a better position to work through them. If they sense that they are working with low-literate parents, for example, they can use telephone calls rather than a printed newsletter to communicate with parents. If they are working with parents whose first language is not English, teachers can seek out people in the community to help them communicate with these parents in their first languages. If they are working with parents who are unlikely to leave home for an evening school meeting primarily because they cannot afford to hire a babysitter, teachers can structure the meetings so that the children can accompany their parents.

There are several ways that parents can be involved with their children's literacy development, including the following:

1. *Observation*—Being read to or seeing adults model reading and writing behavior.
2. *Collaboration*—Having an individual interact with the child to provide encouragement, motivation, and help.
3. *Practice*—Trying out what has been learned; for example, the child writes a story or retells it to another child, stuffed animal, or doll without any help or without being supervised by an adult.
4. *Performance*—Sharing what has been learned with an adult who shows interest and support and gives positive reinforcement.[1]

The checklist shown in Figure 14.1 can be a valuable aid for parents who are interested in helping their young children. It provides parents with a list of parenting behaviors that lead to increased student learning. Parents can use the list as a way of remembering what they should be doing with their children. The International Reading Association publishes several pamphlets related to many of the attributes shown on the checklist. Teachers and parents can access them online by visiting IRA's web site, www.reading.org.

# RESEARCH ON PARENTAL INVOLVEMENT IN THEIR CHILDREN'S EDUCATION

Home support is a major factor in fostering higher achievement; in fact, "one of the clearest predictors of early reading ability is the amount of time spent reading with parents."[2] Researchers also consistently suggest that parents who expect their children to do well and encourage them are enhancing their young children's literacy development.[3] The authors of the National Assessment of Education Progress (NAEP) reports confirm the importance of parental involvement in children's education. They continuously report that those students who have home support for literacy usually have higher average reading achievement than those students without such home support.[4]

[1]Lesley Mandel Morrow and Jeffrey K. Smith, eds., *Assessment for Instruction in Early Literacy* (Boston: Allyn and Bacon, 1990), p. 3.

[2]Scott G. Paris, Barbara A. Wasik, and Julianne C. Turner, "The Development of Strategic Readers," in *Handbook of Reading Research,* Vol. II, eds. Rebecca Barr, Michael L. Kamil, Peter Mosenthal, and P. David Pearson (New York: Longman, 1991), p. 628.

[3]Ibid.

[4]Patricia L. Donahue et al., *NAEP 1998 Reading Report Card for the Nation and the States* (Washington, DC: United States Department of Education, 1999), p. 101.

**FIGURE 14.1    A Parent Checklist**

|  | *Often* | *Seldom* |
|---|---|---|
| I listen to my child. | | |
| I read aloud to my child every day. | | |
| I discuss ideas with my child. | | |
| I explain concepts to my child. | | |
| I spend time with my child. | | |
| I ask my child good questions. | | |
| I ask my child to read picture books to me. | | |
| I watch special TV shows with my child. | | |
| I encourage my child. | | |
| I am patient with my child. | | |
| I take my child to interesting places. | | |
| I do not pressure my child. | | |
| I read and write in the presence of my child. | | |
| I am a good role model for my child. | | |

Go to the Assignments and Activities section of Topic 15: Parents and Families in the MyEducationLab for your course and complete the activity entitled "Positive Communication." As you watch the video and answer the accompanying questions, think about what forms of communication send the most positive messages to parents about their children.

In *The Basic School: A Community for Learning,* the late Ernest Boyer, former president of the Carnegie Foundation for the Advancement of Teaching, stresses that what elementary schools need most is a greater bond between parents and teachers. When interviewed, he stated, "School is a partnership. If education is in trouble, it's not the school that has failed. It's the partnership that has failed." He also stated that "at many schools, parents still feel that they are on the edges. If parents are going to be made partners, schools are going to have to be the ones to reach out. They control the gates."

Boyer then presents examples of schools that give parents realistic ways to become involved. He also shows how employers are getting into the act by giving employees paid time off to volunteer in schools. Edwards mentions several other ways that a community can help parents make time to be in school.[5] For example, she found that in many working-class neighborhoods, parents were working either multiple shifts or shifts that conflicted with school programs. Also, there were many single-parent homes. So to get parents involved in school activities, she had to have the buy-in of many community leaders and proprietors. Among those she found useful were: church leaders, bar and restaurant owners, store proprietors, and employers. These people were interested in children's reading success, because they could see the direct impact of it when employing and involving people from the community. This made it easier for them to give parents permission to leave other concerns behind for important school events—without being penalized. Church leaders agreed to avoid conflicting with school meetings and to promote attendance of the school meetings as a benefit to the congregation. A local bar owner closed down his "happy hour" on parent literacy nights. When community leaders and business owners agree to the value of a more literate community, parents tend to do the same.

---

[5]P. A. Edwards, *Children's Literacy Development: Making It Happen Through School, Family, and Community Involvement* (Boston: Allyn and Bacon, 2004).

# PARENTAL INVOLVEMENT IN REGULAR SCHOOL READING PROGRAMS

Parents sometimes become more involved in school programs when their children have a specific reading need; however, the trend appears to be for increasing parental involvement even for those without reading needs.

The participation of parents in many school districts is often dependent on how aggressive the educators and parents are in demanding such involvement. The presence of the parents in the regular reading program varies from district to district, and even from school to school in some school districts. In one school system, you will find an organized program, and in another you will find that the program is up to the individual teacher in each individual class. The programs that do exist usually are similar in format; they generally include workshops, instructional materials, and book suggestions. What is presented, however, will vary from district to district. Here are some examples:

### Example 1: New Jersey

**Newbery award books**
Books that have received the Newbery Medal, which is given annually to the book in the United States that has been voted "the most distinguished literature" for children.

The following is an example of a program that was developed by employees in a New Jersey school system to incorporate parental involvement in its regular reading program for all children in grades one through five. The program consists of instructional packets, book suggestions, and three workshops. At the first workshop, a reading specialist explains the reading program that is in use in the school system. The parents are acquainted with the reading program and its corresponding terminology. At the second workshop, the parents watch a reading lesson, which shows a teacher and children engaged in a Directed Reading Lesson. The third session, "A Book Talk," provides parents with appropriate children's books at different readability and interest levels. They are also given several suggestions for how to involve their children in reading them.

Another part of the program concerns instructional materials. For those children who have reading needs, teachers construct parent packets that consist of activities based on the skills and strategies that children are learning. Different parent packets are available for different grade levels. For those children who have few reading problems, the packets contain suggestions for ways to extend learning. Yet another packet, which emphasizes more complex books such as several *Newbery Award* winners, is available for parents of children who are able to read such material.

### Example 2: Junior Great Books

**Junior Great Books Program**
Program in which parent–teacher teams work together to plan reading discussion sessions for students; sessions take place in regular classrooms during the reading period and are led by both parent and teacher.

*Junior Great Books* is a program aimed at highly able readers in grades two through six, their teachers, and parents. It involves twelve volunteer parents and twelve teachers. A parent and a teacher are paired up to work together as a team to plan and lead reading discussion sessions for students. The parents who volunteer take the two-day training session, which is conducted by a specialist from the Great Books Foundation, located in Chicago. The training consists primarily of helping parents learn about the kinds of questions they should ask, as well as how to conduct the discussions. The children who participate in the program are considered "good readers" by their teachers. The parent–teacher team meets every week to plan for the reading discussion, which takes place in the regular classroom during the regularly scheduled 45-minute reading period. Both the parent and the teacher lead the discussion with a particular group of children.

### Example 3: Reading Olympics

**Reading Olympics programs**
Programs vary; however, most challenge students to read as many books as they can and to share them in some way with parents.

The structure of *Reading Olympics* programs varies from school system to school system, from school to school, and even from one class to another; however, all include reading books and sharing them in some way with parents. Here is how one such program works in the middle part of the year in a first-grade class.

Children are challenged to read as many books as they can. They must read these books aloud to one of their parents, and after they finish reading the book aloud, the parent asks them questions about the story or has them retell it. Completed books are recorded on a reading record form similar to the one shown in Figure 14.2. Children compete to see who can read the most books. The rewards are manifold. Andrew, the child who won the Read-Aloud Olympics contest in his first-grade class, read 120 books aloud to his parents.

*Example 4: Paired Reading*

**Paired reading**
The child reads aloud simultaneously with another person, usually the parent.

Another helpful practice for parents is *paired reading*. This is a method whereby parents and children read aloud simultaneously. This technique is generally used with children who need additional support when reading, but it can be used with just about any child. At any time during the simultaneous reading, the child can signal that he or she wishes to read alone. The parent praises the child's desire to do so, and allows the child to read

**FIGURE 14.2   Reading Record**

| Day | Title of reading material | Amount of time spent reading / Number of pages read | Comments |
|---|---|---|---|
| Sunday | | | |
| Monday | | | |
| Tuesday | | | |
| Wednesday | | | |
| Thursday | | | |
| Friday | | | |
| Saturday | | | |

alone. As Johnston notes, "The child is encouraged to read alone by lack of criticism and by frequent praise for any independent reading."[6] This technique is powerful because it keeps the focus on reading for enjoyment. Parents need not be concerned with helping their children learn specific reading strategies. They can leave this important aspect of reading instruction to the teacher.

Paired reading was originally designed for parents to use with their children[7] and the growth that children showed in both reading vocabulary and reading comprehension was so startling that it is now used by reading tutors. A demonstration video with accompanying printed information is available from the International Reading Association.

Here are some suggested procedures:[8]

1. Agree on a time that the reading will regularly occur.
2. Provide time for the reader to select the material to be read. This material can be changed from one session to another. That is, if a child selects reading material and decides at the end of the session that he really does not want to continue with it at the next session, he or she can bring another text to the next session.
3. Sit side by side because you will both want to see the text with ease. Make sure that you select a place that is free of all distractions.
4. Agree on a starting signal such as 1, 2, 3. Begin reading together. Also establish a signal for when the reader wants to read solo. A tap on the shoulder is often used. When the reader chooses to read solo, reinforce the reader for taking this risk by saying something such as "Good!"
5. Stop at logical points to talk about the meaning of what is being read.
6. If the reader makes a miscue, wait to see if he or she self-corrects. If not, and if the miscue alters the author's intended meaning, point to the word, say it for the child, and have the child repeat it. Continue reading aloud with the child until the solo signal is again given.

### Example 5: Family Literacy Project

Go to the Assignments and Activities section of Topic 15: Parents and Families in the MyEducationLab for your course and complete the activity entitled "Family Literacy Program." As you watch the video and answer the accompanying questions, consider what kind of knowledge teachers can help parents gain in their classrooms.

Many school district personnel are so interested in parental involvement that they design specific programs for parents. The Family Literacy Project is one such program. Developed by Irvine Unified School District educators, the project aims to provide parents with both encouragement and support in their efforts to instill lifelong reading habits in their children. To accomplish this purpose, they provide numerous tips such as "Tips for Reading to Your Child," "Ten Tips: Helping Your Child Read Effectively," and "Helping Children Develop Oral-Language Skills." All of this information is easily accessible in hard copy form, which is available at the school district's child resource center.

All of these examples show that there are many ways to involve parents. They also show that parents can do much at home to assist their children. They can volunteer right from home! For parents to be partners in learning with educators there has to be equal "give and take." Viewing parents both as parents and as educators "acknowledges the home–school relationship as a rich potential shared among equals, equals who bring important and divergent experiences to bear upon individual and often limited perspectives."[9]

---

[6]Kathy Johnston, "Parents and Reading: A U.K. Perspective," *The Reading Teacher* 42 (February, 1989): 355.

[7]K. Topping, "Paired Reading: A Powerful Technique for Parent Use," *The Reading Teacher* 40 (1987): 604–614.

[8]Ibid.

[9]Gayle Goodman, "Worlds Within Worlds: Reflections on an Encounter with Parents," *Language Arts* 66 (January, 1989): 20.

Regardless of the way teachers choose to involve parents, we offer the following reminders:

- Rather than overwhelming parents by providing them with many activities all at one time, provide them with one idea and include all the reading materials they will need to complete the reading activity with their children. Consider putting both the explanation and the text in a large envelope or backpack.
- Keep communication as jargon-free as possible. Focus on exactly what parents need to do with their children in plain everyday language.
- Remember that many parents are at a loss when it comes to knowing which text or texts their children should be reading. They need help. One way to help them is to provide them with specific titles that are sure to entice their children to practice reading. Many of these titles are listed in this book, as are suitable web sites.
- Many parents will need explicit and welcoming invitations. For example, in many areas of Mexico, schools frown on parents showing up at school. There are many other cultures where parent–teacher interactions are very different from what we expect in the United States. Parents from other cultural backgrounds need to know it is okay to be involved. Also, many US parents did not have positive interactions with school as children, and they need to feel a strong motivation for coming to school.

## TELEVISION, COMPUTERS, PARENTS, CHILDREN, AND READING

### TELEVISION

We would be remiss if we did not discuss the impact of television on children's reading, because most television viewing is done at home. We would also be negligent if we did not consider the computer's impact on children's reading.

The question of the influence of television viewing on children's reading skills has been debated since television was first introduced. The findings have not been definitive. Authors of some studies suggest that "television viewing has a considerable negative impact on reading achievement only for children who watch for relatively many hours—more than 4 to 6 hours a day."[10] Television also seems to affect different groups of children in different ways. The reading achievement of children of high socioeconomic status decreased when they watched greater amounts of television, whereas the converse appeared to be true for low socioeconomic status children; that is, heavier viewing for these children increased their reading achievement.[11]

Although we want children to be engaged with a variety of texts and to develop a habit of reading for a variety of purposes, we need to remember that we live in an information age and as such, there are many ways to obtain information. Parents can use television to stimulate children's reading habits rather than take away from them. Using television to its best advantage can help children to see that there is room for a variety of activities in their lives and that just because they read does not mean that they cannot watch television. The reverse is also true.

Fortunately for parents and teachers alike, there is quite a bit of information about the wise use of television. One source of information is a brochure published by the

[10]Johannes W. J. Beentjes and Tom H. A. Van Der Voort, "Television's Impact on Children's Reading Skills: A Review of Research," *Reading Research Quarterly* 23 (Fall, 1988): 401.

[11]Ibid.

**TABLE 14.1 Using Television to Spur Reading**

| Statement | Rating (1 = low degree, 5 = high degree) |
| --- | --- |
| 1. My child uses good judgment when selecting programs to watch. | 1 2 3 4 5 |
| 2. My child talks to me about some of the ideas gained from television shows. | 1 2 3 4 5 |
| 3. Television is one of several of my child's free time activities. | 1 2 3 4 5 |
| 4. My child appears to be motivated to read about some of the ideas presented on the viewed television shows. | 1 2 3 4 5 |
| 5. My children see me both reading and watching television. | 1 2 3 4 5 |
| 6. Many different kinds of reading materials are available in my home and they are easy for my children to access. | 1 2 3 4 5 |
| 7. Reading gets as much time as television watching. | 1 2 3 4 5 |

International Reading Association entitled, "You Can Use Television to Stimulate Your Child's Reading Habits." Along with several practical suggestions, the authors of the brochure provide a simple checklist that parents can use to determine whether they are teaching their children how to be wise television watchers. Our version of this checklist is shown in Table 14.1.

### Captioned Television

The captions used on television appear to affect students' learning.[12] Watching television shows with accompanying captions appears to improve students' reading. Listening to the script on the television while simultaneously reading the script reinforces the effect on students' word recognition and reading fluency. Teachers can encourage parents to turn on the captioning feature when their children watch television. Parents can lower the volume several decibels so that children have to take a close look at the text to better understand what is happening on the show. Keep in mind, however, that there is often a time delay between when the words are spoken and when the actually appear on the screen. Some words are also deleted and some are misspelled. Despite these shortcomings, captioned television is still a valuable learning tool.

## COMPUTERS

In Chapter 9, we offer information about using computers to assist children's reading. The focus here is to provide some information about several web sites that both children and parents can use to assist reading development.

Many web sites are now available for parents and children. Some of these are created by educators employed in specific school districts (e.g., Irvine Unified School District), whereas others are created by professional organizations and publishers. Several of these are listed here.

---

[12]P. Koskinen, R. Wilson, L. Gambrell, and S. Neuman, "Captioned Video and Vocabulary Learning: An Innovative Practice in Literacy Instruction," *The Reading Teacher* 47(1993): 36–43.

*Web Sites for Parents*

- Professional organizations:

  www.nea.org/parents/index.html (National Education Association)
  www.reading.org (International Reading Association)

  Both of these web sites offer numerous suggestions for ways that parents can get involved in their children's reading education. Specific book titles for different ages and interests are also provided. Information can be downloaded for future reference.

- Publishers:

  www.sfreading.com/ (Scott Foresman)

- Government:

  www.ed.gov/print/parents/academic/help/reader/part1.html

- Other:

  www.rif.org/ (Reading Is Fundamental)
  www.familyeducation.com/home/ (Family Education)
  www.vsarts.org (Visual Arts)

  As with those noted above, these web sites offer suggestions for reading-related activities as well as other important information.

*Web Sites for Children*

  www.umass.edu/aesop (offers Aesop's fables)
  pbskids.org/arthur/ (Marc Brown's Arthur is featured here.)
  www.magickeys.com/books/ (offers children's storybooks online)
  www.guysread.com (offers suggestions especially appealing to boys)

  Several children's authors such as Mem Fox, Jan Brett, Eric Carle, and Janet Stevens also have web sites that children might find interesting.

## REVISITING THE OPENING SCENARIO

Mr. Gonzalez was able to get David's father involved by listening to his concerns and by giving him some specific ideas about ways to help David at home. Now that you have read the chapter, what are some additional suggestions you might give to David's father?

## AUTHORS' SUMMARY

In this chapter, we focused on parental involvement. We explained that parents are partners in education, and that many parents are taking an active role in helping their children to maximize their learning potential. The amount of parental involvement depends in part on the school district in which their children are enrolled. Parental involvement has been triggered by a number of factors. We provided several concrete suggestions and examples to help teachers involve parents in and out of the school setting.

# SUGGESTIONS FOR THOUGHT QUESTIONS AND ACTIVITIES

1. You have been put on a committee in your school district that is looking for ways to involve parents. Using information you gained from this chapter, construct a list of suggestions.
2. You know that your students are involved in a variety of extracurricular activities that could involve reading, but do not. How can you help parents get involved with reading that matches well with what children do outside of school?
3. Choose a school in your area. Schedule an appointment with an administrator to learn how that school involves parents in its reading programs.

# WEB SITES

http://www.readingrockets.org/helping/advocate

This particular link to this site provides numerous articles relating to parents serving as advocates for their children. The articles range in topics, covering steps for parents and narratives by parents for parents, as well as links to other topics. See also http://www.readingrockets.org/guides/readingrockets which provides portable document files (PDF) in Spanish/ English, Hmong/English, Somali/English. These files include family guides containing links for further information.

http://www.colorincolorado.org/

Colorín Colorado is a bilingual site geared toward families and teachers of English language learners (ELL). The site contains both Spanish and English pages with book lists, activities, downloadable guides and projects, and much more.

http://www.teachersfirst.com/getsource.cfm?id=8279

A link from the TeachersFirst web site, this site presents parents with links regarding reading skills, activities around the house, fun games, story time activities, and more. The site provides printable activities, lists of books, and early literacy resource links.

http://www.education-world.com/a_curr/profdev/profdev124.shtml

This page of Education World provides a great article on parents and teachers working together. The links provided offer additional resources and avenues of support.

# SELECTED BIBLIOGRAPHY

Boyer, Ernest L. *The Basic School: A Community for Learning.* Princeton, NJ: Carnegie Foundation for the Advancement of Learning, 1995.

Farkas, Steve, et al. *Playing Their Parts: Parents and Teachers Talk about Parental Involvement in Public Schools.* New York: Public Agenda, 1999.

Guest-Edited Issue. "Family Literacy." *The Reading Teacher* 48 (April, 1995).

Koskinen, P., R. Wilson, L. Gambrell, and S. Neuman. "Captioned Video and Vocabulary Learning: An Innovative Practice in Literacy Instruction." *The Reading Teacher* 47 (1993): 36–43.

Purcell-Gates, Victoria. "Family Literacy," in *Handbook of Reading Research,* Vol. III, edited by Michael L. Kamil et al., 853–870 Mahwah, NJ: Lawrence Erlbaum, 2000.

Rubin, Dorothy. *Your Child Can Succeed in School: 100 Common-Sense Answers to Frequently Asked Questions.* Torrance, CA: Fearon Teacher Aids, 1999.

Thomas, Adele, et al. *Families at School.* Newark, DE: International Reading Association, 1999.

Topping, K. "Paired Reading: A Powerful Technique for Parent Use." *The Reading Teacher* 40 (1987): 604–614.

**PEARSON**
**myeducationlab**

Now go to Topic 15: "Parents and Families" in MyEducationLab (www.myeducationlab .com) for your course, where you can:

- Find learning outcomes for "Parents and Families" along with national standards that connect to these outcomes.
- Complete Assignments and Activities that can help you more deeply understand the chapter content.
- Examine challenging situations and cases presented in the IRIS Center Resources.
- Access video clips of CCSSO National Teacher of the Year award winners responding to the question, "Why Do I Teach?" in the Teacher Talk section.
- Apply and practice your understanding of the core teaching skills identified in the chapter with Building Teaching Skills and Dispositions learning units.

# Putting It All Together

**15**

## CHAPTER OUTLINE

- Scenario: Case Report of Child
- Scenario Explanation
- Five Scenarios

Without a doubt, teachers who subscribe to a reading diagnosis and improvement program have their work cut out for them! There are many considerations to think through when it comes to trying to help children become proficient readers, and this thought process takes time and energy. But with practice, the process becomes easier. This is not to say that figuring out just what might be getting in a child's way of reading becomes any less of a mystery. Nonetheless, as a result of knowing how to select, administer, score, and interpret a variety of reading measures and knowing several instructional strategies, we become more confident because we know where to start. Once started, we have to take our cues from the child to determine the next step. Asking and answering three basic assessment questions helps teachers stay in tune with children's strengths and needs: What do I want to know? Why do I want to know this information? And how can I best discover it?

## CHAPTER OBJECTIVES

After reading this chapter, you should be able to:

- Examine and analyze scenarios.
- Design a plan that shows a child's strengths, needs, and evidence of determining both.
- Develop an instructional plan that shows how you would address each need.
- Articulate why you acted the way you did.

The purpose of this chapter is to provide some simulated experiences to help you to become more skillful in determining children's reading strengths and needs and in designing appropriate instruction that will help children to become proficient readers.

 ## SCENARIO: CASE REPORT OF CHILD

Jason, a student in Mr. Jones's second-grade class, is struggling to become a proficient reader. Mr. Jones is not sure why. He decides to administer some diagnostic assessments to determine exactly what Jason knows and what he needs to know. What follows are some of the assessment instruments and procedures he administered to Jason over a week's time, as well as an analysis of Jason's performance.[1]

*Informal Reading Inventory* (IRI)

*Description*

The purposes of the IRI are to determine a student's reading and listening capacity levels, as well as strengths and needs in word recognition, oral reading comprehension, and silent reading comprehension.

*Analysis of Data*

Jason started the IRI Word List at the Preprimer Level; he made four errors. Therefore, Mr. Jones had Jason start the oral reading passages also at the Preprimer Level.

| Reader Level | Oral Reading WR Errors | Comprehension | Silent Reading Comprehension |
|---|---|---|---|
| PP | 6 (Frust.) | 85% (Instr.) | 85% (Instr.) |
| P | 14 (Frust.) | 25% (Frust.) | |

Listening Capacity = $3^2$ (Reader Level)

---

[1]Case report adapted from Dr. Dallas Cheek, Professor, The College of New Jersey, 2001.

*Qualitative Analysis of IRI*

Mr. Jones analyzed Jason's word reading using the following three criteria:

Meaning: Does the miscue make sense in the text?
Structure: Is the miscue the same part of speech as the text word?
Visual: Does the student's miscue word look similar to the text word?

| Text Word | Student Miscue | Semantic Cue | Syntactic Cue | Visual Cue |
|---|---|---|---|---|
| came | got | yes | no | yes |
| who | how | no | no | no |
| a lot | lots | yes | no | yes |
| who | how | no | no | no |
| sat | asked | no | yes | no |
| her | their | yes | yes | yes |
| string | thing | yes | yes | yes |
| red | already | no | no | yes |
| saw | was | no | yes | yes |
| father | friends | yes | yes | yes |

***Word Lists*** To gain information about Jason's sight vocabulary, word identification, and ability to apply phonics knowledge, Mr. Jones used the following:

- *The Fry Instant Word List.* Mr. Jones had Jason read the words on the Fry Instant Word List. This is a good gauge of a child's sight vocabulary. The first 300 words and their common variants represent 65% of the words used in textbooks in the lower elementary grades. If children have difficulty recognizing these words as sight words, they will have difficulty reading running text with any degree of fluency. Among the first 100 words (see page 259), Jason identified the following words: *they, his, from, or, word, what, were, when, can, each, which, their, other, them, these, her, would, make, into, time, two, more, write, number, way, could, than, first, been, call, now, find, long, come, part.*
- *Names Test.* Mr. Jones also administered Jason this test (see pages 297–299), and he learned that Jason was strong in applying phonics with the exception of controlled vowels.

With the data Mr. Jones has gathered, he feels like he has a clear set of strengths from which to plan engaging reading work that is not likely to frustrate Jason. Now that you have read this entire text and have an expanded knowledge base about reading and reading instruction, how would you answer the following questions about Jason?

1. What conclusions would you draw from looking at the results of the case report?
2. What would you consider to be this child's strengths and needs?
3. Which instructional strategies would you use to help this child?
4. What type of texts would you use?
5. How would you involve parents?

## SCENARIO EXPLANATION

We have worked through one scenario with Mr. Jones and Jason. In the section that follows, we present five additional scenarios. Select at least one scenario and do the following:

1. After reading the scenario, create a list of strengths. You are really forming some hypotheses; you are making your best guess based on the limited information and

your background knowledge. Once you are comfortable with a clear sense of strengths, do the same with the student's needs.

2. Review the different assessment techniques presented throughout this text.

3. Construct a chart that shows each strength and need, and the assessment techniques you will use to test your hypotheses. Use the form shown in Figure 15.1.

4. Create a chart that shows each strength and need listed on your previous chart and write how you would use the strengths to teach the needs. Include instructional suggestions and appropriate texts. Use the form shown in Figure 15.2.

5. State how you would involve parents or primary caregivers. Again, reference the text to show where you located the specific idea(s).

## FIVE SCENARIOS

### Sally, a First-Grader, Age 6

Sally entered first grade knowing letters and sounds in isolation very well and her teacher thought she was going to make very good progress. Now it is the middle of the school year and Sally's teacher is concerned because Sally has not made the anticipated progress. The teacher can't seem to determine Sally's reading levels. Sally can read predictable books very well, yet she has a limited sight vocabulary. Although she can state all consonant sounds and can state the names of the letters, Sally doesn't appear to apply what she knows when she comes to unknown words. Her listening comprehension is very good as is evidenced by her ability to retell stories. She enjoys being read to and chooses to read during her free time.

### Bob, a Sixth-Grader, Age 12

Bob had little trouble with reading throughout his elementary schooling but he always seemed to lag behind others when reading and it took him much longer to write answers to comprehension questions. Now that Bob is in sixth grade, he appears to be struggling with several subjects even though he spends several hours studying each evening. He seems to have trouble remembering what he has read, regardless of the subject. He also gets stomachaches when tests are approaching and usually does not perform well. His instructional level is approximately fifth grade when it comes to reading fiction, but it really drops when reading nonfiction. At one time, Bob read for pleasure, but now he spends so much time on his homework that the last thing he wants to do is read during his free time.

### Mary Beth, a Fourth-Grader, Age 9

Mary Beth is intensely competitive and sees every reading activity as a race. She reads aloud at grade level fairly fluently but when faced with an unfamiliar word, she appears to guess wildly and go right on. She rarely pauses, repeats, or corrects an attempt. In silent reading, she always tries to be the first one done and appears to read only parts of each page. Her comprehension is poor; she appears to make little attempt to predict what might occur next or apply what she already knows to a subject. Consequently, her instructional level is barely at grade level, with an independent level of early second. She urgently desires to be "right" and gets upset with herself when she makes an error, but seems to have few dependable strategies in word recognition or comprehension. She does almost no pleasure reading.

**FIGURE 15.1    Strengths, Needs, and Assessment Techniques to Validate Them**

| Strength | Need | Assessment Technique |
|---|---|---|
| | | |
| | | |
| | | |
| | | |
| | | |
| | | |
| | | |
| | | |
| | | |
| | | |
| | | |
| | | |
| | | |

FIGURE 15.2  Strengths, Needs, Instruction Suggestions, and Texts

| Strengths | Needs | Instructional Suggestions | Appropriate Texts |
|-----------|-------|---------------------------|-------------------|
|           |       |                           |                   |
|           |       |                           |                   |
|           |       |                           |                   |
|           |       |                           |                   |
|           |       |                           |                   |
|           |       |                           |                   |
|           |       |                           |                   |
|           |       |                           |                   |
|           |       |                           |                   |
|           |       |                           |                   |
|           |       |                           |                   |
|           |       |                           |                   |
|           |       |                           |                   |

### *Alan, an Eighth-Grader, Age 14*

Alan had little difficulty with reading in elementary school, although teachers remarked on his slow reading and dogged effort at comprehension. However, in seventh and eighth grades, his subject area work has suffered and his grades are slipping. He is achievement-oriented and conscientious, spending hours every night reading and rereading his assignments. But he has trouble remembering what he reads, panics when faced with a test, and relies on memorization, which usually fails him under pressure. As he experiences more difficulty, he begins to read more and more slowly, trying to remember everything. In ordinary fiction, his instructional level is solid at eighth grade, but in nonfiction of similar difficulty, he can barely manage. His word recognition and decoding skills are good but he often lacks meanings for words he can accurately identify. He spends so much time trying to keep up with required reading that he does little or no reading for pleasure, and shows signs of increasing anxiety and fear of failure.

### *Matt, a Second-Grader, Age 7*

Reading has been a struggle for Matt since the very beginning. He now has an instructional level of mid-first grade, no independent level, and a late-first frustration level. Both oral and silent reading are painfully slow, and oral reading is halting with many substitutions, repetitions, and long pauses. Most miscues are significant and reflect attempts to sound out words. Sounding out is Matt's primary strategy when uncertain of any word. His comprehension is fairly good, at least in getting the gist of what he reads, given his lack of fluency. He is a conscientious boy but avoids reading, especially orally, as much as possible. His self-esteem is suffering badly and he is beginning to show dislike toward school in general. He does enjoy being read to.

Now go to MyEducationLab (www.myeducationlab.com) for your course, where you can:

- Find learning outcomes for each topic along with national standards that connect to these outcomes.
- Complete Assignments and Activities that can help you more deeply understand the chapter content.
- Examine challenging situations and cases presented in the IRIS Center Resources.
- Access video clips of CCSSO National Teacher of the Year award winners responding to the question, "Why Do I Teach?" in the Teacher Talk section.
- Apply and practice your understanding of the core teaching skills identified in the chapter with Building Teaching Skills and Dispositions learning units.

# Appendix A

## CONSTRUCTING AN IRI

## CONSTRUCTING YOUR OWN INFORMAL READING INVENTORY

Although it is time-consuming to construct your own IRI, there are some teachers who would like to do so. This section will present more specific information on the parts of an IRI as well as information on how to construct and score one.

Usually an IRI consists of word lists at varying levels, which have been selected from a traditional basal reader series; passages, which are based on graduated levels of difficulty that have also been selected from a basal reader series, for oral and silent reading; and comprehension questions for both the oral and silent reading passages. A separate set of passages and comprehension questions at graduated levels of difficulty are also usually included to determine the listening capacity level. (The instructions are given for a traditional basal reader program; you can, however, adapt these instructions for use with any reading program that is based on graduated levels of difficulty.)

### GRADED WORD LISTS

The graded word lists usually consist of 20 or 25 words. There is a word list for every reader level of the basal series. The list usually starts at the preprimer level and proceeds to the highest level book available. If the IRI begins at the preprimer level and ends at the eighth-grade level, there would be a word list for each level up to the eighth. (Many traditional basal reader series have two reader levels for certain grades, and some have three or more preprimer reader levels. If there are three or more preprimer reader levels, it's a good idea to use the second one as representative of the three. The IRI in Appendix B is based on a traditional basal reader series.)

The words for the word lists are selected from those introduced in the basal reader for each book level. (At the back of each basal reader there is usually a list of words that have been introduced in the book.) Words for the word lists are based on a random sampling, so that each word introduced at a particular level has an equal and independent chance of being chosen.

If you are constructing your own IRI, an easy way to get a random sampling of the words for the word lists, if there are fewer than 100 words, is to put each word on a slip of paper and put the slips in a small box or hat. (Make sure the slips of paper are well mixed.) Pull 20 words from the hat. (If there are only 20 words that have been introduced at a particular reader level, you obviously would use all the words.) However, at the upper grade levels, where there are more than 100 words presented at each level, you need a method different from the cumbersome "old hat" random sampling method. You need a formula to help you determine the number of random samples of the required sample size for a given word list. The formula for this is as follows:

$$\frac{\text{Word List}}{\text{Sample Size}} = \text{Number of Samples}$$

The number of words you want on your word list is your sample size, and the word list is the total number of words. For example, if you want to select 20 words from a 100-word list, first apply the formula

$$N = \frac{100}{20} = 5$$

Since the number of samples is 5, number the total amount of words sequentially up to 5, that is, 1, 2, 3, 4, 5. To get the 20 words from the 100-word list, select all those words that are numbered either 1, 2, 3, 4, or 5. (Select which number you will use by any method you wish, and then choose all words that have that number.) This procedure will give you a sample of 20 words from the 100-word list covering the entire alphabetical range, if the words are presented alphabetically.

## GRADED ORAL AND SILENT READING PASSAGES

To randomly draw sample passages for your IRI, note the number of pages in each basal reader, and then choose any one of the numbers. For example, if there are 200 pages, choose any number from 1 to 200. Open the book to the number you have chosen. Choose a selection on that page that can be easily excerpted; that is, it can stand alone and make sense. The first sentence of the selection should not have any pronouns that have antecedents in the previous paragraph. If there are no paragraphs on that page that can be easily excerpted, go to the previous page. It may be that you will have to go to the beginning of the story to get a selection that can stand alone.

The sample selections should contain approximately the following sample sizes:

Preprimer level, approximately 40 to 70 words
Primer level, approximately 50 to 85
First-grade level, approximately 70 to 100
Second-grade level, approximately 100 to 150
Third-grade level, approximately 125 to 175
Fourth-grade level, approximately 150 to 200
Fifth-grade level, approximately 175 to 225
Sixth-grade level and up, approximately 175 to 275

The paragraphs that are chosen to comprise your IRI should be representative of the readability level of the basal reader from which they were taken. There are times when this is not so; it's a good idea to double-check the chosen paragraphs with a readability formula. If your selection does not pass the readability formula criterion, repeat the process to choose a different passage. Each selection chosen for the IRI should have a short statement telling something about it.

There is disagreement in the field as to whether the oral and silent reading passages should be from the same or different selections. We prefer to use oral and silent reading passages from the same selection to ensure a greater chance of having a similar difficulty level of concepts and vocabulary. Dissimilarity can be a problem because most basal reader series are literature-based or consist completely of trade books. These kinds of reading programs seem to have a greater variation in vocabulary load between different selections at the same level in the same program than previous basal reader series. It is important to have vocabulary and concepts at the same difficulty level for both oral and silent reading passages because the teacher uses the oral reading passage to determine whether the child should read the silent reading passage.

In addition, we have found that there appears to be a much greater variation in vocabulary load and difficulty among the present literature-based reading programs than in previous series. Often there may be only a few similar words in the glossaries of different reading programs at the same reader grade level. Be aware of these differences if you use selections from different reading programs to construct your IRIs.

## THE COMPREHENSION QUESTIONS

Both the oral and the silent reading passages must have questions based on each passage, and the questions must be text-dependent. These are usually literal comprehension questions, interpretive questions, and word meaning questions. (Some IRIs may contain critical reading questions. These may present a problem because a number of these questions are usually not text-dependent; that is, the student may be able to answer them independently of the text.) Examples of the types of questions that can be asked to assess selected comprehension skills at each level follow.

### *Literal Comprehension Questions*
Literal questions are the easiest to construct, and they are generally the ones most often asked. The answers for literal questions are directly stated in the selection. Here is an example of a selection and some literal comprehension questions based on it:

> Sharon and Carol are sisters.
> They like to play together.
> They play lots of games.
> Their favorite game is Monopoly.

*Literal Questions*

1. Who are sisters? (story detail)
2. What do the sisters like to do? (story detail)
3. What do the sisters play? (story detail)
4. What is their favorite game? (story detail)

### *Interpretive Questions*
Interpretive questions are more difficult to answer because the answers are not directly stated in the selection; they are implied. Interpretive questions are also usually more difficult to construct and are usually not asked as often as literal comprehension questions. Here is an example of a selection and some interpretive questions based on it:

> Do you ever think of the right thing to say too late? I always do, but my friend George always has the right words and answers at the snap of his fingers. Whenever you see George, there's always a crowd around him, and they are always laughing at his jokes. He is never serious about anything. I'm always serious about everything. There's an old saying that definitely explains our friendship.

*Interpretive Questions*

1. What is the main idea of the selection? (main idea)
2. What can you infer about the speaker in the selection? (inference or "reading between the lines")
3. State the old saying that explains the friendship between the two people in the selection and then tell why it explains their relationship. (figurative language; making comparisons)
4. Choose the row with ideas from the story that belong together. (association)

   a. George, unfriendly, crowds
   b. George's friend, friendly, witty
   c. George, witty, crowds
   d. George's friend, serious, witty

5. Choose the word that best completes this analogy: George's friend is to somber as George is to _____ (analogy)
   a. people.
   b. happiness.
   c. grave.
   d. cheerful.

### Critical Reading Questions

Critical reading questions are those that involve evaluation, which is the making of a personal judgment on the accuracy, value, and truthfulness of what is read. The critical thinking questions should be text-dependent. Here is an example of a selection and some critical reading questions based on it:

> Fortunately, the school election will be over soon. I don't think that I can stand another week such as the last one. First, there was John, who told me that I was the only one not voting for his candidate, "True-Blue Tim." Then there was Mary, who told me that if I were a student with lots of school spirit, I'd be out campaigning for her candidate, "Clever Jane." Mary says that the majority of students are supporting her candidate. She says that even the famous local star thinks that Jane is the best person. Personally, I think that both their candidates are creeps, and I don't intend to vote for either one. I'm going to vote for Jennifer because she is so democratic and fair.

### Critical Comprehension Questions

1. State at least five propaganda techniques that are used in the selection, and give examples of them. (propaganda techniques)
2. Determine whether each of the following statements are facts or opinions. (fact or opinion)
   a. The speaker in the selection doesn't think much of the candidates.
   b. The majority of students are voting for Jane.
   c. Jane is clever.

# Appendix B

## INFORMAL READING INVENTORY[*]

**Summary Sheet**

Name _____   Age _____

Grade _____   Teacher _____

| Reader Level | Word Recognition in Isolation (No. of Errors) | Oral Reading | | | Silent Reading | | Listening Capacity | |
|---|---|---|---|---|---|---|---|---|
| | | W.R. | Comp. | | Comp. | | | |
| | | No. of Errors/ Total No. Wds | % Errors | % Correct | % Errors | % Correct | % Errors | % Correct |
| Preprimer | | | | | | | | |
| Primer | | | | | | | | |
| First | | | | | | | | |
| $2^1$ | | | | | | | | |
| $2^2$ | | | | | | | | |
| $3^1$ | | | | | | | | |
| $3^2$ | | | | | | | | |
| 4 | | | | | | | | |
| 5 | | | | | | | | |
| 6 | | | | | | | | |
| 7 | | | | | | | | |
| 8 | | | | | | | | |

[*]The Informal Reading Inventory is based on the Silver Burdett & Ginn series *World of Reading,* 1989

Level at which Word Recognition Inventory
(WRI) was begun                                                    _____

Level at which oral reading was begun                              _____

Oral reading—word recognition
    Independent level                                          _____

    Instructional level                                        _____

    Frustration level                                          _____

Oral reading—comprehension
    Independent level                                          _____

    Instructional level                                        _____

    Frustration level                                          _____

Silent reading—comprehension
    Independent level                                          _____

    Instructional level                                        _____

    Frustration level                                          _____

Listening capacity level                                          _____

Word analysis
    Consonants—single
      initial                                                _____

      medial                                                 _____

      final                                                  _____

    Consonants—double
      blends                                                 _____

      digraphs                                               _____

    Consonants—silent                                          _____

    Vowels—single
      short                                                  _____

      long                                                   _____

    Vowels—double
      digraphs                                               _____

      diphthongs                                             _____

Effect of final *e* on vowel                                       _____

Vowel controlled by *r*                                            _____
    Structural analysis
      prefixes                                               _____

      suffixes                                               _____ combining forms                                    _____

inflectional endings                               _____

Compound words                                     _____

Accent                                             _____

Special Notes on Strengths and Weaknesses

Comments on Behavior During the Testing

Recommendations

## SPECIAL NOTES

Information on the following is given in the body of Chapter 8:

1. Code for marking oral reading errors (p. 154)
2. The scoring of oral reading errors (p. 155)
3. Criteria for estimating the reading levels (p. 164)
4. Administering the IRI (pp. 155–164)
5. Examples (pp. 156–167)

Partial credit may be given for comprehension questions if an answer consists of more than one part. For example, if the answer to a question consists of three names, and the student has named only one, the student should get one-third credit. If the answer to a question consists of two things, and the student gives only one, the student should receive half credit.

Do not count mispronunciations of difficult proper nouns in the oral reading passages as errors. You may pronounce these for the children if necessary. Also, do not count as errors dialectical equivalents (nonstandard dialects); however, these should be noted.

In addition, the term *main idea* is used rather than *central idea,* even though the oral and silent passages are usually more than one paragraph. (See "Finding the Central Idea of a Group of Paragraphs" in Chapter 10, page 222.)

# Word Recognition Inventory (WRI)

| *Preprimer* | | *Primer* | | *First* | |
|---|---|---|---|---|---|
| 1. water | *winter* | 1. blow | ✓ | 1. soup | _____ |
| 2. play | ✓ | 2. little | ✓ | 2. tents | _____ |
| 3. sand | ✓ | 3. many | ✓ | 3. afternoon | _____ |
| 4. look | ✓ | 4. bright | ✓ | 4. baked | _____ |
| 5. wind | ✓ | 5. old | ✗ | 5. family | _____ |
| 6. jump | ✓ | 6. won | *woman* | 6. alone | _____ |
| 7. cave | ✓ | 7. things | ✓ | 7. great | _____ |
| 8. make | ✓ | 8. yellow | ✓ | 8. white | _____ |
| 9. put | ✓ | 9. farm | ✓ | 9. soft | _____ |
| 10. bear | ✓ | 10. friend | ✓ | 10. boy | _____ |
| 11. over | ✓ | 11. more | ✓ | 11. dinner | _____ |
| 12. out | ✓ | 12. thanks | ✓ | 12. does | _____ |
| 13. cap | ✓ | 13. snow | ✓ | 13. wife | _____ |
| 14. could | ✓ | 14. some | ✓ | 14. horse | _____ |
| 15. down | ✓ | 15. cows | ✗ | 15. head | _____ |
| 16. sun | ✓ | 16. game | ✓ | 16. sorry | _____ |
| 17. have | ✓ | 17. please | *planes* | 17. summer | _____ |
| 18. side | ✓ | 18. leaves | ✓ | 18. hungry | _____ |
| 19. top | ✓ | 19. draw | *dark* | 19. drank | _____ |
| 20. surprise | ✓ | 20. work | ✓ | 20. enough | _____ |

# Word Recognition Inventory (WRI) (*Cont.*)

| $2^1$ | $2^2$ | $3^1$ |
|---|---|---|
| 1. brave _____ | 1. office _____ | 1. plow _____ |
| 2. noon _____ | 2. perfect _____ | 2. horn _____ |
| 3. park _____ | 3. patient _____ | 3. hesitate _____ |
| 4. strange _____ | 4. enemy _____ | 4. neglect _____ |
| 5. November _____ | 5. donkey _____ | 5. deaf _____ |
| 6. money _____ | 6. dirt _____ | 6. language _____ |
| 7. library _____ | 7. clever _____ | 7. attention _____ |
| 8. join _____ | 8. company _____ | 8. drawn _____ |
| 9. angry _____ | 9. candle _____ | 9. complain _____ |
| 10. apple _____ | 10. beard _____ | 10. fame _____ |
| 11. carrots _____ | 11. bundle _____ | 11. goal _____ |
| 12. class _____ | 12. address _____ | 12. familiar _____ |
| 13. answer _____ | 13. snowflake _____ | 13. elevator _____ |
| 14. loud _____ | 14. sailors _____ | 14. plunge _____ |
| 15. mouth _____ | 15. score _____ | 15. nature _____ |
| 16. matter _____ | 16. tune _____ | 16. poem _____ |
| 17. hurry _____ | 17. thirsty _____ | 17. stall _____ |
| 18. idea _____ | 18. unload _____ | 18. talent _____ |
| 19. carve _____ | 19. view _____ | 19. worthy _____ |
| 20. clothes _____ | 20. trouble _____ | 20. lung _____ |
| 21. delicious _____ | 21. south _____ | 21. medal _____ |
| 22. below _____ | 22. shy _____ | 22. mistake _____ |
| 23. boil _____ | 23. ambulance _____ | 23. customer _____ |
| 24. built _____ | 24. tiny _____ | 24. courage _____ |
| 25. dragons _____ | 25. hobby _____ | 25. announce _____ |

# Word Recognition Inventory (WRI) (*Cont.*)

| $3^2$ | 4 | 5 |
|---|---|---|
| 1. petal _____ | 1. gracious _____ | 1. tragedy _____ |
| 2. rein _____ | 2. imitate _____ | 2. applause _____ |
| 3. furious _____ | 3. defense _____ | 3. amazement _____ |
| 4. popular _____ | 4. declare _____ | 4. harvest _____ |
| 5. identify _____ | 5. electronics _____ | 5. thaw _____ |
| 6. forecast _____ | 6. punishment _____ | 6. original _____ |
| 7. attach _____ | 7. robot _____ | 7. balcony _____ |
| 8. bought _____ | 8. uniform _____ | 8. marvel _____ |
| 9. admire _____ | 9. twilight _____ | 9. mileage _____ |
| 10. noble _____ | 10. tragedy _____ | 10. cluster _____ |
| 11. migrate _____ | 11. stranger _____ | 11. architect _____ |
| 12. patient _____ | 12. tame _____ | 12. heroine _____ |
| 13. novel _____ | 13. technique _____ | 13. audition _____ |
| 14. ruin _____ | 14. suspect _____ | 14. interrupt _____ |
| 15. rescue _____ | 15. ordinary _____ | 15. landscape _____ |
| 16. unusual _____ | 16. native _____ | 16. petition _____ |
| 17. x-ray _____ | 17. haughty _____ | 17. permission _____ |
| 18. wisdom _____ | 18. hostile _____ | 18. vessel _____ |
| 19. rough _____ | 19. entire _____ | 19. promotion _____ |
| 20. protest _____ | 20. errand _____ | 20. violence _____ |
| 21. persuade _____ | 21. average _____ | 21. voyage _____ |
| 22. influence _____ | 22. appetite _____ | 22. vast _____ |
| 23. prince _____ | 23. radiant _____ | 23. nuisance _____ |
| 24. bandage _____ | 24. prowl _____ | 24. luxury _____ |
| 25. bridge _____ | 25. caution _____ | 25. lonely _____ |

# Word Recognition Inventory (WRI) (*Cont.*)

| 6 | 7 | 8 |
|---|---|---|
| 1. tenement _____ | 1. sham _____ | 1. prospect _____ |
| 2. rebel _____ | 2. scrutiny _____ | 2. quest _____ |
| 3. ease _____ | 3. refuge _____ | 3. scoop _____ |
| 4. exhibit _____ | 4. prestigious _____ | 4. journalism _____ |
| 5. appoint _____ | 5. quarrel _____ | 5. invincible _____ |
| 6. shuttle _____ | 6. nomad _____ | 6. listless _____ |
| 7. unwilling _____ | 7. fault _____ | 7. mirror _____ |
| 8. recede _____ | 8. flattery _____ | 8. circuit _____ |
| 9. wizard _____ | 9. hindrance _____ | 9. defy _____ |
| 10. wrench _____ | 10. imperative _____ | 10. anguish _____ |
| 11. revenge _____ | 11. colleague _____ | 11. augment _____ |
| 12. tiresome _____ | 12. trifle _____ | 12. aristocratic _____ |
| 13. spout _____ | 13. souvenir _____ | 13. formidable _____ |
| 14. strategy _____ | 14. chore _____ | 14. faculty _____ |
| 15. pamphlet _____ | 15. aggressive _____ | 15. seizure _____ |
| 16. persist _____ | 16. barometer _____ | 16. terrace _____ |
| 17. heritage _____ | 17. emigrate _____ | 17. scrabble _____ |
| 18. conquer _____ | 18. verdict _____ | 18. undermine _____ |
| 19. humble _____ | 19. zodiac _____ | 19. sphere _____ |
| 20. arrogant _____ | 20. wrench _____ | 20. naive _____ |
| 21. astronomy _____ | 21. probe _____ | 21. plateau _____ |
| 22. distinguish _____ | 22. momentum _____ | 22. recitation _____ |
| 23. gratitude _____ | 23. mortal _____ | 23. jaunt _____ |
| 24. guarantee _____ | 24. exile _____ | 24. frugal _____ |
| 25. legacy _____ | 25. imitation _____ | 25. hysteria _____ |

# Preprimer

*ORAL READING (64)*[1]

**Introduction: Read this story aloud to find out what a little boy can make. Then I will ask you questions about the story.**

The sun came out.
Bob and Mom came out to play.
Bob said, "Who can play with me?"
Mom said, "Do you see what I see?"
Bob said, "All I see is sand.
I see a lot of sand.
I can make a mountain
with all the sand I see."
Mom said, "Make a sand mountain!
You will see who will come to play."

## Comprehension Questions

|  |  | Points |
|---|---|---|
| (Literal) | 1. Who came out to play? (Bob and Mom) | 20 |
| (Inference) | 2. What did Mom see? (Sand) | 16 |
| (Literal) | 3. How much sand was there? (A lot) | 16 |
| (Literal) | 4. What did Bob say he could make with the sand? (A sand mountain) | 16 |
| (Inference) | 5. What kind of day is it? (Sunny, warm, nice) | 16 |
| (Inference) | 6. What did Mom think the sand mountain would do? (Bring other children to play) | 16 |

## Scoring Scale

| Levels | Word Recognition Errors | Comprehension Errors |
|---|---|---|
| Independent | 0–1 | 0–10 points |
| Instructional | 2–3 | 11–25 points |
| Frustration | 6 or more | 50 points or more |

[1]Level 2, "The Sand Mountain," *Out Came the Sun* (Needham, MA: Silver Burdett & Ginn, 1989), pp. 38–39.

*SILENT READING*[2]

**Introduction: Read this story to find out what Bob and his friends do. Then I will ask you questions about the story. Read it carefully.**

Jane said, "Can I help make it a
big mountain?"
Bob said, "I can put sand here.
You can put sand on the other side."
Fran said, "I came to play.
Can I help make the sand mountain?"
Bob said, "Come on, you can play.
You can help Jane and me."
Jane said, "Will you get water?
The wind is blowing the sand off the mountain."

Comprehension Questions

|  |  | Points |
|---|---|---|
| (Inference) | 1. Who came to play first? (Jane) | 16 |
| (Literal) | 2. What did Jane want to do? (Help Bob make a big mountain) | 16 |
| (Literal) | 3. What did Bob tell Jane she could do? (Put sand on the other side of the mountain) | 16 |
| (Literal) | 4. Whom did Bob say Fran could help? (Jane and him) (water) | 20 |
| (Literal) | 5. Who said, "Will you get water?" (Jane) (Bob) | 16 |
| (Inference) | 6. Why did Jane want water? (To make the sand wet so that the wind would not blow it away) (to make a river) | 16 |

Scoring Scale

| Levels | Comprehension Errors |
|---|---|
| Independent | 0–10 points |
| Instructional | 11–20 points |
| Frustration | 50 points or more |

[2]Ibid., pp. 40–42.

# Primer

*ORAL READING (76)*[3]

> **Introduction: Read this story aloud to find out what Sara wants. Then I will ask you questions about the story.**

Sara sat and sat, looking out at the
big tree. She looked at her mother and asked,
"Mom, do you have some string?"   *something?*
*Somebody*   "Yes, here is some red string,"
said Sara's mother. "Is it for your hair?"
"No," said Sara, "It's not for my hair."
"I know," said Mother, "You   *somebody*
*where* are going to fix something with it."
"No," said Sara. "You'll see."   *you*
Sara saw that her father had   *feather*
some string, too. She asked him for it.

## Comprehension Questions

|  |  | Points |
|---|---|---|
| (Literal) | 1. What was Sara looking at? (The big tree) ✓ | 12.5 |
| (Literal) | 2. What did Sara want from her mother? (String) ✗ | 12.5 |
| (Literal) | 3. What color string did her mother have? (Red) ✓ | 12.5 |
| (Literal) | 4. What did Sara's mother first think the string was for? (Sara's hair) | 12.5 |
| (Inference) | 5. Who thought something was broken? (Sara's mother) ✗ | 12.5 |
| (Inference) | 6. How do we know Sara's mother thought something was broken? (She thought the string was to fix something.) ✗ | 12.5 |
| (Literal) | 7. Who else had string? (Her father) ✓ | 12.5 |
| (Literal) | 8. What did Sara do when she saw her father had some string? (She asked him for it.) ✓ | 12.5 |

## Scoring Scale

| Levels | Word Recognition Errors | Comprehension Errors |
|---|---|---|
| Independent | 0–1 | 0–10 points |
| Instructional | 2–4 | 11–25 points |
| Frustration | 8 or more | 50 points or more |

[3]Jane Mechling, "A Rainbow for Sara," Level 4, *Make a Wish* (Needham, MA: Silver Burdett & Ginn, 1989), pp. 32–34.

*SILENT READING*[4]

**Introduction: Read this story to find out more about Sara and her string. Then I will ask you questions about the story. Read it carefully.**

Sara ran outside to play with Peter
and Anna.
"I am keeping string in a box,"
said Sara.
"I have some green string in my
pocket. You may have it," said Peter.
"You are keeping string?"
said Anna. "What are you going
to do with all that string? Will
you and your cat play with it?"
"No," said Sara. "You'll see."
Soon Sara had all the string she needed.
She had red string, orange string,
green string, and yellow string.

Comprehension Questions

| | | Points |
|---|---|---|
| (Literal) | 1. Where did Sara go? (Outside) | 12.5 |
| (Literal) | 2. Why did Sara go outside? (To play with Peter and Anna) | 12.5 |
| (Literal) | 3. Where was Sara keeping her string? (In a box)  ⌐pocket⌐ | 12.5 |
| (Inference) | 4. Who else was saving string? (Peter)  Anna | 12.5 |
| (Literal) | 5. What color string did Peter have? (Green)  Don remember | 12.5 |
| (Literal) | 6. Where did Peter keep his string? (In his pocket) ✓ | 12.5 |
| (Inference) | 7. Does Sara have a pet? If she does, what is it? (Yes; a cat) ✓ | 12.5 |
| (Literal) | 8. What were the colors of the string Sara had? (Red, orange, green, and yellow) ✓ | 12.5 |

Scoring Scale

| Levels | Comprehension Errors |
|---|---|
| Independent | 0–10 points |
| Instructional | 11–25 points |
| Frustration | 50 points or more |

[4]Ibid., pp. 35–36.

# First Reader

*ORAL READING (88)[5]*

**Introduction: Read this story aloud to find out about Fritz and Anna. Then I will ask you questions about the story.**

Fritz and Anna lived on a farm. It was a small
farm. It was also very dry, and things did not  ~~think~~
grow well. So Fritz and his wife, Anna, were
poor.
   One day there was a tap, tap, tap on the
door. A woman had come to the farm.
She had been walking most of the day,
and she was hungry. She asked Fritz and
Anna to give her something to eat. Fritz and
Anna had a pot of soup. They let the woman
come in to eat.

## Comprehension Questions

| | | Points |
|---|---|---|
| (Literal) | 1. Where did Fritz and Anna live? (On a farm) | 10 |
| (Literal) | 2. What kind of farm was it? (Small, dry) | 10 |
| (Inference) | 3. Why were Fritz and Anna poor? (Things didn't grow well on their farm.) | 10 |
| (Inference) | 4. Why didn't things grow well? (It was too dry.) | 10 |
| (Word meaning) | 5. What does "poor" mean? (Not having money; not having much food to eat) | 10 |
| (Inference) | 6. Who knocked on Fritz and Anna's door? (A woman) | 10 |
| (Literal) | 7. What had the woman been doing? (Walking all day) | 10 |
| (Literal) | 8. How did the woman feel? (Hungry) | 10 |
| Literal) | 9. What did Fritz and Anna have? (A pot of soup) | 10 |
| (Inference) | 10. How do we know Fritz and Anna are kind people? (Even though they are poor, they share their soup with the woman.) | 10 |

## Scoring Scale

| Levels | Word Recognition Errors | Comprehension Errors |
|---|---|---|
| Independent | 0–1 | 0–10 points |
| Instructional | 2–4 | 11–25 points |
| Frustration | 9 or more | 50 points or more |

[5]Verna Aardema, "The Three Wishes," Level 5, *A New Day* (Needham, MA: Silver Burdett & Ginn, 1989), p. 160.

*SILENT READING*[6]

**Introduction: Fritz and Anna are given some wishes by the woman. Read to find out what Fritz and Anna do with one of the wishes. Then I will ask you questions about the story. Read it carefully.**

For most of the day, Fritz and Anna
talked about the three wishes they
would make. They talked long after it was
time to eat again, and they forgot to cook.
They began to get hungry.
   By the time Anna and Fritz made soup,
they were both very, very hungry.
As they sat down to eat, Fritz said,
"I wish we had a sausage to go with this soup."
   And there on the table was a great big
brown sausage!

Comprehension Questions

|  |  | Points |
|---|---|---|
| (Literal) | 1. How many wishes were Fritz and Anna given? (Three) | 10 |
| (Literal) | 2. How long did they talk about the wishes? (For most of the day) | 10 |
| (Literal) | 3. What did they forget to do? (Cook) | 10 |
| (Inference) | 4. Why did they forget to cook? (They were excited about the three wishes; they were busy talking about them.) | 10 |
| (Inference) | 5. How did they know they hadn't eaten? (They became hungry.) | 10 |
| (Literal) | 6. What did they make to eat? (Soup) | 10 |
| (Literal) | 7. How did they feel when the soup was ready? (Very, very hungry) | 10 |
| (Literal) | 8. Who wished for something? (Fritz) | 10 |
| (Literal) | 9. What did Fritz wish for? (A sausage to go with the soup) | 10 |
| (Literal) | 10. What did the wish bring? (A great big brown sausage) | 10 |

Scoring Scale

| Levels | Comprehension Errors |
|---|---|
| Independent | 0–10 points |
| Instructional | 11–25 points |
| Frustration | 50 points or more |

[6]Ibid., p. 163.

# Level 2[1]

*ORAL READING (112)*[7]

**Introduction: Read this story aloud to find out why a farmer needs help. Then I will ask you questions about the story.**

Once there was a farmer who went to the town
wise man because he had a problem, and he did not
know what to do. "How can I help you?" the wise man asked.
"I have a house with one small room," sighed
the farmer.
"That is not a problem," the wise man said.
"It is a problem," the farmer sighed. "I live in this one
small room with my wife and my seven children.
We are always in one another's way, and we are always
talking at the same time. It is so loud that I can hardly
hear myself think. I cannot stand it any longer.
Can you help me?"

## Comprehension Questions

|  |  | Points |
|---|---|---|
| (Literal) | 1. To whom did the farmer go? (To the town wise man) | 10 |
| (Word meaning) | 2. What is a town wise man? (A person who can help others; a man who knows lots of things; he can answer many questions.) | 10 |
| (Literal) | 3. Why did the farmer go to the town wise man? (He had a problem.) | 10 |
| (Literal) | 4. Where does the farmer live? (In a house with one small room) | 10 |
| (Inference) | 5. How many people live in the house? (Nine: seven children, the farmer, and his wife) | 10 |
| (Inference) | 6. Explain whether you think the farmer is rich or poor. (Poor, because he lives in one room with such a large family) | 10 |
| (Inference) | 7. What is the farmer's problem? (It is too noisy in his house.) | 10 |
| (Literal) | 8. What does everyone in the house do at the same time? (Talk) | 10 |
| (Literal) | 9. What is the noise stopping the farmer from doing? (Thinking) | 10 |
| (Inference) | 10. What does the farmer want the town wise man to do? (Help the farmer solve his problem) | 10 |

## Scoring Scale

| Levels | Word Recognition Errors | Comprehension Errors |
|---|---|---|
| Independent | 0–1 | 0–10 points |
| Instructional | 2–6 | 11–25 points |
| Frustration | 11 or more | 50 points or more |

[7]Michael Patrick Hearn, "Not So Wise as You Suppose," Level 6, *Garden Gates* (Needham, MA: Silver Burdett & Ginn, 1989), pp. 94–95.

*SILENT READING*[8]

**Introduction: Read this story to find out what the farmer does to solve his problem. Then I will ask you questions about the story. Read it carefully.**

The wise man stroked his chin and thought.
"Do you have a horse?" the wise man asked.
"Yes, I have a horse," the farmer said.
"Then the answer is simple," the wise man said,
"but you must do as I tell you. Tonight you must bring
the horse into your house to stay with you,
your wife, and your seven children." The farmer was
surprised to hear such a plan, but he did as he was told.
The next morning he returned to the wise man.
He was quite upset.
"You are not so wise as you suppose!" the farmer said,
"Now my house is even louder. The horse just kicks
and neighs morning, noon, and night!
I cannot stand it any longer."

Comprehension Questions

|  |  | *Points* |
|---|---|---|
| (Literal) | 1. What did the wise man stroke? (His chin) | 10 |
| (Literal) | 2. What was the wise man doing when he stroked his chin? (Thinking) | 10 |
| (Literal) | 3. What did the wise man ask the farmer? (If he had a horse) | 10 |
| (Word meaning) | 4. What does "simple" mean? (Easy) | 10 |
| (Literal) | 5. What did the wise man say was simple? (The answer to the farmer's problem) | 10 |
| (Literal) | 6. What did the wise man want the farmer to do? (To bring the horse into the house to stay with the farmer and his family) | 10 |
| (Literal) | 7. When was the farmer supposed to bring the horse into the house? (That night) | 10 |
| (Inference) | 8. Explain how you know whether the wise man's plan worked. (It didn't work because the farmer came in very upset.) | 10 |
| (Literal) | 9. What did the horse do in the house? (Kicked and neighed) | 10 |
| (Literal) | 10. What did the farmer think about the wise man now? (That the wise man was not as wise as he thought he was) | 10 |

Scoring Scale

| *Levels* | *Comprehension Errors* |
|---|---|
| Independent | 0–10 points |
| Instructional | 11–25 points |
| Frustration | 50 points or more |

[8]Ibid., p. 96.

# Level 2[2]

*ORAL READING (131)*[9]

> **Introduction: Read this story aloud to find out what the children's surprise is. Then I will ask you questions about the story.**

The children sat down in a big circle
on the ground. Everyone was excited. Mr. Ortero
(or-te´-rō) had promised them a surprise.

Mr. Ortero walked into the middle of the
circle. He ran the after-school program in the
park.

"I have a mystery today," Mr. Ortero said.
"A treasure is hidden somewhere in the park.
Your job is to solve the mystery and find the
treasure."

Marita (mä-rē´-ta) raised her hand.
"What is the treasure?" she asked.

"That's part of the mystery," Mr. Ortero
answered.

Marita laughed with everyone else.
Mr. Ortero liked to tease them.

"Each of you gets one clue,"
Mr. Ortero said.

He started around the circle, handing out
the clues. Marita was sitting between Jenny
and Mike.

"I'm really a good detective," Mike said.
"I bet I'll find the treasure."

## Comprehension Questions

|  |  | Points |
|---|---|---|
| (Literal) | 1. How were the children sitting? (In a big circle on the ground) | 10 |
| (Literal) | 2. Why were they excited? (Mr. Ortero had promised them a surprise.) | 10 |
| (Literal) | 3. Who was Mr. Ortero? (The person who ran the after-school program in the park) | 10 |
| (Literal) | 4. What did Mr. Ortero have for the children? (A mystery) | 10 |
| (Word meaning) | 5. What is a mystery? (Something that is not known; a secret; a puzzle that has to be solved or figured out) | 10 |

[9]Judith Stamper, "The Treasure Hunt," Level 7, *Going Places* (Needham, MA: Silver Burdett & Ginn, 1989), p. 197.

| (Literal) | 6. What is the mystery Mr. Ortero has for the children? (He has hidden a treasure in the park and wants the children to find it.) | 10 |
| (Literal) | 7. What did Marita want to know? (What the treasure is) | 10 |
| (Inference) | 8. Why didn't Mr. Ortero tell the children what the treasure is? (The treasure is part of the mystery and therefore might give the mystery away; it might make it too easy to solve the mystery.) | 10 |
| (Literal) | 9. What did Mr. Ortero do to help the children find the treasure? (He gave each child a clue.) | 10 |
| (Inference) | 10. Why does Mike think he will find the treasure? (Because he thinks he's a good detective) | 10 |

## Scoring Scale

| Levels | Word Recognition Errors | Comprehension Errors |
|---|---|---|
| Independent | 0–1 | 0–10 points |
| Instructional | 2–7 | 11–25 points |
| Frustration | 13 or more | 50 points or more |

*SILENT READING*[10]

**Introduction: Read this story to find out more about the treasure hunt. Then I will ask you questions about the story. Read it carefully.**

   Jenny looked at Marita and smiled. They both liked Mike, but he bragged a lot.

   Mr. Ortero gave Jenny her clue. Marita was next, and then Mike. Soon, each child had a clue to open and read. Mr. Ortero stepped back into the middle of the circle.

   "Listen to the rules," he said. "First, stay inside the park. The treasure is hidden here. Second, don't harm any plants or trees. Third, you must find the treasure in twenty minutes. Meet me back here in twenty minutes. Good luck!"

   The children jumped to their feet and ran in different directions. Marita read her clue over and over. It said:

   *Thirsty, tired, and very hot?*
   *I'm near what's cool and hits the spot.*

   "Near something to drink," Marita thought. She ran to find the nearest water fountain. She looked all around the fountain, but there was no treasure.

### Comprehension Questions

| | | Points |
|---|---|---|
| (Literal) | 1. How did Jenny and Marita feel toward Mike? (They liked him.) | 10 |
| (Word meaning) | 2. What does "brag" mean? (To boast) | 10 |
| (Inference) | 3. Why did Jenny smile at Marita? (Because Mike is probably always bragging; they were used to his bragging.) | 10 |
| (Literal) | 4. What did Mr. Ortero do after he gave each child a clue? (He gave them rules.) | 10 |
| (Word meaning) | 5. What is a rule? (Something you have to follow) | 10 |
| (Literal) | 6. What were the three rules he gave the children? (Stay inside the park; don't harm any plants or trees; they must find the treasure in twenty minutes.) | 10 |
| (Inference) | 7. How do we know Mr. Ortero is concerned about the park? (He tells children not to harm the plants or trees.) | 10 |

[10]Ibid., p. 198.

| | | |
|---|---|---|
| (Literal) | 8. What did Marita run to find? (The water fountain) | 10 |
| (Inference) | 9. Why did Marita run to the water fountain? (Because of her clue) | 10 |
| (Inference) | 10. What did Marita expect to find at the water fountain? (The treasure) | 10 |

Scoring Scale

| Levels | Comprehension Errors |
|---|---|
| Independent | 0–10 points |
| Instructional | 11–25 points |
| Frustration | 50 points or more |

# Level 3[1]

*ORAL READING (151)*[11]

> **Introduction: Read this story aloud to find out what Jason wants. Then I will ask you questions about the story.**

Every time ten-year-old Jason Hardman wanted a book from a library, he borrowed his sister's bike and pedaled six miles to the next town, Monroe. Since Jason's favorite thing to do was to read books, he spent hours pedaling.

Jason's town of Elsinore, Utah, had only 650 people, too tiny for a library of its own. Elsinore was so small that the children even went to school in Monroe.

One night, Jason said to his parents, "I want to start a library in Elsinore." They were pleased but told him that he would have to talk with the town council.

"What is a town council?" Jason asked.

"It's a group of about eight elected members and the mayor. They run all the town's business," his mom said. "Elsinore, like all towns, collects taxes from its citizens and uses the money for public services, such as fire and police protection," she explained.

## Comprehension Questions

| | | Points |
|---|---|---|
| (Literal) | 1. How old is Jason Hardman? (Ten years old) | 10 |
| (Word meaning) | 2. What does "borrow" mean? (To use something that belongs to someone else after agreeing to return it) | 10 |
| (Literal) | 3. What did Jason borrow? (His sister's bike) | 10 |
| (Inference) | 4. Where did Jason spend a lot of time? (In the Monroe library) | 10 |
| (Literal) | 5. What was Jason's favorite thing? (Reading) | 10 |
| (Literal) | 6. Why didn't Jason's town have a library? (It was too small.) | 10 |
| (Literal) | 7. What did Jason want to do? (Start a library) | 10 |
| (Inference) | 8. Why did Jason want to start a library? (Because he loved to read and didn't want to keep pedaling to Monroe to get library books) | 10 |
| (Literal) | 9. What is a town council? (A group of about eight elected members and a mayor, who run the town's business) | 10 |
| (Main idea) | 10. What is the main idea of the story? (Jason Hardman wants to start a library.) | 10 |

---

[11]Margaret Tuley Patton, "Jason Wants a Library," Level 8, *Castles of Sand* (Needham, MA: Silver Burdett & Ginn, 1989), pp. 184–185.

Scoring Scale

| Levels | Word Recognition Errors | Comprehension Errors |
|---|---|---|
| Independent | 0–2 | 0–10 points |
| Instructional | 3–8 | 11–25 points |
| Frustration | 15 or more | 50 points or more |

*SILENT READING*[12]

**Introduction: Jason meets with the town council and tells them he wants to start a library. Read the story to find out more about Jason and his library. Then I will ask you questions about the story. Read it carefully.**

Another week passed. Every day when Jason came off the school bus, he'd ask his mother: "Did the mayor phone?" Each day, the answer was, "No." Jason phoned the mayor every night for two weeks. Each night, the same answer was given: "The council is still thinking about it." Jason grew tired of waiting. Why can't I use the town hall basement for my library? he thought to himself.

During those weeks, Jason pedaled often to Monroe for library books. "I wonder if I will be biking these six miles forever for a book?" he asked himself sadly. He began to doubt that he would ever get a library for Elsinore.

At last it happened. When he phoned the mayor, Jason was invited to the council's next meeting. The mayor told him they might find space in the town hall basement. It was just too good to be true.

### Comprehension Questions

|  |  | Points |
|---|---|---|
| (Literal) | 1. What did Jason ask his mother when he came home from school? (Did the mayor phone?) | 10 |
| (Inference) | 2. Explain how you know whether Jason lived close to or far from his school. (He didn't live close because he rode a bus to school.) | 10 |
| (Literal) | 3. What did Jason do every night? (He phoned the mayor every night.) | 10 |
| (Literal) | 4. What answer was he always given? (The council is still thinking about it.) | 10 |
| (Literal) | 5. Where did Jason want to have his library? (In the town hall basement) | 10 |
| (Literal) | 6. What did Jason do while he was waiting? (Pedaled often to the library in Monroe) | 10 |
| (Word meaning) | 7. What does "forever" mean? (Always) | 10 |
| (Literal) | 8. What finally happened? (Jason was invited to the council's next meeting. They told him they might find space in the town hall basement for his library.) | 10 |
| (Inference) | 9. How do we know Jason could hardly believe his ears. (In the story it says, "It was just too good to be true.") | 10 |
| (Main idea) | 10. What is the main idea of the story? (After Jason waits a few weeks, the mayor finally tells Jason that he might be able to use the town hall basement for his library.) | 10 |

[12]Ibid., p. 187.

Scoring Scale

| Levels | Comprehension Errors |
|---|---|
| Independent | 0–10 points |
| Instructional | 11–25 points |
| Frustration | 50 points or more |

# Level 3²

*ORAL READING (171)*[13]

> **Introduction: Read this story aloud to find out what King Midas loves. Then I will ask you questions about the story.**

Once upon a time there was a very rich king named Midas. He lived in a fine castle with his daughter, Marygold.
The two things he loved best in life were gold and Marygold.
He loved to go into his treasure room and count his coins.

No one, not even Marygold, was allowed into the king's treasure room.

One day Midas was sitting in the treasure room dreaming about his gold. In his dream, he saw a shadow fall across
the piles of valuable gold coins. He looked up and saw
a stranger standing near him. Since no one was allowed into his treasure room, Midas was surprised. The stranger looked kind, however, so Midas wasn't afraid. He greeted the man, and they began to talk of gold.

"You certainly have a lot of gold," said the stranger.

"It's not so much," said Midas.

The stranger smiled. "Do you want even more gold
than this?" he asked.

"If I had my way, everything I touched would turn
into gold," Midas replied.

### Comprehension Questions

|  |  | Points |
|---|---|---|
| (Literal) | 1. What were the two things that Midas loved best in the world? (Gold and his daughter, Marygold) | 10 |
| (Word meaning) | 2. What is the meaning of "valuable"? (Worth a lot such as gold, money, or jewelry) | 10 |
| (Literal) | 3. Where was no one allowed to go? (In the king's treasure room) | 10 |
| (Literal) | 4. What did King Midas love to do in his treasure room? (Count his coins) | 10 |
| (Inference) | 5. How do we know Midas loves gold very much? (He spends a lot of time sitting in the treasure room counting the coins. He also dreams about the gold.) | 10 |
| (Word meaning) | 6. What is a stranger? (A person who is unknown to you; someone you don't know) | 10 |
| (Literal) | 7. Where did Midas see a stranger? (In his dream while sitting in the treasure room) | 10 |

---

[13]"King Midas and the Golden Touch," retold by Judy Rosenbaum, Level 9, *On the Horizon* (Needham, MA: Silver Burdett & Ginn, 1989), pp. 130–131.

| | | |
|---|---|---|
| (Literal) | 8. Why was Midas surprised when he saw a stranger in his treasure room? (Because no one was allowed in the room) | 10 |
| (Inference) | 9. How do we know Midas is not satisfied with what he has? (Even though he is very rich and has so much gold, he says that it's not so much. He also says he'd like everything he touches to turn into gold.) | 10 |
| (Main idea) | 10. What is the main idea of the story? (Even though King Midas is very rich and has lots of gold, he thinks it's not so much.) | 10 |

## Scoring Scale

| Levels | Word Recognition Errors | Comprehension Errors |
|---|---|---|
| Independent | 0–2 | 0–10 points |
| Instructional | 3–9 | 11–25 points |
| Frustration | 17 or more | 50 points or more |

*SILENT READING*[14]

> **Introduction: The stranger tells King Midas that he will give him the Golden Touch. Everything he touches will turn to gold. Read the story to find out what happens. Then I will ask you questions about the story. Read it carefully.**

Midas was so excited that he could hardly wait until morning. At last the sun rose. Still dreaming, Midas sat up and reached for the water jug by his bed. At once it became gold. Midas was so overjoyed, he got up and danced around the room, touching everything within his reach. Soon he had a room full of gleaming gold objects. When he reached for his clothes, they turned into heavy golden cloth. "Now I shall really look like a king," he said. He got dressed and admired himself in the mirror. Midas was impressed by his golden clothes, though they were so heavy he could hardly move.

His looking glass was more of a problem. He tried to use it to see his new treasures better. To his surprise, he could not see anything through it. He put it on the table and found that it was now gold, but Midas was too excited to worry. He said, "I can see well enough without it. Besides, it is much more valuable now."

Comprehension Questions

|  |  | Points |
|---|---|---|
| (Literal) | 1. What did Midas first do after the sun rose? (He reached for the water jug.) | 10 |
| (Literal) | 2. What happened to the water jug after he touched it? (It turned to gold.) | 10 |
| (Literal) | 3. What did Midas do after the water jug turned to gold? (He got up and danced around the room, touching everything within his reach.) | 10 |
| (Literal) | 4. What happened to everything he touched? (It turned to gold.) | 10 |
| (Inference) | 5. Why were his clothes so heavy? (They too had turned to gold because he had to touch them to put them on.) | 10 |
| (Inference) | 6. Why had his looking glass become gold? (He had touched it.) | 10 |
| (Inference) | 7. Were all these things really happening to Midas? Explain. (No, Midas was dreaming it all.) | 10 |
| (Word meaning) | 8. What does "admire" mean? (To think of someone with approval and respect) | 10 |
| (Literal) | 9. What did Midas say when his looking glass turned to gold? (I can see well enough without it. Besides, it is much more valuable now.) | 10 |
| (Main idea) | 10. What is the main idea of the story? (In his dream, King Midas is very excited because everything he touches turns to gold.) | 10 |

[14]Ibid., p. 132.

Scoring Scale

| Levels | Comprehension Errors |
|--------|----------------------|
| Independent | 0–10 points |
| Instructional | 11–25 points |
| Frustration | 50 points or more |

# Level 4

*ORAL READING (187)*[15]

> **Introduction: Read this story aloud to find out how a writer begins a book for young people. Then I will ask you questions about the story.**

How does a writer such as Mr. Pinkwater begin a novel for young readers? How does he work? "When I'm beginning a new book," he states, "I am almost like an actor getting into character. I listen to music. I watch television. I talk to people. I turn up at a K-Mart store and go through all the motions of being an ordinary citizen.

"When I start a novel, all I'm really doing is waiting for the characters to show up. It's like the movie *Close Encounters of the Third Kind.* The people who have been 'selected' to be in this story show up. It is a very interesting experience."

He does not sit down and write every day. "It would be terrible if I had to work that way. I show up at my office every day in the event that something may want to happen, but if nothing happens, I don't feel that I have failed to perform. If something gets started, fair enough. If it doesn't, and I feel I've given it enough time, I go to K-Mart. I showed up, the story didn't!"

## Comprehension Questions

|  |  | Points |
|---|---|---|
| (Literal) | 1. To whom does Mr. Pinkwater compare himself when he first begins to write? (An actor) | 10 |
| (Literal) | 2. State three things Mr. Pinkwater does when he begins to write. (Listen to music, watch television, talk to people) | 10 |
| (Inference) | 3. What does listening to music, watching television, and talking to people help him do? (Get into character for his book) | 10 |
| (Literal) | 4. When he first starts writing, what is he waiting for? (For his characters to show up) | 10 |
| (Literal) | 5. What place does Mr. Pinkwater visit? (K-Mart) | 10 |
| (Word meaning) | 6. What does "ordinary" mean? (not special; usual; normal) | 10 |
| (Inference) | 7. What does Mr. Pinkwater mean when he says he goes through the motions of being an ordinary person? (He is acting; he is trying to act like the people who go shopping at K-Mart, so he can learn what it feels like.) | 10 |
| (Literal) | 8. What movie does Mr. Pinkwater refer to? (*Close Encounters of the Third Kind*) | 10 |
| (Inference) | 9. What are Mr. Pinkwater's feelings about writing every day? (He doesn't feel he has to. He doesn't feel he is a failure if he doesn't perform every day.) | 10 |
| (Main idea) | 10. What is the main idea of the story? (Mr. Pinkwater describes what he does in beginning to write a book.) | 10 |

[15]Lee Bennett Hopkins, "Daniel Manus Pinkwater," Level 10, *Silver Secrets* (Needham, MA: Silver Burdett & Ginn, 1989), p. 56.

## Scoring Scale

| Levels | Word Recognition Errors | Comprehension Errors |
|---|---|---|
| Independent | 0–2 | 0–10 points |
| Instructional | 3–9 | 11–25 points |
| Frustration | 19 or more | 50 points or more |

*SILENT READING*[16]

> Introduction: Read this story to find out how Daniel Pinkwater feels while he is writing his books. Then I will ask you questions about the story. Read it carefully.

"I love the story as it is being written. Sometimes it's as though it were happening without my doing it. I'll go to bed, excited about what's going to happen tomorrow. I know something's got to happen because I've only got 175 pages done and I've got to do more.

"To me, the beauty in writing is making the words come out as clear as a pane of glass. That I can do, and I'm rather pleased because it took me years to learn how.

"Writing for girls and boys has helped me to remember my own childhood. And since I'm writing books for a specific reader, namely myself at different ages, I've gotten more and more expert at revisiting that person within me at different ages."

He sometimes uses a computer. "The computer allows me to think in a different way. It helps me to be a better, more daring writer. Using a computer was a breakthrough for me."

Comprehension Questions

|  |  | Points |
|---|---|---|
| (Literal) | 1. What does Mr. Pinkwater love? (The story as it is being written) | 10 |
| (Literal) | 2. How does Mr. Pinkwater feel when he goes to bed after working on a story? (Excited) | 10 |
| (Inference) | 3. Why is Mr. Pinkwater excited when he goes to bed after working on his story? (He can't wait to see what will happen or how his story will turn out.) | 10 |
| (Literal) | 4. How does Mr. Pinkwater know something has to happen? (Because he only has 175 pages done and he has to do more.) | 10 |
| (Inference) | 5. What is the beauty in writing for Mr. Pinkwater? (His being able to make words come out as clear as a pane of glass) | 10 |
| (Inference) | 6. What does it mean when he says that his words are as clear as a pane of glass? (That it is easy to understand what he is saying; he gets his ideas across; his words help bring pictures to your mind.) | 10 |
| (Inference) | 7. How do we know it wasn't always easy for him to make his words as clear as a pane of glass? (He said it took him years to learn how.) | 10 |
| (Literal) | 8. What has writing for children helped him to do? (Remember his own childhood) | 10 |

[16]Ibid., pp. 56–57.

(Literal)                9. How does the computer help Mr. Pinkwater? (It allows him to think in a                10
                            different way; it helps him to be a better, more daring writer.)
(Main idea)             10. What is the main idea of the story? (Mr. Pinkwater describes what he                 10
                            does and how he feels while writing a story.)

Scoring Scale

| *Levels* | *Comprehension Errors* |
|---|---|
| Independent | 0–10 points |
| Instructional | 11–25 points |
| Frustration | 50 points or more |

# Level 5

*ORAL READING (208)*[17]

**Introduction: Read this story aloud to find out about how the Davidsons lived years ago. Then I will ask you questions about the story.**

Early in April of 1872, the Davidsons' covered wagon rolled onto their 160-acre land claim in eastern Nebraska. There was no shelter waiting for them. Like most settlers on the Great Plains, the Davidsons had to build their own shelter. At first, the family lived in the covered wagon. That was all right for a while. But by fall, they needed more protection from Nebraska's cold and windy climate.

Back east, the Davidsons had lived in a wooden farmhouse. They would have liked to build a wooden house on the Plains, too. But there wasn't a tree in sight. Lumber for building wasn't available in Nebraska, even if the family had been able to afford it.

There wasn't time for building, anyway. As farmers, the Davidsons knew they had to get on with the all-important work of plowing and planting. Only then would their new land provide enough harvest to see them through the winter.

Rabbits and foxes dig their burrows and dens in hillsides, and that's what the Davidsons did too. The settlers chose the streambank location because it was conveniently close to water. There were no building materials to buy or skilled workers to hire. After two days of digging, the Davidsons' new home was ready.

Comprehension Questions

|  |  | Points |
|---|---|---|
| (Literal) | 1. When did the Davidsons arrive at their destination? (In April of 1872) | 10 |
| (Literal) | 2. What was their destination? (A 160-acre land claim in eastern Nebraska) | 10 |
| (Literal) | 3. Where did they live when they first arrived? (In their covered wagon) | 10 |
| (Literal) | 4. Why did they live in a covered wagon? (There was no shelter waiting for them.) | 10 |
| (Inference) | 5. How do we know that the Davidsons weren't wealthy? (The story said that lumber wasn't available, even if the Davidsons could afford it. Also, they needed the harvest to see them through the winter.) | 10 |
| (Inference) | 6. During what season or seasons of the year did the Davidsons live in their covered wagon? (During the spring and summer; a student may include the beginning of fall as part of the answer. Accept this also.) | 10 |

[17]Duncan Searl, "A Sea of Grass," Level 11, *Dream Chasers* (Needham, MA: Silver Burdett & Ginn, 1989), pp. 423–424.

| | | |
|---|---|---|
| (Inference) | 7. What was the Davidsons' highest priority? (Plowing and planting) | 10 |
| (Inference) | 8. The Davidsons' home was compared to homes built by what two animals? (Rabbits and foxes) | 10 |
| (Word meaning) | 9. What is a burrow? (A hole that an animal digs in the ground) | 10 |
| (Main idea) | 10. What is the main idea of the story? (The Davidsons' only choice to survive the cold and windy climate was for them, themselves, to dig a home in the hillside like the rabbits and foxes.) | 10 |

Scoring Scale

| Levels | Word Recognition Errors | Comprehension Errors |
|---|---|---|
| Independent | 0–2 | 0–10 points |
| Instructional | 3–10 | 11–25 points |
| Frustration | 21 or more | 50 points or more |

*SILENT READING*[18]

**Introduction: Read this story to find out more about how the Davidsons lived years ago. Then I will ask you questions about the story. Read it carefully.**

Most people believe in the old saying, "There's no place like home." The Davidsons, however, might not have felt that way about their dugout. The cramped dwelling was damp and dark, even on sunny days. Dirt from the roof sifted down into bedding and food. Insects and snakes were constant house guests.

Hoping their new shelter would be a temporary one, the Davidsons began to plow and plant. But this wasn't as easy as they had expected. In the early 1870s, more than a foot of thick sod covered almost every inch of the territory. Held together by a mass of tangled roots, this sod was almost impossible to cut through. It could take weeks to plow a single acre. Settlers like the Davidsons became known as "sodbusters."

The sod's toughness gave the settlers an idea. Why not build with it? The new fields were covered with long ribbons of sod that had been plowed up. It would be a simple matter to cut these into smaller pieces and use them as building blocks. The settlers even had a nickname for this unusual building material—"Nebraska marble."

Comprehension Questions

|  |  | Points |
|---|---|---|
| (Literal) | 1. What is the saying that most people believe in? (There's no place like home.) | 10 |
| (Inference) | 2. How would the Davidsons feel about the saying "There's no place like home"? (They would not agree because they lived in a dugout that was not very comfortable.) | 10 |
| (Literal) | 3. State three problems with their dugout. (It was cramped, damp, and dark; dirt from the roof sifted down into bedding and food; and so on.) | 10 |
| (Literal) | 4. Who were the Davidsons' constant guests? (Insects and snakes) | 10 |
| (Inference) | 5. How long had the Davidsons planned on staying in their dugout? (Not long; they hoped their new shelter would be a temporary one.) | 10 |
| (Word meaning) | 6. What is the meaning of "temporary"? (Lasting for a short time; not permanent) | 10 |
| (Literal) | 7. What covered almost every inch of the Davidsons' territory? (More than a foot of thick sod) | 10 |
| (Inference) | 8. Why were the settlers known as "sodbusters"? (Because it was very hard to cut through the sod; however, they did, even though it could take weeks to plow one acre.) | 10 |
| (Literal) | 9. What idea did the sod's toughness give the settlers? (To build with it) | 10 |
| (Main idea) | 10. What is the main idea of the story? (The Davidsons, unhappy with their dugout, come up with the idea to use the tough sod for building material.) | 10 |

[18]Ibid., p. 425.

Scoring Scale

| Levels | Comprehension Errors |
|---|---|
| Independent | 0–10 points |
| Instructional | 11–25 points |
| Frustration | 50 points or more |

# Level 6

*ORAL READING (252)*[19]

**Introduction: Read this story aloud to find out what is special about the Monterey Bay Aquarium. Then I will ask you questions about the story.**

You walk through the door—and immediately freeze. Overhead, to your left, a thresher shark whips its tail. To your right are three huge killer whales. Have you wandered into a nightmare? Hardly. You've just entered the Monterey Bay Aquarium.

The shark and whales, lifesize and hanging from the ceiling, are fiberglass. The other 6,000 creatures you'll meet are not. On a visit to the aquarium, on the shores of California's Monterey Bay, you'll have a chance not only to see them swim, scurry, hunt, and court, but to pick up and handle a few as well.

One of the aquarium's most spectacular exhibits is the three-story-high kelp forest—the world's only kelp forest growing indoors. Clinging to the bottom with a rootlike "holdfast," the yellow-brown kelp reaches up through 28 feet of water, spreading out on the tank's sunlit surface. With "stipes" instead of trunks, and "blades" in place of leaves, the kelp forest resembles an underwater redwood grove. Sunbeams slant down from above, while the kelp sways gently back and forth. With a patient eye, you will begin to spot some of the many creatures that call the kelp forest home.

Long-legged brittle stars and crabs can be seen within the tangled holdfast. Watch for turban snails higher up. The fish of the kelp forest aren't as fast as those of the open ocean, but they're better at playing hide-and-seek. Special air sacs allow some of them to hover in hiding within the maze of blades. Many are completely camouflaged.

## Comprehension Questions

|  |  | Points |
|---|---|---|
| (Literal) | 1. What do you first see when you walk through the door of the Monterey Bay Aquarium? (Overhead to your left a thresher shark and to your right three huge killer whales) | 10 |
| (Inference) | 2. Why would you immediately freeze when you first walk through the door? (Because the thresher shark and three killer whales must look very real, but they aren't.) | 10 |
| (Literal) | 3. How many real creatures are there in the aquarium? (6,000) | 10 |
| (Word meaning) | 4. What does "spectacular" mean? (Of or like a remarkable sight; showy; striking) | 10 |
| (Literal) | 5. What is one of the aquarium's most remarkable exhibits? (The three-story-high kelp forest) | 10 |
| (Inference) | 6. Why is the kelp forest so remarkable? (It's the world's only indoor kelp forest.) | 10 |
| (Literal) | 7. What does the kelp forest resemble? (An underwater redwood grove) | 10 |
| (Inference) | 8. Why are the fish in the kelp forest better at playing hide-and-seek? (They can hover in hiding within the maze of blades so that they blend in with the blades; they are completely camouflaged.) | 10 |
| (Literal) | 9. What allows some of the fish to hover in hiding? (Special air sacs) | 10 |
| (Main idea) | 10. What is the main idea of the story? (The Monterey Sea Aquarium is a very unusual aquarium that houses the world's only kelp forest growing indoors.) | 10 |

[19]Paul Fleischman, "The Monterey Bay Aquarium," Level 12, *Wind by the Sea* (Needham, MA: Silver Burdett & Ginn, 1989), pp. 395–396.

Scoring Scale

| Levels | Word Recognition Errors | Comprehension Errors |
|---|---|---|
| Independent | 0–3 | 0–10 points |
| Instructional | 4–13 | 11–25 points |
| Frustration | 25 or more | 50 points or more |

*SILENT READING*[20]

**Introduction: Read this story to find out about one of the Monterey Bay Aquarium's residents. Then I will ask you questions about the story. Read it carefully.**

Among the animals who depend on the kelp are the aquarium's most playful residents, the sea otters. Floating on their backs, doing somersaults in the water, taking part in high-speed games of tag, these smallest of the marine mammals charm every audience.

Their two-story tank lets you view them from above as well as from below the water's surface. In the wild, though, their home is the kelp beds. They live on creatures who live on the kelp. They depend on it for shelter during storms. Before sleeping, they wrap themselves in it to keep from drifting out to sea.

Why are otters so playful? No one knows, though part of the answer might lie in the fact that their constant motion helps to keep them warm. Unlike the whales and other marine mammals, otters have no layer of blubber between their warm-blooded insides and the cold water outside. So they move around a lot, which requires a lot of energy, which in turn requires a lot of eating. Could you eat 25 hamburgers a day? That's the equivalent of what an otter swallows, eating up to one-quarter of its body weight daily. If you're present at feeding time, you'll be amazed at how much fish, squid, and abalone an otter can eat. Wild otters eat so many purple sea urchins that their bones eventually turn purplish as well.

Otters have another defense against the cold—their coats. When you touch the soft sample of fur on the wall by their tank, you'll understand why they were hunted until they were nearly extinct.

Comprehension Questions

| | | Points |
|---|---|---|
| (Literal) | 1. What animals are the aquarium's most playful residents? (The sea otters) | 10 |
| (Literal) | 2. How do the sea otters charm audiences? (They float on their backs, do somersaults, and play high-speed games of tag.) | 10 |
| (Literal) | 3. Where do the otters live in the aquarium? (In a two-story tank) | 10 |
| (Literal) | 4. Where do the otters live in the wild? (In the kelp beds) | 10 |
| (Literal) | 5. What is the reason given for the otter's playfulness? (Their constant motion keeps them warm.) | 10 |
| (Inference) | 6. Why do the otters have to move around a lot to keep warm? (The otters have no layer of blubber between their warm-blooded insides and the cold water outside.) | 10 |
| (Inference) | 7. What is the effect of the great amount of movement? (The otters have to eat a lot because they use up a lot of energy; they eat one-quarter of their body weight daily.) | 10 |
| (Word meaning) | 8. What does "extinct" mean? (No longer existing; no longer living; having died out) | 10 |
| (Inference) | 9. Why were otters hunted until they almost didn't exist anymore? (For their fur; it is very soft.) | 10 |
| (Main idea) | 10. What is the main idea of the story? (The sea otters are the most playful aquarium residents because they need to move around a lot to keep warm.) | 10 |

Scoring Scale

| Levels | Comprehension Errors |
|---|---|
| Independent | 0–10 points |
| Instructional | 11–25 points |
| Frustration | 50 points or more |

[20]Ibid., p. 397.

# Level 7

*ORAL READING (263)*[21]

**Introduction: Read this story aloud to find out what some courageous children do. (Etienne is pronounced ā-tyen'.) Then I will ask you questions about the story.**

The voice came from out of the sky, "Hey fellows, quick, grab those ropes and pull me into the wind as if I were a kite. Hurry!"

Looking up, the young people were startled to see a man waving wildly at them from a strange banana-shaped flying balloon—a balloon that was about to crash!

Sara reacted quickly and grabbed one of the ropes that dangled near her. But Sara could not even stop the flying contraption, let alone pull it in the other direction. As she attempted to dig her heels into the ground, the balloon nearly toppled her.

"Boys, don't just stand there. Help her," the man in the balloon shouted at Etienne and Louis.

Rushing to help their sister, the boys grabbed other ropes trailing from the balloon and frantically tugged at the runaway flying machine. Finally, the three of them were able to change the direction of the balloon, carrying it into the wind as the aeronaut had requested. The flying machine bobbed up like a kite.

As the young people pulled the balloon down, following the aeronaut's instructions, a crowd began to gather. The moment the flier was safe on the ground, he was surrounded by a large crowd of curious people, all talking at once.

Sara realized that the man she had rescued was the famous Monsieur Santos-Dumont, the wealthy Brazilian inventor and daredevil who predicted people would someday fly like birds.

"Where are the young people? They are the real heroes of this escape from the jaws of death," she heard him shout over the crowd.

## Comprehension Questions

|  |  | *Points* |
|---|---|---|
| (Literal) | 1. Describe what the children saw when they looked up in the sky. (A strange banana-shaped balloon that was about to crash) | 10 |
| (Inference) | 2. How do we know the person in the balloon didn't expect the girl to help him? (He called out to the fellows.) | 10 |
| (Literal) | 3. What did he want the fellows to do? (To grab the ropes and pull him into the wind as if he were a kite) | 10 |
| (Literal) | 4. What happened when Sara tried to help? (She couldn't stop the balloon, let alone pull it in the other direction.) | 10 |
| (Word meaning) | 5. What is an aeronaut? (Someone who navigates in the air, especially a balloon) | 10 |
| (Inference) | 6. What was needed to keep the balloon afloat? (The force of the wind) | 10 |
| (Inference) | 7. What did the young people have to be able to do to pull down the balloon? (Follow the aeronaut's directions) | 10 |
| (Inference) | 8. What kind of person was Monsieur Santo-Dumont? State four characteristics. Give proof for your answer. (Creative—the story said he was an inventor; reckless, adventurous—it said he was a daredevil; well-known—it said he was famous; rich—it said he was wealthy.) | 10 |
| (Literal) | 9. What did Monsieur Santos-Dumont predict people would someday be able to do? (Fly like birds) | 10 |

---

[21]David Fulton, "Through Skies Never Sailed," Level 13, *Star Walk* (Needham, MA: Silver Burdett & Ginn, 1989), pp. 353–354.

(Main idea)  10. What is the main idea of the story? (A courageous girl and her brothers   10
rescue an aeronaut by helping to bring his flying balloon safely to
the ground.)

### Scoring Scale

| Levels | Word Recognition Errors | Comprehension Errors |
|---|---|---|
| Independent | 0–3 | 0–10 points |
| Instructional | 4–13 | 11–25 points |
| Frustration | 26 or more | 50 points or more |

*SILENT READING*[22]

**Introduction: Monsieur Santos-Dumont is very grateful to the children for saving his life. Read the story to see why he comes to the children's home. Then I will ask you questions about the story. Read it carefully.**

"The purpose of my visit in fact is related to the events of this afternoon. I came to invite your family for an excursion in one of my balloons."

Silence filled the Cote parlor as all eyes turned to Sara's father, awaiting his reply. "I don't wish to seem overly conservative or closed minded, Monsieur Santos-Dumont, but I wouldn't consider air travel sufficiently safe to risk my whole family. This afternoon's events are evidence of that."

"I certainly wouldn't ask you to endanger your family, but flying in a balloon, which is merely a big bag filled with hydrogen, has long been demonstrated to be a safe sport.

"I wouldn't suggest taking you in a craft such as the one I was flying this afternoon. That was a 'dirigible.' Its design is the latest breakthrough in the attempt to control the direction of flight. It's a balloon that has a gasoline engine suspended beneath it to direct its movement. Unfortunately, my colleagues and I have yet to work out all the problems. But we will. In any case, the dirigible may soon be obsolete. I recently heard a report at a meeting of the Aero Club, and I understand that some Americans have actually built a glider of some sort that is heavier than the air, and it is said they use a gasoline engine to power it. Now, that is really incredible."

Comprehension Questions

|  |  | *Points* |
|---|---|---|
| (Literal) | 1. What was the purpose of Monsieur Santos-Dumont's visit to the children's family? (To invite them on an excursion in one of his balloons) | 10 |
| (Word meaning) | 2. What is an excursion? (A short pleasure trip) | 10 |
| (Literal) | 3. How does the children's father feel about air travel? (He feels it is not safe.) | 10 |
| (Inference) | 4. What evidence does the children's father give to back up his feelings? (The afternoon's events) | 10 |
| (Literal) | 5. What does Monsieur Santos-Dumont claim is safe? (Flying in a balloon filled with hydrogen) | 10 |
| (Literal) | 6. What kind of machine was Monsieur Santos-Dumont flying in the afternoon? (A dirigible, which has a gasoline engine suspended beneath it to direct its movement) | 10 |
| (Inference) | 7. How do we know Monsieur Santos-Dumont is not working alone on developing the dirigible? (The story says that he and his colleagues have yet to work out the details.) | 10 |
| (Literal) | 8. What does Monsieur Santos-Dumont feel is incredible? (The glider that the Americans have built, which is heavier than air and uses a gasoline engine to power it) | 10 |
| (Inference) | 9. What does Monsieur Santos-Dumont feel the Americans' flying machine will do to the dirigible? (Make the dirigible obsolete, that is, no longer useful or in use) | 10 |
| (Main idea) | 10. What is the main idea of the story? (Monsieur Santos-Dumont tries to persuade the children's father to allow his family to go on a short trip in a balloon Monsieur Santos-Dumont insists is safe.) | 10 |

Scoring Scale

| *Levels* | *Comprehension Errors* |
|---|---|
| Independent | 0–10 points |
| Instructional | 11–25 points |
| Frustration | 50 points or more |

[22]Ibid., p. 356.

# Level 8

*ORAL READING (275)*[23]

**Introduction: Read this story aloud to find out why Lo Tung came to America. Then I will ask you questions about the story.**

Lo Tung leaned against the rattling wall of the freight car. Beneath him the floor moved as the wheels cracked over the rails. It was a long time since he'd sat or walked on anything steady. First there had been the long days and nights on the Pacific Mail Steamship that had brought him from China, then the riverboat from San Francisco to Sacramento, then the train, waiting on the levee.

He hadn't had time for more than a glimpse of the strange, iron monster belching smoke before the boss man had hustled them aboard. It was hard to believe that he was here now, in this freight car along with other Chinese workers, rolling eastward across America.

Lo Tung looked sideways at his friend, Wei. Wei was fifteen years old, too, and as small and thin as Lo Tung.

"Not more than a hundred pounds, either of you," the agent had said in disgust. "You two will not be able to do the heavy railroad work."

"Don't worry. We are strong," Lo Tung had said. He had not added, "Ho Sen was strong, the strongest man in our village. And he was killed building the American railway." Now Ho Sen's bones lay somewhere in this strange country. And Chen Chi Yuen. He had gone and never been heard from again.

Sitting now in the freight car, thinking about the work, Lo Tung flexed his muscles. Strong for the work. Of course, strong and fearless.

It was growing dark. They had been closed in here together for hours, so many of them from the ship. The air was used up and the smells were bad.

## Comprehension Questions

| | | Points |
|---|---|---|
| (Literal) | 1. What kind of car was Lo Tung in? (A freight car) | 10 |
| (Inference) | 2. How do we know Lo Tung has never seen a train before? (Lo Tung thought the locomotive was a strange, iron monster. It wouldn't have been strange if he had seen it before.) | 10 |
| (Inference) | 3. How do we know it has been a long time since Lo Tung was on land? (The story states that it was a long time since he was on anything steady.) | 10 |
| (Literal) | 4. What means of transportation was used to get Lo Tung to his destination? (Steamship, riverboat, and train) | 10 |
| (Inference) | 5. How long did Lo Tung have between getting off the riverboat and boarding the train? (Not long; he only had time to catch a glimpse of the train before he was hustled aboard.) | 10 |
| (Literal) | 6. What was the agent concerned about? (That Lo Tung and his friend were too thin to work on the railroad) | 10 |
| (Literal) | 7. What had happened to Ho Sen? (He had been killed working on the American railroad.) | 10 |
| (Inference) | 8. Why were the smells on the freight train bad? (There was not much air, and there were many people crowded together.) | 10 |
| (Literal) | 9. In what direction was the train rolling across America? (Eastward) | 10 |
| (Main idea) | 10. What is the main idea of the story? (Lo Tung's journey from China to America to work on the American railroad has been long and hard.) | 10 |

[23]Eve Bunting, "It's Not the Great Wall, But It Will Last Forever," Level 14, *Worlds Beyond* (Needham, MA: Silver Burdett & Ginn, 1989), pp. 238–239.

Scoring Scale

| Levels | Word Recognition Errors | Comprehension Errors |
|---|---|---|
| Independent | 0–3 | 0–10 points |
| Instructional | 4–14 | 11–20 points |
| Frustration | 28 or more | 50 points or more |

*SILENT READING*[24]

**Introduction: Agents had advertised in Lo Tung's village for laborers to help build the railroad in California. They offered houses to live in, plenty of food, and thirty dollars a month. The passage to go was fifty-four dollars. Read the story to find out why Lo Tung signed on. Then I will ask you questions about the story. Read it carefully.**

Fifty-four dollars was a fortune, and impossible for his mother! The agent had allowed them to borrow from him. That was when he'd complained of Lo Tung's size.

"Not a penny of your wages will be yours till you pay me back," he had warned.

Lo Tung had agreed. He would have agreed to almost anything. Not that he wanted to go to America. The thought of leaving his home brought tears to his eyes. But it was clearly his duty. He was, after all, the eldest son. Since his father's death the family responsibility had been his. If he went, his debt to the agent would be cleared in two months. Then he could begin sending money home for his mother and his sisters, and his little brother. He had to believe that he could save enough to go home himself some day.

Thinking of home here in the heat of the freight car made loneliness rise in him like water in a swamp. Fear was bad, but loneliness was worse. He would not allow himself to remember.

"We are slowing," Wei said. "I can see through a crack."

Someone else announced, "We are here."

Tired men and boys staggered up, swaying, hoisting their bedrolls. As the train chugged to a stop they waited quietly for what was to come.

When the doors opened Lo Tung saw that it was night outside, the sky filled with a million crystal stars.

"American stars," he whispered to Wei, pointing upward.

"Are they the same that shine over China or …"

"Out! Everyone out!" Men waited beside the train, big, bulky men who cast massive shadows.

"Hurry! Get a move on!"

The words were not in Lo Tung's language but he understood the tone.

Comprehension Questions

|  |  | Points |
|---|---|---|
| (Literal) | 1. How were Lo Tung and his mother able to get enough money for Lo Tung to go to America? (The agent had allowed them to borrow from him.) | 10 |
| (Inference) | 2. Why was Lo Tung going to America? (Because his family needed the money; he couldn't earn the money they needed in his village.) | 10 |
| (Inference) | 3. Why did he feel he had to support his family? (Because his father was dead and he was the eldest son) | 10 |
| (Literal) | 4. How long would it take to clear his debt to the agent? (Two months) | 10 |
| (Inference) | 5. Does Lo Tung expect to stay in America? Explain. (No, the story states that he had to believe that he could save enough to go home himself some day.) | 10 |
| (Literal) | 6. What does Lo Tung feel is worse than fear? (Loneliness) | 10 |
| (Inference) | 7. What simile is used to describe Lo Tung's loneliness? Explain the simile. (Loneliness rose in him like water in a swamp; when it rains, water in a swamp rises very quickly, and that's how fast his loneliness rose.) | 10 |
| (Inference) | 8. How do we know it was a clear night when they arrived at their destination? (The sky was filled with a million crystal stars.) | 10 |

[24]Ibid., p. 240.

(Literal)         9. What kind of men were waiting beside the train? (Big, bulky men who cast massive shadows)    10

(Main idea)      10. What is the main idea of the story? (Even though Lo Tung does not want to leave his family, he goes to America so he can earn money for his family in China.)    10

Scoring Scale

| Levels | Comprehension Errors |
|---|---|
| Independent | 0–10 points |
| Instructional | 11–20 points |
| Frustration | 50 points or more |

# Appendix C

## Teacher's Resource Guide of Language Transfer Issues for English Language Learners

The following chart identifies areas in which speakers of various primary languages may have some difficulty in acquiring English grammar (syntax). The type of transfer error and its cause is outlined for each grammatical category.[1]

### NOUNS

| Grammar Point | Type of Transfer Error in English | Language Background | Cause of Transfer Difficulty |
|---|---|---|---|
| **Plural forms** | omission of plural marker -*s*<br>*I have 5 book.* | Cantonese, Haitian Creole, Hmong, Khmer, Korean, Tagalog, Vietnamese | Nouns do not change form to show the plural in the primary language. |
| **Possessive forms** | avoidance of 's to describe possession<br>*the children of my sister* instead of *my sister's children* | Haitian Creole, Hmong, Khmer, Spanish, Tagalog, Vietnamese | The use of a prepositional phrase to express possession reflects the only structure or a more common structure in the primary language. |
| | no marker for possessive forms<br>*house my friend* instead of *my friend's house* | Haitian Creole, Khmer, Vietnamese | A noun's owner comes after the object in the primary language. |
| **Count versus noncount nouns** | use of plural forms for English noncount nouns<br>*the furniture<u>s</u>, the color of her hair<u>s</u>* | Haitian Creole, Russian, Spanish, Tagalog | Nouns that are count and noncount differ between English and the primary language. |

[1]Charts from "Teacher's Resource Guide of Language Transfer Issues for English Language Learners" in the series *On Our Way to English,* copyright © 2004 Harcourt Achieve, Inc. Reprinted by permission of the publisher.

## ARTICLES

| Grammar Point | Type of Transfer Error in English | Language Background | Cause of Transfer Difficulty |
|---|---|---|---|
| | omission of article<br>*He has job.*<br>*His dream is to become lawyer, not teacher.* | Cantonese, Haitian Creole, Hmong, Khmer, Korean, Russian, Tagalog, Vietnamese | Articles are either lacking or the distinction between *a* and *the* is not paralleled in the primary language. |
| | omission of articles in certain contexts such as to identify a profession<br>*He is teacher.* | Spanish | The article is not used in Spanish in this context, but it is needed in English. |
| | overuse of articles<br>*The honesty is the best policy.*<br>*This food is popular in the Japan.*<br>*I like the cats.* | Arabic, Haitian Creole, Hmong, Spanish, Tagalog | The article is used in the primary language in places where it isn't used in English. |
| | use of <u>one</u> for *a/an*<br>*He is <u>one</u> engineer.* | Haitian Creole, Hmong, Vietnamese | Learners sometimes confuse the articles *a/an* with *one* since articles either do not exist in the primary language or serve a different function. |

## PRONOUNS

| Grammar Point | Type of Transfer Error in English | Language Background | Cause of Transfer Difficulty |
|---|---|---|---|
| **Personal pronouns, gender** | use of pronouns with inappropriate gender<br>*<u>He</u> is my sister.* | Cantonese, Haitian Creole, Hmong, Khmer, Korean, Tagalog | The third person pronoun in the primary language is gender free. The same pronoun is used where English uses masculine, feminine, and neuter pronouns, resulting in confusion of pronoun forms in English. |
| | use of pronouns with inappropriate gender<br>*<u>He</u> is my sister.* | Spanish | In Spanish, subject pronouns are dropped in everyday speech and the verb conveys third-person agreement, effectively collapsing the two pronouns and causing transfer difficulty for subject pronouns in English. |
| | use of inappropriate gender, particularly with neuter nouns<br>*The house is big. <u>She</u> is beautiful.* | Russian, Spanish | Inanimate nouns have feminine and masculine gender in the primary language, and the gender may be carried over into English. |

## PRONOUNS (*continued*)

| Grammar Point | Type of Transfer Error in English | Language Background | Cause of Transfer Difficulty |
|---|---|---|---|
| **Personal pronoun forms** | confusion of subject and object pronoun forms <br> *Him* hit me. <br> I like *she.* <br> Let *we* go. | Cantonese, Hmong, Khmer | The same pronoun form is used for *he/him, she/her,* and in some primary languages for *I/me and we/us.* |
| | use of incorrect number for pronouns <br> *I saw many yellow flowers. It was pretty.* | Cantonese, Korean | There is no number agreement in the primary language. |
| | omission of subject pronouns <br> *Michael isn't here. Is in school.* | Korean, Russian, Spanish | Subject pronouns may be dropped in the primary language and the verb ending supplies information on number and/or gender. |
| | omission of object pronouns <br> *That man is very rude, so nobody likes.* | Korean, Vietnamese | Direct objects are frequently dropped in the primary language. |
| | omission of pronouns in clauses <br> *If not have jobs, they will not have food.* | Cantonese, Vietnamese | A subordinate clause at the beginning of a sentence does not require a subject in the primary language. |
| | use of pronouns with subject nouns <br> *This car, it runs very fast.* <br> *Your friend, he seems so nice.* <br> *My parents, they live in Vietnam.* | Hmong, Vietnamese | This type of redundant structure reflects the popular "topic-comment" approach used in the primary language: The speaker mentions a topic and then makes a comment on it. |
| | avoidance of pronouns by repetition of nouns <br> *Sara visits her grandfather every Sunday, and Sara makes a meal.* | Korean, Vietnamese | It is common in the primary language to repeat nouns rather than to use pronouns. |
| **Pronoun *one*** | omission of the pronoun *one* <br> *I saw two nice cars, and I like the small.* | Russian, Spanish, Tagalog | Adjectives can be used on their own in the primary language, whereas English often requires a noun or *one.* |
| **Possessive forms** | confusion of possessive forms <br> *The book is my.* | Cantonese, Hmong, Vietnamese | Cantonese and Hmong speakers tend to omit final *n,* creating confusion between *my* and *mine.* |

## ADJECTIVES

| Grammar Point | Type of Transfer Error in English | Language Background | Cause of Transfer Difficulty |
|---|---|---|---|
| | position of adjectives after nouns<br>*I read a book interesting.* | Haitian Creole, Hmong, Khmer, Spanish, Vietnamese | Adjectives commonly come after nouns in the primary language. |
| | position of adjectives before certain pronouns<br>*This is interesting something.* | Cantonese, Korean | Adjectives always come before words they modify in the primary language. |
| **Comparison** | omission of markers for comparison<br>*She is smart than me.* | Khmer | Since there are no suffixes or inflections in Khmer, the tendency is to omit them in English. |
| | avoidance of *-er* and *-est* endings<br>*I am more old than my brother.* | Hmong, Khmer, Korean, Spanish | Comparative and superlative are usually formed with separate words in the primary language, the equivalent of *more* and *most* in English. |
| **Confusion of *-ing* and *-ed* forms** | confusion of *-ing* and *-ed* forms<br>*The movie was <u>bored</u>.*<br>*I am very <u>interesting</u> in sports.* | Cantonese, Khmer, Korean, Spanish | The adjective forms in the primary language that correspond to the ones in English do not have active and passive meanings. In Korean, for many adjectives, the same form is used for both active and passive meanings *boring* versus *bored*. |

## VERBS

| Grammar Point | Type of Transfer Error in English | Language Background | Cause of Transfer Difficulty |
|---|---|---|---|
| **Present tense** | Omission of *s* in present tense, third person agreement<br>*She <u>go</u> to school every day.* | Cantonese, Haitian Creole, Hmong, Khmer, Korean, Tagalog, Vietnamese | There is no verb agreement in the primary language. |
| | problems with irregular subject-verb agreement<br>*Sue and Ed <u>has</u> a new house.* | Cantonese, Hmong, Khmer, Korean, Tagalog | Verbs forms do not change to indicate the number of the subject in the primary language. |
| **Past tense** | omission of tense markers<br>*I <u>study</u> English yesterday.*<br>*I <u>give</u> it to him yesterday.* | Cantonese, Haitian Creole, Hmong, Khmer, Korean, Tagalog, Vietnamese | Verbs in the primary language do not change form to express tense. |

**VERBS** *(continued)*

| Grammar Point | Type of Transfer Error in English | Language Background | Cause of Transfer Difficulty |
|---|---|---|---|
| | confusion of present form and simple past of regular verbs<br>*I give it to him yesterday.* | Cantonese, Spanish | Speakers of the primary language have difficulty recognizing that merely a vowel shift in the middle of the verb, rather than a change in the ending of the verb, is sufficient to produce a change of tense in irregular verbs. |
| | incorrect use of present for the future<br>*I come tomorrow.* | Cantonese, Korean | The primary language allows the use of present tense for the future. |
| **In negative statements** | omission of helping verbs in negative statements<br>*I no understand.*<br>*I not get in university.* | Cantonese, Korean, Russian, Spanish, Tagalog | Helping verbs are not used in negative statements in the primary language. |
| **Perfect tenses** | avoidance of present perfect where it should be used<br>*I live here for two years.* | Haitian Creole, Russian, Tagalog, Vietnamese | The verb form either doesn't exist in the primary language or has a different function. |
| | use of present perfect where past perfect should be used<br>*Yesterday I have done that.* | Khmer, Korean | In the primary language, a past marker, e.g., *yesterday,* is inserted to indicate a completed action and no other change is necessary. In English, when a past marker is used, the verb form must change to past perfect instead of present perfect. |
| **Past continuous** | use of past continuous for recurring action in the past<br>*When I was young, I was studying a lot.* | Korean, Spanish, Tagalog | In the primary language, the past continuous form can be used in contexts in which English uses the expression *used to* or the simple past. |
| **Main verb** | omission of main verb<br>*Criticize people not good.* | Cantonese | Unlike English, Cantonese does not require an infinitive marker when using a verb as a noun. |
| | use of two or more main verbs in one clause without any connectors<br>*I took a book went studied at the library.* | Hmong | In Hmong, verbs can be connected without *and* or any other conjunction (serial verbs). |

*(continued)*

## VERBS *(Continued)*

| Grammar Point | Type of Transfer Error in English | Language Background | Cause of Transfer Difficulty |
|---|---|---|---|
| **Linking verbs** | omission of linking verb<br>*He hungry.* | Cantonese, Haitian Creole, Hmong, Khmer, Russian, Vietnamese | The verb *be* is not required in all sentences. In some primary languages, it is implied in the adjective form. In others, the concept is expressed as a verb. |
| **Passive voice** | Omission of helping verb *be* in passive voice<br>*The food finished.* | Cantonese, Vietnamese | Passive voice in the primary language does not require a helping verb. |
| | avoidance of passive constructions<br>*They speak Creole here.*<br>*One speaks Creole here.*<br><br>avoiding the alternate<br>*Creole is spoken here.* | Haitian Creole | Passive constructions do not exist in Haitian Creole. |
| **Transitive verbs versus intransitive verbs** | confusion of transitive and intransitive verbs<br>*He married with a nice girl.* | Cantonese, Korean, Russian, Spanish, Tagalog | Verbs that do and do not take a direct object differ between English and the primary language. |
| **Phrasal verbs** | confusion of related phrasal verbs<br>*I look after the word in the dictionary.*<br>instead of *I look up the word in the dictionary.* | Korean, Russian, Spanish | Phrasal verbs do not exist in the primary language. There is often confusion over their meaning in English. |
| ***have* versus *be*** | use of *have* instead of *be*<br>*I have hunger.*<br>*I have right.* | Spanish | Some Spanish constructions use *have* where English uses *be*. |

## ADVERBS

| Grammar Point | Type of Transfer Error in English | Language Background | Cause of Transfer Difficulty |
|---|---|---|---|
| | use of adjective form where adverb form is needed<br>*Walk quiet.* | Haitian Creole, Hmong, Khmer | There are no suffix-derived adverb forms in the primary language, and the adjective form is used after the verb. |
| | placement of adverbs before verbs<br>*At ten o'clock this morning my plane landed.*<br>avoiding the alternate, My *plane landed at ten o'clock this morning.* | Cantonese, Korean | Adverbs usually come before verbs in the primary language, and this tendency is carried over into English. |

## PREPOSITIONS

| Grammar Point | Type of Transfer Error in English | Language Background | Cause of Transfer Difficulty |
|---|---|---|---|
| | omission of prepositions<br><br>*Money does not grow trees.* | Cantonese | There are no exact equivalents of English prepositions in Cantonese although there are words to mark location and movement. |

## COMPLEX SENTENCES

| Grammar Point | Type of Transfer Error in English | Language Background | Cause of Transfer Difficulty |
|---|---|---|---|
| **Relative clauses** | Omission of relative pronouns<br><br>*My grandfather was a generous man helped everyone.* | Vietnamese | Relative pronouns are not required in Vietnamese. |
| | incorrect pronoun used to introduce a relative clause<br><br>*the house <u>who</u> is big* | Hmong | Hmong uses the same forms of relative pronouns for both personal and inanimate antecedents. |
| **Adverbial clauses** | inclusion of additional connecting word<br><br>*Because he was reckless, <u>so</u> he caused an accident.*<br><br>*Although my parents are poor, <u>but</u> they are very generous.* | Cantonese, Korean, Vietnamese | The primary language sometimes uses a "balancing word" in the main clause. |
| | use of incorrect tenses in time clauses<br><br>*She <u>speaks</u> French before she studied English.*<br><br>*After she <u>comes</u> home, it was raining.*<br><br>*We will go to the beach if the weather <u>will be</u> nice.* | Cantonese, Hmong, Tagalog, Vietnamese | The primary language lacks tense markers so that matching the tenses of two verbs in one sentence correctly can be difficult. Learners may also try to analyze the tense needed in English according to meaning, which in some cases can result in the use of an incorrect tense. |
| ***If* versus *when*** | Confusion of *if* and *when*<br><br>*if you get there, call me!*<br><br>instead of *When you get there, call me!* | Korean, Tagalog | The primary language has one expression that covers the use of English *if* and *when* for the future. |

## INFINITIVES AND GERUNDS

| Grammar Point | Type of Transfer Error in English | Language Background | Cause of Transfer Difficulty |
|---|---|---|---|
| | use of present tense verbs in places where gerunds or infinitives are used in English<br><br>*Stop <u>walk</u>.*<br><br>*I want <u>go</u> there.* | Haitian, Creole, Khmer, Korean | Either the *-ing* form does not exist in the primary language, or learners tend to use present tense verbs instead of gerunds even if they do exist [Haitian Creole]. |
| | use of *for* in infinitive phrases<br><br>*They went <u>for</u> to see the movie.* | Spanish | Spanish uses a prepositional form in similar constructions, which is carried over into English and translated as *for*. |

## SENTENCE STRUCTURE

| Grammar Point | Type of Transfer Error in English | Language Background | Cause of Transfer Difficulty |
|---|---|---|---|
| | omission of object<br><br>*He dyed [his hair].*<br><br>*Yes, I want [some].* | Korean | Korean tends to omit objects and noun phrases after verbs. |
| | lack of variety in the position of clauses<br><br>*Because you weren't at home and I couldn't find [you], I left.*<br><br>avoiding the alternate, *I left because you weren't at home and I couldn't find [you].* | Korean | Since main clauses always come last in Korean, there is a tendency to put the main clause last in English. This is not an error in English, but it leads to a lack of sentence variety. |
| | clauses that describe earlier actions come first<br><br>*After I finish my homework, I will watch TV.*<br><br>avoiding the alternate, *I will watch TV after I finish my homework.* | Cantonese, Korean | The pattern in the primary language is to describe what happens first while later occurrences follow. This is not an error in English, but it leads to a lack of sentence variety. |
| | placement of phrase with the indirect object before the direct object<br><br>*They gave <u>to the girl</u> the book.* | Spanish | The phrase with the indirect object can come before the direct object in Spanish. |
| | placement of modifiers between verb and direct object<br><br>*She speaks <u>very well</u> English.* | Korean, Spanish | Word order, including the placement of adverbials, is freer in the primary language than in English. |

## SENTENCE STRUCTURE *(Continued)*

| Grammar Point | Type of Transfer Error in English | Language Background | Cause of Transfer Difficulty |
|---|---|---|---|
| | use of double negatives <br> *I no see nobody.* | Spanish | Spanish requires double negatives in many sentence structures. |
| | use of clauses for other structures <br> *I want that you help me.* | Russian, Spanish | Verbs that take direct objects versus those that require clauses differ in the primary language and English. |

## QUESTIONS

| Grammar Point | Type of Transfer Error in English | Language Background | Cause of Transfer Difficulty |
|---|---|---|---|
| | avoidance of English inverted question forms in yes/no questions in favor of tag questions or intonation <br> *You come tomorrow, OK?* <br> *He goes to school with you?* | Cantonese, Haitian Creole, Khmer, Korean, Russian, Tagalog, Vietnamese | The primary language doesn't use subject-verb inversion in questions. |
| | lack of subject-verb inversion in questions with helping verbs <br> *When she will be home?* <br> *Where you are going?* | Cantonese, Hmong, Russian, Tagalog | In the primary language, word order is the same in some questions and statements, depending on the context. |
| | omission of *do* or *did* in questions <br> *Where you went?* | Haitian Creole, Hmong, Khmer, Korean, Russian, Spanish, Tagalog | In the primary language, there is no exact counterpart to the *do/did* verb in questions. |
| **Yes/no questions** | incorrect answer form for yes/no questions <br> *A: Do you want more food?* <br> *B: I want.* <br> *A: Do you have a pen?* <br> *B: I not have.* | Cantonese, Hmong, Khmer, Korean, Russian | In the primary language, learners tend to answer yes by repeating the verb in the question. They tend to say no by using *not* and repeating the verb. |
| | positive answer to negative question <br> *A: Aren't you going?* <br> *B: Yes.* when the person is not going | Cantonese, Korean, Russian | The appropriate response pattern differs between the primary language and English. |
| **Tag questions** | incorrect tag questions <br> *You want to go home, are you?* | Cantonese, Khmer, Korean, Vietnamese | The primary language has no exact counterpart to a tag question, forms them differently, or does not add *do/did* to questions. |

# PHONICS TRANSFER ISSUES FOR SEVEN LANGUAGES

*Sound Transfer (Phonology)*

The symbol • identifies areas in which these primary language speakers may have some difficulty pronouncing and perceiving spoken English. The sound may not exist in the primary language, may exist but be pronounced somewhat differently, or may be confused with another sound. Sound production and perception issues affect phonics instruction.

## CONSONANTS

| Sound | Spanish | Vietnamese | Hmong | Cantonese | Haitian Creole | Korean | Khmer |
|---|---|---|---|---|---|---|---|
| /b/ as in bat | | | • | • | | • | |
| /k/ as in cat and kite | | | • | | | | |
| /d/ as in dog | | | | • | | • | |
| /f/ as in fan | | | | | | • | |
| /g/ as in goat | | | • | • | | • | • |
| /h/ as in hen | | | | | • | | |
| /j/ as in jacket | • | • | • | • | | • | |
| /l/ as in lemon | | | | | | • | |
| /m/ as in money | | | | | | | |
| /n/ as in nail | | | | | | | |
| /p/ as in pig | | | • | | | | |
| /r/ as in rabbit | • | | • | • | • | • | |
| /s/ as in sun | | | • | | | | |
| /t/ as in teen | | • | • | | | | |
| /v/ as in video | • | | | • | | • | • |
| /w/ as in wagon | • | | • | | | | • |
| /y/ as in yo-yo | | | | | | | |
| /z/ as in zebra | • | | • | • | | • | • |
| /kw/ as in queen | | | • | | | | |
| /ks/ as in Xray | | | • | • | | | |

## SHORT VOWELS

| Sound | Spanish | Vietnamese | Hmong | Cantonese | Haitian Creole | Korean | Khmer |
|---|---|---|---|---|---|---|---|
| short *a* as in hat | • | • | | • | | • | |
| short *e* as in set | • | | • | • | • | • | |
| short *i* as in sit | • | • | • | • | • | • | |
| short *o* as in hot | • | | • | | | • | |
| short *u* as in cup | • | | • | • | • | • | |

## LONG VOWELS

| Sound | Spanish | Vietnamese | Hmong | Cantonese | Haitian Creole | Korean | Khmer |
|---|---|---|---|---|---|---|---|
| long *a* as in d<u>a</u>te | | | • | • | | | |
| long *e* as in b<u>e</u> | | | | • | | • | |
| long *i* as in <u>i</u>ce | | | | • | | | |
| long *o* as in r<u>oa</u>d | | | • | • | | | |
| long *u* as in tr<u>ue</u> | | | | • | | • | |

## VOWEL PATTERNS

| Sound | Spanish | Vietnamese | Hmong | Cantonese | Haitian Creole | Korean | Khmer |
|---|---|---|---|---|---|---|---|
| *oo* as in b<u>oo</u>k | • | • | • | | • | • | • |
| *aw* as in s<u>aw</u> | • | | | | | • | |

## DIPHTHONGS

| Sound | Spanish | Vietnamese | Hmong | Cantonese | Haitian Creole | Korean | Khmer |
|---|---|---|---|---|---|---|---|
| *oy* as in b<u>oy</u> | | | • | | | | |
| *ow* as in h<u>ow</u> | • | | | | | | |

## *R*-CONTROLLED VOWELS

| Sound | Spanish | Vietnamese | Hmong | Cantonese | Haitian Creole | Korean | Khmer |
|---|---|---|---|---|---|---|---|
| *ir* as in b<u>ir</u>d | • | • | • | • | • | • | • |
| *ar* as in h<u>ar</u>d | • | • | • | • | • | • | • |
| *or* as in f<u>or</u>m | • | • | • | • | • | • | • |
| *air* as in h<u>air</u> | • | • | • | • | • | • | • |
| *ear* as in h<u>ear</u> | • | • | • | • | • | • | • |

## CONSONANT DIGRAPHS

| Sound | Spanish | Vietnamese | Hmong | Cantonese | Haitian Creole | Korean | Khmer |
|---|---|---|---|---|---|---|---|
| *sh* as in <u>sh</u>oe | • | • | | • | | | • |
| *ch* as in <u>ch</u>ain | | • | • | | | | |
| *th* as in <u>th</u>ink | • | • | • | • | • | • | • |
| *ng* as in si<u>ng</u> | • | | • | | • | | |

## CONSONANT BLENDS

| Sound | Spanish | Vietnamese | Hmong | Cantonese | Haitian Creole | Korean | Khmer |
|---|---|---|---|---|---|---|---|
| bl, tr, dr, etc. (start of words) as in black, tree, dress | | • | • | • | • | • | |
| ld, nt, rt, etc. (end of words) as in cold, tent, start | | • | • | • | • | • | • |

# SOUND-SYMBOL TRANSFER (PHONICS)

The following chart identifies sound-symbol transfer issues for four languages that use the roman alphabet. (The remaining three do not.) The symbol • identifies symbols which do not represent the corresponding sound in the writing system of the primary language.

## CONSONANTS

| Sound-Symbols | Spanish | Vietnamese | Hmong | Haitian Creole |
|---|---|---|---|---|
| b as in bat | | | • | |
| c as in cat | | • | • | • |
|    as in cent | | • | • | |
| d as in dog | | | | |
| f as in fish | | | | |
| g as in goat | | | • | |
|    as in giant | • | | • | |
| h as in hen | • | | | |
| j as in jacket | • | • | • | |
| k as in kite | | | • | |
| l as in lemon | | | | |
| m as in moon | | | | |
| n as in nice | | | | |
| p as in pig | | | | |
| qu as in queen | • | | • | • |
| r as in rabbit | • | | • | |
| s as in sun | | | • | |
| t as in teen | | | • | |
| v as in video | • | | | |
| w as in wagon | | • | • | |
| x as in Xray | | • | • | • |
| y as in yo-yo | | | | |
| z as in zebra | • | • | • | |

## CONSONANT DIGRAPHS

| Sound-Symbols | Spanish | Vietnamese | Hmong | Haitian Creole |
|---|---|---|---|---|
| *sh* as in <u>sh</u>oe | • | | | |
| *ch* as in <u>ch</u>air | | | | • |
| *th* as in <u>th</u>ink | • | | | • |
| as in <u>th</u>at | | | | |

## VOWELS AND VOWEL PATTERNS

| Sound-Symbols | Spanish | Vietnamese | Hmong | Haitian Creole |
|---|---|---|---|---|
| *a* as in b<u>a</u>t | • | | • | |
| *aCe* as in d<u>ate</u> | • | • | | |
| *ai* as in r<u>ai</u>n | • | • | • | • |
| *ay* as in d<u>ay</u> | • | | • | • |
| *au* as in <u>au</u>thor | • | • | • | • |
| *aw* as in s<u>aw</u> | • | • | • | • |
| *e* as in b<u>e</u>t | • | | • | • |
| *ee* as in s<u>ee</u>d | • | • | • | • |
| *ea* as in t<u>ea</u> | • | • | • | • |
| *ew* as in f<u>ew</u> | • | • | • | • |
| *i* as in s<u>i</u>t | • | | • | • |
| *iCe* as in p<u>i</u>pe | • | • | • | • |
| *o* as in h<u>o</u>t | • | | • | • |
| *o* as in r<u>o</u>de | • | • | • | • |
| *oo* as in m<u>oo</u>n | • | • | • | • |
| *oo* as in b<u>oo</u>k | • | | • | • |
| *oa* as in b<u>oa</u>t | • | • | • | • |
| *ow* as in r<u>ow</u> | • | • | • | • |
| *ow* as in h<u>ow</u> | • | • | • | • |
| *ou* as in s<u>ou</u>nd | • | • | • | • |
| *oi* as in b<u>oi</u>l | | | • | • |
| *oy* as in b<u>oy</u> | | • | • | • |
| *u* as in c<u>u</u>p | • | • | • | • |
| *uCe* as in J<u>u</u>ne | • | • | | |
| *ui* as in s<u>ui</u>t | • | • | • | • |
| *ue* as in bl<u>ue</u> | • | • | • | • |
| *y* as in tr<u>y</u> | • | • | • | • |
| *ar* as in st<u>ar</u> | | | • | • |
| *er* as in f<u>er</u>n | • | | • | • |
| *ir* as in b<u>ir</u>d | • | | • | • |
| *or* as in t<u>or</u>n | • | | • | |
| *ur* as in b<u>ur</u>n | • | | • | |

# Appendix D

## RESPONSE TO INTERVENTION: GUIDING PRINCIPLES FOR EDUCATORS FROM THE INTERNATIONAL READING ASSOCIATION

## BACKGROUND

Language related to Response to Intervention (RTI) was written into U.S. law with the 2004 reauthorization of the Individuals With Disabilities Education Act (IDEA). This law indicates that school districts are no longer required to take into consideration whether a severe discrepancy exists between a student's achievement and his or her intellectual ability in determining eligibility for learning-disability services. Rather, they may use an alternative approach that determines first whether the student responds to "scientific, research-based" classroom instruction and, if not, then to more intensive and targeted interventions. After receiving this more tailored and intensive instruction, students who do not demonstrate adequate progress are then considered for evaluation for a specific learning disability. This approach has come to be known as RTI, although this precise term is not used in the law.

The concept of RTI builds on recommendations made by the President's Commission on Excellence in Special Education (2002) that students with disabilities should first be considered general education students, embracing a model of prevention as opposed to a model of failure (National Association of State Directors of Special Education and Council of Administrators of Special Education, 2006). A prevention model intends to rectify a number of longstanding problems, including the disproportionate representation of minorities and English-language learners (ELLs) among those identified as learning disabled and the need to wait for documented failure before services are provided. The RTI provision allows local school districts that meet certain criteria to allocate up to 15% of their funding for students with disabilities toward general education interventions designed to prevent language and literacy difficulties. This explains why RTI is often perceived as a special education initiative at the same time as special education organizations describe it as a general education initiative.

The statute and regulations identify eight areas in which low achievement may be the basis for identification of a specific learning disability. Six of these areas are within the domain of language arts: oral expression, listening comprehension, written expression, basic reading skill, reading fluency skills, and reading comprehension. For the purposes of this document, we refer to these six areas as "language and literacy." Because the areas of language and literacy can play such prominent roles in the problems of struggling learners, the International Reading Association (IRA) formed a Commission on Response to Intervention to provide its members with information and opportunities for involvement in articulating IRA's perspective on RTI. In this document, the Commission offers six key principles, adopted by IRA's Board of Directors, to guide thinking and professional work in the area of RTI. These principles are focused specifically on RTI as it intersects with issues of language and literacy and are meant to help classroom teachers, reading/literacy specialists, speech-language pathologists, teachers of ELLs, special educators, administrators, and others as they work toward the goals of preventing language and literacy difficulties and improving instruction for all students.

The Commission embraces the concept of RTI and seeks to clarify it with regard to issues related to language and literacy. The Commission finds it productive to think of RTI as a comprehensive, systemic approach to teaching and learning designed to address language and literacy problems for *all* students through increasingly differentiated and intensified language and literacy assessment and instruction. Qualified professionals with appropriate expertise should provide this instruction. As such, RTI is a process that cuts across general, compensatory, and special education, and is not exclusively a general or special education initiative. The Commission takes the position that carefully selected assessment, dedication to differentiated instruction, quality professional development, and genuine collaboration across teachers, specialists, administrators, and parents are among the factors important for the success of RTI.

The IRA Commission also supports the idea that RTI is not a specific program or model. A paper developed by the National Joint Committee on Learning Disabilities (2005), which includes IRA as a member, emphasizes that there is no one model or approach to RTI and many possible variations can be conceptualized. In fact, the federal government purposely provided few details for the development and implementation of RTI procedures, stating specifically that states and districts should have the flexibility to establish approaches that reflect their communities' unique situations. This means that the widely used three-tier model is neither mandated nor the only possible approach to RTI. Similarly, the statute and regulations do not mandate screening (or any other particular) assessments per se, although they do require data-based documentation of repeated assessments of achievement at reasonable intervals.

Given the context for RTI, the IRA Commission feels it is extremely important that the language used in describing, developing, and implementing an RTI approach reflect its purpose as a systemic initiative rather than a specialized or particular program. More specifically, the language of RTI should reflect the emphasis on optimizing instruction for students who are struggling with language and literacy rather than assuming permanent learning deficits. This may be especially important for English learners or youth living in poverty. For many ELLs, second-language acquisition and development are more uneven than for monolingual English students. For example, some linguistically diverse students with good vocabulary knowledge might still have difficulty with grammar. In order to inform instruction and intervention efforts, we need to avoid characterizing students' profiles in broad terms, such as "low language skills" or "low literacy ability," and instead generate an understanding of students' skills—their strengths and their weaknesses—in specific domains of language and literacy.

To summarize, RTI is not a model to be imposed on schools, but rather a framework to help schools identify and support students before the difficulties they encounter with language and literacy become more serious. According to the research, relatively few students who are having difficulty in language and literacy have specific learning disabilities. Many other factors, including the nature of educational opportunities provided, affect students' academic and social growth. For example, teaching practices and assessment tools that are insensitive to cultural and linguistic differences can lead to ineffective instruction or misjudgments in evaluation. In this document, we assume that instruction and intervention can and will be effective for large numbers of students who are experiencing literacy or other academic difficulties. It is our responsibility to identify students' needs and help students succeed.

Students are often identified as "struggling" or "learning disabled" based on their growth and development in language and literacy. Consequently, IRA takes its responsibility as a professional organization seriously and suggests that its members be active participants in all aspects of RTI in their schools, districts, and states.

To further clarify issues related to RTI with respect to language and literacy, the Commission offers the following set of principles as a guide to IRA members and others concerned with developing and implementing an RTI approach to improving the language and literacy learning of all students.

## GUIDING PRINCIPLES

### 1. INSTRUCTION

RTI is first and foremost intended to prevent problems by optimizing language and literacy instruction.

- Whatever approach is taken to RTI, it should ensure optimal instruction for every student at all levels of schooling. It should prevent serious language and literacy problems through increasingly differentiated and intensified assessment and instruction and reduce the disproportionate number of minority youth and ELLs identified as learning disabled.
- Instruction and assessment conducted by the classroom teacher are central to the success of RTI and must address the needs of all students, including those from diverse cultural and linguistic backgrounds. Evidence shows that effective classroom instruction can reduce substantially the number of students who are inappropriately classified as learning disabled.
- A successful RTI process begins with the highest quality core instruction in the classroom—that is, instruction that encompasses all areas of language and literacy as part of a coherent curriculum that is developmentally appropriate for preK–12 students and does not underestimate their potential for learning. This core instruction may or may not involve commercial programs, and it must in all cases be provided by an informed, competent classroom teacher.
- The success of RTI depends on the classroom teacher's use of research-based practices. As defined by IRA (2002), *research based* means "that a particular program or collection of instructional practices has a record of success. That is, there is reliable, trustworthy, and valid evidence to suggest that when the program is used with a particular group of children, the children can be expected to make adequate gains in reading achievement."
- Research on instructional practices must provide not only information about what works, but also what works with whom, by whom, in what contexts, and on which outcomes. The effectiveness of a particular practice needs to have been demonstrated with the types of students who will receive the instruction, taking into account, for example, whether the students live in rural or urban settings or come from diverse cultural and linguistic backgrounds.
- Research evidence frequently represents the effectiveness of an instructional practice on average, which suggests that some students benefited and others did not. This means that instruction must be provided by a teacher who understands the intent of the research-based practice being used and has the professional expertise and responsibility to plan instruction and adapt programs and materials as needed (see also principle 6, Expertise).
- When core language and literacy instruction is not effective for a particular student, it should be modified to address more closely the needs and abilities of that student. Classroom teachers, at times in collaboration with other experts, must exercise their best professional judgment in providing responsive teaching and differentiation (see also principle 2).

## 2. RESPONSIVE TEACHING AND DIFFERENTIATION

The RTI process emphasizes increasingly differentiated and intensified instruction or intervention in language and literacy.

- RTI is centrally about optimizing language and literacy instruction for particular students. This means that differentiated instruction, based on instructionally relevant assessment, is essential. Evidence shows that small-group and individualized instruction are effective in reducing the number of students who are at risk of becoming classified as learning disabled.
- Instruction and materials selection must derive from specific student–teacher interactions and not be constrained by packaged programs. Students have different language and literacy needs, so they may not respond similarly to instruction—even when research-based practices are used. No single approach to instruction or intervention can address the broad and varied goals and needs of all students, especially those from different cultural and linguistic backgrounds.
- The boundaries between differentiation and intervention are permeable and not clear-cut. Instruction or intervention must be flexible enough to respond to evidence from student performance and teaching interactions. It should not be constrained by institutional procedures that emphasize uniformity.

## 3. ASSESSMENT

An RTI approach demands assessment that can inform language and literacy instruction meaningfully.

- Assessment should reflect the multidimensional nature of language and literacy learning and the diversity among students being assessed. The utility of an assessment is dependent on the extent to which it provides valid information on the essential aspects of language and literacy that can be used to plan appropriate instruction.
- Assessments, tools, and techniques should provide useful and timely information about desired language and literacy goals. They should reflect authentic language and literacy activities as opposed to contrived texts or tasks generated specifically for assessment purposes. The quality of assessment information should not be sacrificed for the efficiency of an assessment procedure.
- Multiple purposes for assessment should be clearly identified and appropriate tools and techniques employed. Not all available tools and techniques are appropriate for all purposes, and different assessments—even in the same language or literacy domain—capture different skills and knowledge. Particular care should be taken in selecting assessments for ELLs and for students who speak an English dialect that differs from mainstream dialects.
- Efficient assessment systems involve a layered approach in which screening techniques are used both to identify which students require further (diagnostic) assessment and to provide aggregate data about the nature of student achievement overall. Initial (screening) assessments should not be used as the sole mechanism for determining the appropriateness of targeted interventions. Ongoing progress monitoring must include an evaluation of the instruction itself and requires observation of the student in the classroom.
- Classroom teachers and reading/literacy specialists should play a central role in conducting language and literacy assessments and in using assessment results to plan instruction and monitor student performance.
- Assessment as a component of RTI should be consistent with the *Standards for the Assessment of Reading and Writing* developed jointly by the International Reading Association and the National Council of Teachers of English (2010).

## 4. COLLABORATION

RTI requires a dynamic, positive, and productive collaboration among professionals with relevant expertise in language and literacy. Success also depends on strong and respectful partnerships among professionals, parents, and students.

- Collaboration should be focused on the available evidence about the needs of students struggling in language and literacy. School-level decision-making teams (e.g., intervention teams, problem-solving teams, RTI teams) should include members with relevant expertise in language and literacy, including second-language learning.
- Reading/literacy specialists and coaches should provide leadership in every aspect of an RTI process—planning, assessment, provision of more intensified instruction and support, and making decisions about next steps. These individuals must embody the knowledge, skills, and dispositions detailed for reading specialists in IRA's (2003) *Standards for Reading Professionals* (and the accompanying revised role definitions from August 2007).
- Collaboration should increase, not reduce, the coherence of the instruction experienced by struggling readers. There must be congruence between core language and literacy instruction and interventions. This requires a shared vision and common goals for language and literacy instruction and assessment, adequate time for communication and coordinated planning among general education and specialist teachers, and integrated professional development.
- Involving parents and students and engaging them in a collaborative manner is critical to successful implementation. Initiating and strengthening collaborations among school, home, and communities, particularly in urban and rural areas, provides the basis for support and reinforcement of students' learning.

## 5. SYSTEMIC AND COMPREHENSIVE APPROACHES

RTI must be part of a comprehensive, systemic approach to language and literacy assessment and instruction that supports all preK–12 students and teachers.

- RTI needs to be integrated within the context of a coherent and consistent language and literacy curriculum that guides comprehensive instruction for all students. Core instruction—indeed, all instruction—must be continuously improved to increase its efficacy and mitigate the need for specialized interventions.
- Specific approaches to RTI need to be appropriate for the particular school or district culture and take into account leadership, expertise, the diversity of the student population, and the available resources. Schools and districts should adopt an approach that best matches their needs and resources while still accomplishing the overall goals of RTI.
- A systemic approach to language and literacy learning within an RTI framework requires the active participation and genuine collaboration of many professionals, including classroom teachers, reading specialists, literacy coaches, special educators, and school psychologists. Given the critical role that language development plays in literacy learning, professionals with specialized language-related expertise such as speech-language pathologists and teachers of ELLs may be particularly helpful in addressing students' language difficulties.
- Approaches to RTI must be sensitive to developmental differences in language and literacy among students at different ages and grades. Although many prevailing approaches to RTI focus on the early elementary grades, it is essential for teachers and support personnel at middle and secondary levels to provide their students with the language and literacy instruction they need to succeed in school and beyond.

- Administrators must ensure adequate resources and appropriate scheduling to allow all professionals to collaborate.
- Ongoing and job-embedded professional development is necessary for all educators involved in the RTI process. Professional development should be context specific and provided by professional developers with appropriate preparation and skill to support school and district personnel. Professional expertise is essential to improving students' language and literacy learning in general as well as within the context of RTI (see also principle 6).

## 6. EXPERTISE

All students have the right to receive instruction from well-prepared teachers who keep up to date and supplemental instruction from professionals specifically prepared to teach language and literacy (IRA, 2000).

- Teacher expertise is central to instructional improvement, particularly for students who encounter difficulty in acquiring language and literacy. RTI may involve a range of professionals; however, the greater the literacy difficulty, the greater the need for expertise in literacy teaching and learning.
- Important dimensions of teachers' expertise include their knowledge and understanding of language and literacy development, their ability to use powerful assessment tools and techniques, and their ability to translate information about student performance into instructionally relevant instructional techniques.
- The exemplary core instruction that is so essential to the success of RTI is dependent on highly knowledgeable and skilled classroom teachers (IRA, 2003).
- Professionals who provide supplemental instruction or intervention must have a high level of expertise in all aspects of language and literacy instruction and assessment and be capable of intensifying or accelerating language and literacy learning.
- Success for culturally and linguistically diverse students depends on teachers and support personnel who are well prepared to teach in a variety of settings. Deep knowledge of cultural and linguistic differences is especially critical for the prevention of language and literacy problems in diverse student populations.
- Expertise in the areas of language and literacy requires a comprehensive approach to professional preparation that involves preservice, induction, and inservice education. It also requires opportunities for extended practice under the guidance of knowledgeable and experienced mentors.

# Glossary

**Accommodation.** Developing new categories for stimuli that do not fit into into existing ones—another aspect of what Piaget refers to as cognitive development.

**Affective domain.** Part of the reading process that involves an individual's feelings and emotions.

**Affixes.** Prefixes and suffixes.

**Analogy.** A comparison of relationships between words or ideas.

**Analytic phonics instruction.** The teacher presents students with a whole word and asks them to break it into its sounds and letters.

**Anecdotal record.** A record of observed behavior over a period of time.

**Antonyms.** Words opposite in meaning.

**Assessment.** Asking questions about students' knowledge and skills, and the process of getting answers.

**Assimilation.** A continuous process that helps the individual to integrate new incoming stimuli into existing concepts—one aspect of what Piaget refers to as cognitive development.

**Astigmatism.** A defect of vision that causes blurred vision.

**Auditory acuity.** Physical response of the ear to sound vibrations.

**Auditory discrimination.** Ability to distinguish differences and similarities between sound symbols.

**Auditory memory span.** Amount of information able to be stored in short-term memory for immediate use or reproduction.

**Authentic assessment.** Using authentic, "real-life" materials to assess students' reading.

**Binaurality.** The ability of listeners to direct both ears to the same sound.

**Bottom-up reading models.** Models that consider the reading process as one of grapheme-phoneme correspondences; code emphasis or subskill models.

**Buffer zone.** The area that falls between the instructional and frustration levels.

**Categorizing.** A thinking skill involving the ability to classify items into general and specific categories.

**Central idea.** The main idea of a larger chunk of text.

**Checklist.** A means for systematically and quickly recording behavior; the observer checks items as present or absent.

**Classroom tests.** Teacher-made tests; also called informal tests.

**Cloze procedure.** A technique that helps teachers gain information about a variety of language facility and comprehension ability skills.

**Cloze test.** A reader must supply words which have been systematically deleted from a passage.

**Cognitive domain.** Hierarchy of objectives ranging from simplistic thinking skills to the more complex ones.

**Combining forms.** Roots borrowed from another language combine with each other or with affixes to form a word.

**Comparison.** A demonstration of the similarities between persons, ideas, things, and so on.

**Comprehension.** Understanding; the effort and process used to get the meaning of something.

**Concentration.** Sustained attention. It is essential for both studying and listening to lectures.

**Concept.** A group of stimuli with common characteristics.

**Concept development.** Refers to development of thinking.

**Consonant blends.** A combination of consonant sounds blended together so that the identity of each sound is retained.

**Consonant digraph.** Two consonant letters that represent one sound.

**Content domain.** Term that refers to subject matter covered.

**Context clue.** An item of information from the words surrounding a particular word in the form of a synonym, antonym, example, definition, description, explanation, and so on, that helps shed light on the meaning of that particular word.

**Contrast.** A demonstration of the differences between persons, ideas, things, and so on.

**Creative reading.** Uses divergent thinking skills to go beyond the literal comprehension, interpretation, and critical reading levels.

**Criterion-referenced tests.** Based on an extensive inventory of objectives in a specific curriculum area; they are used to help assess an individual student's performance with respect to his or her mastery of specified objectives in a given curriculum area.

**Critical reading.** A high-level reading skill that involves evaluation—making a personal judgment on the accuracy, value, and truthfulness of what is read.

**Derivatives.** Combinations of root words with prefixes or suffixes, or both.

**Developmental reading.** Reading skills and strategies that are systematically and sequentially developed to help students become effective readers.

**Developmental spelling.** Learning to spell is ongoing and based on the cognitive development of the child.

**Diagnosis.** The act, process, or result of identifying the nature of a disorder or disability through observation and examination. In education, it often includes the planning of instruction and an assessment of the strengths and weaknesses (i.e., needs) of the student.

**Diagnostic pattern.** Consists of three steps: identify, assess and set goals.

**Diagnostic reading tests.** Provide subscores discrete enough that specific information about a student's reading behavior can be obtained and used for planning instruction.

**Diagnostic teaching.** The practice of continuously trying a variety of instructional strategies and materials based on the current needs of students.

**Diphthongs.** Blends of vowel sounds written with two letters.

**Directed listening/thinking approach.** Requires teachers to ask questions before, during, and after a talk; consists of a number of steps; requires students to be active participants.

**Directed Reading–Thinking Activity (DRTA).** Requires teachers to nurture the inquiry process and students to be active participants and questioners; includes prediction and verification.

**Divergent thinking.** The many different ways to solve problems or to look at things.

**Educational factors.** Those factors that come under the domain or control of the educational system and influence learning.

**Emergent literacy.** The development of the association of print with meaning that begins early in a child's life and continues until the child reaches the stage of conventional reading and writing.

**Emergent writing.** Nonconventional writing that includes scribbling and nonphonetic letterings.

**Equilibrium.** According to Piaget, a balance between assimilation and accommodation in cognitive development.

**Evaluation.** Evaluation is interpreting evidence.

**Example.** Something representative of a whole or a group.

**Explicit instruction.** Instruction guided by a teacher, who uses various strategies to help students understand what they are reading.

**Frustration reading level.** The child reads with many word recognition and comprehension errors. It is the lowest reading level and one to be avoided.

**Grade equivalents.** Description of the year and month of school for which a given student's level of performance is typical.

**Group tests.** Administered to a group of students at the same time.

**High-frequency words.** Words that appear most often in texts.

**Home environment.** Socioeconomic class, parents' education, and the neighborhood in which children live are some factors that shape children's home environments.

**Homonyms.** Words that are spelled and sound the same but have different meanings.

**Hypermetropia.** Farsightedness; difficulty with close-up vision.

**Identification.** Part of diagnostic pattern; the act of determining the student's present level of performance in word recognition and comprehension for screening purposes.

**Independent reading level.** Level at which a child reads words without any assistance and comprehends the text.

**Individual tests.** Administered to one person at a time.

**Inference.** Understanding that is not derived from a direct statement but from an indirect suggestion in what is stated; understanding of what is implied.

**Informal interviews.**  Teachers converse with students to learn about their interests and feelings.

**Informal Reading Inventory (IRI).**  A valuable aid in helping teachers determine a student's reading levels and his or her strengths and needs. It usually consists of oral and silent reading passages and comprehension questions.

**Informal tests.**  Teacher-made tests.

**Initial consonant.**  One stopped speech sound represented by one letter at the beginning of a word.

**Instructional reading level.**  The teaching level.

**Interactive reading models.**  Models that consider the top-down processing of information as dependent on the bottom-up processing, and vice versa.

**Interest inventory.**  A statement or questionnaire method that helps teachers learn about students' likes and dislikes.

**Interpretation.**  A reading level that demands a higher level of thinking ability because the material it involves is not directly stated in the text but only suggested or implied.

**Junior Great Books Program.**  Program in which parent–teacher teams work together to plan reading discussion sessions for students; sessions take place in regular classrooms during the reading period and are led by both parent and teacher.

**Listening capacity level.**  The highest level at which a learner can understand material when it is read aloud to him or her.

**Listening capacity test.**  Given to determine a child's comprehension through listening. The teacher reads aloud to the child and then asks questions about the selection.

**Listening vocabulary.**  The words one knows the meaning of when they are said aloud.

**Literal comprehension.**  The ability to obtain a low-level type of understanding by using only information that is explicitly stated.

**Literature webbing.**  A story map technique to help guide children in using predictable trade books.

**Locator test.**  Used to determine at what level a student should begin testing.

**Main idea.**  The central thought of a paragraph. All the sentences in the paragraph develop the main idea.

**Masking.**  Factor inhibiting hearing as other sounds interfere with the spoken message.

**Maze procedure.**  The reader must choose the correct word from three choices for words which have been systematically selected from a passage.

**Mean.**  Arithmetical average.

**Measurement.**  Ways of gathering evidence for evaluation.

**Metacognition.**  Thinking critically about thinking; refers to students' knowledge about their thinking processes and ability to control them.

**Miscue analysis.**  A process that helps teachers learn how readers use language cues to construct meaning.

**Miscue.**  Unexpected response to print.

**Myopia.**  Nearsightedness; difficulty with distance vision.

**Newbery award books.**  Books that have received the Newbery Medal, which is given annually to the book in the United States that has been voted "the most distinguished literature" for children.

**Noneducational factors.**  Those factors that do not come under the domain or control of the educational system and that supposedly cannot be influenced by it.

**Normal curve.**  Scores are symmetrically distributed around the mean.

**Norm-referenced tests.**  Standardized tests with norms so that comparisons can be made to a sample population.

**Norms.**  Average scores for a given group of students, which allow comparisons to be made among different students or groups of students.

**Note taking.**  A useful tool for studying and writing papers.

**Objective.**  Desired educational outcome.

**Objectivity.**  The same score must result regardless of who grades the test.

**Observation.**  A technique that helps teachers collect data about students' behavior.

**Overlearning.**  Helps people retain information over a long period of time; occurs when individuals continue to practice even after they think they have learned the material.

**Paired reading.**  The child reads aloud simultaneously with another person, usually the parent.

**Percentile.**  A point on the distribution below which a certain percentage of the scores fall.

**Perception.** A cumulative process based on an individual's background of experiences. It is defined as giving meaning to sensations or the ability to organize stimuli on a field.

**Perceptual domain.** Part of the reading process that depends on an individual's background of experiences in using the body's sensory receptors and interpreting sensory input.

**Performance assessment.** Using a situation or project where learners can demonstrate knowledge.

**Phonemic awareness.** Awareness that words are made up of individual sounds.

**Phonics.** The study of the relationships between sounds and letters in a language.

**Phonogram.** Sets of letters with the same phonetic value in a number of words, that is, word families.

**Phonological awareness.** Awareness of spoken words, syllables, and phonemes.

**Portfolio assessment.** Material in a portfolio is evaluated in some way.

**Portfolio.** A storage system that represents samples of students' reading and writing over a period of time.

**Practice test.** Ensures that the actual test measures what students know rather than their test-taking ability; it familiarizes students with the test.

**Prefix.** A letter or a sequence of letters added to the beginning of a root word.

**Pre-reading.** Precursor to reading; before formal reading begins.

**Projective technique.** A method in which the individual puts himself or herself into a situation and reveals how he or she feels.

**Question–Answer Relationships (QARs).** Helps students distinguish between "what they have in their heads" and information that is in the text.

**Questions.** A good way for students to gain better insight into a subject; questioning also gives the teacher feedback.

**Rating scale.** An evaluative instrument used to record estimates of particular aspects of a student's behavior.

**Raw score.** The number of items that a student answers correctly on a test.

**Reading autobiography.** Students write or tell about their feelings and attempt to analyze their reading problems.

**Reading comprehension taxonomy.** A hierarchy of reading comprehension skills ranging from the more simplistic to the more complex ones; a classification of these skills.

**Reading comprehension.** A complex intellectual process involving a number of abilities. The two major abilities involve knowing word meanings and reasoning with verbal concepts.

**Reading diagnosis and improvement.** Reading instruction interwoven with diagnosis and intervention.

**Reading Olympics programs.** Programs vary; however, most challenge students to read as many books as they can and to share them in some way with parents.

**Reading process.** Concerned with the affective, perceptual, and cognitive domains.

**Reading readiness.** Children demonstrate behaviors that show they are ready for reading instruction.

**Reading.** A dynamic, complex act that involves bringing meaning to and getting meaning from the printed page.

**Reciprocal reading instruction.** A teacher-directed technique consisting of four steps: summarizing, questioning, clarifying, and predicting.

**Recite or recall.** The process of answering a question from memory, without rereading the text or notes.

**Reliability.** The extent to which a test instrument consistently produces similar results.

**Remedial reading program.** Takes place inside or outside the regular classroom and is handled by special personnel.

**Repeated reading.** Similar to paired reading; the child reads along (assisted reading with model or tape) until he or she gains confidence to read alone.

**Root.** Smallest unit of a word that can exist and retain its basic meaning.

**Running record.** Documentation of a child's reading.

**Schema theory.** Deals with relations between prior knowledge and comprehension.

**Schemata.** These structured designs are the cognitive arrangements by which the mind is able to categorize incoming stimuli.

**Schwa.** The unstressed vowel sound, which does not have a common letter.

**Self-fulfilling prophecy.** Teacher assumptions about children become true, at least in part, because of the attitude of the teachers, which in turn becomes part of the children's self-concept.

**Semantic mapping (graphic organizer).** A graphic representation used to illustrate concepts and relationships among concepts such as classes, properties, and examples.

**Sight words.** Words readers can identify instantaneously.

**Silent consonant digraphs.** Two adjacent consonant letters, one of which is silent, for example, *kn* (know), *pn* (pneumonia).

**Skimming.** Reading rapidly to find or locate information.

**SQ3R.** A widely used study technique that involves five steps: survey, question, read, recite or recall, and review.

**Standard deviation.** Deals with how widely scores vary from the mean.

**Standard scores.** Used to compare test takers' assessment scores. Presented in terms of standard deviations.

**Standardized tests.** Tests that have been published by experts in the field and have precise instructions for administration and scoring.

**Story sense.** The understanding that there is a structure used to tell stories and that stories are written to be understood.

**Study procedures.** (1) Build good habits, (2) devise a system that works for you, (3) keep at it, (4) maintain a certain degree of tension, and (5) concentrate.

**Suffix.** A letter or a sequence of letters added to the end of a root word.

**Suitability.** The appropriateness of a test for a specific population of students.

**Summary.** A brief statement of the essential information in a longer piece.

**Supporting details.** Additional information that supports, explains, or illustrates the main idea. Some of the ways that supporting details may be arranged are as cause and effect, examples, sequence of events, descriptions, definitions, comparisons, or contrasts.

**Survey.** To gain an overview of the text material.

**Syllable.** A vowel and the consonants around it.

**Synonyms.** Words similar in meaning.

**Synthetic phonics instruction.** Each sound associated with letters in a word is pronounced in isolation, and then the sounds are blended together.

**Teacher-made tests.** Tests prepared by the classroom teacher for a particular class and given by the classroom teacher under conditions of his or her own choosing.

**Test.** An assigned set of tasks to be performed.

**Top-down reading models.** Models that depend on reader's background of experiences and language ability in constructing meaning from the text.

**Validity.** The degree to which a test instrument leads to valid inferences—that is, the degree to which it really measures what it claims to measure.

**Visual discrimination.** The ability to distinguish differences and similarities between written symbols.

**Vocabulary consciousness.** An awareness that words may have different meanings based on their context and a desire to increase one's vocabulary.

**Vowel digraph.** Two vowel letters that represent one speech sound.

**Word identification.** A twofold process that includes both pronunciation and knowledge of word meaning.

# Name Index

## A

Aardema, Verna, 371
Adams, Marilyn Jager, 180, 256, 313
Adler, David, 193, 205, 250, 252, 277, 283
Adoff, Arnold, 277, 283
Afflerbach, Peter, 15, 216, 229, 306
Agee, Jon, 277, 283
Alborough, Jez, 190, 205
Alexander, P. A., 184
Allen, J., 260, 283
Allen, Vernon L., 204
Allen, Virginia G., 59
Allington, Richard L., 6, 15, 19, 47, 48, 183, 204
Almasi, J. F., 204
Anastasi, Anne, 37
Anderson, Richard C., 15, 19, 238
Anderson, Virgil A., 56
Appelt, Kathi, 277, 283
Armbruster, Bonnie B., 239
Armstrong, Tom, 68
Arnold, Katya, 191, 205
Arnold, Tedd, 277, 283
Asbridge, M., 52
Ashton-Warner, Sylvia, 32
Askov, Eunice N., 19, 316
Auch, Herm, 250, 252
Auch, Mary Jane, 250, 252

## B

Baer, G. Thomas, 313
Baker, Keith, 309, 314
Ballard, Robin, 277, 283
Bardhan-Quallen, Sudipta, 194, 205
Barr, Rebecca, 15, 204, 255, 257, 339
Barrentine, Shelby J., 64, 90
Barrett, Judi, 127, 145
Barron, Rex, 129, 145
Bartlett, B. J., 211
Bass, Hester, 277, 283
Bauer, Marion D., 129, 145, 309, 314
Baumann, James F., 32, 131–132, 139–140, 250, 252, 283, 332
Beaver, J., 172, 180
Beck, Isabel L., 204, 255, 280, 313
Bee, William, 278, 284
Beentjes, Johannes W. J., 344
Beers, James W., 136
Bennett, Christine I., 59
Bennett, J., 67

Berglund, R., 280
Bett, Jan, 346
Bettencourt, Edward M., 48
Betts, Emmett A., 149, 150–153, 180
Bidwell, Charles E., 19
Blachowicz, Camille L. Z., 251, 255, 257, 264, 268, 281, 283, 313
Black, Cathy Collins, 211
Blanchfield, C., 283
Block, C. C., 251
Bloom, Benjamin, 213
Bolt, Sara, 41, 101
Bond, Guy L., 19, 129
Bormuth, John R., 231
Boyer, Ernest L., 340, 347
Boyles, N. N., 251
Bratcher, Suzanne, 64, 90
Bredekamp, Sue, 108
Brink, Carol Ryrie, 197
Brown, Ann L., 239
Brown, Marc, 346
Brown, Margaret Wise, 277
Brown, Ruth, 250, 252
Bryant, B. R., 124
Bunting, Eve, 250, 252, 401
Burger, Douglas, 278, 284
Burgstahler, S., 204
Burleigh, Robert, 129, 145
Burns, M. Susan, 287
Burns, Paul C., 180
Burns, S. M., 108
Buros, Oscar, 95
Buss, Kathleen, 251
Butter, K. G., 281
Bynum, Janie, 128, 145
Byrnes, James P., 50

## C

Cabrera, 195, 206
Calfee, Robert C., 300
Cammack, D., 202, 205
Camourne, B., 107
Carle, Eric, 309, 314, 346
Carpenter, Robert D., 57–58
Carr, Jan, 185, 205
Carter, David, 190, 205
Castle, Marrietta, 251
Chall, Jeanne S., 12, 19, 283, 313
Chambers, Veronica, 195, 205

Chandler-Olcott, K., 204
Charles, C. M., 204
Cheek, Dallas, 350
Chernick, Eleanor, 53
Choate, J., 67
Cianciolo, Patricia, 251
Clay, Marie, 110, 116, 130, 138, 142, 170,
      180, 300, 310
Cleary, Beverly, 215, 252
Clymer, Theodore, 287
Coffelt, Nancy, 278, 284
Cohen, Caron Lee, 309, 314
Cohen, Dorothy H., 90, 118, 277
Cohen, E., 204
Cohen, Peter, 278, 284
Coiro, J., 202, 204, 205
Cole, A., 251
Cole, Nancy S., 52, 59
Cole, Robert, 196
Collicut, Paul, 129, 145, 191, 205
Coltheart, Max, 108
Conrad, Kim, 181
Cooper, J. D., 12, 13
Cramer, Eugene H., 251
Creech, Sharon, 195, 205
Crelin, Bob, 191, 205
Crimi, Carolyn, 278, 284
Crowley, 240
Crowther, Robert, 278, 284
Cullinan, Bernice E., 5, 15, 205
Cunningham, James W., 216, 310
Cunningham, Patricia M., 295, 310, 313
Curlee, Lynn, 191, 205
Curtis, Christopher, 195, 205
Curtis, M. E., 283, 313

**D**
Daneman, Meredyth, 255
Davey, B., 238
Davis, Charlotte E., 213
Davis, Lillie Smith, 287
Davis, Robin L., 213
Dawson, Mildred A., 50
Day, Alexandra, 138, 145
DeFord, D., 205
DeGross, Monalisa, 278, 284
Dewdney, Anna, 250, 252
Diakiw, Jerry Y., 196
Dickinson, D., 142
Diez, M. E., 19, 28
Dion, G. S., 49
Dole, Janice A., 210
Donahue, Patricia L., 32, 49, 183, 339
Dorn, L. J., 251
Dorris, Michael, 197

Dow, Roger S., 313
Dowhower, Sarah L., 239
Downley, Lynne, 129, 145
Dr. Seuss, 128
Dreyer, Lois G., 106
Druse, A. E., 295
Duffelmeyer, Barbara Blakely, 180
Duffelmeyer, Frederick A., 180, 295
Duffy-Hester, Ann M., 32, 304, 313
Duke, N. K., 9
Duncan, Pamela, 129, 145
Dunphy, Madeline, 278, 284
Dunsmore, K. L., 258
Durkin, Dolores, 23, 32, 271, 313
Dykstra, Robert, 19, 129
Dymock, Susan, 211

**E**
Easley, Shirley-Dale, 64, 90
Edwards, P. A., 49, 340
Ehlert, Lois, 309, 314
El-Hindi, A., 204
Elley, Warwick B., 118, 145
Elliot, Emerson, J., 49
Elya, Susan, 278, 284
Emberley, Adrian, 309, 314
Emberley, Ed, 278, 284, 309, 314
Emberley, Rebecca, 309, 314
Enderle, Judith Ross, 309, 314
Enright, B., 67
Erekson, James, 78, 199, 204, 273, 307
Erickson, Gina, 309, 314
Erickson, John, 193, 205
Ervin, Criss, 181
Escamilla, Kathy, 50
Estice, Rose Mary, 15
Ets, Marie Hall, 309, 314

**F**
Fargstrup, A. E., 9
Farkas, Steve, 347
Fawson, Parker C., 240
Feldman, Eve, 129, 145
Feldman, Virginia Simon, 210
Fisher, Peter, 255, 257, 264, 268, 281, 283, 313
Fleischman, Paul, 395
Flippo, R. F., 164
Florence, M. D., 52
Florian, Douglas, 194, 205
Flurkey, A., 10
Ford, Michael P., 32, 173, 181, 184, 199, 201,
      204, 205
Forell, Elizabeth, 180
Foster, Kelli, 309, 314
Fountoukidis, D., 259

Fox, Barbara J., 313
Fox, Mem, 346
Franklin, S. H., 49
Frasier, Debra, 278, 284
Frayer, D., 276
Frazee, Marla, 128, 145
Frederick, W., 276
Freeman, Ann E., 7, 15
Freeman, D. E., 11, 12
Freeman, Y. S., 11, 12
French, M., 280
Fresch, Mary Jo, 204
Fried Mary D., 15
Fry, E., 259, 294, 313
Fulton, David, 398
Futrell, Mynga K., 204
Fyfe, S. A., 295

**G**

Gaiman, Neil, 195, 205
Galda, Lee, 252
Gambrell, L. B., 202, 205, 345, 347
Garan, Elaine M., 47
Gardner, Howard, 51
Gates, Arthur I., 204
Gavelek, J. R., 258
Geisert, Paul G., 204
Gentile, Lance M., 19
Gentry, J. Richard, 136
George, Lindsay Barrett, 250, 252
George, Margaret, 192, 206
Gerstein, Mordicai, 250, 252
Gillespie, Cindy S., 90
Gillingham, Mark G., 108
Gillis, M. K., 181
Giovanni, Nikki, 195, 206
Glass, G. V., 6
Glassman, Peter, 278, 284
Goforth, F., 193
Goldman, S. R., 204
Goodman, Gayle, 343
Goodman, Kenneth S., 10, 110, 167–168
Goodman, Yetta, 168
Goodrich, Heidi, 90
Graber, Janet, 195, 206
Graves, M., 255, 271
Greenburg, Dan, 193, 206
Griffin, Peg, 108, 287
Grohens, Joe, 59
Grover, Mary, 133, 145
Grover, Max, 278, 284
Gruber, Barbara, 313
Guccione, L. M., 11, 273
Gunning, T., 312, 313
Guralnick, Elissa, 278, 284

**H**

Haggard, M., 279
Hall, Donald, 250, 252
Hall, Leigh, 21, 51
Hall, Zoe, 185, 206
Halliday, M., 121
Hamilton, Kersten, 129, 145
Hammond, H., 271
Hampston, J., 19
Hansen, J., 138
Hanushek, Eric, 19
Hare, Victoria Chou, 216
Harkins, Peggy, 204
Harley, Avis, 278, 284
Harris, Albert J., 3, 15, 19, 48, 52, 53
Harris, T., 105, 204
Hart, B., 256
Hartill, M., 283
Hatcher, Catherine W., 211, 212
Hawkins, Colin, 309, 314
Hawkins, Jacqui, 309, 314
Hearn, Michael Patrick, 373
Heath, Shirley Brice, 49
Hegamin, Cozbi, 195, 206
Heilman, Arthur W., 313
Heimlich, J., 280
Henderson, Edmund H., 136
Hepworth, Cathi, 309, 314
Hickman, P., 256
Hiebert, Elfrieda H., 15, 19, 204
Hillerich, Robert L., 108
Hirschi, Ron, 278, 284
Hirschmann, Kris, 193, 206
Hoban, Tana, 121, 278, 284
Hoberman, Mary, 129, 145
Hochberg, Julian E., 7
Hodges, Richard E., 3, 105, 135, 204
Hoffman, James V., 57–58, 201, 204
Hoffman, Sybil M., 210
Holland, D., 164
Hopkins, Lee Bennett, 194, 206, 387
Horgan, Dianne D., 59
Hoyt, L., 252
Hughes, John P., 50
Hughes, Kay E., 106
Hull, Marion A., 313

**I**

Irvin, Judith L., 336
Isadora, Rachel, 195, 206

**J**

Jackobson, Julie, 204
Jackson, Phillip W., 32
Jacobson, Lenore, 21, 32

Jacobson, Michael G., 213
Janeczco, Paul, 194, 206
Jenkins, J. R., 145
Jeppson, Ann-Sofie, 278, 284
Johns, Jerry L., 86, 137, 145
Johnson, B., 283
Johnson, Dale D., 283, 313
Johnson, Marjorie Seddon, 151, 181
Johnson, Peter, 19, 47
Johnson, R. B., 251
Johnston, Kathy, 343
Johnston, Peter H., 15
Johnston, Tony, 309, 314
Jolly, Thomas, 210
Jones, William O., 55
Josephine, Sister, C.S.J., 263

K

Kalman, Maira, 278, 284
Kame'Enui, E., 283
Kamii, Constance, 108
Kamil, Michael L., 15, 201, 204, 252, 255, 257, 271, 283, 313, 339, 347
Kara-Soteriou, J., 204, 205
Karchmer, R. A., 204, 205
Karweit, Nancy L., 21
Kasarda, John D., 19
Kelty, Annette P., 210
Kendal, J., 11
Khuon, O., 11
Kiger, N., 12, 13
Killgallon, Patsy A., 149
Kim, H. S., 201, 204
Kinney, Jeff, 193, 206
Kintsch, Walter, 210
Kinzer, C. K., 202, 205
Kirk, Daniel, 278, 284
Kiss, Andrew, 278, 284
Klausmeier, H., 276
Koch, Lisa, 205
Koskinen, P., 345, 347
Kozminsky, Ely, 210
Krashen, S., 11
Kress, Roy A., 151, 181
Kruel, M., 204
Kucan, L., 255
Kucer, Steven, 8, 136, 168, 210, 252, 291

L

Labbo, L., 202, 205
Labov, William, 51
Lane, D., 201, 204
Lasky, Kathryn, 278, 284
Leedy, Loreen, 278, 284
Le Guin, Ursula K., 309, 314

Lehr, Fran, 108
Lenski, Susan Davis, 86
Leu, D. J., Jr., 202, 205
Levitt, Paul, 278, 284
Lewin, Ted, 278, 284
Lewis, J. Patrick, 250, 252
Lewison, Wendy C., 309, 314
Lipson, Marjorie Y., 51, 58
Loban, Walter D., 49, 113
Lobel, Arnold, 129, 145, 194, 206
London, Jonathan, 129, 145
Long, Melinda, 215, 252
Lowry, Lois, 195, 206
Luckie, William R., 336
Lupica, Mike, 193, 206
Lyons, C., 205

M

Macdonald, Suse, 250, 252
MacGillivray, Laurie, 118
MacGinitie, Ruth, 106
MacGinitie, Walter, 106, 255
Mack, 195, 206
MacKinnon, G. E., 108
Mahar, D., 204
Mallette, M. H., 204, 205
Malloy, J. A., 205
Mandl, Heinz, 239
Mann, Bethany, 191, 206
Mantione, R., 252
Manzo, A. V., 243
Manzo, K., 215
Maria, Katherine, 106
Marriott, D., 252
Marshak, Samuel, 129, 145
Martin, Bill, 129, 145
Martin, Jacqueline Briggs, 250, 252
Martin-Lara, Susan G., 181
Marzollo, Jean, 191, 206
Mather, Nancy, 300
Mayer, Richard E., 8
Mazano, R., 283
McCabe, A., 142
McCarthy, M., 164
McClain-Ruelle, Leslie, 251
McDonnell, Flora, 133, 145
McKenna, M., 202, 205
McKeown, M. G., 204, 255, 280, 283, 313
McMillan, James H., 41, 101
McMillan, Merna, 19
McVee, M. B., 258
Mechling, Jane, 369
Meister, Cari, 309, 314
Melmed, Laura, 191, 206
Merkley, D. J., 295

Mesmer, Heidi Anne E., 205
Milgrim, David, 309, 314
Miller, L., 67
Miller, William, 195, 206
Mills, Claudia, 192, 206
Minarik, Else, 194, 206
Miranda, Anne, 127, 145
Mitchell, Joyce Slayton, 278, 284
Mitchell, Kay, 64, 90
Mitton, Tony, 309, 314
Moe, A., 271
Moore, David W., 216
Morris, Ann, 278, 284
Morris, Darrell, 181
Morrison, Coleman, 19
Morrow, Barbara Olenyik, 129, 145
Morrow, Lesley Mandel, 202, 339
Mosenthal, Peter B., 15, 204, 255, 257, 339
Most, Bernard, 121
Mugford, Simon, 192, 206
Munsch, Robert, 215, 252
Muth, K. D., 184

**N**

Nagy, William E., 283, 313
Neuman, S., 345, 347
Nickerson, L., 268
Nishizuka, Koko, 195, 206
Norman, Kimberly A., 300
Norworth, Jack, 129, 145

**O**

Obrochta, C., 283
O'Connor, R. E., 145
Oczkus, L., 252
Ogle, D., 251
Ohanian, S., 283
Olivo, Richard, 278, 284
Olson, Mary W., 181
Opitz, Michael F., 11, 23, 28, 32, 53, 77, 78, 85, 117, 119,
    120, 123, 124, 126, 131–132, 139–140, 145, 168,
    169, 171, 173, 174, 175, 181, 184, 199, 201, 204,
    205, 212, 215, 250, 252, 273, 332
Osborn, Jean, 108
Otto, Wayne, 93
Outsen, N., 252
Owocki, G., 252

**P**

Page, William D., 231
Palatini, Margie, 129, 145
Palincsar, Annemarie Sullivan, 239
Paris, Scott G., 57–58, 229, 306, 339
Parish, Herman, 250, 252
Parry, Florence, 250, 252

Patton, Margaret Tuley, 379
Paulson, Eric J., 7, 15
Pavey, Peter, 129, 145
Pearson, P. David, 9, 15, 204, 229, 255, 257, 306, 339
Peterson, Barbara, 186, 205
Piaget, Jean, 59, 112–113
Pickering, D., 283
Pierce, Cathryn M., 252
Pikulski, John J., 151, 181
Pinnel, G., 205
Pinnell, Gay Su, 15
Pittelman, S., 280
Pleasants, H. M., 49
Polacco, Patricia, 190, 206
Polk, J., 259
Pollard-Durodola, S., 256
Pollatsek, Alexander, 51
Popham, James W., 36, 41, 90, 101
Post, Arden Ruth, 252
Poteet, J., 67
Potter, Alicia, 309, 314
Pressley, Michael, 19, 202, 211, 252
Price, Gary Glen, 108
Priceman, Marjorie, 309, 314
Prosek, James, 191, 206
Pulver, Robin, 309, 314
Purcell-Gates, Victoria, 49, 347

**R**

Rabinowitz, Mitchell, 216
Rakestraw, J. A., Jr., 204
Raledy, T., 67
Rampey, B. D., 49
Raphael, Taffy E., 242, 280, 283
Rasinski, T. V., 168, 169, 171, 181, 215
Raths, J. D., 19, 28
Rathvon, N., 110, 130
Rayner, Keieth, 51
Readence, J., 276
Reed, J. H., 184
Reeves, Harriet Ramsey, 205
Reilly-Giff, Patricia, 192, 206
Reinhart, Matthew, 278, 284
Reinking, D., 202, 205
Reutzel, D. Ray, 240
Richards, John P., 211, 212
Rigg, Pat, 59
Risley, T. R., 256
Robb, Laura, 131–132, 139–140, 250, 252, 283, 332
Robinson, Susan R., 180
Rockwell, Anne, 190, 206
Rodgers, L. L., 251
Roe, Betty D., 180
Rogers, Sally, 127–128, 145
Roller, C., 11, 29, 50

Root, Phyllis, 116
Rose, Elaine D., 336
Rosenbaum, Judy, 383
Rosenshine, Barak V., 48
Rosenthal, Robert, 21, 32
Ross, Stewart, 191, 206
Rotner, Shelly, 121, 278, 284
Rowe, Deborah W., 118
Rowling, J. K., 193, 206
Rubin, Dorothy, 145, 252, 260, 283, 313, 336, 347
Rudell, Robert, 202, 205, 210
Ryan, Linda, 64, 90
Rycik, James A., 313
Rycik, Mary T., 313
Ryder, Joanne, 191, 206
Rylant, Cynthia, 129, 145, 194, 195, 206

S
Sabuda, Robert, 133, 145
Sachar, Louis, 195, 206
Sadler, C., 252
Salvia, John, 23, 41, 90, 101
Sammons, Janice, 300
Samoyault, Tiphanie, 278, 284
Samuels, S. Jay, 9, 15
Satcher, D., 52
Savage, John F., 313
Say, Allen, 195, 206
Schaefer, Lola M., 250, 252
Schallert, Diane L., 57–58, 184, 201, 204
Scheinfeld, Amram, 52
Schertle, Alice, 129, 145
Schieble, Karen Magnus, 216
Schmitt, 234
Schwartz, Jonathan, 300
Schwartz, R., 280, 283
Scieszka, Jon, 129, 145
Scott, Judith A., 15, 19, 283, 313
Scrimshaw, Nevin S., 53
Searfoss, L., 276
Searl, Duncan, 391
Segal, Lore, 309, 314
Shake, Mary C., 6, 15, 48
Shapiro, Zachary, 129, 145
Shaw, D., 252
Shaw, Nancy, 309, 314
Shea, Pegi Deitz, 191, 206
Sibberson, Franki, 205
Siebert, Diane, 278, 284
Silvaroli, J. Nicholas, 181
Silverstein, Shel, 278, 284
Singer, Eliot A., 78
Singer, Marilyn, 309, 314
Sipay, Edward R., 15, 48, 52, 53
Slavin, Robert E., 21, 51, 64

Smalls, Irene, 195, 206
Smead, S., 252
Smethurst, Wood, 336
Smith, B., 50
Smith, Charles R., Jr., 278, 284
Smith, Dora V., 196
Smith, Jeffrey K., 339
Smith, M. L., 6
Smith, Nila Banton, 59, 213
Snicket, Lemony, 250, 252
Snow, Catherine E., 15, 108, 252, 287
Sobel, June, 278, 284
Soffos, C., 251
Solomon, G., 205
Spence, Amy, 127, 145
Spence, Rob, 127, 145
Spiegel, D., 252
Spinelli, Jerry, 215, 252
Spires, Elizabeth, 278, 284
Sprague, K., 142
Squier, Susan E., 180
Stahl, K., 304, 313
Stahl, Steven A., 108, 213, 304, 313
Stamper, Judith, 375
Stauffer, Russell G., 238
Stead, Tony, 205
Stephens, Sarah Hines, 191, 206
Stern, Virginia, 90
Stevens, Janet, 346
Stevenson, Robert Louis, 129, 145, 194, 206
Sticht, Thomas, 210
Stilton, Geronimo, 193, 206
Stojic, Manya, 278, 284
Stokes, Sandra M., 64, 90
Stoll, D., 197
Strang, Ruth, 4, 34
Sturges, Philemon, 194, 206
Stuve-Bodeen, Stephanie, 195, 206
Sutton, Christine, 59
Swan, M., 50
Sweet, A., 252
Swinburne, Stephen, 121, 250, 252
Swinning, E. A., 164
Szymusiak, Karen, 205

T
Talbott, Hudson, 191, 206
Tatham, Betty, 191, 206
Taylor, Barbara M., 211
Taylor, Mildred, 196
Taylor, Wilson, 231
Teague, Mark, 309, 314
Teale, W., 105
Terrell, T., 11
Tessler, Stephanie Gordon, 309, 314

Thaler, M., 280
Thogmartin, M. B., 190
Thomas, Adele, 347
Thorndike, Edward L., 211
Tiedt, Iris M., 59
Tiedt, Pamela L., 59
Tobias, Tobi, 278, 284
Tobin, Jim, 129, 145
Tompkins, G. E., 283
Topping K., 343, 347
Torgesen, J. K., 124
Tractenberg, P., 313
Trussell-Cullen, A., 281
Turner, Julianne C., 339
Tyre, Peg, 52

**U**
Unrau, N., 202, 205
Usher, M. D., 192, 206
Utterback, L., 204

**V**
Van Allsburg, Chris, 250, 252
Van Der Voort, Thom H. A., 344
Vaughn, S., 256
Veugelers, P. J., 52
Viorst, Judith, 250, 252

**W**
Waczisko, M., 19, 28
Wallach, G. P., 281
Waller, T. Gary, 108
Walsh, Daniel J., 108
Wasik, Barbara A., 339
Wasik, Barbara M., 21, 50
Watson, 240
Wedwick, Linda, 205
Weinstein, Claire E., 8
Weinstein, Ellen Slusky, 129, 145, 190, 206

Weitzman, David, 191, 206
Wepman, Joseph M., 56
West, Tracey, 193, 206
Wharton-McDonald, R., 19, 48
Wheelock, Warren H., 181
Whitman, Walt, 194, 206
Wilbur, Richard, 309, 314
Wilder, Laura Ingalls, 197
Wilhelm, Hans, 309, 314
Wilhelm, J., 252
Wilkinson, Ian A. G., 15, 19
Willems, Mo, 192, 206
Williams, Laura Ellen, 133, 145
Wilson, R., 345, 347
Wittrock, Merlin C., 8, 15, 53
Wixson, Karen K., 51, 58
Wood, Audry, 190, 206
Woolfolk, Anita E., 32, 42, 59, 96, 101
Wooten, Deborah, 205
Wormell, Mary, 190, 206
Wutz, Jessica Ann, 205

**Y**
Yaden, David B., Jr., 118
Yoe, Craig, 278, 284
Yolen, Jane, 194, 195, 206, 250, 252, 309, 314
Yopp, H., 110
Young, Ed, 195, 206
Young, William E., 210
Ysseldyke, James E., 23, 41, 90, 101
Yulga, S., 252

**Z**
Zabaracki, M., 212
Ziefert, Harriet, 309, 314
Zieky, Michael, 92, 98
Zollinger, Miriam, 50
Zuckerman, Andrew, 309, 314

# Subject Index

## A

*ABC Disney* (Sabuda), 133, 145
*ABC Kids* (Williams), 133, 145
*The Absentminded Fellow* (Marshak), 129, 145
Abstract words, 258
*The Accidental Zucchini* (Grover), 133, 145
Accommodation, 112
Active readers, 9
Adjectives, 258
  foreign languages, transfer issues for, 408
Administering
  Early Names Test for assessing phonics, 300
  Informal Reading Inventory (IRI), 155–164
  letter identification test, 130
  listening capacity test, 159
  Modified Miscue Analysis, 168
  Names Test, 295, 297, 300
  phonics assessments, 295, 297, 300
  phonological awareness test, 124
  running records, 172–176
  Word Recognition Inventory of IRI, 157–158
Adverbs, language transfer issues for, 410
Advertisement texts, 199–200
Aesops's fables, web site for, 346
Affective domain, 7
Affixes, 259
  breaking apart affixes, teaching, 271
*African Acrostics* (Harley), 278, 284
Ages of literacy development, 12–14
*All About Where* (Hoban), 278, 284
All Children Survey, 29
*Alligator Baby* (Munsch), 215, 252
Alliteration books, 129
Almost proficient reading and writing, 13
Alphabet books for letter identification, 133
*Alphabetical Order: How the Alphabet Began* (Samoyault), 278, 284
Alphabetic principle and early literacy, 108
Alternative assessment, 64
*Altoona Baboona* (Bynum), 128, 145
*Amelia Bedelia's First Day of School* (Parish), 250, 252
*American Girl*, 197
Analogies
  phonics, analogies for teaching, 310
  teaching students to make, 276–277
  vocabulary and, 263
Analytic phonics instruction, 304, 306
Anecdotal records, 69–72
  example of, 81

*Animal Opposites* (Reinhart), 278, 284
*An Island Grows* (Schaefer), 250, 252
*Antics* (Hepworth), 309, 314
Antonym context clues, 261–262
*The Apple Pie Tree* (Hall), 185, 206
Appreciative listening, 212
*Arthur* series web site, 346
Articles, grammar transfer issues for, 406
Assessment. *See also* Pre-reading assessment;
    Tests and testing
  authentic, performance-based assessment, 63–66
  defined, 35–36
  hierarchy, 35
  interests inventories and, 82–84
  interviews, informal, 79–82
  of letter identification, 130
  observation and, 67–69
  of phonics, 295–303
  of phonological awareness, 124
  portfolio assessment, 66–67
  projective techniques, 84, 87
  reading autobiography, 87–88
  of reading comprehension, 229–235
  of story sense, 138–140
  strengths, needs, and assessment techniques, chart of,
    353–354
  of vocabulary, 264
  of writing, 136–138
Assimilation, 112
Assumptions, hidden, 21
Astigmatism, 53
At-risk children, 45
Attitude
  performance and, 58
  reading attitude surveys, 82, 85–86
Auditory acuity, 54–56
Auditory discrimination, 56, 287, 288
Auditory memory span, 56–57
Auditory perception, 54–57
Authentic, performance-based assessment, 63–64
Authentic assessment, 64
Authentic literature, 185
Autobiography, reading, 87–88

## B

*Babu's Song* (Stuve-Bodeen), 195, 206
*Baby Sea Otter* (Tatham), 191, 206
Balanced reading, 5
Basal readers, 185–186, 188

*The Basic School: A Community for Learning* (Boyer), 340

*A Beasty Story* (Martin), 129, 145

*The Beckoning Cat* (Nishizuka), 195, 206

*Becoming a Nation of Readers* (Anderson et al.), 19

Beginning reading, 13, 105

Betts Reading Levels, 151–153

*Beyond the Great Mountains* (Young), 195, 206

Biases
  objective testing and, 38–39
  reliability of test and, 39

*Big, Bigger, Biggest* (Coffelt), 278, 284

*Billy & Milly Short & Silly* (Feldman), 129, 145

Binaurality, 56

*Bird, Butterfly, Eel* (Prosek), 191, 206

Birth order and performance, 50

*B Is for Bulldozer: A Construction ABC* (Sobel), 278, 284

*Bless Us All: A Child's Yearbook of Blessings* (Rylant),
      129, 145

*Block City* (Stevenson), 194, 206

Bloom's taxonomy of educational objectives, 213

*Boehm Test of Language concepts,* 116

Boldface type, use of, 281

*Boo-Hoo Moo* (Palatini), 129, 145

Books. *See also* Children's Literature Index
  basal readers, 185–186, 188
  chapter books, 194–195
  commercial books, 187–189
  information books, 190–191
  little books, 187–188
  multicultural books, 195–197
  multilevel books, 191–192
  Newberry Award books, 341
  phonics, teaching, 307–309
  predictable books, 189–190
  reference books, 334–335
  series books, 192–193
  trade books, 185
  vocabulary, books for teaching, 277–278, 281–282
  web sites for children's books, 346

*Boris's Glasses* (Cohen), 278, 284

Bottom-up reading models, 10

Brainstorming for teaching phonics, 306–307

Bridging language proficiency, 11

*Bud, Not Buddy* (Curtis), 195, 205

Buffer zone. *See* Informal Reading Inventory (IRI)

*Bug Off!* (Hepworth), 309, 314

*A Butterfly Grows* (Swinburne), 250, 252

*Button Up!* (Schertle), 129, 145

*Buzz Said the Bee* (Lewison), 309, 314

**C**

*Caddie Woodlawn* (Brink), 197

Calendars as texts, 200

Cambourne's Conditions of Learning, 107

*Cam Jansen* (Adler), 193, 205

*Carnival* (Ballard), 277, 283

Case report of child, 350–351

*Cat Dreams* (Le Guin), 309, 314

Categorizing words, 262–263
  chart for, 273
  teaching strategies, 272–276

*Celia Cruz, Queen of Salsa* (Chambers), 195, 205

Chapter books, 194–195

Characteristics of good teachers, 20–21

Checklists
  comprehension observation checklist, 78
  group checklists, 72–76
  group performance checklist, 77
  individual checklists, 74–76
  for observations, 67
  observations and, 72–78
  portfolio checklist, 68
  rating scales and, 76–78
  for self-evaluation by teacher, 29, 30
  speech problems, diagnostic checklist of, 74
  whole class language concepts checklist, 75

Children's literature. *See* Books; Children's
      Literature Index

Children's Reading Room, 201

Children's Storybooks Online: Stories of Kids
      of All Ages, 202

Chunking, 8

Churches and parental involvement, 340

*Clang! Clang! Beep! Beep! Listen to the City*
      (Burleigh), 129, 145

Classroom tests, 99

C letter sounds, 291

*Clickety Clack* (Spence & Spence), 127, 145

*Close, Closer, Closest* (Rotner & Olivo), 278, 284

Closed word sorts, 309–310

Cloze procedure, 231–234

Cloze tests
  example of, 233–234
  maze procedure compared, 234–235

Cognitive Academic Language Proficiency (CALP)
      and ELLs, 12

Cognitive domain, 7–8

Collaboration, parent/child, 339

*Color Me a Rhyme* (Yolen), 250, 252

*Colors* (Crowther), 278, 284

Combining forms, 259–260
  teaching use of, 270–272

*Comeback Kids* (Lupica), 193, 206

*Come Rhyme with Me!* (Wilhelm), 309, 314

Commercial books, 187–189

Community and parental involvement, 340

Comparison/contrast context clues, 260–261

Complex sentences, transfer issues for, 411

*The Composer Is Dead* (Snicket), 250, 252

Compound words, 258

Comprehension. *See also* Listening comprehension;
    Reading comprehension
  defined, 209
  observation checklist, 78
Computers. *See also* Internet
  influence of, 345–346
Concentration and studying, 325–326
Concepts
  defined, 111–112
  development of, 112–113
  and early literacy, 111–122
  informal inventory test for concept development,
    114–116
  language, concept development and, 113
  oral language concept assessment, 113–116
  Piagetian concept development, 112–113
  print concepts, assessment of, 116–122
*Concepts About Print* (Clay), 110, 116–117
Concrete words, 258
Confused students, testing for, 38
Connections, strategy for making, 244, 250
Consonant blends, 290–291
  foreign languages, transfer issues for, 415
Consonant digraphs, 290–291
  foreign languages, transfer issues for, 415, 417
  silent consonant digraphs, 291
  sound-symbol transfers, 417
Consonants, 287, 289–291
  C letter sounds, 291
  final consonants, 289
  foreign languages, transfer issues for, 414, 416
  G letter sounds, 291
  initial consonants, 289
  Q letter sounds, 291
  sound-symbol transfers, 416
Content domain of criterion-referenced tests, 98
Context clues. *See* Vocabulary
Contextually-defined words, using, 282
Context-Use for vocabulary, 268
Contrast context clues, 260–261
Correspondence as texts, 200
Council for Exceptional Children, 10
*Crazy Like a Fox - A Simile Story* (Leedy), 278, 284
Creative reading. *See* Reading comprehension
*Creature* (Zuckerman), 309, 314
*Cricket Magazine,* 197
Criterion-referenced tests, 97–98
  limitations of, 98
Critical listening, 212
Critical reading. *See* Reading comprehension
*Crunch Munch* (London), 129, 145
Culture
  intelligence and, 51
  multicultural books, 195–197
Cybertext, reading, 21

**D**
*Dappled Apples* (Carr), 185, 205
*The Day of Ahmed's Secret* (Parry), 250, 252
*The Dead Bird* (Brown), 277
*Dear Mr. Henshaw* (Cleary), 215, 252
Decoding and reading models, 10
*The Deep Blue Sea: A Book of Colors* (Wood), 190, 206
Deep structure and comprehension, 211
Definition context clues, 260
Derivatives of words, 259–260
Description context clues, 260
Developing language proficiency, 11
Developmental reading, 5–6
*Developmental Reading Assessment (DRA),* 172
Developmental spelling, 135–136
Diagnosis
  close procedure and comprehension diagnosis,
    231–234
  considerations for, 6–7
  defined, 2–3
  portfolios and, 67
  teacher's role in, 18
  ten principles of, 3–4
Diagnostic pattern, defined, 4
Diagnostic reading tests, 100
*Diagnostic Survey* (Clay), 138, 142
Diagnostic teaching, 23
Dialects, 50–51
*Diary of a Wimpy Kid* (Kinney), 193, 206
Dictionaries, 334
"Digits Forward"/"Digits Backward," 57
*Dinothesaurus* (Florian), 194, 205
Diphthongs, 293
  foreign languages, transfer issues for, 415
*Directed Reading-Thinking Activity (DRTA),* 238
  and story sense, 141
Directions, following, 326–327
Discriminative listening, 212
Dispositions of teachers, 19
  human relations incidents (HRIs) for, 28
Divergent thinking, questions stimulating, 241
Divorce and performance, 49
Dolch list of high-frequency words, 258
*Donovan's Word Jar* (DeGross), 278, 284
*Don't Talk to Me About the War* (Adler), 250, 252
*Down to the Sea in Ships* (Sturges), 194, 206
*Dynamic Indicators of Basic Early Literacy Skills
  (DIBELS),* 110

**E**
Early emergent readers, 12
Early intervention, 141–142
Early literacy, 103–146
  beginning stages of, 105–106
  components of, 108

Early literacy (*continued*)
  concepts and, 111–122
  current assessment methods, 109–111
  early intervention and, 141–142
  letter identification, 128–133
  phonological awareness, 123–128
  pre-reading assessment, 106–109
  story sense, 138–141
  summary of test results, 143
  what, why, and how of, 111
  writing, emergent, 133–138
Early Names Test for phonics assessment, 300–303
*Earthsong* (Rogers), 127–128, 145
Educational factors, 45–46, 47–49
  instructional materials, 47–48
  instructional time, 49
  reading models, 47
  school environment, 49
  teachers, 48
Educational Testing Service (ETS) on gender and reading, 52
*The Eensy-Weensy Spider* (Hoberman), 129, 145
Electronic texts, 201–203
*Elephant and Piggie* (Willems), 192, 206
*Elephant in a Well* (Ets), 309, 314
*Elephants Can Paint, Too* (Arnold), 191, 205
ELLs (English language learners), 11–12
  performance and, 50–51
  tests for, 37
*Elvis Lives! And Other Anagrams* (Agee), 277, 283
Emergent literacy, 12–13, 105
Emergent writing, 133–138
Emerging language proficiency, 11
Emotional health and performance, 57–58
End of unit exercises, using, 282
English language learners. *See* ELLs
    (English language learners)
Entertainment texts, 199
Equilibrium, 112–113
*Erika-San* (Say), 195, 206
Evaluation, defined, 36–37
Evaluative readers, 9
*Everywhere the Cow Says Moo!* (Weinstein), 129, 145, 190, 206
Example context clues, 260–261
*Excellent Reading Teachers* (IRA), 3–4
Expanding language proficiency, 11
Expectations of teachers, 21–22
Explanation context clues, 260
Explicit reading, teacher's role in, 24–25
Explicit teaching, 25
  drill and, 30–31
  of print concepts, 122
  of vocabulary, 256, 268
Eye movements, 7

**F**

*Faces in the Forest* (Hirschi), 278, 284
*Faces Magazine,* 197
*Faces of the Moon* (Crelin), 191, 205
*Fair!* (Lewin), 278, 284
Families. *See also* Parental involvement
  divorce and performance, 49
  performance and, 49–50
  phonological awareness and, 128
  tests for students with problems, 38
Family Education web site, 346
Family Literacy Project, 343
*Farmer Joe and the Music Show* (Mitton), 309, 314
Farsightedness, 53
*Fed Up! A Feast of Frazzled Foods* (Barron), 129, 145
Financial transaction texts, 200
*The Flea's Sneeze* (Downley), 129, 145
*Flora McDonnell's A B C* (McDonnell), 133, 145
Fluency
  of letter recognition (LRF), 110
  reading comprehension and, 214–215
*Flying Eagle* (Bardhan-Quallen), 194, 205
Focused teaching of print concepts, 122
Following directions, 326–327
*A Foot in the Mouth: Poems to Speak, Sing, & Shout* (Janeczco), 194, 206
Foreign languages. *See also* ELLs (English language learners)
  grammar, transfer issues for, 405–413
  phonics, transfer issues for, 414–417
  sound-symbol transfers, 416–417
Frayer Model for categorizing words, 276
*Fritz Danced the Fandango* (Potter), 309, 314
*Frog and Toad* series (Lobel), 194, 206
*Froggie Went A-Courting* (Priceman), 309, 314
*The Frogs and Toads All Sang* (Lobel), 129, 145
*From Head to Toe* (Carle), 309, 314
Frustration reading level, 151, 152
  listening capacity test and, 159
  reporting, 153
Fry Instant Word List, 258, 259
  in case report of child, 351
Functional level testing, 95

**G**

Games
  categorizing words and, 274
  concept development and, 113
  print concepts, teaching, 121
  Yea/Nay game for teaching vocabulary, 280
Games We Know file, 2742
*Gates-MacGinitie Reading Tests,* 93–94
  for pre-reading assessment, 106

Gender, 46
as noneducational factor, 51–52
Generalizations in phonics, 286–287
*Geronimo Stilton* (Stilton), 193, 206
Gerunds, grammar transfer issues for, 412
*The Giver* (Lowry), 195, 206
*Glad Monster, Sad Monster* (Emberly), 278, 284
G letter sounds, 291
Glossaries
of textbooks, 325
use of, 281
*The Gold Cadillac* (Taylor), 196
*Good Dog, Carl* (Day), 138, 145
*Good Morning, Digger* (Rockwell), 190, 206
Good readers, attributes of, 9
Goofy books, 129
Government web sites, 346
Grad equivalents, defined, 96–97
Grammar, transfer issues for, 405–413
Grapheme-phoneme correspondences, 211
*The Graveyard Book* (Gaiman), 195, 205
Groups
checklists for, 72–76
guided reading experiences, size for, 27
performance checklist, 77
tests, administering, 99–100
Guided reading
group size for, 27
phonological awareness and, 127
*Gus and Grandpa* (Mills), 192, 206
Guys Read web site, 346

**H**
Halliday's Functions of Language, 122
*Hank, the Cowdog* (Erickson), 193, 205
*Hansel and Gretel* (Isadora), 195, 206
Harcourt Archive's Literacy by Design little books, 187
*Harry Potter* (Rowling), 193, 206
Health
emotional health and performance, 57–58
as noneducational factor, 52–53
*Health Behaviors* (Reed & Lang), 224–225
Hearing
listening and, 211
performance and, 54–57
problems, symptoms of, 55
*Heart of Texas* (Melmed), 191, 206
*Hello World! Greetings in 42 Languages Around the Globe!* (Stojic), 278, 284
*Henry and Mudge* series (Rylant), 194, 206
*Here Comes Pontus!* (Jeppson), 278, 284
*Here Is the Arctic Winter* (Dunphy), 278, 284
*Here Is the Southwestern Desert* (Dunphy), 278, 284
*Here Is the Tropical Rain Forest* (Dunphy), 278, 284

Hertz (Hz), 55
Heuristic function of language, 122
Hidden assumptions, 21
High-frequency words, 258
High-stakes tests, 93
"Hokey Pokey," 121
*Holes* (Sachar), 195, 206
Home environment. *See* Families; Parental involvement
Homographs, 258
as context clues, 262
Homonyms, 258
as context clues, 262
Homophones, 258
as context clues, 262
Houghton Mifflin
Pair-It Extreme little books, 187
Reading basal readers, 188
*How Do Dinosaurs Say Good Night?* (Yolen & Teague), 309, 314
*How Many Days to America* (Bunting), 250, 252
*How Many Fish?* (Cohen), 309, 314
*How Tall, How Short, How Far Away?* (Adler), 277, 283
*Hug* (Alborough), 190, 205
Human relations incidents (HRIs) for teacher dispositions, 28
Humorous poetry, 193
*The Hungry Monster* (Root), 116
*Hush Little Baby* (Frazee), 128, 145
Hypermetropia, 53

**I**
Identification. *See also* Letter identification
defined, 4–5
Illness and performance, 52
Imaginative function of language, 122
Implied statements, understanding, 225–226
*I'm Your Bus* (Singer), 309, 314
Independent reading level, 151, 152
phonological awareness and, 127
reporting, 153
Independent writing
phonological awareness and, 127
Indexes of textbook, 325
Individuals, checklists for, 74–76
Individuals with Disabilities Education Improvement Act (IDEIA), 4
Individual tests, 99
Individual work, 27
Inferences. *See* Reading comprehension
Infinitives, grammar transfer issues for, 412
Informal Reading Inventory (IRI), 149–167. *See also* Listening capacity test; Word Recognition Inventory (WRI)

Informal Reading Inventory (*continued*)
　administering, 155–164
　Betts Reading Levels, 151–153
　buffer zone, 153, 160
　　listening capacity test and, 160
　capacity levels, determining, 151–153
　in case report of child, 350–351
　custom IRI, constructing, 356–359
　defined, 149–150
　errors, codes for marking and scoring, 150, 154
　first reader level questions, 371–372
　level 2 questions, 373–378
　level 3 questions, 379–386
　level 4 questions, 387–390
　level 5 questions, 391–394
　level 6 questions, 395–397
　level 7 questions, 398–400
　level 8 questions, 401–404
　normal reading inventory, 360–404
　oral reading passages, administering, 158
　preprimer level questions, 367–368
　primer level questions, 369–370
　purposes of, 151
　rapport with student, establishing, 155
　reporting reading levels, 153–154
　running records compared, 170–172
　scoring oral reading errors, 154–155
　selection criteria, 164–167
　silent reading passages, administering, 158
　special notes for normal IRI, 362
　strengths and needs, sample note on, 163, 167
　student feedback and, 151
　summary sheet for, 161–162, 165–166, 360
　word recognition formula, 155
Informal student interviews, 79–82
Informal tests, 99
Informative function of language, 122
*In 1776* (Marzollo), 191, 206
Instructional materials, 47–48
Instructional reading level, 151, 152
　reporting, 153
Instructional time, 48
Instrumental function of language, 122
Intelligence
　malnutrition and, 53
　memory span and, 57
　as noneducational factor, 51
Interactional function of language, 122
Interactive reading models, 10
Interactive writing and phonological awareness, 127
Interest inventories, 73
　assessment with, 82–84
International Reading Association (IRA)
　early literacy, assessment of, 109–110
　early literacy, use of term, 105

Guiding Principles on RtI, 4
　on paired reading, 343
　on phonological awareness, 124
　on television, 345
　ten principles of diagnosis, 3–4
　web site, 346
Internet
　children, web sites for, 346
　parental involvement and, 345–346
　parents, web sites for, 346
　texts on, 201–203
　vocabulary, web sites for teaching, 278–279
Interpretation. *See also* Reading comprehension
　of running records, 178
　of Word Recognition Inventory of IRI, 158
Intervention, 4–5
Interviews
　informal student interviews, 79–82
　protocol for student interview, 79–80
　suggestions for managing, 80, 82
　summary for student interview, 81
*In the Garden: Who's Been Here?* (George), 250, 252
*In the Swim* (Florian), 194, 205
*Into the Ice: The Story of the Arctic Exploration* (Curlee), 191, 205
Invented spelling, 126, 135–136
Inventories. *See also* Informal Reading Inventory (IRI); Interest inventories
　for concept development, 114–116
Irvine Unified School District, 343
*Is it Larger? Is it Smaller?* (Hoban), 278, 284
Italics, use of, 281
*It's About Dogs* (Johnston), 309, 314

**J**
*Jen the Hen* (Hawkins & Hawkins), 309, 314
*Journal of Adolescent & Adult Literacy,* 95
Journals on standardized tests, 95
Junior Great Books program, 341
*Just How Long Can a Long String Be?* (Baker), 309, 314

**K**
Kindergarten. *See also* Early literacy
　readers, 13
Knowledge Rating vocabulary, teaching, 268, 281

**L**
Labels, reading, 199
*Ladybug Magazine,* 197
Language. *See also* Foreign languages; Oral language
　concepts checklist, 75
　Halliday's Functions of Language, 122
　proficiency, levels of, 11
Learned helplessness, 57

Learning, Cambourne's Conditions of, 107
*Leaving the Nest* (Gerstein), 250, 252
Less proficient readers, 8
Letter identification, 128–133
    alphabet books and, 133
    assessment of, 130
    defined, 128, 130
    early literacy and, 108
    names and, 130
    pretests, 131–132
    teaching, 130, 133
Leveled books, 185–186
*Liberty Rising: The Story of the Statue of Liberty* (Shea),
    191, 206
*Linking Testing to Teaching: A Classroom Resource for
    Reading Assessment and Instruction,* 195
Listening. *See also* Informal Reading Inventory (IRI)
    concentration and, 325–326
    levels of, 212
    to read alouds, 210
    vocabulary, 210–211, 256
Listening capacity test, 150, 151, 152–153
    administering, 159
    criteria for giving, 159–164
    frustration reading level and, 159
    strengths and needs, sample note on, 163, 167
    summary sheets for, 161–162, 165–166
Listening comprehension, 209–211
    diagnostic checklist for, 236
    reading comprehension compared, 212
    teaching, 235–250
List-Group-Label method for categorizing words, 276
Literacy by Design little books, 187
Literal comprehension. *See* Reading comprehension
Literature webbing, 240
Literature webbing strategy lesson (LWSL), 240
*Little Bear* series (Minarik), 194, 206
Little books, 187–188
*Little House in the Big Woods* (Wilder), 197
*Llama Llama Mad at Mama* (Dewdney), 250, 252
Locator tests, 95
Long vowels, 292
    foreign languages, transfer issues for, 415
*Lucille Lost* (George & Murphy), 192, 206
Lyric poetry, 193

**M**

Macrostructure and comprehension, 211
Magazines, 197–198
    encouraging readers with, 21
Magic Keys web site, 346
Main ideas. *See* Reading comprehension
Malnutrition and performance, 52–53
Manager role for teachers, 25–26
*Maniac Magee* (Spinelli), 215, 252

Masking, 56
*Max's Wacky Taxi Day* (Grover), 278, 284
Maze procedure, 234–235
Mean, defined, 96
Meaning and reading models, 10
Measurement, defined, 36
Media center, using, 333–335
Memory span, 56–57
*Mental Measurements Yearbooks,* 95
*Meow: Cat Stories from Around the World* (Yolen),
    195, 206
Metacognition, 8
    and comprehension, 211
    training, 9
*Meta-Comprehension Strategy Index,* 234
*Metropolitan Achievement Tests,* 94
*Metropolitan Readiness Tests,* 108
Microstructure and comprehension, 211
*Mighty Book of Jokes* (Yoe), 278, 284
*Mike Mulligan and His Steam Shovel,* 277
Miscue analysis, 167–170
    Modified Miscue Analysis, 168–170
    uses of, 168
*Miss Alaineus* (Frasier), 278, 284
*Missing May* (Rylant), 195, 206
Modeled writing and phonological awareness, 127
Models of reading, 10
Modified Miscue Analysis, 168–170
    form for, 169
    summary of observations, 171
*Mommies Say Shhh!* (Polacco), 190, 206
Monitoring understanding, strategy for, 246, 250
*Moon: Science, History, and Mystery* (Ross), 191, 206
*A Mop for Pop* (Foster & Erickson), 309, 314
*More Parts* (Arnold), 277, 283
*Most Loved in All the World* (Hegamin & Cabrera),
    195, 206
Motivation and performance, 57–58
*A Mountain Alphabet* (Kiss), 278, 284
*Mr. Mosquito Put on His Tuxedo* (Morrow), 129, 145
*Muktar and the Camels* (Graber & Mack), 195, 206
Multicultural books, 195–197
Multilevel books, 191–192
Multiple intelligences theory, 51
Music. *See also* Songs
    texts, 199
*My Dad's Job* (Glassman), 278, 284
*My Nana and Me* (Smalls), 195, 206
Myopia, 53
*My Shadow* (Stevenson), 129, 145

**N**

Names and letter identification, 130
Names Test for phonics assessment, 295, 297–299
*The Napping House* (Wood), 190, 206

Narrative poetry, 193
National Assessment of Educational Progress (NAEP), 49
  on fluency, 215
  on parental involvement, 339
National Association for the Education of Young Children
    (NAEYC)
  early literacy, assessment of, 109
National Center for Research on Teacher Learning
    (NCRTL), 19
National Education Association (NEA) web site, 346
*National Geographic Kids,* 197
National Reading Panel on phonological awareness,
    124, 126
Nation's Report Cards, 183
Naturalistic assessment, 64
Nearsightedness, 53
Newberry Award books, 341
*A New House for Mole and Mouse* (Ziefert),
    309, 314
New Jersey reading program, 341
Newspapers, 198–199
  letter identification and, 133
Noneducational factors, 45–46, 49–58
  ELLs (English language learners), 50–51
  gender, 51–52
  health, 52–53
  home environment, 49–50
  intelligence, 51
  perceptual factors, 53–57
Nonsense poetry, 193
Normal curve, defined, 96
Norm-referenced tests, 92–93
  limitations of, 93
Norms, defined, 92
Note taking, 329–330
Nouns, 258
  foreign languages, transfer issues for, 405
Nursery rhymes for teaching phonics, 307–308
Nutrition and performance, 52–53

**O**
Obesity and performance, 53
Objectives
  Bloom's taxonomy of educational objectives, 213
  for criterion-referenced tests, 97
Objective testing, 38–39
Objectivity of observations, 67–69
Objects, letter identification and, 133
Observation, 67–69
  anecdotal records and, 69–72
  checklists for, 72–78
  class observation form, 70
  objectivity of, 67–69
  parents, observation by, 339
  phonics assessment by, 295, 296

*Observation Survey* (Clay), 130
Official documents as texts, 200
*Oh No, Gotta Go!* (Elya), 278, 284
*On Earth* (Karas), 191, 206
*One Dragon's Dream* (Pavey), 129, 145
*One Red Dot* (Carter), 190, 205
Ongoing teacher improvement, 20–21
Only children and performance, 50
Open-ended reading autobiography, 87
Open word sorts, 310
Oral language
  concepts, assessment of, 113–116
  early literacy and, 108
  phonological awareness and, 128
  teaching, 118, 121–122
Oral reading. *See also* Informal Reading
    Inventory (IRI)
  administering oral reading passages of IRI, 158
  books for practicing, 215
  comprehension and, 214–215
  for custom IRI, 357–358
  diagnostic checklist for, 155, 156
  listening and, 210
  phonological awareness and, 127–128
  principles of, 215
  print concepts, development of, 118, 121
  what, why, and how of, 149
Organizer role for teachers, 25–26
Outlines and semantic mapping, 330–331
*Outside, Inside* (Adoff), 277, 283
*Outside, Inside* (Crimi), 278, 284
*Over, Under, Through* (Hoban), 121
Overlearning, 317
*Ox-Cart Man* (Hall), 250, 252

**P**
Paired reading, 342–343
Pair-It Extreme little books, 187
*A Pair of Protoceratops* (Most), 121
*Palindromania* (Agee), 277, 283
*Panda Kindergarten* (Ryder), 191, 206
Paragraphs. *See also* Reading comprehension
  central idea, 222–225
    informal assessment of, 222–223
  main idea, comprehension of, 216–222
  organized/disorganized paragraphs, 220–222
Parental involvement, 337–348
  beginning levels for Word Recognition Inventory (WRI),
    361–362
  checklist for, 340
  computers and, 345–346
  Family Literacy Project, 343
  Junior Great Books program, 341
  New Jersey reading program, 341
  paired reading, 342–343

Reading Olympics, 341–342
in school reading programs, 341–344
television and, 344–345
Partners, working with, 27
*Parts* (Rotner), 121
PBS Kids, 201–202
Percentiles, defined, 97
Perception, 7
Perceptual domain, 7
Perceptual factors, 53–57
Performance
    assessment, 64–66
    attitude and, 58
    authentic, performance-based assessment, 63–64
    individual performance checklist, 76
    motivation and, 57–58
    and parental involvement, 339
Persistent readers, 9
Personal function of language, 122
Personality of students, 46
Phonemes
    blending, 124
    manipulation, 124
    segmentation, 124
    smatching, 123
Phonemic awareness, 123
    tasks of, 123–124
Phonetic stage of spelling, 136
Phonics, 285–314
    administering assessments, 295, 297, 300
    analogies for teaching, 310
    analytic phonics instruction, 304, 306
    assessing, 295–303
    auditory discrimination, 287, 288
    books for teaching, 307–309
    consonant blends, 290–291
    consonants, 287, 289–291
    content in phonics programs, 287–288
    defined, 287
    developmental sequence of, 287–295
    diagnostic checklist for word recognition skills, 206
    Early Names Test for assessing, 300–303
    exemplary instruction guidelines, 303–304
    foreign languages, transfer issues for, 414–417
    generalizations in, 286–287
    guidelines for teaching, 303–304
    Names Test for assessing, 295, 297–299
    nursery rhymes for teaching, 307–308
    observation for assessing, 295, 296
    phonograms, 288, 294–295
    poetry for teaching, 307–308
    prompts for teaching, 310, 312
    running records for assessing, 300
    syllables, 288, 295
    synthetic phonics instruction, 304, 306

teaching strategies, 303–312
Tile Test for assessing, 300, 305
visual discrimination, 287, 289
vowels, 288, 291–293
whole-part-whole instruction, 307–309
word-building for teaching, 310, 311
word identification for teaching, 306–307
wordness and, 308
word sorts for teaching, 309–310
writing for teaching, 310
Phonograms, 287, 294–295
    common phonograms, list of, 294
Phonological awareness, 123–128
    assessment of, 124
    defined, 123
    early literacy and, 108
    reading aloud and, 127–128
    reading/writing experiences promoting, 126–127
    scoring test on, 124–126
    stages of, 123
    teaching, 124–128
Phonological processing, 53–54
Phonology, foreign languages and, 414–417
Piagetian concept development, 112–113
*Piggies in a Polka* (Appelt), 277, 283
*The Pig in the Spigot* (Wilbur), 309, 314
*Pignic* (Miranda), 127, 145
Place for study, 317
*Planet Earth* (Hirschmann), 193, 206
*Planet Earth* (West), 193, 206
Planned, intentional instruction, 23
Planner role for teachers, 22–24
Play, books inviting, 129
*The Plot Chickens* (Auch & Auch), 250, 252
Poetry, 193–194. *See also* Rhyme
    books, 129
    *Earthsong* (Rogers), 127–128, 145
    examples of, 194
    phonics, teaching, 307–308
    phonological awareness and, 127–128
*Police Officers on Patrol* (Hamilton), 129, 145
*Polk Street Kids* (Reilly-Giff), 192, 206
*Pond Year* (Lasky), 278, 284
Portfolios, 64–65
    assessment of, 66–67
    checklist for, 68
Practices of good teachers, 20–21
Practice tests, 95
Practicing, parents involved with, 339
Precise listening, 212
Precommunicative stage of spelling, 136
Predictable books, 189–190
    examples of, 190
Predictions, strategy for making, 245, 250
Preface of textbooks, 3234

Prefixes, 258–259
   teaching about, 271–272
Pre-kindergarten readers, 12
Prentice-Hall textbooks, 189
Prepositions, transfer issues for, 411
Pre-reading assessment, 106–109
   standardized tests for, 110–111
   suggestions for choosing and using, 109
Primary reading survey, 85
Print concepts
   assessment of, 116–122
   books for reading aloud, 121
   class profile sheet for, 120
   early literacy and, 108
   explicit teaching of, 122
   focused teaching of, 122
   games and teaching, 121
   reading aloud and, 118, 121
   summary sheet for, 119
   teaching, 118, 121–122
*Print Concepts Test,* 116–118
Printed directions, following, 326–327
Productive readers, 9
Proficient readers, 8, 13
   characteristics of, 8–10
Projective techniques, 84, 87
Prompts
   for phonics teaching, 310, 312
   skimming prompts, 328
Pronouns, transfer issues for, 406–407
Pronunciation guides, use of, 281
Pull-out programs, 6
Purposeful readers, 9
Put upon children, 44

**Q**
Q letter sounds, 291
Question-Answer Relationships (QARS), 242–243
Questionnaire reading autobiography, 87
Questions. *See also* Reading comprehension
   foreign languages, grammar transfer issues for, 413
   in SQ3R technique, 318
   study skill, asking questions as, 328–329
   tips for asking, 328–329

**R**
*Rain* (Bauer), 309, 314
Rating scales, checklists using, 76–78
Raw score, defined, 96
R-controlled vowels, 293
   foreign languages, transfer issues for, 415
*Reader's Guide to Periodical Literature,* 334
Reading. *See also* Diagnosis
   defined, 6–7
   improvement, defined, 2–3

   as integrative process, 7–8
   models, 47
   models of, 10
   parental involvement in programs, 341–344
   process, 7
   readiness, 105
   in SQ3R technique, 318
Reading aloud. *See* Oral reading
Reading autobiography, 87–88
Reading comprehension
   Analyzing My Reading example, 239
   assessment of, 229–235
   categorization and, 262–263
   central idea, 222–225
      intermediate grades, instructional suggestions for, 224
      upper primary grades, instructional suggestions for, 223–224
   Cloze procedure for assessing, 231–234
   cloze tests, 231–234
   connections, strategy for making, 244, 250
   context clues and, 260–262
   creative reading, 214
      questions for, 241
   critical reading, 214
      custom IRI, creating questions for, 359
      questions for, 241
   custom IRI, comprehension questions for, 358–359
   defined, 211–213
   diagnostic checklist for, 237
   *Directed Reading-Thinking Activity (DRTA),* 238
   divergent thinking, questions requiring, 241
   fluency and, 214–215
   implied statements, understanding, 225–226
   inferences, drawing, 225–229
      informal assessment of inference, 227–228
      intermediate grades, instructional suggestions for, 226, 229
      primary grades, instructional suggestions for, 226
   interpretation, 214
      custom IRI, creating questions for, 358–359
      questions for, 241
   listening comprehension compared, 212
   literal comprehension, 213
      custom IRI, creating for, 358
      questions for, 241
   literature webbing, 240
   main ideas, 216–222
      finding, 216–217
      guidelines for finding, 217–218
      "hand" method for finding, 220
      informal assessment of, 218, 221
      intermediate grades, instructional suggestions for, 219–222

primary grades, instructional suggestions for, 218–219
    visuals and, 224
maze procedure, 234–235
*Meta-Comprehension Strategy Index,* 234
monitoring understanding, strategy for, 246, 250
oral reading and, 214–215
organized/disorganized paragraphs, 220–222
predictions, strategy for making, 245, 250
Question-Answer Relationships (QARS), 242–243
questioning
    as diagnostic technique, 230–231
    Question-Answer Relationships (QARS), 242–243
    Re-Quest method, 243
    strategies for teaching, 248, 250
    as teaching strategy, 240–241
reciprocal reading instruction, 239–240
repeated reading, 239
Re-Quest method, 243
retelling/summarizing, strategies for, 249, 250
strategies for, 229
supporting details, determining, 218
taxonomies of, 213–214
teaching strategies for, 235–250
thinking aloud approach, 238
topic sentences, guidelines on, 217–218
visualizing, strategy for, 247, 250
visuals and main ideas, 224–225
what, why, and how of, 230
Reading Is Fundamental web site, 346
Reading Miscue Inventory (RMI), 168
Reading Olympics, 341–342
Reading record, sample of, 342
*Reading Recovery,* 142
Reading survey tests, 93–97
    locator tests, 95
    practice tests, 95
*The Reading Teacher,* 95
    reading comprehension assessment strategies, 234
Reading vocabulary, 256
Real-life texts, 199–201
Reasoning and comprehension, 211–212
Recalling in SQ3R technique, 321
Reciprocal reading instruction, 239–240
Reciting in SQ3R technique, 321
Record keeping and assessment, 66
Reference books, 334–335
Regional dialects, 50–51
Regulatory function of language, 122
Reliability of tests, 39
Remedial reading, 6
*Rent Part Jazz* (Miller), 195, 206
Repeated reading for comprehension, 239
Repetition books, 129
Re-Quest method, 243
Response to intervention (RtI), 4

Retelling
    running records, retelling form for, 175
    strategies for, 249, 250
    summarizing compared, 331, 332
Reviewing in SQ3R technique, 321–322
Rhyme
    books, 129
    phoneme awareness and, 123
    phonics, nursery rhymes for teaching, 307–308
    in predictable books, 190
*Rhyming Dust Bunnies* (Thomas), 129, 145
*Riddle Road: Puzzles in Poems and Pictures* (Spires),
    278, 284
RIF Reading Planet, 202
*River of Dreams - Story of the Hudson River* (Talbott),
    191, 206
Root words, 259–260
*Rosa* (Giovanni), 195, 206
Rubrics, 65
*Ruby Bridges* (Cole), 196
Running records, 170–172
    administering, 172–176
    example of, 177
    Informal Reading Inventory (IRI) compared, 170–172
    interpreting, 178
    for phonics assessment, 300
    purposes of, 170
    repeated errors, recording, 176
    retelling form, 175
    sample form, 173
    scoring, 176–178
    summary of, 174, 179
*Runny Babbit: A Billy Sook* (Silverstein), 278, 284

**S**
Scanning as study skill, 327
*The Scarecrow's Dance* (Yolen), 194, 206
Scenarios
    case report of child, 350–351
    explanation of, 351–352
    five scenarios, comparison of, 352–355
    strengths, needs, and assessment techniques, chart of,
        353–354
Schedules as texts, 200
Schemata, 112
    and comprehension, 211
Schema theory of reading comprehension, 212–213
*Scholastic*
    *News,* 198
    textbooks, 189
School environment, 49
School media center, 333–335
    for intermediate and upper grades, 334–335
    for primary grades, 334
*School Supplies: A Book of Poems* (Hopkins), 194, 206

Schwa sound, 293
Scoring
    cloze tests, 232
    Early Names Test for assessing phonics, 300–303
    letter identification test, 130, 132
    Modified Miscue Analysis, 168–170
    Names Test for phonics assessment, 297–299
    oral reading errors, 154–155
    phonological awareness test, 124–126
    for *Print Concepts Test,* 118
    running records, 176–178
    for standardized tests, 95–97
    story sense tests, 140
Scott Foresman
    Reading Street basal readers, 188
    web site, 346
*The Secret World of Walter Anderson* (Bass), 277, 283
Seeing, reading and, 211
*See Pip Point* (Milgrim), 309, 314
*Sees Behind Trees* (Dorris), 197
Self-awareness and student interviews, 79
Self-concept and performance, 57
Self-evaluation
    checklist for, 29, 30
    by teachers, 26–27, 29
Self-extending system, developing, 310
Self-fulfilling prophecy, 21
Self-selection, 58
    vocabulary, strategy for teaching, 279–280
Semantic feature analysis for teaching vocabulary, 280
Semantic mapping, 330–331
Semantic networks and comprehension, 211
Semiphonetic stage of spelling, 136
Sentences
    completion test, 84, 87
    foreign languages, grammar transfer issues for, 411–413
Series books, 192–193
*Sesame Street Magazine,* 197
*Seventeenth Mental Measurements Yearbook,* 95
Sex roles, 46
*Shape by Shape* (Macdonald), 250, 252
*Shapes, Shapes, Shapes* (Hoban), 278, 284
Shared reading and phonological awareness, 127
*Sharks and Other Dangers of the Deep* (Mugford), 192, 206
*Sheep Take a Hike* (Shaw), 309, 314
*Shiloh* (Naylor), 195, 206
*Shoes, Shoes, Shoes* (Morris), 278, 284
*Short Takes* (Smith), 278, 284
Short vowels, 292
    foreign languages, transfer issues for, 414
*Show Off: How to Do Absolutely Everything One Step at a Time* (Stephens & Mann), 191, 206
Siblings and performance, 50

Sight vocabulary, 258
Signs as texts, 200
Silent consonant digraphs, 291
*Silent Letters Loud and Clear* (Pulver), 309, 314
Silent reading
    administering silent reading passages of IRI, 158
    comprehension score, 153
    for custom IRI, 357–358
    diagnostic checklist for, 155, 156
Silver/Burdett/Ginn textbooks, 189
"Simon Says," 121
Single-parent homes
    parental involvement and, 340
    performance and, 49
*Six Creepy Sheep* (Enderle & Tessler), 309, 314
Skimming
    index of textbook, 325
    as study skill, 327–328
*Sky Magic* (Hopkins), 194, 206
*Sleep, Little One, Sleep* (Bauer), 129, 145
Small groups, 27
Snellen charts, 53
*Snowflake Bentley* (Martin), 250, 252
Socioeconomic status (SES) and performance, 49–50
*So Many Circles, So Many Squares* (Hoban), 278, 284
Songs
    books, 129
    phonological awareness and, 128
Sound-symbol transfers in foreign languages, 416–417
Speaking vocabulary, 256
Special letters and sounds, 288
Speech problems, diagnostic checklist of, 74
Spelling
    developmental spelling, 135–136
    invented spelling, 126, 135–136
    stages of development, 136
*Sports Illustrated for Kids,* 197
*Spot the Plot: A Riddle Book of Book Riddles* (Lewis), 250, 252
SQ3R technique, 318, 321–323
    modeling approach, scenario for, 323–324
    note taking, scenario for, 329–330
    teaching, 324
Stages of literacy development, 12–14
Standard deviation, defined, 96
Standard English, 50–51
Standardized tests, 39, 91–102
    criterion-referenced tests, 97–98
    locator tests, 95
    norm-referenced tests, 92–93
    practice tests, 95
    for pre-reading assessment, 106–109, 110–111
    reading survey tests, 93–97

what, why, and how of, 264, 265
    word chains for teaching, 268, 281
    word maps for teaching, 280–281
    word part clues, teaching, 270–272
    word riddles for teaching, 280
    word walls for teaching, 279
    writing vocabulary, 256
    Yea/Nay game for teaching, 280
Vocabulary consciousness, 257
Vowel digraphs, 293
Vowels, 287, 291–293
    diphthongs, 293
    foreign languages, transfer issues for, 414–415, 417
    schwa sound, 293
    sound-symbol transfers, 417

**W**

*The Wacky Wedding: A Book of Alphabet Antics* (Duncan), 129, 145
*Walk Two Moons* (Creech), 195, 205
Web sites. *See* Internet
*Weekly Reader,* 198
*The Weighty Word Book* (Levitt, Burger & Guralnick), 278, 284
*Wepman Auditory Discrimination Test,* 56
*We're All in the SAME BOAT* (Shapiro), 129, 145
*Whatever* (Bee), 278, 284
*What Pete Ate from A to Z* (Kalman), 278, 284
*What's Opposite* (Swinburne), 121
*When I Heard the Learn'd Astronomer* (Whitman), 194, 206
*When Papa Snores* (Long), 215, 252
*When Tiny Was Tiny* (Meister), 309, 314
Whole class, 27
    language concepts checklist, 75
Whole-part-whole instruction for phonics, 307–309
*Who Ordered the Jumbo Shrimp? And Other Oxymorons* (Agee), 277, 283
*Why Not?* (Wormell), 190, 206
*The Widow's Broom* (Van Allsburg), 250, 252

*Wise Guy: The Life and Philosophy of Socrates* (Usher), 192, 206
Wish test, 87
Word-building for teaching phonics, 310, 311
Word chains for teaching vocabulary, 268, 281
Word identification for teaching phonics, 306–307
Wordless picture stories, 138–140
Word lists, 262–266, 356–357. *See also* Fry Instant Word List
Word maps for teaching vocabulary, 280–281
Word Recognition Inventory (WRI), 155, 157–158
    administering, 157–158
    beginning levels for, 361–362
    interpretation of results, 158
    word lists for, 262–266, 356–357
Word riddles for teaching vocabulary, 280
Words. *See* Vocabulary
Word sorts for teaching phonics, 309–310
Word walls for teaching vocabulary, 279
*A World of Words: An ABC of Quotations* (Tobias), 278, 284
Writing. *See also* Spelling
    assessment of, 136–138
    emergent writing, 133–138
    environment for, 138
    observation form, 137
    phonics, teaching, 310
    teaching writing, 138
    time for, 138
    vocabulary, 256

**Y**

Yahooligans!, 201
Yea/Nay game for teaching vocabulary, 280
*Yopp-Singer Test of Phonemic Segmentation,* 110

**Z**

*Zack Files* (Greenburg), 193, 206
Zone of proximal development (ZPD), 152
*Zoobooks,* 197